Essential Concepts and Applications

Fundamentals of Management

Second Edition

Stephen P. Robbins
San Diego State University

David A. De Cenzo
Towson State University

PRENTICE HALL Upper Saddle River, New Jersey 07458

Vice President/Editorial Director: *James Boyd*
Editor-in-Chief: *Natalie Anderson*
Associate Editor: *Lisamarie Brassini*
Editorial Assistant: *Crissy Statuto*
Marketing Manager: *Stephanie Johnson*
Production Editor: *Judith Leale*
Managing Editor: *Dee Josephson*
Manufacturing Supervisor: *Arnold Vila*
Manufacturing Manager: *Vincent Scelta*
Senior Designer: *Ann France*
Design Director: *Patricia Wosczyk*
Interior Design: *Ginidir Marshall*
Cover Design: *Wendy Helft*

A Simon & Schuster Company
Upper Saddle River, New Jersey 07458

Library of Congress Cataloging-in-Publication data

Robbins, Stephen P.,
Fundamentals of management: essential concepts and applications / Stephen P. Robbins, David A. De Cenzo.—2nd ed.
p. cm.
Includes bibliographical references.
ISBN 0-13-578600-2
1. Management. I. De Cenzo, David A. II. Title.
HD31.R5643 1997
658—dc21 96–45064
CIP

Prentice-Hall International (UK) Limited, London
Prentice-Hall of Australia Pty. Limited, Sydney
Prentice-Hall Canada, Inc., Toronto
Prentice-Hall Hispanoamericana, S.A., Mexico
Prentice-Hall of India Private Limited, New Delhi
Prentice-Hall of Japan, Inc., Tokyo
Simon & Schuster Asia Pte. Ltd., Singapore
Editoria Prentice-Hall do Brasil, Ltda., Rio de Janeiro

Printed in the United States of America

10 9 8 7 6 5 4 3 2 1

Brief Contents

Contents

Preface

To the Instructor

In the first edition of this book, we said we thought there was a market for a "different" kind of management textbook. Not different just for the sake of being different but a book that was truly reflective of the "reengineering" efforts in the world of business. To us, that meant a book that focused on the foundations of management—one that covered the essential concepts in management, provided a sound foundation for understanding the key issues, had a strong practical focus, and yet also covered the latest research studies in the field. It could be completed in a one-term course. Perhaps most important, a book that provided significant value both in relevance and cost to its readers. Our first edition sought to fill that need. The revision you have before you continues this tradition.

We address four critical questions in this preface.

- **1.** What assumptions guided the development of this book?
- **2.** What important features are continued from the previous edition?
- **3.** What's new in this revision?
- **4.** How does the book encourage learning for the reader?

Let's try to answer each.

What Were Our Assumptions in Writing This Book?

Every author who sits down to write a book has a set of assumptions—either explicit or implicit—that guide what is included and what is excluded. We want to state ours up front.

Management is an exciting field. The subject matter encompassed in an introductory management text is inherently exciting. We're talking about the real world. We're talking about why Nucor Steel is revolutionizing the worldwide steel-producing industry; how Autodesk, a relatively new software company, develops multimedia products in its creative and innovative corporate culture; how a company like Apple Computer, once a fairy-tale start-up company, must now struggle to survive; how to redesign an entire company in teams, cut waste, control costs, and increase productivity; and techniques that can make a university more efficient and responsive to its students. A good management text should capture this excitement. How? Through a crisp and conversational writing style, elimination of nonessential details, a focus on issues that are relevant to the reader, and inclusion of lots of examples and visual stimuli to make concepts come alive.

It's our belief that management shouldn't be studied solely from the perspective of "top management," "billion-dollar companies," or "U.S. corporations." The subject matter in management encompasses everyone from the lowest supervisor to the chief executive officer. The content should give as much attention to the challenges and opportunities in supervising fifteen clerical workers as those in directing a staff of MBA-educated vice presidents. Similarly, not everyone wants to work for a Fortune 500 company. Readers who are interested in working in small businesses or not-for-profit organizations should find the descriptions of management concepts applicable to their needs. Finally, organizations operate today in a global village. Readers must understand how to adjust their practices to reflect differing cultures.

Content should emphasize relevance. Before we committed anything to paper and included it in this book, we made sure it met our "so what?" test. Why would someone need to know this fact or that? If the relevance isn't overtly clear, either the item should be omitted or its relevance should be directly explained. In addition, content must be timely. We live in dynamic times. Changes are taking place at an unprecedented pace. A textbook in a dynamic field such as management must reflect this fact by including the latest concepts and practices. Our does!

This book is organized around the four traditional functions of management—planning, organizing, leading, and controlling. It is supplemented with material that addresses current issues affecting managers. For example, we take the reader through the Changing Face of Management (Chapter 2), Technology and the Design of Work Processes (Chapter 6), and Managing Teams (Chapter 11) and integrate throughout the text such contemporary topics as reengineering, empowerment, diversity, and continuous improvements. The text is divided into five parts: Part 1: Introduction; Part 2: Planning; Part 3: Organizing; Part 4: Leading; and Part 5: Controlling. There are a total of sixteen chapters, plus two appendixes that describe the evolution of management thought and provide some special information to students regarding how to build their management careers.

Bringing an introductory management text in at sixteen chapters required us, for the first edition, to make some difficult decisions regarding the cutting and reshaping of material. After a lot of review and considerable discussion, we felt we identified the essential elements students need in an introductory management course. Of course, the choice of "right topics" was a judgment call. We believe the tremendous success enjoyed by the first edition of this book confirms that the critical issues instructors typically expect in an introductory management text have been included. The same care shown in the first edition has been carried over to this revision.

What Important Features Were Kept from the First Edition?

The first edition contained a number of topics and features that adopters considered unique, useful, and/or particularly popular with students. We have retained those, and they include the following:

Classic research studies. Achieving our goal of writing a reengineered text required some major changes. In addition to cutting material that we considered to be marginally relevant to the introductory students, we concluded that much of the research that is covered in the management text of 700+ pages was not critical for introductory students. In fact, we cut through the theory where possible and emphasized the practical aspects of management. But we respect the fact that there are classic studies that many instructors want their students to know about. Unfortunately, most students aren't interested in the details behind these classics. In response, we created boxed vignettes called Details on a Management Classic. Although the research implications are discussed in the body of the text, the background on the research is reserved for the Details boxes.

Management skills. Today's typical student is more likely to someday be an entrepreneur, a senior executive in a small business, a manager in a not-for-profit organization, or a mid-level manager in a large company rather than CEO of a Fortune 500 firm. Success in these jobs will require practical skills. So we've included skill boxes throughout the text that provide step-by-step guidelines for handling specific elements of a manager's job. We call these Developing a Management Skill.

Practical applications. Our experience has led us to conclude that students like to see and read about people who have had a significant influence on their organization's performance. So we have included Managers Who Made a Difference boxes. All the managers are new to this edition; they include men and women from organizations ranging in size from small to large and located throughout the world.

Self-assessment exercises. We also are aware that students like to get feedback about themselves that they can use in their development. Toward this end, we have included a self-assessment in each chapter. These are called Understanding Yourself. Some examples of the questions asked include: What kind of organization design do you want to work for? How do you define life success? How ready are you for managing in a turbulent world? What needs are most important for you? What is your preferred leadership style?

Video case. Each chapter includes a video case. These are based on videos from the ABC News/Prentice Hall Video Library. We've also written these cases so they could be used as stand-alone case applications for those not wanting to show the video.

Writing style. This revision continues our commitment to present material in a lively and conversational style. Our goal continues to be to present material in an interesting and relevant manner—rich with examples to reinforce the point.

Headings designed around questions. When we were designing the layout for the first edition, we wanted something that was "student-friendly." We created headings that read as questions. This format allows readers to identify what important concept they should have gotten from that section or where they can go to get the answers to something they failed to grasp.

What's New for the Second Edition?

Several new features and content topics have been included in this revision.

Expanded coverage. In the second edition, look for more on reengineering, downsizing, contingent workers, work force diversity, boundaryless organizations, training, and management information systems.

Updated research foundation. You will also find a sound and current research base in this edition. We have done an extensive literature review to include many 1995 and 1996 citations from business periodicals and academic journals.

Two new chapters. We added two chapters to this edition: Technology and the Design of Work Processes (Chapter 6) and Managing Teams (Chapter 11). Rather than simply adding two additional chapters, we combined the organizing and organizational design material into one chapter and the chapters on foundations of individual and group behaviors into another.

Several new topics. Highlights include:

- the information age (Chapter 2)
- managing chaos (Chapter 2)
- criticism of planning (Chapter 3)
- types of strategies (Chapter 3)
- downside of management by objectives (Chapter 3)
- heuristics in decision making (Chapter 5)
- team-based structures (Chapter 7)
- contemporary career development (Chapter 8)
- compensation and benefits (Chapter 8)
- safety and health (Chapter 8)
- stress and employee assistance programs (Chapter 9)
- "big-five" personality factors and Myers-Briggs (Chapter 10)
- pay for performance and employee stock option programs (Chapter 12)
- trust and credibility in leadership (Chapter 13)
- men and women leadership styles (Chapter 13)
- interpersonal skills (Chapter 14)
- employee monitoring and privacy (Chapter 15)
- tips for developing a successful managerial career (Appendix B)

At the end of each chapter, we feature our home page address ⟨**www.prenhall.com/robbinsfom**⟩. Given the information age in which we live, it's important for students—if they aren't already on the Net—to have exposure to using the Internet for educational purposes. At our Web site, you will find chapter-specific Internet exercises, author biographies, and links to PHLIP—Prentice Hall's Learning on the Internet Partnership. PHLIP contains a number of useful professor and student resources. These include a "Management Web Site of the Week" and biweekly current-events articles tied directly to our book.

Inclusion of SCANS material and emphasis on skills, knowledge, and abilities across the curriculum. Several years ago, business schools began taking a hard look at themselves. What they found was that curriculum changes were warranted, business programs needed to be more mission-driven, and more infusion of the liberal arts was required. These changes translated into a need to emphasize skill, knowledge, and abilities across the curriculum. This need was reinforced in another forum when the Secretary of Labor published the *Secretary's Committee on Acquiring Necessary Skills* (SCANS). What did these two have in common? Both highlighted the need for business programs to cover the basic skill areas of communications, critical thinking, computer technology, globalization, diversity, ethics and values, and personal qualities (such as personality traits). Within each of these areas, there also exist several levels of understanding. They can be addressed from the simple to the complex. At the lower end of the spectrum, instructors are concerned with imparting knowledge, assisting comprehension, and encouraging application. Higher-order thinking, on the other hand, requires students to demonstrate that they can analyze, synthesize, and evaluate.[1]

This edition of *Fundamentals of Management* has been designed to facilitate increasing levels of thinking from knowledge to comprehension, and finally to applica-

[1]See, for example, F. Goodhart, P. Verdi, and S. Kennedy, "Assuring Quality in Health Education," paper presented at the Mid-Atlantic College Health Association, October 25, 1991.

Exhibit P-1
Critical Skills Coverage

CRITICAL SKILLS, KNOWLEDGE, ABILITIES	TOPIC AND LOCATION*	INTENDED LEVEL OF REINFORCEMENT
Critical Thinking	Chapter Objectives	Knowledge
	Chapter Summaries	Knowledge
	Review and Discussion Questions	Comprehension, application, analysis
	Case Applications	Application, analysis
	Testing Your Comprehension	Comprehension
Communication Skills	Applying the Concepts	Applications
	Interpersonal Skills (Chapter 14)	Knowledge
	Applying the Concepts	Application
Computer Technology	Technology (Chapter 6)	Knowledge
	At the Net	Knowledge, comprehension, application
Globalization	Global Village (pp. 34)	Knowledge
	ISO 9000 (pp. 101, 107, 108)	Knowledge
	and motivation (pp. 374, 375)	Knowledge
	and control (pp. 476, 477)	Knowledge
Diversity	Cultural diversity (pp. 199)	Knowledge
	in decision-making (pp. 154)	Knowledge
	in recruiting (pp. 237)	Knowledge
	managing diverse individuals	Knowledge
	in teams (pp. 411, 413)	Knowledge
	in motivation	Knowledge
	gender and cultural differences in leading (pp. 411, 413)	Knowledge
	in communications (pp. 431, 433)	Knowledge
Ethics/Values	Ethics and Social Responsibility (pp. 40, 42, 56, 57)	Knowledge
	Value judgment	Applications, analysis, evaluation
Personal Qualities	Foundations of Individual Behavior (pp. 391-397)	Knowledge
	Understanding Yourself	Applications, analysis, synthesis, evaluation

*A location not referenced by specific page numbers indicates a major section included in each chapter.

tion. We convey relevant management knowledge to students, give them an opportunity to reinforce their comprehension, and demonstrate that they can apply the concepts. For example, at the end of each chapter we have included multiple choice questions that have been specifically written to reinforce all the chapter objectives. These classroom-tested questions have been used previously to assess students' knowledge and comprehension of management topics. Exhibit P-1 summarizes how this book covers critical skills.

How Have We Encouraged Understanding with In-Text Learning Aids?

Just what do students need to facilitate their learning? We began to answer that question by pondering some fundamental issues: Could we make this book both "fun" to read and pedagogically sound? Could it motivate students to read on and facilitate learning? Our conclusion was that an effective textbook should teach as well as present ideas. Toward that end, we designed this book to be a quality learning tool. Let us specifically point out some pedagogical features—in addition to what we've mentioned previously—that we included to help students better assimilate the material.

Learning objectives. Before you start a trip, it's valuable to know where you're headed. That way, you can minimize detours. The same holds true in reading a text. To make learning more efficient, we open each chapter of this book with a list of objectives that describe what the student should be able to do after reading the chapter. These objectives are designed to focus students' attention on the major issues within each chapter.

Chapter summaries. Just as objectives clarify where one is going, chapter summaries remind you where you have been. Each chapter of this book concludes with a concise summary organized around the opening learning objectives.

Review and discussion questions. Every chapter in this book ends with a set of ten review and discussion questions. If students have read and understood the contents of a chapter, they should be able to answer the review questions. These review questions are drawn directly from the material in the chapter.

The discussion questions go beyond comprehending chapter content. They're designed to foster higher-order thinking skills. That is, they require the reader to apply, integrate, synthesize, or evaluate management concepts. The discussion questions will allow students to demonstrate that they not only know the facts in the chapter but also can use those facts to deal with more-complex issues.

Class exercises. Today's students are tomorrow's employees, and they will undoubtedly be working at times in teams. To help facilitate being part of a team, we've included a number of in-class group exercises. These class exercises, which we have called Applying the Concepts, are also tied to content in their respective chapters.

Case applications. Each chapter contains three case applications. The first application involves an ethical dilemma. The case is designed to get students to apply their values to an actual business situation. The second case is an actual case of an organization. This case gives students an opportunity to use one or more concepts discussed in the chapter and apply them to actual problems faced by managers. Also, as previously mentioned, each chapter contains a video case that can be used as a stand-alone case application or with the video provided.

Supplements package. This book is accompanied by the full complement of support material that you expect. Adopters of this text can obtain the following classroom aids: an Instructor's Manual with video guide available in hard copy or on disk; a comprehensive Test Item File, also available on disk in both Macintosh and Windows versions; color transparencies with teaching notes; an electronic version of the transparencies in PowerPoint; and an ABC News Video Library to complement cases within the text. Additionally, adopters will have access to a web site of activities and information specifically designed for *Fundamentals of Management 2/e* at:

⟨**www.prenhall.com/robbinsfom**⟩.

Acknowledgments

Writing a textbook is often the work of a number of people whose names generally never appear on the cover. Yet, without their help and assistance, a project like this would never come to fruition. We'd like to recognize some special people who gave so unselfishly to making this book a reality.

First are our friends at Prentice Hall. Granted, there are so many people who should be recognized here that the list is almost unending. Nevertheless, a few deserve special recognition—our acquisition and production editors. Our acquisition editor, Natalie Anderson, continues to support our ideas for projects like this—even though at times we must come close to driving her crazy. Natalie, thank you and know we appreciate the hard work and effort you give to us. Judy Leale, our production editor had the challenge of pulling all the pieces together. She worked diligently in bringing the final product to completion. Thanks, Judy, for being a vital part of our team.

In addition to Natalie and Judy, there are several others we'd like to recognize. We are grateful to the following for their efforts on our behalf (in alphabetical order): Jim Boyd, Lisamarie Brassini, Mary Helen Fitzgerald, Stephanie Johnson, Bill Oldsey, Margo Quinto, Crissy Statuto, Sandy Steiner, and Teri Stratford. We apologize to anyone we may have inadvertently omitted.

We thank all our reviewers who gave us their constructive comments and suggestions on how we could improve the book.

Finally, we'd like to add a personal note. Each of us has some special people we'd like to recognize.

From Steve's corner: I thank my new bride, Laura. You are making great strides in helping me balance my life. Every day is better because you're in it.

From Dave's: I'd like to recognize my family. Through thick and thin, they're always there. To Teri, my lovely wife, here's hoping that all our dreams are fulfilled. To Mark, Meredith, Gabriella, Natalie—and the dog and the cat—thanks. You've always been my inspiration and ever so special to me. Always remember that I am there—even if it is in my office "playing" on my computer.

To the Student

Now that our writing chores are over, we can put our feet up on the table and offer a few brief comments to those of you who will be reading and studying this book. First, this text provides you exposure to the fundamentals of management. As you'll see in our first chapter, *fundamentals* implies coverage of the basic functions of management. We've made every effort to give you the essential information a student will need to solidly build a knowledge foundation about this dynamic, exciting, and often chaotic field. A knowledge base, however, is not easily attained unless you have a text that is straightforward, timely, and interesting to read. We have made every effort to achieve those goals with a writing style that tries to capture the conversational tone that you would get if you were personally attending one of our lectures. That means logical reasoning, clear explanations, and lots of examples to illustrate concepts.

A book, in addition to being enjoyable to read and understand, should help you learn. Reading for reading's sake, without comprehension or understanding of what you've just read, is a waste of your time and effort. So, we've done a couple of things in this book to assist your learning. We've introduced major topic headings in each chapter. These you'll find as headings in the purple boxes. Those number one heads, as they are called, provide exposure to a broad management concept. Most of those number one heads are followed by questions. Each "question" head was carefully chosen to reinforce understanding of very specific information. Accordingly, as you read each of these sections, material presented will address the question posed. Thus, after reading a chapter (or a section for that matter), you should be able to return to those headings and respond to the question. If you can't answer a question or are unsure of your response, you'll know exactly what sections need to be reread or reviewed or where more of your effort needs to be placed. All in all, this format provides a self-check on your reading comprehension.

We've added other check points that you should find useful. Our review and discussion questions are designed to reinforce the chapter objectives from two perspectives. First, review questions focus on material covered in the chapter. These are another way to reinforce the important concepts in the chapter. The discussion questions require you to go one step further. Rather than requiring that you recite facts, discussion questions require you to integrate, synthesize, or apply a management concept. True understanding of the material is revealed when you can deal with these more complex issues.

Often, even after going through review and discussion questions, our students have told us that they have found something missing. Why can't the book have multiple choice questions like the questions on exams? We thought the students were on to something. So we added a section called Testing Your Comprehension. Each chapter contains multiple choice questions that test the chapter's material. In the back of the book, we've provided the answers. These are questions that we've used previously with our students. If you can correctly answer these multiple choice questions, then you're one step closer to demonstrating your understanding of that material. Recognize, of course, that these questions are designed to be only a learning aid. They don't, nor are they intended to, replace careful reading or intensive studying. And don't assume that getting a question right means you fully understand the concept covered. Why? Any set of multiple choice questions can test only a limited range of information. So don't let correct answers lull you into a false sense of security. However, if you miss a question or don't fully understand why you got the correct response, go back to the corresponding pages in the chapter and reread the material. To help in this, we've provided in the answer section a cross-reference to the page in the text related to the question.

There is another element of this text that we hope you'll share our excitement about. These are our Developing a Management Skill boxes. Practicing management today requires sound competencies—competencies that can be translated into specific skills. In this book, we've taken a major concept and developed a series of specific steps (skills) that, if practiced and mastered, can make you more effective as a manager. This includes such skills as building a power base, interviewing candidates, building trust, and providing performance feedback. We hope that you carefully review each of these, focus on the central behaviors we are explaining, and keep these handy for later reference in your career.

Now that we've given our ideas behind the text, we'd also like to extend an open invitation to you. That is, if you'd like to give us some feedback, we encourage you to write. Send all correspondence to Dave De Cenzo at the Department of Management, Towson State University, Towson, Maryland 21204–7097. Dave is also available on e-mail. His address is ⟨decenzo@towson.edu⟩. Good luck this semester, and we hope you enjoy reading this book as much as we did preparing it for you.

Steve Robbins

Dave De Cenzo
decenzo@towson.edu

• PART 1 •

Introduction

Managers and Management

1

LEARNING OBJECTIVES

What will I be able to do after I finish this chapter?

1. **DESCRIBE** the difference between managers and operative employees.
2. **EXPLAIN** what is meant by the term *management*.
3. **DIFFERENTIATE** between efficiency and effectiveness.
4. **DESCRIBE** the four basic functions of management.
5. **CLASSIFY** the three levels of managers and identify the primary responsibility of each group.
6. **IDENTIFY** the roles performed by managers.
7. **DESCRIBE** the four skills necessary for becoming a successful manager.
8. **EXPLAIN** whether the manager's job is generic.
9. **DESCRIBE** the value of studying management.
10. **EXPLAIN** the process, systems, and contingency approaches to the study of management.

THERE'S AN OLD ADAGE THAT SAYS "ONLY the strong survive." In business, survival means being better than the competition and doing things that others can't. In today's fiercely competitive markets, survival requires organizations to produce quality products and services and to ensure that those products and services meet customers' expectations. But how does an organization achieve these ends? By having a vision created and implemented by individuals committed to the organization.

These individuals are called managers, and they come from all walks of life. They differ in terms of shape, color, age, and gender. They work to produce a profit or to achieve some social good. But managers don't accomplish those goals by themselves. Rather, their goals are completed through the efforts of others. One such manager is Carol Bartz.

Carol is the CEO of Autodesk, Inc., a San Rafael, California, design-software manufacturer.[1] Before Bartz arrived at Autodesk in 1992, the organization was best described as operating chaotically. Decisions were made without any coordinated focus. Decision makers often acted on whims—without any set goals in mind. The result? Confusion, uncertainty, and financial problems for the company. The organization was barely surviving! So the owners decided to bring in a professional management team headed by Carol Bartz.

Carol Bartz, CEO of Autodesk, Inc., understands the importance of good management in today's organizations. Since Bartz and her professional management team took over the ailing company in 1992, they have made decisions that have more than doubled company sales to $600 million a year in just under three years.

Carol Bartz had been in the software development business long enough to know what worked and what didn't. Upon joining Autodesk, she immediately began to assess where there were problems and set in action a course for correcting them. She opened up communications among organizational members, seeking their input into matters that affected them. Likewise, she asked customers what they wanted but were not getting from Autodesk and made sweeping changes to overcome the deficiencies. For example, Bartz noticed that different customers had different software needs, and treating them all alike wasn't working. So she changed how employees in the organization were grouped so that each segment could serve a particular customer base—creating a company-customer partnership in such areas as computer-aided design, multimedia, data management, and geographic information systems. Now, each market group has the ability to solve its customers' problems, as well as responsibility for developing new products for those and future customers. For instance, Bartz strongly encourages creative thinking for innovating new products. She understands that the volatility of technology can render any product obsolete overnight. So Autodesk is moving forward with new 3-D technology software that will revolutionize how surgeons diagnose illnesses, how engineers design products, how cartographers map the land, and how computer games will be played. Bartz has also opened up communications between senior management and employees. As a result, her employees are committed to the organization because they are involved in what affects them. Meeting frequently with management at brown-bag lunches, they have an opportunity to exchange information—they ask questions and receive "state of the business" information. Similar communications with market groups and customers have also enabled Autodesk to accurately and quickly respond to changing market needs.

Have Carol Bartz's efforts been successful for Autodesk? The answer is a resounding Yes! In three years under Bartz's leadership, Autodesk has more than doubled sales, to more than $600 million. It's these results that have earned Carol Bartz the distinction of being one of the leading female managers in the rapidly growing software development business.

Carol Bartz provides an good example of the efforts of a successful manager today. The key word, however, is example. There is no universally accepted model of what a successful manager looks like. Managers today can be found from under age eighteen to over eighty. Nowadays, they are as frequently women as they are men.[2] They manage large corporations, small businesses, government agencies, hospitals, museums, schools, and such nontraditional organizations as cooperatives. Some hold positions at the top of their organizations; others are first-line supervisors overseeing operating personnel. And today's managers can be found doing their work in every country on the globe.

This book is about the work activities that Carol Bartz and the tens of millions of other managers like her do. In this chapter, we introduce you to managers and management by answering, or at least beginning to answer, these questions: Who are managers, and where do they work? What is management, and what do managers do? Why should you spend your time studying management? And how do we study this subject?

Who Are Managers, and Where Do They Work?

Managers work in places we call an organization. Therefore, before we identify who managers are and what they do, we must clarify what we mean by the term *organization.*

An **organization** is a systematic arrangement of people brought together to accomplish some specific purpose. Your college or university is an organization. So are sororities, charitable agencies, churches, your neighborhood convenience store, the Montreal Canadiens hockey team, the Home Depot Corporation, the Australian Dental Association, and British Petroleum. These are all organizations because each comprises three common characteristics.

organization
A systematic arrangement of people to accomplish some specific purpose.

What Three Common Characteristics Do All Organizations Have?

It takes people to make decisions . . . to make the goal a reality.

Every organization has a purpose and is made up of people who are grouped in some fashion (see Exhibit 1-1). The distinct purpose of an organization is typically expressed in terms of a goal or set of goals. For example, Wolfgang Schmitt, the head of Rubbermaid Corporation, has set his sights on achieving

How does an organization like the Dallas Cowboys become successful? By having in place a systematic arrangement of quality people—both on and off the field—all focusing their efforts on achieving some goal. For them, that's winning the Super Bowl!

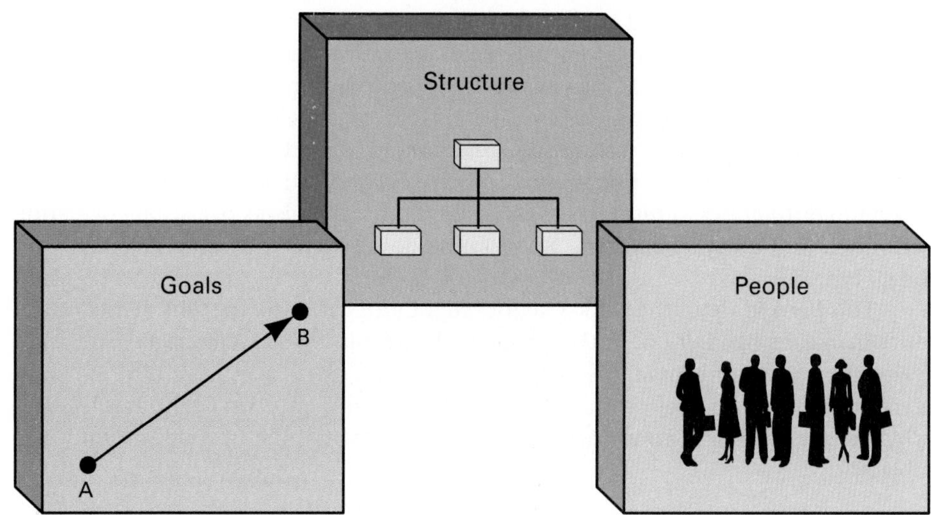

Exhibit 1-1
Common Characteristics of Organizations

15 percent annual growth in revenues (the goal) for his company.[3] Second, no purpose or goal can be achieved by itself. It takes people, to make decisions to establish the purpose and to perform a variety of activities to make the goal a reality. Third, all organizations develop a systematic structure that defines and limits the behavior of its members. Developing structure may include, for example, creating rules and regulations, giving some members supervisory control over other members, forming work teams, or writing job descriptions so that organizational members know what they are supposed to do. The term *organization* therefore refers to an entity that has a distinct purpose, has people or members, and has a systematic structure.

How Are Managers Different from Operative Employees?

operatives
People who work directly on a job or task and have no responsibility for overseeing the work of others.

managers
Individuals in an organization who direct the activities of others.

Managers work in organizations, but not everyone who works in an organization is a manager. For simplicity's sake, we can divide organizational members into two categories: operatives and managers. **Operatives** are people who work directly on a job or task and have no responsibility for overseeing the work of others. The people who attach gas tanks on the Harley Davidson motorcycle assembly line, make your burrito at Taco Bell, or process your course registration in your college's registrar office are all operatives. In contrast, **managers** direct the activities of other people in the organization. Customarily classified as top, middle, or first-line, these individuals supervise both operative employees and lower-level managers (see Exhibit 1-2). That does not mean, however, that managers don't work directly on tasks. Some managers also have operative responsibilities themselves. For example, district sales managers for Frito Lay also have basic responsibilities to service some accounts in addition to overseeing the activities of the other sales associates in their district. The distinction, then, between the two groups—operatives and managers—is that managers have employees who report directly to them.

What Titles Do Managers Have in Organizations?

first-line managers
Supervisors; responsible for directing the day-to-day activities of operative employees.

Identifying exactly who managers are in an organization is often not a difficult task, although you should be aware that management positions come with a variety of titles. **First-line managers** are usually called supervisors. They are responsible for directing the day-to-day activities of operative employees. In your college, for example,

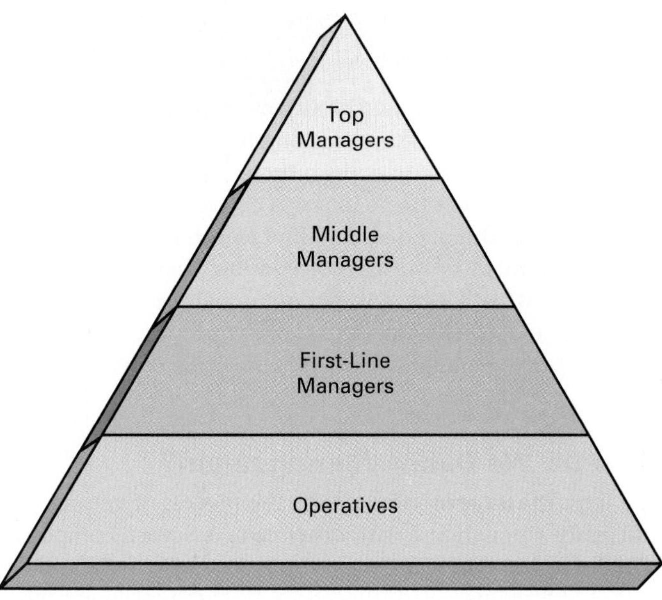

Exhibit 1-2
Organizational Levels

the Department Chair would be a first-line supervisor overseeing the activities of the departmental faculty (the operatives). **Middle managers** represent levels of management between the first-line manager (the supervisor) and top management. These individuals manage other managers—and possibly some operative employees—and are typically responsible for translating the goals set by top management into specific details that lower-level managers can perform. In organizations, middle managers may have such titles as department or agency head, project leader, unit chief, district manager, dean, bishop, or division manager.

middle managers Individuals at levels of management between the first-line manager and top management.

At or near the top of an organization are **top managers.** These individuals, like Carol Bartz, are responsible for making decisions about the direction of the organization and establishing policies that affect all organizational members. Top managers typically have titles such as vice president, president, chancellor, managing director, chief operating officer, chief executive officer, or chairperson of the board.

top managers Individuals who are responsible for making decisions about the direction of the organization and establishing policies that affect all organizational members.

Not all managers are chief executive officers. Few, in fact, actually reach that top spot. Instead, the majority of managers, and those closest to operative employees, are called first-line supervisors. This supervisor discusses quality issues with her employees.

What Is Management, and What Do Managers Do?

Just as organizations have common characteristics, so, too, do managers. Despite the fact that their titles vary widely, there are several common elements to their jobs—regardless of whether the manager is a head nurse in the intensive care unit of Cedars-Sinai Hospital who oversees a staff of eleven critical care specialists or the president of the 115,000-member Boeing Corporation, the Seattle-based aircraft manufacturer.[4] In this section we will look at these commonalities as we define management, present the classical management functions, review recent research on managerial roles, and consider the universal applicability of managerial concepts.

How Do We Define Management?

management
The process of getting things done, effectively and efficiently, through and with other people.

The term **management** refers to the process of getting things done, effectively and efficiently, through and with other people. Several components in this definition warrant discussion. These are the terms *process, effectively,* and *efficiently.*

The term *process* in the definition of management represents the primary activities managers perform. In management terms, we call these the functions of management. We explore these functions in the next section.

efficiency
Means doing the thing right; refers to the relationship between inputs and outputs. Seeks to minimize resource costs.

Effectiveness and efficiency deal with what we are doing and how we are doing it. **Efficiency** means doing the task right and refers to the relationship between inputs and outputs. For instance, if you get more output for a given input, you have increased efficiency. So, too, do you increase efficiency when you get the same output with fewer resources. Since managers deal with input resources that are scarce—money, people, equipment—they are concerned with the efficient use of those resources. Management, therefore, is concerned with minimizing resource costs.

effectiveness
Means doing the right thing; goal attainment.

Although minimizing resource costs is important, it is not enough simply to be efficient. Management is also concerned with completing activities. In management terms, we call this ability **effectiveness.** Effectiveness means doing the right task. In an organization, that translates into goal attainment (see Exhibit 1-3).

Although efficiency and effectiveness are different terms, they are interrelated. For instance, it's easier to be effective if one ignores efficiency. AlliedSignal could produce more-sophisticated and longer-lasting Fram oil filters if it disregarded labor and material input costs. Similarly, some government agencies have been regularly attacked on the grounds that they are reasonably effective but extremely inefficient. That is, the agency accomplishes its goals, but it does so at a very high cost. Our conclusion: Good management is concerned with both attaining goals (effectiveness) and doing so as efficiently as possible.

Effectiveness and efficiency deal with what managers do and how they do it.

Can organizations be efficient and yet not be effective? Yes, by doing the wrong things well! A number of colleges have become highly efficient in processing students. Through the use of computer-assisted learning, distance learning programs, or a heavy reliance on part-time faculty, administrators may have significantly cut the cost of educating each student. Yet some of these colleges have been criticized by students, alumni, and accrediting agencies for failing to educate students properly. Of course, high efficiency is associated more typically with high effectiveness. And poor management is most often due to both inefficiency and ineffectiveness or to effectiveness achieved through inefficiency.

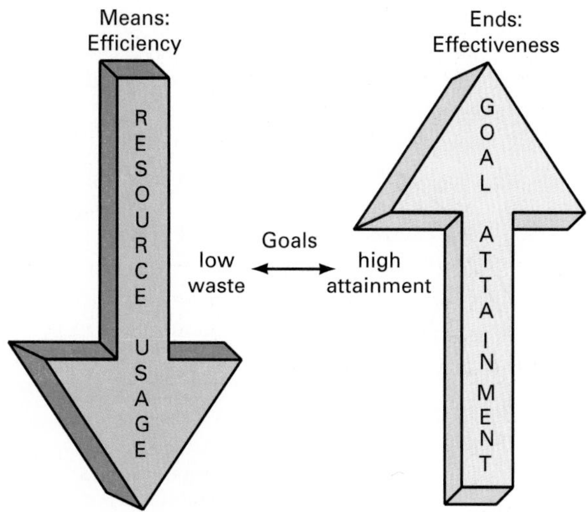

Exhibit 1-3
Efficiency and Effectiveness

What Are the Four Functions of Management?

In the early part of this century, a French industrialist by the name of Henri Fayol wrote that all managers perform five management functions. They plan, organize, command, coordinate, and control.[5] In the mid-1950s, two professors at UCLA used the functions of planning, organizing, staffing, directing, and controlling as the framework for a textbook on management that for twenty years was unquestionably the most widely sold text on the subject.[6] The most popular textbooks still continue to be organized around **management functions,** though these have generally been condensed to the basic four: planning, organizing, leading, and controlling (see Exhibit 1-4). Let us briefly define what each of these functions encompasses. Keep in mind before we begin, however, that, although we will look at each as an independent function, managers must be able to perform all four functions simultaneously and that each function has an effect on the others. That is, these functions are interrelated and interdependent.

management functions
Planning, organizing, leading, and controlling.

planning
Includes defining goals, establishing strategy, and developing plans to coordinate activities.

organizing
Includes determining what tasks are to be done, who is to do them, how the tasks are to be grouped, who reports to whom, and where decisions are to be made.

leading
Includes motivating employees, directing the activities of others, selecting the most effective communication channel, and resolving conflicts.

controlling
The process of monitoring performance, comparing it with goals, and correcting any significant deviations.

If you don't much care where you want to get to, then it doesn't matter which way you go, as the Cheshire cat explained to Alice in Wonderland. Since organizations exist to achieve some purpose, someone has to define that purpose and the means for its achievement. A manager is that someone. The **planning** function encompasses defining an organization's goals, establishing an overall strategy for achieving those goals, and developing a comprehensive hierarchy of plans to integrate and coordinate activities. Setting goals keeps the work to be done in its proper focus and helps organizational members keep their attention on what is most important.

Managers like Carol Bartz are also responsible for designing an organization's structure. We call this management function **organizing.** Organizing includes determining what tasks are to be done, who is to do them, how the tasks are to be grouped, who reports to whom, and where decisions are to be made.

We know that every organization contains people. And it is part of a manager's job to direct and coordinate those people. Performing this activity is the **leading** function of management. When managers motivate employees, direct the activities of others, select the most effective communication channel, or resolve conflicts among members, they are engaging in leading.

The final function managers perform is **controlling.** After the goals are set, the plans formulated, the structural arrangements determined, and the people hired,

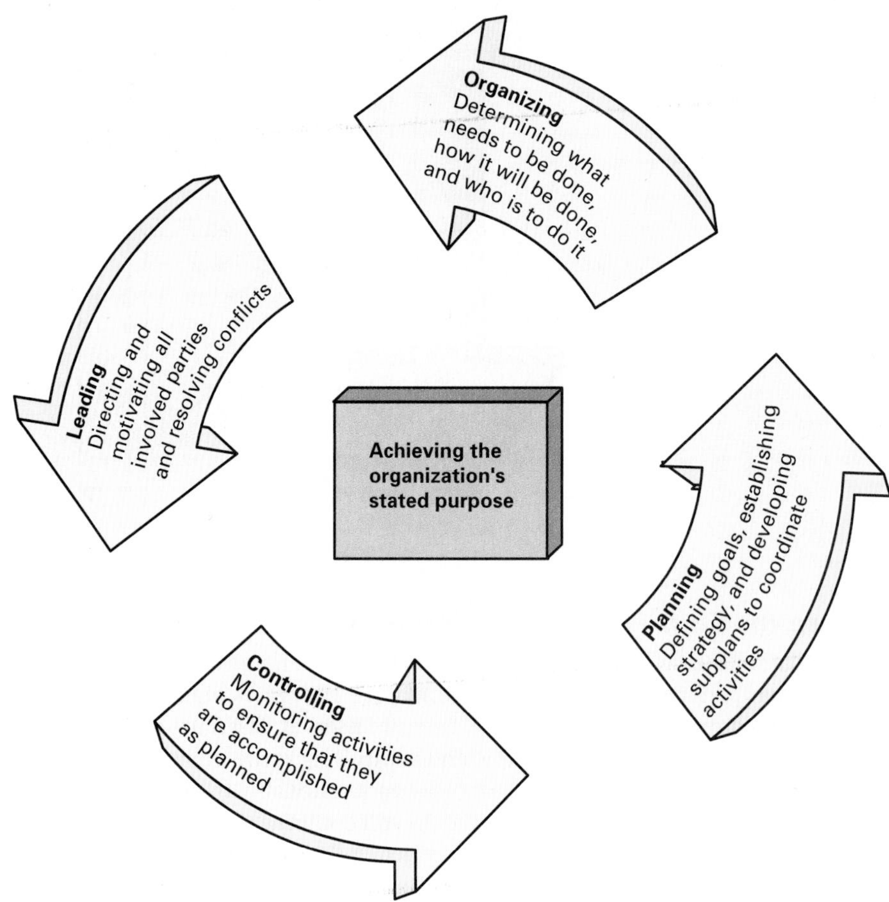

Exhibit 1-4
Management Functions

trained, and motivated, something may still go amiss. To ensure that things are going as they should, a manager must monitor the organization's performance. Actual performance must be compared with the previously set goals. If there are any significant deviations, it is the manager's responsibility to get the organization back on track. This process of monitoring, comparing, and correcting is what we mean when we refer to the controlling function.

The continued popularity of the functional approach is a tribute to its clarity and simplicity. But is it an accurate description of what managers actually do?[7] Following the functional approach, it is easy to answer the question What do managers do? They plan, organize, lead, and control. But is this really true of all managers? Fayol's original functions were not derived from a careful survey of thousands of managers in hundreds of organizations. Rather, they merely represented observations based on his experience in the French mining industry. In more recent years, there have been additional efforts at trying to classify what managers do. The following describes several of those efforts.

What Are Management Roles?

In the late 1960s, Henry Mintzberg undertook a careful study of five chief executives at work.[8] What he discovered challenged several long-held notions about the manager's job. For instance, in contrast to the predominant views at the time that managers were reflective thinkers who carefully and systematically processed information before making decisions, Mintzberg found that the managers he studied engaged in a large number of varied, unpatterned, and short-duration activities. There was little time for reflective thinking because the managers encountered constant interruptions. Half of these managers' activities lasted less than nine minutes. But in addition to these insights, Mintzberg provided a categorization scheme for defining what managers do on the basis of actual managers on the job. These are commonly referred to as Mintzberg's managerial roles.

Whenever a manager, like Larry Bossidy of AlliedSignal, represents the organization to the community at large, that individual is performing the management role of spokesperson.

Mintzberg concluded that managers perform ten different but highly interrelated roles. The term **management roles** refers to specific categories of managerial behavior. These ten roles, as shown in Exhibit 1-5, can be grouped under three primary headings—interpersonal relationships, the transfer of information, and decision making.

management roles Specific categories of managerial behavior; often grouped under three primary headings: interpersonal relationships, transfer of information, and decision making.

How Are These Roles Evident in Managers' Jobs?

All managers are required to perform duties that are ceremonial and symbolic in nature. These duties require **interpersonal roles.** When Herb Kelleher, president of Southwest Airlines, gives a speech to members of the Federal Aviation Administration, or the shift supervisor of Utz Potato Chips gives a group of elementary school students a tour of the plant, they are acting in *figurehead roles.* All managers have a role as a *leader.* This role includes hiring, training, motivating, and disciplining employees. The third role within the interpersonal grouping is the *liaison role.* Mintzberg described this activity as contacting external sources who provide the manager with information. These sources are individuals or groups outside the manager's unit and may be inside or outside the organization. The computer operations manager at a Nissan plant who obtains information from the plant's human resources manager has an internal liaison relationship. When that computer operations manager has contacts with other computer executives through a common trade association, she has an outside liaison relationship.

interpersonal roles Management roles that include figurehead, leader, and liaison activities.

All managers will, to some degree, receive and collect information from organizations and institutions outside their own. Performing these activities is part of **informational roles.** Typically, information is gathered through reading periodicals and talking with others to learn of changes in the public's tastes, what competitors may be planning, and the like. Mintzberg called this the *monitor role.* Managers also act as a conduit to transmit information to organizational members. This is the *disseminator role.* When they represent the organization to outsiders, managers also perform a *spokesperson role.*

informational roles Management roles that include monitor, disseminator, and spokesperson activities.

Finally, Mintzberg identified four roles that revolve around the making of choices—**decisional roles.** As *entrepreneurs,* managers initiate and oversee new projects that will improve their organization's performance. As *disturbance handlers,* managers take some action in response to previously unforeseen events—for example, quickly appointing a replacement when a senior manager suddenly dies. As *resource allocators,* managers are responsible for allocating human, physical, and monetary resources by, for instance, creating budgets. Last, managers perform as *negotiators* when

decisional roles Management roles that include entrepreneur, disturbance handler, resource allocator, and negotiator.

Exhibit 1-5
Mintzberg's Managerial Roles

Source: From *The Nature of Managerial Work* by H. Mintzberg. Copyright © 1973 by Henry Mintzberg. Reprinted by permission of Addison Wesley Educational Publishers, Inc.

ROLE	DESCRIPTION	IDENTIFIABLE ACTIVITIES
Interpersonal		
Figurehead	Symbolic head; obliged to perform a number of routine duties of a legal or social nature	Greeting visitors; signing legal documents
Leader	Responsible for the motivation and activation of employees; responsible for staffing, training, and associated duties	Performing virtually all activities that involve employees
Liaison	Maintains self-developed network of outside contacts and informers who provide favors and information	Acknowledging mail; doing external board work; performing other activities that involve outsiders
Informational		
Monitor	Seeks and receives wide variety of special information (much of it current) to develop thorough understanding of organization and environment; emerges as nerve center of internal and external information about the organization	Reading periodicals and reports; maintaining personal contacts
Disseminator	Transmits information received from other employees to members of the organization—some information is factual, some involves interpretation and integration of diverse value positions of organizational influencers	Holding informational meetings; making phone calls to relay information
Spokesperson	Transmits information to outsiders on organization's plans, policies, actions, results, etc.; serves as expert on organization's industry	Holding board meetings; giving information to the media
Decisional		
Entrepreneur	Searches organization and its environment for opportunities and initiates "improvement projects" to bring about change; supervises design of certain projects as well	Organizing strategy and review sessions to develop new programs
Disturbance handler	Responsible for corrective action when organization faces important, unexpected disturbances	Organizing strategy and review sessions that involve disturbances and crises
Resource allocator	Responsible for the allocation of organizational resources of all kinds—in effect, the making or approval of all significant organizational decisions	Scheduling; requesting authorization; performing any activity that involves budgeting and the programming of employees' work
Negotiator	Responsible for representing the organization at major negotiations	Participating in union contract negotiations or in those with suppliers

Details on a Management Classic

MINTZBERG'S ROLES

A number of follow-up studies have tested the validity of Mintzberg's role categories across different types of organizations and at different levels within given organizations.[9] The evidence generally supports the idea that managers—regardless of the type of organization or level in the organization—perform similar roles. However, the emphasis that managers give to the various roles seems to change with hierarchial level.[10] Specifically, the roles of disseminator, figurehead, negotiator, liaison, and spokesperson are more important at the higher levels than at the lower ones. Conversely, the leader role is more important for lower-level managers than it is for either middle- or top-level managers.

Have Mintzberg's ten roles, which are derived from actual observations of managerial work, invalidated the more traditional functions of planning, organizing, leading, and controlling? Do they diminish the importance placed on those four traditional functions or negate the reasons we study them? No! First, the functional approach still represents the most useful way of conceptualizing the manager's job. "The classical functions provide clear and discrete methods of classifying the thousands of activities that managers carry out and the techniques they use in terms of the functions they perform for the achievement of organizational goals."[11] Second, although Mintzberg may offer a more detailed and elaborate classification scheme of what managers do, these roles are substantially reconcilable with the four management functions.[12] Many of Mintzberg's roles align smoothly with one or more of the management functions.

For instance, resource allocation is part of planning, as is the entrepreneurial role. All three of the interpersonal roles are part of the leading function. Most of the other roles fit into one or more of the four management functions, but not all of them do. The difference is substantially explained by Mintzberg's intermixing management activities and pure managerial work.[13]

All managers do some work that is not purely managerial. The fact that Mintzberg's executives spent time in public relations or raising money attests to the precision of Mintzberg's observational methods but shows that not everything a manager does is necessarily an essential part of the manager's job. Thus, some activities were included in Mintzberg's schema that, perhaps, should not have been.

Do the comments above mean that Mintzberg's role categories are invalid? Not at all! Mintzberg clearly offered new insights into what managers do. The attention his work has received is evidence of the importance of defining management roles. Future research comparing Mintzberg's roles with the four functions of management will continue to expand our understanding of the manager's job.

they discuss and bargain with other groups to gain advantages for their own units. (If you want to learn more about managers' roles, see Details on a Management Classic.)

Are Effective Managers Also Successful Managers?

Fred Luthans and his associates looked at the issue of what managers do from a somewhat different perspective.[14] They asked whether managers who advance most quickly in an organization do the same activities and with the same emphasis as those managers who do the best job? You would tend to think that those managers who were the most effective in their jobs would also be the ones who were promoted the fastest. But that's not what appears to happen.

Luthans and his associates studied more than 450 managers. What they found was that these managers all engaged in four managerial activities.

- **1.** *Traditional management.* Decision making, planning, and controlling
- **2.** *Communication.* Exchanging routine information and processing paperwork
- **3.** *Human resource management.* Motivating, disciplining, managing conflict, staffing, and training
- **4.** *Networking.* Socializing, politicking, and interacting with outsiders

The managers studied spent 32 percent of their time in traditional management activities, 29 percent communicating, 20 percent in human resource management activities, and 19 percent networking. However, the amount of time and effort that different managers spent on these four activities varied a great deal. Specifically, as shown in Exhibit 1-6, managers who were successful (defined in terms of the speed of promotion within their organization) had a very different emphasis than managers who were effective (defined in terms of the quantity and quality of their performances and the satisfaction and commitment of their subordinates). Networking made the biggest relative contribution to the successful managers' success, while human resource management activities made the least relative contribution. Among effective managers, communication made the largest relative contribution and networking the least.

The Luthans study adds several important insights to our knowledge of what managers do. On average, managers spend approximately 20 to 30 percent of their time on each of the four activities of traditional management, communication, human resource management, and networking. However, successful managers do not give the same emphasis to activities as do effective managers. In fact, they do almost the opposite. This study challenges the historical assumption that promotions are based on performance and vividly illustrates the importance that social and political skills play in getting ahead in organizations.

Is the Manager's Job Universal?

Previously, we mentioned the universal applicability of management functions. So far, we have discussed management as if it were a generic activity. That is, a manager is a

Exhibit 1-6
Distribution of Time per Activity by Average, Successful, and Effective Managers

Source: Based on *Real Managers* by F. Luthans, R.M. Hodgetts, and S.A. Rosenkrantz. Copyright © 1988 by Ballinger Publishing Company. Reprinted by permission of HarperCollins Publishers Inc.

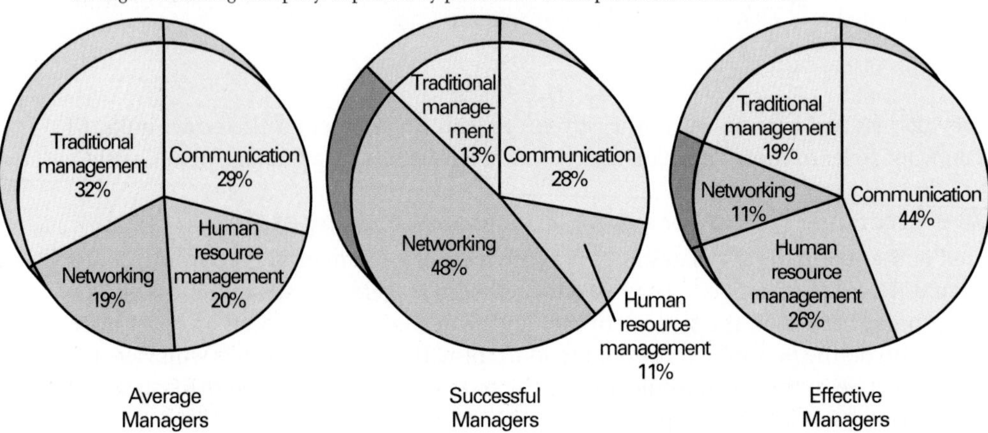

manager regardless of where he or she manages. If management is truly a generic discipline, then what a manager does should be essentially the same regardless of whether he or she is a top-level executive or a first-line supervisor; in a business firm or a government agency; in a large corporation or a small business; or located in Paris, France, or Paris, Texas. Let's take a closer look at the generic issue.

We have already acknowledged that the importance of managerial roles varies depending on the manager's level in the organization. But the fact that a supervisor in a research laboratory at Merck Pharmaceuticals doesn't do exactly the same things that the president of Merck does should not be interpreted to mean that their jobs are inherently different. The differences are of degree and emphasis but not of function.

Managers must possess conceptual, human, technical, and political competencies.

In functional terms, as managers move up the organization, they do more planning and less direct overseeing of others. This distinction is visually depicted in Exhibit 1-7. All managers, regardless of level, make decisions. They perform planning, organizing, leading, and controlling functions. But the amount of time they give to each function is not necessarily constant. In addition, the content of the managerial functions changes with the manager's level. For example, as we will demonstrate in Chapter 7, top managers are concerned with designing the overall organization's structure, whereas lower-level managers focus on designing the jobs of individuals and work groups.

Even though we recognize that all managers perform some degree of the four basic functions of management, a more crucial question becomes, What are the critical areas that are related to managerial competence? In the 1970s, management researcher Robert L. Katz attempted to answer that question.[15] What Katz and others have found is that successful managers must possess four critical competencies. These are conceptual, human, technical, and political capabilities.

Conceptual competencies refer to one's mental ability to coordinate all of the organization's interests and activities. **Human competencies** address the manager's ability to work with, understand, and motivate other people. **Technical competencies** require one to use the tools, procedures, and techniques of a specialized field. Finally, **political competencies** refer to one's ability to enhance one's power, build a power base, and establish the "right" connections. Undoubtedly, as we are becoming more "skills-oriented" in our pursuit of organizational goals, it becomes clear that possessing and demonstrating these skills are important to one's success as a manager. (To find out whether you might be management material, see Understanding Yourself.)

Two final perspectives need to be considered regarding what managers do. They are: Managers make decisions, and managers are agents of change. Almost everything

conceptual competencies A manager's mental ability to coordinate all of the organization's interests and activities.

human competencies A manager's ability to work with, understand, and motivate other people.

technical competencies A manager's ability to use the tools, procedures, and techniques of a specialized field.

political competencies A manager's ability to build a power base and establish the "right" connections.

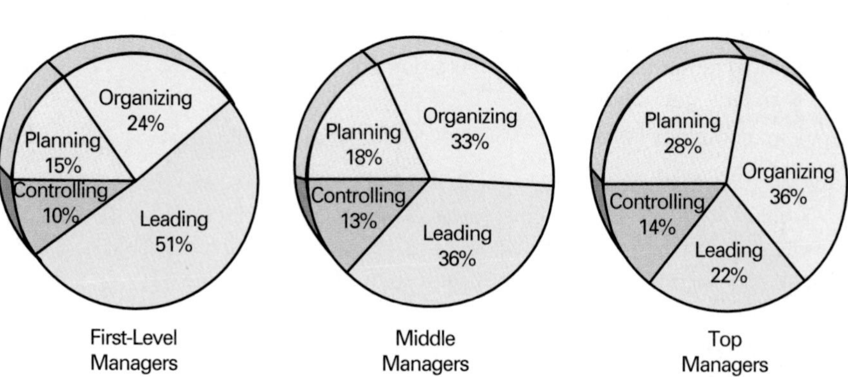

Exhibit 1-7
Distribution of Time per Function by Organizational Level

Source: Adapted from T. A. Mahoney, T. H. Jerdee, and S. J. Carroll, "The Job(s) of Management," *Industrial Relations* 4, No. 2 (1965), p. 103.

Understanding Yourself

Are You Management Material?

Managing in organizations is different today than at any time in organizational history. Although many want to manage because of the excitement, status, power, or rewards, managing is not something that comes automatically; it requires certain skills and competencies as well as a desire to manage.

Below are twenty questions designed to provide insight into your aptitude for management. Rate each question according to the following scale:

ML = *Most like me* SU = *Somewhat unlike me*
SL = *Somewhat like me* MU = *Most unlike me*
NS = *Not sure*

	ML	SL	NS	SU	MU
1. I can get others to do what I want them to do.	ML	SL	NS	SU	MU
2. I frequently evaluate my job performance.	ML	SL	NS	SU	MU
3. I prefer not to get involved in office politics.	ML	SL	NS	SU	MU
4. I like the freedom that open-ended goals provide me.	ML	SL	NS	SU	MU
5. I work best when things are orderly and calm.	ML	SL	NS	SU	MU
6. I enjoy making oral presentations to groups of people.	ML	SL	NS	SU	MU
7. I am confident in my abilities to accomplish difficult tasks.	ML	SL	NS	SU	MU
8. I don't like to write.	ML	SL	NS	SU	MU
9. I like solving difficult puzzles.	ML	SL	NS	SU	MU
10. I am an organized person.	ML	SL	NS	SU	MU
11. I have difficulty telling others they made a mistake.	ML	SL	NS	SU	MU
12. I like to work set hours each day.	ML	SL	NS	SU	MU
13. I view paperwork as a trivial task.	ML	SL	NS	SU	MU
14. I like to help others learn new things.	ML	SL	NS	SU	MU
15. I prefer to work alone.	ML	SL	NS	SU	MU
16. I believe it's who you know, not what you know, that counts.	ML	SL	NS	SU	MU
17. I enjoy doing several things at once.	ML	SL	NS	SU	MU
18. I am good at managing money.	ML	SL	NS	SU	MU
19. I would rather back down from an argument than let it get out of hand.	ML	SL	NS	SU	MU
20. I am computer-literate.	ML	SL	NS	SU	MU

Scoring: For statements 1, 2, 4, 6, 7, 9, 10, 11, 13, 14, 16, 17, 18, and 20, give yourself 5 points for every ML; 4 points for SL; 3 points for NS; 2 points for SU; and 1 point for MU. For statements 3, 5, 8, 12, 15, and 19, reverse the scoring. That is, give yourself 1 point for each ML, 2 points for SL, and so on. Total your score.

What the Assessment Means: In this assessment, a total of 100 points is possible. A score ranging between 80 and 100 demonstrates that you may possess many of the skills and competencies that successful managers need. It also may indicate that you have a high desire to manage others. A score between 40 and 79 indicates that you may have some of the skills and competencies to manage successfully, but you need some fine-tuning. Learning new management skills and experiencing "managing" techniques may serve you well. A score below 40 indicates that your management skills are dormant or that you have a low desire to manage others. Someone in this category who wants to manage should pay particular attention to the management skills, competencies, and techniques in which he or she feels weakest.

Source: The idea for this assessment came, in part, from J. B. Miner and N. R. Smith, "Decline and Stabilization of Managerial Motivation Over a 20-Year Period," *Journal of Applied Psychology,* June 1982, p. 298.

managers do requires them to make decisions. Whether it involves setting goals in the organization, deciding how to structure jobs, determining how to motivate and reward employees, or determining where significant performance variances exist, a manager must make a decision. The best managers, then, are the ones who can identify critical problems, assimilate the appropriate data, make sense of the information, and decide the best course of action to take for resolving the problem.

Organizations today also operate in a world of dynamic change. Managing chaos has become the rule—not the exception. Successful managers acknowledge the rapid changes around them and are flexible in adapting their practices to deal with those changes. For instance, successful managers recognize the importance technological improvements can have on a work unit's performance. But they also realize that people often resist change. Accordingly, managers need to be in a position to "sell" the benefits of the change while, simultaneously, helping their employees deal with the uncertainty and anxiety that the changes may bring. This example illustrates how managers act as agents of change. We'll look at this change phenomenon in greater detail in Chapter 9.

Is Managing the Same in Profit and Not-for-Profit Organizations?

Does a manager who works for the U.S. Internal Revenue Service, the Canadian Armed Forces, or the Goodwill Industries do the same things that a manager in a business firm does? Put another way, is the manager's job the same in both profit and not-for-profit organizations? The answer is, for the most part, Yes.[16] Regardless of the type of organization a manager works in, the job has commonalities with all other managerial positions. All managers make decisions, set objectives, create workable organization structures, hire and motivate employees, secure legitimacy for their organization's existence, and develop internal political support in order to implement programs. Of course, there are some noteworthy differences. The most important is measuring performance. Profit, or the "bottom line," acts as an unambiguous measure of the effectiveness of a business organization. There is no such universal measure in not-for-profit organizations. Measuring the performance of schools, museums, government agencies, or charitable organizations, therefore, is more difficult. But don't interpret this difference to mean that managers in those organizations can ignore the financial side of their operation. Even not-for-profit organizations need to make money to survive. It's just that making a profit for the "owners" of not-for-profit organizations is not the primary focus. Consequently, managers in these organizations generally do not face a profit-maximizing market test for performance.

Our conclusion is that, while there are distinctions between the management of profit and not-for-profit organizations, the two are far more alike than they are different. They are similarly concerned with planning, organizing, leading, and controlling.

Is the Manager's Job Any Different in a Small Organization Than in a Large One?

Would you expect the job of a manager in a print shop that employs twelve people to be different from that of a manager who runs a 1,200-person printing plant for the *New York Times?* This question is best answered by looking at the job of managers in small business firms and comparing them with our previous discussion of managerial roles. First, however, let's define small business and the part it plays in our society.

small business
Any independently owned and operated profit-seeking enterprise that has fewer than 500 employees.

There is no commonly agreed-upon definition of a small business because of different criteria used to define *small.* For example, an organization can be classified as a **small business** using such criteria as number of employees, annual sales, or total assets. For our purposes, we will call a small business any independently owned and operated profit-seeking enterprise that has fewer than 500 employees. Small businesses may be little in size, but they have a major effect in world economy. Statistics tell us that small businesses account for about 97 percent of all nonfarm businesses in the United States; they employ over 60 percent of the private work force; they dominate such industries as retailing and construction; and they will generate half of all new jobs during the next decade. Moreover, small businesses are where the job growth has been in recent years. Between 1980 and 1995, Fortune 100 companies cut several million jobs. But companies with fewer than 500 employees have created more than 20 million jobs.[17] This phenomenon is not confined solely to the United States. Similar small business start-ups have been witnessed in such countries as China, Japan, and Great Britain.[18]

Now to the question at hand: Is the job of managing a small business different from that of managing a large one? A study comparing the two found that the importance of roles differed significantly.[19] As illustrated in Exhibit 1-8, the small business manager's most important role is that of spokesperson. The small business manager spends a large amount of time doing such outwardly directed things as meeting with customers, arranging financing with bankers, searching for new opportunities, and stimulating change. In contrast, the most important concerns of a manager in a large organization are directed internally—toward deciding which organizational units get what available resources and how much of them. According to this study, the entrepreneurial role—looking for business opportunities and planning activities for performance improvement—is least important to managers in large firms.

Tomina Edmark, owner of Topsy Tails in Dallas, Texas, has built a $35 million company that sells, among other products, a device that flips ponytails inside out. She and her three employees continuously look for new products that they can make and sell through the mail—including the Topsy Tail doll and their two-piece hair bow.

Compared with a manager in a large organization, a small business manager is more likely to be a generalist. His or her job will combine the activities of a large corporation's chief executive with many of the day-to-day activities undertaken by a first-line supervisor. Moreover, the structure and formality that characterize a manager's job in a large organization tend to give way to informality in

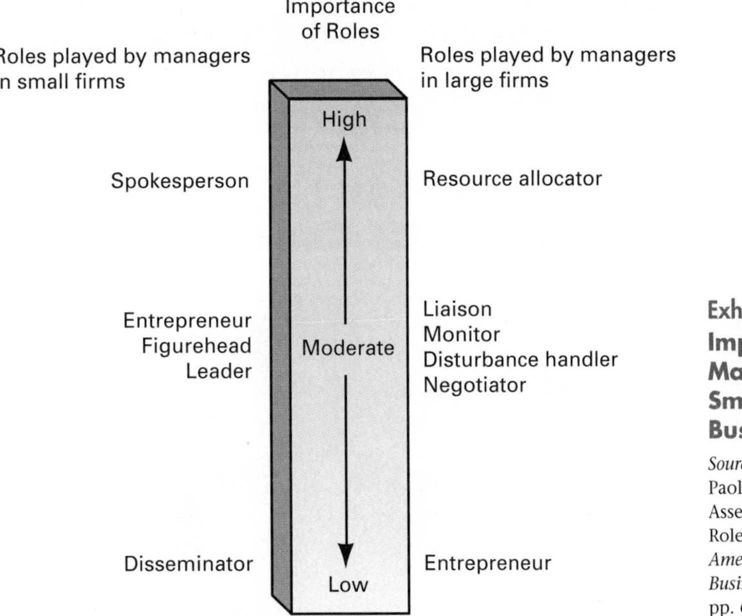

Exhibit 1-8
Importance of Managerial Roles in Small and Large Businesses

Source: Adapted from J. G. P. Paolillo, "The Manager's Self Assessments of Managerial Roles: Small vs. Large Firms," *American Journal of Small Business,* January–March 1984, pp. 61–62.

small firms. Planning is less likely to be a carefully orchestrated ritual. The organization's design will be less complex and structured. And control in the small business will rely more on direct observation than on sophisticated computerized monitoring systems.[20]

Again, as with organizational level, we see differences in degree and emphasis, but not in function. Managers in both small and large organizations perform essentially the same activities; only how they go about them and the proportion of time they spend on each are different.

Are Management Concepts Transferable across National Borders?

If managerial concepts were completely generic, they would also apply universally in any country in the world, regardless of economic, social, political, or cultural differences. Studies that have compared managerial practices between countries have not generally supported the universality of management concepts.[21] In Chapter 2, we will examine some specific differences between countries and describe their effect on managing. At this point, it is sufficient to say that most of the concepts we will be discussing in future chapters primarily apply to the United States, Canada, Great Britain, Australia, and other English-speaking democracies. We should be prepared to modify these concepts if we want to apply them in India, China, Chile, or other countries whose economic, political, social, or cultural environment differs greatly from that of the so-called free-market democracies (see Managers Who Made a Difference).

How Much Importance Does the Marketplace Put on Managers?

Good managers can turn straw to gold. Poor managers can do the reverse. This realization has not been lost on those who design compensation systems for organizations. Managers tend to be more highly paid than operatives. As a manager's authority and

Managers Who Made a Difference

MILTON KIM OF SSANGYONG INVESTMENT & SECURITIES COMPANY

Milton Kim is the managing director of Ssangyong Investment & Securities Company in Seoul, Korea.[22] The firm is part of one of South Korea's most profitable conglomerates. In fact, the organization was tied with Daewoo Securities as the top brokerage firm in terms of foreign revenue. How did Ssangyong achieve this distinction? In many respects, it was through Milton Kim's sound managerial skills and willingness to implement changes.

Kim is often regarded as being radical for his introduction of Western management practices. Milton advocates competition, innovation and risk, and performance pay for solid performers. And even though his record speaks for itself, he has recognized that it is difficult to bring change in his organization when colleagues see no need for change. For example, Milton Kim believes that the best workers should be promoted—irrespective of gender. So "if a woman is capable and aggressive and willing to make a career out of this business," he makes every effort to hire her. Kim also recognizes that, for an organization to be successful, employees need to be rewarded. For him, that means implementing merit-based career promotions and incentive-driven wages.

Many of the business practices Milton Kim advocates appear commonplace in Western cultures. But in Seoul, Korea, they are not. Rather, Seoul's culture is one of egalitarianism, consensus-building, and compromise. What Milton Kim has done is to attempt to find those things in Western management that may work well and to find a way to implement them. Of course, showing organizational members how these concepts will improve their overall situation and being patient in their implementation are generating positive results.

responsibility expand, so typically does his or her pay. Moreover, many organizations willingly offer extremely lucrative compensation packages to get and keep good managers.

If you were privy to the compensation paid employees at such large toy-manufacturing firms such as Mattel and Fisher Price, you would discover an interesting fact. Their best sales associates rarely earn more than $95,000 a year. In contrast, the annual income of their senior managers is rarely less than $225,000, and, in some cases, it may exceed $750,000. The fact that these firms pay their managers considerably more than their nonmanagers is a measure of the importance placed on effective management skills. What is true at these toy-manufacturing firms is true in most organizations. Good managerial skills are a scarce commodity, and compensation packages are one measure of the value that organizations place on them.

Do All Managers Make Six-Figure Incomes?

Not all managers make six-figure incomes. Such salaries are usually reserved for senior executives. What, then, could you expect to earn as a manager? The answer depends on your level in the organization, your education and experience, the type of business the organization is in, comparable pay standards in the community, and how effective a manager you are. Most first-line supervisors earn between $25,000 and $50,000 a year. Middle managers often start near $35,000 and top out at around $110,000. Senior managers in large corporations can earn $1 million a year or more. In 1994, for instance, the average cash compensation (salary plus annual bonus) for chief executives at the 371 largest publicly held U.S. corporations was $2.8 million.[23] In many cases, this compensation was enhanced by other means. For instance, Linda Wachner earned $3.5 million in salary as the CEO of Warnaco and Authentic Fitness Corporation. But she made another $7.7 million from long-term incentives and stock options.[24] Management salaries reflect the market forces of supply and demand. Management superstars, like superstar athletes in professional sports, are wooed with signing bonuses, interest-free loans, performance incentive packages, and guaranteed contracts. Of course, as in the case of athletes, some controversy surrounds the large dollar amounts paid to these executives.[25]

Who is one of the highest paid women executives in organizations today? Linda Wachner, CEO of Warnaco and Authentic Fitness Corporation, whose 1996 salary exceeded $11 million.

Why Study Management?

Management, as an academic field of study, offers a number of insights into many aspects of our daily organizational lives. Consequently, there are several reasons why we may want to study this topic.

The first reason for studying management is that we all have a vested interest in improving the way organizations are managed. Why? Because we interact with them every day of our lives. Does it frustrate you when you have to spend a couple of hours in a Department of Motor Vehicles office to get your driver's license renewed? Are you perplexed when none of the salespeople in a department store seem interested in helping you? Are you angered when you call an airline three times and their representatives quote you three different prices for the same trip? As a taxpayer, doesn't it seem as if something is wrong when you read about companies that have overbilled the federal government for defense-related equipment? These are all examples of problems that can largely be attributed to poor management. Organizations that are well managed—such as Wal-Mart, Siemens, Southwest Airlines, Motorola, Merck Pharmaceuticals, Toys 'R' Us, and Ssangyong Investment and Securities Company—develop a loyal constituency, grow, and prosper. Those that are poorly managed often find themselves with a declining customer base and reduced revenues. Eventually, the survival of poorly managed organizations becomes threatened. Thirty years ago, Gimbels, W.T. Grant, and Eastern Airlines were thriving corporations. They employed tens of thousands of people and provided goods and services on a daily basis to hundreds of thousands of customers. But weak management did them in. Today those companies no longer exist.

The second reason for studying management is the reality that once you graduate from college and begin your career, you will either manage or be managed. For those who plan on careers in management, an understanding of the management process forms the foundation upon which to build their management skills. But it would be naive to assume that everyone who studies management is planning a career in management. A course in management may only be a requirement for a degree you want, but that needn't make the study of management irrelevant. Assuming that you will have to work for a living and recognizing that you will almost certainly work in an organization, you will be a manager or work for a manager. You can gain a great deal of insight into the way your boss behaves and the internal workings of organizations by studying management. The point is that you needn't aspire to be a manager to gain something valuable from a course in management.

How Do We Study Management?

Before the mid-twentieth century, a number of diversified approaches to management were suggested (see Appendix, p. A-1). In recent years, however, three integrative frameworks have evolved that can help you organize the subject matter of management. These are the process, systems, and contingency approaches.

What Is the Process Approach?

In December 1961, Professor Harold Koontz published an article in which he carefully detailed the diversity of approaches to the study of management—things such as functions, quantitative emphasis, human relations approaches—and concluded that there existed a "management theory jungle."[26] Koontz conceded that each of the diverse approaches had something to offer management theory, but he then proceeded to demonstrate that many were only tools to be used by managers. He felt that a **process approach** could encompass and synthesize the diversity of the day. The process approach, originally introduced by Henri Fayol, is based on the management functions we discussed earlier. The performance of these functions—planning, organizing, leading, and controlling—is seen as circular and continuous (see Exhibit 1-4, p. 8).

Although Koontz's article stimulated considerable debate, most management teachers and practitioners held fast to their own individual perspectives.[27] But Koontz had made a mark. The fact that most current management textbooks follow the process approach is evidence that it continues to be a viable integrative framework.

process approach
A conceptual framework to help organize the subject matter of management; based on the functions planning, organizing, leading, and controlling.

systems approach
A conceptual framework to help organize the subject matter of management that views an organization as a set of interrelated and interdependent parts arranged in a manner that produces a unified whole.

closed system
A system (or organization) that is not influenced by and does not interact with its environment.

open system
A system (or organization) that is influenced by and does interact with its environment.

How Can a Systems Approach Integrate Management Concepts?

The mid-1960s began a decade in which the idea that organizations could be analyzed in a systems framework gained a strong following. The **systems approach** defines a system as a set of interrelated and interdependent parts arranged in a manner that produces a unified whole. Societies are systems, and so too are computers, automobiles, organizations, and animal and human bodies.

There are two basic types of systems: closed systems and open systems. **Closed systems** are not influenced by and do not interact with their environment. In contrast, an **open systems** approach recognizes the dynamic interaction of the system with its environment (see Exhibit 1-9). Today, when we talk of organizations as systems, we mean open systems. That is, we acknowledge the organization's constant interaction with its environment.

An organization (and its management) is a system that interacts with and depends upon its environment. In management terms, we call this relationship dealing

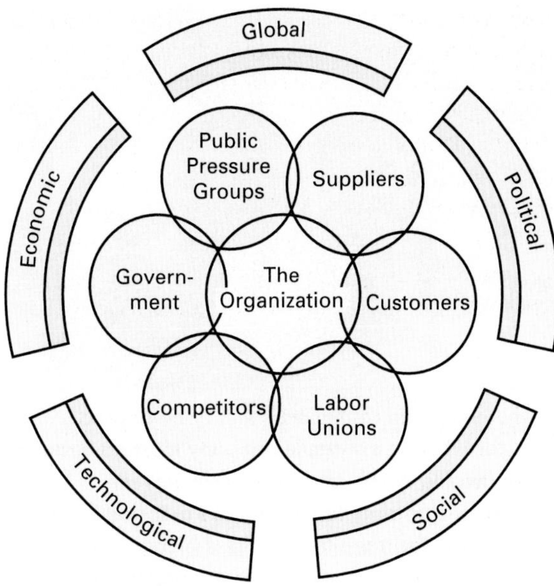

Exhibit 1-9
The Organization and Its Environment

with the organization's stakeholders. **Stakeholders** represent any group that is affected by organizational decisions and policies. These can include government agencies, labor unions, competing organizations, employees, suppliers, customers and clients, local community leaders, or public interest groups. The manager's job is to coordinate all these parts in an effort to achieve the organization's goals. For example, most organizational members realize that customers are the lifelines of organizations. But bringing a new product to market without first ensuring that it is needed, and desired, by customers could lead to disaster. Failing to anticipate what customers want can lead to a reduction in revenues. As a result, there may be less financial resources to pay wages and taxes, buy new equipment, or repay loans. The systems approach recognizes that such relationships exist and that management must understand them and the potential constraints that they may impose.

stakeholders
Any group that is affected by organizational decisions and policies.

The systems approach also recognizes that organizations do not operate in isolation. Instead, organizational survival often depends on successful interactions with the external environment.[28] These include economic conditions, the global marketplace, political activities, technological advancements, and social customs. Ignoring any of these over a long period of time can have a detrimental effect on the organization.

Organizational survival often depends on successful interactions with the external environment.

What Is a Contingency Approach to the Study of Management?

Management, like life itself, is not based on simplistic principles. Health insurance companies know that not all people have the same probability of becoming seriously ill. Factors such as age, fitness, and the use of alcohol or tobacco products are contingencies that influence one's health. Similarly, you cannot say that students always learn less in a course using computer-based software than in one where a professor holds weekly classes. An extensive body of research tells us that contingency factors such as course content and the way in which individuals learn influence learning effectiveness.

contingency approach A conceptual framework to help organize the subject matter of management; recognizes differences among organizations and categorizes variables that affect an organization's performance. Sometimes called situational approach.

In what ways can contingency theory be applied? Consider what an insurance company must go through in determining health insurance premiums for employees. Knowing the health risks associated with smoking and the more-frequent and higher medical costs for smokers, many health insurance companies charge one rate for insurance premiums for those employees who do not smoke and another, higher, rate for those who do smoke.

The **contingency approach** (sometimes called the *situational approach*) has been used in recent years to replace simplistic principles of management and to integrate much of management theory.[29] A contingency approach to the study of management is intuitively logical. Since organizations are diverse—in size, objectives, tasks being done, and the like—it would be surprising to find that there would be universally applicable principles that would work in all situations. But, of course, it is one thing to say "It all depends" and another to say what it depends upon. Advocates of the contingency approach—a group that includes most management researchers and practitioners—have been trying to identify the "what" variables. Exhibit 1-10 describes four popular contingency variables. This list is not comprehensive—there are at least 100 different variables that have been identified—but it represents those most widely used and gives you an idea of what we mean by the term *contingency variable.*

Exhibit 1-10
Four Popular Contingency Variables

Organization size. The number of people in an organization is a major influence on what managers do. As size increases, so do the problems of coordination. For instance, the type of organization structure appropriate for an organization of 50,000 employees is likely to be inefficient for an organization of fifty employees.

Routineness of task technology. In order for an organization to achieve its purpose, it uses technology; that is, it engages in the process of transforming inputs into outputs. Routine technologies require organizational structures, leadership styles, and control systems that differ from those required by customized or nonroutine technologies.

Environmental uncertainty. The degree of uncertainty caused by political, technological, sociocultural, and economic changes influences the management process. What works best in a stable and predictable environment may be totally inappropriate in a rapidly changing and unpredictable environment.

Individual differences. Individuals differ in terms of their desire for growth, autonomy, tolerance for ambiguity, and expectations. These and other individual differences are particularly important when managers select motivational techniques, leadership styles, and job designs.

Summary

How will I know if I fulfilled the Learning Objectives found on page 1? You will have fulfilled the Learning Objectives if you understand the following.

1. **Describe the difference between managers and operative employees.** Managers are individuals in an organization who direct the activities of others. They have such titles as supervisor, department head, dean, division manager, vice president, president, and chief executive officer. Operatives are nonmanagerial personnel. They work directly on a job or task and have no responsibility for overseeing the work of others.
2. **Explain what is meant by the term *management*.** Management refers to the process of getting activities completed efficiently with and through other people. The process represents the functions or primary activities of planning, organizing, leading, and controlling.
3. **Differentiate between efficiency and effectiveness.** Efficiency is concerned with minimizing resource costs in the completion of activities. Effectiveness is concerned with getting activities successfully completed—that is, goal attainment.
4. **Describe the four basic functions of management.** The four basic functions of management are planning (setting goals), organizing (determining how to achieve the goals), leading (motivating employees), and controlling (monitoring activities).
5. **Classify the three levels of managers and identify the primary responsibility of each group.** The three levels of management are first-line supervisors, middle managers, and top managers. First-line supervisors are the lowest level of management and are responsible for directing the day-to-day activities of operative employees. Middle managers represent the levels of management between the first-line supervisor and top management. These individuals—who manage other managers and possibly some operative employees—are typically responsible for translating the goals set by top management into specific details that lower-level managers can perform. Top managers, at or near the pinnacle of the organization, are responsible for making decisions about the direction of the organization and establishing policies that affect all organizational members.
6. **Identify the roles performed by managers.** Henry Mintzberg concluded that managers perform ten different roles or behaviors. He classified them into three sets. One set is concerned with interpersonal relationships (figurehead, leader, liaison). The second set is related to the transfer of information (monitor, disseminator, spokesperson). The third set deals with decision making (entrepreneur, disturbance handler, resource allocator, negotiator).
7. **Describe the four skills necessary for becoming a successful manager.** Fred Luthans and his associates found that successful managers—those who got promoted most quickly—emphasized networking activities over human resource management skills. In contrast, effective managers—those who performed best—emphasized communication. This finding suggests the importance of social and political skills in getting ahead in organizations.
8. **Explain whether the manager's job is generic.** Management has several generic properties. Regardless of level in an organization, all managers perform the same four functions; however, the emphasis given to each function varies with the manager's position in the hierarchy. Similarly, for the most part, the manager's job is the same regardless of the type of organization he or she is in. The generic properties of management are found mainly in the world's English-speaking democracies. One should be careful in assuming that management practices are universally transferable outside so-called free-market democracies.
9. **Describe the value of studying management.** People in all walks of life have come to recognize the important role that good management plays in our society. For those who aspire to managerial positions, the study of management provides the body of knowledge that will help them to be effective managers. For those who do not plan on careers in management, the study of management can give them considerable insight into the way their bosses behave and into the internal activities of organizations.
10. **Explain the process, systems, and contingency approaches to the study of management.** All three approaches seek to integrate management concepts. The process approach was proposed as a way to synthesize what managers do by presenting management around the functions of planning, organizing, leading, and controlling. The systems ap-

proach recognizes the interdependency of internal activities in the organization and between the organization and its external environment. The contingency approach isolates situational variables that affect managerial actions and organizational performance.

Review & Discussion Questions

1. What is an organization? Why are managers important to an organization's success?
2. Are all effective organizations also efficient? Discuss. If you had to choose between being effective or being efficient (although both are needed), which one would you select? Why?
3. What four common functions do all managers perform? Briefly describe each of them.
4. Contrast the four functions of management with Henry Mintzberg's ten roles.
5. What are the four managerial activities identified by Luthans? Contrast the emphasis placed on these four activities by average, successful, and effective managers.
6. How does a manager's job change with his or her level in the organization?
7. Is your college instructor a manager? Discuss in terms of both Fayol's managerial functions and Mintzberg's managerial roles.
8. In what ways would the activities of an owner of a bicycle repair shop that employs two people and the president of Schwinn Bicycle's job be similar? In what ways would they be different?
9. Some individuals today have the title of project leader. They manage projects of various size and duration and must coordinate the talents of many people to accomplish their goals. But none of the workers on their projects report directly to them. Can these project leaders really be considered managers if they have no employees over whom they have direct authority? Discuss.
10. How is the process approach to management an integrative approach?
11. Explain what is meant by the term *contingency approach,* and describe how practicing managers can benefit by using it.

Testing Your Comprehension • • • 

Circle the correct answer, then check yourself on page AK-1.

1. An organization is commonly considered a
   a) systematic arrangement of people to sell goods or services
   b) structural grouping of people to accomplish a set of objectives
   c) structural grouping of managers and subordinates who are attempting to increase profits
   d) systematic grouping of people to establish procedures, rules, and regulations

2. Operatives can BEST be described as
   a) those who actually do the tasks of an organization
   b) those who work anonymously behind the scenes
   c) manual laborers
   d) those who supervise others

3. Which one of the following titles is usually associated with a middle manager position?
   a) receptionist/typist
   b) chairperson of the board
   c) dean of students at a state university
   d) chief financial officer

4. Management is BEST described as the process of
   a) personally completing tasks in an efficient manner
   b) efficiently completing tasks with the help of others
   c) using scarce resources to minimize output
   d) organizing activities over a long period of time

5. When managers perform management functions such as organizing and planning, they are applying the teachings of
   a) Henry Mintzberg
   b) Henri Fayol
   c) Milton Kim
   d) Carol Bartz

6. The managerial concept that focuses on task completion is
   a) efficiency
   b) of little concern for first-line managers
   c) mostly the job of top managers
   d) effectiveness

7. Which one of the following BEST demonstrates the concept of efficient management?
   a) getting activities completed
   b) maximizing output
   c) maintaining output with fewer resources
   d) increasing output and input

8. When a manager fails to complete the department's tasks but has used the resources sparingly and wisely, the results are said to be
   a) efficient and effective
   b) efficient and ineffective
   c) inefficient and effective
   d) inefficient and ineffective

9. The planning function of management includes
   a) directing the activities of others
   b) monitoring an organization's performance
   c) comparing actual results with plans
   d) establishing an organization's goals

10. The organizing function of management includes
    a) how tasks are to be grouped
    b) conflict resolution among subordinates
    c) comparison of actual results with a budget
    d) definition of an organization's goals

Continued

11. The activities of motivating employees, directing others, selecting the most effective communication channels, and resolving conflicts refer to which management function?
    a) planning
    b) organizing
    c) leading
    d) controlling

12. When a famous speaker, such as the President of the United States, addresses a college graduating class, he or she is exhibiting Mintzberg's role of
    a) liaison
    b) disturbance handler
    c) disseminator
    d) figurehead

13. When Lisa Wilson, the sales manager of Acme Corporation, reviews actual sales and compares them with the annual forecast, she is demonstrating the management function of
    a) planning
    b) leading
    c) controlling
    d) organizing

14. Concerning Mintzberg's managerial roles, which of the following statements is MOST accurate?
    a) Managers perform essentially different roles in different types of organizations.
    b) Managers perform essentially different roles at different levels of an organization.
    c) The emphasis managers give the various roles differs with various organizational levels.
    d) Roles of figurehead, disseminator, and liaison seem to be most appropriate for first-line managers.

15. Which of the following statements is MOST correct?
    a) Decisions in public organizations reflect political considerations, whereas business decisions are politically neutral.
    b) Both public and business organizations have essentially the same managerial functions.
    c) Managers in public organizations are constrained by procedures, but business decision makers rarely have procedural constraints.
    d) Compared with their business counterparts, public employees are more security-driven than involved with their work.

16. Which of the following statements is LEAST accurate?
    a) Regardless of the organizational level, managers perform essentially the same functions.
    b) Most managerial functions are the same throughout the world.
    c) Small or large organizations perform essentially the same functions.
    d) The entrepreneurial role is more prevalent in small organizations than in large ones.

17. Which of the following would not be considered a stakeholder of an organization?
    a) retired employees of an organization
    b) customers
    c) fluctuations of the U.S. dollar
    d) public pressure groups

18. The view that management involves recognizing and responding to variables as they arise is known as the
    a) systems approach
    b) functional approach
    c) process approach
    d) contingency approach

Applying the Concepts

A New Beginning

One of the more unnerving aspects of beginning a new semester is gaining an understanding of what is expected in each class.[30] By now, your instructor has probably provided you with a course syllabus, which gives you some necessary information about how the class will function. Understandably, this information is important to you. Yet, there is another component: giving your instructor some indication of what you want or expect from the class. Specifically, there are some data that can be useful for providing insight into your taking this class. To collect these data, you will need to answer some questions. First, take out a piece of paper and place your name at the top; then respond to the following:

1. What do I want from this course?
2. Why is this class important to me?
3. How does this course fit into my career plans?
4. How do I like an instructor to "run" the class?
5. What is my greatest challenge in taking this class?

When you have finished answering these questions, pair up with another class member (preferably someone you do not already know) and exchange papers. Get to know one another (using the information on these sheets as a starting point). Prepare an introduction of your partner, and share your partner's responses to the five questions with the class and your instructor.

Take It to the Net

We invite you to visit the Robbins/De Cenzo page on the Prentice Hall Web site at:

http://www.prenhall.com/robbinsfom

for this chapter's World Wide Web exercise.

You can also visit the Web sites for these companies and agencies featured within this chapter:

Allied Signal
http://www.alliedsignal.com

Autodesk Inc.
http://www.autodesk.com.au/

Daewoo Securities
http://www.dwe.co.kr/emain.htm

Federal Aviation Administration
http://www.faa.com

Good Will Industries
http://www.goodwill.org

Harley Davidson
http://harleydavidson.com

Montreal Canadiens Hockey Team
http://www.nhl.com/teampage/mon

Ssangyong Investment and Securities Company
http://tfsys.co.kr/musso/ssang.html

Taco Bell
http://vcomm.net/~smartax/tacobell

U.S. Internal Revenue Service
http://www.irs.ustreas.gov

Thinking Critically

Making a Value Judgment: Telling the Truth

A college instructor might find it difficult to change the value systems of students, but he or she can teach students how to analyze situations so that they can be better prepared to deal with decisions they will make that require moral judgments. By the time you reach college, you undoubtedly have an idea of what you would do in a given situation and what behaviors are unacceptable to you. You have a sense of what is right and what is wrong. But are you as comfortable with your actions when right and wrong are not clear-cut and you have to do something in that proverbial "gray zone"? Do you live by a rule of "Do unto others as you would have them do unto you"? Or do you ask yourself several questions like the following before you take some action: How would I feel about explaining what I did to my family? How would I feel if my decisions were described, in detail, on the front page of my local newspaper? Is there an appearance of a conflict of interest in my decision?

Let's begin our look at ethical dilemmas in management by asking: Is it wrong to withhold information? A manager communicates with members in the organization. Occasionally, the facts that the manager must transmit and explain are not particularly pleasant. This situation presents the dilemma of whether it is unethical to withhold information.

For example, assume that one of your employees has just been diagnosed with a treatable form of cancer. He has confided in you about the status of his health. He has also asked you not to say a word to anyone because he considers his health to be a personal matter. Over the next few months, this employee is absent frequently, especially during his radiation treatments. His absences are not a major problem because some of his duties involve direct computer work, which he can do while at home and forward electronically to appropriate people in the organization. However, your employees are wondering what's wrong. Many have come to you to find out. You simply, and politely, decline to discuss the issue about this employee. However, a number of them think that this individual is getting special treatment, and they are ready to go to your boss to complain. You know that if they only knew what was going on they would understand. But you cannot reveal the reason for his absence. On the other hand, if some employees begin to make trouble for this employee, they could create more problems for him. And that is something he doesn't need right now in his life.

Questions

1. Should you tell your employees the whole story regarding their coworker's absence? Why or why not?
2. Do you explain to your boss what's really going on? Discuss.
3. How would you handle this situation?

Making a Goal at TSI Soccer

Just how far can someone go with a great enthusiasm for the sport of soccer? For a select few, becoming a professional soccer player is the goal. For others, it is the love of the sport that encourages them to pass on their knowledge by coaching the next generation of soccer players. Evan Jones translated his knowledge of soccer into a successful business venture.[31]

Evan Jones was a good athlete—but his sport was tennis. In fact, his prowess on the tennis courts earned him a scholarship to Duke University. After earning an M.B.A. from Duke, Jones joined the firm of Prudential-Bache Capital Funding in New York City where he worked on corporate mergers and acquisitions. During his stay in Raleigh-Durham, Evan had frequent contact with a locally run soccer equipment mail-order business, Sports Endeavor. The organization was profitable, but he felt that Sports Endeavor was successful in spite of the owner's lack of management ability. Sports Endeavor was being run by a soccer fanatic—who hired individuals who shared the owner's love for the game and were soccer players but were often marginally qualified to properly meet customers' needs. Jones believed he could compete well against this company. He resigned from Prudential-Bache and returned to the Durham, North Carolina, area. There, he started the TSI Soccer Corporation.

He developed an outstanding business plan and used it to entice investors into his venture. In 1989, he rented space in a local warehouse, where he and his employees filled mail orders. Unlike his competitor, who has four persons serving as an executive management team and making decisions, Jones runs his company autocratically. He hires and trains each employee in how to do his or her job most efficiently—all the while stressing customer satisfaction. Although he doesn't require employees to be soccer players, he encourages them to keep on top of the sport by reading *Soccer America*, a magazine specializing in soccer issues.

He wants everyone in the organization to know what is "hot" in the sport and how the business may have to transform itself to reflect changing trends. For example, on the basis of such data, Jones feels that a mail-order soccer business alone is not enough to be successful in the future. He feels that, for the business to grow, it must expand into retail stores. By late 1995, Jones had opened four retail stores—two in Baltimore and two in Atlanta. He has set his sights on having twenty retail stores by 1998 in an effort to make the transition from a mail-order business to a national retail chain retailer with projected revenues of $40 million. Doing so will make him the number one soccer retailer in the United States. He is currently number two, one slot behind Sports Endeavor!

Questions

1. Describe how Evan Jones performs the four functions of management. Cite specific examples from the case.
2. What management roles did Jones "play" in starting TSI Soccer Corporation? Do you believe any of these roles have changed over the past few years in running a successful business? Explain.
3. Describe the management competencies Evan Jones must possess to become the number one soccer retailer in the United States. Give examples from the case.

Video Case ABCNEWS

Managing in the Federal Government

She tried to "make a difference" in the way the U.S. federal government operates and in the way the public perceive it. She championed change and inspired confidence both within and outside her department. Who is she? She's Hazel O'Leary—former Secretary of Energy in President Clinton's first administration. Although she managed only one department in the vast and cumbersome federal bureaucracy, O'Leary attempted to bring in a new look to the way her small corner of the government was managed.

Her main goal for managing the Department of Energy was to make sure that the department was accountable for what it accomplished. O'Leary also attempted to change the way the department does its work. She crusaded for opening the department's activities to the public. In the past, its work had been shrouded in secrecy. For example, O'Leary learned that her department had secretly carried out radiation experiments on Americans for nearly forty years. As she said, "To look in the eyes of one who clearly has been a victim or believes that he or she has clearly been a victim and to find those individuals shocked because anyone in government gives a damn is what drives me."

O'Leary recognized how important it is to be a visionary, dynamic leader. Soon after taking the position as Secretary of Energy, she told her senior staff to be prepared to change. She also told them to make plans for what changes needed to be made and how to bring about those changes. The type of dramatic change effort that O'Leary spearheaded meant negotiating with and bringing together dozens of departmental "fiefdoms" that would have preferred to keep things as they were. In "opening up" her Department of Energy, O'Leary also took her message beyond Washington, D.C. She talked to top scientists throughout the United States about the need to abandon weapons technology research and instead focus on finding ways to apply this expertise to the business world and peace-time applications.

Hazel O'Leary vividly demonstrated the varied roles that managers must play and the types of functions they must engage in as they get important activities completed effectively and efficiently with and through other people. She is a good example of the new look of management in the federal government.

Questions

1. How might Hazel O'Leary's former job managing the Department of Energy be similar to the job of an individual who manages in a for-profit organization? How might the jobs be different?
2. Which of Mintzberg's roles did you see O'Leary performing? Cite specific examples.
3. What management functions do you think O'Leary might have been engaging in as she attempted to change the Department of Energy? Discuss.

Source: "Hazel O'Leary: Person of the Week," *ABC World News Tonight,* January 28, 1994.

The Changing Face of Management

2

LEARNING OBJECTIVES

What will I be able to do after I finish this chapter?

1. **EXPLAIN** the importance of viewing management from a global perspective.
2. **DESCRIBE** how technology is changing the manager's job.
3. **DEFINE** social responsibility and social responsiveness.
4. **EXPLAIN** what is meant by the term *entrepreneurial spirit.*
5. **DESCRIBE** the management implications of a diversified work force.
6. **DEFINE** TQM and identify its five primary components.
7. **EXPLAIN** why corporations downsize.
8. **EXPLAIN** the increased popularity of managers' performing a coaching role and empowering their employees.
9. **DEFINE** ethics.
10. **DESCRIBE** why contemporary managers must be able to "thrive on chaos."

WHO WOULD YOU BELIEVE SELLS the most bikes in the New Haven, Connecticut, area? If you guessed Sears, K-Mart, or the local toy store you'd be wrong. The honor goes to Zane's Cycles, an independent bicycle shop run by its thirty-year-old founder, Chris Zane, who had sales of $1.2 million in 1995.[1] To many people, Chris Zane is the epitome of today's manager. Chris wanted to control his destiny by being his own boss. So he started his own business, and, from the beginning, had a vision of what he wanted the business to become. After mustering up the necessary resources to get the operation up and running, he entered into a highly competitive, and risky, retail venture. He understood, too, that being satisfied with any success today could lead to doom tomorrow. The interesting thing was that Chris began this process at the ripe old age of twelve!

As a young lad, Chris had an affinity for fixing bikes. He would help his friends, as well as grown-up neighbors, repair any problems they had with their bikes. By the time he was thirteen, his home repair business had grown to a $400 a week after-school hobby. He became the talk of the town and the most desired bike repair person in the area. By age sixteen, he wanted to expand his business and convinced his parents to sign for a loan that would allow him to open up a bike shop in town. Hiring his mother to run the "shop" while he was in school, Chris tended to the business every afternoon and on weekends.

Zane had a lot of faith in his ability to be successful. He knew, though, that to be successful he would have to take some risks. After all, a small bike shop competing against large retailers appeared to offer him little chance to survive. But Chris would not accept failure. He learned all he could in college about running a business—particularly focusing on satisfying customers and implementing new and creative techniques to achieve his goals. For instance, when two main competitors in town offered ninety-day warranties on bike sales and repairs, Zane offered a one-year warranty. When they matched him, he raised the ante—giving a lifetime guarantee on all transactions at the store. He will even come and pick up the bike at a customer's house. When those two competitors went out of business, he negotiated a deal with the phone company. He agreed to pay the remainder of the two companies' Yellow Page advertising. Callers to either of those numbers heard not only, "The number you are calling is no longer in service," but also, "If you are in need of a bicycle dealer, Zane's Cycles will be happy to serve you." By pressing zero, the caller is automatically transferred to Chris!

Amenities such as complimentary coffee and a juice bar at Zane's Cycles help create a positive shopping experience for customers. Chris Zane's creative management actions like this one have helped Zane's Cycles to increase revenues by more than 25 percent annually.

Even with fewer competitors, Zane realized he couldn't stop moving forward. He had to contend with the large discount retailers and a growing bicycle mail-order business. Chris recognized that he had to give the appearance of being a larger business—especially if he wanted to expand nationwide and possibly abroad. But he wanted to do so without hurting his "small" business appeal. To that end, he contracted with a marketing co-op firm to develop a thirty-two-page mail-order catalog. By using the co-op, Zane customized several pages specifically to his shop, while advertising and offering for sale many of the same items that other mail-order bike dealers do. And his newly installed computer tracking system can tell him precisely what zip code areas are producing the highest sales volumes.

Although his creativity had boosted sales, Zane recognized that most of his business came from customers who visited the shop. And he wanted them to feel special. Now, while customers browse, they can enjoy free refreshments at his in-store coffee and juice bar. Even the kids have a toy corner, so parents can shop at their own pace without being distracted. He has hired sales representatives and given them the freedom to make whatever decisions they need to please the customer and make a sale. But ringing up an "immediate" sale is not the primary focus. For example, Chris recognizes that, in his business, some customers feel nickled-and-dimed to death for having to purchase the most mundane things. So Chris does not charge for any item in his store that sells for less than $1. If customers need a bike part—a tire valve cap or a chain link—salespeople simply give it to them. The store also gives away cellular phones so bike riders can keep in touch with others or be prepared to make a call for assistance if needed.

Zane also believes that any successful business owes its success to the community that supports it. It's a relationship that must be nurtured. So, for example, when a Connecticut law was passed requiring helmets to be worn by all bicyclers, Zane supported the cause by selling his bike helmets to customers at cost. And to give even more back to the community, he established five $1000 annual scholarships for local high school students who wanted to go to college. Do these expenditures have a bearing on his success? You bet they do. For instance, he calculates that his "cheap parts" giveaway, lifetime warranties, and coffee and juice bar concept have resulted in a 700 percent return on his investment—and a committed and loyal clientele.

Chris Zane's bicycle business has been growing annually by more than 25 percent. By any definition that is success! Yet he's aware that competitors are carefully eyeing his success. Discount retailer Wal-Mart and Ski Market, a large sporting goods discount chain, have recently opened stores a few miles from Chris's shop, and both sell bikes. Is Chris scared? No! Given that "there will be more less-expensive bikes that will need to be fixed" in the community, he's shifting emphasis toward expanding his repair business.

A generation ago, successful managers valued stability, predictability, and efficiency achieved through economies of large size. But many of yesterday's stars—for instance, IBM and CBS—have faded because they did not adapt to what was happening around them. In Exhibit 2-1, we have identified the 1960s star and the current star in a number of industries.

What common factors characterize the stars of the 1990s? They are lean, fast, and flexible. They are dedicated to quality, organize work around teams, create ethical work environments, minimize hierarchical overhead, and, like Chris Zane, exhibit entrepreneurial skills when facing change.

Exhibit 2-1
Corporate Stars: 1960 Versus 1990

INDUSTRY	1960s STAR	1990s STAR
Airlines	Pan Am	Southwest
Automobiles	General Motors	Toyota
Broadcasting	CBS	CNN
Cameras	Bell & Howell	Minolta
Computers	IBM	Gateway 2000
Cosmetics	Revlon	L'Oreal
Credit cards	Visa	AT&T Universal
Film	Eastman Kodak	Fuji
General retailing	Sears	Wal-Mart
Information access	Local public library	America Online
Mail delivery	U.S. Post Office	Federal Express
Newspapers	*New York Times*	*USA Today*
Steel	USX (U.S. Steel)	Nucor Steel

In this chapter, we will establish a foundation for understanding this changing world of work. No successful organization, or its management, can operate without understanding and dealing with the dynamic environment that surrounds it. We will look at the forces that are causing organizations to change, what contemporary organizations are like, and how managers in these contemporary organizations are expected to act.

Forces of Change in the Environment

The histories of our 1960s stars in Exhibit 2-1 demonstrate that organizations that remain stagnant and highly bureaucratic are increasingly fading from the limelight. Why? Because one of the biggest problems in managing an organization today is trying to hold on to the past. Economies throughout the world are going through turbulent change. To better understand the current change, let us look back on the road we have taken.

One of the biggest problems in managing an organization today is trying to hold on to the past.

Futurist Alvin Toffler has written extensively about social change.[2] Classifying each period of social history, Toffler has argued that modern civilization has evolved over three "waves." With each wave came a new way of doing things. Some groups of people gained from the new way; others lost.

The first wave was driven by *agriculture,* which dominated work through the early 1890s. Individuals were their own boss and were responsible for performing a variety of tasks. Their success—or failure—was contingent on how well they produced.

Imagine if you were traveling and needed to take computer support with you. Twenty years ago, you would have had to take along something very similar to this IBM ES/9000 system. Today, technology makes it possible to do on a laptop computer what once took these large machines. Employees can be more efficient and have better and continuous computer access wherever they go. And they won't upset the passengers sitting next to them on the plane when they try to place their computer on the seat between them!

Industrialization, the second wave, began an unprecedented economic revolution near the start of the 1900s. Work left the fields and moved into formal organizations. The industrial wave forever changed the lives of skilled craftsmen. No longer did they grow something or produce a product in its entirety. Instead, workers were hired into tightly structured and formal workplaces. Mass production, specialized jobs, and authority relationships became the mode of operation. It gave rise to a new group of workers—the blue-collar industrial worker—individuals who were paid for performing routine work that relied almost exclusively on physical stamina. This industrial structure was successful. It paved the way for some countries, such as the United States and England, to become world leaders in manufacturing products such as steel, tires, and rubber. But the industrial wave, too, would pass.

By the start of the 1970s, the *information* wave was gaining momentum. Technological advancements were eliminating many low-skilled, blue-collar jobs. Moreover, the information wave was transforming society from a manufacturing focus to one of service. People were increasingly moving from jobs on the production floor to clerical, technical, and professional jobs. The economy needed software programmers, accountants, market researchers, and fast-food service workers.

As these waves influenced society, so too, have they affected how we do business (see Exhibit 2-2). International markets, technological improvements, changes in work force composition, and the like, are giving rise to new organizational issues. In the following section—as well as throughout this chapter—we will explore some of the more important forces that are creating challenges for contemporary managers.

Is There Global Competition?

Part of the rapidly changing environment that managers face is the globalization of business. Management is no longer constrained by national borders. BMW, a German-owned firm, builds cars in South Carolina. Similarly, McDonald's sells hamburgers in China. Exxon, a so-called American company, receives more than three-fourths of its revenues from sales outside the United States. Toyota makes cars in Kentucky; General Motors makes cars in Brazil. And the Maserati sports car is produced by Chrysler Corporation. Parts for Ford Motor Company's Crown Victoria come from all over the world: Mexico (seats, windshields, and fuel tanks), Japan (shock absorbers), Spain (electronic engine controls), Germany (antilock brake systems), and England (key axle parts). These examples illustrate that the world has become a **global village.** To be effective in this boundaryless world, managers need to adapt to cultures, systems, and techniques that are different from their own.

global village
Refers to the concept of a boundaryless world; the production and marketing of goods and services worldwide.

In the 1960s, Canada's prime minister described his country's proximity to the United States as analogous to sleeping with an elephant: "You feel every twitch the animal makes." In the 1990s, we can generalize this analogy to the entire world. A rise in interest rates in Japan, for example, instantly affects managers and organizations throughout the world. The fall of communism in Eastern Europe and the collapse of the Soviet Union created exciting opportunities for business firms throughout the free world.

International businesses have been with us for a long time. Siemens, Remington, and Singer, for instance, were selling their products in many countries in the nineteenth century. By the 1920s, some companies, including Fiat, Ford, Unilever, and Royal Dutch/Shell, had gone multinational. But it was not until the mid-1960s that **multinational corporations (MNCs)** became commonplace. These corporations—which maintain significant operations in two or more countries simultaneously but are based in one home country—initiated the rapid growth in international trade. To-

multinational corporations (MNCs)
Companies that maintain significant operations in two or more countries simultaneously but are based in one home country.

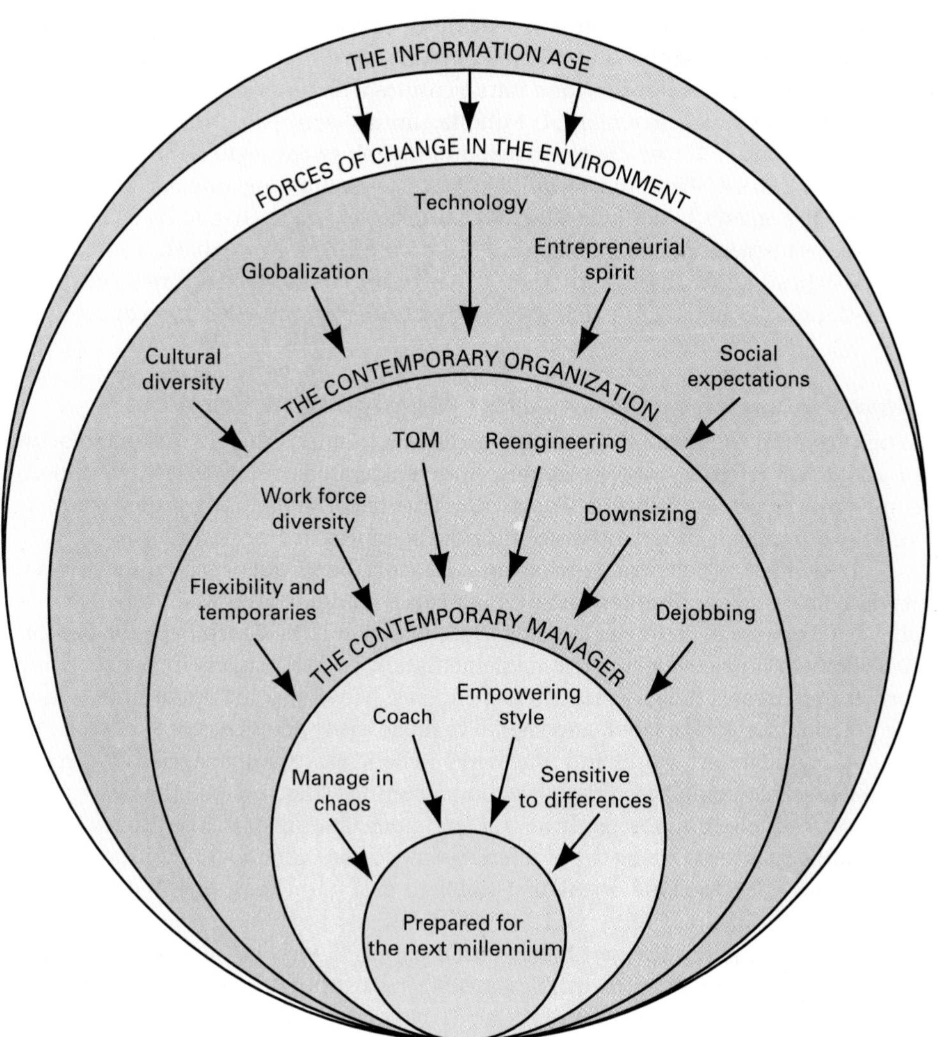

Exhibit 2-2
Forces of Change: The Environment, Organization, and Manager

day, companies such as Aflac, Mobil Oil, and Citicorp are among a growing number of firms that earn more than 60 percent of their revenues from foreign operations.[3]

The reach and goals of MNCs are being expanded to create an even more extensive organization—the **transnational corporation (TNC).** This type of organization does not seek to replicate its domestic successes by managing foreign operations from home. Instead, decisions in TNCs are made at the local level. Nationals (individuals born and raised in a specific country) typically are hired to run operations in each country. The products and marketing strategies for each country are tailored to that country's culture. Nestlé's, for example, is a transnational. With operations in almost every country on the globe, it is the world's largest food company, yet its managers match their products to their consumers. Nestlé's sells products in parts of Europe, for instance, that are not available in the United States or Latin America.

transnational corporation (TNC)
A company that maintains significant operations in more than one country simultaneously and decentralizes decision making in each operation to the local country.

How does an organization go global? One way is to simply export its products to foreign countries. Others are to hire foreign representatives or to contract with foreign manufacturers. In the clothing industry in the United States, this latter method is quite popular. Companies contract with foreign manufacturers and import the final goods back to the U.S. markets for retail sales. Another option for going global includes licensing or franchising a company's name or specialized process to another firm. Pharmaceutical companies and fast-food chains have found this option to be very profitable. Companies can also form joint ventures with firms in different lands. Many high-tech firms—such as Polaroid, Minolta, British Aerospace, Daimler Benz Aerospace, and France's Aerospatiale—have found the joint venture to be an excellent way to increase market share and to build synergy by combining valuable company resources. And Spain's CASA found the joint venture to be effective in its dealings with the European plane maker Airbus.[4] Finally, a company can establish a foreign subsidiary—either by purchasing an existing foreign firm or by starting a new one. Acura, a free-standing company fully owned by Honda, is an example of a foreign subsidiary.

How Does Globalization Affect Management Practices?

When you hear the name Whirlpool, what comes to mind? A large U.S. manufacturer of appliances such as washers, dryers, and refrigerators, right? That description is somewhat correct. But Whirlpool's activities are not confined to the United States. It is also the top manufacturer and distributor of appliances in Europe and Asia.[5]

In terms of the changing global environment, the spread of capitalism makes the world a smaller place. Business has new markets to conquer. And well-trained and reliable workers in such countries as Hungary, Slovakia, and the Czech Republic become a rich source of low-cost labor. The implementation of free markets in Eastern Europe further underscores the growing interdependence between countries of the world and the potential for goods, labor, and capital to move easily across national borders.

A boundaryless world introduces new challenges for managers. One specific challenge is managing in a different national culture. These include the views a manager has of people from foreign lands and an understanding of their cultures. The specific challenge is recognizing the differences that might exist and finding ways to make interactions effective. One of the first issues to deal with, then, is the perception of "foreigners."

U.S. managers in the past held a rather parochial view of the world of business. **Parochialism** is a narrow focus; these managers saw things solely through their own eyes and within their own perspectives.[6] They believed that their business practices were the best in the world. They did not recognize that people from other countries had different ways of doing things or that they lived differently from Americans. In essence, parochialism is an **ethnocentric view.** That is, U.S. managers viewed their practices as being better than those in other cultures. Of course this view cannot succeed in a global village—nor is it the dominant view held today. But changing U.S. managers' perception first required understanding of the different cultures and their environments.

parochialism
Refers to a narrow focus, in which one sees things solely through one's own eyes and within one's own perspective.

ethnocentric view
A parochial view in which one sees one's own culture as better than any other.

All countries have different values, morals, customs, political and economic systems, and laws. Traditional approaches to studying international business have sought to advance general principles of cultural behavior. However, a strong case is being made that organizational forms and goals need to be understood within their social context. This research supports the idea that organizational success can come from a variety of managerial and organizational structures—each of which is derived from a different business environment.[7] For example, status is perceived differently in different countries, partly because the value systems of the countries differ. In France, for instance, status is often the result of factors important to the organization, such as seniority, education, and the like. This emphasis is called ascribed status.[8] In the United States, status is more a function of what individuals have personally accomplished (achieved status). Managers need to understand societal issues (such as status) that might affect operations in another country.

Countries also have differences in their laws. In the United States, laws guard against employers' taking action against employees solely on the basis of an employee's age. Similar laws do not exist in all other countries. For instance, an employee of SmithKline Beecham, Plc., a British firm that operates in the United States, was denied a promotion for jobs outside the United States because company officials determined him to be "too old." Such action would be discriminating and illegal in the United States, but the law was not applicable to the England-based company.[9] Of course, if SmithKline officials had made that same decision about an employee for a job in the United States, they would have been breaking the law.

Since World War II, virtually no country has followed the U.S. economic example. Instead, the pattern of choice has been Japan, where business and government relationships are close and emphasis is placed on protectionism. So viewing the global environment from any single perspective provides too narrow an explanation. A more promising approach is to study a country's culture. Understanding **cultural environments** is critical to the success of managing others in the global village.

cultural environment
The attitudes and perspectives shared by individuals from a specific culture, or country, that shape their behavior and the way they see the world.

Details on a Management Classic

Hofstede's Cultural Variables

To date, the most valuable framework to help managers understand differences between national cultures is the one developed by Geert Hofstede.[10] He surveyed over 116,000 employees in forty countries; they all worked for IBM. What did he find? His huge data base indicated that, in general, national culture has a major impact on employees' work-related values and attitudes. More important, Hofstede was able to classify those values and attitudes into four specific dimensions of national culture: (1) **individualism** versus **collectivism,** (2) **power distance,** (3) **uncertainty avoidance,** and (4) **quantity** versus **quality of life.**[11]

Individualism refers to a loosely knit social framework in which people are supposed to look after their own interests and those of their immediate family. They are able to do so because such a society allows individuals a large amount of freedom. Collectivism is characterized by a tight social framework in which people expect others in their group (such as family or organization) to look after them and to protect them. In exchange, they feel they owe absolute allegiance to the group.

Power distance is a measure of the extent to which a society accepts the fact that power in institutions and organizations is distributed unequally. A high power distance society accepts wide differences in power in organizations. Employees show a great deal of respect for those in authority. Titles and rank carry a lot of weight. In contrast, a low power distance society plays down inequalities as much as possible. Supervisors still have authority, but employees are not fearful or in awe of the boss.

A society that is high in uncertainty avoidance is characterized by a high level of anxiety among its people, which manifests itself in great nervousness, stress, and aggressiveness. Because people in these societies feel threatened by uncertainty and ambiguity, mechanisms are created to provide security and reduce risk. Their organizations are likely to have formal rules; there will be little tolerance for deviant ideas and behaviors; and members will strive to believe in absolute truths. Not surprisingly, in organizations in countries with high uncertainty avoidance, employees demonstrate relatively low job mobility, and lifetime employment is a widely practiced policy.

Hofstede's Cultural Variables Continued

Quantity versus quality of life, like individualism and collectivism, represents a dichotomy. Some cultures emphasize the quantity of life and value things such as assertiveness and the acquisition of money and material goods. Other cultures emphasize the quality of life, placing importance on relationships and showing sensitivity and concern for the welfare of others.

Into which countries will U.S. managers fit best? Where are they likely to have the biggest adjustment problems? All we have to do is identify those countries that are most and least like the United States on the four dimensions. The United States is strongly individualistic but low on power distance. This same pattern was exhibited in Hofstede's study by England, Australia, Canada, the Netherlands, and New Zealand. Those least similar to the United States on these two dimensions were Venezuela, Colombia, Pakistan, Singapore, and the Philippines.

The United States scored low on uncertainty avoidance and high on quantity of life. This same pattern was shown by Ireland, England, Canada, New Zealand, Australia, India, and South Africa. Those least similar to the United States on these dimensions were Chile and Portugal.

These results empirically support part of what many of us suspected—that the U.S. manager transferred to London, Toronto, Melbourne, or a similar Anglo city would have to make the fewest adjustments. Hofstede's results allow us to identify the countries in which "culture shock" is likely to be the greatest. In those countries, one would probably have to radically modify one's managerial style.

individualism
A cultural dimension in which people are supposed to look after their own interests or those of their immediate families.

collectivism
A cultural dimension in which people expect others in their group to look after them and protect them when they are in trouble.

power distance
A cultural measure of the extent to which society accepts the unequal distribution of power in institutions and organizations.

uncertainty avoidance
A cultural measure of the degree to which people tolerate risk and unconventional behavior.

quantity of life
A national culture attribute describing the extent to which societal values are characterized by assertiveness and materialism.

quality of life
A national culture attribute that reflect the emphasis placed upon relationships and concern for others.

One illuminating study of the differences of cultural environments was conducted by Geert Hofstede.[12] By analyzing various dimensions of a country's culture, Hofstede was able to provide a framework for understanding what one might find when managing in the global village (see Details on a Management Classic).

Hofstede's findings allow managers to characterize countries according to such cultural variables as individualism, perceptions of status, anxiety, and materialism. These variables are an integral part of how a country's government deals with its people and indicate how the people see themselves. For example, in an individualistic society, people are primarily concerned with their own family. On the contrary, in a collectivist society, people care for all individuals who are part of the group, whether the group is a company or an entire nation. Thus, a strong individualistic U.S. manager may not succeed in a Pacific Rim country where collectivism dominates—unless that manager adapts his or her management practices to that country's culture. What's the message? Flexibility and adaptability are key components for managers who cross national borders.

Flexibility and adaptability are key components for managers who cross national borders.

But not all dealings with individuals from other cultures occur when managers cross national borders. Most such encounters are likely to involve interactions between managers in the United States and individuals who come to work here. What then can these managers do? When working with individuals from different cultures, a manager must understand that individuals informally learn about their cultures and that most such learning is unconscious. The Mars Company (the candy maker), for example, recognizes and builds on this informal development. It provides formalized training to its U.S. employees that focuses on the "major differences which may lead to problems," such as communication barriers and how differences can be resolved.[13] Managers need to be flexible in their dealings with their foreign-born employees. Because of cultural differences, these employees just may not understand you. Managers must, therefore, recognize and acknowledge that differences do exist in their backgrounds, customs, work schedules, and the like.[14] In organizations such as Nucor, Levi-Strauss, Motorola, and Avon, managers are provided extensive training to help them recognize these differences and "change the way they think about people from different lands."[15]

Why the Emphasis on Technology?

Suppose you need information on how well your unit is meeting production standards. Thirty years ago, it may have taken as long as a month to obtain that information. Today, however, a few keystrokes on your computer will get that information almost instantaneously!

Since the 1970s, U.S. companies such as General Electric, Wal-Mart, and 3M have been using automated offices, robotics in manufacturing, computer-assisted design software, integrated circuits, microprocessors, and electronic meetings. These technological advances make the organizations more productive and, it is hoped, help them create and maintain a competitive advantage.[16]

Technology includes any equipment, tools, or operating methods that are designed to make work more efficient. Technological advances reflect integrating any technology into any process for changing inputs into outputs. For example, to sell its goods or services, an organization must first take certain inputs, or raw materials, and transform them into outputs. In years past, many of these transforming operations were performed by human labor. Technology, however, has made it possible to enhance this production process by replacing human labor with electronic and computer equipment. For instance, assembly operations at General Motors rely heavily on ro-

Technology has enabled workers to become more efficient and more customer-oriented. In the control room of a Lukens Inc. steel mill, an employee operates an advanced control system that manufactures specialty steel products at a higher level of quality. With a few changes on the computer, the company can manufacture customized steel products much more cheaply today than a decade ago.

botics. Robots perform repetitive tasks—such as spot welding and painting—much more quickly than humans can. And the robots are not subject to health problems caused by exposure to chemicals or other hazardous materials. Technology, however, is not being used just in manufacturing enterprises. The banking industry, for instance, has been able to replace thousands of bank tellers by installing ATM machines and electronic bill-paying systems. Technology, too, is making it possible to better serve customers. For example, state-of-the-art steelmaking technology enables Lukens, Inc. to customize customer orders such that "making a one-of-a-kind product" can be done as efficiently as producing a whole shipload of the same product.[17]

Technological advancements are also used to provide better, more-useful information. Most cars built in the 1990s, for example, have an on-board computer circuit that a technician can plug into to determine problems with the automobile—saving countless diagnostic hours for a mechanic. And at Frito-Lay, technology has meant getting better and more-timely information. Sales representatives enter inventory and sales data into a hand-held computer; the data are then transmitted daily to company headquarters. As a result, company officials have complete information on 100 product lines in more than 400,000 stores within twenty-four hours.[18]

Undoubtedly, technology has had a positive effect on the internal operations of organizations. But how has it changed the manager's job? To answer that question, we need to look no further than how the typical office is set up. Organizations today have become integrative communication centers. By linking computers, telephones, fax machines, copiers, printers, and the like, managers can get complete information quickly. With that information, managers can better formulate plans, make faster decisions, more clearly define the jobs that workers need to perform, and monitor work activities as they happen. In essence, technology today has enhanced a manager's ability to more effectively and efficiently perform the four functions of management!

Technology is also changing how a manager's work is performed. Historically, the work site was located close to a source of skilled labor, so employees were near their bosses. Management could observe what work was being done and could easily communicate with employees face to face. Through the advent of technological advancements, managers are able to supervise employees in remote locations, and face-to-face interaction has decreased dramatically. Work, for many, occurs where their computers are. **Telecommuting** capabilities—linking a worker's computer and modem with those of coworkers and management at an office—have made it possible for employees to be located anywhere in the global village. Consequently, effectively communicating with individuals in remote locations, as well as ensuring that performance objectives are being met, have become two of managers' biggest challenges.[19]

telecommuting
The linking of a worker's computer and modem with those of coworkers and management at an office.

What Does Society Expect from Managers?

The issue of corporate social responsibility drew little attention before the 1960s, when the activist movement began questioning the singular economic objective of business. For instance, were large corporations irresponsible because they discriminated against women and minorities, as shown by the obvious absence of female and minority managers at that time? Was the Dow Chemical Company ignoring its social responsibility by marketing breast implants when data existed indicating that leaking silicone could be a health hazard? Before the 1960s, few people asked such questions. Even today, good arguments can be made for both sides of the social responsibility issue (see Exhibit 2-3). Arguments aside, times have changed. Managers are now regularly confronted with decisions that have a dimension of social responsibility; philanthropy, pricing, employee relations, resource conservation, product quality, and operations in

The major arguments for the assumption of social responsibilities by business are:

- ▶ **1. Public expectations.** Social expectations of business have increased dramatically since the 1960s. Public opinion in support of business pursuing social as well as economic goals is now well solidified.
- ▶ **2. Long-run profits.** Socially responsible businesses tend to have more-secure long-run profits. This is the normal result of the better community relations and improved business image that responsible behavior brings.
- ▶ **3. Ethical obligation.** A business firm can and should have a conscience. Business should be socially responsible because responsible actions are right for their own sake.
- ▶ **4. Public image.** Firms seek to enhance their public image to gain more customers, better employees, access to money markets, and other benefits. Since the public considers social goals to be important, business can create a favorable public image by pursuing social goals.
- ▶ **5. Better environment.** Involvement by business can solve difficult social problems, thus creating a better quality of life and a more desirable community in which to attract and hold skilled employees.
- ▶ **6. Discouragement of further government regulation.** Government regulation adds economic costs and restricts management's decision flexibility. By becoming socially responsible, business can expect less government regulation.
- ▶ **7. Balance of responsibility and power.** Business has a large amount of power in society. An equally large amount of responsibility is required to balance it. When power is significantly greater than responsibility, the imbalance encourages irresponsible behavior that works against the public good.
- ▶ **8. Stockholder interests.** Social responsibility will improve the price of a business's stock in the long run. The stock market will view the socially responsible company as less risky and open to public attack. Therefore, it will award its stock a higher price-earnings ratio.
- ▶ **9. Possession of resources.** Business has the financial resources, technical experts, and managerial talent to provide support to public and charitable projects that need assistance.
- ▶ **10. Superiority of prevention over cures.** Social problems must be dealt with at some time. Business should act on them before they become serious and costly to correct and take management's energy away from accomplishing its goal of producing goods and services.

The major arguments against the assumption of social responsibilities by business are:

- ▶ **1. Violation of profit maximization.** This is the essence of the classical viewpoint. Business is most socially responsible when it attends strictly to its economic interests and leaves other activities to other institutions.
- ▶ **2. Dilution of purpose.** The pursuit of social goals dilutes business's primary purpose: economic productivity. Society may suffer as both economic and social goals are poorly accomplished.
- ▶ **3. Costs.** Many socially responsible activities do not pay their own way. Someone has to pay these costs. Business must absorb these costs or pass them on to consumers in higher prices.
- ▶ **4. Too much power.** Business is already one of the most powerful institutions in our society. If it pursued social goals, it would have even more power. Society has given business enough power.
- ▶ **5. Lack of skills.** The outlook and abilities of business leaders are oriented primarily toward economics. Business people are poorly qualified to cope with social issues.
- ▶ **6. Lack of accountability.** Political representatives pursue social goals and are held accountable for their actions. Such is not the case with business leaders. There are no direct lines of social accountability from the business sector to the public.
- ▶ **7. Lack of broad public support.** There is no broad mandate from society for business to become involved in social issues. The public is divided on the issue. In fact, it is a topic that usually generates a heated debate. Actions taken under such divided support are likely to fail.

Exhibit 2-3
Arguments For and Against Social Responsibility

Source: Based on R. J. Monsen Jr., "The Social Attitudes of Management," in J. M. McGuire, ed. *Contemporary Management: Issues and Views* (Englewood Cliffs, N.J.: Prentice Hall, 1974), p. 616; and K. Davis and W. Frederick, *Business and Society: Management, Public Policy, Ethics,* 5th ed. (New York: McGraw Hill, 1984), pp. 28–41.

countries with oppressive governments are some of the more obvious. To help managers make such decisions, let us begin by defining social responsibility.

Few terms have been defined in as many different ways as *social responsibility.* Some of the more popular meanings include "profit making only," "going beyond profit making," "voluntary activities," "concern for the broader social system," and "social responsiveness."[20] Most of the debate has focused at the extremes. On one side, there is the classical—or purely economic—view that management's only social responsibility is to maximize profits.[21] On the other side stands the socioeconomic position, which holds that management's responsibility goes well beyond making profits to include protecting and improving society's welfare.

social responsibility
A firm's obligation, beyond that required by the law and economics, to pursue long-term goals that are good for society.

From Obligations to Responsiveness. Now it's time to narrow in on precisely what we mean when we talk about **social responsibility.** It is a business firm's obligation, beyond that required by the law and economics, to pursue long-term goals that are good for society.[22] Note that this definition assumes that business obeys the law and pursues economic interests. We take as a given that all business firms—those that are socially responsible and those that are not—will obey all laws that society imposes. Also note that this definition views business as a moral agent. In its effort to do good for society, it must differentiate between right and wrong.

social obligation
The obligation of a business to meet its economic and legal responsibilities and no more.

We can understand social responsibility better if we compare it with two similar concepts: social obligation and social responsiveness.[23] **Social obligation** is the foundation of a business's social involvement. A business has fulfilled its social obligation when it meets its economic and legal responsibilities and no more. It does the minimum that the law requires. A firm pursues social goals only to the extent that they contribute to its economic goals. In contrast to social obligation, both social responsibility and social responsiveness go beyond merely meeting basic economic and legal standards. For example, both might mean respecting the community in which the company operates, treating all employees fairly, being friendly to the environment, supporting career goals and special work needs of women and minorities, or not doing business in countries where there are human rights violations.

social responsiveness
The ability of a firm to adapt to changing societal conditions.

Social responsibility also adds an ethical imperative to do those things that make society better and not to do those that could make it worse. **Social responsiveness** refers to the capacity of a firm to adapt to changing societal conditions.[24] As Exhibit 2-4 describes, social responsibility requires business to determine what is right or wrong and thus seek fundamental ethical truths. Social responsiveness is guided by social norms. The value of social norms is that they can provide managers with a meaningful guide for decision making.

	SOCIAL RESPONSIBILITY	SOCIAL RESPONSIVENESS
Major consideration	Ethical	Pragmatic
Focus	Ends	Means
Emphasis	Obligation	Responses
Decision framework	Long-term	Medium- and short-term

Exhibit 2-4
Social Responsibility versus Social Responsiveness

Source: Adapted from S. L. Wartick and P. L. Cochran. "The Evolution of the Corporate Social Performance Model," *Academy of Management Review,* October 1985, p. 766.

Examples of Social Responsiveness. When a company meets pollution-control standards established by the federal government or does not discriminate against employees over the age of thirty-nine in promotion decisions, it is meeting its social obligation and nothing more. The law says that the company may not pollute or practice age discrimination. When Bayfront Medical Center, Inc. provides on-site childcare facilities for employees; Procter & Gamble declares that Tide "is packaged in 100 percent recycled paper"; and the head of the world's largest tuna canner says "StarKist will not purchase, process, or sell any tuna caught in association with dolphins," these firms are being socially responsive. Why? Pressure from working mothers and environmentalists make such practices pragmatic. Of course, if these same companies had provided child care, offered recycled packaging, or sought to protect dolphins back in the early 1970s, their actions probably would have been accurately characterized as socially responsible (see Managers Who Made a Difference).

Managers Who Made a Difference

Fran Sussner Rogers, Founder, Work/Family Directions

Fran Sussner Rogers has a nameplate on her office door: "President Fran's Office—Otherwise Known as Mom." This nameplate was made by her son and is done in felt-tip pen.[25]

Fran Rogers has always believed that meeting the needs of employees required more than simply paying them and offering a slate of employee benefits. She recognized that balancing the realities of one's work and personal life is difficult. More important, she knew that problems employees face in their personal lives will ultimately show up on their performance at work. She believed that companies had to help—getting involved before the employees cracked. That, to Fran, was the humane thing to do. It was also a way for an organization to give something back to its community. Helping employees would not only demonstrate social responsibility but was also a way to enhance worker performance and profitability.

Work/Family Directions, in Boston, Massachusetts, began in 1983. Working with a client organization, IBM, Rogers attempted to help the organization's employees find quality child care in the Boca Raton, Florida, area. Rogers succeeded in helping these IBM employees—and Work/Family Directions was off and running. Today, the company has grown to 247 employees and has annual revenues of $50 million. Its client list now boasts corporations such as Xerox, American Express, and NationsBank.

Fran Sussner Rogers may have found a secret to socially responsible behavior—she helps companies recognize that giving to their employees can reap many benefits for all involved. She continues her crusade for organizations to make significant investments in work- and family-related issues. She wants organizations to do more by helping individuals with all kinds of personal problems, not only with day care and elder care, and by helping with work-related problems arising from restructuring, reengineering, and going global.

Why the Emphasis on the Entrepreneurial Spirit?

In Chapter 1, we introduced the small business. Although some differences between managing in a small business and a large one were noted, the issue before us was primarily one of size. But, as the environment surrounding business continues to change, one trend becomes evident: many individuals are starting their own businesses.

Whether they are reacting to being laid off or do not want to deal any more with the "rat race" of corporate America, many individuals are choosing to control their own destiny by being their own boss. Some are simply taking their skills and transforming them into a viable business venture. Others, to lessen some of the start-up risks, are buying franchises—the Coffee Beanery, Super 8 Motels, or Meineke Discount Mufflers.[26] For whatever reason, all these individuals are exhibiting the **entrepreneurial spirit.** That is, they are independent workers who initiate a business venture, who have a tendency to take calculated risks, and who, at the same time, accept the fact that mistakes occur.[27]

entrepreneurial spirit
The qualities possessed by independent workers who initiate a business venture, have a tendency to take calculated risks, and accept the fact that mistakes occur.

The entrepreneurial spirit is not limited solely to the small business. Some companies are attempting to model the activities of the entrepreneur. Why? In general, entrepreneurs are better able to respond to a changing environment than are managers in a traditional hierarchical organization. The owner-manager is involved in the day-to-day operations and, like Chris Zane, is usually close to the customer. Furthermore, the owner-manager is the main decision maker, and all employees report to him or her. The result is a "flat" organization—one that contains very few, if any, layers of hierarchy.

In large organizations, people who demonstrate entrepreneurial characteristics are called **intrapreneurs.**[28] They have been known, in some cases, to help increase the speed with which work gets done. Should this imply then that entrepreneurs can exist in every large, established organization? The answer depends on one's definition of *entrepreneur.* The noted management guru Peter Drucker, for instance, argues that they can.[29] He describes an entrepreneurial manager as someone who is confident in his or her abilities, who seizes opportunities for change, and who not only expects surprises but capitalizes on them. He contrasts that with the traditional manager, who feels threatened by change, is bothered by uncertainty, prefers predictability, and is inclined to maintain the status quo. Drucker's use of the term *entrepreneurial,* however, is misleading. By almost any definition of good management, his entrepreneurial type would be preferred over the traditional type. Yet intrapreneurship can never capture the autonomy and riskiness inherent in true entrepreneurship, because intrapreneurship takes place within a larger organization: All financial risks are carried by the parent company; rules, policies, and other constraints are imposed by the parent company; intrapreneurs report to bosses; and the payoff for success is not financial independence but career advancement.[30] We will come back to entrepreneurs in the next chapter.

intrapreneurs
Persons within an organization who demonstrate entrepreneurial characteristics.

The Contemporary Organization

Just as the environment in which businesses operate has changed drastically over the past few decades, so too have organizations. The changes reflect the need for organizations to be more flexible and more responsive to the radical changes occurring around them. In this section, we will explore some of the more prominent changes "reshaping" the contemporary organization.

What Will the Work Force of 2005 Look Like?

Earlier, we described how cultural diversity is changing the makeup of the work force. That discussion focused primarily on culture from a global perspective. The composition of an organization's work force today, however, reflects more change than simply an influx of people from foreign lands. The bulk of the pre-1980s work force in North America consisted primarily of male Caucasians working full-time to support a non-employed wife and school-aged children. Such employees are now true minorities in organizations. For instance, 56 percent of the 23,000 U.S. employees at Levi-Strauss are minorities. The top management is 14 percent nonwhite and 30 percent female. Today's organizations are characterized by **work force diversity**—that is, workers are heterogeneous in terms of gender, race, and ethnicity, and they include the physically disabled, gays and lesbians, the elderly, and even those who are significantly overweight.

work force diversity Refers to the heterogeneous nature of today's work force, which includes people of both genders, of different races and enthnicities, with physical disabilities, and of all ages and sexual orientations.

Until very recently, managers took a "melting-pot" approach to differences in organizations. They assumed that people who were different would somehow automatically want to assimilate. But today's managers have found that employees do not set aside their cultural values and lifestyle preferences when they come to work. The challenge for managers, therefore, is to make their organizations more accommodating to diverse groups of people by addressing different lifestyles, family needs, and work styles. The melting-pot assumption is being replaced by the recognition and celebration of differences (see Understanding Yourself).[31]

If there is one certainty in business today, it is that our work force has changed over the past thirty years. Today, managers are likely to manage employees of all races, of all ages, of both genders, from any nation, and with disabilities and different sexual orientations. These employees bring to the job a variety of needs. At AT&T for example, councils composed of African Americans, Asians, Latinos, women, and gays help managers learn about issues facing each group.

Understanding Yourself

How Informed Are You About Diversity?

Today's work force is more diverse than ever before. Success for both managers and employees depends on being able to address issues of cultural diversity effectively. How aware are you of the following issues? Circle the correct answer.

1. The "Glass Ceiling" in corporations refers to
   - *a.* The feeling that many minorities and women experience of being constantly watched and supervised by those above them
   - *b.* The hiring of female entry-level employees with the clear opportunity for future promotions based upon performance
   - *c.* The high expectations, but frustrating limits, that women and minorities experience in promotions
   - *d.* The effect of indirect lighting on employee motivation
2. You can tell who is gay or lesbian by
   - *a.* Their mannerisms
   - *b.* Whom they associate with at work
   - *c.* The jobs they prefer
   - *d.* The kind of personal stories they share
   - *e.* None of the above
3. Provisions of the Disabilities Act prohibit an employer from inquiring into a job applicant's disability with questions concerning
   - *a.* Mental illness
   - *b.* Age
   - *c.* Past work experience
   - *d.* Religious affiliation
4. As of October 1994, women constituted 46 percent of the total U.S. work force. The percentage of women occupying top executive-level jobs is
   - *a.* 40 *c.* 12
   - *b.* 25 *d.* 5
5. By the year 2000, which one of the following ethnic minority groups is predicted to be the largest in the United States?
   - *a.* African Americans
   - *b.* Hispanics
   - *c.* Native Americans
   - *d.* Asian Americans
6. Among full-time workers 25 and older, whites earn more than blacks at all levels, and the difference is greater than the wage disparities between men and women, regardless of race.
   - *a.* True *b.* False
7. For every dollar men earn, women earn approximately
   - *a.* 50 cents *c.* 60 cents
   - *b.* 90 cents *d.* 70 cents
8. Women in blue-collar, male-dominated occupations are physically sexually harassed more often than their female white-collar counterparts, and they are likely to be
   - *a.* Less assertive in resisting and reporting it
   - *b.* More assertive in resisting and reporting it
   - *c.* Equally assertive in resisting and reporting it
   - *d.* More assertive in resisting, but less likely to report it
9. None of the Fortune 500 companies below has ever had a woman on the board of directors, except for which company?
   - *a.* Microsoft
   - *b.* Rite Aid
   - *c.* Ocean Spray Cranberries
   - *d.* Rubbermaid
10. One of the most common complaints of employees with a physically disabling condition is
    - *a.* They are constantly taken care of
    - *b.* They are treated as though they are invisible
    - *c.* They are asked to perform duties beyond their capabilities
    - *d.* They are regularly asked about their condition
11. According to a 1993 American Bar Foundation study of bargaining at new-car dealerships, the average profit that dealers made on an automobile was
    - *a.* $225 from white male customers, $419 from black male customers
    - *b.* $564 from white male customers, $1,665 from black male customers
    - *c.* $540 from white male customers, $826 from black male customers
    - *d.* $330 from white male customers, $380 from black male customers

12. Affirmative Action programs are designed to
   a. Give preference to female and minority candidates who may be somewhat less qualified in order to make their numbers in the workplace equal to white males
   b. Open access to potential employees who have previously been excluded from equal competition for jobs within particular organizations
   c. Fill a predetermined quota of women and minorities in an organization
   d. Have organizations look more affirmatively on women and minorities in job evaluations than they look upon white males

13. An employer can be held responsible if a customer, contractor or other non-employee sexually harasses one of its own employees.
   a. True   b. False

14. In one four-category description of the different "social styles" of people, (1) Analytic, (2) Driver, (3) Amiable, (4) Expressive, the most effective managers tend to be from
   a. The Analytic category
   b. The Driver category
   c. The Amiable category
   d. The Expressive category
   e. All of the above

15. Placing persons with disabilities in a separate seating area at public events is often experienced by people with disabilities as
   a. The same as segregation
   b. A reasonable accommodation
   c. Neither a nor b
   d. Both a and b

16. In the "Glass Ceiling" Report of the U.S. Department of Labor, women and minorities who were in higher management positions were almost always in
   a. Line positions such as operations and production
   b. Line positions such as sales
   c. Staff positions such as human resources and public relations
   d. Temporary positions

17. Between January of 1977 and August of 1991, no whites were executed for the killing of an African American.
   a. True   b. False

18. In 1994 what percentage of experts and sources named in business magazines and newspapers were women?
   a. 53%   c. 13%
   b. 29%   d. 4%

19. Which positive stereotype of Asian and Pacific Islander Americans is not a major barrier to their advancement into top leadership positions?
   a. They are good at science, engineering, and technology
   b. They are highly educated
   c. They are nonconfrontational
   d. All of the above

20. According to the 1995 Fact-finding Report of the Federal Glass-Ceiling Commission, what are the three major differences that lead to discomfort in the workplace and hence discrimination?
   a. Cultural, gender, and color-based differences
   b. Socioeconomic, gender, and color-based differences
   c. Educational, cultural, and color-based differences

21. A Japanese-American male executive with a bachelor's degree who works for a private for-profit company earns on average how much more than his white male counterpart?
   a. $22,400
   b. $5,600
   c. $13,800
   d. A Japanese male doesn't earn more than a white male

22. If maternity leave is controlled for, more men in senior management positions take leaves of absence than women at the same level.
   a. True   b. False

23. Over the past five years, the stock-market performance of firms that have good glass-ceiling records was approximately how many times higher than that of firms with poor glass-ceiling records?
   a. 9.7
   b. 2.4
   c. 0.5
   d. The stocks of companies with good glass-ceiling records did not perform better than the stocks of companies with poor ones

24. The percentage of Americans with assets of $500,000 or more who are women is approximately
   a. 10%   c. 40%
   b. 25%   d. 65%

Scoring

1. c; **2.** e; **3.** a; **4.** d; **5.** a; **6.** a; **7.** d; **8.** d; **9.** d; **10.** d; **11.** b; **12.** b; **13.** a; **14.** e; **15.** d; **16.** c; **17.** a; **18.** c; **19.** b; **20.** *a*; **21.** a; **22.** a; **23.** b; **24.** c;

Continued

What the Assessment Means: Give yourself 4 points for each correct response (for a total of 96 points). You get 4 points for just taking the assessment! Scoring is handled as in a typical 100-point test. That is, 90 or above means that you are well informed about diversity. Below 60, however, means that you are not as well informed as you could be about diversity issues in today's society. However, the key word is *informed.* Reading texts such as this, as well as being exposed to diversity issues in many of your classes and life experiences, will help to increase your awareness.

Source: D. P. Tulin and P. Watts, "What's Your Multicultural IQ?" *Executive Female,* May/June 1995, pp. 17–19. Used with permission.

As Exhibit 2-5 illustrates, growth in the U.S. work force from 1990 to 2000 will be occurring most rapidly among women and Hispanics. Almost two-thirds of all new entrants to the work force will be women.[32] And with them will come a need for organizations to change some of their practices. More emphasis will have to be placed on employee training, and employee benefit programs will have to be modified in such a way that the organization will be better able to meet the diverse work force's needs.

In an effort to attract and maintain a diversified work force, organizations such as Levi-Strauss, Seagrams Ltd., and Xerox have implemented diversity programs.[33] These programs are designed to help all employees change their attitudes, perceptions, and prejudices to adjust to the differences diverse people bring to the workplace. To better meet the needs of the diverse work force, some organizations, such as AT&T, the Prudential Insurance Company, and Hewlett-Packard, are also offering family-friendly benefits.[34] **Family-friendly benefits** include a wide range of work and family programs such as on-site day care, child and elder care, flexible work hours, job sharing, part-time employment, relocation programs, adoption benefits, and parental leave.[35] With more dual-career couples and single working parents, family-friendly benefits are a means of helping employees balance their work and family lives. And they may help organizations, too. For example, Nyloncraft, Inc. significantly reduced its turnover rates by offering on-site child care. Now it retains more employees, and productivity is up, too![36]

family-friendly benefits A wide range of work and family programs to help employees; include on-site day care, child and elder care, flexible work hours, job sharing, part-time employment, relocation programs, adoption benefits, parental leave, and other programs.

Exhibit 2-5

A Decade of Change: Percent Increase in the Number of New U.S. Workers, 1990 to 2000

Source: S. Pedigo, "Diversity in the Work Force: Riding the Tide of Change," *The Wyatt Communicator,* Winter 1991, p. 9.

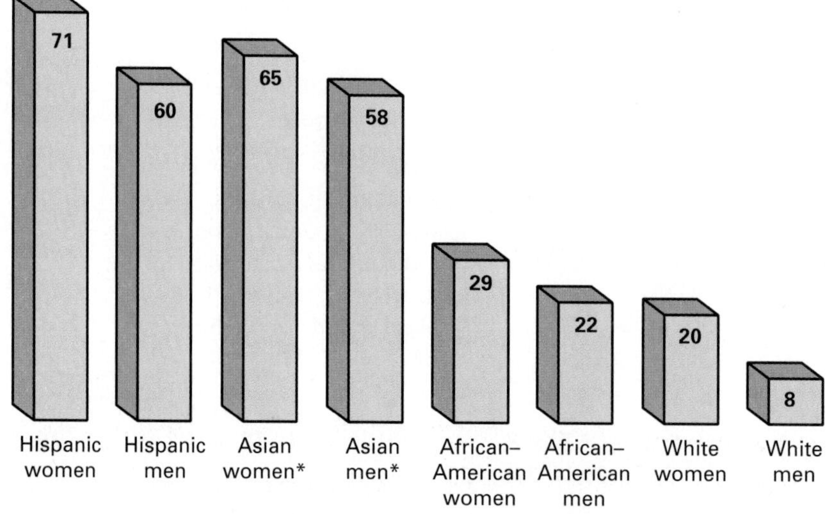

Why the Increased Concern with Quality?

There is a quality revolution taking place in both the private and the public sectors.[37] The generic term that has evolved to describe this revolution is **total quality management,** or **TQM** for short. The revolution was inspired by a small group of quality experts, the most prominent of whom was the late W. Edwards Deming.[38]

total quality management (TQM)
A philosophy of management that is driven by customer needs and expectations and that is committed to continuous improvement.

An American, Deming found few managers in the United States interested in his ideas. Consequently, in 1950, he went to Japan and began advising many top Japanese managers on how to improve their production effectiveness. Central to his management methods was the use of statistics to analyze variability in production processes. A well-managed organization, according to Deming, was one in which statistical control reduced variability and resulted in uniform quality and predictable quantity of output. Deming developed a fourteen-point program for transforming organizations. (We will take a closer look at this program in Chapter 16, when we discuss control techniques.) Today, Deming's original program has been expanded into a philosophy of management that is driven by customer needs and expectations[39] (see Exhibit 2-6). Importantly, however, TQM expands the term *customer* beyond the traditional definition to include everyone involved with the organization, either internally or externally. So TQM encompasses employees and suppliers as well as the people who buy the organization's products or services.[40] The objective is to create an organization committed to continuous improvement, or as the Japanese call it, ***kaizen.***

The objective of TQM is to create an organization committed to continuous improvement.

kaizen
The Japanese term for continuous improvement.

TQM represents a counterpoint to earlier management theories, which purported that low costs were the only road to increased productivity. The U.S. automobile industry, in fact, represents a classic case of what can go wrong when attention is focused solely on trying to keep costs down. Throughout the 1970s and 1980s, companies such as General Motors, Ford, and Chrysler ended up building products that a large part of the car-buying public rejected. Moreover, when the costs of rejects, repairing shoddy work, recalls, and expensive controls to identify quality problems were factored in, the U.S. manufacturers actually were less productive than many foreign

Exhibit 2-6
Components of Total Quality Management

1. Intense focus on the *customer.* The customer includes not only outsiders who buy the organization's products or services but also internal customers (such as shipping or accounts payable personnel) who interact with and serve others in the organization.
2. Concern for *continuous improvement.* TQM is a commitment to never being satisfied. "Very good" is not good enough. Quality can always be improved.
3. Improvement in the *quality of everything* the organization does. TQM uses a very broad definition of quality. It is related not only to the final product but also to how the organization handles deliveries, how rapidly it responds to complaints, how politely the phones are answered, and the like.
4. Accurate *measurement.* TQM uses statistical techniques to measure every critical variable in the organization's operations. These are compared against standards, or benchmarks, to identify problems, trace them to their roots, and eliminate their causes.
5. *Empowerment of employees.* TQM involves the people on the line in the improvement process. Teams are widely used in TQM programs as empowerment vehicles for finding and solving problems.

competitors. The Japanese demonstrated that it was possible for the manufacturers of the highest-quality products to also have the lowest costs. Beginning in the mid-1980s, U.S. auto manufacturers realized the importance of TQM and implemented many of its basic components, such as quality control groups, process improvement, teamwork, improved supplier relations, and listening to the needs and wants of customers. TQM, or at least the recognition that the continuous improvement in quality is necessary for an organization to compete effectively, is not just a fad. It is here to stay!

Why Must Managers Think in Terms of Quantum Changes Rather Than Incremental Change?

Although TQM is a positive start in many of our organizations, it focuses on continuous improvement or ongoing incremental change. Such action—a constant and permanent search to make things better—is intuitively appealing. Many of our companies, however, operate in an environment of rapid and dynamic change. As the elements around them change ever so quickly, a continuous improvement process may keep them behind the times.

The problem with a focus on continuous improvements is that it may provide a false sense of security. It may make managers feel as if they are actively doing something positive, which is somewhat true. Unfortunately, ongoing incremental change may avoid facing up to the possibility that what the organization may really need is radical or quantum change, commonly referred to as **reengineering.**[41] Continuous change may also make managers feel as if they are taking progressive action while, at the same time, avoiding having to implement quantum changes that will threaten organizational members. The incremental approach of continuous improvement, then, may be the 1990s version of rearranging the deck chairs on the *Titanic.*[42]

reengineering
Radical, quantum change in an organization.

If you have been reading this chapter closely, you may be asking yourself, "Aren't these authors contradicting what they said a few paragraphs ago about TQM?" On the surface, it may appear so, but consider this. While TQM is important for organizations and can often lead to improvements, TQM may not always be the right thing initially. For example, if what you are producing is outdated, a new improved version of the product may not be helpful to the company. Instead, a complete overhaul might be required. After that has occurred, then continuous improvement can have its rightful place. Let's see how this may be so.

Assume that you are the manager responsible for implementing some type of change in your roller skate manufacturing process. If you took the continuous improvement approach, your frame of reference would be a high-toe leather shoe on top of a steel carriage with four wooden wheels. Your continuous improvement program may lead you to focus on things such as using a different grade of cowhide for the shoe, adding speed laces to the uppers, or using a different type of ball bearing in the wheels. Of course, your skate may be better than the one you previously made, but is that enough? Compare your action with that of a competitor who reengineers the process.

To begin, your competitor poses the following question: How can we design a skate that is safe, fun, fast, and provides greater mobility? Starting from scratch, and not being constrained by her current manufacturing process, your competitor completes her redesign with something that looks like today's popular inline skates. Instead of leather and metal skates, you are now competing against a molded boot, similar to that used in skiing. Your competitor's skate is better than one made from leather and has no laces to tie. In addition, it uses four to six high-durability plastic wheels, which are placed in line for greater speed and mobility.

In this contrived example, both companies made progress. But which do you believe made the most progress given the dynamic environment they face? Our example clearly demonstrates why companies such as Thermos, Hoechst Celanese, Seiko, and Ryder Trucks opted for reengineering rather than incremental change.[43] It is imperative in today's business environment that all managers consider the challenge of reengineering their organizational processes. Why? Because reengineering can lead to "major gains in cost, service, or time."[44] For example, through reengineering efforts, General Motors cut the assembly times for its Chevrolet Cavalier from thirty-one to twenty-one hours.[45] In a similar fashion, Yokogawa Electric—makers of industrial testing and measuring equipment—now produce a one-piece temperature recorder cover. Previously, the recorder cover included thirty-one components. As a result of their improvement, Yokogawa's material costs decreased 96 percent, assembly time fell 96 percent, and the overall cost of producing the item decreased by 45 percent.[46] It is these kinds of gains that will make companies more competitive as they enter the twenty-first century—gains made from properly designing their operations, reducing waste, and eliminating inefficient ways of getting work done.

Why Do Organizations Lay Off Workers?

There was a time in corporate America when organizations followed a relatively simple rule. In good times you hire employees; in bad times, you fire them. That "rule" no longer holds true, at least for most of the largest companies in the world. Since 1991, more than 2.2 million workers have been laid off in the United States alone.[47] For instance, du Pont has eliminated 37,000 jobs. The National Aeronautics and Space Administration (NASA) cut 25,000 jobs. At AT&T, more than 80,000 jobs were lost; Sears cut 50,000 employees; and AlliedSignal, 13,000.[48] But this **downsizing** phenomenon is not going on just in the United States. Jobs are being eliminated in almost all industrialized nations. For example, Peugeot (France) has cut nearly 10 percent of its work force in the last five years; Renault (France) has eliminated 17 percent of its jobs; Daimler Benz (Germany) cut 5,100 positions; and Volkswagen (Germany) is eliminating about 30,000 jobs and cutting the remaining employees' pay by 16 percent.[49]

downsizing
An activity in an organization designed to create a more-efficient operation through extensive layoffs.

Why this trend for downsizing? Organizations are attempting to maintain some flexibility to deal with the changes around them. As a result of TQM and reengineering efforts, they are creating flatter structures and redesigning the way work is to be carried out. This means "delayering" the organization so that there are fewer levels of management between employees and senior management. Downsizing also promotes greater use of outside firms for providing necessary products and services, called **outsourcing,** and redesigning work processes to increase productivity.

outsourcing
An organization's use of outside firms for providing necessary products and services.

Are we implying that big companies are disappearing? Absolutely not! It is how they are operating that is changing. Big isn't necessarily inefficient. Companies such as PepsiCo, Home Depot, and Motorola manage to blend large size with agility by dividing their organization into smaller, more-flexible units. And for them, this setup is proving to be successful—not only for their "bottom line" but also for the 73,000 new jobs these three organizations created in 1994.[50] The success of these large companies does not indicate that downsizing is "over" as a business strategy. Rather, at issue for organizations is staffing their ranks properly—according to their strategic goals. This means that when organizations become overstaffed, they will likely cut jobs. At the same time, they are likely to increase staff when doing so adds value to the organization. A better term, then, might be **rightsizing**—or linking staffing levels to organizational goals. For example, American Airlines cut about 5,000 jobs between 1991 and 1992, but it also added more than 2,000 employees to its information services depart-

rightsizing
Linking staffing levels to organizational goals.

Outsourcing is a troubling issue for union members. In fact, the March 1996 General Motors–United Auto Workers strike occurred primarily over GM's desire to outsource some of their work. For example, GM wants to be able to purchase quality parts from a variety of sources—from both internal and external suppliers—on the basis of price. Company officials find this step necessary to remain competitive in the global marketplace. The UAW, on the other hand, sees outsourcing as a potential threat to unionized jobs at GM.

ment at the same time. Overall, the organization improved productivity by 26 percent.[51]

Why the Emphasis on Flexibility and Temporaries?

Bob Singleton worked full-time for more than fourteen years for the Bank of America. He was a credit specialist—a productive individual who had been loyal and committed to the bank's goals. Then one day, Bob was approached and given the following choices: cut his work hours to nineteen hours a week and receive no employee benefits or be laid off permanently.[52] In fact, by 1994, only 19 percent of Bank of America's employees worked full-time.[53] The Bank of America, and thousands of organizations in the global village, have decided they could save money and increase their flexibility by converting many jobs, like Bob's, into temporary or part-time positions—giving rise to what is commonly referred to as the **contingent work force** (see Exhibit 2-7).[54] Today, temporary workers can be found in secretarial, nursing, accounting, assembly-line, legal, dentistry, computer programming, engineering, marketing, and even senior management positions.[55] Why the organizational emphasis on this trend?

contingent work force
Part-time, temporary, and contract workers who are available for hire on an as-needed basis.

Organizations facing a rapidly changing environment must be in a position to adjust rapidly to those changes. Having a large number of permanent full-time employees limits management's ability to react. For example, an organization that faces significantly decreased revenues during an economic downturn may have to cut staff. Deciding who is to be laid off and what effect the layoffs will have on productivity and on the rest of the organization will be extremely complex in organizations that have a large permanent work force. On the other hand, organizations that rely heavily on contingent workers will have greater flexibility because workers can be easily added or taken off as needed. In addition, staffing shortages, opportunities to capitalize on new markets, obtaining someone who possesses a special skill for a particular project, and the like, all point to a need for the organization to be able to rapidly adjust its staffing level.

Temporaries, and the flexibility they foster, present special challenges for managers. Each contingent worker may need to be treated differently in terms of practices and "policies." For instance, one worker may have to be on site, while another may be able, given the nature of the work, to work at home. Managers must also make sure that contingent workers do not perceive themselves as second-class workers. Because they often do not receive many of the amenities—such as health and paid-leave benefits—that full-time employees do, contingent workers may tend to view their work as not being critically important. Accordingly, they may not be as loyal, as committed to the organization, or as motivated on the job as permanent workers are. That tendency may be especially relevant to those individuals, like Bob, who have been forced to join the temporary work force. Today's managers must recognize that it will be their responsibility to motivate their entire work force—full-time and temporary employees—and to build their commitment to doing good work!

Exhibit 2-7
Contingent Workers

Part-time employees	Part-time employees are those employees who work fewer than forty hours a week. In general, part-timers are afforded few, if any, employee benefits. Part-time employees are generally a good source of employees for organizations to staff their peak hours. For example, the bank that expects its heaviest clientele between 10 A.M. and 2 P.M. may bring in part-time tellers for those four hours. Part-time employees may also be involved in job sharing, in which two employees split one full-time job.
Temporary employees	Temporary employees, like part-timers, are generally employed during peak production periods. Temporary workers also fill in for employees who are off work for an extended period of time. For example, a secretarial position may be filled by a "temp" while the secretary is off work during his twelve-week unpaid leave of absence for the birth of his daughter. Temporary workers create a fixed cost to an employer for labor "used" during a specified period.
Contract workers	Contract workers, subcontractors, and consultants (may be referred to as freelance individuals) are hired by organizations to work on specific projects. These workers, typically very skilled, perform certain duties for an organization. Often their fee is set in the contract and is paid when the organization receives particular deliverables. Organizations use contract workers because their labor cost is fixed, and they do not incur any of the costs associated with a full-time employee population. In addition, some contract arrangements may exist because the contractor can provide virtually the same good or service in a more efficient manner than could a permanent employee.

Are Jobs, as We Know Them, Disappearing?

What do TQM, reengineering, downsizing, rightsizing, and outsourcing, have in common? In many cases, one or more of these actions are eliminating jobs as we know them.[56]

Almost 200 years ago, very few people had a "job." Sure, they worked, and worked hard, raising food or building things. They did so, however, without scheduled work hours, without bosses and job descriptions, and without employee benefits. Instead, they performed a variety of tasks, guided by the weather or when people would gather at the market to buy what they had made. It was the Industrial Revolution that introduced individuals to large manufacturing organizations, which helped create what we know today as the job—centralized work locations, formalized job requirements, and being responsible to a "boss." But now, some 100 years after the Industrial Revolution changed America, things are changing again. Customized production is replacing mass production. Employees today are more likely to be processing information than to be producing physical products. And, as mentioned earlier, organizations face a more dynamic environment, such as increased competition from the global village.[57] As a result, the United States is being dejobbed! What does that mean for workers?

Yesterday's workers had the luxury of having a job description that defined what work they needed to do. Their tasks were relatively routine—even when they performed "other work as assigned." Employees today, however, may not have that luxury. Tasks change too frequently to be accurately captured in a job description. Sure, job descriptions can be rewritten, but not every week. For many jobs, the job description may become obsolete.[58]

Rather than having a routine job, employees will work on tasks as they are needed. They will not be specialists in one area but rather will be multifunction specialists. They will work with other employees for a period of time, then move on to another project. Workers will perform their duties as members of project teams. They will be assigned to these teams because of the skills they possess, not because they represent a particular department. They will have changing schedules, work in several places, and perform a wide variety of tasks. And some of these project team members will be contingent workers—the temporary, contractual, and consultant "hired-guns" brought in to assist.

Clearly, not all jobs in the United States are being dejobbed. Yet the trends are pointing in that direction. Actual numbers of workers might not decrease drastically. Rather, dejobbing will reflect the degree of connectedness employees have to an organization. That is, dejobbing is creating two primary work groups. There will be a small group of **core employees,** the full-time employees of the organization who provide some essential job tasks for the organization. Employees who hold these core jobs will enjoy a full slate of employee benefits and job security that workers enjoyed three decades ago. Beyond this core group, will be the contingent work force. These individuals will make up the bulk of an organization's work force. They will work as needed and will continue working for an organization as long as their performance is satisfactory, and as long as a project lasts. Job security for these individuals, then, will last only for the duration of the project on which they work. Survival for many contingent workers will become a function of their entrepreneurial abilities.

core employees
The small group of full-time employees of an organization who provide some essential job tasks for the organization.

The Contemporary Manager

If you stop for a moment and digest what you have been reading in this chapter so far, you must be thinking that organizations and managers as we described them in Chapter 1 no longer exist. That is, it may be no longer appropriate to accept the status quo or to manage the company from a traditional, hierarchical position. The fact is that managers, like organizations, must change with the times. In the next section, we will explore some of the implications these changes have for managers.

How Do Managers Become Empowering Coaches?

Frederick Taylor, the "Father of Scientific Management" (see Appendix A), argued nearly a century ago for the division of work and responsibility between management and workers. He wanted managers to do the planning and thinking. Workers were just to do what they were told. That prescription might have been good advice at the turn of the century, but workers today are far better educated and trained than they were in Taylor's day. In fact, because of the complexity and changing nature of many jobs, today's workers may be considerably more knowledgeable than those who manage them about how best to do their jobs. This fact is not being ignored by management. Managers are transforming themselves from bosses into team leaders. Instead of telling people what to do, an increasing number of managers are finding that they become more effective when they focus on motivating, coaching, and cheerleading. Managers also recognize that they can often improve quality, productivity, and employee commitment by redesigning jobs in order to increase the decision-making discretion of workers. We call this process **empowering** employees.[59]

empowering
The redesigning of jobs in order to increase the decision-making discretion of workers.

Empowerment builds on ideas originally made by early management writers who promoted the well-being of employees. For many years, a lot of organizations stifled the capabilities of their work force. They overspecialized jobs and demotivated employees by treating them like unthinking machines. Recent successes at empowering employees in companies such as Colgate-Palmolive, Fiat, Wal-Mart, and Quad/Graphics, Inc. suggest that the future lies in expanding the worker's role in his or her job rather than in practicing Taylor's segmentation of responsibilities.[60]

The empowerment movement is being driven by two forces. First is the need for quick decisions by those people who are most knowledgeable about the issues. That requires moving decisions to individuals closest to the problems. If organizations are to successfully compete in a global village, they have to be able to make decisions and implement changes quickly. Second is the reality that the large layoffs in the middle-management ranks that began in the late 1980s have left many managers with considerably more people to supervise than they had in the past. And they may not have formal control over the work activities of some of these individuals.

Downsizing efforts at IBM have resulted in company managers' having to become empowering coaches. These IBM employees know they have more work in store for them, but their manager Ted Childs (top center), recognizes that he has to let all of his employees have some control over their daily work activities while at the same time encouraging them to do the best they can.

The same manager who today oversees a staff of thirty-five cannot micromanage in the ways that were possible when he or she supervised ten people. For example, one manager at AT&T, which had undergone extensive downsizing, had to assume responsibilities for three areas that previously had been handled by three managers. This manager had to empower her people, "because you can't know every data system and every policy. It's been a letting-go process and stretching."[61] That letting go and stretching process can be likened to the role of a sports team **coach.**

coach
A manager who motivates, empowers, and encourages his or her employees.

Consider the job of head coach of a football team. This individual is the one who establishes the game plan for an upcoming game and readies the players for the task. Even though the coach prepares the plans and the players, the fact remains that the coach cannot go out on Saturday and play the game. Instead, it is the players who execute the game plan. So what does the coach do during the game? It depends on how well the plan is working. When the competition is doing something that is counter to the game plan, the coach must quickly formulate new plans to give the players another competitive advantage. Thus, the coach deals with the exceptions. And, regardless of the game's outcome, as the players play the game, the coach becomes one of the major cheerleaders—recognizing outstanding performance toward fulfilling the plan and boosting player morale. This coaching role is increasingly becoming an accurate description of today's managers!

How Do We Make Managers More Sensitive to Differences?

The diversity that exists in the work force requires managers to be more sensitive to the differences each group brings to the work setting. Managers should recognize that this diversity will carry with it important implications for them. For example, they will have to shift their philosophy from treating everyone alike to recognizing individual differences and responding to those differences in ways that will ensure employee retention and greater productivity. They must be in a position to recognize and deal with the different values, needs, interests, and expectations that employees have. They must avoid any practice or action that can be interpreted as being sexist, racist, or offensive to minorities. Of course, at the same time, they must not illegally discriminate against any of their employees.

Such organizations as Levi-Strauss, Hewlett-Packard, Lotus Development, and U.S. West are providing sophisticated diversity training programs for their managers to help them better communicate, motivate, and lead. These training programs are designed to raise diversity consciousness among current employees. For example, Hewlett-Packard conducts training on cultural differences between American Anglos, Mexicans, Indochinese, and Filipinos at a San Diego plant. Monsanto's two-day diversity program directly addresses racial, ethnic, and gender stereotypes.[62] Lotus Development Corporation also offers training to its employees to help heterosexual and homosexual employees address stereotypes and issues that affect their work relationships.[63]

How Do Managers Improve Their Ethics?

Many observers believe that we are currently suffering an ethics crisis. Behaviors that were once thought of as reprehensible—lying, cheating, misrepresenting, covering up mistakes—have become, in many people's eyes, acceptable or necessary practices. Some managers have profited from illegal use of insider information. Others have covered up information about the safety of their products. Some government contractors overcharge for their work. Price fixing, polluting the environment, and pirating software are further illustrations of ethical lapses. Even college students seem to have become caught up in this wave. A Rutgers University study of over 6,000 students found that, among those anticipating careers in business, 76 percent admitted to having cheated on at least one test and 19 percent acknowledged having cheated on four or more tests.[64]

Concern over this perceived decline in ethical standards is being addressed at two levels. First, ethics education is being widely expanded in college curriculums. For instance, the primary accrediting agency for business schools now requires all its member programs to integrate ethical issues throughout their business curriculum.[65] Second, organizations are creating codes of ethics and introducing ethics training programs.[66] Let's look closer at this issue of ethics.

Is it ethical for a salesperson to offer an expensive gift to a purchasing agent as an inducement to buy? What if the gift comes out of the salesperson's commission? Does that make it any different? Is it ethical for managers to require their employees to participate in mandatory drug testing? Is it ethical for someone to "whistleblow" on a company practice to an external agency without first consulting company officials? How about using the company telephone for personal long-distance calls? Is it ethical to ask a company secretary to type personal letters?[67]

ethics
The rules or principles that define right and wrong conduct.

Ethics commonly refers to the rules or principles that define right and wrong conduct.[68] But understanding ethics may be difficult, depending on the view that one holds of the topic (see Developing a Management Skill). Exhibit 2-8 presents three views of ethical standards.[69] Regardless of one's view of ethics, whether a manager acts ethically or unethically will depend on several factors. These factors include the individual's morality, values, personality, and experiences; the organization's culture; and the issue that is being called into question.[70] People who lack a strong moral sense are much less likely to do the wrong things if they are constrained by rules, policies, job descriptions, or strong cultural norms that discourage such behaviors. Conversely, very moral people can be corrupted by an organizational structure and culture that permits or encourages unethical practices. For example, someone in your class is sell-

Exhibit 2-8
Three Views of Ethics

Source: G. F. Cavanaugh, D. J. Moberg, and M. Valasquez, "The Ethics of Organizational Politics," *Academy of Management Journal,* June 1981, pp. 363–74.

Utilitarian view of ethics	Refers to a situation in which decisions are made solely on the basis of their outcomes or consequences. The goal of utilitarianism is to provide the greatest good for the greatest number. On one side, utilitarianism encourages efficiency and productivity and is consistent with the goal of profit maximization. On the other side, however, it can result in biased allocations of resources, especially when some of those affected lack representation or voice.
Rights view of ethics	Refers to a situation in which the individual is concerned with respecting and protecting individual liberties and privileges, including the rights to privacy, freedom of conscience, free speech, and due process. The positive side of the rights perspective is that it protects individuals' freedom and privacy. But it has a negative side in organizations: It can present obstacles to high productivity and efficiency by creating an overly legalistic work climate.
Theory of justice view of ethics	Refers to a situation in which an individual imposes and enforces rules fairly and impartially. A manager would be using a theory of justice perspective in deciding to pay a new entry-level employee $1.50 an hour over the minimum wage because that manager believes that the minimum wage is inadequate to allow employees to meet their basic financial commitments. Imposing standards of justice also comes with pluses and minuses. It protects the interests of those stakeholders who may be underrepresented or lack power, but it can encourage a sense of entitlement that reduces risk taking, innovation, and productivity.

Developing a Management Skill
GUIDELINES FOR ACTING ETHICALLY

About the Skill: *Making ethical choices can often be difficult for managers. Obeying the law is mandatory, but acting ethically goes beyond mere compliance with the law. It means acting responsibly in those "gray" areas, where right and wrong are not defined. What can you do to enhance your managerial abilities in acting ethically? We offer some guidelines.*

Steps in practicing the skill

1 ***Know your organization's policy on ethics.*** Company policies on ethics, if they exist, describe what the organization perceives as ethical behavior and what it expects you to do. This policy will help you to clarify what is permissible and the managerial discretion you will have. This becomes your code of ethics to follow!

2 ***Understand the ethics policy.*** Just having the policy in your hand does not guarantee that it will achieve what it is intended to do. You need to fully understand it. Behaving ethically is rarely a cut-and-dried process. But the policy can act as a guiding light, providing a basis from which you will do things in the organization. Even if a policy does not exist, there are still several steps you can take before you deal with the difficult situation.

3 ***Think before you act.*** Ask yourself, "Why am I going to do what I'm about to do? What led up to the problem? What is my true intention in taking this action? Is my reason valid? Or are there ulterior motives behind it—such as demonstrating organizational loyalty? Will my action injure someone? Would I disclose to my boss or my family what I'm going to do?" Remember, it's your behavior and your actions. You need to make sure that you are not doing something that will jeopardize your role as a manager, your organization, or your reputation.

4 ***Ask yourself what-if questions.*** If you are thinking about why you are going to do something, you should also be asking yourself what-if questions. For example, the following questions may help you shape your actions. "What if I make the wrong decision: what will happen to me? to my job?" "What if my actions were described, in detail, on the local TV news show or in the newspaper: would it bother or embarrass me or those around me?" "What if I get caught doing something unethical: Am I prepared to deal with the consequences?"

5 ***Seek opinions from others.*** If it is something major that you must do, and about which you are uncertain, ask for advice from other managers. Maybe they have been in a similar situation and can give you the benefit of their experience. Or maybe they can just listen and act as a sounding board for you.

6 ***Do what you truly believe is right.*** You have a conscience, and you are responsible for your behavior. Whatever you do, if you truly believe it was the right action to take, then what others say, or what the "Monday morning quarterbacks" say is immaterial. You need to be true to your own internal ethical standards. Ask yourself: Can I live with what I've done?

ing a copy of the final exam for $50. Rumors abound in the department, but nothing is being done. Do you buy a copy because without it you'll be disadvantaged, or do you do without it and try your best? A faculty member who suspects that a copy is floating around and does nothing is doing little to dissuade cheating. In that case, you may rationalize getting a copy for yourself.

The example of the final exam illustrates how ambiguity about what is ethical can be a problem for employees. Codes of ethics are an increasingly popular tool for reducing that ambiguity.[71] A code of ethics is a formal document that states an organization's primary values and the ethical rules it expects employees to follow.[72] Ideally, these codes should be specific enough to guide employees in what they are supposed to do yet loose enough to allow for freedom of judgment.[73] Nearly 80 percent of Fortune 500 companies have a stated code of ethics.[74]

Will Chaos Dominate a Manager's Activities?

Today's managers confront an environment in which change is taking place at an unprecedented rate; new competitors spring up overnight and old ones disappear through mergers, acquisitions, or failure to keep up with the changing marketplace. The organization has downsized, leaving fewer workers to complete the necessary work. Constant innovations in computer and telecommunications technologies are making communications instantaneously. These factors, combined with the globalization of product and financial markets, have created chaos. As a result, many past traditional management practices—created for a world that was far more stable and predictable—no longer apply.

Today's managers must turn disasters into opportunities.

Successful managers today must change, too. They must be able to make sense out of a situation when everything appears futile. Managers must be able to turn disasters into opportunities. To do so, they must be more flexible in their styles, smarter in how they work, quicker in making decisions, more efficient in managing scarce resources, better at satisfying customers, and more confident in enacting massive and revolutionary changes. As management writer Tom Peters captured in one of his best-selling books, today's managers must be able to thrive on change and uncertainty.[75]

Preparing for the New Millennium

Change, newness, uncertainty? What do they mean for tomorrow's managers? Although making predictions can be viewed as an exercise in futility, there is plenty of evidence suggesting what managers will need to concern themselves with. The key to success, if it can be narrowed down to one statement is: Be prepared to make adjustments. Opportunities will abound for those prepared to accept and deal with the information age. Realize that as little as twenty years ago, almost no one had a fax machine, cellular phone, or personal pager. Computers were still too large to fit on desks. E-mail, modems, and the Internet weren't everyday words spoken by the general public. Sophisticated gadgetry was often left to the *James Bond* movies!

But information technology, supported by the creation of the silicon chip, has permanently altered a manager's life. Electronic communications, optical character and voice recognition, as well as storage and retrieval of data bases, among other things, are significantly influencing how information is created, stored, and used.[76] And that influence is affecting managers. Telecommunications technologies, as we mentioned earlier in the chapter, are creating the need for managers to develop processes for "controlling" off-site operations.

Equally as important, though, is the constantly evolving list of skills and competencies managers must possess. Those who embrace knowledge and continuously learn new skills will be the ones who survive in the high-tech world.

Summary

How will I know if I fulfilled the Learning Objectives found on page 30? You will have fulfilled the Learning Objectives if you understand the following.

1. **Explain the importance of viewing management from a global perspective.** Competitors are no longer defined within national borders. New competition can suddenly appear at any time, from anywhere in the world. Managers must think globally if their organizations are to succeed over the long term.
2. **Describe how technology is changing the manager's job.** Technology is changing a manager's job in several ways. Managers will have immediate access to information that will help them in making decisions. In addition, through the advent of technological advancements, managers may be supervising employees in remote locations, reducing the face-to-face interaction with these individuals. Consequently, effectively communicating with individuals in remote locations, as well as ensuring that performance objectives are being met, will become major challenges.
3. **Define social responsibility and social responsiveness.** Social responsibility refers to an obligation, beyond that required by law and economics, for a firm to pursue long-term goals that are good for society. Social responsiveness is the capacity of the firm to adapt to changing societal conditions.
4. **Explain what is meant by the term *entrepreneurial spirit.*** *Entrepreneurial spirit* refers to individuals who possess such characteristics as (1) being independent workers who initiate a business venture, (2) having a tendency to take calculated risk, and (3) accepting the fact that mistakes occur in business.
5. **Describe the management implications of a diversified work force.** The work force of 2001 will witness heterogeneity of gender, race, and ethnicity. It will also include the physically disabled, gays and lesbians, the elderly, and those who are significantly overweight. The most important implication for managers is a requirement of being sensitive to the differences among individuals. That means they must shift their philosophy from treating everyone alike to recognizing differences and responding to those differences in ways that will ensure employee retention and greater productivity.
6. **Define TQM and identify its five primary components.** TQM is a philosophy of management that is driven by customer needs and expectations. Its five primary components are focus on the customer; seek continual improvement; strive to improve the quality of work; seek accurate measurement; and empower employees.
7. **Explain why corporations downsize.** Corporate downsizing has occurred in response to global competition. Downsizing is an attempt to make companies more responsive to customers and more efficient in their operations. Incremental change refers to change that is constant and continuous; it is usually associated with TQM. Quantum change, or reengineering, is radical change in determining new processes for the organization.
8. **Explain the increased popularity of managers' performing a coaching role and empowering their employees.** The complexity and changing nature of today's jobs may result in workers' being considerably more knowledgeable about how best to do their jobs than are those who manage them. As a result, instead of telling employees what to do, many managers are finding that they can become more effective when they focus on coaching and encouraging their employees. Many of these same managers also recognize that they can often improve quality, productivity, and employee commitment by redesigning jobs in order to increase the decision-making discretion of workers through a process called empowering.
9. **Define ethics.** Ethics refers to rules or principles that define right or wrong conduct.
10. **Describe why contemporary managers must be able to "thrive on chaos."** Managers must accept that they will be responsible for turning disasters into opportunities. In contrast to traditional managers, they must be more flexible in their styles, smarter in how they work, quicker in making decisions, more efficient in managing scarce resources, better at satisfying the customer, and more confident in enacting massive and revolutionary changes.

Review & Discussion Questions

1. Describe how the three "waves" identified by Alvin Toffler changed the way individuals work.
2. Why must managers pay attention to the global village?
3. What are the managerial implications of Hofstede's research on cultural environments? In what countries do you believe the United States is likely to have to make the fewest adjustments? In what countries do you believe the United States is likely to have to make the most adjustments?
4. "Individuals are born with the characteristics associated with the entrepreneurial spirit. They either have them, or they don't." Do you agree or disagree with the statement? Explain.
5. Given that tomorrow's organizations will comprise all different kinds of people, what managerial implication will this diversity bring about?
6. "TQM includes contributions from all management approaches." Do you agree or disagree with this statement? Discuss.
7. "Reengineering for better customer service and more efficiency was just a ruse by large companies to reduce their payrolls and increase their profits." Do you agree or disagree with this statement? Explain.
8. Identify the characteristics and behaviors of what you would consider an ethical manager.
9. "Coaching must replace the traditional management functions. Success for the organizations will demand it." Do you agree or disagree with this statement? Explain.
10. How can learning to manage chaos better prepare individuals for managing in the next millennium?

Testing Your Comprehension • • • 

Circle the correct answer, then check yourself on page AK-1.

1. When we find organizations with employees who are heterogeneous in terms of gender, race, ethnicity, sexual preference, or other characteristics,
   a) it indicates that successful hiring practices exist in the organization
   b) we have work force diversity
   c) we have an example of the contingency approach in hiring in the global village
   d) it indicates that the teachings of Geert Hofstede are being followed

2. In terms of total quality management, the customer is
   a) always right
   b) the party actually using the good or service
   c) any internal or external party who interacts with the organization
   d) the party who buys an organization's products or services

3. Institutions and forces outside an organization that affect its performance
   a) are collectively called environmental forces
   b) create an organization's culture
   c) have a minor impact on management's options
   d) define an organization's structure

4. Which of the following statements demonstrates that the world is becoming a global village?
   a) The family is becoming more important throughout the world.
   b) With the fall of communism, capitalism is becoming more widespread as an economic system.
   c) Companies are no longer constrained by national borders.
   d) Students are being required to learn foreign languages in schools.

5. In his work, Hofstede attempted to
   a) encourage the fall of communism and replace it with a more "pro-business" system
   b) stabilize international exchange rates to encourage easy transition of money transfers
   c) establish foreign trade zones to facilitate regional cooperation
   d) provide a framework for analyzing cultural differences

6. Organizations today are gaining more flexibility by eliminating layers of hierarchy. This delayering is best reflective of
   a) reengineering
   b) controlling the environment
   c) downsizing
   d) none of the above

7. Which of the following statements is TRUE about reengineering?
   a) Reengineering focuses on incremental change.
   b) Reengineering is the new TQM buzz word.
   c) Reengineering implies making major changes.
   d) Reengineering provides a false sense of security.

8. A code of ethics is NOT
   a) formal
   b) an increasingly popular response
   c) aimed at encapsulating an organization's primary values
   d) required by law

9. Which of the following is FALSE regarding contemporary managers?
   a) Many managers are transforming themselves from bosses into coaches.
   b) Managers must be considerably more knowledgeable than their employees about how the employees' jobs should be done.

c) Technological improvements are making the manager's job more complex in terms of dealing with employees.

d) Managers must be prepared to make opportunities out of chaos.

---

10. Which of the following is NOT an attribute associated with entrepreneurial spirit?
   a) taking risks
   b) learning from mistakes
   c) controlling one's own destiny
   d) accepting the status quo

---

11. Which of the following individuals is BEST associated with fostering a total quality management environment in organizations?
   a) Edwards Deming
   b) Alvin Toffler
   c) Geert Hofstede
   d) Chris Zane

---

12. Which of the following is NOT a characteristic associated with TQM?
   a) continuous improvement
   b) predictability
   c) customer focus
   d) accurate measurement

---

13. Which of the following statements is TRUE?
   a) Multinational corporations are based in several countries.
   b) Multinational corporations gained popularity in the 1980s.
   c) Transnational corporations encourage major decisions to be made at the local site.
   d) Transnational corporations often do not hire locally.

---

14. Which of the following statements about social responsibility is TRUE?
   a) Social responsibility often lacks broad public support.
   b) Social responsibility involves doing things to make society better and not to harm it.
   c) Social responsibility refers to the capacity of a firm to respond to social pressures.
   d) Social responsibility and an organization's social obligations are the same thing.

---

15. Which of the following statements is FALSE regarding how technology has affected the manager's job?
   a) Technology allows managers to supervise employees in remote locations.
   b) Technology has increased the face-to-face interaction between managers and employees.
   c) Technology allows for managers to get better performance data much faster.
   d) Technology will continue to change the way managers manage.

---

16. The use of outside firms for providing necessary products and services to an organization is called
   a) outsourcing
   b) reengineering
   c) delayering
   d) total quality management

---

17. Which of the following statements is LEAST correct regarding the contingent work force?
   a) Using contingent workers helps an organization respond to changes in its environment.
   b) Using contingent workers helps an organization determine who will be laid off in economic downturns.
   c) Using contingent workers helps an organization to more easily fill staffing shortages.
   d) Using contingent workers helps an organization create more loyal and committed employees.

Applying the Concepts

Understanding Cultural Differences

Work force diversity has become a major issue for managers. Although there are often similarities among individuals, obvious differences do exist. A means of identifying some of those differences is to get to know individuals from the diverse groups. For this exercise, you will need to contact people from a different country. If you don't know any, the office of your college that is responsible for coordinating international students can give you a list of names. Interview at least three people to get responses to such questions as:

1. What country do you come from?
2. What is your first language?
3. Describe your country's culture in terms of, for example, form of government, emphasis on individual versus group, role of women in the work force, benefits provided to employees, how managers treat their employees, and so on.
4. What were the greatest difficulties in adapting to your new culture?
5. What advice would you give me if I had a management position in your country?

In groups of three to five class members, discuss your findings. Are there similarities in what each of you found? If so, what are they? Are there differences? Describe them. What implications for managing in the global village has this exercise generated for you and your group?

Take It to the Net

We invite you to visit the Robbins/De Cenzo page on the Prentice Hall Web site at:

http://www.prenhall.com/robbinsfom

for this chapter's World Wide Web exercise.

You can also visit the Web sites for these companies featured within this chapter:

BMW
http://www.bmw.com

Daimler Benz Aerospace
http://www.dasa.com
Fiat: http://www.fiatusa.com

Mars Company
http://www.cbl.com.au/mfr/welcome.html

Maserati
http://stone.america.com/maserati/

Nestlé's:
http://www.nestle.com

Royal Dutch/Shell
http://www.srtca.shell.nl/anthology/index.html

USA Today
http://www.usatoday.com

Zane's Cycles
http://www.inc.com/incmagazine/archives/029603/html/

Thinking Critically

Making a Value Judgment: The Contingent Work Force

Hiring contingent workers can be a blessing for both organizations and individuals. Contingent workers provide employers with a rich set of diverse skills on an as-needed basis. In addition, hiring precisely when the specific work is to begin is very cost-effective. Moreover, individuals who desire to work less than full time are also given the opportunity to keep their skills sharp. Simultaneously, being contingent workers permits them to balance their commitment to personal matters and their careers.

Many of the blessings for individuals, however, revolve around a central theme: that an individual *chooses* to be a contingent worker. Unfortunately, that is not always the case. Jobs in the United States have been shifted, and that trend is expected to continue. Consequently, the involuntary contingent work force will be expected to grow in the years ahead.

Being part of the contingent work force—even if not by choice—might not be so bad if employees received benefits typically offered to full-time employees. Although hourly rates sometimes are higher for the contingent workers, these individuals have to pay themselves for the benefits that organizations typically provide to their full-time permanent employees. For instance, as a contract worker, you are required to pay all of your social security premiums. For core and some part-time employees, the employee and the employer share in this "tax." So some of that "extra" hourly rate of the contingent worker is taken away as an expense. Added to social security are such things as paying for one's health insurance. Buying health insurance through an organization that receives group rates is generally cheaper than having to buy the insurance yourself. This is yet another added expense to the contingent worker. So too is having to pay for one's office supplies and equipment. As for time off with pay benefits, forget about it. Vacation, holidays, sick leave? It's simple. Take all you want. But remember, when you don't work, you don't get paid!

Questions:

1. Does hiring contingent workers who would rather have permanent employment connote exploitation by management?
2. Should organizations be legally required to provide some basic level of benefits—such as health insurance, vacation, sick leave, and retirement—to contingent workers?

Shocking News at General Electric

Ask 100 managers and 100 business professors who they believe are the top ten managers in the world, and the list will vary widely. But common on both is surely to be one name—Jack Welch, CEO of General Electric. Jack Welch is highly regarded as one of the world's most admired leaders. He has taken General Electric to new heights—simultaneously becoming one of Wall Street's noted superstars. He has developed his people, and many of his protégés have ascended to top leadership positions in other Fortune 100 companies. Stories about him, and many outstanding practices developed at GE, have appeared in almost every business-related journal. What he touches often turns to gold—not instantly, but through the hard work and market focus he exhibits. In fact, the General Electric "rule" of business is often repeated—Be number one or number two in the market, or get out!

Of course, people of this stature like the press. News coverage elevates their esteem among their peers, and it gives them a tremendous sense of personal accomplishment. Jack Welch is no exception. But what Welch would prefer not to see in print or on television are stories about the nightmares he has faced during his tenure with the organization![77]

Over the past eighteen years under his leadership, General Electric has been involved in six major scandals. In 1995, the organization pleaded guilty for overcharging the Air Force on the *Minuteman* missile. In 1989, GE paid $3.5 million as a penalty for falsifying time cards on a government contract and $30 million for other fraudulent practices involved in an Army and other Department of Defense contracts. In 1992, General Electric pleaded guilty and paid out $69 million for inappropriate practices involving the sale of jet engines to Israel—a sale that involved employee bribes. And, in 1993, a staged crash test of GM vehicles that was aired on an NBC news program (NBC is a division of GE) led to GE's agreeing to pay General Motors more than $1 million in legal fees.

Maybe Welch's greatest embarrassment came from GE's Kidder Peabody investment subsidiary. Kidder Peabody's Chief Government Bond Trader, Joseph

Jett, was allegedly involved in a scheme that produced about $350 million in phony profits. Compounding the scheme was the fact that top managers at Kidder Peabody—including a Welch protégé who was put in charge of the organization after an insider-trading scandal in the mid-1980s—disregarded standard operating procedures. The organization's profitability was not recovering as expected. In fact, there is speculation that questions about Jett's practices were either answered incorrectly, ignored, or simply evaded because of Jett's "importance to the bottom line." This, despite General Electric's and Welch's emphatic assertion that a "commitment to integrity" was one of the organization's top goals.

Welch, however, knows that integrity requires more than tough talk. It requires action—especially when a problem arises. So, in response, Welch commissioned an investigation of the Kidder Peabody scandal. And when the inquiry was complete, Welch took swift action. He pressured his close friend and Kidder's top manager, Michael Carpenter, to resign. Jett's immediate supervisor was also pressured to resign. General Electric also took a $210 million charge against profits to absorb the loss created by the false profit results.

Questions:

1. Do you think that GE's goal of being number one or number two in every one of its markets had any influence on the Kidder Peabody scandal? Explain your position.
2. Do you think that Jack Welch handled the Kidder scandal ethically? Why or why not?
3. How can an idolized corporate leader who heads a large organization—one who emphasizes a commitment to integrity—prevent scandals, or other unethical practices, from happening again in the organization? Do you think that Jack Welch is ultimately responsible for what happens in "his" organization?
4. General Electric has a code of ethics, but it doesn't appear to work. What do you think might be the reason?

Video Case ABCNEWS

Heroes or Villains?

The recovery is resounding. Corporate profits are increasing. The Dow Jones Industrial Average stands at an all time high. There is strong competitiveness in a global marketplace. Do these statements indicate a return to prosperity? Maybe. But don't say this around the thousands of employees who continue to lose their jobs. In fact, since 1993 over 1.6 million employees have lost their jobs. If you thought downsizing would end when "times got better," think again! The layoffs continue—about 100,000 a month.

Days appear to be long gone where a company takes care of its employees. That's not to say that there aren't exceptions to this "rule." There are still some people like Aaron Feurstein left in business. In December 1994, a fire destroyed Feurstein's textile mill in Massachusetts. Being the area's primary employer, Feurstein could have "done things right," instead he created havoc in his community. For example, he could have taken his insurance money and closed the business down. Or, he could have sent workers home—and to the unemployment lines—until the factory was rebuilt. What he did, though, was nothing short of miraculous. Feurstein pledged to his employees and the community that he would rebuild the plant. And while this was ongoing, he promised to keep the employees on the payroll—so that they would keep getting a paycheck and their benefits even though they weren't working. Because of his actions, many regard Feurstein a true socially responsible employer.

Stories like Aaron Feurstein's, while they make news, are frequently overshadowed by the questionable actions of some businesses. It appears that many have given into greed. From the 1950s through the 1970s, massive layoffs only happened when an organization's survival was at risk. Today it appears companies are "laying off lots of workers in order to fatten the bottom line," and their own pockets. And their practices are pleasantly received by those on Wall Street. When a CEO announces that the organization is going to make massive layoffs, it's interpreted by investors that the company is controlling its costs—and shifting its priorities to ensure survival, even growth. And if you're a stockholder in that company—like the CEO frequently is—your investment can benefit from this reaction. Making moves like this has become a "trademark" of Albert Dunlap—irreverently referred to as Chainsaw Al—former chairman of Scott Paper Company.

Dunlap considers himself a turnaround specialist. He has taken over as CEO of several companies and made significant cuts to keep these companies alive. At

Scott Paper, for example, he took an ailing company and eliminated 11,000 jobs. As a result, Scott's stock price nearly doubled. When Dunlap left Scott some two years later, he walked away with a "cool" $100 million. Was he justified in getting this amount of money on the "backs of the workers?"

Consider that in most cases, Dunlap had taken over companies on the verge of bankruptcy. Scott paper, for instance, had losses exceeding $227 million, and its future prospects looked grim. By cutting 35 percent of Scott's work force, Dunlap "protected the job security of the remaining 65 percent." To him, it was better to save the jobs of the majority than to have 100 percent of the employees out of work. Is he a hero or a villain?

Questions:

1. Do you believe there is a difference between downsizing for organizational survival and downsizing for "economic reasons?" Discuss.
2. Explain how Aaron Feurstein's actions could be considered socially responsible behavior.
3. Do you believe Al Dunlap is a hero or a villain? Discuss. Does the fact that he benefitted immensely from his actions influence your perception of him? Explain.

Source: "Corporate Layoffs and the Fate of American Workers," *ABC News Nightline,* February 14, 1996.

• PART 2 •
Planning

Foundations of Planning

3

LEARNING OBJECTIVES

What will I be able to do after I finish this chapter?

1. **DEFINE** planning.
2. **EXPLAIN** the potential benefits of planning.
3. **IDENTIFY** potential drawbacks to planning.
4. **DISTINGUISH** between strategic and tactical plans.
5. **STATE** when directional plans are preferred over specific plans.
6. **DEFINE** management by objectives and identify its common elements.
7. **OUTLINE** the steps in the strategic management process.
8. **DESCRIBE** the four grand strategies.
9. **EXPLAIN** SWOT analysis.
10. **COMPARE** how entrepreneurs and bureaucratic managers approach strategy.

ALLEN CHAO GREW UP IN TAIWAN.[1] His parents owned and operated a large pharmaceutical manufacturing business. Their dream was for Allen to be educated in pharmacy sciences at a U.S. institution and then to return home to succeed his father. But along the way, their plans changed. After earning a doctorate degree from Purdue University in 1973 in industrial and physical pharmacy, Allen chose to work as a researcher for G. D. Searle & Company. Five years later, after being recognized for his creative abilities, Chao was promoted to director of new product and new pharmaceutical technology development. Meanwhile, Allen's parents had sold their business and decided to relocate to California. In 1983, Chao followed in his parents' footsteps and started his own company, naming it after his mother's family name, Hwa, and adding the word *son* to it. Americanizing the name, he formed Watson Pharmaceuticals. His company would specialize in the manufacturing of generic drugs.

Like many entrepreneurs, Allen Chao found that starting a company is difficult. He needed more than $4 million just to set up labs—yet no lenders would invest in him. It was too risky in the fiercely competitive pharmaceutical business—especially for a company specializing in manufacturing generic drugs. But, like a true entrepreneur, Chao was not deterred by setbacks. He knew he could be successful, so he turned to his family and friends in Taiwan—giving up almost 90 percent of the equity in the business in exchange for start-up capital.

Allen Chao has combined entrepreneurial skills and a strong focus to build a successful corporation. His business is centered on generic drugs. Watson Pharmaceuticals has reached annual sales nearing $100 million, producing profits of more than $12 million annually.

Chao's strategy was unlike most other strategies in the generic drug business. Large competitors targeted multimillion dollar markets and high-volume drugs such as Tagamet and Valium. Watson Pharmaceuticals specialized in producing generic equivalents of hard-to-copy medicines such as Lederle's Asendin brand of antidepressants and Loxitane's Loxapine brand of tranquilizers. Furthermore, most of Chao's competition sought to compete in the generic markets where annual sales were at least $150 million, and they went after named drugs. Chao, on the other hand, chose to go after market segments where sales rarely exceeded $10 million and where little drug name recognition existed.

Has his strategy paid off? You bet! Since introducing its first generic drug in 1985, Watson Pharmaceuticals now has fifty-nine products on the market. And fourteen of them have no direct competition. In fact, Chao's niche of going after the smaller markets has led Watson Pharmaceuticals to control almost 50 percent of those markets. His strategy has resulted in annual revenues approaching $100 million and profits exceeding $12 million.

This chapter presents the basics of planning. In the following pages, you will learn the difference between formal and informal planning, why managers plan, and the various types of plans managers use. We will explore the strategic planning process and will look at the various strategies available to organizations and ways they can develop and maintain a competitive advantage. Finally, we will discuss entrepreneurship and how it is a special type of strategic planning.

Planning Defined

What is meant by the term *planning?* As we stated in Chapter 1, planning encompasses defining the organization's objectives or goals, establishing an overall strategy for achieving those goals, and developing a comprehensive hierarchy of plans to integrate and coordinate activities. It is concerned, then, with *ends* (what is to be done) as well as with *means* (how it is to be done).

Planning can be further defined in terms of whether it is *informal* or *formal.* All managers engage in planning, but it might be only the informal variety. In informal planning, very little, if anything, is written down. What is to be accomplished is in the head of one or a few people. Furthermore, the organization's objectives are rarely verbalized. This generally describes planning in many small businesses; the owner-manager has a private vision of where he or she wants to go and how he or she expects to get there. The planning is general and lacks continuity. Of course, informal planning exists in some large organizations, and some small businesses have very sophisticated formal plans.

When we use the term *planning* in this book, however, we are implying formal planning. Specific objectives that cover a period of years are formulated. These objectives are written down and made available to organization members. Finally, specific action programs exist for the achievement of these objectives. This means that management clearly defines the path it wants to take to get from where it is to where it wants to be.

Planning in Uncertain Environments

If managers performed their jobs in organizations that never faced changes in the environment, there would be little need for planning. What a manager did today, and well into the future, would be precisely the same as it was decades ago. There would be no need to think about what to do. It would be spelled out in some manual. In such a world, planning efforts would be unnecessary. But we know that that world doesn't exist today. Technological, social, political, economic, and legal changes are ever-present. The environment managers face is too dynamic and has too great an effect on an organization's survival to be left to chance events. Accordingly, contemporary managers must plan—and plan effectively.

If . . . organizations . . . never faced changes in the environment, there would be little need for planning.

Why Should Managers Formally Plan?

Managers should engage in planning for several reasons. Four of the more popular justifications are that planning provides direction, reduces the impact of change, minimizes waste and redundancy, and sets the standards to facilitate control (see Exhibit 3-1).

Planning establishes coordinated effort. It gives direction to managers and nonmanagers alike. When all organizational members understand where the organization is going and what they must contribute to reach the objectives, they can begin to coordinate their activities. When they do, cooperation and teamwork are fostered. On the other hand, a lack of planning can cause various organizational members or their units to work against one another. Consequently, the organization may be prevented from moving efficiently toward its objectives.

By forcing managers to look ahead, anticipate change, consider the impact of change, and develop appropriate responses, planning reduces uncertainty. It also

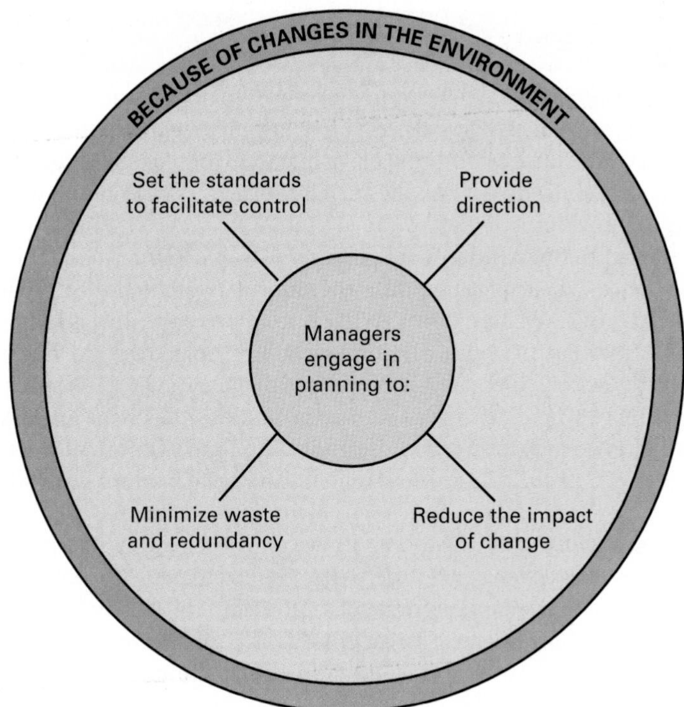

Exhibit 3-1
Reasons for Planning

clarifies the consequences of the actions managers might take in response to change. Planning, then, is precisely what is needed when managing in a chaotic environment.

Planning also reduces overlapping and wasteful activities. Coordination before the fact is likely to uncover waste and redundancy. Furthermore, when means and ends are clear, inefficiencies become obvious.

Finally, planning establishes objectives or standards that facilitate control. If organizational members are unsure of what they are attempting to achieve, how can they determine whether they have achieved it? In planning, objectives are developed. In the controlling function of management, performance is compared against the established objectives. If and when significant deviations are identified, corrective action can be taken. Without planning, then, there truly cannot be effective control.

What Are Some Criticisms of Formal Planning?

Formalized planning became very popular in the 1960s. And, for the most part, it still is today! It makes sense to establish some direction. After all, as the Cheshire cat said to Alice in the *Alice in Wonderland* story, the way you ought to go "depends a good deal on where you want to get to." But critics have begun to challenge some of the basic assumptions underlying planning. Let's look at the major arguments that have been offered against formal planning (see Managers Who Made a Difference).

Planning may create rigidity.[2] Formal planning efforts can lock an organization into specific goals to be achieved within specific timetables. When these objectives were set, the assumption may have been made that the environment wouldn't change during the time period the objectives cover. If that assumption is faulty, managers who follow a plan may have trouble. Rather than remaining flexible—and possibly scrapping the plan—managers who continue to do the things required to achieve the originally set objectives may not be able to cope with the changed environment. Forcing a course of action when the environment is fluid can be a recipe for disaster. When that occurred at the Toronto-based business-form company Moore Corporation, Ltd., the result was a loss of several million dollars in annual revenues.[3]

Plans can't be developed for a dynamic environment.[4] As we mentioned a few sentences ago, most organizations today face dynamic change in their environments. If a basic assumption of making plans—that the environment won't change—is faulty, then how can one make plans at all? We have described today's business environment as chaotic. By definition, that means random and unpredictable. Managing chaos and turning disasters into opportunities requires flexibility. And that may mean not being tied to formal plans.

Not all strategies work well. Beech Aircraft, the makers of this jet, bet that their innovative airplane, the *Starship*, would be a huge success. They built the fuselage and wings out of materials that are 350 percent stronger than aluminum and 15 to 20 percent lighter. The plane should have been much more fuel-efficient and less costly to operate than less-innovative planes. But problems with the design added significantly more weight to the plane. There also were problems with FAA regulations. Sales were dismal. All told, this innovative aircraft project ended up being a $750 million failure.

Formal plans can't replace intuition and creativity.[5] Successful organizations are typically the result of someone's vision. But these visions have a tendency to become formalized as they evolve. Formal planning efforts typically follow a methodology that includes a thorough investigation of the organization's capabilities and opportunities and a mechanistic analysis that reduces the vision to a programmed routine. That can spell disaster for an organization. For instance, the rapid rise of Apple Computer in the late 1970s and throughout the 1980s was attributed, in part, to the creativity and anticorporate attitudes of one of its cofounders, Steven Jobs. But as the company grew, Jobs felt a need for more-formalized management—something he was uncomfortable performing. He hired a CEO, who ultimately ousted Jobs from his own company. With Jobs's departure came increased organizational formality—the same thing Jobs despised so much because it hampered creativity. By 1996, this one-time leader of its industry had lost much of its creativity and was struggling for survival.[6]

Planning focuses managers' attention on today's competition, not on tomorrow's survival.[7] Formal planning has a tendency to focus on how to best capitalize on existing business opportunities within the industry. It often does not allow for managers to consider creating or reinventing the industry. Consequently, formal plans may result in costly blunders and incur catch-up costs when others take the lead. On the other hand, companies such as Intel and ABB (Asea Brown Boveri) have found much of their success coming from forging into uncharted waters, designing and developing new industries as they go![8]

Formal planning reinforces success, which may lead to failure.[9] We have been taught that success breeds success. That has been an American "tradition." After all, if it's not broken, don't fix it. Right? Well, maybe not! Success may, in fact, breed failure in an uncertain environment. It is hard to change or discard successful plans—leaving the comfort of what works for the anxiety of the unknown. Successful plans, however, may provide a false sense of security—generating more confidence in the formal plans than they deserve. Managers often won't deliberately face that unknown until they are forced to do so by changes in the environment. But by then, it may be too late!

The Bottom Line: Does Planning Improve Organizational Performance?

Do managers and organizations that plan outperform those that don't? Or have the critics of planning won the debate? Let's look at the evidence.

Contrary to the reasons the critics of planning cite, the evidence generally supports the position that organizations should have formal plans. But that's not to be interpreted as a blanket endorsement of planning. We cannot say that organizations that

Managers Who Made a Difference

Anita Roddick, Founder of Body Shop International

Some people just have a knack for being successful! Those words couldn't apply more to Anita Roddick, founder of Body Shop International, based in Littlehampton, Sussex, England.[10] In 1976, Anita founded this natural soap and lotions company in Brighton, England. From the very beginning, Roddick's strategy was to build a successful company that was environmentally friendly. Her mission was to create a company of "character and cause," driven by principles not by profits. She wanted her product line to include products that were made from only natural ingredients and none of which had been tested on animals.

Anita Roddick knows that when you're "queen of the hill" competitors will come after you. But just knowing about competitors isn't enough. The organization must be able to change, but not so much that it loses sight of its primary way of doing business. In Roddick's case, after losing market share, she returned Body Shop International to its basic, more flexible plans and structure and is once again seeing profits rise.

Through the years, Anita has never lost sight of her initial vision. The company grew from its single store in Brighton to 1,366 stores in forty-six countries. In fact, by 1995, Body Shop International was Britain's most successful company, with annual sales of approximately $360 million. This kind of success, however, doesn't go unrecognized. Other organizations look at what is being achieved, and those with the abilities enter the market. One such organization is the U.S.-based Bath and Body Works.

What distinguished the Bath and Body Works from Body Shop International was that it had the backing of a major U.S. Corporation, the Limited. Because of the Limited's stronghold in mall retailing, they have been able to successfully take business away from Roddick's company. In fact, while Body Shop International has had significant growth in Asia, South Korea, and the Philippines and has maintained a healthy market share in Britain, its stores in the United States have lost money. Why? There are always many reasons associated with a decline. One reason, obviously, is that there is now formidable competition in the United States. But evidence indicates that Roddick let her company become too much of a bureaucracy. She knew competition would come after her. That's all part of business. So she set into motion rigid strategic plans and organizational structures. But as her organization became more formalized, it also became slow in its ability to react to the environment. For example, early in the organization's formative years, Roddick could get a new product to market in a matter of a few months. More recently, it has taken well over a year to accomplish the same feat. Rigidity and formality at the Body Shop have "squashed a lot of the entrepreneurial spirit."

Sometimes competition brings an organization back to reality. Will rekindling the entrepreneurial spirit work? Roddick recognizes that it will take a couple of years to answer that question. So far, though, her actions appear to be working; profits are beginning to rise and U.S. losses have been curtailed.

formally plan *always* outperform those that don't. That statement would be inaccurate.

Many studies have been undertaken to test the relationship between planning and performance.[11] On the basis of those studies, we can draw the following conclusions. First, where formal planning exists in an organization, there are generally higher profits, higher return on assets, and other positive financial results. Second, the *quality* of the planning process and the appropriate *implementation* of the plans probably contribute more to high performance than does the *extent* of planning. Finally, in those organizations in which formal planning did not lead to higher performance, the environment was typically the culprit. For instance, government regulations and similar environmental constraints reduce the impact of planning on an organization's performance. Why? Because managers will have fewer viable alternatives to choose from. For example, planning efforts by Rebecca Mark and her staff at Enron Corporation (a Houston-based energy company) suggested that it was a good decision to enter into an agreement to build a power plant in Dabhol, India. However, when the Indian government abruptly canceled the $2.8 billion contract as a result of "a rising backlash against foreign investments," the value of Enron's planning effort was significantly reduced.[12] When uncertainty is high, there's no reason to anticipate that organizations that plan will outperform those that do not.

Rebecca Mark, chairman and CEO of Enron Corporation, has witnessed firsthand the volatility of doing business globally. The uncertainty surrounding her company's $2.8 billion contract in Dabhol, India, finally came to light as Enron's contract was canceled by Indian government officials.

Types of Plans

The most popular ways to describe plans are by their *breadth* (strategic versus tactical), *time frame* (long term versus short), *specificity* (directional versus specific), and *frequency of use* (single use versus standing). Keep in mind, however, these planning classifications are not independent of one another. For instance, there is a close relationship between the short- and long-term categories and the strategic and tactical categories. Exhibit 3-2 illustrates the relationship of types of plans.

How Do Strategic and Tactical Planning Differ?

Plans that apply to the entire organization, that establish the organization's overall objectives, and that seek to position the organization in terms of its environment are called **strategic plans.** It is the strategic plans that drive the organization's efforts to achieve its goals. As these plans filter down in the organization, they serve as a basis for

strategic plans
Plans that are organizationwide, establish overall objectives, and position an organization in terms of its environment.

Exhibit 3-2
Types of Plans

BREADTH	TIME FRAME	SPECIFICITY	FREQUENCY OF USE
Strategic	Long-term	Directional	Single use
Tactical	Short-term	Specific	Standing

tactical plans
Plans that specify the details of how an organization's overall objectives are to be achieved.

forming the tactical plans. **Tactical plans** specify the details of how the overall objectives are to be achieved. How do strategic and tactical plans differ? Strategic and tactical plans differ in three primary ways—their time frame, scope, and whether they include a known set of organizational objectives.[13] Tactical plans tend to cover shorter periods of time. For instance, an organization's monthly, weekly, and day-to-day plans are almost all tactical. On the other hand, strategic plans tend to include an extended time period—usually five years or more. They also cover a broader area and deal less with specifics. Finally, strategic plans include the formulation of objectives, whereas tactical plans assume the existence of objectives. Tactical plans describe how those objectives will be attained.

In What Time Frame Do Plans Exist?

Financial analysts traditionally describe investment returns as short- and long-term. The short term covers less than one year. Any time frame beyond five years is classified as long-term. Managers have adopted the same terminology to describe plans. For clarity, we will emphasize **short-term plans** and **long-term plans** in this discussion.

short-term plans
Plans that cover less than one year.

long-term plans
Plans that extend beyond five years.

The difference between short- and long-term plans is important given the length of future commitments and the degree of variability organizations face. For example, the more an organization's current plans affect future commitments, the longer the time frame for which management should plan. That is, plans should extend far enough to see through those commitments that are made today. Planning too long or too short a period is inefficient.

With respect to the degree of variability, the greater the uncertainty, the more plans should be of the short-term variety. That is, if rapid or important technological, social, economic, legal, or other changes are taking place, well-defined and precisely chartered routes are more likely to hinder an organization's performance than to aid it. Shorter-term plans allow for better accommodation of changes by providing more flexibility.

Strategic plans include the formulation of objectives.

What Is the Difference between Specific and Directional Plans?

It appears intuitively correct that specific plans are always preferable to directional, or loosely guided, plans. **Specific plans** have clearly defined objectives. There is no ambiguity, and there are no problems with misunderstandings. For example, a manager who seeks to increase her firm's sales by 16 percent over a given twelve-month period might establish specific procedures, budget allocations, and schedules of activities to reach that objective. These actions represent specific plans.

specific plans
Plans that have clearly defined objectives and leave no room for misinterpretation.

However, specific plans are not without drawbacks. They require clarity and a predictability that often does not exist. When uncertainty is high, and management must maintain flexibility in order to respond to unexpected changes, then directional plans are preferable.[14] As shown in Exhibit 3-3, both directional and specific plans can lead you from point A to point B. If there were a detour on Sussex Road, however, the specific plans might create confusion. **Directional plans,** on the other hand, identify general guidelines. They provide focus but do not lock managers into specific objectives or specific courses of action. A specific plan might aim to cut costs by 10 percent and increase revenues by 8 percent in the next six months; a directional plan might aim at improving corporate profits by 6 to 12 percent during the next six months. The flexibility inherent in directional plans is obvious. This advantage must be weighed against the loss in clarity provided by specific plans.

directional plans
Flexible plans that set out general guidelines.

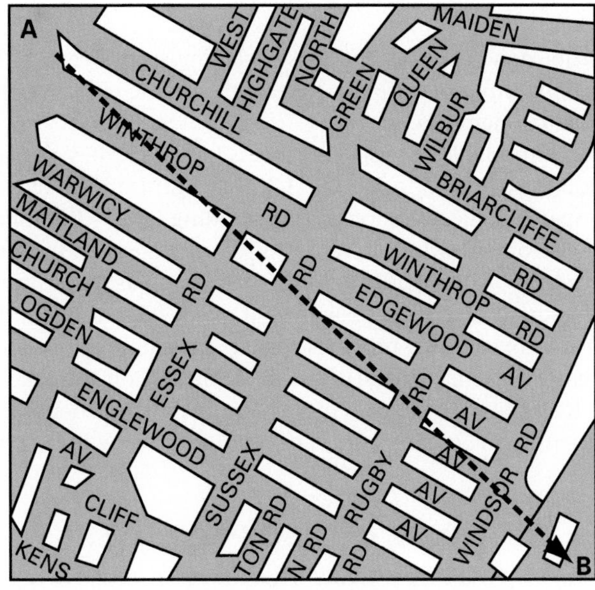

Directional plan

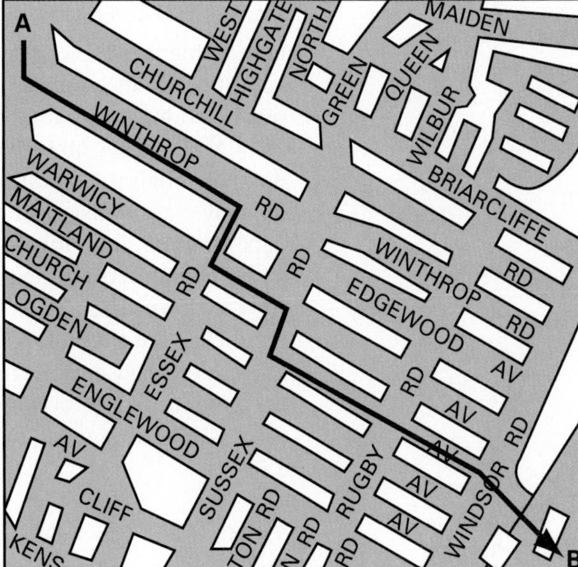

Specific plan

Exhibit 3-3
Directional versus Specific Plans

How Do Single-Use and Standing Plans Differ?

Some plans are meant to be used only once; others are used repeatedly. A **single-use plan** is used to meet the need of a particular or unique situation. For example, in 1996 when SBC Communications Inc. purchased the Pacific Telis Group, top managers devised a single-use plan to guide the acquisition.[15]

single-use plan
A plan that is used to meet the needs of a particular or unique situation.

Standing plans, in contrast, are ongoing. They provide guidance for repeatedly performed actions in the organization. For example, when you register for classes for the coming semester, you are experiencing a standing "registration" plan at your college or university. The dates have changed, but the process works in the same way semester after semester.

standing plan
A plan that is ongoing and provides guidance for repeatedly performed actions in an organization.

Management by Objectives

At Cypress Semiconductor Corporation, a computer chip manufacturer in San Jose, California, every employee defines specific, quantifiable objectives for which he or she will be responsible.[16] When T. J. Rogers took over as president, he wanted an objective-setting program that would specify exactly what his managers and employees were expected to accomplish and that would motivate rather than intimidate. What he installed was a system of participatory objective setting.

Rogers was using **management by objectives (MBO).** It is a system in which specific performance objectives are jointly determined by subordinates and their superiors, progress toward objectives is periodically reviewed, and rewards are allocated on the basis of that progress. Rather than using goals to control, MBO uses them to motivate.

management by objectives (MBO)
A system in which specific performance objectives are jointly determined by subordinates and their superiors, progress toward objectives is periodically reviewed, and rewards are allocated on the basis of that progress.

What Is MBO?

Management by objectives is not new. The concept goes back almost fifty years.[17] Its appeal lies in its emphasis on converting overall objectives into specific objectives for organizational units and individual members.

MBO makes objectives operational by devising a process by which they cascade down through the organization. As depicted in Exhibit 3-4, the organization's overall objectives are translated into specific objectives for each succeeding level—divisional, departmental, individual—in the organization. Because lower-unit managers jointly participate in setting their own goals, MBO works from the bottom up as well as from the top down. The result is a hierarchy that links objectives at one level to those at the next level. For the individual employee, MBO provides specific personal performance objectives. Each person, therefore, has an identified specific contribution to make to his or her unit's performance. If all the individuals achieve their goals, then their unit's goals will be attained. Subsequently, the organization's overall objectives will become a reality.

What Are the Common Elements to an MBO Program?

There are four ingredients common to MBO programs. These are goal specificity, participative decision making, an explicit time period, and performance feedback.

The objectives in MBO should be concise statements of expected accomplishments. It is not adequate, for example, merely to state a desire to cut costs, improve service, or increase quality. Such desires need to be converted into tangible objectives that can be measured and evaluated. To cut departmental costs by 12 percent, to improve service by ensuring that all insurance claims are processed within seventy-two hours after receipt, or to increase quality by keeping returns to less than 0.05 percent of sales are examples of specific objectives.

In MBO, the objectives are not unilaterally set by the boss and assigned to employees, as is characteristic of traditional objective setting. MBO replaces these imposed goals with participatively determined goals. The manager and employee jointly choose the goals and agree on how they will be achieved.

Each objective has a concise time period in which it is to be completed. Typically, the time period is three months, six months, or a year. The final ingredient in an MBO program is feedback on performance. MBO seeks to give continuous feedback on progress toward goals. Ideally, this is accomplished by giving ongoing feedback to in-

Exhibit 3-4
Cascading of Objectives

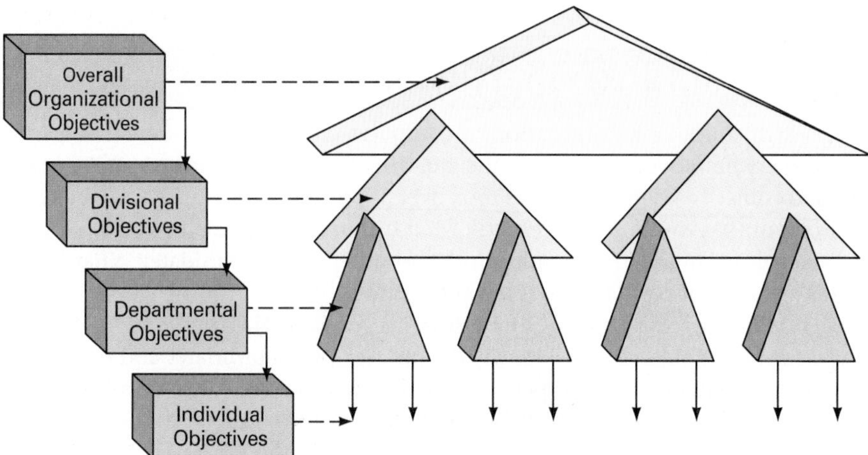

dividuals so they can monitor and correct their own actions. This is supplemented by periodic formal appraisal meetings in which superiors and subordinates can review progress toward goals and further feedback can be provided.

Does MBO Work?

Assessing the effectiveness of MBO is a complex task. Let's briefly review a growing body of literature on the relationship between goals and performance.[18] If factors such as a person's ability and acceptance of goals are held constant, evidence demonstrates that more-difficult goals lead to higher performance. Although individuals with very difficult goals achieve them far less often than those with very easy goals, they nevertheless perform at a consistently higher level.

Moreover, studies consistently support the finding that specific hard goals produce a higher level of output than do no goals or generalized goals such as "do your best." Feedback also favorably affects performance. Feedback lets a person know whether his or her level of effort is sufficient or needs to be increased. It can induce a person to raise his or her goal level after attaining a previous goal and can inform a person of ways in which to improve his or her performance.

The results cited above are all consistent with MBO's stress on specific goals and feedback. MBO implies, rather than explicitly states, that goals must be perceived as feasible. Research on goal setting indicates that MBO is most effective if the goals are difficult enough to require the person to do some stretching (see Developing a Management Skill).

But what about participation? MBO strongly advocates that goals be set participatively. Does the research demonstrate that participatively set goals lead to higher performance than those assigned by a manager? Somewhat surprisingly, the research comparing participatively set and assigned goals on performance has not shown any strong or consistent relationships.[19] When goal difficulty has been held constant, assigned goals frequently do as well as participatively determined goals, contrary to MBO ideology. Therefore, it is not possible to argue for the superiority of participation as MBO proponents advocate. One major benefit from participation, however, is that it appears to induce individuals to establish more-difficult goals.[20] Thus, participation may have a positive effect on performance by increasing one's goal-aspiration level.

Participation may have a positive effect on performance by increasing one's goal-aspiration level.

Studies of actual MBO programs confirm that MBO effectively increases employee performance and organizational productivity. A review of seventy programs, for example, found organizational productivity gains in sixty-eight of them.[21] This same review also identified top management commitment to MBO as critical for it to reach its potential. When top managers had a high commitment to MBO and were personally involved in its implementation, the average gain in productivity was 56 percent. When commitment and involvement were low, the average gain in productivity dropped to only 6 percent.

Is There a Downside to Objectives?

Despite some strong evidence indicating that specific employee goals are linked to higher performance, not everyone supports the value of setting objectives. One of the most vocal critics of processes like MBO was the late W. Edwards Deming.[22] Deming argued that specific goals may, in fact, do more harm than good. He felt that employees tend to focus on the goals by which they will be judged, so they may direct their efforts toward quantity of output (what's being measured) and away from quality. Specific goals also, say some critics, encourage individual achievement rather than

Developing a Management Skill

STEPS IN GOAL SETTING

About the Skill: *Employees should have a clear under-standing of what they're attempting to accomplish. Further, managers have the responsibility for seeing that this task is achieved by helping employees set work goals. These two statements appear to be common sense. Managers frequently think that, too. But that's not the case. Setting goals is a skill that every manager must perform well. The steps below, when applied, can lead to better performance by employees who know what is expected.*

Steps in practicing the skill

1. ***Identify an employee's key job tasks.*** Goal setting begins by defining what it is that you want your employees to accomplish. The best source for this information is each employee's job description.

2. ***Establish specific and challenging goals for each key task.*** Identify the level of performance expected of each employee. Specify the target for the employee to hit.

3. ***Specify the deadlines for each goal.*** Putting deadlines on each goal reduces ambiguity. Deadlines, however, should not be set arbitrarily. Rather, they need to be realistic given the tasks to be completed.

4. ***Allow the employee to actively participate.*** When employees participate in goal setting, they are more likely to accept the goals. However, it must be sincere participation. That is, employees must perceive that you are truly seeking their input, not just going through the motions.

5. ***Prioritize goals.*** When you give someone more than one goal, it is important for you to rank the goals in order of importance. The purpose of prioritizing is to encourage the employee to take action and expend effort on each goal in proportion to its importance.

6. ***Rate goals for difficulty and importance.*** Goal setting should not encourage people to choose easy goals. Instead, goals should be rated for their difficulty and importance. When goals are rated, individuals can be given credit for trying difficult goals, even if they don't fully achieve them.

7. ***Build in feedback mechanisms to assess goal progress.*** Feedback lets employees know whether their level of effort is sufficient to attain the goal. Feedback should be both self- and supervisor-generated. In either case, feedback should be frequent and recurring.

8. ***Link rewards to goal attainment.*** It's natural for employees to ask "What's in it for me?" Linking rewards to the achievement of goals will help answer that question.

promote a team focus.[23] In addition, Deming believed that, when objectives are set, employees tend to view them as ceilings rather than as floors. That is, after setting a goal and achieving it, employees will tend to relax. Consequently, specific goals tend to limit employees' potential and discourage efforts for continuous improvement.

The criticisms of objectives are potentially correct. However, they can be overcome.[24] One means for managers to assist in this matter is to ensure that employees have multiple goals—all of which have a quality component. For instance, an insurance claims adjuster could be evaluated not only on the total number of claims processed but also on the number of errors made. Managers should also treat MBO as an ongoing activity. This means that they should regularly review goals with employees and make changes when warranted. Furthermore, managers should reward employees for setting difficult goals—even if they aren't fully achieved. In doing so, managers reduce or eliminate the perception that failing to achieve goals results in punishment. If fear of reprisal dominates employees' thinking, employees are likely to try to set easier, attainable goals. As a result, employees won't stretch themselves by setting ambitious goals, and, ultimately, productivity will be reduced.

Using MBO-like measures, Harley-Davidson is responding to its customer demand by increasing production capacity from 115,000 to 200,000 motorcycles by 2003. That production goal and management's desire to improve dealerships and expand into global markets have given this "heavy bike" manufacturer some standards against which it can measure its progress.

The Importance of an Organizational Strategy

Before the early 1970s, managers who made long-range plans generally assumed that better times lay ahead. Plans for the future were merely extensions of where the organization had been in the past. However, the energy crisis, deregulation, accelerating technological change, and increasing global competition, as well as other environmental shocks of the 1970s and 1980s, undermined this approach to long-range planning.[25] These changes in the rules of the game forced managers to develop a systematic means of analyzing the environment, assessing their organization's strengths and weaknesses, and identifying opportunities where the organization could have a competitive advantage. The value of thinking strategically began to be recognized.[26]

One recent survey of business owners found that 69 percent had strategic plans, and, among those who had plans, 89 percent responded that they had found their plans to be effective.[27] They said, for example, that strategic planning gave them specific goals and provided their staffs with a unified vision. Other studies have also supported the premise that companies that plan strategically have better financial measurements than those without plans.[28]

Today, strategic planning has moved beyond the private sector to include government agencies, hospitals, and educational institutions. For example, the skyrocketing costs of a college education, competition from companies offering alternative educational forums, and cutbacks in federal aid for students and research have led many university administrators to assess their colleges' aspirations and identify a market niche in which they can survive, prosper, and implement an effective strategy.[29]

A Strategic Framework: Choosing a Niche

When an organization attempts to develop its strategy, senior management goes through an activity called the strategic management process. The **strategic management process,** as illustrated in Exhibit 3-5, is a nine-step process that involves strategic planning, implementation, and evaluation. Strategic planning encompasses the first seven steps, but even the best strategies can go awry if management fails either

strategic management process
A nine-step process that involves strategic planning, implementation and evaluation.

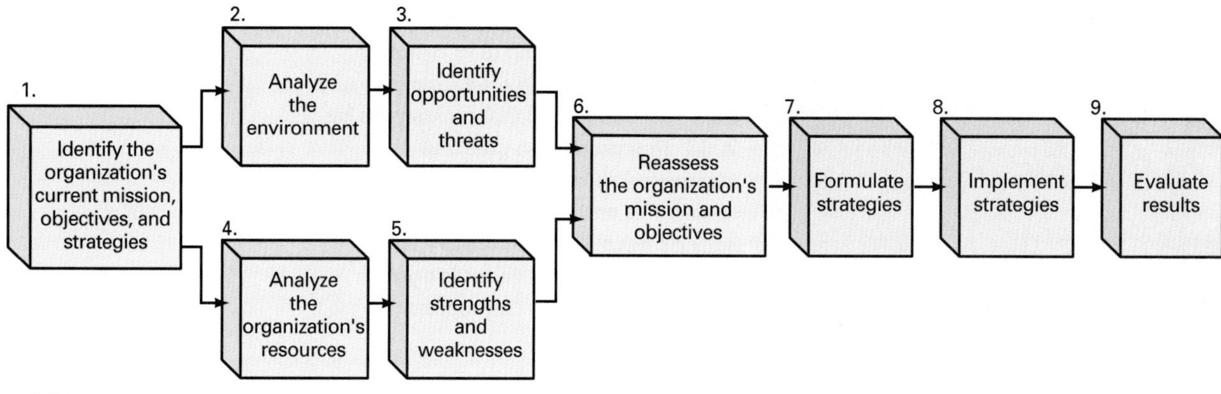

Exhibit 3-5
The Strategic Management Process

to implement them properly or to evaluate their results. Let's look at the various steps in the strategic management process.

How Does the Strategic Management Process Operate?

In order to develop their strategy, organizational members must first identify the organization's current mission, objectives, and strategies (step 1). Every organization has a **mission** that defines its purpose and answers the question What business or businesses are we in? Defining the organization's mission forces management to identify the scope of its products or services carefully. For example, Oticon Holding A/S of Hellerup, Denmark, set its sights on becoming the world premier hearing-aid manufacturer. Achieving that mission "drives the business, mobilizes the workers, and gets the high-quality product to the market."[30]

mission
The purpose of an organization.

Determining the nature of one's business is as important for not-for-profit organizations as it is for business firms. Hospitals, government agencies, and colleges must also identify their missions. For example, is a college training students for the professions, training students for particular jobs, or educating students through a well-rounded, liberal education? Is it seeking students from the top 5 percent of high school graduates, students with low academic grades but high aptitude test scores, or students in the vast middle ground? Answers to questions such as these clarify the organization's current purpose (see Applying the Concepts, at the end of the chapter). Once its mission has been identified, the organization can begin to look outside the company to ensure that its strategy aligns well with the environment.[31] As a case in point, Panasonic is a major producer of home entertainment systems. But beginning in the mid-1980s, technological breakthroughs in miniaturization and the social trend toward living in smaller homes dramatically increased the demand for powerful, but highly compact, sound systems. The success of Panasonic's home audio strategy depends on understanding the technological and social changes that are taking place in its environment.

Management of every organization needs to analyze its environment (step 2). In the Netherlands, by law, proprietary information is public. But organizations in other countries—such as the United States—must obtain that information on their own.[32] That means that these organizations need to find out, for instance, what their competition is up to, what pending legislation might affect them, what their customers desire, and what the supply of labor in locations where they operate is like. By analyzing the external environment, managers are in a better position to define the available strategies—those that best align with their environment.[33] For example, to address a customer desire for an environmentally friendly grill, Thermos, the Schaumburg, Illinois, bottle and lunch box company[34] developed an electric barbecue grill that cooked foods that tasted like foods cooked on gas and charcoal grills. But Thermos's grill did not have the potential for creating air pollution. By understanding their environment, Thermos was able to capitalize on a product that increased its total revenues by more than 13 percent. That's what understanding an organization's environment is all about!

Step 2 of the strategy process is complete when management has an accurate grasp of what is taking place in its environment and is aware of important trends that might affect its operations.

What Are the Primary Steps in the Strategic Management Process?

After analyzing the environment, management needs to evaluate what it has learned in terms of **opportunities** that the organization can exploit and **threats** that the organization faces (step 3).[35] In a very simplistic way, opportunities are positive external environmental factors, while threats are negative ones.

opportunities
Positive external environmental factors.

threats
Negative external environmental factors.

Keep in mind, however, that the same environment can present opportunities to one organization and pose threats to another in the same or a similar industry because of their different resources or different focus. Take communications, for example. Telecommuting technologies have enabled organizations that sell computer modems, fax machines, and the like to prosper. But organizations such as the U.S. Post Office and even Federal Express, whose business it is to get messages from one person to another, have been adversely affected by this environmental change.

Karl Vuursteen, CEO of Heineken, sees U.S. beer makers as great threats to his Amsterdam-based company. Although Heineken's market is larger than either Miller's or Anheuser-Busch's, some of their movement in Asia, Latin America, and Europe is making Vuursteen pay close attention to his competitors' actions.

Next, in step 4, we move from looking outside the organization to looking inside.[36] That is, we are evaluating the organization's internal resources. What skills and abilities do the organization's employees have? What is the organization's cash flow? Has it been successful at developing new and innovative products? How do customers perceive the image of the organization and the quality of its products or services?

This fourth step forces management to recognize that every organization, no matter how large and powerful, is constrained in some way by the resources and skills it has available. A small automobile manufacturer, such as Volvo, cannot start making minivans simply because its management sees opportunities in that market. Volvo does not have the resources to successfully compete against the likes of Chrysler, Ford, Toyota, and Nissan. On the other hand, Renault and a Peugeot-Fiat partnership can, and they may begin expanding their European markets by selling minivans in North America.[37]

The analysis in step 4 should lead to a clear assessment of the organization's internal resources—such as capital, worker skills, patents, and the like. It should also indicate organizational departmental abilities such as training and development, marketing, accounting, human resources, research and development, and management information systems. Internal resources that are available or things that the organization does well are called its **strengths.** And any of those strengths that represent unique skills or resources that can determine the organization's competitive edge are

strengths
Internal resources that are available or things that an organization does well.

distinctive competence Unique skills or resources that can determine an organization's competitive edge.

weaknesses Resources that an organization lacks or activities that it does not do well.

called its **distinctive competence.** Black & Decker, for instance, bought General Electric's small-appliances division—which made coffeemakers, toasters, irons, and the like—renamed them, and capitalized on Black & Decker's reputation for quality and durability to make these appliances far more profitable than they had been under the GE name. In a similar fashion, Calgary's Big Rock Brewery has built a distinctive competence simply by creating a special taste for its beers and giving them "ugly names like Warthog and Grasshopper."[38] On the other hand, those resources that an organization lacks or activities that the firm does not do well are its **weaknesses** (step 5).

An understanding of the organization's culture and the strengths and weaknesses of its culture is a crucial part of step 5 that has only recently been getting the attention it deserves.[39] Specifically, managers should be aware that strong and weak cultures have different effects on strategy and that the content of a culture has a major effect on the content of the strategy.

In a strong culture, for instance, almost all employees will have a clear understanding of what the organization is about. In a strong culture, it should be easy for management to convey to new employees the organization's distinctive competence. A department store chain such as Nordstrom, which has a very strong culture that embraces service and customer satisfaction, should be able to instill its cultural values in new employees in a much shorter time than can a competitor with a weak culture. The negative side of a strong culture, of course, is that it is difficult to change. A strong culture may act as a significant barrier to acceptance of a change in the organization's strategies. In fact, the strong culture at Wang Labs undoubtedly kept top management from perceiving the need to adopt a new corporate strategy in the 1980s in response to changes in the computer industry—and led, in part, to the demise of the organization. Successful organizations with strong cultures can become prisoners of their own past successes.

SWOT analysis Analysis of an organization's strengths, weaknesses, opportunities, and threats in order to identify a strategic niche that the organization can exploit.

What Is SWOT Analysis?

A merging of the externalities (steps 2 and 3) with the internalities (steps 4 and 5) results in an assessment of the organization's opportunities (see Exhibit 3-6). This merging is frequently called **SWOT analysis** because it brings together the organization's **S**trengths, **W**eaknesses, **O**pportunities, and **T**hreats in order to identify a strategic niche that the organization can exploit. Having completed the SWOT analysis, the or-

Exhibit 3-6
SWOT: Identifying Organizational Opportunities

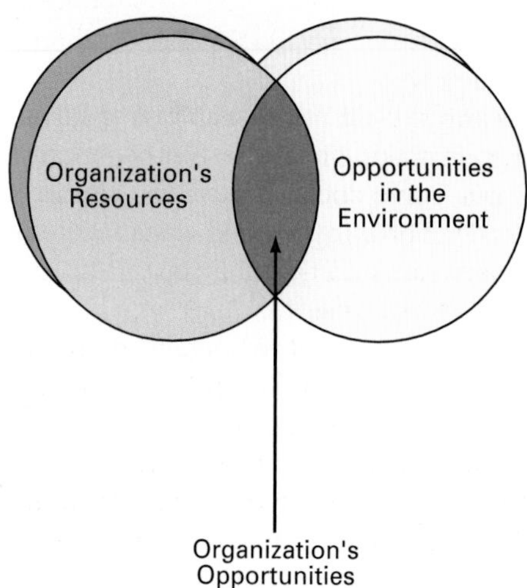

ganization reassesses its mission and objectives (Exhibit 3-5, step 6). For example, as the demand for film continues to rise worldwide, managers at Kodak have developed plans to begin selling "yellow boxes of film" in such countries as Russia, India, and Brazil, where many of the "people . . . have yet to take their first picture."[40] Although there is risk associated with this venture, company executives feel that they have to exploit this strategic niche and take advantage of an opportunity in the external environment.

In light of the SWOT analysis and identification of the organization's opportunities, management reevaluates its mission and objectives. Are they realistic? Do they need modification? If changes are needed in the organization's overall direction, this is where they are likely to originate. On the other hand, if no changes are necessary, management is ready to begin the actual formulation of strategies.

How Do You Formulate Strategies?

Strategies need to be set for all levels in the organization (step 7). Management needs to develop and evaluate alternative strategies and then select a set that is compatible at each level and will allow the organization to best capitalize on its resources and the opportunities available in the environment. For most organizations, four primary strategies are available. Frequently called the **grand strategies,** they are growth, stability, retrenchment, and combination strategies.

grand strategies
The four primary types of strategies: growth, stability, retrenchment, and combination.

The Growth Strategy. If management of an organization believes that bigger is better, then it may choose a growth strategy. A **growth strategy** is one in which an organization attempts to increase the level of the organization's operations.[41] Growth can take the form of having more sales revenues, having more employees, or achieving more market share. Many "growth" organizations achieve this objective through direct expansion or by diversifying—merging with or acquiring other firms.

growth strategy
A strategy in which an organization attempts to increase the level of its operations; can take the form of increasing sales revenue, number of employees, or market share.

Growth through direct expansion involves increasing company size, revenues, operations, or work force. This effort is internally focused and does not involve other firms. For example, Dunkin' Donuts is pursuing a growth strategy when it expands. As opposed to purchasing other "donut" chains, Dunkin' Donuts expands by opening restaurants in new locations or by franchising to entrepreneurs who are willing to accept and do business the "Dunkin'" way. Growth, too, can also come from creating businesses within the organization. When Northwest Airlines decided to create and supply its own in-flight meals—as opposed to contracting with an external vendor—the airline was exhibiting a growth strategy by expanding its operations to include food distribution.

Companies may also grow by merging with other companies or acquiring similar firms. A **merger** occurs when two companies—usually of similar size—combine their resources to form a new company. For example, when the Lockheed and Martin-Marietta Corporation merged to form Lockheed-Martin, they did so to compete more effectively in the aerospace industry. Organizations can also acquire another firm. An **acquisition,** which is similar to a merger, usually happens when a larger company "buys" a smaller one—for a set amount of money or stocks, or both—and incorporates the acquired company's operations into its own. Examples include PepsiCo's acquisition of KFC, Pizza Hut, 7-Up International, and Taco Bell;[42] Samsung Electronic's acquisition of Array, Harris Microwave Semiconductors, Lux, Integrative Telecom Technologies, and AST Research;[43] and Seagram Company's acquisition of MCA (a film, television, and record company).[44] These acquisitions demonstrate a growth strategy whereby companies expand through diversification.

merger
Occurs when two companies, usually of similar size, combine their resources to form a new company.

acquisition
Occurs when a larger company buys a smaller one and incorporates the acquired company's operations into its own.

The Stability Strategy. A stability strategy is almost best known for what it is not. That is, the **stability strategy** is characterized by an absence of significant changes. This means that an organization continues to serve its same market and customers and maintains its market share. When is a stability strategy most appropriate? It is most appropriate when several conditions exist: a stable and unchanging environment, satisfactory organizational performance, an absence of valuable strengths and critical weaknesses, and only nonsignificant opportunities and threats.

stability strategy
A strategy that is characterized by an absence of significant change.

Talk about growth! Baby Superstore president, Linda Robertson, left a $55 a week part-time job as a legal secretary for attorney Jim Tate. Robertson and Tate joined forces and opened up Baby Superstore, now 155 stores strong. In just ten years, the company has grown from a start-up company to one with $1 billion in annual revenues.

Are there examples of organizations that are successfully employing a stability strategy? Yes. But most do not get the "press" that companies using other strategies get. One reason might be that no change means no news. Another might be that the company itself wants to keep a low profile; stakeholders may consider maintaining the status quo to be inappropriate, or the strategy may be an indication of rigidity of the planning process. Nonetheless, a company such as Kellogg's does use the stability strategy very well. Kellogg's, intent on exploiting its unique niche, has not moved far from its breakfast food market emphasis. The company also has not demonstrated a desire to diversify into other food markets as some of its competitors have.

The Retrenchment Strategy. Before the 1980s, very few North American companies ever had to consider anything but how to grow or maintain what they currently had. But, because of technological advancements, global competition, other environmental changes, mergers, and acquisitions growth and stability strategies are no longer viable for some companies. Instead, organizations such as Sears, AlliedSignal, General Motors, the U.S. Army, and Apple Computer have had to pursue a **retrenchment strategy.** This strategy is characteristic of an organization that is reducing its size. For management, it means setting a strategy in an environment of decline.[45]

retrenchment strategy
A strategy characteristic of a company that is reducing its size, usually in an environment of decline.

The Combination Strategy. A **combination strategy** is the simultaneous pursuit of two or more strategies described above. That is, one part of the organization may be pursuing a growth strategy while another is retrenching. For example, Pennzoil has sold off (retrenchment) declining business operations such as its Purolator oil-filter business. Simultaneously, it has expanded (growth) its oil marketing efforts into foreign markets and is developing new exploration efforts in such areas as Azerbaijan and Qatar.[46]

combination strategy
The simultaneous pursuit by an organization of two or more of growth, stability, and retrenchment strategies.

Determining a Competitive Strategy. The selection of a grand strategy sets the stage for the entire organization. Subsequently, each unit within the organization has to translate this strategy into a set of strategies that will give the organization a competitive advantage. That is, to fulfill the grand strategy, managers will seek to position their units so that they can gain a relative advantage over the company's rivals. This positioning requires a careful evaluation of the competitive forces that dictate the rules of competition within the industry in which the organization operates.

One of the leading researchers into strategy formulation is Michael Porter of Harvard's Graduate School of Business.[47] His competitive strategies framework demonstrates that managers can choose among three generic competitive strategies (see Details on a Management Classic). According to Michael Porter, no firm can successfully perform at an above-average profitability level by trying to be all things to all people. Rather, Porter proposed that management must select a **competitive strategy** that will give its unit a distinct advantage—by capitalizing on the strengths of the organization and the industry it is in. These three strategies are: **cost-leadership** (low-cost producer), **differentiation** (uniqueness in a broad market), and **focus** (uniqueness in a narrow market). Which strategy management chooses depends on the organization's strengths and its competitors' weaknesses. Management should avoid a position in which it has to slug it out with everybody in the industry. Rather, the organization should put its strength where the competition isn't. Success, then, depends on selecting the right strategy, the one that fits the complete picture of the organization and the industry of which it is a part. In so doing, organizations can gain the most favorable competitive advantage.

competitive strategy A strategy to position an organization in such a way that it will have a distinct advantage over its competition; three types are cost-leadership, differentiation, and focus strategies.

cost-leadership strategy The strategy an organization follows when it wants to be the lowest-cost producer in its industry.

differentiation strategy The strategy an organization follows when it wants to be unique in its industry within a broad market.

focus strategy The strategy an organization follows when it wants to establish an advantage in a narrow market segment.

What if an organization cannot use one of these three strategies to develop a competitive advantage? Porter uses the term *stuck in the middle* to describe that situation. Organizations that are stuck in the middle often find it difficult to achieve long-term success. If and when they do succeed, it is usually a result of competing in a highly favorable market or having all their competitors similarly stuck in the middle. Porter notes, too, that successful organizations may get into trouble by reaching beyond their competitive advantage and ending up stuck in the middle. For example, Mercedes' entry into the "microcompact" auto market may cause it to get stuck in the middle. Its plan is to sell a mass market "A" sedan for less than $15,000. Doing so may detract from the company's focused competitive strategy of building "class" cars and blur the public image of Mercedes.[48] The wisdom of Mercedes' decision remains to be seen.

Sustaining a Competitive Advantage. Long-term success with any one of Porter's competitive strategies requires that the advantage be sustainable. That is, it must withstand both the actions of competitors and the evolutionary changes in the industry. That isn't easy, especially in environments that are as dynamic as the ones organizations face today. Technology changes. So too, do customers' product preferences. And competitors frequently try to imitate an organization's success. Managers need to create barriers that make imitation by competitors difficult or reduce the competitive opportunities. The use of patents, copyrights, or trademarks may assist in this

"Billions and billions served." We see that familiar phrase whenever we pass a McDonald's restaurant sign. You'd think with that success, McDonald's management could relax. But that's the farthest from the truth. Rather than sitting idly, the fast-food chain is always looking for new ways to expand its market. Whether it's the new "Arch Deluxe" hamburger, introduced in May 1996, or placing McDonald's restaurants in gas stations, one thing is certain: McDonald's is not complacent!

Details on a Management Classic

Michael Porter's Generic Strategies

According to Michael Porter, when an organization sets out to be the low-cost producer in its industry, it is following a cost-leadership strategy. Success with this strategy requires that the organization be the cost leader and not merely one of the contenders for that position. In addition, the product or service being offered must be perceived as comparable to that offered by rivals, or at least acceptable to buyers.

How does a firm gain such a cost advantage? Typical means include efficiency of operations, economies of scale, technological innovation, low-cost labor, or preferential access to raw materials. Firms that have used this strategy include Wal-Mart, Canadian Tire, Gallo wines, and Southwest Airlines.[49]

The firm that seeks to be unique in its industry in ways that are widely valued by buyers is following a differentiation strategy. It might emphasize high quality, extraordinary service, innovative design, technological capability, or an unusually positive brand image. The key is that the attribute chosen must be different from those offered by rivals and significant enough to justify a price premium that exceeds the cost of differentiating. There is no shortage of firms that have found at least one attribute that allows them to differentiate themselves from competitors. Intel (technology), Maytag (reliability), Mary Kay Cosmetics (distribution), and L.L. Bean (service) are a few.

The first two strategies sought a competitive advantage in a broad range of industry segments. The focus strategy aims at a cost advantage (cost focus) or differentiation advantage (differentiation focus) in a narrow segment. That is, management will select a segment or group of segments in an industry (such as product variety, type of end buyer, distribution channel, or geographical location of buyers) and tailor the strategy to serve them to the exclusion of others. The goal is to exploit a narrow segment of a market. Of course, whether a focus strategy is feasible depends on the size of a segment and whether it can support the additional cost of focusing. Stouffer's used a cost-focus strategy in its Lean Cuisine line to reach calorie-conscious consumers seeking both high-quality products and convenience.

effort. For example, to protect its "environmentally friendly computer chip process" the Radiance Service Company has secured patents in thirty-seven countries.[50] Similarly, Kendall-Jackson has trademarked its packaging of its Turning Leaf chardonnay wine and has used that trademark in an effort to keep E & J Gallo Winery from selling its chardonnay in like packaging.[51]

In addition, when there are strong efficiencies from economies of scale, reducing price to gain volume is a useful tactic. Organizations can also "tie up" suppliers with exclusive contracts that limit their ability to supply materials to rivals. Or organizations can encourage and lobby for government policies that impose import tariffs that are designed to limit foreign competition.

The one thing management cannot do is to become complacent. Resting on past successes may be the beginning of serious troubles for the organization. Sustaining a competitive advantage requires constant action by management in order to stay one step ahead of the competition.

What Happens after Strategies Are Formulated?

The next-to-last step in the strategic management process is implementation (step 8). No matter how good a strategic plan is, it cannot succeed if it is not implemented properly. Top management leadership is a necessary ingredient in a successful strategy. So, too, is a motivated group of middle- and lower-level managers to carry out senior management's specific plans.

Finally, results must be evaluated (step 9). How effective have the strategies been? What adjustments, if any, are necessary? In Chapter 15, we will review the control process. The concepts and techniques that we introduce in that chapter can be used to assess the results of strategies and to correct significant deviations.

TQM as a Strategic Weapon

TQM . . . can result in a competitive advantage others cannot steal.

An increasing number of organizations are applying total quality management as a way to build a competitive advantage. As we discussed in Chapter 2, TQM focuses on quality and continuous improvement. To the degree that an organization can satisfy a customer's need for quality, it can differentiate itself from the competition and attract and hold a loyal customer base. Moreover, constant improvement in the quality and reliability of an organization's products or services can result in a competitive advantage others cannot steal.[52] Product innovations, for example, offer little opportunity for sustained competitive advantage. Why? Because usually they can be quickly copied by rivals. But incremental improvement, which is an essential element of TQM, is something that becomes an integrated part of an organization's operations and can develop into a considerable cumulative advantage. To illustrate how TQM can be used as a strategic tool, let's look at the Watsonville, California, Granite Rock Company, winners of a prestigious U.S. award for quality.

Granite Rock is a company that "produces and sells crushed stone, mixes concrete and asphalt products, and does some highway paving."[53] There did not appear to be a serious need for Granite to change its operations. But its management team, headed by Bruce and Steve Woolpert, would not sit still. They knew they had to continuously get to know their customers in terms of what quality meant to them. What they found was startling. They learned that each product line had special customers' needs tied to it. For example, in its concrete operations, customers demanded "on time delivery," which meant that Granite had to be prepared to deliver its product whenever the customer wanted. This required an around-the-clock operation—the beginning of Granite Xpress. Granite Xpress is now open twenty-four hours a day, seven days a week. How does it work? Customers simply drive their trucks under a loader, insert a card, and tell the machine how much of a product they want. It is then automatically dispensed, and a bill is sent to the customer later. The Woolperts implemented this change simply because they recognized that it was needed to satisfy their customers. This strategic innovation, as well as some others, not only helped them weather the construction recession in the early 1990s but also led them to double their market share!

Using TQM for developing a competitive advantage does not apply only to firms in industries like Granite Rock. Organizations worldwide—from Whirlpool in the United States to Daewoo in South Korea to educational institutions such as Oregon State University—are recognizing the value of TQM as a competitive advantage.[54]

Entrepreneurship: A Special Case of Strategic Planning

You have heard the story dozens of times. With only an idea, a few hundred dollars, and use of the family garage, someone starts what eventually becomes a multibillion dollar global corporation. In the case of Packard Bell, the only deviation is that Israeli-born entrepreneur Beny Alagem began the business in his dorm room at the California State Polytechnic University.[55]

Beny Alagem had been fascinated by electronics since his early childhood. By 1983, he formed Cal-Abco, a company that specialized in wholesaling memory chips. The early days of the business had problems. High debts and poor component quality—and a name no one recognized—almost ended the company. Alagem, however, was unwilling to give up. Instead, in 1985 he purchased the name Packard Bell from a defunct electronics company. Immediately, it gave the organization name recognition beyond Alagem's wildest dreams. Was the company part of the radio manufacturer of the 1920s? Or was it a spin-off business of Hewlett-Packard or Ma Bell? Alagem and his partners wouldn't say. They just capitalized on this perceived strength. Ten years later, with emphasis on market niches and quality, Packard Bell has grown to an organization employing more than 3,000 people and having annual revenues nearing $3 billion. What differentiates Packard Bell from its competitors? High-quality hardware, comprehensive service and technical support, and low prices. Packard Bell sells its computers in department stores such as Sears, Wal-Mart, Best Buy, and Circuit City, and today it enjoys the honor of selling more personal computers than any other computer manufacturer.

Strategic planning often carries a "big business" bias. It implies a formalization and structure that fits well with large, established organizations that have abundant resources. But the primary interest of many students is not in managing large and established organizations. Like Beny Alagem, or Dave Thomas of Wendy's, or Stan Smith of Acer Computer International, they are excited about the idea of starting their own business from scratch—an action that is called entrepreneurship (see Understanding Yourself).

What is an entrepreneur and how does one differ from "traditional" managers? For people like Beny Alagem that question is easy to answer. He's bold and innovative. He takes initiative and calculated risks to move into new ventures. All this in his effort to pursue opportunities—and to control his own destiny!

Understanding Yourself

Do You Have Entrepreneurial Characteristics?

This assessment is designed to see if you have the characteristics frequently associated with highly successful entrepreneurs. Rate each of the following twenty-two characteristics using the following scale:

−2 = *I don't have this characteristic*
−1 = *I don't have very much of this characteristic*
0 = *Neutral, or I don't know*
+1 = *I have this characteristic a little bit*
+2 = *I am very strong in this characteristic*

CHARACTERISTIC	−2	−1	0	+1	+2
Self-confidence	___	___	___	___	___
Energy, diligence	___	___	___	___	___
Ability to take calculated risks	___	___	___	___	___
Creativity	___	___	___	___	___
Flexibility	___	___	___	___	___
Positive response to challenges	___	___	___	___	___
Dynamism, leadership	___	___	___	___	___
Ability to get along with people	___	___	___	___	___
Responsiveness to suggestions	___	___	___	___	___
Responsiveness to criticism	___	___	___	___	___
Knowledge of market	___	___	___	___	___
Perseverance, determination	___	___	___	___	___
Resourcefulness	___	___	___	___	___
Need to achieve	___	___	___	___	___
Initiative	___	___	___	___	___
Independence	___	___	___	___	___
Foresight	___	___	___	___	___
Profit orientation	___	___	___	___	___
Perceptiveness	___	___	___	___	___
Optimism	___	___	___	___	___
Versatility	___	___	___	___	___
Knowledge of product and technology	___	___	___	___	___

Scoring: Total your score for the twenty-two characteristics. Remember to add the +s and subtract the −s. Your score will fall between +44 and −44.

Continued

What the Assessment Means: High positive scores demonstrate that you strongly share many of the characteristics commonly associated with highly successful entrepreneurs. Very low positive scores and negative scores indicate that you may not currently possess or rely on these characteristics. But don't take a low score to mean that you couldn't be an entrepreneur. It simply implies that you may need to focus more on developing yourself in many of these areas.

Source: R. Marx, T. Jick, and P. Frost, *Management Live: The Video Book* (Englewood Cliffs, N.J.: Prentice Hall, 1991), p. 291.

What Is Entrepreneurship?

There is no shortage of definitions of *entrepreneurship.*[56] Some, for example, apply it to the creation of any new business. Others focus on intentions, claiming that entrepreneurs seek to create wealth, which is different from starting businesses merely as a means of income substitution (that is, working for yourself rather than working for someone else). When most people describe entrepreneurs, they use adjectives such as bold, innovative, taking initiatives, venturesome, and risk-taking. They also tend to associate entrepreneurs with small businesses. We will define entrepreneurship as a process by which individuals pursue opportunities, fulfilling needs and wants through innovation, without regard to the resources they currently control.[57]

It is important not to confuse managing a small business with entrepreneurship. Why? Because not all small business managers are entrepreneurs.[58] Many do not innovate. A great many managers of small businesses are merely scaled-down versions of the conservative, conforming bureaucrats who staff many large corporations and public agencies.

Do Entrepreneurs Possess Similar Characteristics?

One of the most researched topics in entrepreneurship has been the search to determine what, if any, psychological characteristics entrepreneurs have in common. A number of common characteristics have been found. These include hard work, self-confidence, optimism, determination, a high energy level,[59] and even good luck.[60] But three factors regularly sit on the top of most lists that profile the entrepreneurial personality. Entrepreneurs have a high need for achievement, believe strongly that they can control their own destinies, and take only moderate risks.[61] The research allows us to draw a general description of entrepreneurs. They tend to be independent types who prefer to be personally responsible for solving problems, for setting goals, and for reaching those goals by their own efforts. They value independence and particularly do not like being controlled by others. They are not afraid of taking chances, but they are not wild risk takers. They prefer to take calculated risks where they feel that they can control the outcome.

The evidence on entrepreneurial personalities leads us to several conclusions. First, people with this personality makeup are not likely to be contented, productive employees in the typical large corporation or government agency. The rules, regulations, and controls that these bureaucracies impose on their members frustrate entrepreneurs. Second, the challenges and conditions inherent in starting one's own business mesh well with the entrepreneurial personality. Starting a new venture, which they control, appeals to their willingness to take risks and determine their own destinies. But, because entrepreneurs believe that their future is fully in their own hands, the risk they perceive as moderate is often seen as high by nonentrepreneurs. Finally,

	TRADITIONAL MANAGERS	ENTREPRENEURS
Primary motivation	Promotion and other traditional corporate rewards such as office, staff, and power	Independence, opportunity to create, financial gain
Time orientation	Achievement of short-term goals	Achievement of five- to ten-year growth of business
Activity	Delegation and supervision	Direct involvement
Risk propensity	Low	Moderate
View toward failures and mistakes	Avoidance	Acceptance

Source: Based on D. Hisrich, "Entrepreneurship/Intrapreneurship," *American Psychologist,* February 1990, p. 218.

Exhibit 3-7
Comparison of Entrepreneurs and Traditional Managers

the cultural context in which individuals were raised will have an effect.[62] For instance, in eastern Germany, where the cultural environment exhibits high power distance and high uncertainty avoidance (see Geert Hofstede, Chapter 2), many of the associated entrepreneurial characteristics—such as initiative and risk taking—are lacking.

How Do Entrepreneurs Compare with Traditional Managers?

Exhibit 3-7 summarizes some key differences between entrepreneurs and traditional bureaucratic managers. While the latter tend to be custodial, entrepreneurs actively seek change by exploiting opportunities. When searching for these opportunities, entrepreneurs often put their personal financial security at risk. The hierarchy in large organizations typically insulates traditional managers from these financial wagers and rewards them for minimizing risks and avoiding failures.

Summary

How will I know if I fulfilled the Learning Objectives found on page 69? You will have fulfilled the Learning Objectives if you understand the following.

1. **Define planning.** Planning is the process of determining objectives and assessing the way those objectives can best be achieved.
2. **Explain the potential benefits of planning.** Planning gives direction, reduces the impact of change, minimizes waste and redundancy, and sets the standards to facilitate controlling.
3. **Identify potential drawbacks to planning.** Planning is not without its critics. Some of the more noted criticisms of planning are: it may create rigidity; plans cannot be developed for a dynamic environment; formal plans cannot replace intuition and creativity; planning focuses managers' attention on today's competition not on tomorrow's survival; and, because formal planning reinforces success it may lead to failure.
4. **Distinguish between strategic and tactical plans.** Strategic plans cover an extensive time period (usually five or more years), cover broad issues, and include the formulation of objectives. Tactical plans cover shorter periods of time, focus on specifics, and assume that objectives are already known.
5. **State when directional plans are preferred over specific plans.** Directional plans are preferred over specific plans when managers face uncertainty in their environments and desire to maintain flexibility in order to respond to any unexpected changes.

6. **Define management by objectives and identify its common elements.** Management by objectives is a system in which specific performance objectives are jointly determined by employees and their bosses, progress toward objectives is periodically reviewed, and rewards are allocated on the basis of the progress. The four ingredients common to MBO programs are goal specificity, participative decision making, explicit time periods, and performance feedback.
7. **Outline the steps in the strategic management process.** The strategic management process is made up of nine steps: (1) identify the organization's current mission, objectives, and strategies; (2) analyze the environment; (3) identify opportunities and threats in the environment; (4) analyze the organization's resources; (5) identify the organization's strengths and weaknesses; (6) reassess the organization's mission and objectives on the basis of its strengths, weaknesses, opportunities, and threats; (7) formulate strategies; (8) implement strategies; and (9) evaluate results.
8. **Describe the four grand strategies.** The four grand strategies are growth (increasing the level of the organization's operations), stability (making no significant change in the organization), retrenchment (reducing the size or variety of operations), and combination (using two or more grand strategies simultaneously).
9. **Explain SWOT analysis.** SWOT analysis refers to analyzing the organization's internal strengths and weaknesses as well as external opportunities and threats in order to identify a niche that the organization can exploit.
10. **Compare how entrepreneurs and bureaucratic managers approach strategy.** Entrepreneurs approach strategy by first seeking out opportunities that they can exploit. Bureaucratic managers approach strategy by first determining the availability of their resources.

Review & Discussion Questions

1. Contrast formal with informal planning.
2. "Organizations that fail to plan are planning to fail." Do you agree or disagree with the statement? Explain your position.
3. Under what circumstances are short-term plans preferred? Under what circumstances are specific plans preferred?
4. What is MBO, and where do you believe it is most useful?
5. Compare an organization's mission with its objectives.
6. Describe the nine-step strategic management process.
7. What is a SWOT analysis?
8. Using the generic strategies of Michael Porter, describe the strategy used by each of the following companies to develop a competitive advantage in its industry: Target Stores, BMW, Toys "R" Us.
9. "The primary means of sustaining a competitive advantage is to adjust faster to the environment than your competitors do." Do you agree or disagree with the statement? Explain your position.
10. How can TQM provide a competitive advantage? Give an example.
11. What differentiates small business managers from entrepreneurs? Explain your answer.

Testing Your Comprehension • • • 

Circle the correct answer, then check yourself on page AK-1.

1. The term *planning* implies all of the following EXCEPT
   a) defining an organization's goals and objectives
   b) establishing an overall strategy for goal achievement
   c) providing directions for ethical behaviors
   d) developing a series of plans to coordinate activities

---

2. A lack of planning can
   a) foster cooperation among employees
   b) reduce wasteful activities
   c) ensure the coordination of activities
   d) none of the above

---

3. A manager once quipped, "Though I hate it, formulating the annual business plan forces me to think through every single aspect of my business in advance." This BEST illustrates which benefit of planning?
   a) reduces overlapping and wasteful activities
   b) establishes standards to facilitate control
   c) reduces uncertainty by anticipating change
   d) establishes coordinated effort

---

4. Which of the following statements is MOST accurate?
   a) Many studies confirm the positive relationship between planning and performance.
   b) All organizations that plan extensively outperform those that plan less formally.
   c) All organizations that plan outperform those that do not.
   d) Many studies confirm that planning does not lead to greater performance because labor unions are weak.

---

5. Plans that determine specific details about organizational objectives that are to be achieved are called
   a) strategic plans
   b) tactical plans
   c) long-term plans
   d) detailed plans

---

6. Plans are commonly described according to all of the following EXCEPT
   a) breadth
   b) time frame
   c) length
   d) specificity

---

7. Which of the following statements is NOT a criticism of planning?
   a) Planning creates rigidity.
   b) Planning assists in dealing with changes in a dynamic environment.
   c) Planning reinforces success.
   d) Planning focuses managers' attention on today's competition not on tomorrow's survival.

---

8. Management by objectives
   a) uses a top-down goal-setting process
   b) uses goals that indicate the general direction desired
   c) has a hierarchy of objectives that are closely linked between organizational levels
   d) was first proposed in the late 1970s

---

9. According to the philosophy of MBO,
   a) feedback occurs at the annual performance review
   b) goals follow a top-down approach
   c) goals typically are broad, general statements of intent
   d) constant feedback is provided

Continued

10. MBO assists in answering "What's in it for me as an employee" by
   a) linking rewards to goal attainment
   b) identifying employees' key job tasks
   c) allowing employees to participate actively
   d) prioritizing goals

11. The mission of a nonprofit organization is MOST accurately described by which of the following phrases?
   a) the set of traditions in an organization
   b) a physical location remote from the main operation
   c) a statement of what business the organization operates
   d) a detailed plan of expected resources for a set time period

12. When an organization seeks to identify environmental opportunities and match them with its strengths, it is
   a) seeking to develop its mission statement
   b) determining its distinctive competence
   c) identifying environmental uncertainties
   d) creating a multinational corporation

13. SWOT analysis
   a) matches the organization's competencies with its environmental forces
   b) sometimes involves industrial espionage tactics
   c) occurs during the mission statement formulation
   d) is most useful for helping an organization sustain its competitive advantage

14. Which of the following is NOT a grand strategy that an organization can use for defining its all-encompassing focus?
   a) stability strategy
   b) market gain strategy
   c) growth strategy
   d) combination strategy

15. The type of organizational strategy that emphasizes increasing market share or the level of an organization's operations is called
   a) stability strategy
   b) combination strategy
   c) market gain strategy
   d) none of the above

16. According to Michael Porter, the goal of the focus strategy is to
   a) exploit a narrow segment of the market
   b) seek competitive advantages in large market segments
   c) use technological innovation to target customers more accurately
   d) bring suppliers and distributors together and combine efforts

17. Which of the following is NOT a strategic implication of TQM?
   a) TQM can assist an organization in differentiating itself from the competition.
   b) TQM can assist an organization in forecasting product sales in the global village.
   c) TQM can assist an organization in attracting and holding a loyal customer base.
   d) TQM can assist an organization in sustaining its competitive advantage.

18. Which of the following is a characteristic associated with an entrepreneur?
   a) focuses on the opportunity to create
   b) refuses to accept failures and mistakes
   c) emphasizes direct supervision of employees
   d) emphasizes achievement of short-term goals

Applying the Concepts

Your College's Mission

Students might not pay much attention to their college's goals and objectives since they are focusing on their studies. But your college had to carve out its niche in an effort to provide something of value to its students and must continue to monitor its performance. For this exercise, break up into small groups. The charge of each small group is to prepare responses to the following questions and present its findings to the class.

1. What do you think is your college's mission? What resources does your college have that support its mission?
2. How would you describe your college's environment in terms of technology and of government regulations?
3. What do you believe are the strengths and weaknesses of your college?
4. Which grand strategy is your college following? Which of Porter's generic strategies is evident at your college?
5. What do you believe to be your college's competitive advantage? What do you think your college should do to sustain its competitive advantage?

Take It to the Net

We invite you to visit the Robbins/De Cenzo page on the Prentice Hall Web site at:

http://www.prenhall.com/robbinsfom

for this chapter's World Wide Web exercise.

You can also visit the Web sites for these companies featured within this chapter:

Calgary's Big Rock Brewery
http://www.bigrockbeer.com

Dunkin' Donuts
http://www.franchise1.com/comp/dunkin1.html

E & J Gallo Winery
http://kj.com

L.L. Bean
http://www.llbean.com

Mercedes
http://www.mercedes-benz.com/

Oregon State University
http://www.orst.edu

PepsiCo.
http://www.pepsi.com

Toys "R" Us
http://www.toysrus.com

Thinking Critically

Making a Value Judgment: Strategically Going Bankrupt

What do Texaco, Continental Airlines, and Southland Corporation have in common? Their managements have all used Chapter 11 of the U.S. Bankruptcy Code as a corporate strategy.[63] The 1978 Bankruptcy Reform Act and its amendments were intended to make it easier for corporations to reorganize. The logic was that the use of Chapter 11 would allow declining companies to nurse themselves back to financial health. In the interim, managers and employees would keep their jobs, companies would be saved, and the economy would benefit. But the law no longer required that a company be insolvent before it could file for reorganization. Therefore, it gave management considerable leeway in determining the circumstances and timing of a bankruptcy filing. Congress did not intend for the new law to turn the Chapter 11 decision into a strategic option, but that is essentially what it did. The discretionary nature of the act allowed organizations, almost at will, to escape from almost any financial obligations. And some companies did just that.

Texaco, for instance, was found to have interfered in Pennzoil's attempt to buy Getty Oil. The courts gave Pennzoil a $10.5 billion judgment against Texaco. Texaco's management responded by filing for bankruptcy even though the company was enormously profitable. The strategy allowed Texaco to cut its obligation to Pennzoil down to $3 billion. Continental Airlines' management used bankruptcy as a means to break the company's union agreements and other contractual obligations. In and out of bankruptcy several times in the past decade, Continental has been able to continue to operate and aggressively compete for airline customers. Many of Continental's passengers are completely unaware that they are flying on a "bankrupt" airline. Southland Corporation, which operates the Seven-Eleven convenience store chain, "prepackaged" its bankruptcy. It negotiated a deal with its creditors before filing its bankruptcy petition. The result: Creditors took a reduced payment and Southland emerged out of bankruptcy in just four months.

Questions:

1. Is it wrong for managers to use bankruptcy as a strategy, even though it allows the company to continue to operate and save employees' jobs?
2. A debtor's going bankrupt can place undue hardship on creditors and other claimants. Creditors are forced to settle for a few cents on the dollar, and landlords are left holding broken leases. Does knowing that change your view of bankruptcy?
3. Do you believe that bankruptcy should be permitted to be used so that an organization can evade responsibility and liability? Why or why not?

Setting Strategies at Drypers Corporation

When you're king of the hill, there's always someone who wants to knock you down. And, if you're not careful, removing you can easily be done. Consider that David slew Goliath, that Wal-Mart replaced Sears as America's number one retailer, and that little Microsoft Corporation has consistently outsmarted IBM. How were these feats accomplished? Through careful planning.

Years ago, companies like Procter & Gamble and Kimberly-Clark dominated the U.S. market for disposable diapers. Their big brand sellers, Pampers and Huggies, respectively, were the clear winners in the $4 billion a year disposable diaper industry, holding some 85 percent of the market share between them.[64] Today, however, competition is getting fierce, and much of the chase of the big two is coming from Dave Pitassi and Wally Klemp, cofounders of Drypers Corporation. The two college buddies from Portland, Oregon, dreamed up their business idea while students. Although their venture was not highly regarded by those around them, they never gave up hope. They knew from their research that there had to be a market for a quality, off-market diaper. But they had to have a focused plan to go up against the likes of Procter & Gamble.

In 1988, at age twenty-three, the two developed a business plan designed to show financial backers how they would become a low-cost producer of quality disposable diapers. Although they ran into several roadblocks along the way, the two persevered. Pitassi and Klemp's main thrust was to use materials from local businesses in their production of disposable diapers. This approach enabled them to manufacture a cheap but good-quality diaper. In its first year, Drypers generated just over $100,000 in sales. Then the world opened up. Because of careful long-term planning and several marketing ploys, Drypers sales jumped to $35 million by the end of the third year. And, with a careful analysis of how to expand even more, Drypers acquired two regional diaper manufacturers. By the end of 1996, sales had reached over $150 million. Today, Drypers continues its strong growth and now accounts for more than 6 percent of the disposable diaper market.

Questions:

1. What type of grand strategy is Drypers pursuing? Cite specific examples.
2. Michael Porter identified three generic strategies that companies can follow to develop a competitive advantage. Which one of the three do you believe Drypers is using? Discuss and support your choice.
3. How would you recommend they exploit their competitive advantage? How can they sustain it?

Video Case ABCNEWS

Missing the Mark at Denver International Airport

Federico Peña, then Mayor of Denver, had a vision—to build a "state of the art" airport. During his tenure as mayor, Peña noticed that Denver's current airport, Stapleton, was almost at capacity. By 1985, Stapleton handled nearly 30 million passengers a year. Forecasts by Federal Aviation Administration sources indicated that by 1995, passenger service would increase by more than 160 percent in Denver. Furthermore, congestion in downtown Denver caused by the traffic at Stapleton was creating a need for action. A new facility needed to be built. Although there were some questions raised about the forecasts, and Denver's citizens would have to travel an extra half-hour to get to the new airport, Peña moved forward with the $1.7 billion construction plan. That action was taken even though local analysts projected that the costs of building an airport would exceed $5 billion. If Peña and his planners had been able to look ten years into the future, they'd have seen that nearly every one of their projections was wrong. In fact, by 1995, as the Denver International was putting last-minute touches on its grand opening, the project was "overdue, over budget, and under investigation."

Initially, Denver International was regarded as one of the biggest public works projects ever undertaken in the United States. It was supposed to be a high-tech facility, spanning some 53 square miles outside of the city of Denver. That's bigger than the airport at Dallas-Fort Worth and Chicago's O'Hare Airport combined. Denver International was to become the first airport in the world that was so technologically advanced that air traffic controllers would be able to land three planes at the same time on parallel runways. The systems used were also designed to keep runways unclogged, avert crashes, and keep the airport open in the worst of Colorado's snowstorms. A computer-controlled subway system, traveling along a 6,000-foot-long tunnel was supposed to transport passengers to various locations in the airport's terminals. But the highlight of it all was to be a completely automated baggage-handling system. This system would handle up to 60,000 pieces of luggage an hour, routing it along some 22 miles of underground railroad track from the aircraft to the appropriate baggage claim spot. No human hands would touch the luggage once it left the plane! But all of this high technology became high trouble for Peña and the citizens of Denver.

Denver International Airport finally opened, nearly two years later than planned. Its costs skyrocketed, ending up approximately two and one-half times the initial projections. The high-tech systems—especially the baggage-handling one—became nightmares. In many cases, allegations were made that shoddy construction of these systems contributed to both their delays and additional costs. And the projections for passenger usage? They too were significantly off. No one could have predicted that management at Continental Airlines would decide that they could no longer compete with United Airlines at Denver; they took their business to East Coast airports and opened hubs in cities such as Baltimore.

Questions:

1. Given that a lot of planning went into this airport construction project, yet nearly every projection was wrong, what should Peña have done to ensure that the project would be on time and within budget?
2. Do you believe that Denver city officials should have anticipated Continental Airline's departure from the Denver area? Why or why not? Do you believe they could have done anything to prevent it?
3. When plans go as wrong as they did in building Denver International, is it an indictment against planning as a function or against those who engaged in the planning? Support your position.

Source: "The Storm over Denver International Airport," *ABC News Nightline,* February 27, 1995. Some data also from L. Kaufman-Rosen and D. Glick, "Finally, It's Here!" *Newsweek,* March 6, 1995, pp. 44–46.

Planning Tools and Techniques

LEARNING OBJECTIVES

What will I be able to do after I finish this chapter?

1. **DESCRIBE** techniques for scanning the environment.
2. **CONTRAST** quantitative and qualitative forecasting.
3. **EXPLAIN** why budgets are popular.
4. **LIST** two approaches to budgeting.
5. **DIFFERENTIATE** Gantt and load charts.
6. **IDENTIFY** the steps in a PERT network.
7. **STATE** the factors that determine a product's break-even point.
8. **DESCRIBE** the requirements for using linear programming.
9. **EXPLAIN** how queuing theory can be a planning tool.
10. **LIST** five steps for better time management.

RENZO ROSSO IS A MODERN-DAY RAGS-TO-riches story. Rosso was born in the farming community of Brugine, Italy. His early life was best described as humble, but he learned the value of hard work.[1]

In the 1970s, Renzo took a job as a supervisor in a sportswear clothing store. Although he was unknowingly learning the clothing business, his low-paying, low-status supervisory job didn't provide Rosso the kind of opportunities he wanted, but he didn't let such difficulties get the best of him. Instead, of complaining about what life had dealt him, he did something about it. He began to learn everything he could about the business. He took on a variety of jobs, worked long and hard, and eventually started to be recognized as a valuable employee in the organization.

Then in 1985, Renzo Rosso purchased the company he had labored in for a decade—establishing the Milvena, Italy, Diesel Apparel Company. In just over ten years, the jeans, sweatshirt, and tee shirt business has grown significantly throughout Europe and is continuing its expansion in the United States. Company profits during this same period rose, too, reaching $35 million in 1995 on sales of $150 million.

Renzo Rosso, owner of Diesel Apparel, uses a variety of planning tools to assist him in managing his business. With proper scheduling, budgets, and the like, Renzo has built a $150 million dollar business, generating more than $35 million in profits each year.

How does Renzo succeed in managing these retail shops spread over two continents? Rosso has a system. He knows when inventories need to be replaced. He understands how many employees are needed to staff each store and when to add extra personnel to meet peak sales demands. He helps each store develop budgets and controls to ensure that budgets are adhered to. And Rosso does thorough forecasting. Through forecasts, he is able to accurately predict what trends he will face in the next fashion season.

In this chapter, we will discuss some basic planning tools and techniques. We will begin by looking at four planning techniques that help managers assess their environment: scanning, forecasting, benchmarking, and the ISO 9000 standards. We will review the most popular planning tool used by managers—budgets—and then discuss scheduling, break-even analysis, and other practical planning tools. Finally, we will conclude by providing some time-management concepts to help you in your personal, day-to-day planning.

Assessing the Environment

In the preceding chapter, we introduced planning and the strategic management process. In this section, we review several techniques that have been developed to help managers with one of the most challenging aspects of the process: assessing their organization's environment. Twenty years ago, environmental analysis was an informal endeavor based on intuitive judgments. Today, using structured techniques such as environmental scanning, forecasting, and benchmarking, a manager can analyze an organization's environment much more accurately.

What Is Environmental Scanning?

Russell Boss, CEO of A.T. Cross, knows firsthand about the importance of environmental scanning.[2] Makers of luxury Cross pens, the organization had enjoyed much success in the 1970s and 1980s. This success was attributed primarily to Cross's slender, thin-profiled pens. By the late 1980s, however, customers' preferences had changed. They wanted fatter, sturdier writing instruments. A.T. Cross failed to recognize that trend. Competing pens, such as Gillette Company's Waterman S.A. fountain pens and Germany's Montblanc pen took over the luxury pen market; Cross was moved to the middle of the pack. Boss recognizes the company's error in failing to scan the environment and must now play catch-up.

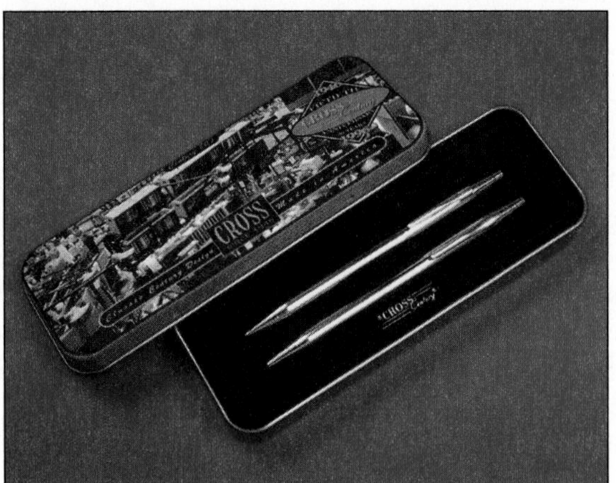

Cross pens and pencils were once the industry standards. But the failure of Cross's management to scan the environment led to significant losses in the market. If they had scanned, Cross would have produced the fatter, sturdier pen that customers wanted.

Managers like Roger Penske (see Managers Who Made a Difference), in both small and large organizations, are increasingly turning to **environmental scanning** to anticipate and interpret changes in their environment.[3] The term, as we use it, refers to screening large amounts of information to detect emerging trends and create a set of scenarios. There is some evidence to support the position that companies that scan the environment achieve higher profits and revenue growth than companies that don't.[4]

environmental scanning The screening of large amounts of information to detect emerging trends and create a set of scenarios.

The importance of environmental scanning was first recognized (outside of national security agencies such as the Central Intelligence Agency or National Security Agency) by firms in the life insurance industry in the late 1970s.[5] Life insurance companies found that the demand for their product was declining even though all the key environmental signals they were receiving strongly favored the sale of life insurance. The economy and population were growing. Baby boomers were finishing school, entering the labor force, and taking on family responsibilities. The market for life insurance should have been expanding. But it wasn't. What the insurance companies had failed to recognize was a fundamental change in family structure in the United States.

Young families, who represented the primary group of buyers of new insurance policies, tended to be dual-career couples who were increasingly choosing to remain childless. The life insurance needs of a family with one income, a dependent spouse, and a houseful of kids are much greater than those of a two-income family with few, if any, children. That a multibillion dollar industry could overlook such a fundamental social trend underscored the need to develop techniques for monitoring important environmental developments.

How Does Competitive Intelligence Help?

One of the fastest growing areas of environmental scanning is **competitive intelligence.**[6] It seeks basic information about competitors: Who are they? What are they doing? How will what they are doing affect us? As managers at A.T. Cross should have recognized, accurate information on the competition can allow managers to anticipate competitors' actions rather than merely react to them.

competitive intelligence An environmental scanning activity that seeks to identify who competitors are, what they are doing, and how their actions will affect the focus organization.

Managers Who Made a Difference

Roger Penske at the Penske Corporation

Managers with good planning tools can make a difference in an organization's performance! Some make their mark by proceeding cautiously, taking one step at a time. Others achieve their goals rapidly. The latter description accurately fits Roger S. Penske. He is CEO of the Penske Corporation, the Michigan-based transportation company that manufactures diesel engines (Detroit Diesel), leases trucks, owns car dealerships, and is involved in auto racing.[7]

Roger Penske began his racing career while studying marketing and business at Lehigh University in Pennsylvania. He was a weekend race enthusiast whose forte was getting the checkered flag. But Penske wanted more out of life than going in circles at a high rate of speed. He wanted to own his own company. And from a single car dealership purchased in 1964, he has "grown" his business into a $3.6 billion empire. One of his more remarkable stories began in 1988 when he purchased the Detroit Diesel Company from General Motors. Under the direction of managers at GM, Detroit Diesel had a paltry 3 percent of the market for heavy-truck engines, and the floundering company was losing money. But Penske saw something others didn't. Keeping most of the existing employees, Penske immediately began instituting changes that transformed Detroit Diesel into a small, focused, market-driven organization—even teaming with such other organizations as Daimler Benz (makers of the Mercedes), and Bosche (auto parts).

Penske understood a couple of important aspects of running a successful business. Employees are rarely the cause of poor organizational performance. More often, the cause is a lack of effective planning, which results in a company's simply going through the motions without achieving results. Correcting the problem starts with setting the corporate direction and ensuring that those goals are met! With proper guidance, an organization can become committed to excellence. For Penske, that meant determining what the company needed to do to be on top of its field. And that information had to be understood by everyone in the company.

Penske has succeeded in invigorating Detroit Diesel and making it a major competitor in the truck-engine market. The company's market share has risen to an impressive 25 percent and is still climbing. Proper planning is helping to make the company more profitable. Roger Penske is happy. And his employees are happy too; they benefit directly from their work because Penske rewards them with profit-share bonuses.

One individual who has closely studied competitive intelligence suggests that 95 percent of the competitor-related information an organization needs to make crucial strategic decisions is available and accessible to the public.[8] In other words, competitive intelligence isn't organizational espionage. Advertisements, promotional materials, press releases, reports filed with government agencies, annual reports, want ads, newspaper reports, information placed on the Internet, and industry studies are examples of readily accessible sources of information. Trade shows and the debriefing of your own sales staff can be other good sources of information on competitors. Many organizations even regularly buy competitors' products and have their own employees evaluate them to learn about new technical innovations.

The techniques and sources listed above can reveal a number of issues and concerns that can affect an organization. But in a global business environment, environmental scanning becomes more complex.[9] Because global scanning must gather information from around the world, many of the previously mentioned information sources may be too limited. One means of overcoming this difficulty is for management to subscribe to news services that review newspapers and magazines from around the globe and provide summaries to client companies.

Competitive intelligence seeks basic information about who the competition is and what they are doing.

Is There Any Way to Help Predict the Future?

scenario
A visualization of what the future is likely to be.

A **scenario** is a visualization of what the future is likely to be. If, for instance, scanning uncovers increasing interest in Congress for raising the national minimum wage, Popeye's Chicken could create a multiple set of scenarios to assess the possible consequences of such an action. What would be the implications for its labor supply if the minimum wage were raised to $5.75 an hour? What if it were raised to $6.20 an hour? What effect would these changes have on labor costs? How might competitors respond? Different assumptions would lead to different outcomes. The intention of this exercise is not to try to predict the future but to reduce uncertainty by playing out potential situations under different specified conditions.[10] Popeye's could, for example, develop a set of scenarios ranging from optimistic to pessimistic in terms of the minimum-wage issue. It would then be better prepared to initiate changes in its strategy to gain and hold a competitive advantage.

What Are the Different Types of Forecasts?

Environmental scanning creates the foundation for forecasts. Information obtained through scanning is used to form scenarios. These, in turn, establish premises for forecasts, which are predictions of future outcomes. Two popular outcomes for which management is likely to seek forecasts are future revenues and new technological breakthroughs. But virtually any component in the organization's general and specific environment can receive forecasting attention.

General Mills's sales level drives purchasing requirements, production goals, employment needs, inventories, and numerous other decisions. Similarly, the University of North Dakota's income from tuition and state appropriations will deter-mine course offerings, staffing needs, salary increases for faculty, and the like. Both of these examples illustrate that predicting future revenues—**revenue forecasting**—is a critical element of planning for both profit and not-for-profit organizations.

revenue forecasting
Predicting future revenues.

Where Does Management Get Data for Developing Revenue Forecasts? Typically, management obtains data for developing revenue forecasts by reviewing historical revenue figures. For example, what were last quarter's or the previous year's revenues? This figure can then be adjusted for trends. What revenue patterns have evolved over recent years? What changes in social, economic, or other factors in the general environment might alter the pattern in the future? In the specific environment, what actions can an organization expect from its competitors? Answers to questions like these provide the basis for revenue forecasts.

What Is Technological Forecasting? Technological forecasting attempts to predict changes in technology and the time frame in which new technologies are likely to be economically feasible. Rapidly changing technologies have included innovations in lasers, biotechnology, robotics, data processing, and telecommunications that have dramatically changed surgery practices, pharmaceutical offerings, and the processes used for manufacturing almost every mass-produced product. Few organizations are exempt from the possibility that technological innovation will dramatically change the demand for their current products or services. The environmental scanning techniques discussed earlier can provide data on potential technological innovations.

technological forecasting Predicting changes in technology and the time frame in which new technologies are likely to be economically feasible.

An example of technological forecasting can be seen in the music industry. Between 1986 and 1990, some firms, including Columbia and MCA, saw the demand for one of their basic products—vinyl long-playing records—almost disappear. Consumers still wanted to listen to music, but they preferred a new technology: compact disks. The record companies that successfully forecasted this technology and foresaw its impact on their business were able to convert their production facilities, adopt the technology, and beat their competition to the record store racks. Ironically, CDs are already under attack from digital tape technology. Again, those in the music business who accurately forecast when, or if, this technology will become the preferred music medium are likely to score big in the market.

What Are the Different Types of Forecasting Techniques?

Forecasting techniques fall into two categories: quantitative and qualitative. **Quantitative forecasting** applies a set of mathematical rules to a series of past data to predict future outcomes. These techniques are preferred when management has sufficient hard data from which to work. **Qualitative forecasting,** on the other hand, uses the judgment and opinions of knowledgeable individuals. Qualitative techniques typically are used when precise data are scarce or difficult to obtain. Exhibit 4-1 lists some of the better-known quantitative and qualitative forecasting techniques.

quantitative forecasting Applies a set of mathematical rules to a series of past data to predict future outcomes.

qualitative forecasting Uses the judgment and opinions of knowledgeable individuals to predict future outcomes.

How Can Benchmarking Help?

Another planning tool is **benchmarking.** This is the search for the best practices among competitors or noncompetitors that lead to their superior performance.[11] The basic idea underlying benchmarking is that management can improve quality by analyzing and then copying the methods of the leaders in various fields. As such, benchmarking is a very specific form of environmental scanning.

benchmarking The search for the best practices among competitors or noncompetitors that lead to their superior performance.

In 1979, Xerox undertook what is widely regarded as the first benchmarking effort in the United States. Until then, the Japanese had been aggressively copying the successes of others by traveling around, watching what others were doing, and then applying their new knowledge to improve their products and processes. Xerox's management couldn't figure out how Japanese manufacturers could sell midsize copiers in the United States for considerably less than Xerox's production costs. So the company's head of manufacturing took a team to Japan to make a detailed study of their competition's costs and processes. They got most of their information from Xerox's own joint venture, Fuji-Xerox, which knew its competition well. What the team found was shocking. Their Japanese rivals were light-years ahead of Xerox in efficiency. Benchmarking those efficiencies marked the beginning of Xerox's recovery in the copier field. Today, in addition to Xerox, companies such as Southwest Airlines, Du Pont, Alcoa, Ford, Eastman Kodak, and Motorola use benchmarking as a standard tool in their quest for quality improvement.

TECHNIQUE	DESCRIPTION	EXAMPLE OF APPLICATION
Quantitative		
Time-series analysis	Fits a trend line to a mathematical equation and projects into the future by means of the equation	Predicting next quarter's sales on the basis of four years of previous sales data
Regression model	Predicts one variable on the basis of known or assumed other variables	Seeking factors that will predict a certain level of sales (for example, price, advertising expenditures)
Econometric model	Uses a set of regression equations to simulate segments of the economy	Predicting change in car sales as a result of changes in tax laws
Economic indicators	Use one or more economic indicators to predict a future state of the economy	Using change in GNP to predict discretionary income
Substitution-effect	Uses a mathematical formulation to predict how, when, and under what circumstances a new product or technology will replace an existing one	Predicting the effect of microwave ovens on the sale of conventional ovens
Qualitative		
Jury of opinion	Combines and averages the opinions of experts	Polling all the company's personnel managers to predict next year's college recruitment needs
Sales-force composition	Combines estimates from field sales personnel of customers' expected purchases	Predicting next year's sales of industrial lasers
Customer evaluation	Combines estimates from established customers of expected purchases	Surveying of major dealers by a car manufacturer to determine types and quantities of products desired

Exhibit 4-1
Forecasting Techniques

To illustrate benchmarking's use in practice, let's look at its application at Ford Motor Company. Ford used benchmarking in the early 1980s in developing its highly successful Taurus. The company compiled a list of some 400 features that its customers said were the most important and then set about finding the car with the best of each. Then it tried to match or top the best of the competition. For instance, the door handles on the Taurus were benchmarked against the Chevrolet Lumina; the easy-to-change taillight bulbs, against the Nissan Maxima; and the tilt steering wheel, against the Honda Accord. The Taurus has been the best-selling passenger vehicle since 1992 in the United States.[12] When the Taurus was redesigned for 1996, Ford benchmarked all over again. This time, however, the Taurus was repositioned to compete more directly with the Toyota Camry in a more expensive market niche.

Benchmarking for kids' products? You bet! John Rogers, president of Educational Teaching Devices, Inc., looked at what other companies were doing in developing educational tools. In doing so, he found a profitable niche: making giant foam jigsaw puzzles of the United States and mounting them on Velcro. Rogers's products have been instrumental in helping students learn about geography. The puzzles are also generating over $500,000 in annual revenues for the Newport Beach, California, company.

What Is the ISO 9000 Series?

During the 1980s, there was an increasing push among global corporations to improve their quality. They knew that, to compete in the global village, they had to offer some assurances to purchasers of their products and services that what they were buying was of the quality they expected. In years past, purchasers had to accept individual "guarantees" that what was being sold met their needs and standards. That individual guarantee changed in 1987, with the formation of the **ISO 9000 series,** designed by the International Organization for Standardization, based in Geneva, Switzerland.[13] The ISO standards reflect a process whereby "independent auditors attest that a company's factory, laboratory, or office has met quality management requirements."[14] These standards, once met, assure customers that a company uses specific steps to test the products it sells; continuously trains its employees to ensure they have up-to-date skills, knowledge, and abilities; maintains satisfactory records of its operations; and corrects problems when they occur.[15] Some of the multinational and transnational companies that have met these standards are Texas Petrochemical; British Airways; Shanghai-Foxboro Company, Ltd.; Braas Company; Betz Laboratories; Hong Kong Mass Transit Railway Corporation; BP Chemicals International Ltd.; Cincinnati Milacron's Electronic Systems Division; and Taiwan Synthetic Rubber Corporation.

ISO 9000 series
A series of standards designed by the International Organization for Standardization, based in Geneva, Switzerland, that reflects a process whereby "independent auditors attest that a company's factory, laboratory, or office has met quality management requirements."

A company that obtains an ISO certification can boast that it has met stringent international quality standards and is one of a select group of companies worldwide to achieve that designation. Certification can be more than just a competitive advantage; it also permits entry into some markets not otherwise accessible. For example, eighty-nine nations have adopted the ISO standards. Uncertified organizations attempting to do business in those countries may be unable to successfully compete against certified companies. Many customers in the global village want to see the certification, and it becomes a dominant customer need. And in 1997, ISO 14000 went into effect. Companies achieving this certification will have demonstrated that they are environmentally responsible.[16]

ISO 9000 certifies that an organization has met stringent international quality standards.

Achieving ISO certification is far from cost-free. Most organizations that want certification spend nearly one year and incur several hundreds of thousands of dollars to achieve that goal.[17] For example, Betz Laboratories in Trevor, Pennsylvania, spent over eight months and more than $500,000 to obtain their ISO certification. But Betz company officials, as well as hundreds of individuals like them, recognize that obtaining such certification is quickly becoming a necessity to export goods to any organization in the nations that support the ISO 9000 series standards.

Budgets

Most of us are familiar with budgets. We learned about them at an early age, discovering that unless we allocated our "revenues" carefully, we would consume our weekly allowance before half the week was out. A **budget** is a numerical plan for allocating resources to specific activities. Managers typically prepare budgets for revenues, expenses, and such capital expenditures as machinery and equipment. It is not unusual, though, for budgets to be used for improving time, space, and the use of material resources. These latter types of budgets substitute nondollar numbers for dollar terms. Such items as person-hours, capacity utilization, or units of production can be budgeted for daily, weekly, or monthly activities. However, we will emphasize dollar-based budgets.

budget
A numerical plan for allocating resources to specific activities.

Why Are Budgets So Popular?

Budgets are popular probably because they are applicable to a wide variety of organizations and units within an organization. We live in a world in which almost everything is expressed in monetary units. Dollars, pesos, francs, yen, and the like are used as a common denominator within a country. Even human life has a monetary value. Insurance actuaries regularly compute the value of a lost eye, arm, or leg. Although most people argue that life is priceless, U.S. insurance companies and juries regularly convert the loss of human body parts or life itself into dollars and cents. It seems logical, then, that monetary budgets make a useful common denominator for directing activities in such diverse departments as production and marketing research or at various levels in an organization. Budgets are one planning device that most managers, regardless of level in the organization, help to formulate.

What Are the Primary Types of Budgets?

There is no shortage of items or areas for which budgets can be used. Exhibit 4-2 provides an overview of the various types of budgets that managers are most likely to use.

How Do Incremental Budgets Differ from Zero-Based Budgets? There are essentially two approaches managers can take to budgeting. By far the most popular approach is the incremental, or traditional, budget. But in recent years, managers in some organizations have been trying to make budgets more effective by experimenting with the zero-based budget. Let's look at each of these approaches.

The **incremental** (or traditional) **budget** has two identifying characteristics. First, funds are allocated to departments or organizational units. The managers of these units then allocate funds to activities as they see fit. Second, an incremental budget develops out of the previous budget. Each period's budget begins by using the last period as a reference point. Only incremental changes in the budget request are reviewed. Each of these characteristics, however, creates a problem.

incremental budget
A budget that allocates funds to departments according to allocations in the previous period.

Revenue budget	A budget that projects future sales
Expense budget	A budget that lists the primary activities undertaken by a unit and allocates a dollar amount to each
Profit budget	A budget used by separate units of an organization that combines revenue and expense budgets to determine the units
Cash budget	A budget that forecasts how much cash an organization will have on hand and how much it will need to meet expenses
Capital expenditure budget	A budget that forecasts investments in property, buildings, and major equipment
Fixed budget	A budget that assumes a fixed level of sales or production
Variable budget	A budget that takes into account those costs that vary with volume

Exhibit 4-2
Types of Budgets

When funds are allocated to organizational units, it becomes difficult to differentiate activities within units. Why? Because organizational units typically have multiple goals and hence engage in a number of activities. Incremental budgets do not take this diversity of activities into consideration. They focus on providing funds for units rather than for activities within the units. Given that units have multiple goals, it seems reasonable to conclude that (1) some goals are more important than others and (2) unit managers have varying degrees of success in achieving their multiple goals. Incremental budgets throw everything into the same pot. Thus, as planning devices, they lack sufficient focus and specificity.

Zero-based budgeting (ZBB), originally developed by Texas Instruments, requires managers to justify their budget requests in detail from scratch, regardless of previous appropriations.[18] It is designed to attack one of the drawbacks of incremental budgets: Activities have a way of becoming immortal because the incremental budget is based on the previous year. Once established, organizational activities can take on lives of their own. This is especially true in public organizations, where task forces and commissions frequently are self-perpetuating even if they were designed to be temporary.[19]

zero-based budgeting (ZBB)
A system in which budget requests start from scratch, regardless of previous appropriations.

ZBB shifts the burden of proof to the manager to justify why his or her unit should get any budget at all. The ZBB process reevaluates all organizational activities to see which should be eliminated, funded at a reduced level, funded at the current level, or increased (see Details on a Management Classic).

Why Isn't Zero-Based Budgeting Appropriate for All Organizations?

The difficulty and expense of implementing ZBB suggest that it is not for every organization. The politics of large organizations often undermine any potential gain that ZBB might produce. It tends to be most effective in small public organizations and in support-staff units in business firms (or in declining organizations). For example, because the resource requirements of staff units in business firms, which include areas such as market research and human resource management, are rarely related directly to the firm's output, it is difficult to determine whether their budgets are realistic or denote efficient operation. Thus, for this type of unit, ZBB may be a valuable planning and control device. Also, ZBB is compatible with managing declining resources.[20] When organizations face cutbacks and financial restraints, their managers particularly look for devices that allocate limited resources effectively. ZBB can be just such a device.

Details on a Management Classic

Texas Instruments's Zero-Based Budgeting Technique

When Texas Instruments originally developed its zero-based budgeting system, the company decided on a three-part process. The three steps were:

1. Each discrete departmental activity is broken down into a decision package.
2. The individual decision packages are ranked according to their benefit to the organization during the budget period.
3. Budget resources are allocated to the individual packages according to preferential rank in the organization[21] (see Exhibit 4-3).

The decision package is a document that identifies and describes a specific activity. Usually prepared by operating managers, it includes a statement of the expected result or purpose of the activity, its costs, personnel requirements, measures of performance, alternative courses of action, and an evaluation of the benefits from performance and consequences of nonperformance from an organizationwide perspective. In more specific terms, each package lists a number of alternative methods of performing the activity, recommends one of those alternatives, and delineates effort levels. The effort levels identify spending targets—for instance, how the activity would be completed at 70, 90, and 110 percent of the current budget level. Any large organization

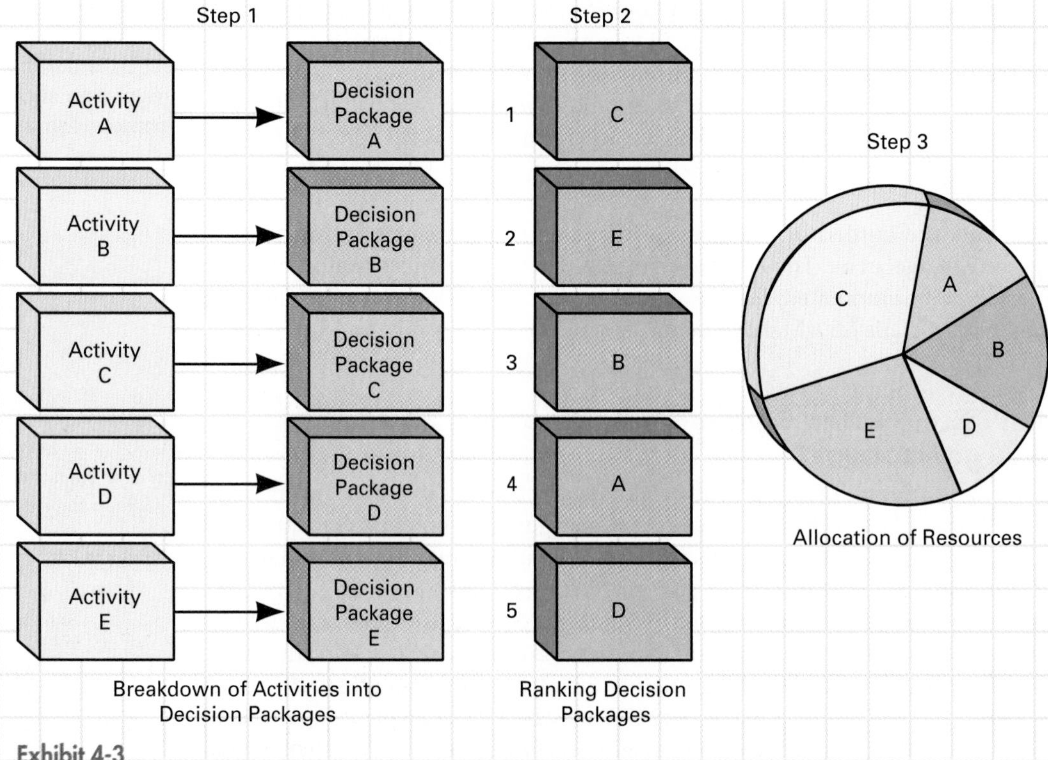

Exhibit 4-3
The Zero-Based Budget Process

that adopts ZBB will have literally thousands of these packages.

Once departmental managers have completed the decision packages, the packages are forwarded to the top executive group, which determines how much to spend and where to spend it. They make this determination by ascertaining the total amount to be spent by the organization and then by ranking all packages in order of decreasing benefits to the organization. Packages are accepted down to the spending level. When properly executed, the ZBB process carefully evaluates every organizational activity, assigns it a priority, and results in either the continuation, modification, or termination of the activity.

ZBB is no panacea. Like incremental budgeting, it has drawbacks.[22] It increases paperwork and requires time to prepare; the important activities that managers want funded tend to have their benefits inflated; and, unfortunately, the eventual outcome rarely differs much from what would have occurred through an incremental budget.

Tactical Planning Tools

Clean and Shine is a small, highly successful car wash in St. Louis, Missouri. Bridget Collins, who owns and manages the car wash, spends much of her time setting up work schedules for the twelve people she employs, deciding how many employees to have on hand throughout the day and solving similar day-to-day problems. In the following pages, we will discuss some operational planning tools that can help managers like Bridget to be more effective.

How many employees does Bridget Collins need at any given time when her Clean and Shine car wash is open? Using scheduling techniques, Bridget can determine the answer, so her customers get fast service.

What Is Scheduling?

If you were to observe a group of supervisors or department managers for a few days, you would see them regularly detailing what activities have to be done, the order in which they are to be done, who is to do each, and when they are to be completed. The managers are doing what we call **scheduling.** The following discussion reviews some useful scheduling devices.

scheduling
A listing of what activities have to be done, the order in which they are to be done, who is to do each, and when they are to be completed.

How Do You Use a Gantt Chart?

The **Gantt chart** is a planning tool developed around the turn of the century by Henry Gantt (see the Appendix). The idea behind the Gantt chart is relatively simple. It is essentially a bar graph, with time on the horizontal axis and the activities to be scheduled on the vertical axis. The bars show output, both planned and actual, over a period of time. The Gantt chart visually shows when tasks are supposed to be done and compares that with the actual progress on each. It is a simple but important device that allows managers to detail easily what has yet to be done to complete a job or project and to assess whether it is ahead of, behind, or on schedule.

Gantt chart
A bar graph that shows the relationship between work planned and completed on one axis and time elapsed on the other.

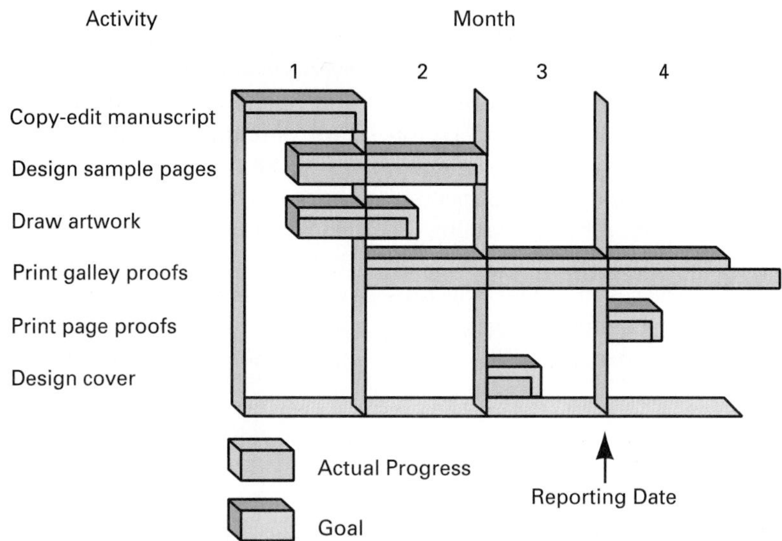

Exhibit 4-4
A Sample Gantt Chart

Exhibit 4-4 shows a Gantt chart that was developed for book production by a manager in a publishing firm. Time is expressed in months across the top of the chart. Major activities are listed down the left side. The planning comes in deciding what activities need to be done to get the book finished, the order in which those activities need to be done, and the time that should be allocated to each activity. The purple shading represents actual progress that is being made in completing each activity. A Gantt chart, then, actually becomes a managerial control device as the manager looks for deviations from the plan. In this case, most activities were completed on time. However, if you look at the "print galley proofs" activity, you will notice that "actual progress" took two weeks longer than planned. Given this information, the manager might want to take some corrective action—either to make up for the lost two weeks or to ensure that no further delays will occur. At this point, the manager can expect that the book will be published at least two weeks late if no corrective action is taken.

load chart
A modified Gantt chart that schedules capacity by work stations.

A modified version of the Gantt chart is called a **load chart.** Instead of listing activities on the vertical axis, load charts list either whole departments or specific resources. This information allows managers to plan and control for capacity utilization. In other words, load charts schedule capacity by work stations. For example, Exhibit 4-5 shows a load chart for six production editors at the same publishing firm. Each editor supervises the design and production of several books. By reviewing the load chart, the executive editor who supervises the six production editors can see who is free to take on a new book. If everyone is fully scheduled, the executive editor might decide not to accept any new projects, to accept new projects and delay others, to ask the editors to work overtime, or to employ more production editors.

What Is a PERT Network Analysis?

Gantt and load charts are helpful as long as the activities or projects being scheduled are few and independent of each other. But what if a manager had to plan a large project—such as a complex reorganization, the launching of a major cost-reduction campaign, or the development of a new product—that required coordinating inputs from marketing, production, and product design personnel? Such projects require coordinating hundreds or thousands of activities, some of which must be done simulta-

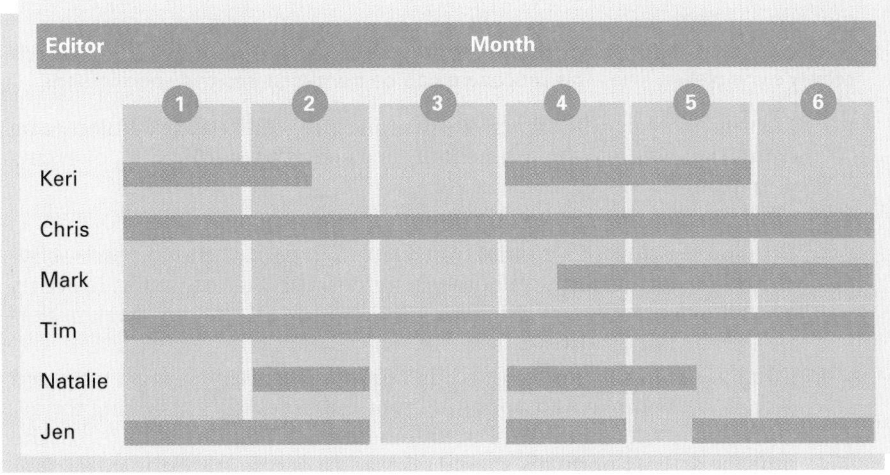

Exhibit 4-5
A Sample Load Chart

neously and some of which cannot begin until earlier activities have been completed. If you are constructing a shopping mall you obviously cannot start erecting walls until the foundation has been laid. How, then, can you schedule such a complex project? You could use the program evaluation and review technique.

PERT (program evaluation and review technique)
A method of scheduling large, complex projects.

PERT network
A flowchart-like diagram that depicts the sequence of activities needed to complete a project and the time or costs associated with each activity.

events
End points that represent the completion of major activities in a PERT network.

activities
The time or resources needed to progress from one event to another in a PERT network.

critical path
The longest or most time-consuming sequence of events and activities in a PERT network that are required to complete the project in the shortest amount of time.

The **program evaluation and review technique**—usually just called **PERT,** or the PERT network analysis—was originally developed in the late 1950s for coordinating the more than 3,000 contractors and agencies working on the *Polaris* submarine weapon system.[23] This project was incredibly complicated, with hundreds of thousands of activities that had to be coordinated. PERT is reported to have cut two years off the completion date for the *Polaris* project.

A **PERT network** is a flowchart-like diagram that depicts the sequence of activities needed to complete a project and the time or costs associated with each activity. With a PERT network, a project manager must think through what has to be done, determine which events depend on one another, and identify potential trouble spots (see Exhibit 4-6). PERT also makes it easy to compare the effects alternative actions will have on scheduling and costs. PERT has been used to design and construct facilities, prepare environmental studies, conduct research and development, design software, and even plan large conferences.[24] PERT allows managers to monitor a project's progress, identify possible bottlenecks, and shift resources as necessary to keep the project on schedule. NASA and its many contractors—Rockwell and AlliedSignal, for example—use PERT to schedule Space Shuttle flights and in the engineering design of NASA's space station. It is also used in product design activities at such companies as Samsung.[25]

What Are the Key Components of PERT? To understand how to construct a PERT network, you need to know three terms: *events, activities,* and *critical path.* Let us define those terms, outline the steps in the PERT process, and then develop an example. **Events** are end points that represent the completion of major activities. Sometimes called *milestones,* events indicate that something significant has happened (such as receipt of purchased items) or an important component is finished. In PERT, events represent a point in time. **Activities,** on the other hand, are the actions that take place. Each activity consumes time, as determined on the basis of the time or resources required to progress from one event to another. The **critical path** is the longest or

Developing a PERT network requires the manager to identify all key activities needed to complete a project, rank them in order of dependence, and estimate each activity's completion time. This procedure can be translated into five specific steps:

- **1.** Identify every significant activity that must be achieved for a project to be completed. The accomplishment of each activity results in a set of events or outcomes.
- **2.** Ascertain the order in which these events must be completed.
- **3.** Diagram the flow of activities from start to finish, identifying each activity and its relationship to all other activities. Use circles to indicate events and arrows to represent activities. The result is a flowchart diagram that we call the PERT network.
- **4.** Compute a time estimate for completing each activity, using a weighted average that employs an optimistic time estimate (t_o) of how long the activity would take under ideal conditions, a most-likely estimate (t_m) of the time the activity normally should take, and a pessimistic estimate (t_p) that represents the time that an activity should take under the worst possible conditions. The formula for calculating the expected time (t_e) is then

$$t_e = \frac{t_o + 4t_m + t_p}{6}$$

- **5.** Finally, using a network diagram that contains time estimates for each activity, the manager can determine a schedule for the start and finish dates of each activity and for the entire project. Any delays that occur along the critical path require the most attention because they delay the entire project. That is, the critical path has no slack in it; therefore, any delay along that path immediately translates into a delay in the final deadline for the completed project.

Exhibit 4-6
Developing PERT Charts

most time-consuming sequence of events and activities required to complete the project in the shortest amount of time. Let's apply PERT to a construction manager's task of building a 5,500 square foot custom home.

As a construction manager, you recognize that time really is money in your business. Delays can turn a profitable job into a money loser. Accordingly, you must determine how long it will take to complete the house. You have carefully dissected the entire project into activities and events. Exhibit 4-7 outlines the major events in the construction project and your estimate of the expected time required to complete each activity. Exhibit 4-8 depicts the PERT network based on the data in Exhibit 4-7.

Engineers at Samsung Group use PERT networks to keep control of major projects. When interdependent activities are required, in projects such as these engineers' product-development tasks, PERT network techniques help bring the project in on time, within budget, and up to quality standards.

Your PERT network tells you that if everything goes as planned, it will take just over thirty-two weeks to build the house. This time is calculated

EVENT	DESCRIPTION	TIME (WEEKS)	PREDECESSOR ACTIVITY
A	Approve design and get permits	3	None
B	Perform excavation/lot clearing	1	A
C	Pour footers	1	B
D	Erect foundation walls	2	C
E	Frame house	4	D
F	Install windows	0.5	E
G	Shingle roof	0.5	E
H	Install brick front and siding	4	F, G
I	Install electrical, plumbing, and heating and A/C rough-ins	6	E
J	Install insulation	0.25	I
K	Install sheetrock	2	J
L	Finish and sand sheetrock	7	K
M	Install interior trim	2	L
N	Paint house (interior and exterior)	2	H, M
O	Install all cabinets	0.5	N
P	Install flooring	1	N
Q	Final touch-up and turn over house to homeowner	1	O, P

Exhibit 4-7
Major Activities in Building a Custom Home

by tracing the network's critical path: A-B-C-D-E-I-J-K-L-M-N-P-Q. Any delay in completing the events along this path will delay the completion of the entire project. For example, if it took six weeks instead of four to frame the house (event E), the entire project would be delayed by two weeks (or the time beyond that expected). But a one-week delay for installing the brick (event H) would have little effect because that event is not on the critical path. By using PERT, the construction manager would know that no corrective action would be needed. Further delays in installing the brick, however, could present problems—for such delays may, in actuality, result in a new critical path. Now back to our original critical path dilemma.

Notice that the critical path passes through activities N, P, and Q. Our PERT chart (Exhibit 4-7) tells us that these three activities take four weeks. Wouldn't path N-O-Q be faster? Yes. The PERT network shows that it takes only 3.5 weeks to complete that path. So why isn't N-O-Q on the critical path? Because activity Q cannot begin until both activities O and P are completed. Although activity O takes half a week, activity P

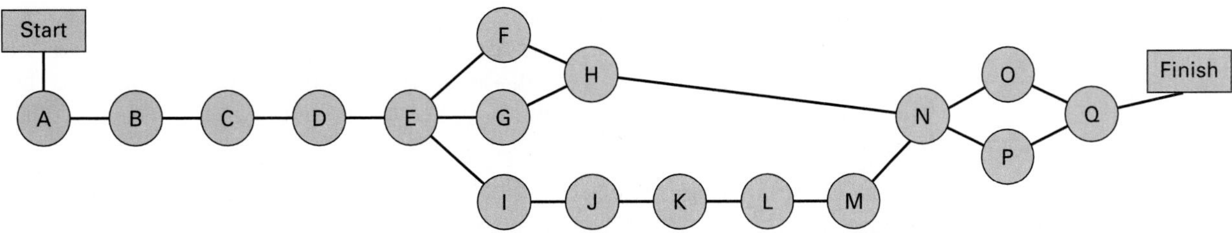

Exhibit 4-8
A PERT Network for Building a Custom Home

takes one full week. So, the earliest we can begin Q is after one week. What happens to the difference between the critical activity (activity P) time and the noncritical activity (activity O) time? The difference, in this case one-half week, becomes slack time. **Slack time** is the time difference between the critical path and all other paths. What use is there for slack? If the project manager notices some slippage on a critical activity, perhaps slack time from a noncritical activity can be borrowed and temporarily assigned to work on the critical one.

slack time
The time difference between the critical path and all other paths.

How Is PERT Both a Planning and a Control Tool? Not only does PERT help us to estimate the times associated with scheduling a project, it also gives us clues about where our controls should be placed. Because any event on the critical path that is delayed will delay the overall project (making us not only late but probably also over budget), our attention needs to be focused on the critical activities at all times. For example, if activity F (installing windows) is delayed by a week because supplies have not arrived, that is not a major issue. It's not on the critical path. But if activity P (installing flooring) is delayed from one week to two weeks, the entire project will be delayed by one week. Consequently, anything that has the immediate potential for delaying a project (critical activities) must be monitored very closely.

What Is Break-Even Analysis?

How many units of a product must an organization sell in order to break even—that is, to have neither profit nor loss? A manager might want to know the minimum number of units that must be sold to achieve his or her profit objective or whether a current product should continue to be sold or be dropped from the organization's product line. **Break-even analysis** is a widely used technique for helping managers make profit projections.[26]

break-even analysis
A technique for identifying the point at which total revenue is just sufficient to cover total costs.

Break-even analysis is a simplistic formulation, yet it is valuable to managers because it points out the relationship among revenues, costs, and profits. To compute the break-even point *(BE)*, the manager needs to know the unit price of the product being sold *(P)*, the variable cost per unit *(VC)*, and the total fixed costs *(TFC)*.

An organization breaks even when its total revenue is just enough to equal its total costs. But total cost has two parts: a fixed component and a variable component. Fixed costs are expenses that do not change, regardless of volume. Examples include insurance premiums and property taxes. Fixed costs, of course, are fixed only in the short term because, in the long run, commitments terminate and are thus subject to variation. Variable costs change in proportion to output and include raw materials, labor costs, and energy costs.

The break-even point can be computed graphically or by using the following formula:

$$BE = \left(\frac{TFC}{P - VC}\right)$$

This formula tells us that (1) total revenue will equal total cost when we sell enough units at a price that covers all variable unit costs, and (2) the difference between price and variable costs, when multiplied by the number of units sold, equals the fixed costs.

When Is Break-Even Useful? To demonstrate, assume that, at Todd's Seattle Espresso, Todd charges $1.75 for a cup of coffee. If his fixed costs (salary, insurance, etc.) are $47,000 a year and the variable costs for each cup of espresso are $0.40, Todd can compute his break-even point as follows: $47,000/(1.75 − 0.40) = 34,815 (about

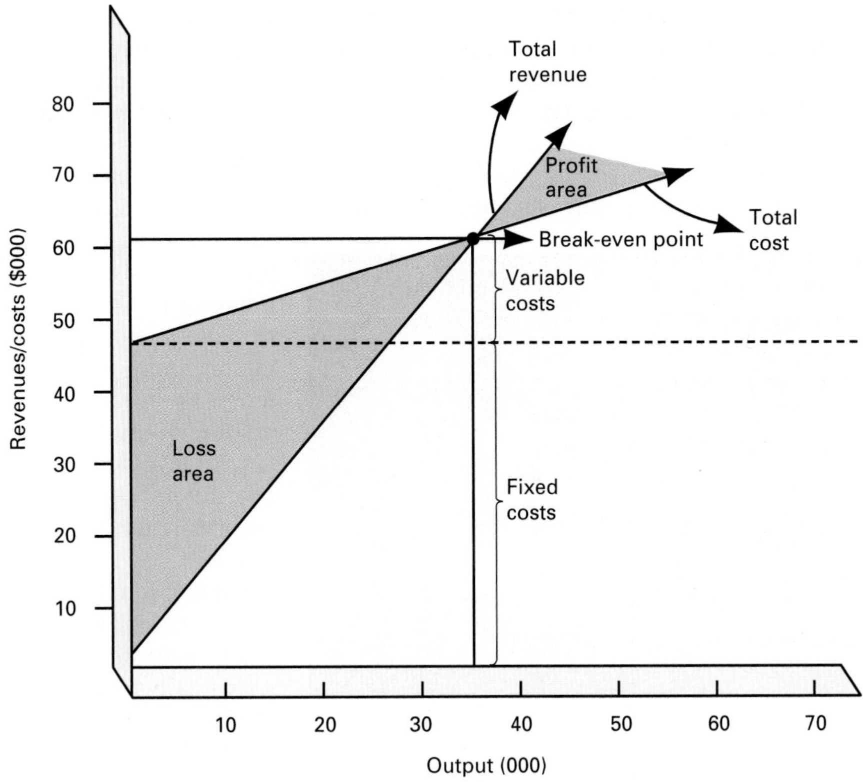

Exhibit 4-9
The Break-Even Analysis

670 cups of espresso sold each week), or when annual revenues are approximately $60,926. This same relationship is shown graphically in Exhibit 4-9.

How Can Break-Even Serve as a Planning Tool? As a planning tool, break-even analysis could help Todd set his sales objective. For example, he could establish the profit he wants and then work backward to determine what sales level is needed to reach that profit. Break-even analysis could also tell Todd how much volume has to increase to break even if he is currently operating at a loss or how much volume he can afford to lose and still break even if he is currently operating profitably. In some cases, such as the management of professional sports franchises, break-even analysis has shown the projected volume of ticket sales required to cover all costs to be so unrealistically high that the best action for management to take is to sell or close the business.

What Is Linear Programming, and What Kinds of Problems Lend Themselves to It?

Erica Kapenski owns a software developing company. One product line involves designing and producing software that detects and removes viruses. The software comes in two formats: DOS and MAC versions. She can sell all of these products she can produce. That, however, is her dilemma. The two formats go through the same production departments. How many of each type should she make to maximize her profits?

A close look at Erica's operation tells us she can use a mathematical technique called **linear programming** to solve her resource allocation dilemma. As we will show, linear programming is applicable to Erica's problem, but it cannot be applied to all resource allocation situations. Besides requiring limited resources and the objective of optimization, it requires that there be alternative ways of combining resources to

linear programming
A mathematical technique for solving resource allocation problems that attempts to minimize costs or maximize profits with limited resources and numerous options.

produce a number of output mixes. There must also be a linear relationship between variables.[27] This means that a change in one variable will be accompanied by an exactly proportional change in the other. For Erica's business, this condition would be met if it took exactly twice the time to produce two diskettes—irrespective of format—as it took to produce one.

Many different types of problems can be solved using linear programming. Selecting transportation routes that minimize shipping costs, allocating a limited advertising budget among various product brands, making the optimum assignment of personnel among projects, and determining how much of each product to make with a limited number of resources are just a few. To give you some idea of how linear programming is useful, let's return to Erica's problem and see how linear programming could help her solve it. Fortunately, Erica's problem is relatively simple, so we can solve it rather quickly. For complex linear programming problems, there is computer software that has been designed specifically to help develop solutions.

Suzanne Bernard Leclair, founder of the Leval, Quebec, Les Fourgons Transit, Inc., uses linear programming in determining production resource allocation for her customized truck-box manufacturing process.

First, we need to establish some facts about Erica's business. She has computed the profit margins to be \$18 for the DOS format and \$24 for the MAC. She can therefore express her objective function as: maximum profit = \$18 R + \$24 S, where R is the number of DOS diskettes produced and S is the number of MAC diskettes. In addition, Erica knows how long it takes to produce each format and the monthly production capacity for virus software [2,400 hours in design and 900 hours in production] (see Exhibit 4-10). The production capacity numbers act as constraints on her overall capacity. Now Erica can establish her constraint equations:

$$4R + 6S \leq 2{,}400$$

$$1.5R + 1.5S \leq 900$$

Of course, because a software format cannot be produced in a volume less than zero, Erica can also state that $R > 0$ and $S > 0$. Erica has graphed her solution as shown in Exhibit 4-11. The blue shaded area represents the options that do not exceed the ca-

Exhibit 4-10
Production Data for Virus Software

	NUMBER OF HOURS REQUIRED PER UNIT		
DEPARTMENT	DOS VERSION	MAC VERSION	MONTHLY PRODUCTION CAPACITY (HOURS)
Design	4	6	2,400
Manufacture	1.5	1.5	900
Profit per unit	$18	$24	

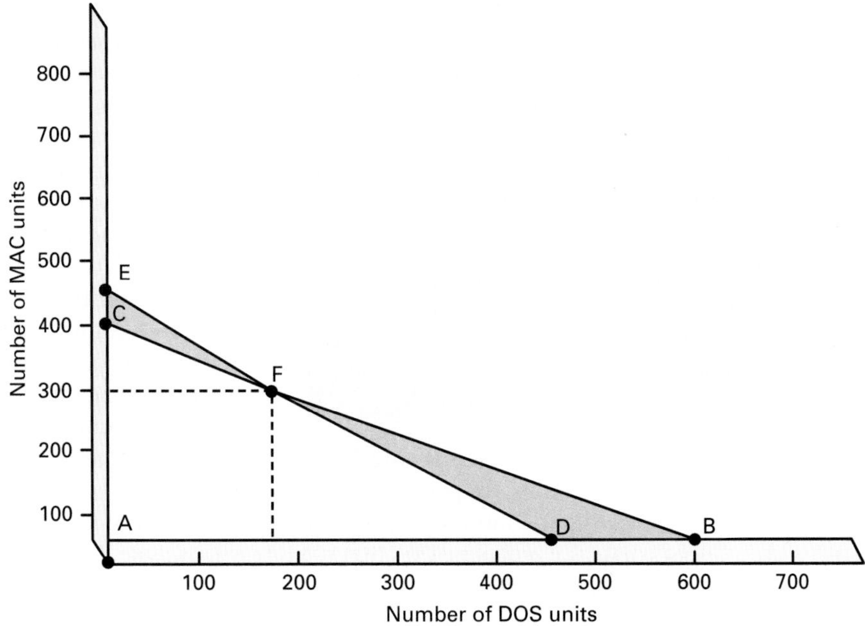

Exhibit 4-11
Graphical Solution to Erica Kapenski's Linear Programming Problem

pacity of either department. What does this mean? We know that total design capacity is 2,400 hours. So if Erica decides to design only DOS format, the maximum number she can produce is 600 (2,400 hours ÷ 4 hours of design for each DOS). If she decides to produce all MAC versions, the maximum she can produce is 400 (2,400 hours ÷ 6 hours of design for MAC). This design constraint is shown in Exhibit 4-11 as line BC. The other constraint Erica faces is that of production. The maximum of either format she can produce is 450, since each takes 1.5 hours to copy, verify, and package. This production constraint is shown in the exhibit as line DE. Erica's optimal resource allocation will be defined at one of the corners of this feasibility region (area ACFD). Point F provides the maximum profits within the constraints stated. At point A, profits would be zero because neither virus software version is being produced. At points C and D, profits would be $9,600 (400 units @ $24) and $8,100 (450 units @ $18), respectively. At point F profits would be $9,900 (150 DOS units @ $18 + 300 MAC units @ $24).

What Is Queuing Theory, and When Is It Useful?

You are a supervisor for a branch of NationsBank outside Atlanta. One of the decisions you have to make is how many of the nine cashier stations you should keep open at any given time. **Queuing theory,** or what is frequently referred to as waiting-line theory, could help you decide.

queuing theory
A technique that balances the cost of having a waiting line against the cost of service to maintain that line; also called waiting-line theory.

Whenever a decision involves balancing the cost of having a waiting line against the cost of service to maintain that line, it can be made easier with queuing theory. This includes such common situations as determining how many gas pumps are needed at gas stations, tellers at bank windows, toll takers at toll booths, or check-in lines at airline ticket counters. In each situation, management wants to minimize cost by having as few stations open as possible yet not so few as to test the patience of customers. In our teller example, on certain days (such as the first of every month and Fridays) you could open all nine windows and keep waiting time to a minimum, or you could open only one, minimize staffing costs, and risk a riot.

Queuing theory is designed to keep customers, like these at Costco's Kirkland, Washington, warehouse store, from waiting too long in line to check out. If the wait becomes too frustrating, customers may take their business elsewhere.

The mathematics underlying queuing theory is beyond the scope of this book. But you can see how the theory works in our simple example. You have nine tellers working for you, but you want to know whether you can get by with only one window open during an average morning. You consider twelve minutes to be the longest you would expect any customer to wait patiently in line. If it takes four minutes, on average, to serve each customer, the line should not be permitted to get longer than three deep (12 minutes ÷ 4 minutes per customer = 3 customers). If you know from past experience that, during the morning, people arrive at the average rate of two per minute, you can calculate the probability *(P)* that the line will become longer than any number *(n)* of customers as follows:

$$P_n = \left(1 - \frac{\text{Arrival rate}}{\text{Service rate}}\right) \times \left(\frac{\text{Arrival rate}}{\text{Service rate}}\right)^n$$

where $n = 3$ customers, arrival rate = 2 per minute, and service rate = 4 minutes per customer. Putting these numbers into the above formula generates the following:

$$P_n = \left(1 - \frac{2}{4}\right) \times \left(\frac{2}{4}\right)^3 = \left(\frac{1}{2}\right) \times \left(\frac{8}{64}\right) = \left(\frac{8}{128}\right) = 0.0625$$

What does a P of 0.0625 mean? It tells you that the likelihood of having more than three customers in line during the average morning is 1 change in 16. Are you willing to live with four or more customers in line 6 percent of the time? If so, keeping one teller window open will be enough. If not, you will have to assign more tellers to staff them.

Planning on a Personal Level: Managing Your Time

What is time? It's something that can be your best friend in that it gives you an opportunity to accomplish your goals. Of course, it can also be your worst enemy, for there never appears to be enough of it to get everything done. Time therefore, is a scarce resource. Time wasted can never be replaced. Time, too, can never be saved. When a second passes, it is gone forever.

time management
A way of scheduling time effectively.

Time management is a tool any individual can use to schedule time effectively. It is a way of planning one's personal activities. Time management is also a self-discipline that keeps an individual's attention focused on those things that need to be accomplished. Unfortunately, there are no hard and fast rules for managing time that will work in every case. A perfect solution has yet to be found—if one ever could be.

Developing a Management Skill

TECHNIQUES FOR MANAGING YOUR TIME

About the Skill: *The essence of time management is to use your time effectively. This means you must know the goal you want to accomplish, the required activities that, when accomplished, will help you meet your goal, and the urgency of each activity.*

Steps in practicing the skill

1. ***Identify your objectives.*** What specific objectives have you set for yourself or for your unit? If you work in an organization that uses MBO or some other goal-setting method, these objectives may already exist.

2. ***Prioritize your objectives.*** Not all objectives you have are equally important. Given limitations that exist on your time, you want to give highest priority to the objectives that are most important.

3. ***List the activities that must be done to accomplish your objectives.*** Planning is really the key here. You must identify the specific actions you need to take to achieve your goals. Record these activities on a sheet of paper, an index card, or even a computer-generated schedule. These activities become your To-Do list. Your To-Do list should cover, at a minimum, those things that need to be done over the next few days. The list should be reviewed throughout the day and updated when necessary. Items completed should be crossed out.

4. ***Prioritize your To-Do list.*** This step involves imposing a second set of priorities. Here, you need to emphasize both importance and urgency. If the activity is not important, you should consider delegating it to someone else. If it is not urgent, it can usually wait. Completing this step helps you identify activities you *must* do, activities you *should* do, those you'll do *when you can,* and those you can *get others to do for you.*

5. ***Schedule your day.*** After prioritizing your activities, develop a daily plan. Each morning (or the night before) identify what you want to accomplish during the day. This list should identify five to seven things you want to do during the day. Work first on any activity that you must do. Then follow with those you should do, and so forth. But be realistic in your schedule. Given the nature of your activities, you may be unable to complete everything. Be realistic in what you can accomplish. The key, however, is to concentrate on the "must-do's," making sure they do get done. Fifteen minutes here, a half-hour there, add up in getting a must-do done. Don't make the mistake of working on the "when you can" activities just because they are easier to accomplish. You'll be spending time on activities that really won't add to your effectiveness.

Nonetheless, there are several time-management techniques that, when applied, can make an individual a better time manager (see Developing a Management Skill).

Remember, time management is not something that generally comes easily. It takes a dedicated effort to be a good time manager. Individuals who are good at this technique often appear to have more time than others. They don't! After all, they face the same twenty-four-hour constraint that everyone else faces in a day. What they do have going for them is that they know how to use those twenty-four hours effectively. For instance, they understand their productivity cycle. Some people are most productive in the mornings, others in the evening. Once you know your productivity cycle, you should schedule your most important activities when you are able to give them the most effort (see Understanding Yourself).

Understanding Yourself

Determining Your Daily Productivity Cycle

Are you a morning or an evening person? This assessment is designed to provide you with some information that will help you make that determination. For each of the thirteen statements that follow, choose, by circling the letter, the response that best describes you.

1. If you were free to choose, (and you were not constrained by having to work) at what time would you prefer to get up each day?
   a. 5:00–6:30 A.M.
   b. 6:30–7:45 A.M.
   c. 7:45–9:45 A.M.
   d. 9:45–11:00 A.M.
   e. 11:00 A.M.–noon
2. If you were free to choose, at what time would you prefer to go to bed each night?
   a. 8:00–9:00 P.M.
   b. 9:00–10:15 P.M.
   c. 10:15 P.M.–12:30 A.M.
   d. 12:30–1:45 A.M.
   e. 1:45–3:00 A.M.
3. Under normal circumstances, how easy is it for you to wake up in the morning?
   a. not at all easy
   b. slightly easy
   c. fairly easy
   d. very easy
4. How alert do you feel during the first half-hour after you awake in the morning?
   a. not at all alert
   b. slightly sluggish
   c. fairly alert
   d. very alert
5. During the first half-hour after you awake, how do you feel?
   a. very tired
   b. fairly tired
   c. fairly refreshed
   d. very refreshed
6. You join a friend in exercising two mornings a week between 7:00 and 8:00 A.M. Do you think you would find the exercise
   a. very refreshing
   b. somewhat refreshing
   c. somewhat difficult
   d. very difficult

7. At what time in the evening do you feel tired and, as a result, in need of sleep?
   a. 8:00–9:00 P.M.
   b. 9:00–10:15 P.M.
   c. 10:15 P.M.–12:30 A.M.
   d. 12:30–1:45 A.M.
   e. 1:45–3:00 A.M.
8. You wish to be at your peak for a mentally exhausting test that will last two hours. If you had a choice, at which time would you prefer to take the test?
   a. 8:00–10:00 A.M.
   b. 11:00 A.M.–1:00 P.M.
   c. 3:00–5:00 P.M.
   d. 7:00–9:00 P.M.
9. Which of the following statements best reflects how you view yourself?
   a. I am definitely a morning type.
   b. I am more a morning than an evening type.
   c. I am more an evening than a morning type.
   d. I am definitely an evening type.
10. Given that you have eight hours of work ahead of you, when would you prefer to get up?
    a. before 6:30 A.M.
    b. 6:30–7:30 A.M.
    c. 7:30–8:30 A.M.
    d. 8:30 A.M. or later
11. If you had to get up every morning at 6:00 A.M. (even on your days off), what do you think it would be like?
    a. very difficult and unpleasant
    b. rather difficult and unpleasant
    c. a little unpleasant but no great problem
    d. easy and not unpleasant
12. How long does it take you to recover your senses after a night's sleep?
    a. 0–10 minutes
    b. 11–20 minutes
    c. 21–40 minutes
    d. more than 40 minutes
13. Indicate your level of activity in the morning versus in the evening.
    a. I am mostly active in the morning and tired in the evening.
    b. I am somewhat more active in the morning.
    c. I am somewhat more active in the evening.
    d. I am mostly active in the evening and tired in the morning.

Continued

Scoring: Circle your response selected for the thirteen statements.

1. a = 5	5. a = 1	8. a = 4	11. a = 1
b = 4	b = 2	b = 3	b = 2
c = 3	c = 3	c = 2	c = 3
d = 2	d = 4	d = 1	d = 4
e = 1			
2. a = 5	6. a = 4	9. a = 4	12. a = 4
b = 4	b = 3	b = 3	b = 3
c = 3	c = 2	c = 2	c = 2
d = 2	d = 1	d = 1	d = 1
e = 1			
3. a = 1	7. a = 5	10. a = 4	13. a = 4
b = 2	b = 4	b = 3	b = 3
c = 3	c = 3	c = 2	c = 2
d = 4	d = 2	d = 1	d = 1
4. a = 1	e = 1		
b = 2			
c = 3			
d = 4			

Now total your circled numbers.

What the Assessment Means: Score totals range from 13 to 55. Scores of 22 or less indicate that you are most productive in the evening. Scores of 23 to 43 indicate an intermediate range. This means you can function well during both the morning and the evening, depending on the circumstances. Scores of 44 and above indicate that you are most productive in the morning. If you don't already do this, you should adjust your activities so that your most important, urgent, and challenging activities are undertaken when your cycle is high.

Source: Adapted from C. S. Smith, C. Reilly, and K. Midkiff, "Evaluation of Three Circadian Questionnaires with Suggestions for an Improved Measure of Morningness," *Journal of Applied Psychology,* October 1989, p. 374. Copyright © 1989 by the American Psychological Assn. Reprinted with permission.

Good time managers also know how to minimize disruptions, called time wasters, that will steal a person's time. These include interruptions, phone calls, and the like. During your most productive time, you need to insulate yourself from the time wasters. Go somewhere, if possible, where you won't be disturbed. Have calls screened, or let them roll over to the answering machine. Close your door to keep interruptions to a minimum. Obviously, the degree of insulating yourself will depend on your organization's policies, your boss, and your employees. However, you must attempt to protect your productive time at all costs. Remember though, if you are disturbed, take it in stride. Deal with the issue, then return to your task as soon as you can.

Finally, as a manager, you will be attending many meetings. If it is your meeting, have a reason for it. Meeting just to meet is often a waste of time. Set an agenda for the meeting, describing its purpose and what you want to accomplish. Then stick to it. Efficiently run meetings are time-effective. If it is not your meeting, ask for an agenda if one hasn't been sent. If you can, find out why you need to attend. Maybe someone on your staff could represent you. If that's not possible, try to attend only the part of the meeting that requires your presence. And if that fails, just go. Don't fret, and don't waste more time chitchatting after the meeting. Do what you need to do, then return to your priority tasks!

Summary

How will I know if I fulfilled the Learning Objectives found on page 100? You will have fulfilled the Learning Objectives if you understand the following.

1. **Describe techniques for scanning the environment.** Techniques for scanning the environment include reading newspapers, magazines, books, and trade journals; reading competitors' ads, promotional materials, and press releases; attending trade shows; debriefing sales personnel; and analyzing competitors' products.

2. **Contrast quantitative and qualitative forecasting.** Quantitative forecasting applies a set of mathematical rules to a set of past data to predict future outcomes. Qualitative forecasting uses judgments and the opinions of knowledgeable individuals to predict outcomes.

3. **Explain why budgets are popular.** Budgets are popular planning devices because money is a universal common denominator that can be used in all types of organizations and by managers at all levels.

4. **List two approaches to budgeting.** Two popular approaches to budgeting are the traditional (incremental) and the zero-based budgeting approaches. The traditional budget is based on past allocations. Zero-based budgets are established each budgeting period and make no reference to past allocations.

5. **Differentiate Gantt and load charts.** Gantt and load charts are scheduling devices. Both are bar graphs. Gantt charts monitor planned and actual activities over time; load charts focus on capacity utilization by monitoring whole departments or specific resources.

6. **Identify the steps in a PERT network.** The five steps in developing a PERT network are (1) identify every significant activity that must be achieved for a project to be completed; (2) determine the order in which these activities must be completed; (3) diagram the flow of activities in a project from start to finish; (4) estimate the time needed to complete each activity; and (5) use the network diagram to determine a schedule for the start and finish dates of each activity and for the entire project.

7. **State the factors that determine a product's break-even point.** A product's break-even point is determined by the unit price of the product, its variable cost per unit, and its total fixed costs.

8. **Describe the requirements for using linear programming.** For linear programming to be applicable, a problem must have limited resources, constraints, an objective function to optimize, alternative ways of combining resources, and a linear relationship between variables.

9. **Explain how queuing theory can be a planning tool.** Queuing theory can be used as a planning tool when the cost of having a waiting line is balanced against the costs incurred in maintaining that line.

10. **List five steps for better time management.** Five steps for better time management include: (1) identify your objectives; (2) prioritize your objectives; (3) list the activities that must be done to accomplish your objectives; (4) prioritize your To-Do list; and (5) schedule your day.

Review & Discussion Questions

1. How is scanning the environment related to forecasting?
2. What effects have improvements in technology had on planning tools and techniques? Cite specific examples.
3. Assume that you manage the ticket sales for the Chicago Sports Authority. Your hours of operation are 7:00 A.M. until 11:00 P.M. You want to know the number of sales representatives to have on each shift. What type of planning tool(s) do you think will be useful to you? What type of environmental scanning, if any, would you likely do in this management job?
4. How can benchmarking improve the quality of an organization's products or processes?
5. What is ISO 9000, and how does it affect an organization?
6. Describe how budgets can be used as both a planning and a control tool.
7. Explain how a Gantt chart can be used for writing a college term paper.
8. What is the significance of the critical path in a PERT network?
9. How can break-even analysis be used as a planning tool?
10. In what situations is queuing theory applicable? In what situations is linear programming applicable?
11. How can managers assess how well they are currently managing their time?

Testing Your Comprehension • • • 

Circle the correct answer, then check yourself on page AK-1.

1. Which of the following is NOT a technique for assessing the environment?
   a) forecasting
   b) environmental scanning
   c) national weather service long-range outlook
   d) benchmarking

2. The technique by which managers identify competitors and attempt to determine what those competitors are doing is
   a) scenario analysis
   b) illegal for most organizations
   c) called organizational espionage
   d) none of the above

3. A company predicts the possibility that certain legislation will be passed and considers the possible consequences to its business. This is an example of
   a) environmental scanning
   b) benchmarking
   c) building scenarios
   d) forecasting

4. The search for the best practice among other organizations is
   a) forecasting
   b) benchmarking
   c) TQM
   d) substitution effect

5. A budget that combines the revenue and expense budgets is a
   a) profit budget
   b) cash budget
   c) fixed budget
   d) variable budget

6. Which of the following is NOT true of the incremental budget?
   a) Each budget is a modified extension of past budgets.
   b) It is probably the most widely used budget today.
   c) Funds are appropriated for each division or unit; managers then use their discretion in the actual use of their unit's funds.
   d) It is essentially the same as a zero-based budget.

7. The zero-based budget
   a) requires managers to justify all proposed expenditures
   b) can provide continuity by automatically expanding budgets over the years
   c) relies heavily on an extension of the prior budget
   d) was developed by the Rockwell Corporation for the Space Shuttle program

8. When managers determine what is to be done, who is to do it, and when it is to be completed, they are exhibiting some of the components of
   a) budgeting
   b) scheduling
   c) linear programming
   d) simulation

9. If fixed costs are $8,000 and variable costs are $70 per unit, how many units must be sold at a price of $870 in order for the business to break even?
   a) 9.2
   b) 114.3
   c) 10
   d) 100

Continued

10. A bar graph showing time on the horizontal axis and activities to be completed on the vertical axis is a
   a) simulation chart
   b) zero-base budget
   c) Gantt chart
   d) break-even analysis

---

11. A load chart is a
   a) modified simulation method showing critical paths
   b) modified Gantt chart showing capacity utilization
   c) method of budgeting in an uncertain environment
   d) control devise designed to minimize extreme weight on certain bridges

---

12. When would a PERT network NOT provide much help?
   a) when sequencing is important
   b) for complicated jobs
   c) for independent projects
   d) for jobs with many steps involved

---

13. After all significant activities of a PERT network have been identified,
   a) a time estimate for each activity is prepared
   b) a diagram of all activities and events is prepared
   c) the entire schedule is determined
   d) the order of all activities is determined

---

14. After the manager has determined the time estimates for each activity in a PERT network,
   a) the order of events must be determined
   b) the critical path can be determined
   c) a diagram of the flow of activities can be completed
   d) a funding request is prepared

---

15. The difference between the duration of a critical activity and that of a noncritical activity is the
   a) break-even point
   b) critical path
   c) linear program
   d) slack time

---

16. The operational planning technique that attempts to minimize costs or maximize profits with limited resources and numerous options is called
   a) linear programming
   b) simulation techniques
   c) PERT network
   d) break-even analysis

---

17. As the "front-end" manager of a Target Store, part of your responsibilities include deciding how many check-out lines to have open during any given hour. To help you decide, you could use
   a) break-even analysis
   b) linear programming
   c) queuing theory
   d) time-management analysis

---

18. Which of the following is recommended as the final step in time management?
   a) prioritize objectives
   b) list goals
   c) list the activities that will accomplish your objectives
   d) prepare daily plan

Applying the Concepts

Managing Your Time and Money

Have you ever thought about how you spend your time and money in a typical week? Do you know who or what "wastes" your time? Do you know where you have spent your money? Can you account for your expenditures? Or has your money just disappeared?

For this exercise, develop a time log for each day for the next week. Starting at 7:00 A.M. and in fifteen-minute increments, list what you do and who you interact with until 11:00 P.M. Fill in each time period as it ends—don't wait until later and attempt to complete it by memory. In a similar fashion, develop an expense budget, listing all your expenditures during the week.

When you have tracked data for the week, review the time log and the expense budget. Develop responses to the following questions. In the time log, can you identify areas in which (1) you were most productive? (2) you wasted time? Are there consistencies in these time wasters—time, place, individual?

Do a similar analysis of your expenditures. What did you spend most of your money on? Do you spend your money on things you need, or do you buy on impulse? Do you believe that having a weekly budget could benefit you in managing your money? Explain.

After you have compiled these data, exchange papers with two classmates. Look for similarities between their lists and yours. Make two recommendations for each of your two classmates that could help them manage their time and their money better. Share these recommendations with the group. Discuss your reactions to their recommendations, and answer any questions they may have about the recommendations you made. Finally, as a group, discuss what changes you are willing to make to better manage your time and money.

Take It to the Net

We invite you to visit the Robbins/De Cenzo page on the Prentice Hall Web site at:

http://www.prenhall.com/robbinsfom

for this chapter's World Wide Web exercise.

You can also visit the Web sites for these companies and agencies featured within this chapter:

Braas Company
http://www.vaccon.com/distrib/braas.htm

Central Intelligence Agency
http://www.odci.gov/cia

Ford Motor Company
http://www.ford.com

General Mills, Inc.
http://www.genmills.com

Montblanc
http://www.icanect.net/montb/

NASA
http://www.nasa.gov

National Security Agency
http://www.nsa.gov:8080

Penske Corporation
http://www.pensketoyota.com

Thinking Critically

Making a Value Judgment: Gathering Competitive Intelligence

All business operations need to gather information about their competitors in an effort to remain competitive. For many, it's a game—but one that must be taken seriously. Some organizations, too, pride themselves on being able to obtain competitive data in some of the must unusual ways. This may involve "surfing the Net" in order to see what new products are being released or checking court record data bases to determine what, if any, lawsuits or civil cases have been brought against a competitor. For the most part, these organizations are obtaining public information. But other tactics are used, too. For example, one can call a competitor's office and ask very specific questions about the company's mission and strategic direction. Answers may not be forthcoming, but there is a chance that the person on the other end of the line will be quite talkative.

Other tactics may include buying some stock shares in a competitor's organization so that you can get annual reports and other information about the company that normally isn't available to the general public. An organization may even encourage one of its employees to take a job with a competitor and then to quit and return to his or her old job after getting some "company private" data. Furthermore, an organization may interview or hire managers from a competing firm, in the hope that they will bring with them a wealth of "inside" information.[28]

Questions:

1. From your point of view, when does competitive intelligence become corporate espionage?
2. If you were an employee of A.T. Cross and were asked to get some information about Montblanc pens, how would you go about it? Just how far would you go, and what kind of tactics would you use, to get the data? Would your position change if you knew that getting some "critical" data could result in your receiving a $25,000 bonus?
3. Do you believe that ethical guidelines should be established to deal with competitive intelligence activities? Explain.

Larry Harmon at DeMar Plumbing

Larry Harmon is owner of DeMar Plumbing, Heating, and Air Conditioning, a Clovis, California, company. He runs one of the fastest-growing small businesses in the United States.[29] Many individuals might wonder why so much attention is being paid to a plumbing firm. The answer is simple. Harmon has shown that applying planning tools can and does work—no matter what the business is.

Harmon's success comes from some basic business concepts. He's on the job by 5 A.M., carefully scheduling his employees and the day's work. Furthermore, Larry makes sure that the necessary inventory for each job is readily available. This means that each of his mechanics knows exactly what customers he or she will see that day and the reason for the service call. The mechanics also have all the necessary parts to correct the problem. But these preliminaries are only part of the success of Demar Plumbing. The other, as Larry states, is not to think like a plumber. For example, if a customer has a leaky toilet, a plumber might go in and fix the problem. Larry, on the other hand, not only wants the problem corrected but also wants his customers to "feel so good about his work they'll keep coming back." In other words, Larry's team will correct what doesn't work and provide outstanding customer service. His mechanics are polite, take the necessary time to answer each customer question, and make sure that the work site is as clean or cleaner when they leave it than it was when they arrived. This customer service is something few, if any, of Harmon's competitors offer.

In short, Harmon is successful because he has not lost sight of one basic fact. Any plumber can fix a leak, unplug a stopped-up toilet, or recharge a heat pump compressor. But can they do it in such a way that the customer is happy—not only with the job but also with the company that did the work? In the case of DeMar Plumbing, Heating, and Air Conditioning, Larry Harmon makes sure that customer satisfaction comes first. That's a competitive advantage that has translated into a multimillion dollar operation.

Questions:

1. How can environmental scanning help an organization like DeMar Plumbing? What might be some of the areas of interest for Larry Harmon?
2. If Larry Harmon came to you asking for assistance on developing competitive intelligence, what suggestions would you make that would provide DeMar Plumbing with accurate and timely data?
3. Why are scheduling and time-management tools critical for DeMar's success? What other planning tools could you suggest Larry Harmon use? Why?

Video Case ABCNEWS

Winning by Planning

Every toy company hopes that the new creations it's preparing for the holiday buying season will be the ones that kids are screaming for and parents are scrambling to find in the toy stores. We're talking a huge potential market here. During 1993, for example, more than $17 billion was spent on toys in the United States alone, and about two-thirds of that amount was spent during the last quarter of the calendar year. So the stakes and potential payoff for developing the year's "hot toy" are high.

Yet these toy companies don't leave the development of a winner to chance. The planning tools and techniques used in the long process to get a product from the creative spark in the mind of a toy inventor to a lineup of kids crawling into Santa's lap asking for that specific toy are carefully orchestrated. At Tyco Toy's headquarters in Mount Laurel, New Jersey, for instance, marketing and product design managers had been working on the Dr. Dreadful Drinklab for over two years. Every facet of the Dr. Dreadful toy had been endlessly discussed and debated in the company's attempt to eventually earn the maximum sales revenues. The Dr. Dreadful toy started when the marketing team at Tyco noticed a trend in kids' candies—a trend of "in-your-face," pushing the limits of the sourest, hottest, and grossest. A Tyco vice president recalls that one of his favorites was candy snot that came in a nose container and dripped out through the nostrils. Company managers decided to tie this trend of kids' infatuation with gross food into a theme area that has been perennially popular with children—monsters. So the line of monster toys that made food that looked gross, but tasted great, was born.

Getting the product line from an idea to an actual packaged toy isn't always a smooth process. For instance, some Tyco executives were concerned about whether boys, particularly, would want to play with toys that involved cooking. Also, there was some concern about whether gross food that excited children would be too gross for parents. To investigate some of these concerns over the planned product, Tyco executives held numerous focus group interviews with kids and parents to get their comments and feedback about the idea. At the same time, company chemists at a lab in New Jersey played at being mad scientists in order to come up with products that would be "manageably gross." When the market testing was done, the product team proceeded to the next step of selling the Dr. Dreadful toy. They took it to the annual toy fair, held in February, where manufacturers introduce their latest products to buyers and the public. The Dr. Dreadful booth was a huge hit, and Tyco implemented its advertising campaign push. The long campaign—over two years' worth of work—seems to have paid off. Tyco expects the Dr. Dreadful toy to bring in $50 million in domestic and international sales.

Questions:

1. Although it's not specifically mentioned in the case above, how would break-even analysis be useful to the product managers at Tyco in the development of a new toy line?
2. What type(s) of forecasting is evident in the development of the Dr. Dreadful toy?
3. What other tools and techniques that were discussed in this chapter might be used by Tyco executives as they plan a new toy? Explain.

Source: "The Business of Toys (at Christmas Time)," *ABC News Nightline,* December 22, 1994.

Foundations of Decision Making

5

LEARNING OBJECTIVES

What will I be able to do after I finish this chapter?

1. **EXPLAIN** the steps in the decision-making process.
2. **IDENTIFY** the assumptions of the rational decision-making model.
3. **EXPLAIN** the limits to rationality.
4. **DEFINE** certainty, risk, and uncertainty as they relate to decision making.
5. **DESCRIBE** the actions of the bounded-rational decision maker.
6. **IDENTIFY** the two types of decision problems and the two types of decisions that are used to solve them.
7. **DEFINE** heuristics and explain how they affect the decision-making process.
8. **IDENTIFY** four decision-making styles.
9. **DESCRIBE** the advantages and disadvantages of group decisions.
10. **DESCRIBE** three techniques for improving group decision making.

Research over the past few decades has shown us the need for understanding the sociocultural factors among people from different countries. Individuals from countries where power distance is high, for example, are frequently accustomed to a condition in those societies where there are "Haves" and "Have-nots." Being part of the Haves gives individuals in this group significant power to make decisions. Yet, when these Haves leave the comforts of their homeland, they, too, often must make some adjustments in their decision-making styles. That's precisely what Loida Nicolas Lewis did.[1]

Loida grew up in the Philippines. She was born into a politically well-connected family that still operates the country's largest and most successful furniture company. Her early years were filled with all the privileges and amenities that are often associated with "high society." These included attending the best schools, foreign travel, and having a large base of support and assistance. One thing that her upbringing did not include, however, was having decisions made for her.

Loida has always been an independent woman, making choices that she wanted and not those her family wanted her to make. For example, her father attempted to "make" Loida a lawyer and a politician and to have her become an instrumental member of the ruling class in the Philippines. Loida rejected that alternative. Instead, she wanted to dedicate her life to two goals—raising a family and helping others less fortunate than herself. In this latter case, she wanted to help other Filipinos get into the United States so that they could get out from under the political repression in the Philippines. For the former, she married Reginald F. Lewis, the major owner and chairman of Beatrice International Holdings, Inc. the New York–based global supermarket and specialty foods company.

Growing up in a country where power distance is high didn't directly influence Loida Nicolas Lewis's management style. Since taking over the top spot of Beatrice, upon her husband's sudden passing, Loida has used sound decision making to move the company forward. Under her direction, company revenues have grown by more than 17 percent in just a few years.

Loida was living her dream—raising a family and helping others. Her life was uncomplicated. At least until 1993, when Reginald Lewis—who by then had earned the title of the world's richest African-American man and had become a national role model—passed away. In his will, he left the job of running Beatrice to his wife. On his death, Loida inherited a $1.7 billion company—a company that was stagnating.

Lewis did not have the business acumen or the experience of her late husband. In fact, this soft-spoken, petite woman has a persona that was directly opposite of Reginald's "macho, bruising style." Rightfully anxious, she nevertheless took over the company and began molding it in her image.

She recognized that the company was losing money. Its tremendous growth through diversification in the 1980s was hurting Beatrice. Many of the "status" symbols her late husband had accumulated—a corporate jet, high-priced New York real estate, and the like—were now viewed as being a financial drain leading in part to a $17 million loss. So she made several major decisions. She pared down the company to enhance its four core business operations—making ice cream in the Canary Islands, making consumer food products in Spain, making snack foods in Ireland, and running its private-label operations based in France. She also decided to sell off the company limousine and the corporate jet, cut headquarter staff in half, and sell off many of the less-profitable ice cream companies that Beatrice held in Denmark, Germany, and Italy. She also focused on reducing Beatrice's debt in an effort to take the company public.

One would think that following a strong leader like Reginald would have posed problems for Loida. It didn't. Although her style is very different from her husband's, she has achieved remarkable success. She involves her inner group in decisions and uses compassion to develop a "focused, disciplined, sensitive, and collegial atmosphere." And the numbers support that her approach is working. Her actions so far have led to a 17 percent increase in sales to $2.1 billion, have increased market share in the four core business operations, and have significantly increased profits.

Loida Nicolas Lewis, like all managers, makes a lot of decisions—some small and some large. The overall quality of those decisions goes a long way in determining her organization's success or failure.[2] In this chapter, we examine the foundations of decision making.

In the last two chapters, we addressed how companies plan—for both the long-term survival of the organization and the short-term day-to-day operations. Implied in those planning activities were the decisions managers make. Plans should not come out of thin air. They should be the result of careful analyses. After weighing the advantages and disadvantages of various alternatives, managers select the ones that will best serve the interests of the organization. This selection process is called decision making. What kinds of planning decisions do managers like Loida Nicolas Lewis make? We have listed a few in Exhibit 5-1.

The Decision-Making Process

decision-making process
A set of eight steps that includes identifying a problem, selecting a solution, and evaluating the effectiveness of the solution.

Decision making is typically described as "choosing among alternatives." But this view is overly simplistic. Why? Because decision making is a process rather than the simple act of choosing among alternatives. Exhibit 5-2 illustrates the **decision-making process** as a set of eight steps that begins with identifying a problem, moves through selecting an alternative that can alleviate the problem, and concludes with evaluating the decision's effectiveness. This process is as applicable to your personal decision about what you're going to do on spring break as it is to McDonald's decision to introduce the Arch Deluxe burger. The process can also be used to describe both individual and group decisions. Let's take a closer look at the process in order to understand what each step encompasses.

What Defines a Decision Problem?

problem
A discrepancy between an existing and a desired state of affairs.

The decision-making process begins with the existence of a **problem** (step 1) or, more specifically, a discrepancy between an existing and a desired state of affairs.[3] Let's develop an example that illustrates this point and that we can use throughout this section. For the sake of simplicity, let's make the example something to which most of us can relate: the decision to buy a new car. Take the case of a new-product manager for

Exhibit 5-1
Examples of Planning-Function Decisions

What are the organization's long-term objectives?
What strategies will best achieve those objectives?
What should the organization's short-term objectives be?
What is the most efficient means of completing tasks?
What might the competition be considering?
What budgets are needed to complete department tasks?
How difficult should individual goals be?

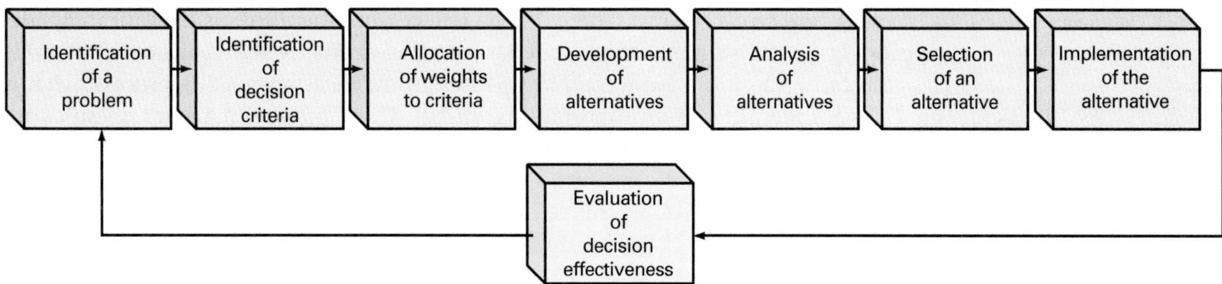

Exhibit 5-2
The Decision-Making Process

the French-based chemical and pharmaceuticals company Phone-Poulenc. The manager has spent several hundred dollars on auto repairs over the past few years. Now the car has a blown engine. Repair estimates indicate that it is not economical to repair the car. Furthermore, convenient public transportation is unavailable.

So now we have a problem. There is a disparity between the manager's need to have a car that runs and the fact that her current one doesn't. Unfortunately, this example doesn't tell us much about how managers identify problems. In the real world, most problems don't come with neon signs identifying them as such. A blown engine is a clear signal to the manager that she needs a new car, but few problems are so obvious. Instead, problem identification is subjective. Furthermore, the manager who mistakenly solves the wrong problem perfectly is likely to perform just as poorly as the manager who fails to identify the right problem and does nothing. Problem identification is neither a simple nor an unimportant part of the decision-making process.[4] How do managers become aware that they have a discrepancy? Managers have to make a comparison between their current state of affairs and some standard. What is that standard? It can be past performance, previously set goals, or the performance of some other unit within the organization or in other organizations. In our car-buying example, the standard is a previously set goal—having a car that runs.

Wouldn't it be nice if all problems jumped out at us like this one? But even then, is it a blown engine or a burst radiator hose? Like this car, problems may not be what they appear to be. The first thing one needs to do in decision making is to identify the true problem.

What Is Relevant in the Decision-Making Process?

Once a manager has identified a problem that needs attention, the **decision criteria** that will be important in solving the problem must be identified (step 2).

decision criteria
Factors that are relevant in a decision.

In our car-buying example, the product manager has to assess what factors are relevant in her decision. These might include criteria such as price, model (two-door or four-door), size (compact or intermediate), manufacturer (French, German, American), optional equipment (automatic transmission, side protection impact system, leather interior), and repair records. These criteria reflect what she thinks is relevant in her decision. Every decision maker has criteria—whether explicitly stated or not—that guide his or her decision. Note that, in this step in the decision-making process, what is not identified is as important as what is. If the product manager doesn't consider fuel economy to be a criterion, then it will not influence her final choice of car. Thus, if a decision maker does not identify a particular matter in this second step, then it is treated as irrelevant to the decision maker.

Decision criteria indicate what are important factors in making a decision.

Why Does the Decision Maker Need to Weight the Criteria?

The criteria listed above are not all equally important. It is necessary, therefore, to weight the items listed in step 2 in order to give them their relative priority in the decision. We call this step allocating weights to the decision criteria (step 3).

A simple approach is merely to give the most important criterion a weight of ten and then assign weights to the rest against that standard. Thus, in contrast to a criterion that you gave a five, the highest-rated factor would be twice as important. The idea is to use your personal preferences to assign priorities to the relevant criteria in your decision as well as to indicate their degree of importance by assigning a weight to each. Exhibit 5-3 lists the criteria and weights that our manager developed for her car-replacement decision. Price is the most important criterion in her decision, with such factors as performance and handling having low weights.

The next step requires the decision maker to list the alternatives that could succeed in resolving the problem (step 4). No attempt is made in this step to appraise these alternatives, only to list them. Let's assume that our manager has identified twelve vehicles as viable choices. They are Jeep Cherokee, Ford Taurus, Mercedes C230, Saab 900, Mazda 626, Dodge Intrepid, Ford Explorer, Isuzu Rodeo, Volvo 850, Audi 90, Toyota Camry, and the Volkswagen Passat.

Once the alternatives have been identified, the decision maker must critically analyze each one (step 5). The strengths and weaknesses of each alternative become evident as they are compared with the criteria and weights established in steps 2 and 3. Each alternative is evaluated by appraising it against the criteria. Exhibit 5-4 shows the assessed values that the manager put on each of her twelve alternatives after she had test driven each car. Keep in mind that the ratings given the twelve cars shown in Exhibit 5-4 are based on the assessment made by the new-product manager. Again, we are using a one-to-ten scale. Some assessments can be achieved in a relatively objective fashion. For instance, the purchase price represents the best price the manager can get from local dealers, and consumer magazines report data from owners on frequency of repairs. But the assessment of handling is clearly a personal judgment. The point is that most decisions contain judgments. They are reflected in the criteria chosen in step 2, the weights given to the criteria, and the evaluation of alternatives. This

CRITERION	WEIGHT
Price	10
Interior comfort	8
Durability	5
Repair record	5
Performance	3
Handling	1

Exhibit 5-3
Criteria and Weight in Car-Buying Decision (Scale of 1 to 10)

ALTERNATIVES	INITIAL PRICE	INTERIOR COMFORT	DURA-BILITY	REPAIR RECORD	PERFOR-MANCE	HANDLING	TOTAL
Jeep Cherokee	2	10	8	7	5	5	37
Ford Taurus	9	6	5	6	8	6	40
Mercedes C230	8	5	6	6	4	6	35
Saab 900	9	5	6	7	6	5	38
Mazda 626	5	6	9	10	7	7	44
Dodge Intrepid	10	5	6	4	3	3	31
Ford Explorer	4	8	7	6	8	9	42
Isuzu Rodeo	7	6	8	6	5	6	38
Volvo 850	9	7	4	4	4	5	33
Audi 90	5	8	5	4	10	10	42
Toyota Camry	6	5	10	10	6	6	43
Volkswagen Passat	8	6	6	5	7	8	40

Exhibit 5-4
Assessment of Car Alternatives

explains why two vehicle buyers with the same amount of money may look at two totally distinct sets of alternatives or even look at the same alternatives and rate them differently.

Exhibit 5-4 represents only an assessment of the twelve alternatives against the decision criteria. It does not reflect the weighting done in step 3. If one choice had scored 10 on every criterion, you wouldn't need to consider the weights. Similarly, if the weights were all equal, you could evaluate each alternative merely by summing up the appropriate lines in Exhibit 5-4. For instance, the Saab 900 would have a score of 38, and the Toyota Camry, a score of 43. If you multiply each alternative assessment against its weight, you get Exhibit 5-5. For instance, the Isuzu Rodeo scored a 40 on durability, which was determined by multiplying the weight given to durability (5) by the manager's appraisal of Isuzu on this criterion (8). The summation of these scores represents an evaluation of each alternative against the previously established criteria and weights. Notice that the weighting of the criteria has changed the ranking of alternatives in our example. The Mazda 626, for example, has gone from first to third. From our analysis, both initial price and interior comfort worked against the Mazda.

What Determines the "Best" Choice?

The sixth step is the critical act of choosing the best alternative from among those enumerated and assessed. Since we have determined all the pertinent factors in the decision, weighted them appropriately, and identified the viable alternatives, we merely have to choose the alternative that generated the highest score in step 5. In our car example (Exhibit 5-5), the decision maker would choose the Toyota Camry. On the basis of the criteria identified, the weights given to the criteria, and the decision maker's assessment of each vehicle's achievement on the criteria, the Toyota scored highest (224 points) and thus became the best alternative.

decision implementation
Putting a decision into action; includes conveying the decision to the persons who will be affected by it and getting their commitment to it.

What Is Decision Implementation?

Although the choice process is completed in the previous step, the decision may still fail if it is not implemented properly (step 7). Therefore, this step is concerned with putting the decision into action. **Decision implementation** includes conveying the

ALTERNATIVES	INITIAL PRICE (10)		INTERIOR COMFORT (8)		DURA-BILITY (5)		REPAIR RECORD (5)		PERFOR-MANCE (3)		HANDLING (1)		TOTAL
Jeep Cherokee	2	**20**	10	**80**	8	**40**	7	**35**	5	**15**	5	**5**	**195**
Ford Taurus	9	**90**	6	**48**	5	**25**	6	**30**	8	**24**	6	**6**	**223**
Mercedes C230	8	**80**	5	**40**	6	**30**	6	**30**	4	**12**	6	**6**	**198**
Saab 900	9	**90**	5	**40**	6	**30**	7	**35**	6	**18**	5	**5**	**218**
Mazda 626	5	**50**	6	**48**	9	**45**	10	**50**	7	**21**	7	**7**	**221**
Dodge Intrepid	10	**100**	5	**40**	6	**30**	4	**20**	3	**9**	3	**3**	**202**
Ford Explorer	4	**40**	8	**64**	7	**35**	6	**30**	8	**24**	9	**9**	**202**
Isuzu Rodeo	7	**70**	6	**48**	8	**40**	6	**30**	5	**15**	6	**6**	**209**
Volvo 850	9	**90**	7	**56**	4	**20**	4	**20**	4	**12**	5	**5**	**203**
Audi 90	5	**50**	8	**64**	5	**25**	4	**20**	10	**30**	10	**10**	**199**
Toyota Camry	6	**60**	5	**40**	10	**50**	10	**50**	6	**18**	6	**6**	**224**
Volkswagen Passat	8	**80**	6	**48**	6	**30**	5	**25**	7	**21**	8	**8**	**212**

Exhibit 5-5
Weighting of Vehicles (Assessment × Criteria Weight)

decision to those affected and getting their commitment to it. As we will demonstrate later in this chapter, groups or committees can help a manager achieve commitment. The people who must carry out a decision are most likely to enthusiastically endorse the outcome if they participate in the decision-making process.

Why Evaluate Decision Effectiveness?

The last step in the decision-making process (step 8) appraises the result of the decision to see whether it has corrected the problem. Did the alternative chosen in step 6 and implemented in step 7 accomplish the desired result? The evaluation of the results of decisions is detailed in Chapters 15 and 16, where we will look at the control function.

Making Decisions: The Rational Model

rational
Describes choices that are consistent and value-maximizing within specified constraints.

certainty
The implication that, in making a decision, the decision maker knows the outcome of every possible alternative.

Managerial decision making is assumed to be **rational.** By that we mean that managers make consistent, value-maximizing choices within specified constraints.[5] In this section, we take a close look at the underlying assumptions of rationality and then determine how valid those assumptions actually are.

A decision maker who was perfectly rational would be fully objective and logical. He or she would define a problem carefully and would have a clear and specific goal. Moreover, the steps in the decision-making process would consistently lead toward selecting the alternative that maximizes that goal. Exhibit 5-6 summarizes the assumptions of rationality.

An important aspect to remember is that the assumptions of rationality often do not hold true, because there rarely exists the level of certainty that the rational model demands. That is, **certainty** implies that a manager can make an accurate decision because the outcome of every alternative is known. In the real world, we know that

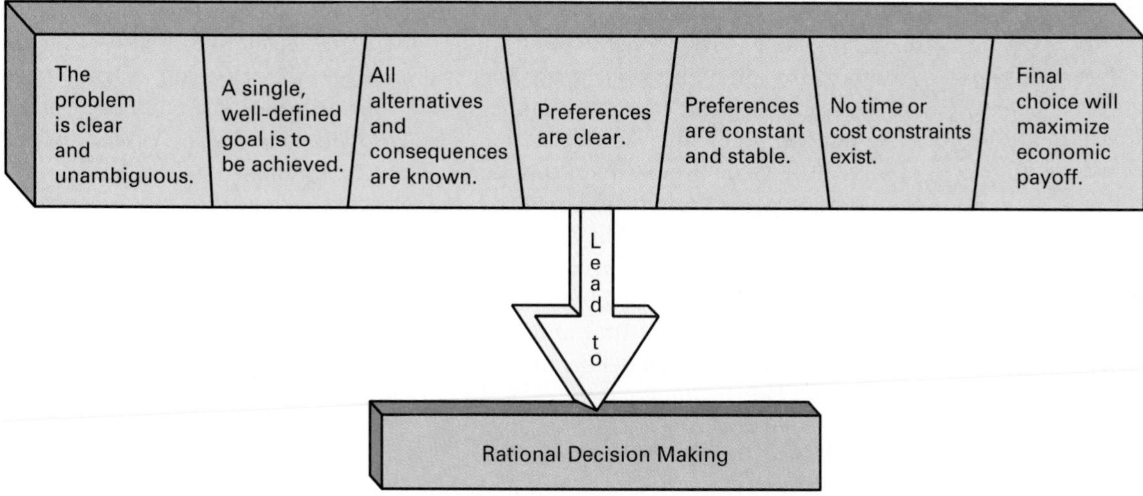

Exhibit 5-6
Assumptions of Rationality

is not the case. Most managers, then, must try to assign probabilities to outcomes that may result. We call this process dealing with **risk.** When decisions must be made with limited information because decision makers do not have full knowledge of the problem they face and cannot determine even a reasonable probability of alternative outcomes, they must make their decisions under a condition of **uncertainty.**

risk
The probability that a particular outcome will result from a given decision.

uncertainty
A condition in which managers do not have full knowledge of the problem they face and cannot determine even a reasonable probability of alternative outcomes.

The Real World of Managerial Decision Making: Modification of the Rational Model

When you were considering attending college, did you obtain catalogs from the more than 10,000 colleges and universities that exist throughout the world? Obviously not! Did you carefully identify all the relevant criteria—tuition costs, scholarships offered, location, majors offered, and so forth—in making your decision? Did you evaluate each potential college against these criteria in an effort to make an optimum selection? The answer, again, is undoubtedly No. But don't take this as an indictment of you. Most of us make decisions on the basis of incomplete information. Why? When we are faced with complex problems, most of us respond by reducing the problem to something we can readily understand. People often have limited abilities in processing and assimilating massive amounts of information to reach an optimal solution. As a result, they *satisfice.* That is, they seek solutions that are satisfactory and sufficient—or just good enough.

People . . . often seek solutions . . . that are just good enough.

Do managers engage in satisficing behavior? Or do they act rationally by carefully assessing problems, identifying all the relevant criteria, using their creativity to identify all viable alternatives, and, after a meticulous review of each alternative, find the one that is the optimum choice? In some situations—when managers are faced with a simple problem having few alternatives, when time pressures are minimal, and when the cost of seeking out and evaluating alternatives is low—the rational model provides a good description of the decision-making process.[6] But such situations are the exception rather than the rule.

Hundreds of studies have sought to improve our understanding of managerial decision making.[7] Individually, these studies often challenge one or more of the assumptions of rationality. Taken together, they suggest that decision making often veers from the logical, consistent, and systematic process that rationality implies. Do these limits to rationality mean that managers ignore the eight-step decision process we described at the beginning of this chapter? Not necessarily. Why? Because despite the limits to perfect rationality, managers are expected to appear to follow the rational process.[8] They know that "good" decision makers are supposed to do certain things: identify problems, consider alternatives, gather information, behave thoughtfully, and act decisively but prudently. By doing so, managers signal to their bosses, peers, and employees that they are competent and that their decisions are the result of intelligent and rational deliberation. The process they follow is frequently referred to as *bounded rationality.*

What Is Bounded Rationality?

bounded rationality
Behavior that is rational within the parameters of a simplified model that captures the essential features of a problem.

In **bounded rationality,** decision makers construct simplified models that extract the essential features from the problems they face without capturing all their complexity. Then, given information-processing limitations and constraints imposed by the organization, managers attempt to behave rationally within the parameters of the simple model. The result is a satisficing decision rather than a maximizing one; that is, a decision in which the solution is "good enough." As a result, instead of optimizing a choice, you selected an alternative that satisficed.[9]

Herbert Simon recognized that decisions made often do not follow the rational decision-making model. But that wasn't an indictment of the model itself. Although environmental factors may act as barriers to the rational model, decision makers still can act rationally. They do this in what Simon called bounded rationality.

The implications of bounded rationality on the manager's job cannot be overlooked. In situations in which the assumptions of perfect rationality do not apply (including many of the most important and far-reaching decisions that a manager makes), the details of the decision-making process are strongly influenced by the decision maker's self-interest, the organization's culture, internal politics, and power considerations (see Details on a Management Classic).

Are There Common Errors Committed in the Decision-Making Process?

heuristics
Judgmental shortcuts.

availability heuristic
The tendency for people to base their judgments on information that is readily available to them.

When individuals have to make decisions, they must make choices. But doing so requires careful thought—and a lot of information. Complete information for any of us, however, would overload us. Consequently, we often engage in behaviors that speed up the process. That is, in order to avoid information overload, we rely on judgmental shortcuts—called **heuristics.**[10] Heuristics commonly can be found to exist in two forms—availability and representative. Both types create biases in a decision maker's judgment. Another bias that exists is the decision maker's tendency to escalate commitment to a failing course of action.

Availability Heuristic. Availability heuristic is the tendency for people to base their judgments on information that is readily available to them. Events that invoke

Details on a Management Classic

Herbert Simon and Bounded Rationality

Management theory is built on the premise that individuals act rationally, and the essence of their job revolves around the rational decision-making process. However, the assumptions of rationality are rather extreme. Few people actually behave rationally. Given this fact, how do managers make decisions if it is unlikely that they are perfectly rational? Herbert Simon, an economist and management scholar, provided the answer. Simon found that within certain constraints, managers do act rationally. Because it is impossible for human beings to process and understand all the information necessary to meet the test of rationality, what they do is construct simplified models that extract the essential features from problems without capturing all their complexities.[11] Consequently, they can behave rationally (the rational decision-making model) within the limits of the simplified or bounded model.

How do managers' actions within these boundaries differ from actions within the rational model? Once a problem is identified, the search for criteria and alternatives begins. But this list of criteria is generally limited and made up of the more conspicuous choices. That is, Simon found that the decision maker will focus on easy-to-find choices—those that tend to be highly visible. In many instances, this means developing alternatives that vary only slightly from decisions that have been used in the past to deal with similar problems.

Once this limited set of alternatives is identified, the decision maker will begin reviewing them. But that review will not be exhaustive. Rather, the manager will proceed to review the alternatives only until he or she identifies an alternative that is sufficient, or good enough, to solve the problems at hand. Thus, the first alternative to meet the "good enough" criterion ends the search, and the decision maker can then proceed to implement this acceptable course of action.

strong emotions, that are vivid to the imagination, or that have recently occurred create a strong impression on us. As a result, we are likely to overestimate the frequency of the occurrence of unlikely events. For instance, many people have a fear of flying. Although traveling in commercial aircraft is statistically safer than driving a car, accidents in the former get much more attention. ValueJet's crash in the Florida Everglades on May 11, 1996, and the death of 110 people got much more attention than fatal auto accidents that occurred on that Mother's Day weekend.[12] The media coverage of the ValueJet air disaster, and others like it, results in individuals' overstating the risk in flying and understating the risk of driving. For managers, availability heuristic can also explain why, when conducting performance appraisals (see Chapter 8), they tend to give more weight to more-recent behaviors of an employee than behaviors of six or nine months ago.

representative heuristic The tendency for people to base judgments of probability on things with which they are familiar.

Representative Heuristic. Literally millions of Little Leaguers dream of becoming a professional baseball player one day. In reality, most of these youngsters have a better chance of becoming medical doctors than they do of ever playing in the Major Leagues. These dreams are examples of what we call **representative heuristic.**

Representative heuristic causes individuals to match the likelihood of an occurrence with something that they are familiar with. For example, our young ballplayers may think about someone from their local sports club league who fifteen years ago went on to play in the big leagues. Or they think, while watching players on television, that they could perform as well.

In organizations, we can find several instances where representative heuristic occurs. Decision makers may predict the future success of a new product by relating it to a previous product's success. Managers may also be affected by representative heuristic when they no longer hire college graduates from a particular college program because the last three hired from that program were poor performers.

Escalation of commitment represents the tendency to "stay the course," despite negative data.

Escalation of Commitment. A popular strategy in playing blackjack is to "guarantee" you can't lose. When you lose a hand, double your next bet. This strategy, or decision rule, may appear innocent enough, but if you start with a $5 bet and lose six hands in a row (not uncommon for many of us), you will be wagering $320 on your seventh hand merely to recoup your losses and win $5.

We know an individual who had been dating a woman for about four years. Although he admitted things weren't going too well in the relationship, he stated that he was going to marry his "significant other." A bit surprised about his intended plans, we asked him why. He responded, "I have a lot invested in this relationship."

escalation of commitment
An increased commitment to a previous decision despite negative information.

The blackjack strategy and the marriage decision just described illustrate a phenomenon called **escalation of commitment.** Specifically, it is defined as an increased commitment to a previous decision despite negative information. That is, the escalation of commitment represents the tendency to "stay the course," despite negative data that suggest one should do otherwise.[13]

Some of the best-recorded events involving escalation of commitment were decisions made by presidents of the United States.[14] For example: Lyndon Johnson's administration increased the tonnage of bombs dropped on North Vietnam, despite continual information that bombing was not bringing the war any closer to conclusion. Richard Nixon refused to destroy his secret White House tapes. George Bush believed that, given his popularity after Operation Desert Storm and the fall of the Soviet Union, he had only to pay attention to foreign affairs to win the 1992 presidential election. History now tells us that staying the course proved detrimental to Johnson, Nixon, and Bush. More recently, David Peterson, the premier of Ontario, committed an additional $4 billion to complete the Darlington nuclear plant even though there was evidence that consumption, and thus revenue projections, were too optimistic. Rather than cut his losses, Peterson continued to commit funds to the project—eventually spending double the original estimate. Meanwhile, consumption and revenue estimates proved to have been significantly overstated.[15]

Go to many Little League baseball games and you probably will find one thing in common. Someone playing shortstop is probably wearing the number 8. Why? Because many of these ballplayers are trying to be like Cal Ripken of the Baltimore Orioles. After all, wearing his number and playing baseball like him will get them to the big leagues, right? That dream is what we call a representative heuristic.

In organizations, managers like David Peterson may recognize that there is evidence that their previous solution is not working. But rather than search for new alternatives, they further increase their commitment to the original solution. Why do they do this? In many cases, it's an effort to demonstrate that their initial decision was not wrong.[16]

Decision Making: A Contingency Approach

The types of problems managers face in decision-making situations often determine how a problem is treated. In this section, we present a categorization scheme for problems and for types of decisions. Then we show how the type of decision a manager uses should reflect the characteristics of the problem.

How Do Problems Differ?

Some problems are straightforward. The goal of the decision maker is clear, the problem familiar, and information about the problem easily defined and complete. Examples might include a supplier's being late with an important delivery, a customer's wanting to return a mail-order purchase, a news program's having to respond to an unexpected and fast-breaking news event, or a university's handling of a student who is applying for financial aid. Such situations are called **well-structured problems.** They align closely with the assumptions underlying perfect rationality.

well-structured problems Straightforward, familiar, easily defined problems.

Many situations faced by managers, however, are **ill-structured problems.** They are new or unusual. Information about such problems is ambiguous or incomplete. The decision to enter a new market segment or to hire an architect to design a new office park are examples of ill-structured problems. So too is the decision to invest in a new, unproven technology.

ill-structured problems New problems in which information is ambiguous or incomplete.

What Is the Difference between Programmed and Nonprogrammed Decisions?

Just as problems can be divided into two categories, so too can decisions. As we will see, programmed, or routine, decision making is the most efficient way to handle well-structured problems. However, when problems are ill-structured, managers must rely on nonprogrammed decision making in order to develop unique solutions.

A Goodyear mechanic breaks an alloy wheel rim while installing new tires on a vehicle. What does the manager do? There is probably some standardized routine for handling this type of problem. For example, the manager replaces the rim at the company's expense. This is a **programmed decision.** Decisions are programmed to the extent that they are repetitive and routine and to the extent that a definite approach has been worked out for handling them. Because the problem is well-structured, the manager does not have to go to the trouble and expense of working up an involved decision process. Programmed decision making is relatively simple and

programmed decision A repetitive decision that can be handled by a routine approach.

Programmed decisions are designed to deal with structured problems. Stocking shelves in this Ho Chi Minh City, Vietnam, grocery store doesn't require a new plan each time shelves become bare. Instead, restocking shelves occurs at predetermined times—it is a programmed decision.

tends to rely heavily on previous solutions. The "develop-the-alternatives" stage in the decision-making process is either nonexistent or given little attention. Why? Because once the structured problem is defined, its solution is usually self-evident or at least reduced to very few alternatives that are familiar and that have proved successful in the past. In many cases, programmed decision making becomes decision making by precedent. Managers simply do what they and others have done previously in the same situation. The broken wheel rim does not require the manager to identify and weight decision criteria or to develop a long list of possible solutions. Rather, the manager falls back on a systematic procedure, rule, or policy.

What Are Procedures, Rules, and Policies, and When Are They Best Used?

procedure
A series of interrelated sequential steps that can be used to respond to a well-structured problem.

A **procedure** is a series of interrelated sequential steps that a manager can use for responding to a well-structured problem. The only real difficulty is in identifying the problem. Once the problem is clear, so is the procedure. For instance, a purchasing manager receives a request from engineering for five neural network software packages. The purchasing manager knows that there is a definite procedure for handling this decision. Has the requisition been properly filled out and approved? If not, send the requisition back with a note explaining what is deficient. If the request is complete, the approximate costs are estimated. If the total exceeds $7,500, three bids must be obtained. If the total is $7,500 or less, only one vendor need be identified and the order placed. The decision-making process is merely the execution of a simple series of sequential steps.

rule
An explicit statement that tells managers what they ought or ought not to do.

A **rule** is an explicit statement that tells a manager what he or she ought or ought not to do. Rules are frequently used by managers when they confront a well-structured problem because they are simple to follow and ensure consistency. In the illustration above, the $7,500 cutoff rule simplifies the purchasing manager's decision about when to use multiple bids.

policy
A general guide that establishes parameters for making decisions.

A third guide for making programmed decisions is a **policy.** It provides guidelines to channel a manager's thinking in a specific direction. The statement that "we hire from within, whenever possible," is an example of a policy. In contrast to a rule, a policy establishes parameters for the decision maker rather than specifically stating what should or should not be done. As an analogy, think of the Ten Commandments as rules and the U.S. Constitution as policy. The latter requires judgment and interpretation, the former do not.

What Do Nonprogrammed Decisions Look Like?

nonprogrammed decisions
Decisions that must be custom-made to solve unique and nonrecurring problems.

Deciding whether to acquire another organization, which global markets offer the most potential, how to reengineer operations to improve efficiency, or whether to sell off an unprofitable division are examples of **nonprogrammed decisions.** Such decisions are unique and nonrecurring. When a manager confronts an ill-structured problem, there is no cut-and-dried solution. A custom-made, nonprogrammed response is required (see Managers Who Made a Difference).

The creation of a marketing strategy for a new product or, as in the case of Loida Lewis, deciding which businesses to sell off at Beatrice International Holdings, Inc. are examples of nonprogrammed decisions. These decisions are different from previous organizational decisions because the problem is new, a different set of environmental factors exists, and other conditions that may have existed when previous products were introduced years earlier have changed. For example, IBM's introduction of a personal computer in the early 1980s was unlike any other marketing decision the company had previously made. Clearly, IBM had a wealth of experience selling computers—but these

Managers Who Made a Difference

Michael F. Lamorte of Applied Engineering Software, Inc.

If you were to read a list of some of the greatest thinkers of our time, you'd likely find names of individuals such as Sir Isaac Newton, Galileo, Albert Einstein, and Michael F. Lamorte. Michael F. Lamorte? Yes, that's correct. This engineer has developed a scientific decision-making model that has the potential to significantly change our world.[17]

Michael F. Lamorte, founder of Applied Engineering Software, Inc., in Durham, North Carolina, has developed a decision-making process that uses math and computer power to mimic nature. The holder of twelve patents—from computer chips to solar cells—he has invented an "equation" that can predict solutions to complex problems society faces. Many of these problems, in fact, cannot be solved today. Called CLAMP, an acronym for "closed-form solutions applied to a mesh-point field," Lamorte's model generates predictions for what may occur at any point in a grid. In essence, CLAMP views problem-solving from a unique perspective. Rather than take a complex problem and divide it into multiple parts, Lamorte's model places the problem on a "virtual grid." Then, through the use of a complex mathematical model, each point of the grid is analyzed and is linked to all other grid points before an "optimum" solution is achieved. Other current problem-solving models do not link one complex part to another. Consequently, maximizing solutions are unlikely.

Michael's system could revolutionize how decisions are made in the future, but not everyone is convinced of his claims. For instance, many corporate research laboratory personnel, such as James Cavendish of General Motors, view Lamorte's model as being laughable. It's not just the fact that, to coordinate all the grid points, CLAMP's equation—if it were laid out end to end—would be more than 200 feet long; it's the belief that CLAMP is akin to "turning lead into gold." But the Army Research Laboratory in Hampton, Virginia, thinks otherwise. Using CLAMP to simulate metal stress, Lamorte was able to generate in about six seconds a solution for the time it would take metal to bend and snap. Traditional calculations—to get the same result—took thirty minutes. Although in this experiment CLAMP was not dealing with an "unsolvable" problem, its efficiency cannot be overlooked.

Will Michael F. Lamorte be regarded as advancing science in the twenty-first century? Many of his supporters think so. CLAMP is more realistic and much faster than traditional problem-solving methods—even those using the most sophisticated supercomputers. According to Lamorte, CLAMP may result, for example, in "enhancing the ability of engineers to design planes, cars, and bridges, create new drugs, and find oil."

were primarily large mainframe varieties. The company also had previously sold to small businesses and general consumers through its typewriter division. But it had no substantive experience in mass marketing relatively low-cost personal computers. It faced such aggressive competitors as Apple, Hewlett-Packard, and Digital Equipment. The needs and sophistication of personal computer customers differed from those of buyers who purchased multimillion-dollar systems for their corporate headquarters.

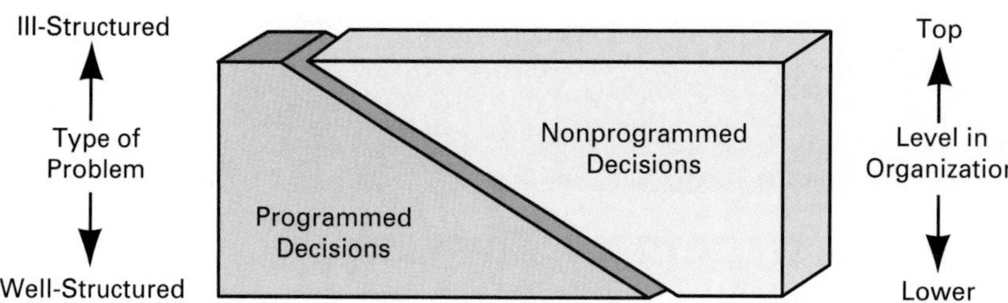

Exhibit 5-7
Types of Problems, Types of Decisions, and Level in the Organization

The hundreds of decisions that went into IBM's marketing strategy for personal computers had never been made before; they were clearly of the nonprogrammed variety.

How Can You Integrate Problems, Types of Decisions, and Level in the Organization?

Exhibit 5-7 describes the relationship between types of problems, types of decisions, and level in the organization. Well-structured problems are responded to with programmed decision making. Ill-structured problems require nonprogrammed decision making. Lower-level managers essentially confront familiar and repetitive problems; therefore, they most typically rely on programmed decisions such as standard operating procedures. However, the problems confronting managers are more likely to become ill-structured as the managers move up the organizational hierarchy. Why? Because lower-level managers handle the routine decisions themselves and pass upward only decisions that they find unique or difficult. Similarly, managers pass down routine decisions to their employees in order to spend their time on more problematic issues.

Few managerial decisions in the real world are either fully programmed or fully nonprogrammed. These are the extremes, and most decisions fall somewhere in between. Few programmed decisions are designed to eliminate individual judgment completely. At the other extreme, even the most unusual situation requiring a nonprogrammed decision can be helped by programmed routines.

At last point on this topic is that organizational efficiency is facilitated by the use of programmed decision making—a fact that may explain its wide popularity. Whenever possible, management decisions are likely to be programmed. Obviously, this approach is not too realistic at the top of the organization, since most of the problems that top management confront are of a nonrecurring nature. But there are strong economic incentives for top management to create policies, standard operating procedures, and rules to guide other managers.

Programmed decisions minimize the need for managers to exercise discretion. This benefit is important because discretion costs money. The more nonprogrammed decision making a manager is required to do, the greater the judgment needed. Since sound judgment is an uncommon quality, it costs more to acquire the services of managers who possess it.

Decision-Making Styles

Every decision maker brings a unique set of personal characteristics to his or her problem-solving efforts. For example, a manager who is creative and comfortable with uncertainty is likely to develop decision alternatives differently from someone who is more conservative and less likely to accept risk. As a result of this information, research has sought to identify different decision-making styles.[18]

The basic premise for this decision-making model is the realization that individuals differ along two dimensions. The first is the way they *think*.[19] Some decision makers are logical and rational. Being such, they process information in a sequential manner. In contrast, there are some individuals who think creatively and use their intuition.[20] These decision makers have a tendency to see matters from a "big picture" perspective. The second dimension focuses on individuals' *tolerance for ambiguity*. Some individuals have a high need for consistency and order in making decisions so that ambiguity is minimized. Others, however, are able to tolerate high levels of uncertainty and can process many thoughts at the same time. When we diagram these two dimensions, four decision-making styles are formed. These styles are *directive, analytic, conceptual,* and *behavioral* (see Exhibit 5-8).

The directive style represents a decision-making style characterized by low tolerance for ambiguity and a rational way of thinking. These individuals are logical and efficient and typically make fast decisions that focus on the short run. The analytic decision-making style is characterized by high tolerance for ambiguity combined with a rational way of thinking. These individuals prefer complete information before making a decision. As a result, they typically carefully consider many alternatives. The conceptual style of decision-making represents someone who tends to be very broad in outlook and typically will look at many alternatives. These decision makers tend to focus on the long run and often look for creative solutions. The behavioral style reflects an individual who thinks intuitively but has a low tolerance for uncertainty. These decision makers work well with others, are open to suggestions, and are concerned about the individuals who work for them.

Although the four decision-making styles appear independent, most managers possess characteristics of more than one style. That is, while they usually have a dominant style, the other three styles can be considered as alternatives—to be used when a situation may be best resolved by using a particular style. Do you have an idea of your dominant decision-making style? Do the Understanding Yourself exercise to gain some insight about how you approach making decisions.

Exhibit 5-8
Decision-Making Styles

Source: S. P. Robbins, *Supervision Today* (Englewood Cliffs, N.J.: Prentice Hall, 1995), p. 111.

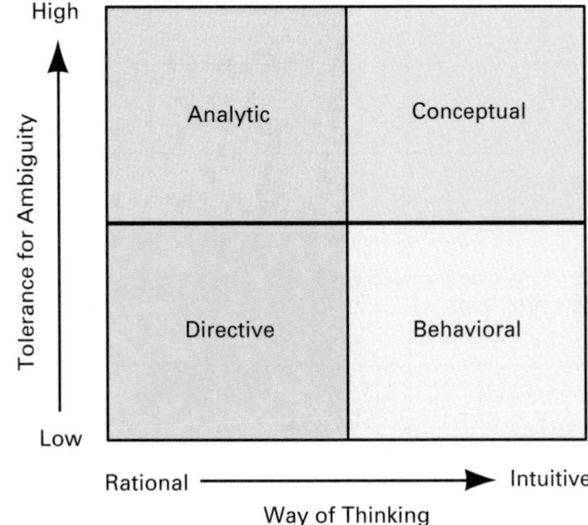

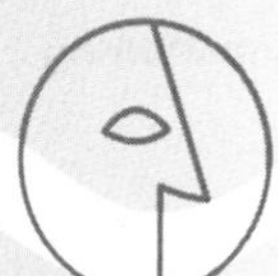

Understanding Yourself

What Is Your Dominant Decision-Making Style?

1. Use the following numbers to rate the answers to each question:

   8 = *when the question is MOST like you.*
   4 = *when the question is MODERATELY like you.*
   2 = *when the question is SLIGHTLY like you.*
   1 = *when the question is LEAST like you.*

2. One of the numbers must be inserted in each box following the answers to each question.
3. DO NOT repeat any number on a given line.
4. For example, the numbers you might use to answer a given question could look as follows: **8 2 1 4**
5. In answering the questions, think of how you NORMALLY act in your work situation.
6. Use the first thing that comes to your mind when answering the question.
7. There is no time limit in answering the questions, and there are no right or wrong answers.
8. Your responses should reflect how you feel about the questions and what you prefer to do, not what you think might be the right thing to do.

Please score the following questions according to the instructions given. Your score reflects how *you see yourself,* not what you believe is correct or desirable, as related to *your work situation.* It covers *typical decisions* that you make in your work environment.

		I		*II*		*III*		*IV*
1. My prime objective is to	have a position with status		be the best in my field		achieve recognition for my work		feel secure in my job	
2. I enjoy jobs that	are technical and well defined		have considerable variety		allow independent action		involve people	
3. I expect people working for me to be	productive and fast		highly capable		committed and responsive		receptive to suggestions	
4. In my job, I look for	practical results		the best solutions		new approaches or ideas		good working environment	
5. I communicate best with others	in a direct one-to-one basis		in writing		by having a group discussion		in a formal meeting	
6. In my planning I emphasize	current problems		meeting objectives		future goals		developing people's careers	
7. When faced with solving a problem, I	rely on proven approaches		apply careful analysis		look for creative approaches		rely on my feelings	

		I		II		III		IV
8. When using information, I prefer	specific facts		accurate and complete data		broad coverage of many options		limited data that are easily understood	
9. When I am not sure about what to do, I	rely on intuition		search for facts		look for a possible compromise		wait before making a decision	
10. Whenever possible, I avoid	long debates		incomplete work		using numbers or formulas		conflict with others	
11. I am especially good at	remembering dates and facts		solving difficult problems		seeing many possibilities		interacting with others	
12. When time is important, I	decide and act quickly		follow plans and priorities		refuse to be pressured		seek guidance or support	
13. In social settings, I generally	speak with others		think about what is being said		observe what is going on		listen to the conversation	
14. I am good at remembering	people's names		places we met		people's faces		people's personality	
15. The work I do provides me	the power to influence others		challenging assignments		achieving my personal goals		acceptance by the group	
16. I work well with those who are	energetic and ambitious		self-confident		open-minded		polite and trusting	
17. When under stress, I	become anxious		concentrate on the problem		become frustrated		am forgetful	
18. Others consider me	aggressive		disciplined		imaginative		supportive	
19. My decisions typically are	realistic and direct		systematic or abstract		broad and flexible		sensitive to the needs of others	
20. I dislike	losing control		boring work		following rules		being rejected	
Totals								

Scoring: Add the points in each of the four columns—I, II, III, IV. The sum of the four columns should be 300 points. If your sum does not equal 300 points, check your addition and your answers.

What the Assessment Means: The column with the highest score is your dominant decision-making style. Column I = Directive; Column II = Analytic; Column III = Conceptual; Column IV = Behavioral.

Source: A.J. Rowe, R. Mason, and K. Dickel, *Strategic Management and Business Policy.* (Reading, Mass.: Addison-Wesley, 1982), p. 217. Reproduced by permission of Alan J. Rowe.

Making Decisions in Groups

Do managers make a lot of decisions in groups? You bet they do! Many decisions in organizations, especially important decisions that have far-reaching effects on organizational activities and personnel, are made in groups. It's a rare organization that doesn't at some time use committees, task forces, review panels, work teams, or similar groups as vehicles for making decisions. Why? In many cases, these groups represent people who will be most affected by the decisions being made. As such, their input can be valuable.

Studies tell us that managers spend up to 40 percent or more of their time in meetings[21] (see Developing a Management Skill). Undoubtedly, a large portion of that time is involved with defining problems, arriving at solutions to those problems, and determining the means for implementing the solutions. It is possible, in fact, for groups to be assigned any of the eight steps in the decision-making process.

Developing a Management Skill

CONDUCTING AN EFFECTIVE MEETING

About the Skill: *As a manager, you will spend a large portion of your workday in meetings. And, undoubtedly, there will be instances when you will be responsible for running meetings. Below are some suggestions for making sure your meetings run properly.*

Steps in practicing the skill

1. ***Prepare and distribute an agenda well in advance of the meeting.*** An agenda defines the meeting's purpose for participants and the boundaries between relevant and irrelevant discussion topics. Also, the agenda can serve as an important vehicle for premeeting discussions with participants.

2. ***Consult with participants before the meeting to ensure proper participation.*** Let all participants know that their input is valuable and that you welcome their speaking up at the meeting when they have something to offer.

3. ***Establish specific time parameters for the meeting; specify when it will start and end.*** This step helps keep the meeting on time and focused on the important matters.

4. ***Maintain focused discussion during the meeting.*** Items not on the agenda should not be given substantial time during the meeting. If an issue is important, maybe another meeting, with its own agenda, should be held to address that issue.

5. ***Encourage and support participation by all members.*** If you have done a good job in the second step, participants should come prepared to talk but still may need some encouragement at the meeting. Sometimes, direct questions about what they think will get them to talk.

6. ***Encourage the clash of ideas.*** Remember, you want as much information about a topic to surface as possible. Disagreements are fine. They indicate that different voices are being heard. Better to work the differences out now than to have them surface later.

7. ***Discourage the clash of personalities.*** Disagreements can enhance the process, but they should be substantive disputes. Differences due to personal dislikes are a disaster in a meeting.

8. ***Bring closure by summarizing accomplishments and allocating follow-up assignments.*** This step lets participants understand what occurred in the meeting and what they may have to do before the next meeting. This is, in essence, planning.

What Are the Advantages to Group Decision Making?

Individual and group decisions have their own set of strengths. Neither is ideal for all situations. Let's begin by reviewing the advantages that group decisions have over individual decisions.

Group decisions provide more complete information than do individual ones. There is often truth to the axiom that two heads are better than one. A group will bring a diversity of experience and perspectives to the decision process that an individual, acting alone, cannot. Groups also generate more alternatives. Because groups have a greater quantity and diversity of information, they can identify more alternatives than can an individual. Quantity and diversity of information are greatest when group members represent different specialties. Furthermore, group decision making increases acceptance of a solution. Many decisions fail after the final choice has been made because people do not accept the solution. However, if the people who will be affected by a certain solution and who will help implement it get to participate in the decision making itself, they will be more likely to accept the decision and to encourage others to accept it. And last, this process increases legitimacy. The group decision-making process is consistent with democratic ideals; therefore, decisions made by groups may be perceived as more legitimate than decisions made by a single person. The fact that the individual decision maker has complete power and has not consulted others can create a perception that a decision was made autocratically and arbitrarily.

What Are the Disadvantages to Group Decision Making?

If groups are so good, how did the phrase "a camel is a racehorse put together by a committee" become so popular? The answer, of course, is that group decisions are not without their drawbacks. There are several major disadvantages of group decisions. First, they are time-consuming. It takes time to assemble a group. In addition, the interaction that takes place once the group is in place is frequently inefficient. The result is that groups almost always take more time to reach a solution than it would take an individual making the decision alone. There may also be a situation in which there is minority domination. Members of a group are never perfectly equal. They may differ in rank in the organization, experience, knowledge about the problem, influence on other members, verbal skills, assertiveness, and the like. This imbalance creates the opportunity for one or more members to use their advantages to dominate others in the group. A minority that dominates a group frequently has an undue influence on the final decision.

Another problem focuses on the pressures to conform. There are social pressures to conform in groups. They can lead to what has been called **groupthink.**[22] This is a form of conformity in which group members withhold deviant, minority, or unpopular views in order to give the appearance of agreement. Groupthink undermines critical thinking in the group and eventually harms the quality of the final decision (see Details on a Management Classic). And, finally, there is ambiguous responsibility. Group members share responsibility, but who is actually responsible for the final outcome? In an individual decision, it is clear who is responsible. In a group decision, the responsibility of any single member is watered down.

groupthink
The withholding by group members of different views in order to appear to be in agreement.

When Are Groups Most Effective?

Whether groups are more effective than individuals depends on the criteria you use for defining effectiveness. Group decisions tend to be more accurate. The evidence indicates that, on the average, groups make better decisions than individuals.[23] However, if decision effectiveness is defined in terms of speed, individuals are superior. If creativity is important, groups tend to be more effective than individuals. And if

Details on a Management Classic

Irving L. Janis and Groupthink

Have you ever been in a situation in which several people were sitting around discussing a particular item, and, in the course of that discussion, you had something to say that ran contrary to the consensus views that dominated the group but you remained silent? Were you surprised to learn later that others shared your views and also had remained silent? What you experienced is what Irving Janis termed groupthink.[24]

Groupthink applies to a situation in which a group's ability to appraise alternatives objectively and arrive at a quality decision is jeopardized. Because of pressures for conformity, groups often deter individuals from critically appraising unusual, minority, or unpopular views. Consequently, there is a deterioration of an individual's mental efficiency, reality testing, and moral judgment.

How does groupthink occur? The following are examples in which groupthink is evident:

1. Group members rationalize any resistance to the assumptions they have made.
2. Members apply direct pressures on those who momentarily express doubts about any of the group's shared views or who question the validity of arguments favored by the majority.
3. Those members who have doubts or hold differing points of view seek to avoid deviating from what appears to be group consensus.
4. There is an illusion of unanimity. If someone does not speak, it is assumed that he or she is in full accord.

Does groupthink really hinder decision making? Yes. Several research studies have found that groupthink symptoms were associated with poorer-quality decision outcomes.[25] But, groupthink can be minimized if the following conditions exist in group decision making: the group is cohesive, fosters open discussion, and is lead by an impartial leader who seeks input from all members.

effectiveness means the degree of acceptance the final solution achieves, the nod again goes to the group.[26]

The effectiveness of group decision making is also influenced by the size of the group. The larger the group, the greater the opportunity for heterogeneous representation. On the other hand, a larger group requires more coordination and more time to allow all members to contribute. What this means is that groups probably should not be too large: A minimum of five to a maximum of about fifteen is best. Evidence indicates, in fact, that groups of five and, to a lesser extent, seven are the most effective.[27] Because five and seven are odd numbers, strict deadlocks are avoided. Effectiveness should not be considered without also assessing efficiency. Groups almost always stack up a poor second in efficiency to the individual decision maker. With few exceptions, group decision making consumes more work hours than does individual decision making. In deciding whether to use groups, then, primary consideration must be given to assessing whether increases in effectiveness are more than enough to offset the losses in efficiency.

Groupthink undermines critical thinking and harms the final decision.

How Can You Improve Group Decision Making?

When members of a group meet face to face and interact with one another, they create the potential for groupthink. They can censor themselves and pressure other group members into agreement. Three ways of making group decision making more creative have been suggested: brainstorming, the nominal group technique, and electronic meetings.

What Is Brainstorming? Brainstorming is a relatively simple technique for overcoming pressures for conformity that retard the development of creative alternatives.[28] It does this by utilizing an idea-generating process that specifically encourages any and all alternatives while withholding any criticism of those alternatives. In a typical brainstorming session, a half-dozen to a dozen people sit around a table. The group leader states the problem in a clear manner that is understood by all participants. Members then "freewheel" as many alternatives as they can in a given time. No criticism is allowed, and all the alternatives are recorded for later discussion and analysis. Brainstorming, however, is merely a process for generating ideas. The next method, the nominal group technique, goes further by helping groups arrive at a preferred solution.[29]

brainstorming
An idea-generating process that encourages alternatives while withholding criticism.

How Does the Nominal Group Technique Work? The **nominal group technique** restricts discussion during the decision-making process, hence the term. Group members must be present, as in a traditional committee meeting, but they are required to operate independently. They secretely write a list of general problem areas or potential solutions to a problem. The chief advantage of this technique is that it permits the group to meet formally but does not restrict independent thinking, as so often happens in the traditional interacting group.

nominal group technique
A decision-making technique in which group members are physically present but operate independently.

How Can Electronic Meetings Enhance Group Decision Making? The most recent approach to group decision making blends the nominal group technique with sophisticated computer technology.[30] It is called the **electronic meeting.**

electronic meeting
A type of nominal group technique in which participants are linked by computer.

Once the technology for the meeting is in place, the concept is simple. Up to fifty people sit around a horseshoe-shaped table that is empty except for a series of computer terminals. Issues are presented to participants, who type their responses onto their computer screens. Individual comments, as well as aggregate votes, are displayed on a projection screen in the room.

Companies such as Minolta and IBM use electronic meetings to bring people from all over the world together to have input into decisions that are being made. This process permits anonymity, honesty, and speed.

The major advantages of electronic meetings are anonymity, honesty, and speed. Participants can anonymously type any message they want, and it will flash on the screen for all to see at the push of a board key. It also allows people to be brutally honest with no penalty. And it is fast—chitchat is eliminated, discussions do not digress, and many participants can "talk" at once without interrupting the others.

Experts claim that electronic meetings are as much as 55 percent as fast as traditional face-to-face meetings.[31] Phelps Dodge Mining, for instance, used the approach to cut its annual planning meeting from several days down to twelve hours. However, there are drawbacks. Those who can type quickly can outshine those who may be verbally eloquent but are lousy typists; those with the best ideas don't get credit for them; and the process lacks the informational richness of face-to-face oral communication. But this technology is currently only in its infancy;

the future of group decision making is very likely to include extensive usage of electronic meetings.

National Culture and Decision-Making Practices

Research shows that, to some extent, decision-making practices differ from country to country.[32] The way decisions are made—whether by group, by team members, participatively, or autocratically by an individual manager—and the degree of risk a decision maker is willing to take are just two examples of decision variables that reflect a country's cultural environment. For example, in India, power distance and uncertainty avoidance (see Chapter 2) are high. There, only very senior-level managers make decisions, and they are likely to make safe decisions. In contrast, in Sweden, power distance and uncertainty avoidance are low. Swedish managers are not afraid to make risky decisions. Senior managers in Sweden also push decisions down in the ranks. They encourage lower-level managers and employees to take part in decisions that affect them. In countries such as Egypt, where time pressures are low, managers make decisions at a slower and more deliberate pace than managers in the United States. And in Italy, where history and traditions are valued, managers tend to rely on tried and proven alternatives to resolve problems.

Decision making in Japan is much more group-oriented than in the United States.[33] The Japanese value conformity and cooperation. Before making decisions, Japanese CEOs collect a large amount of information, which is then used in consensus-forming group decisions called *ringisei*. Because employees in Japanese organizations have high job security, managerial decisions take a long-term perspective rather than focusing on short-term profits, as is often the practice in the United States.

Senior managers in France and Germany also adapt their decision styles to their country's culture. In France, for instance, autocratic decision making is widely practiced, and managers avoid risks. Managerial styles in Germany reflect the German culture's concern for structure and order. Consequently, there are extensive rules and regulations in German organizations. Managers have well-defined responsibilities and accept that decisions must go through channels.

These examples are meant to remind you that managers need to modify their decision styles to reflect the national culture of the country in which they live.

Summary

How will I know if I fulfilled the Learning Objectives found on page 132? You will have fulfilled the Learning Objectives if you understand the following.

1. **Explain the steps in the decision-making process.** Decision making is an eight-step process: (1) identify a problem, (2) identify decision criteria, (3) allocate weights to the criteria, (4) develop alternatives, (5) analyze alternatives, (6) select an alternative, (7) implement the alternative, and (8) evaluate decision effectiveness.
2. **Identify the assumptions of the rational decision-making model.** The rational decision model assumes that the decision maker can identify a clear problem, has no goal conflict, knows all options, has a clear preference ordering, keeps all preferences constant, has no time or cost constraints, and selects a final choice that maximizes his or her economic payoff.
3. **Explain the limits to rationality.** Rationality assumptions do not apply in many situations because problems are not simple, goals are not clear, alternatives are many, and there are time and cost constraints. In addition, decision makers sometimes

increase commitment to a previous choice to confirm its original correctness, prior decision precedents constrain current choices, and most organizational cultures discourage taking risks and searching for innovative alternatives.

4. **Define certainty, risk, and uncertainty as they relate to decision making.** Certainty implies that a manager can make an accurate decision because the outcome of every alternative is known. Because this is often not the case, risk involves assigning probabilities to outcomes that may result. When decision makers have neither full knowledge of the problem they face nor a reasonable probability of something that may happen, they must make their decisions under a condition of uncertainty.
5. **Describe the actions of the bounded-rational decision maker.** In the bounded-rational decision-making process, decision makers construct simplified models that extract essential features from the problems they face without capturing all their complexity. They then attempt to act rationally within this simplified model.
6. **Identify the two types of decision problems and the two types of decisions that are used to solve them.** Managers face well- and ill-structured problems. Well-structured problems are straightforward, familiar, easily defined, and solved using programmed decisions. Ill-structured problems are new or unusual, involve ambiguous or incomplete information, and are solved using nonprogrammed decisions.
7. **Define heuristics and explain how they affect the decision-making process.** Heuristics are shortcuts decision makers can take to speed up the decision-making process. Heuristics commonly exist in two forms—availability and representative. Both types create biases in a decision maker's judgment.
8. **Identify four decision-making styles.** The four decision-making styles are the directive style (characterized by low tolerance for ambiguity and a rational way of thinking), the analytic style (characterized by high tolerance for ambiguity combined with a rational way of thinking), the conceptual style (characterized by a very broad outlook and a tendency to look at many alternatives), and the behavioral style (characterized by intuitive thinking and a low tolerance for uncertainty).
9. **Describe the advantages and disadvantages of group decisions.** Groups offer certain advantages: more-complete information, more alternatives, increased acceptance of a solution, and greater legitimacy. On the other hand, groups are time-consuming, can be dominated by a minority, create pressures to conform, and cloud responsibility.
10. **Describe three techniques for improving group decision making.** Three ways of improving group decision making are brainstorming (utilizing an idea-generating process that specifically encourages any and all alternatives while withholding any criticism of those alternatives), the nominal group technique (a technique that restricts discussion during the decision-making process), and electronic meetings (most recent approach to group decision making, blends the nominal group technique with sophisticated computer technology).

Review & Discussion Questions

1. Explain how decision making is related to the planning process.
2. Describe a decision you have made that closely aligns with the assumptions of perfect rationality. Compare this with the process you used to select your college. Is there a departure from the rational model in your college decision? Explain.
3. How is implementation important to the decision-making process?
4. What is a satisficing decision? How does it differ from a maximizing decision?
5. How do certainty, risk, and uncertainty affect individuals when they make a decision?
6. How does escalation of commitment affect decision making?
7. What is the difference between a rule and a policy?
8. Is the order in which alternatives are considered more critical under assumptions of perfect rationality or bounded rationality? Why?
9. What is groupthink? What are its implications for decision making?
10. Why do you think organizations have increased the use of groups for making decisions during the past twenty years? When would you recommend using groups to make decisions?

Testing Your Comprehension • • • 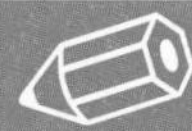

Circle the correct answer, then check yourself on page AK-1.

1. Which of the following sequences is correct for the decision-making process?
   a) identify decision criteria, analyze alternatives, allocate weights to criteria
   b) analyze alternatives, select an alternative, implement the alternative
   c) select an alternative, evaluate decision effectiveness, weight the criteria
   d) analyze alternatives, develop alternatives, allocate weights to criteria

2. Which of the following is NOT a prerequisite for identifying a problem?
   a) managers must be rational
   b) managers must be aware of some discrepancy
   c) managers must be under pressure to take action
   d) managers must have the resources to be able to act

3. When British Airway's U.S. manager observed that her market share had slipped in relation to Avianca Air, she was
   a) recognizing a discrepancy by comparison with another unit in the organization
   b) analyzing alternatives
   c) recognizing a discrepancy by comparison with past performance
   d) identifying decision criteria

4. Once a problem is formulated, the next step is to
   a) select an alternative
   b) list all possible solutions
   c) observe a discrepancy
   d) decide what is critical in the decision

5. The decision criteria are
   a) factors that determine what is important
   b) used to implement a decision
   c) what we use to spot a discrepancy
   d) guidelines for deciding who can make a decision

6. When a manager who is contemplating all the features a new purchase should have prioritizes the most important, he or she is practicing
   a) selection of criteria
   b) problem formulation
   c) weighting of criteria
   d) analyzing alternatives

7. After implementation has been accomplished
   a) the decision-making process is complete
   b) the control function of management becomes important
   c) the alternatives are ranked
   d) the manager must complete written evaluation forms

8. Bounded rationality refers to the idea that
   a) managers are bound by ethical considerations to be rational
   b) managers will promote rationalization as an aid to decision making
   c) managers employ model construction to simplify decision making
   d) managers are to behave according to rational guidelines within the bounds of their authority in the workplace

9. The tendency for decision makers to base their judgments on information that is readily accessible to them is best referred to as
   a) escalation of commitment
   b) representative heuristic
   c) bounded rationality
   d) none of the above

10. Well-structured problems are
   a) new
   b) closely aligned with the assumptions of perfect rationality
   c) ambiguous
   d) characterized by limited information

11. When a decision maker relies on a programmed decision, he or she
   a) may fall back on rules, procedures, or policies
   b) will develop many alternatives from which to select a solution
   c) will spend considerable time on the decision
   d) must be dealing with a unique or unusual problem

12. A procedure can be defined as a
   a) method to guide a manager's thinking in one general direction
   b) hierarchy of authority relationships in an organization
   c) series of interrelated sequential steps for problem solving
   d) collection of explicit statements about what a manager can or cannot do

13. A rule is BEST described by which of the following?
   a) a general guideline designed to direct a manager's focus
   b) a series of interrelated sequential steps
   c) a prohibition against desired activity
   d) an explicit and specific statement of correct behavior

14. A policy typically contains
   a) parameters to constrain behavior, not specific rules
   b) nothing but explicit, unambiguous terminology
   c) a sequence of steps to follow for approved decision making
   d) specific rules

15. A conceptual style of decision-making reflects an individual who
   a) thinks intuitively and has a low tolerance for ambiguity
   b) thinks rationally and has a high tolerance for ambiguity
   c) thinks intuitively and has a high tolerance for ambiguity
   d) thinks rationally and has a low tolerance for ambiguity

16. Group decisions will usually be superior to individual decisions when
   a) speed is a concern
   b) accuracy is critical
   c) minimizing the tendency of groupthink is important
   d) flexibility is needed

17. Which of the following is NOT an example of a situation in which groupthink occurs?
   a) Group members rationalize any resistance to the assumptions they have made.
   b) Group members apply direct pressure on those who express doubts.
   c) Group members avoid openly showing lack of consensus.
   d) Group members question those who are silent and try to sway them.

18. Which of the following statements is correct regarding national culture and decision making?
   a) In Sweden, employees are empowered to make decisions on matters that directly affect them.
   b) In Japan, ringisei reflects an efficient way for managers to make individual decisions regarding strategic directions.
   c) In Egypt, time pressure in making decisions promotes individual rather than group decision making.
   d) In France, risk avoidance is best achieved through participative decision making.

Applying the Concepts

Individual versus Group Decisions

Objective: *To contrast individual and group decision making.*

Time: *Fifteen minutes.*

Step 1: *You have five minutes to read the following story and individually respond to each of the eleven statements as either* true, false, *or* unknown *(indicated by a question mark). Begin.*

The Story: *A salesclerk had just turned off the lights in the store when a man appeared and demanded money. The owner opened a cash register. The contents of the cash register were scooped up, and the man sped away. A member of the police force was notified promptly.*

Statements about the Story

1. A man appeared after the owner had turned off his store lights. T F ?
2. The robber was a man. T F ?
3. The man did not demand money. T F ?
4. The man who opened the cash register was the owner. T F ?
5. The store owner scooped up the contents of the cash register and ran away. T F ?
6. Someone opened a cash register. T F ?
7. After the man who demanded the money scooped up the contents of the cash register, he ran away. T F ?
8. The cash register contained money, but the story does *not* state how much. T F ?
9. The robber demanded money of the owner. T F ?
10. The story concerns a series of events in which only three persons are referred to: the owner of the store, a man who demanded money, and a member of the police force. T F ?
11. The following events in the story are true: Someone demanded money; a cash register was opened; its contents were scooped up; a man dashed out of the store. T F ?

Step 2: *After you have answered the eleven questions individually, form groups of four or five members each. The groups have ten minutes to discuss their answers and agree on the correct answers to each of the eleven statements.*

Step 3: *Your instructor will give you the actual correct answers. How many correct answers did you get at the conclusion of step 1? How many did your group achieve at the conclusion of step 2? Did the group outperform the average individual? The best individual? Discuss the implications of these results.*

Take It to the Net

We invite you to visit the Robbins/De Cenzo page on the Prentice Hall Web site at:

http://www.prenhall.com/robbinsfom

for this chapter's World Wide Web exercise.

You can also visit the Web sites for these companies featured within this chapter:

Adidas
http://www.adidas.com

Puma
http://www.newout.com/pumahome.html

Bausch & Lomb
http://www.bausch.com

Reebok
http://www.planetreebok.com

Phelps Dodge Mining
http://www.irin.com/pd/

ValueJet
http://www.valuejet.com

Thinking Critically

Making a Value Judgment: Plant Closing at Bausch & Lomb

Bausch & Lomb, the Rochester, New York, eyewear company, made some major changes in early 1996 that have a number of western Maryland citizens seeing red. A Bausch & Lomb sunglass-lens plant in the area has been targeted for closure. As a result, approximately 600 jobs will be lost.[34] Company representatives have indicated that they decided to close the plant because it would be too expensive to maintain the current operation in the Maryland area. They have decided to shift the operations to plants in San Antonio, Texas, and Hong Kong.

Is Bausch & Lomb justified in its actions? Company officials certainly have a right to manage the operations in the most profitable way they can. Bausch & Lomb had watched profits fall from $171.4 million in 1992 to $31.1 million in 1994. The company's chief executive was ousted, but that change was not enough to boost profits. Moving to areas where employee pay is lower is a good way to reduce costs. Therefore, the "bottom line" warrants their actions. Furthermore, management could argue that the company brought more to the community—specifically, high-paying jobs that allowed the community to grow and prosper—than the community gave back. And, in today's global economy, hometown loyalties cannot override economic considerations.

Although the frequency of downsizing—in companies such as U.S. Steel (now USX Corporation), R. J. Reynolds Tobacco, and General Motors—has increased in the past decade, Bausch & Lomb's action will create significant problems for its former employees and the surrounding community, because the company is the largest employer in the region. When the biggest employer in an area makes such a change, it affects not only employees who will be laid off but also other businesses. When income levels in a region drop significantly, less money is spent in the local economy. And when there is nothing to replace that economic loss, problems arise. For instance, restaurants that opened and served a good portion of Bausch & Lomb employees may have to close because of a lack of patronage. Likewise, schools and other town-supported organizations may also suffer as tax revenues drop significantly.

One reason for the company's actions is related to how much employees are paid in the Maryland plant. When a company such as Bausch & Lomb establishes an operation in an area, it does so to attract a skilled, dedicated, and committed work force. But, because Bausch & Lomb was the primary employer in the region, turnover was almost nonexistent and pay levels kept climbing upward. At the San Antonio plant, in contrast, turnover is significant, and new employees can be hired at lower wage rates than the person who left the job. As a result of the longevity, the average hourly wage rate in Maryland is about 33 percent as high as it is in Texas; the percentage is even higher when the Maryland plant is compared with the Hong Kong plant.

Employees in the Maryland plant do make more money than their counterparts in Texas and Hong Kong, but they have given the company something that other plants have not—high-recognition quality products. Over the years, this western Maryland plant has been recognized by several independent groups for producing some of the highest-quality sunglass lenses in the world. In fact, employees have been awarded a prestigious international designation of quality that few organizations anywhere in the world achieve. In addition, this western Maryland plant received a productivity award from the U.S. government.

Questions:

1. What role, if any, should social responsibility play in Bausch & Lomb's decision to close its western Maryland plant?
2. Do you believe that companies like Bausch & Lomb should have a legal right to move to another area simply to cut costs, knowing it will create an economic hardship? Would you respond differently knowing that a company received tax incentives to relocate to the new area?
3. Should organizations develop any procedures, rules, or policies to deal with situations like this? If so, what should they be like? If not, why not?

Philip Knight and the Nike Revolution

During the physical fitness boom of the 1970s, millions of previously unathletic people became interested in exercise. During that time, the fastest-growing segment of the physical fitness market was joggers. In fact, it was estimated that by the late 1970s, almost 30 million people were jogging and another 10 million wore running shoes for leisure wear. For most of those 40 million people, there was only one real choice in athletic shoes—Nike.[35]

Nike was founded by Philip Knight, a track star from the University of Oregon. Importing shoes to the United States, Nike's big breakthrough came in 1975 with the development of the "waffle" sole—soles with tiny rubber studs that made the shoe spongier than any other shoe—even those from Adidas, Puma, and Converse—on the market. From that point on, Nike's sales skyrocketed. Today, Nike has annual sales in excess of $3.8 billion, almost a 30 percent share of the U.S. market, and nearly a 25 percent market share globally.

Nike's success can be traced to several core values Knight holds. First, the company emphasizes research and development to continually look for ways to improve its products. Second, the company provides a variety of styles and models to "satisfy" everyone's taste—from the professional athlete to the elderly looking for a comfortable pair of walking shoes. But most notably, behind Knight's actions is his desire for the company to be on the "hearts, minds, and feet" of every individual. To achieve that goal, Nike has relied heavily on a phenomenal marketing campaign.

Being an athlete, Knight recognized that professional sports heroes could influence a lot of people. He believed that if you could get high-profile athletes—such as Michael Jordan, Charles Barkley, Ken Griffey Jr., Troy Aikman, and André Agassi—to become part of the Nike team, the company could "build new product lines and marketing campaigns around them." The athletes' dominating presence and the consumers' passion for imitating their idols would enable Knight to achieve his goal of being the number one athletic shoe and apparel company in the world. That formula seems to have worked! But success is not something that Knight, or Nike, can take for granted. When you are number one, everyone else is "after" you!

Reebok is currently number two in the U.S. market—and they are trying harder. With revenues of $3.3 billion in 1994, Reebok is in a good position to overtake Nike. Its president, Paul Fireman, has been successful in filling niches that Nike once overlooked. For instance, while Nike was producing jogging and other athletic shoes primarily for men, Reebok recognized that a large segment of the population was being ignored. Accordingly, Reebok developed its white-leather shoes for women who needed good aerobics and exercise shoes—and the market exploded. In fact, by the late 1980s, Reebok had a greater market share than Nike. That lasted until Nike started its "Air Jordan" line of shoes—and once again it took the revenue lead from Reebok.

Fireman, however, was not to be outdone. Seeing what success Nike was having with its professional athletes as sponsors, Reebok signed a few of its own—including Frank Thomas, Michael Chang, and Emmett Smith. Their greatest athlete signing, however, came when they got Shaquille O'Neal under contract. He is a role model for many of the under-eighteen males who are the primary purchasers of Nike's products.

Questions:

1. What decisions did Nike's management make that helped lead to its success?
2. By the late 1980s, Nike had missed a large part of the market and gave Reebok the opportunity to become the number one athletic shoe company in the world. How did poor decision making lead to Nike's reduced market share? Do you think that uncertainty played a role in Nike's decision? Explain.
3. Now that Nike has regained world dominance in the athletic shoes and apparel market, what, if anything do you think Reebok's management can do to knock it back down to number two?

Video Case ABCNEWS

Making Tough Choices

What do Mary Bravo, Scott Bradely, and Pete Barrera have in common? Each was caught up in a life-or-death situation. Mary, Scott, and Pete had serious illnesses that required organ transplants. But, because of a number of bureaucratic constraints, their transplants were either significantly delayed or didn't happen at all.

Mary Bravo, fifty-eight years old, faced a fate that no human should be subjected to. She needed a new heart. Her diseased heart was able to pump only 20 percent of the blood necessary to keep her alive. Mary knew she had little time left—perhaps only a week. Unfortunately, Mary Bravo was not a candidate for a new heart, because she had neither health insurance nor the $100,000 she would need to pay for the heart transplant.

Scott Bradely faced a similar fate. His heart had been damaged by a virus, and Scott had congestive heart failure. Because Scott had worked for years, he was qualified for federal disability insurance in the amount of $719 a month. But the fact that he was getting disability payments disqualified him from his state's program that would have paid for the surgery.

Pete Barrera never dreamed he would have to face what happened to him. Oh sure, he knew anyone could get sick. But he had health insurance through his employer. Unfortunately, his health insurance did not cover liver transplants. Pete and his family waged a gallant battle, but it was all for naught. Pete died before a decision could be made on how to "finance" his new liver. Ironically, during Pete's last week, he had to be hospitalized in the intensive care unit. This specialized care and the medications he was given—which his health insurance plan did cover—cost nearly $100,000. That money "spent letting Mr. Barrera die would have nearly paid for the transplant he needed."

What's happening in a society when individuals without health insurance, or who get caught in a bureaucratic web, die? Upwards of 60,000 people like Mary, Scott, and Pete find themselves in such a situation. They need an organ transplant—certifiable by a physician—but can't get one. That's because there are loopholes. For instance, Medicare makes heart and liver transplant patients wait for approximately two and one-half years before it will pay for the procedure. Moreover, poor working-class individuals won't even get Medicare coverage. So if they work some, and are just barely above poverty levels, they are not considered indigent under Medicare regulations and thus are ineligible for help. Furthermore, hospitals are big business—as are health insurance companies. To be effective, they have to follow certain guidelines and policies. Many hospitals, for example, have rigid financial screening requirements before an individual is placed on an organ transplant list. Individuals who are unable to pay for an organ transplant—either through health insurance or private means—just won't get one.

Fortunately, Mary Bravo and Scott Bradely found individuals who would take up their cause. They got their transplants and are healthy today. Pete Barrera was not as fortunate. The individuals who had his fate in their hands failed him—in essence pronouncing on him a death sentence.

Questions:

1. Do you believe that life-or-death situations—such as deciding who will get an organ transplant—should have costs as a highly weighted factor? Why or why not? Support your position.
2. Should hospital administrators ignore the financial ability of their patients and allow medical procedures to be performed without concern for "the bottom line"? Would your view change if you knew that such an action would lead to the hospital's having to close due to bankruptcy? Discuss.
3. What role does social responsibility play in determining candidates for organ transplants?

Source: "Who Lives and Who Dies—Organ Transplants," *ABC PrimeTime,* September 20, 1995.

• PART 3 •
Organizing

Technology and the Design of Work Processes

6

LEARNING OBJECTIVES

What will I be able to do after I finish this chapter?

1. **DESCRIBE** the formula for calculating productivity.
2. **EXPLAIN** how technology can improve productivity.
3. **DESCRIBE** the advantages of computer-aided design.
4. **EXPLAIN** what is meant by the term *just-in-time inventory systems.*
5. **IDENTIFY** why management might consider introducing flexible manufacturing systems.
6. **DEFINE** and describe the three key elements in reengineering.
7. **EXPLAIN** how information technology is providing managers with decision support.
8. **IDENTIFY** the five key dimensions in a job.
9. **DESCRIBE** how managers can design individual jobs to maximize employee performance.
10. **EXPLAIN** how flextime, job sharing, and telecommuting increase organizational flexibility.

HENRY DUIGNAN, CHIEF OPERATING OFFIcer at Ross Operating Valve Company of Troy, Michigan, is building "a whole new business for the twenty-first century."[1] Although most of Ross's current business is producing high-volume, standardized valves, the company has invested $30 million since the late 1980s on sophisticated computer-aided design (CAD) systems and automated production equipment so they can produce customized valves practically overnight.

"We're selling 'virtual products' to our customers," says Duignan. By that he means unique products that don't exist until a customer needs them—as opposed to something out of a catalog.

At Ross's Lavonia, Georgia, facility, there are no manufacturing engineers, machinists, or inspectors. A fifteen-person team of multiskilled engineers works closely with customers to design sophisticated pneumatic valve assemblies to serve specialized needs. These engineers can put working prototypes of customized valves in a customer's hands in as little as seventy-two hours. And continuous design refinements can be made by the customer at very little cost. Once the valve has been designed, the Lavonia unmanned production plant produces the final product using a Japanese-built flexible manufacturing system. This state-of-the-art design and production system allows Ross to deliver custom valves in about one-hundredth of the time and at one-tenth the cost of traditional methods.

The designs created in Lavonia also can be transmitted in seconds, using satellite communications, to the firm's plants in Germany, Japan, England, and Michigan. With flexible manufacturing equipment similar to that in use in Georgia now installed in the Frankfurt and Tokyo facilities, Ross is developing its capability to meet customers' needs worldwide.

Companies such as Ross Operating Valve Company are using technology to automate their production processes. This employee is making a circuit board that, when installed in machinery, will eliminate many costly person-hours of production.

Duignan sums up the future for Ross: "Down the road, we plan to give our customers an access number that will allow them to directly access our Intergraph CAD terminal and design their own valve system on our terminal. We'll apply all the pneumatic technology and send the information back to them—then we'll build it for them at the plant closest to them and deliver it the next day."

Technology has completely changed Henry Duignan's business. And it is having a similar impact on most organizations. In this chapter, we focus on how operations and information technologies are influencing management and work processes, the affect of technology on worker obsolescence, and how managers can design jobs and work schedules to maximize employee performance.

Technology and Productivity

technology
How an organization transforms its inputs into outputs.

We briefly introduced the term *technology* in the Chapter 2 discussion of information processing. It is now time to focus on this phenomenon that is sweeping through companies. In its purest form, **technology** is how an organization transforms its inputs into outputs. In recent years, the term has become widely used by economists, managers, consultants, and business analysts to describe machinery and equipment that use sophisticated electronics and computers to produce those outputs.

The common feature of new technologies in the workplace is that they substitute machinery for human labor in transforming inputs into outputs. This substitution of capital for labor has been going on essentially nonstop since the Industrial Revolution in the mid-1800s. For instance, the introduction of electricity allowed textile factories to introduce mechanical looms that could produce cloth far faster and more cheaply than was previously possible when the looms were powered by individuals. But it is the computerization of equipment and machinery in the last quarter-century that has been the prime mover in reshaping the twentieth-century workplace. Automated teller machines, for example, have replaced tens of thousands of human tellers in banks. Ninety-eight percent of the spot welds on new Ford Tauruses are performed by robots not by people. Many cars now come equipped with on-board computers that diagnose in seconds problems that mechanics used to take hours to diagnose. IBM has built a plant in Austin, Texas, that can produce laptop computers without a single worker. Everything from the time parts arrive at the IBM plant to the final packing of finished products is completely automated. An increasing number of companies, small and large alike, are turning to multimedia and interactive technology for employee training. And literally millions of organizations have utilized personal computers to decentralize decision making and generate enormous increases in productivity (see Managers Who Made a Difference).

productivity
An organization's outputs divided by its inputs (labor plus capital plus materials).

Productivity is the name of the game! It is technology's ability to significantly increase productivity that is driving the technology "bandwagon." In its simplest form, productivity can be expressed in the following ratio:

$$\text{Productivity} = \frac{\text{Outputs}}{\text{Labor} + \text{Capital} + \text{Materials}}$$

The above formula can be applied in its total form or broken down into subcategories.[2] For instance, output per labor-hour is perhaps the most common partial measure of productivity. Industrial engineers, who conduct time-and-motion studies in factories, are largely focused on generating increases in labor productivity. IBM's automated plant in Austin, Texas, is an example of increasing productivity by substituting capital (i.e., machinery and equipment) for labor. Materials productivity is concerned with increasing the efficient use of material inputs and supplies. A meatpacking plant, as an illustrative case, improves its materials productivity when it finds additional uses for by-products that were previously treated as waste.

Productivity can also be applied at three different levels—the individual, the group, and the total organization. Word-processing software, fax machines, and e-mail have made secretaries more productive by allowing them to generate more output during their workday. The use of self-managed teams has increased the productivity of

Managers Who Made a Difference

BRENDA FRENCH, FOUNDER OF FRENCH RAGS

Brenda French is using technology to totally reinvent her business.[3] Starting in 1978, French had built French Rags into a $10 million a year business manufacturing women's knitwear. Her garments were being sold at leading department stores such as Neiman Marcus, Bonwit Teller, and Bloomingdale's. From an outsider's perspective, the business looked healthy. But French knew otherwise. Retailers' slowness in paying for merchandise put pressures on her limited financial resources. In addition, she was frustrated by department store buyers who were often choosing to sell just a few of her styles, sizes, and colors. She felt that her knitwear product line was reaching only a small percentage of its potential market.

Her financial and distribution problems were solved, and her business completely reshaped, by two isolated events in 1989. First, a friend introduced her to an expert in knitting equipment who just happened to have acquired a German-made Stoll computerized knitting machine. The sleek Stoll knitting machine uses thousands of precisely angled needles to do things the old-fashioned way—one stitch at a time—but it churns out garments at a breathtaking pace. This one machine can produce as many as twenty-four garments for each one produced by a hand knitter. Second, French's cash crunch had forced her to cut back production and sell only to the few stores who were willing to pay COD (cash on delivery). One loyal customer, frustrated by not being able to buy her favored French Rags garments, called French on the phone. On learning of French's money problems, the customer said, "You bring your clothes to my house, and I know twenty people who'll buy them." Desperate, French went to the customer's home. To her surprise, she took an order for $80,000 worth of products (with a 50 percent deposit).

These two events—the availability of a knitting expert with a computerized knitting machine and access to a new marketing channel—led Brenda French to reinvent her business. Today, French Rags mass produces custom-made knitwear and sells it directly to customers. Her distribution system no longer includes retail stores. Her sales force is now composed of customers who sell her goods out of their homes. She supplies them with order forms, sample garments, and fabric snippets of thirty color choices. After customers select their style and color combinations, individual measurements are taken, a 50 percent down payment is secured, and the order form is faxed to the French Rags factory. It is at this point that French's high-tech operation kicks into gear.

French now owns eleven of the Stoll machines. Using custom software that produces knit-by-number templates for fast and easy switching from one garment to another and a Silicon Graphics work station for designing the knitwear—combined with the new, low-cost home-distribution system—French Rags is able to produce quality, custom-made knitwear and sell it at off-the-rack prices. For example, a software program on a personal computer produces portable templates with instructions about which color yarns should be loaded on which spools atop a knitting machine as the machine is about to knit a particular garment. An elaborate knit jacket that used to take a skilled craftsperson a day and a half to knit by hand can be produced on this equipment in less than an hour. Another jacket, in

Continued

Brenda French, Founder of French Rags Continued

another style and color combination, can then be made in the following hour with a different knit-by-number template.

French can offer her customers more than 50,000 style and color combinations, allowing them to wear custom-made outfits that fit perfectly and are exactly like no other. French ships her merchandise directly to customers, usually within four to six weeks. And best of all, for a business that had consistently had money problems, French no longer has to worry about carrying inventories or accounts receivables. "We have no inventory problems because we have no inventory," says French. "Everything we make is presold."

many work groups at companies such as Honeywell, Coors Brewing, and Aetna Life. And Southwest Airlines is overall a more productive organization than rivals such as American Airlines or USAir because Southwest's cost per available seat-mile is 30 to 60 percent lower than theirs.

The above analysis brings us to the following conclusion. Since technology is the means by which inputs are turned into outputs, it is the primary focus of any management's efforts to improve productivity.

Operations Technology

High-tech manufacturing is going global. Satyan Pitroda, for instance, believes that developing countries, such as India and Mexico, can leapfrog into the upper ranks of high-tech manufacturing.[4] By using technology developed elsewhere (called technology transfer), these countries can bypass stages of development. To illustrate, Pitroda used an all-Indian team to design a phone switch suited to India's heat, humidity, dust, and frequent power failures. Inside the switch are chips from Motorola, Intel, and Texas Instruments, but Indian firms are designing and exporting the switches.

In this section, we look at key issues related to operations technology—design, production, customer service, distribution, continuous improvement processes, and reengineering work processes (see Exhibit 6-1).

How Can Products Be Designed More Efficiently?

Technology is redefining how the design of products is done. For instance, computer-aided design is generating substantial improvements in design productivity. And sophisticated computer networks are allowing designers to collaborate as never before.

computer-aided design (CAD)
The use of computational and graphics software that allows the geometry of a product or component to be graphically displayed and manipulated on video monitors.

Computer-aided design (CAD) essentially has made manual drafting obsolete. Computational and graphics software allow the geometry of a product or component to be graphically displayed and manipulated on video monitors. Alternative designs can be created and evaluated quickly, and the cost of developing mockups and prototypes is often eliminated.[5] CAD enables engineers to develop new designs in as little as a third of the time required for manual drafting. Eagle Engine Manufacturing, for instance, used its CAD system to design a new race-car engine in nine months instead of the traditional two-plus years.[6]

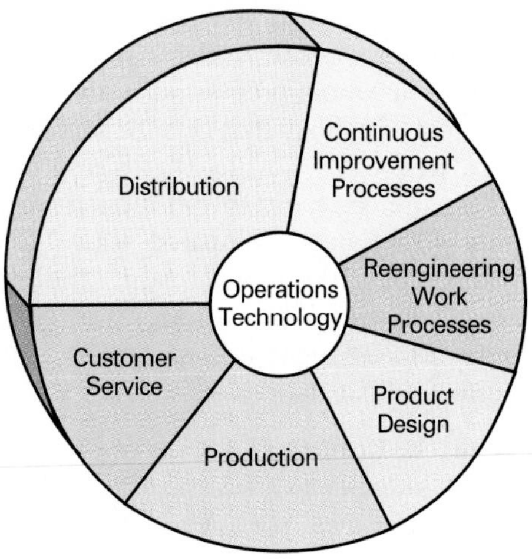

Exhibit 6-1
Components of Operations Technology

The best CAD software lets engineers plan products, test them on-screen, and even design tools to make them. Designers at Caterpillar have one of the most sophisticated design systems anywhere. It's a virtual-reality proving ground where designers can test-drive huge earthmoving machines before they are built.[7] It is a surround-screen, surround-sound cube about 10 feet on each side that creates the illusion of reality for anyone inside by projecting supercomputer-generated 3-D graphics onto the walls. Designers operate imaginary controls and make adjustments as needed. A recent Caterpillar backhoe and wheel loader incorporate visibility and performance improvements based on data from these virtual test drives.

CAD enables engineers to develop new designs in as little as a third of the time.

Ford Motor Co. has developed an international network that allows its designers around the world to work together as if they were in the same room.[8] Ford's corporate design organization combines design sites in Dearborn, Michigan; Dunton, England; Cologne, Germany; Turin, Italy; Valencia, California; Hiroshima, Japan; and Melbourne, Australia. The network enables a Ford engineer in Dunton, for example, to transmit to Dearborn massive CAD files of 3-D drawings for a future model car. In Michigan, a designer can bring up the drawings on a work station, phone his English colleague, and work simultaneously with that colleague in making on-screen revisions, even rotating the 3-D images to view them from all sides. A few hours later, the data files might be sent through satellite or fiber-optic circuits to Turin, where a computerized milling machine can turn out a clay or plastic-foam model in a matter of hours. The Ford Contour, the Mercury Mystique, and Ford's European Mondeo were all designed using this network approach.

In What Ways Can Production Processes Be Enhanced?

Technological advances over the past twenty years have completely revolutionized the way products are manufactured. First there were robotics and just-in-time inventory systems. Today we have entered the stage of mass customization called flexible manufacturing systems. Of course, there have also been important breakthroughs in the basic technologies of manufacturing. For instance, consider the success Finarvedi Spa has had with its new sheet steel plant in Cremona, Italy.[9]

Traditional steelmaking uses a technology, called hot and cold rolling, that wastes a lot of energy and floor space. Coils of steel about a twelfth of an inch thick are made by casting steel slabs, lugging them to giant ovens for reheating, and then flattening them out under a series of monstrous rollers that stretch for up to two miles. The whole process takes about three hours. The Cremona mill uses a revolutionary technology that gets the same results in fifteen minutes, uses one-third the energy, and requires a line that measures a little under 600 feet! The new technology allows the company to roll molten metal directly into thin steel. The mill employs only 400 people, compared with 1,200 workers needed to generate comparable volume in a traditional plant. And not only does this new technology provide Finarvedi with a $25 a ton advantage over its rivals, it can now produce steel to order. Management can guarantee delivery within three days, versus the industry norm of about three weeks.

robotics
Computer-controlled machines that manipulate materials and perform complex functions.

just-in-time (JIT) inventory systems
Systems in which inventory items arrive when they are needed in the production process instead of being stored in stock.

kanban
The Japanese word for "card" or "sign"; the basis of JIT inventory systems.

What Is Robotics? Robots are machines that act like human beings. By the late 1970s, manufacturing firms began adding robots to assembly lines. General Dynamics, for instance, used a robot in its Fort Worth, Texas, plant to drill more than 500 holes in the tail fins of its F-16 jet fighter. The robot was able to do in three hours what previously had taken workers twenty-four hours![10] From those basic robots came industrial **robotics**—computer-controlled machines that manipulate materials and perform complex functions. The leaders of this move to industrial robotics were the Japanese. In 1990, they had more than 2 million manufacturing robots in use.[11]

But robots were not without their problems. They were good at handling simple jobs, but they failed when tasks became more complicated. Today, robots are playing more of a support role in a larger computer-based manufacturing system.

How Do Just-in-Time Inventory Systems Operate? Large companies, such as Boeing, Toyota, and General Electric, have billions of dollars tied up in inventories. It is not unusual for even small firms to have a million dollars or more tied up in inventories. So anything management can do to significantly reduce the size of its inventory will improve its organization's productivity.

Just-in-time (JIT) inventory systems change the technology around which inventories are managed. Inventory items arrive when they are needed in the production process instead of being stored in stock.[12]

Robotics are computer-controlled machines that manipulate materials and perform complex functions. They are great for handling simple jobs—especially those that present hazards to humans.

In Japan, JIT systems are called *kanban,* a word that gets to the essence of the just-in-time concept. ***Kanban*** is Japanese for "card" or "sign." Japanese suppliers ship parts in containers. Each container has a card, or kanban, slipped into a side pocket. When a production worker at the manufacturing plant opens a container, he or she takes out the card and sends it back to the supplier. Receipt of the card initiates the shipping of a second container of parts that, ideally, reaches the production worker just as the last part in the first container is being used up. The ultimate goal of a JIT inventory system is to eliminate raw material inventories by coordinating production and supply deliveries precisely. When the system works as designed, it results in a number of positive benefits for a manufacturer: reduced inventories, reduced setup time, better work flow, shorter manufacturing time, less space consumption, and even higher quality. Of course, suppliers who can be depended on to deliver quality materials on time must be found. Because there are no inventories, there is no slack in the system to compensate for defective materials or delays in shipments.

An illustration of how JIT works in the United States can be seen in the relationship that has developed between Lear Seating Corp. and Chrysler.[13] Lear is a rapidly growing manufacturer of car seats. They make seats for most of the major auto makers. To supply Chrysler's Detroit "Dodge City" plant with seats for Dodge pickup trucks,

Lear built a 200-worker facility thirty-eight miles away in Romulus, Michigan. When a pickup starts down Dodge City's line, an electronic message calling for the particular seats for that truck is flashed to Romulus, which can produce the seats and deliver them to Chrysler in ninety minutes. The seats are built and shipped in the sequence in which they will be used, saving both Chrysler and Lear large amounts of working capital that was once tied up in seat inventories. In essence, Lear's Romulus plant has become an extension of Chrysler's Dodge City plant. And because Chrysler concentrates its seat orders with Lear, the seat manufacturer gains efficiencies of scale that it can pass on to Chrysler in lower costs.

At Ryder Trucks, a just-in-time system helps management control its operations. This inventorying system makes it possible to schedule deliveries appropriately—having parts and vehicles delivered on an as-needed basis.

What Are Flexible Manufacturing Systems? Flexible manufacturing systems look like something out of a science fiction movie in which remote-controlled carts deliver a basic casting to a computerized machining center. With robots positioning and repositioning the casting, the machining center calls upon its hundreds of tools to perform varying operations that turn the casting into a finished part. Completed parts, each a bit different from the others, are finished at a rate of one every ninety seconds. Neither skilled machinists nor conventional machine tools are used. Nor are there any costly delays for changing dies or tools in this factory. A single machine can make dozens or even hundreds of different parts in any order management wants. This is the world of **flexible manufacturing systems.**[14]

flexible manufacturing systems
Systems that, by integrating computer-aided design, engineering, and manufacturing, can produce low-volume, customized products at a cost comparable to that of high-volume, standardized products.

In a global economy, those manufacturing organizations that can respond rapidly to change have a competitive advantage. They can, for instance, better meet the diverse needs of customers and deliver products faster than their competitors. When customers were willing to accept standardized products, fixed assembly lines made sense. But nowadays, flexible technologies are increasingly necessary to compete effectively.

The unique characteristic of flexible manufacturing systems is that, by integrating computer-aided design, engineering, and manufacturing, they can produce low-volume products for customers at a cost comparable to what had been previously possible only through mass production. Flexible manufacturing systems are, in effect, repealing the laws of economies of scale. Management no longer has to mass produce thousands of identical products to achieve low per-unit production costs. With flexible manufacturing, when management wants to produce a new part, it does not change machines—it just changes the computer program. So management is able to respond to each customer's unique taste, specification, and budget.

Flexible technologies are increasingly necessary to compete effectively.

Some automated plants can build a wide variety of flawless products and switch from one product to another on cue from a central computer. John Deere, for instance, has a $1.5 billion automated factory that can turn out ten basic tractor models with as many as 3,000 options without plant shutdowns for retooling. National Bicycle Industrial Co., which sells its bikes under the Panasonic brand, uses flexible manufacturing to produce any of 11,231,862 variations on eighteen models of racing, road, and mountain bikes in 199 color patterns and an almost unlimited number of sizes. So Panasonic can provide almost-customized bikes at mass-produced prices.[15]

In What Ways Can Customer Service Be Improved?

In the midst of the Christmas rush, a frazzled customer came into Silverman's, a men's apparel chain in North and South Dakota.[16] "Do you know Frank Sauer?" she asked the saleswoman. "What does he like? What size does he wear? Help!" From a computer terminal on the sales floor, the saleswoman confidently checked Frank Sauer's record: He wears size large, looks best in Polo rugby shirts and Levi Dockers (items he looked at recently but didn't buy), works as a lawyer, and enjoys boating. "No problem," the saleswoman said. "I can take care of this gift for you. Sit down and have a cup of coffee." A few minutes later the relieved customer left the store with her gift and the satisfaction of knowing that Frank Sauer was going to get a Christmas gift he wanted and in the right size.

Consistent with the quality movement, technology can be used to revitalize customer service.[17] It can provide the ability to identify and track individual customers, to monitor service levels by company representatives, and to assist customers in specifying, acquiring, fixing, or returning products.

Managers are using technology to improve their customer service strategies in three ways.[18] First, technology can *personalize* service that previously was standardized. It can allow management to individualize service for each customer's unique needs. For instance, if you are a previous customer of Domino's Pizza or L.L. Bean, when you call to place an order, their computer system will already have data about your personal preferences recorded. Having this information enables the company to treat people as individuals rather than as objects, and it speeds the order-taking process.

Second, technology can *augment* service by providing the customer with additional support related to the acquisition or use of the product. Hertz used this strategy when it created its Gold Card service. Their computer system has your credit card number for billing, your car style and size preference, insurance data, and driver's license information. One short phone call makes your car reservation. Then when you arrive at your destination, an electronic sign with your name on it indicates where your car is located. The paperwork is already done and your contract is sitting in your awaiting car. When your trip is complete and you drop the car off, you bypass the line at the checkout counter. All you have to do is hand the keys and contract to the lot attendant, who records the time, date, and mileage in his hand-held computer, and you're off to your next destination in a couple of minutes.

Third, technology can *transform* your business. That is, it can allow an organization to fundamentally develop new business practices and reinvent itself. That is essentially what Henry Duignan did with his business (see opening vignette). He uses computer technology to provide his customers with custom-made valves.

How Does Technology Enhance Product Distribution?

Traditional distribution technology relied heavily on sales agents or brokers, wholesalers, and retailers. It was not unusual for a product to go through two or three intermediaries before getting into the consumer's hands. New technologies are increasingly cutting out those intermediaries.[19] Management has been investing heavily in multiple-distribution technologies to get closer to the customer, while also cutting costs, providing quicker deliveries and better service, and better meeting the needs of a diverse customer base. The two most recent breakthroughs in distribution technology are home shopping through television and electronic shopping via the Internet. Each of these technologies allows manufacturers to directly reach customers.

Cable television channels such as the Home Shopping Network, Cable Value Network, and the QVC channel have created a multibillion-dollar industry. Most of the products sold on these channels are bought from manufacturers. As such, they merely create a new mechanism for manufacturers to reach customers. However, some manufacturers are using these channels to directly sell their products to customers and paying the channels a commission for air time. Joan Rivers, for example, can sell tens of thousands of dollars' worth of her jewelry products in a few minutes by appearing on one of these cable channels.

How can technology enhance product distribution? With the capabilities and opportunities made available, for instance, on cable television, individuals like Joan Rivers can sell tens of thousands of dollars' worth of merchandise.

Infomercials are another vehicle by which manufacturers can directly take their product to the consumer. These programs—which typically last half-an-hour and present product testimonials in an entertainment format—allow makers of products as diverse as car waxes, kitchen appliances, cosmetics, and self-help courses to sell merchandise without having to go through wholesalers or retailers.

The latest and potentially most exciting distribution channel made possible by computer technology is marketing products directly to customers on the Internet.[20] Just about every major business firm, educational institution, and not-for-profit organization is setting up sites on the World Wide Web and creating a home page. Why? Because it's a relatively cheap way to reach over 20 million consumers. If you want to learn about the latest offerings from General Motors and Dell Computer, or review the latest exhibits at the Smithsonian Institute, you can merely tap into their web site and review their home page. Toronto Dominion Bank, for instance, has turned its web site into a one-stop financial shopping center. Its web site contains 300 "pages" of general financial information about savings plans, mortgages, and other financial products and services.[21]

Is 99.9 Percent Good Enough?

In Chapter 2, we described total quality management as a philosophy of management that is driven by the constant attainment of customer satisfaction through the continuous improvement of all organizational processes. Managers in many organizations, especially in North America, have been criticized for accepting a level of performance that is below perfection. TQM, however, argues that *good* isn't *good enough!* To dramatize this point, assume that a 99.9 percent error-free performance represents the highest standard of excellence. By that standard, the U.S. Post Office would lose 2,000 pieces of mail an hour, hospitals would give twelve babies to the wrong parents each day, 6,800 books would be shipped each day with the wrong covers, U.S. doctors would perform 500 incorrect surgical operations a week, and there would be two plane crashes a day at O'Hare Airport in Chicago![22]

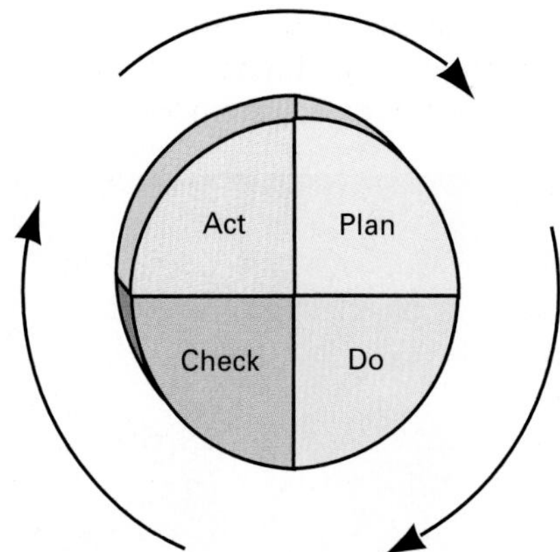

Exhibit 6-2
The PDCA Cycle

TQM programs seek to achieve continuous process improvements so that variability is constantly reduced. When you eliminate variations, you increase the uniformity of the product or service. Uniformity, in turn, results in lower costs and higher quality. For instance, Advanced Filtration Systems Inc., of Champaign, Illinois, recently cut the number of product defects—as determined by a customer quality audit—from 26.5 per 1,000 units to zero over four years. And that occurred during a period when monthly unit production tripled and the number of workers declined by 20 percent.

Continuous improvement runs counter to the more-typical American management approach of seeing work projects as being linear—with a beginning and an end. For example, American managers traditionally looked at cost cutting as a short-term project. They set a goal of cutting costs by 20 percent, achieved it, and then said: "Whew! Our cost cutting is over." The Japanese, on the other hand, have regarded cost control as something that never ends. The search for continuous improvement creates a race without a finish line.

The search for never-ending improvement requires a circular approach rather than a linear one, as illustrated in the plan-do-check-act (PDCA) cycle in Exhibit 6-2.[23] Management plans a change, does it, checks the results, and, depending on the outcome, acts to standardize the change or begin the cycle of improvement again with new information. This cycle treats all organizational processes as being in a constant state of improvement.

Eaton Corporation, a major manufacturer of automobile components, has adopted the PDCA cycle throughout the company.[24] Management encourages its workers to take thousands of small steps to incrementally improve the products they make and the processes used to make them. This policy extends to office workers who haggle over utility rates, challenge local tax assessments, scrutinize inventories, and eliminate paperwork. Continuous improvement helped Eaton increase its annual productivity between 1983 and 1992 by 3 percent a year compared with the U.S. average of 1.9 percent.

Will Reengineering Enhance Work Processes?

We also introduced reengineering in Chapter 2. We described it as considering how things would be done if you could start all over from scratch.

The term *reengineering* comes from the historical process of taking apart an electronics product and designing a better version. Michael Hammer coined the term for organizations. When he found companies using computers simply to automate outdated processes rather than finding fundamentally better ways of doing things, he realized that the principles of reengineering electronics products could be applied to business. So, as applied to organizations, reengineering means starting with a clean sheet of paper, rethinking and redesigning the processes by which the organization creates value and does work, and eliminating operations that have become antiquated in the computer age.[25]

What Are the Key Elements of Reengineering? Three key elements of reengineering are identifying an organization's distinctive competencies, assessing core processes, and reorganizing horizontally by process.

As discussed in Chapter 3, an organization's distinctive competencies are the unique skills and resources that determine its competitive weapons. Distinctive competencies define what it is that the organization can do better than its competition can. It might have superior store locations, a more efficient distribution system, higher-quality products, more-knowledgeable sales personnel, or superior technical support. Dell Computer, for instance, differentiates itself from its competitors by emphasizing high-quality hardware, comprehensive service and technical support, and low prices. Why is identifying distinctive competencies so important? Because it guides decisions regarding what activities are crucial to the organization's success.

Management also needs to assess the core processes that clearly add value to the organization's distinctive competencies. These are the processes that transform materials, capital, information, and labor into products and services that the customer values. When the organization is viewed as a series of processes, ranging from strategic planning to after-sales customer support, management can determine to what degree each adds value. Not surprisingly, this **process value analysis** typically uncovers a whole lot of activities that add little or nothing of value and whose only justification is "we've always done it this way."

process value analysis Analysis of the core processes that add value to an organization's distinctive competencies by transforming materials, capital, information, and labor into products and services that customers value.

Reengineering requires management to reorganize around horizontal processes. This orientation means using cross-functional and self-managed teams. It means focusing on processes rather than on functions. So, for instance, the vice president of marketing might become the "process owner of finding and keeping customers."[26] It also means cutting out levels of middle management. As Hammer points out, "Managers are not value-added. A customer never buys a product because of the caliber of management. Management is, by definition, indirect. So if possible, less is better. One of the goals of re-engineering is to minimize the necessary amount of management."[27]

Why Reengineering Now? Isn't reengineering something management should have been doing all along? Why has it become such a hot topic in the 1990s? The answers, according to Michael Hammer, are a changing global environment and organizational structures that had gotten top heavy.[28]

Traditional bureaucratic organizations worked fine in times of stable growth. Activities could be fragmented and specialized to gain economic efficiencies. That description fits the environment faced by most North American organizations in the 1950s, 1960s, and much of the 1970s. But most organizations today operate in a very different environment. Customers are much more informed and sophisticated than they were thirty years ago. Moreover, markets, production, and capital can be moved all over the world. Investors in Australia, for example, can put their money into opportunities in Japan, Canada, or anywhere else in the world if they see better returns than they can get at home. Customers worldwide now demand quality, service, and low cost. If you can't provide it, they will get it from someone else.

Work specialization, bureaucratic departments, managers' supervising few employees, and the like drove down direct labor costs, but the bureaucracies they created had massive overhead costs. To coordinate all the fragmentation and specialization, the organization needed numerous levels of middle management. So, although bureaucracies drove down costs at the operating level, they required increasingly expensive coordinating systems. Organizations that introduced teams, drove decisions down to the people closest to the problems, made managers supervise more employees, and eliminated layers of management challenged the traditional ways of doing things.

Information Technology

Advances in equipment and software technology have made telemedicine a reality. For instance, emerging information technologies have created a whole new way for rural hospitals to offer radiology services that were previously not financially feasible.[29] In Durham, North Carolina, Team Radiology is able to analyze medical scans over telephone lines from anywhere in the United States, twenty-four hours a day. Just a few years ago, that wasn't possible. But, because of recent breakthroughs in compression technology, x-ray images can be sent over phone lines, and the images can be accurately scanned with laser technology. Rural hospitals, consequently, can offer patients fast and competent readings of x-rays without having a radiologist on staff. Similarly, Team Radiology's outsourcing service provides a backup alternative for big-city hospitals' in-house radiologists.

That is yet another example of how information technology is revolutionizing the way organizations operate. In this section, we will highlight how technology is reshaping office work flows, changing the way internal communications are handled, and providing high-tech support for organizational decision making.

What Is Workflow Automation?

In the typical office, information spends most of its life moving from desk to desk.[30] For instance, consider the creation of a marketing plan. The marketing director approves the creation of the plan. A product manager is given responsibility for overseeing the plan's development. Staff marketing researchers gather the necessary data. A senior researcher then writes a first draft and sends it on to the product manager. This whole process requires documents to be passed along from one desk to another as the plan is developed, reviewed, edited, and rewritten, until eventually a final document is agreed upon and approved. This process can take weeks or even months because the document can sit on someone's desk for days. In fact, it is estimated that gathering and transferring paper documents can take up as much as 90 percent of the time needed to finish typical office tasks.

workflow automation
Use of computer software to automatically process and route documents and information through an organization.

Workflow automation can solve much of this delay. It greatly improves the process of creating and transferring documents by automating the flow of information. Workflow automation begins by examining how documents, business forms, and other information wend their way through an organization. It looks for bottlenecks and outdated procedures that slow things down and add to costs. Once new routes are laid out, workflow software is installed on computer networks to instantly convey to the right desk all information—whether it's a digital image of an invoice or an e-mail question from a customer. This software makes the movement of documents automatic, eliminating the need for a human to figure out who should get the information next, collapsing the travel times, and avoiding misrouting. The system can also be programmed to send documents along different paths depending on content.

Workflow automation greatly improves the process of creating and transferring documents.

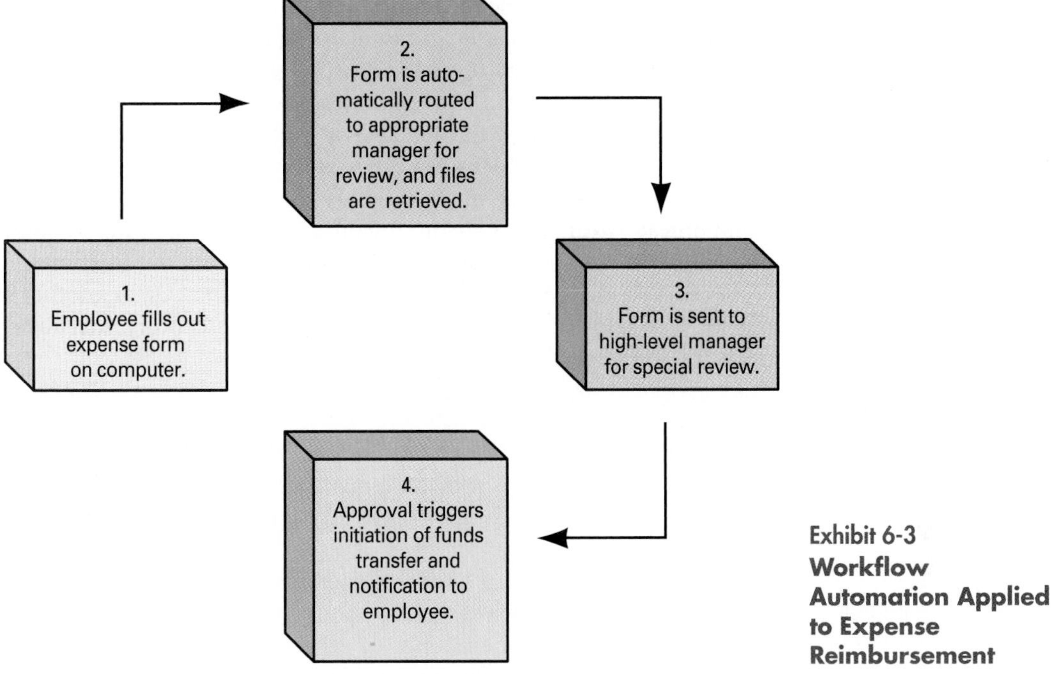

Exhibit 6-3
Workflow Automation Applied to Expense Reimbursement

Exhibit 6-3 illustrates how workflow automation has improved one firm's information flow in the processing of an employee's expense reimbursement request. In step 1, the employee fills out an expense form on her computer. The software then routes the form over a network to the appropriate decision maker for initial review (step 2). The form's arrival triggers the retrieval of employee files that might be needed. In step 3, the software recognizes that the transaction involves more than $5,000, so the form is automatically sent to an upper-level manager for special review. Upon final sign-off, in step 4, the software sends a copy of the form to another computer, which processes payment; an electronic note is sent to notify the employee that her reimbursement check is ready (or that an automatic transfer of funds to her bank account has been completed). Then the form is automatically stored on an archival laser disk.

How Does Technology Enhance Internal Communications?

Information technology is reshaping communications within organizations. For example, it is significantly improving management's ability to monitor organizational performance and is allowing employees to have more-complete information to make faster decisions. But if we had to identify the two most important developments in information technology, in terms of their impact on internal organizational communications, it would probably be digitalization and the wireless phenomenon.[31]

Organizations are converting internal information from analog language to digital. Telephones, for instance, have historically used an analog signal—an electric wave-form representation of sound. Computers, on the other hand, use a digital language—combinations of 1s and 0s—to communicate. Organizations are aggressively changing all their internal communication systems to the digital format. Why? Analog is slower, less accurate, and prone to interruptions and distortions. Moreover, any information—numbers, words, voice, or pictures—can be digitized. So, by converting to a completely digital format, organizations will have put in place a system that can permit managers and employees to communicate in any form. Anything can be delivered to any instrument capable of displaying it. A television, for instance, can receive and display computer text, or a radio can receive a phone call.

Now combine digitalization with wireless networks and you have revolutionized internal communications. Wireless products—such as personal pagers, cellular telephones, and computers with modems—are making it possible for people in organizations to be fully accessible to each other, at any time, regardless of where they are. Employees won't have to be at their desk with their computer plugged in in order to communicate with others in the organization. "I think wireless communications is probably the last communications breakthrough in our lifetimes," says Kenneth Forbes III, president and CEO of Mobile Digital Corp.[32] Or, as another senior manager put it, "The last 100 years have been the wireline century. We have just embarked upon the wireless century."[33]

In What Ways Does Technology Assist Decision Making?

Information technology is providing managers with a wealth of decision-making support. Examples include expert systems, neural networks, groupware, and specific problem-solving software.

expert systems
Software programs that use the encoded relevant experience of a human expert to analyze and solve ill-structured problems.

Expert systems use software programs to encode the relevant experience of a human expert and allow a system to act like that expert in analyzing and solving ill-structured problems.[34] The essence of expert systems is that (1) they use specialized knowledge about a particular problem area rather than general knowledge that would apply to all problems; (2) they use qualitative reasoning rather than numerical calculations; and (3) they perform at a level of competence that is higher than that of non-expert humans.[35] They guide users through problems by asking them a set of sequential questions about the situation and drawing conclusions based on the answers given. The conclusions are based on programmed rules that have been modeled on the actual reasoning processes of experts who have confronted similar problems before. Once in place, these systems are allowing employees and lower-level managers to make high-quality decisions that previously could have been made only by senior managers. Expert systems are being used in such diverse areas as medical diagnosis, mineral and oil explorations, equipment-fault locating, credit approvals, and financial planning.[36] For instance, IDS Financial Services has encoded the expertise of its best financial-planning account managers in an expert systems program. "Now even the worst of our 6,500 planners is better than our average planner used to be," said the company's chairman.[37]

neural networks
Computer software that imitates the structure of brain cells and connections among them and that can distinguish patterns and trends too subtle or complex for human beings.

Neural networks are the next step beyond expert systems.[38] They use computer software to imitate the structure of brain cells and connections among them. Neural networks have the ability to distinguish patterns and trends too subtle or complex for human beings. For instance, people can't easily assimilate more than two or three variables at once, but neural networks can perceive correlations among hundreds of variables. As a result, they can perform many operations simultaneously, recognizing patterns, making associations, generalizing about problems they haven't been exposed to before, and learning through experience. For instance, Mellon Bank uses neural networks to flag potential credit card fraud.[39] The bank previously had an expert system to keep track of its 1.2 million Visa and MasterCard accounts. But this system could look at only a few factors, such as the size of a transaction. As such, it would frequently generate as many as a thousand potential defrauding incidents a day, most of which were false positives. Meanwhile, all these potential fraud cases were overwhelming Mellon's investigative staff. Since Mellon replaced its expert system with a neural network, it deals with only one-tenth as many suspicious transactions, and they are much more likely to be actual cases of fraud. And, with the expert system, investigators usually did not get around to checking on a questionable transaction for a couple of days. With the new neural network system, investigators are on top of most problems in less than two hours.

Videoconferencing equipment, like this setup at Compression Labs, is helping companies cut costs. Bringing people together electronically, rather than physically, saves time and eliminates travel expenses.

In the previous chapter, we introduced the concept of electronic meetings as one means of improving group decision making. Although electronic meetings have assisted in the decision-making process, today, groups are interacting electronically for a number of reasons.[40] **Groupware** is a term used to describe the multitude of software programs that have developed to facilitate group interaction and decision making. Other applications of groupware are videoconferencing group meetings, disseminating presentations, augmenting face-to-face customer visits, and even conducting preliminary interviews of job candidates.[41] In 1995, more than 40 percent of the largest companies in the United States used video-conferencing; the 3M Company, which led the pack, makes more than 22,000 videoconferencing calls each year.[42] Conferencing allows participants to communicate over networks or telephone lines with others at different locations at the same time.[43] If you have participated in chat-room sessions on the Internet or on one of the commercial on-line services, you are already familiar with conferencing.

groupware Computer software programs that facilitate group interaction and decision making by persons at different locations.

The latest wrinkle in decision support software is the growing supply of unique problem-solving programs to help managers do their jobs more effectively. Consider a few of the latest offerings: Forecast Pro analyzes data and enables managers with minimal background in statistics to run simple forecasts. Business Insight helps managers brainstorm about "big picture" issues such as strategic planning. Performance Now! provides a framework for managers to evaluate an employee's performance and then guides the manager through the steps in writing up a specific performance review. Negotiator Pro prepares a manager for any negotiation by helping prepare a psychological profile of the manager and the opponent and then helps the manager create a detailed negotiation plan.[44]

Technology and Worker Obsolescence

Rob Hanc is only twenty-eight, but he has already come face to face with the new reality—his skills don't match what employers need.[45] Rob graduated high school and followed in his father's footsteps by taking a job at the Dofasco steel foundry in Hamilton, Ontario. His job? He was a heavy laborer—doing lifting and carrying. At twenty-one, Rob was making $47,000 a year. But Dofasco couldn't compete paying such high wages for someone to do unskilled labor. Hanc lost his job. "My biggest problem is lack of education," says Rob. "Me and school don't go together. I need to work with my hands." But, as Rob now knows, "heavy labor is a dying breed."

Glenna Cheney also has only a high school education.[46] But, unlike Rob Hanc, Glenna has been changing with the times. Glenna went to work for Fingerhut Co., a Minneapolis-based catalog company, in 1965. She answered the telephone, took orders, and wrote customer orders and payment schedules on index cards. When Fingerhut replaced the index cards with a mainframe computer, Glenna learned about computers. She learned so well, in fact, that she got promoted to supervisor. When the mainframe system was recently replaced with a group of work stations, Glenna enthusiastically took training classes to learn the new technology. She was recently promoted to a business analyst position, in which she advises Fingerhut's computer specialists on how to further develop the work stations to fit workers' needs.

Changes in technology have cut the shelf-life of most employees' skills. A factory worker or clerical employee in the 1950s could learn one job and be reasonably sure that his or her skills would be adequate to do that job for most of his or her work life. That certainly is no longer true. New technologies driven by computers, reengineering, TQM, and flexible manufacturing systems are changing the demands of jobs and the skills employees need to do them.

Repetitive tasks—such as those traditionally performed on assembly lines and by low-skilled office clerks—will continue to be automated. And a good number of jobs will be upgraded. For instance, as most managers and professionals take on the task of writing their own memos and reports using word-processing software, the traditional secretary's job will be upgraded to become more of an administrative assistant position. Secretaries who are not equipped to take on these expanded roles will be displaced. Other white-collar jobs that are disappearing or being reshaped as a result of technology include bank teller, telephone operator, meter reader, and travel agent.

Reengineering, as we previously noted, is producing significant increases in employee productivity. The redesign of work processes is achieving higher output with fewer workers. And these reengineered jobs require different skills. Employees who are computer illiterate, have poor interpersonal skills, or can't work autonomously will increasingly find themselves ill-prepared for the demands of new technologies.

Keep in mind that the obsolescence phenomenon does not exclude managers. Middle managers who merely acted as conduits in the chain of command between top management and the operating floor are being eliminated. And new skills—for example, coaching, negotiating, and building teams—are becoming absolute necessities for every manager.

Finally, software is changing the jobs of many professionals, including lawyers, doctors, accountants, financial planners, and librarians.[47] Software programs will allow laypeople to use specialized knowledge to solve routine problems themselves or opt for a software-armed paraprofessional. Particularly vulnerable are those professionals who do standardized jobs. A lot of legal work, for instance, consists of writing standard contracts and performing other routine activities. These tasks will be done inside law firms by computers or paralegals, or by clients themselves, using software designed to prepare wills, trusts, incorporations, and partnerships. Software packages, such as Turbo Tax, will continue to take a lot of work away from professional accountants. And hospitals are using software to help doctors make their diagnoses. Punch in a patient's age, sex, lab results, and symptoms, answer a set of structured questions, and a $995 program called Iliad will draw on its knowledge of nine subspecialties of internal medicine to diagnose the patient's problem. These examples demonstrate that even the knowledge of highly trained professionals can become obsolete. As the world changes, professionals will also need to change if they are to survive.

As the world changes, professionals will also need to change if they are to survive.

Work Design

If you walk into the headquarters of the Pittsburgh-based Aluminum Company of America (ALCOA), you'll be in for a surprise.[48] There are no executive suites, permanent work cubicles or desks, filing cabinets, or other trappings typically associated with an office. Why? Because ALCOA has redesigned its offices into a **virtual workplace.** Employees are free to work where they please. Many of them choose to telecommute from home. The only space at headquarters that employees can call their own are the high school style lockers where they can stow their personal belongings. Employees who choose to go into the office on any given day stop in the lobby and pick up laptop computers and portable phones, which can be programmed with their extension number. Then they head for any one of a dozen or so open spaces, pull over a desk-on-wheels, plug into nearby modem jacks, and begin their work. All documents once stored in filing cabinets are now available electronically. And for the occasional meetings of work groups, communications centers are scattered around the building.

virtual workplace
Office characterized by open space, movable furniture, portable phones, laptop computers, and electronic files; designed for occasional use by telecommuting employees.

ALCOA's virtual office, staffed by mobile employees, is just one way that business firms can redesign work to meet changing demands. The message in this example is that in times of dynamic change, don't expect the design of jobs, work spaces, and work schedules to remain intact. In this section, we will identify the primary dimensions of jobs, describe how those dimensions can be mixed and matched to maximize employee performance, and review innovative work-scheduling options that managers might consider to further improve employee performance.

What Are the Key Dimensions in a Job?

What differentiates one job from another? We know that a traveling salesperson's job is different from that of an emergency-room nurse. And we know that both of those jobs have little in common with the jobs of an editor in a newsroom or a component assembler on a production line. But what is it that allows us to draw these

What does a virtual workplace look like? Open space, and furniture that's mobile. That's exactly the situation at this Minneapolis ad agency.

job characteristics model (JCM)
A framework for analyzing and designing jobs; identifies five core job dimensions—skill variety, task identity, task significance, autonomy, and feedback—their interrelationships, and impact on outcome variables.

skill variety
The degree to which a job requires a variety of activities that call for different skills and talents.

task identity
The degree to which a job requires completion of a whole and identifiable piece of work.

task significance
The degree to which a job affects the lives or work of other people.

autonomy
The degree to which a job provides freedom, independence, and discretion to an individual in scheduling and carrying out his or her work.

feedback
The degree to which carrying out the work activities required by a job results in the individual's obtaining direct and clear information about the effectiveness of his or her performance.

distinctions? Currently, the best answer is something called the **job characteristics model (JCM).**[49]

According to the researchers who developed the JCM (see Details on a Management Classic), any job can be described in terms of five core job dimensions, defined as follows:

- ▶ **1. Skill variety.** The degree to which the job requires a variety of activities so the worker can use a number of different skills and talents
- ▶ **2. Task identity.** The degree to which the job requires completion of a whole and identifiable piece of work
- ▶ **3. Task significance.** The degree to which the job affects the lives or work of other people
- ▶ **4. Autonomy.** The degree to which the job provides freedom, independence, and discretion to the individual in scheduling the work and in determining the procedures to be used in carrying it out
- ▶ **5. Feedback.** The degree to which carrying out the work activities required by the job results in the individual's obtaining direct and clear information about the effectiveness of his or her performance

Exhibit 6-4 (page 182) offers examples of job activities that rate high and low for each characteristic. Exhibit 6-5 (page 183) presents the model. As Exhibit 6-5 shows, the links between the job dimensions and the outcomes are moderated or adjusted by the strength of the individual's growth need; that is, by the employee's desire for self-esteem and self-actualization. This means that individuals with a high growth need are more likely to experience the psychological states when their jobs are enriched than are their counterparts with a low growth need. Moreover, they will respond more positively to the psychological states when they are present than will low-growth-need individuals (see also Understanding Yourself).

The job characteristics model has been well researched. Most of the evidence supports the general framework of the theory—that is, there is a set of multiple job characteristics, and these characteristics affect behavioral outcomes.[50] But there is still considerable debate around the five specific core dimensions in the JCM and the validity of growth-need strength as a moderating variable.

There is some question whether task identity adds to the model's predictive ability,[51] and there is evidence suggesting that skill variety may be redundant with autonomy.[52] In addition, the strength of an individual's growth needs as a meaningful moderating variable has recently been called into question.[53] Other variables—such as the presence or absence of social cues, perceived equity with comparison groups, and likelihood to integrate work experience[54]—may be more valid in moderating the job characteristics–outcome relationship. Given the current state of research on moderating variables, one should be cautious in unequivocally accepting growth-need strength as originally included in the JCM.

Where does this leave us? We can make the following statements with relative confidence: (1) The JCM provides a reasonably valid framework for defining the core characteristics in a cross section of jobs. (2) People who work on jobs with high core job dimensions are generally more motivated, satisfied, and productive than are those who do not. (3) Job dimensions operate through the psychological states in influencing personal and work outcome variables rather than influencing them directly.[55]

Are Job Dimensions Perception or Reality?

Ronni Anderson teaches math classes at Crossland High School. She has been teaching the same calculus, algebra, and geometry courses at the school for fourteen years. "This job is driving me crazy," says Ronni. "It's boring. I talk about the same concepts,

Details on a Management Classic

J. Richard Hackman and Greg R. Oldham: The Job Characteristics Model

The dominant framework today for defining task characteristics and understanding their relationships to employee motivation is J. Richard Hackman and Greg R. Oldham's job characteristics model (JCM).[56] Research on the JCM has found that the first three dimensions—skill variety, task identity, and task significance—combine to create meaningful work. That is, if these three characteristics exist in a job, we can predict that the person will view his or her job as being important, valuable, and worthwhile. Jobs that possess autonomy give the job incumbent a feeling of personal responsibility for the results, and jobs that provide feedback let the employee know how effectively he or she is performing.

From a motivational standpoint, the JCM says that internal rewards are obtained when one *learns* (knowledge of results) that one *personally* (experienced responsibility) has performed well on a task that one *cares about* (experienced meaningfulness).[57] The more these three conditions are present, the greater will be the employee's motivation, performance, and satisfaction.[58]

The core dimensions can be combined into a single index called the Motivating Potential Score (MPS). The MPS is calculated as follows:

$$\text{Motivating potential} = \left[\frac{\text{Skill variety} + \text{Task identity} + \text{Task significance}}{3}\right] \times \text{Autonomy} \times \text{Feedback}$$

What does the JCM tell us? Jobs will score high on motivating potential if they are high on at least one of the three factors that lead to experiencing meaningfulness (skill variety, task identity, or task significance). They must also be high on both autonomy and feedback. Creating jobs that meet these requirements will result in a high motivating potential score. In doing so, motivation, performance, and satisfaction will be positively affected, and the likelihood of absenteeism and turnover will be lessened.[59]

to a similar bunch of sixteen- and seventeen-year-olds, semester after semester. I know the answers to their questions before they get the fifth word out of their mouths. I've heard it all before. I can teach these classes with my brain turned off! I'm burned out! I'm sick of this job. I've decided that this is going to be my last year of teaching."

Kris Driscoll also teaches math classes at Crossland High School. She and Ronni joined the faculty at the same time, right out of college. But listening to Kris, you would think she was doing an entirely different job than Ronni. "I've loved my job from day one," says Kris. "It's as interesting and challenging this term as it was the first. The students change every year, but they're still young and optimistic. I have a unique opportunity to shape their attitudes about math. In less than ten years, some of these young people will be working, designing new products and technologies—and quite possibly changing the world! And I'll have had a major part in that! I don't think I'll ever tire of what I do."

The above illustrates that people can look at the same job and evaluate it differently. The fact that people respond to their jobs as they perceive them rather than to

JOB CHARACTERISTIC	EXAMPLE JOB
Skill Variety	
High variety	The owner-operator of a garage who does electrical repair, rebuilds engines, does bodywork, and interacts with customers
Low variety	A body shop worker who sprays paint eight hours a day
Task Identity	
High identity	A cabinetmaker who designs a piece of furniture, selects the wood, builds the object, and finishes it to perfection
Low identity	A worker in a furniture factory who operates a lathe solely to make table legs
Task Significance	
High significance	Nursing the sick in a hospital intensive care unit
Low significance	Sweeping hospital floors
Autonomy	
High autonomy	A police detective who schedules his or her own work for the day, makes contacts without supervision, and decides on the most effective techniques for solving a case
Low autonomy	A police telephone dispatcher who must handle calls as they come according to a routine, highly specified procedure
Feedback	
High feedback	An electronics factory worker who assembles a modem and then tests it to determine if it operates properly
Low feedback	An electronics factory worker who assembles a modem and then routes it to a quality control inspector who tests it for proper operation and makes needed adjustments

Exhibit 6-4
Examples of High and Low Job Characteristics

Source: Adapted from G. Johns, *Organizational Behavior: Understanding and Managing Life at Work,* 4th ed. (New York: Harper Collins, 1996), p. 204. With permission.

social information processing (SIP) model A framework for analyzing employee motivation and job satisfaction; based on the premise that employees adopt attitudes and behaviors in response to the social cues provided by others with whom they have contact.

the objective jobs themselves is the central premise of the **social information processing (SIP) model.**[60]

The SIP model argues that employees adopt attitudes and behaviors in response to the social cues provided by others with whom they have contact. These others can be coworkers, supervisors, friends, family members, or customers. For instance, Garth Connolley got a summer job working in a British Columbia sawmill. Since jobs were scarce and this one paid particularly well, Garth arrived on his first day of work highly motivated. Two weeks later, however, his motivation was quite low. What happened was that his coworkers consistently bad-mouthed their jobs. They said the work was boring, that having to clock in and out proved management didn't trust them, and that supervisors never listened to their opinions. The objective characteristics of Garth's job had not changed in the two-week period; rather, Garth had reconstructed reality on the basis of messages he had received from others.

A number of studies generally confirm the validity of the SIP model.[61] For instance, it has been shown that employee motivation and satisfaction can be manipulated by such subtle actions as a coworker or boss commenting on the existence or ab-

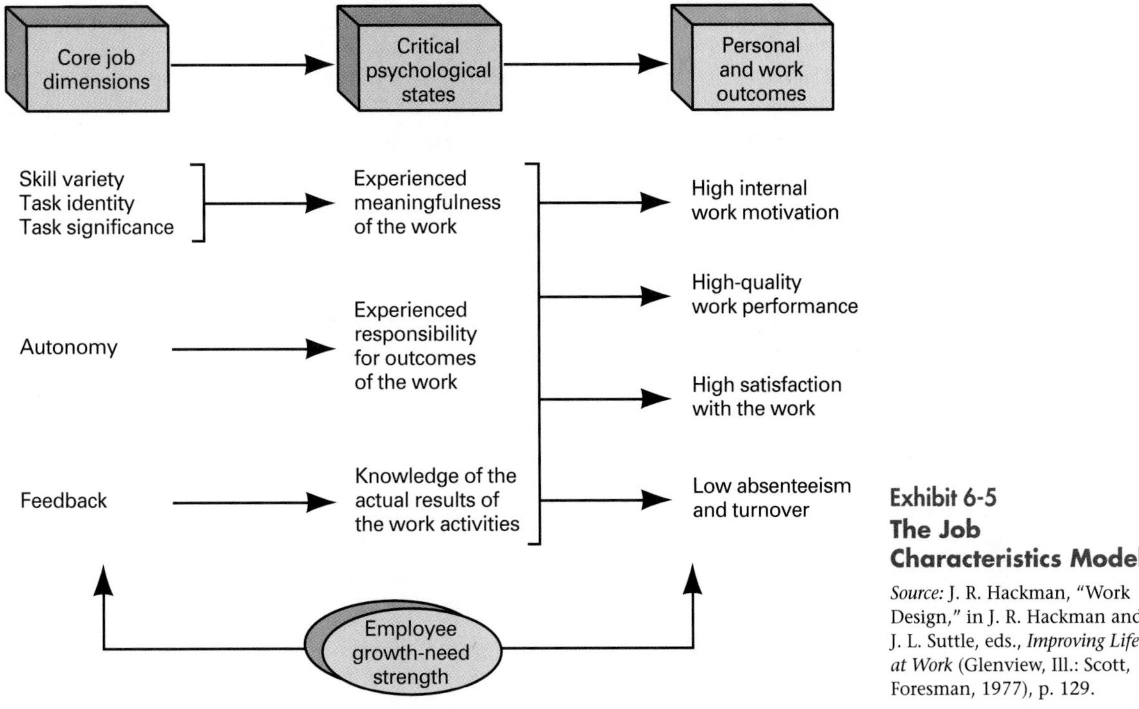

Exhibit 6-5
The Job Characteristics Model

Source: J. R. Hackman, "Work Design," in J. R. Hackman and J. L. Suttle, eds., *Improving Life at Work* (Glenview, Ill.: Scott, Foresman, 1977), p. 129.

sence of job features such as difficulty, challenge, and autonomy. So managers should give as much (or more) attention to employees' perceptions of their jobs as they give to the actual characteristics of those jobs. They might spend more time telling employees how interesting and important their jobs are. And managers should also not be surprised that newly hired employees and people transferred or promoted to a new position are more likely to be receptive to social information than are those with greater seniority.

Can Work Design Ideas Be Used with Groups?

Most of the emphasis on work design has focused on individual jobs. However, employees are increasingly working in groups and teams. What, if anything, can we say about the design of group-based work to try to improve employee performance in those groups?

We know a lot more about individual-based job design than we do about design at the group level.[62] This lack of data on group work design is mostly due to the fact that the wide popularity of teams—specifically assigning tasks to a group of individuals instead of to a single person—is a relatively recent phenomenon. That said, the best work in this area offers two sets of suggestions.[63]

First, the JCM recommendations seem to be as valid at the group level as they are at the individual level. Managers should expect a group to perform at a high level when: (1) the group task requires members to use a variety of relatively high-level skills; (2) the group task is a whole and meaningful piece of work, with a visible outcome; (3) the outcomes of the group's work on the task have significant consequences for other people; (4) the task provides group members with substantial autonomy for deciding about how they do the work; and (5) work on the task generates regular, trustworthy feedback about how well the group is performing (see Developing a Management Skill).

Understanding Yourself

Is an Enriched Job for You?

People differ in what they like and dislike in their jobs. Listed below are twelve pairs of jobs. For each pair, indicate which job you would prefer. Assume that everything else about the jobs is the same—pay attention only to the characteristics actually listed for each pair of jobs. If you would prefer the job in the left-hand column (Column A), indicate how much you prefer it by circling a number to the left of the Neutral point (4). If you prefer the job in the right-hand column (Column B), circle one of the numbers to the right of Neutral. Circle number 4 (Neutral) only if you find the two jobs equally attractive or unattractive. Try to use the number 4 (Neutral) rarely.

COLUMN A	Scale (Strongly prefer A — Neutral — Strongly prefer B)	COLUMN B
1. A job that offers little or no challenge.	7 | 6 | 5 | 4 | 3 | 2 | 1	A job that requires you to be completely isolated from coworkers.
2. A job that pays very well.	7 | 6 | 5 | 4 | 3 | 2 | 1	A job that allows considerable opportunity to be creative and innovative.
3. A job that often requires you to make important decisions.	1 | 2 | 3 | 4 | 5 | 6 | 7	A job in which there are many pleasant people to work with.
4. A job with little security in a somewhat unstable organization.	1 | 2 | 3 | 4 | 5 | 6 | 7	A job in which you have little or no opportunity to participate in decisions that affect your work.
5. A job in which greater responsibility is given to those who do the best work.	1 | 2 | 3 | 4 | 5 | 6 | 7	A job in which greater responsibility is given to loyal employees who have the most seniority.
6. A job with a supervisor who sometimes is highly critical.	1 | 2 | 3 | 4 | 5 | 6 | 7	A job that does not require you to use much of your talent.
7. A very routine job.	7 | 6 | 5 | 4 | 3 | 2 | 1	A job in which your coworkers are not very friendly.
8. A job with a supervisor who respects you and treats you fairly.	7 | 6 | 5 | 4 | 3 | 2 | 1	A job that provides constant opportunities for you to learn new and interesting things.
9. A job that gives you a real chance to develop yourself personally.	1 | 2 | 3 | 4 | 5 | 6 | 7	A job with excellent vacations and fringe benefits.
10. A job in which there is a real chance you could be laid off.	1 | 2 | 3 | 4 | 5 | 6 | 7	A job with very little chance to do challenging work.

COLUMN A		COLUMN B
11. A job with little freedom and independence to do your work in the way you think best.	7 | 6 | 5 | 4 | 3 | 2 | 1 Strongly prefer A — Neutral — Strongly prefer B	A job with poor working conditions.
12. A job with very satisfying teamwork.	7 | 6 | 5 | 4 | 3 | 2 | 1 Strongly prefer A — Neutral — Strongly prefer B	A job that allows you to use your skills and abilities to the fullest extent.

Scoring: Each item on the questionnaire yields a score from 1 to 7. To obtain your individual growth-need strength score, average the twelve items by summing the numbers you have circled and dividing that total by 12.

What the Assessment Means: This assessment is designed to assess the degree to which you desire complex and challenging work. A high need for growth suggests that you are more likely to experience the desired psychological states in the job characteristics model when you have a job that gives you freedom and autonomy to act (called enrichment). Research indicates that if you score high on this measure (4.5 or greater) you will respond positively to an enriched job. Conversely, if you score low (2.5 or less), you will not find enriched jobs satisfying or motivating. Scores from 2.5 to 4.5 indicate that some enrichment is satisfying to you, but that some structure and managerial control of the job are also preferred.

Source: J. R. Hackman, and G. R. Oldham, *The Job Diagnostic Survey: An Instrument for the Diagnosis of Jobs and the Evaluation of Job Redesign Projects,* Technical Report No. 4 (New Haven, Conn.: Yale University, Department of Administrative Sciences, 1974). Used with permission.

Second, group composition is critical to the success of the work group. Managers should try to ensure that the following four conditions are met: (1) individual members have the necessary task-relevant expertise to do their work; (2) the group is large enough to perform the work; (3) members possess interpersonal as well as task skills; and (4) membership is moderately diverse in terms of talents and perspectives. In Chapter 10, we will elaborate on these group-composition factors.

Work Schedule Options

Brett Richardson is the classic "morning person." He rises each day at 5 A.M. sharp, full of energy. On the other hand, as he puts it, "I'm usually ready for bed right after the 7 P.M. news."

Brett's work schedule as a claims processor at Allstate Insurance is flexible. It allows him some degree of freedom as to when he comes to work and when he leaves. His office opens at 6 A.M. and closes at 7 P.M. It's up to him how he schedules his eight-hour day within this thirteen-hour period. Because Brett is a morning person, shares childcare responsibility with his wife, who works the evening shift at a local food-processing plant, and has a seven-year-old son who gets out of school at 3 P.M., a flexible schedule motivates him. He's at the job when he's mentally most alert, and can be home to take care of his son after he gets out of school.

Most people continue to work an eight-hour day, five days a week. They are full-time employees who report to a fixed organizational location and start and leave at a fixed time. But, consistent with managers' attempts to increase their organizations' flexibility, a number of new scheduling options are being introduced to give management and employees more flexibility.[64] In addition to an increased use of temporary workers, which has been around for a long time, these include flextime, job sharing, and telecommuting.

Developing a Management Skill
DESIGNING JOBS

About the Skill: *As a manager, what can you do regarding job design so as to maximize your employees' performance? On the basis of the JCM and SIP models, we suggest that you improve the five core job dimensions.*

Steps in Practicing the Skill

1 ***Combine tasks.*** As a manager, you should put existing fractionalized tasks back together to form a new, larger module of work. This step increases skill variety and task identity.

2 ***Create natural work units.*** You should design tasks that form an identifiable and meaningful whole. This step increases employee "ownership" of the work and encourages your employees to view their work as meaningful and important rather than as irrelevant and boring.

3 ***Establish client relationships.*** The client is the user of the product or service that your employees work on. Whenever possible, you should establish direct relationships between your workers and their clients. This step increases skill variety, autonomy, and feedback for the employee.

4 ***Expand jobs vertically.*** Vertical expansion means giving employees responsibilities and controls that were formerly reserved for you, the manager. It partially closes the gap between the "doing" and "controlling" aspects of the job, and it increases employee autonomy.

5 ***Open feedback channels.*** Feedback tells employees not only learn how well they are performing their jobs but also whether their performances are improving, deteriorating, or remaining at a constant level. Ideally, employees should receive performance feedback directly as they do their jobs rather than from you on an occasional basis.[65]

How Does Flextime Work? Flextime is a scheduling option that allows employees, within specific parameters, to decide when to go to work. Brett Richardson's work schedule at AllState Insurance is an example of flextime. But what specifically is flextime?

flextime
Flexible work hours; usually arranged around six core hours and giving employees the freedom to decide for themselves when they will complete the remaining two hours of an eight-hour work day.

Flextime is short for flexible work hours. Employees have to work a specific number of hours a week, but they are free to vary the hours of work within certain limits. As shown in Exhibit 6-6, each day consists of a common core, usually six hours, with a flexibility band surrounding the core. For example, exclusive of a one-hour lunch break, the core may be 9:00 A.M. to 3:00 P.M., with the office actually opening at 6:00 A.M. and closing at 6:00 P.M. All employees are required to be at their jobs during the common core period, but they are allowed to accumulate their other two hours before or after the core time. Some flextime programs allow extra hours to be accumulated and turned into a free day off each month. Flextime has become an extremely popular scheduling option. For instance, a recent study of firms that have more than 1,000 employees found that 53 percent offered employees the option of flextime.[66]

The potential benefits from flextime are numerous. They include improved employee motivation and morale, reduced absenteeism as a result of enabling employees to better balance work and family responsibilities, and the ability of the organization to recruit higher-quality and more-diverse employees.[67]

Flextime's major drawback is that it is not applicable to every job. It works well with clerical tasks in which an employee's interaction with people outside his or her department is limited. It is not a viable option when key people must be available during standard hours, when work flow requires tightly determined scheduling, or when specialists are called upon to maintain coverage of all functions in a unit.[68]

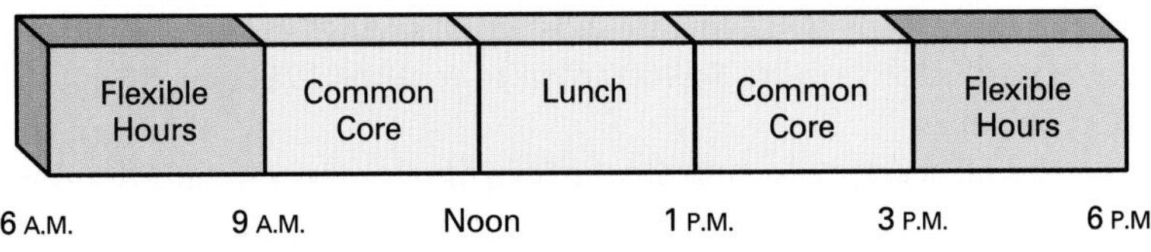

Exhibit 6-6
A Sample Flextime Schedule

Can Employees Share Jobs? Job sharing is a special type of part-time work. It allows two or more individuals to split a traditional forty-hour-a-week job. So, for example, one person might perform the job from 8 A.M. to noon, while another performs the same job from 1 P.M. to 5 P.M.; or the two could work full, but alternate, days.

job sharing
A special type of part-time work that allows two persons to split a traditional forty-hour-a-week job.

Job sharing is growing in popularity, but it is less widespread than flextime. Only about 30 percent of large organizations offer job sharing.[69] Xerox is one such organization. Laura Meier and Lori Meagher, for instance, share a sales management position at Xerox.[70] Both are mothers of preschoolers and wanted greater flexibility. But they did not want to give up their managerial careers at Xerox. So now Laura oversees their eight sales reps on Thursdays and Fridays, Lori has the job on Mondays and Tuesdays, and the two women work alternate Wednesdays.

Job sharing allows the organization to draw upon the talents of more than one individual for a given job. A bank manager who oversees two job sharers describes it as an opportunity to get two heads while "paying for one."[71] It also opens up the opportunity to acquire skilled workers—for instance, women with young children and retirees—who might not be available on a full-time basis.[72] The major drawback, from management's perspective, is finding compatible pairs of employees who can successfully coordinate the intricacies of one job.[73]

What Is Telecommuting? It might be close to the ideal job for many people. No commuting, flexible hours, freedom to dress as you please, and little or no interruptions from colleagues. It's called *telecommuting* and refers to employees who do their work at home on a computer that is linked to their office.[74] Currently, about 8.4 million people work at home in the United States doing things such as taking orders over the phone, filling out reports and other forms, and processing or analyzing information.[75] It is presently the fastest growing trend in work scheduling; one projection, for instance, predicts that more than 80 percent of all U.S. organizations will have at least 50 percent of their staff participating in some form of telecommuting by 1999.[76]

American Express Travel Services is one organization whose experience with telecommuting has been very positive.[77] In 1993, 100 AmEx travel agents in fifteen locations were telecommuters. The company can connect these people's homes to American Express's phone and data lines for a modest one-time expense of $1,300 each, including hardware. Once the connections are in place, calls to AmEx's reservation service are seamlessly routed to workers at home, where they can look up fares and book reservations on PCs. The typical telecommuting agent at AmEx handles 26 percent more calls at home than at the office. Why? One agent thinks it is due to an absence of distractions: "I don't feel like I'm working any harder. It's just that I don't have Suzy next to me telling me her husband is a jerk. I'm not worried about who's going into the boss's office, or noticing who's heading to the bathroom for the tenth time today." In addition, as more agents become telecommuters and free up office space, the company will generate substantial savings in rent. For instance, in New York City, it costs AmEx nearly $4,400 a year to rent the 125 square feet of space each travel agent occupies.

Not all employees embrace the idea of telecommuting. After the massive Los Angeles earthquake in January 1994, many L.A. firms began offering telecommuting for their workers.[78] It was popular for a week or two, but its popularity soon faded. Many workers complained that they were missing out on important meetings and informal interactions that led to new policies and ideas. The vast majority were willing to put up with two- and three-hour commutes while bridges and freeways were being rebuilt in order to maintain their social contacts at work.

The long-term future of telecommuting depends on some questions for which we do not yet have definitive answers. For instance, will employees who do their work at home be at a disadvantage in office politics? Might they be less likely to be considered for salary increases and promotions? Is being out of sight equivalent to being out of mind? Will non-work-related distractions, such as children, neighbors, and the proximity of the refrigerator, significantly reduce productivity for those without superior willpower and discipline?

Summary

How will I know if I fulfilled the Learning Objectives found on page 162? You will have fulfilled the Learning Objectives if you understand the following.

1. **Describe the formula for calculating productivity.** In its simplest form, productivity can be expressed in terms of the following ratio: outputs divided by labor plus capital plus materials.
2. **Explain how technology can improve productivity.** By substituting computerized equipment and machinery for human labor and traditional machinery, technology allows organizations to achieve increased levels of output with less labor, capital, and materials.
3. **Describe the advantages of computer-aided design.** Computer-aided design has essentially made manual drafting obsolete. It allows designers to create and evaluate alternative designs quickly, and it dramatically cuts the costs of developing prototypes. CAD lets engineers plan products, test them on the computer screen, and design tools to make the product.
4. **Explain what is meant by the term *just-in-time inventory systems.*** Just-in-time inventory systems change the technology around which inventories are managed. Inventory items arrive when they are needed in the production process instead of being stored in stock.
5. **Identify why management might consider introducing flexible manufacturing systems.** Flexible manufacturing systems provide management with the technology to meet customers' unique demands by producing nonstandardized products but with the efficiency associated with standardization.
6. **Define and describe the three key elements in reengineering.** The three key elements of reengineering are: (1) identifying an organization's distinctive competencies—the unique skills and resources that determine an organization's competitive weapons; (2) assessing core processes—the processes that customers value; and (3) reorganizing horizontally by process—this requires flattening the structure and relying more on teams.
7. **Explain how information technology is providing managers with decision support.** Expert systems, neural networks, groupware, and specific managerial problem-solving software are examples of information technologies that have been created to support and improve organizational decision making.

8. **Identify the five key dimensions in a job.** The five key dimensions in a job are skill variety, task identity, task significance, autonomy, and feedback.
9. **Describe how managers can design individual jobs to maximize employee performance.** Managers can design individual jobs to maximize employee performance by combining tasks, creating natural work units, establishing client relationships, expanding jobs vertically, and opening feedback channels.
10. **Explain how flextime, job sharing, and telecommuting increase organizational flexibility.** Flextime allows employees some discretion in choosing their work hours. Job sharing allows the organization to hire people who might not be available on a full-time basis, and it gives the organization two heads for the price of one. Telecommuting cuts the costs of maintaining a permanent work area for an employee and increases employee flexibility by cutting out commuting time and allowing workers to better balance work and family responsibilities.

Review & Discussion Questions

1. Explain how just-in-time systems improve productivity.
2. Describe how technology can improve an organization's customer service.
3. How might the Internet change organizations and management practice?
4. How do you think information technology will have reshaped the office by the year 2010?
5. What downside, if any, do you see for (a) the organization and (b) employees from replacing humans with computerized technology?
6. What are the implications of worker obsolescence on (a) society, (b) management practice, and (c) you, as an individual planning your career?
7. "Everyone wants a job that scores high on the five JCM dimensions." Build an argument to support this statement. Then negate that argument.
8. What is the managerial relevance of the Motivating Potential Score?
9. What can management do to improve employees' perceptions that their jobs are interesting and challenging?
10. Many managers see employees involved in job sharing as a burden—something that just makes their job more difficult to do. Why? What, if anything, can be done to minimize this disadvantage of job sharing?

Testing Your Comprehension • • • 

Circle the correct answer, then check yourself on page AK-1.

1. Technology is best defined as
   a) substituting machinery for human labor
   b) transferring inputs into outputs
   c) increasing the use of multimedia and interactive software
   d) none of the above

2. Increasing the efficient use of material inputs and supplies can be measured by
   a) cost per labor-hour productivity
   b) organizational productivity
   c) materials productivity
   d) outputs divided by labor plus capital plus materials

3. Which of the following statements is a benefit of computer-aided design?
   a) Computer-aided design has made manual drafting obsolete.
   b) Computer-aided design enhances customization in manufacturing.
   c) Computer-aided design involves computer-controlled machines and materials manipulation.
   d) All of the above are benefits of computer-aided design.

4. The Japanese word *kanban* is best associated with which of the following operations-technology concepts?
   a) robotics
   b) computer-aided design
   c) flexible manufacturing systems
   d) just-in-time inventory systems

5. Which of the following statements is correct regarding flexible manufacturing systems?
   a) Flexible manufacturing systems ensure that inventory items arrive when they are needed in the production process rather than being stored in stock.
   b) Flexible manufacturing systems permit organizations to rapidly change their production setups to more fully meet customers' needs.
   c) Flexible manufacturing systems permit an organization to more effectively meet customer needs, but do so at an increased cost per unit produced.
   d) Flexible manufacturing systems can be used to enhance information technology.

6. What is the point of the question "Is 99.9% good enough"?
   a) Sometimes good isn't good enough.
   b) Continuous process improvement will never reach perfection.
   c) TQM efforts have lost their luster in manufacturing corporations.
   d) TQM without reengineering will not achieve corporate goals of 100 percent effectiveness.

7. The process by which an organization improves how it creates documents and transfers the flow of information is best defined as
   a) information technology
   b) neural networks
   c) workflow automation
   d) computer-assisted information design

8. Expert systems
   a) use software programs to model how someone analyzes and solves an ill-structured problem
   b) use software programs to imitate the structure of the brain cells and the connections among them
   c) is a term used to describe software programs that help to facilitate group decision making
   d) enable managers with minimal statistical background to solve organizational problems that require quantitative techniques

9. You are a senior manager of a global manufacturing company. You would like to obtain input from several of your plant managers regarding the advantages and disadvantages of installing the newest robotic technology. Several thousand miles separate you and your plant managers, who are working on four continents. Given this background information, and your desire to involve them in making a decision, which of the following information technology support systems would you use to most efficiently get your managers' input?
   a) an expert system
   b) a neural network
   c) electronic mail
   d) groupware

10. Why have some workers' skills become obsolete in today's organizations?
   a) Reengineering has resulted in many employees' losing their jobs and thus not being given the opportunities to upgrade their skills on new equipment.
   b) Changes in technology are changing the demands of jobs and the skills employees need to do them.
   c) Repetitive tasks, once manually done, have been eliminated in most organizations.
   d) All of the above are reasons why some workers' skills have become obsolete in today's organizations.

11. What term describes a situation in which employees are free to work where they please and traditional office settings have been restructured to include more open spaces as opposed to formal offices?
   a) virtual reality
   b) office automation
   c) virtual workplace
   d) telecommuting

12. The degree to which the job requires an assortment of different activities so the worker can use a number of different skills and talents is best defined as
   a) autonomy
   b) task identity
   c) task significance
   d) none of the above

13. Which of the following was NOT identified in the job characteristics model as a core job dimension?
   a) skill ability
   b) task identity
   c) autonomy
   d) feedback

14. An inspector working at a nuclear plant recognizes that her job is important to members of the surrounding community. Given this perception, which of the five core job dimensions of the job characteristics model is being affected?
   a) autonomy
   b) task identity
   c) task significance
   d) feedback

15. The social information processing model argues that
   a) information technology contributes extensively to worker obsolescence
   b) employees adopt attitudes and behaviors in response to cues provided by others around them
   c) employees process information about the job's actual requirements and form their likes and dislikes about the job on the basis of factual data
   d) employee motivation and satisfaction are not affected by challenging or autonomous work

16. Requiring full-time employees to be in the office between 9:00 and 2:00 each day but permitting them to schedule the remaining work hours to match their individual needs represents which type of work schedule option?
   a) worker autonomy
   b) core work hours
   c) job sharing
   d) flextime

Applying the Concepts

Designing Motivating Jobs

Break into groups of four or five. You are a consulting team that has been hired by Indas, SA, a hygiene-related (e.g., diapers and sanitary napkins) product manufacturer located in Posuelo de Alarcon, Spain.[79] Indas has asked you to help solve a motivation/performance problem.

Indas is a family-owned business with annual revenues exceeding U.S. $63 million. The company employs 337 people in its production facility. Many of these jobs have been split up so that each person performs a single, routine task over and over again. For instance, there are employees whose responsibility it is to package the wrapped products into cases. Others push buttons and load plastic wrap into the automatic product wrapper. Employees have become dissatisfied with these mundane jobs, and this dissatisfaction shows in their work. Severe backlogs have developed, and error rates are unacceptably high. Your team's tasks are to (a) make suggestions for work redesign for the production employees and (b) identify how these changes are likely to affect production supervisors.

Your team has 30 minutes to complete these tasks.

Take It to the Net

We invite you to visit the Robbins/De Cenzo page on the Prentice Hall Web site at:

http://www.prenhall.com/robbinsfom

for this chapter's World Wide Web exercise.

You can also visit the Web sites for these companies featured within this chapter:

Bloomingdale's
http://www.bloomingdales.com

Coors Brewing
http://www.catalogsite.com/Gen/Coors_p1.html

Domino's Pizza
http://www.dominos.com

John Deere
http://www.arends–sons.com

Neiman Marcus
http://www.neimanmarcus.com

Turbo Tax
http://www.intuit.com/turbotax

Thinking Critically

Making a Value Judgment: Using Technology to Monitor Employees' Behavior

Technological advancements have provided managers in organizations many opportunities to become more efficient in their operations and more effective in attaining their strategic goals. But some of these technologies may also have some other uses. For instance, if you work for Nissan Motors in almost any of their jobs and use their e-mail system, your computer messages may be routinely read by your manager.[80] And he or she has every right to do so! Suppose that, in the past, you made some derogatory e-mail comments about your manager to friends both inside and outside of the organization. And your manager is using that information against you. Or suppose that your are a loyal employee of the Boston Sheraton Hotel. Would you be upset to know that you are being secretly videotaped in the restroom at the hotel? Would you feel differently if the videotaping were designed to monitor "bathroom" behavior in hopes of ridding from the premises substance abusers and drug dealers? Technology today makes it possible, even easy, for companies to monitor their employees' behavior. And many do so in the hopes that it will help all organizational members to become more productive and more quality-oriented. But an appropriate question for employees is: When does this high-tech snooping become unethical?

Just how pervasive is this practice of monitoring employees? Exact numbers are not known, but guesstimates in the millions appear reasonable. For example, call most 800 customer service numbers, like that of Gateway 2000, and you'll likely hear a message telling you that calls are monitored for quality. Or recognize that networked computer stations can be monitored from a central location to assess "real time" productivity. Under such an arrangement, however, employers generally issue an "employee monitoring" policy, which details what is monitored, when, and how the information is used. In such instances, employees appear more tolerant of being monitored. Yet, these same employees appear to exhibit more stress-related symptoms than employees who are not monitored.

Are managers overstepping the bounds of decency and respect for employees? Consider that it is almost kids' play to monitor cellular phone conversations or to intercept and copy fax transmissions. Or take the case of Olivetti, which has employees wearing "smart badges." These identification devices can track the whereabouts of an employee. That can be helpful in having messages transferred to your location, but it also means that Olivetti managers are capable of knowing your every move.

Questions:

1. Technological advancements in information processing in the workplace can help enhance performance and provide valuable feedback to both the manager and the employee. But at what point do you believe a manager's need for information violates your right to privacy? Discuss.
2. How would you feel about working for a manager who reads your computer messages? What advice could you give to a coworker who doesn't know that this monitoring is taking place?

Reengineering at Greyhound: A Dog-Gone Shame!

Greyhound Lines Inc. benefited greatly when its new management team sought to reengineer the company. But the benefit wasn't in any fundamental improvement in the organization. The only thing that really benefited was the company's stock, and then only in the short term. The following highlights a three-year period in the life of Greyhound.[81]

The Greyhoud saga begins in October 1991. Greyhound was emerging from bankruptcy brought on by a decline in the bus industry. For instance, because of increased automobile ownership and discounted airline seats, the bus industry's share of interstate travel dropped from 30 percent to 6 percent between 1960 and 1990. The company was now being largely run by CEO Frank Schmieder, a former merchant banker, and the company's chief financial officer, J. Michael Doyle. Schmieder and Doyle believed that Greyhound could survive only by undertaking a massive reorganization. So that's what they did. They began by cutting the work force, cutting routes and services, and reducing the bus fleet by one-third. Then they committed the company to "Trips," a custom-designed computerized reservation system. Wall Street was so impressed by management's reengineering plan that the company's stock more than doubled in the first month following emergence from bankruptcy.

But there were problems aplenty that Wall Street never saw. What were those problems? Lousy customer service and a failed reservation system top the list. Cutbacks had quickly hurt customer service. Experienced regional executives were being fired and replaced with part-time workers and "customer-service associates," who, whether sweeping floors or selling tickets, were paid about $6 an hour. Management reasoned that if people stayed too long, they would get sour and cynical. The result: Turnover approached 100 percent annually. And customer surveys began regularly identifying employee discourtesy as a major problem. Random checks by management, for instance, found terminal workers making fun of customers and ignoring them.

Meanwhile, as ridership faltered and customer service deteriorated, management and Wall Street analysts spoke as if a turnaround was a sure thing. Trips was the primary source of this optimism. Trips would replace Greyhound's antiquated manual methods for allocating buses and drivers. It would dramatically increase productivity and cut operating costs. At least that's what was promised. But the Trips development team was unable to deal with the program's complexity and management's pressure to bring the system on-line. Technicians estimated that the system had to be capable of managing as many as 1,800 vehicle stops a day, more than ten times those of the average airline. And, while American Airlines spent years and several hundred million dollars perfecting its Sabre reservation system, Greyhound's management provided its development team only $6 million to do the job and expected the system to be up and running by April 1993. The team did the best it could to meet management's unrealistic deadline. But, not surprisingly, the final product was a disaster. It took far more training than terminal workers were given; it didn't include all Greyhound destinations; and because of the data overload, the system regularly crashed. The typical time it took a worker to issue a ticket doubled.

Meanwhile, during all this chaos, Wall Street analysts were still optimistic—more out of ignorance than anything else. Greyhound stock continued to rise throughout 1992 and into the summer of 1993. The stock's demise began in August 1993, when the company announced that ridership had fallen 12 percent in the previous month and earnings were down. Schmieder was forced to resign later that month, and three weeks later Doyle resigned. From a high of $22.75 a share in May 1993, the company's stock was selling for just over $2 a share by October 1994. As one bondholder put it, "They [Greyhound's management] reengineered that business to hell."

Questions:

1. "There is a tendency in business these days to applaud anything resembling reengineering. Comprehensive change is seen as always good." Relate this comment to the Greyhound case.
2. Are reengineering and first-rate customer service compatible goals? Discuss.
3. If you had been the CEO at Greyhound, would you have done anything differently than Schmieder did? Explain.

Video Case — ABCNEWS

Policing the Information Highway

The information age has quickly become a major component in sharing data among many different peoples in all parts of the global economy. One tool of the information age, the Internet, is quickly becoming a staple for anyone needing information on almost any subject. The Internet, too, is providing jobs for thousands of individuals. It's giving people opportunities to reach others anywhere on the globe. It's creating opportunities that a decade ago were considered unimaginable. But it's also creating a major legal quagmire for David LaMacchia.

LaMacchia is what many people would refer to as a computer hacker. As a student at MIT, LaMacchia developed a bulletin board that was designed to provide an array of services. One of them was to review software, give those contacting the bulletin board an opportunity to exchange information about software programs, trade software, or even download certain software programs. LaMacchia believed that his service would fulfill a particular need—giving individuals substantial information about a software product or even the chance to see what the program could do. The problem LaMacchia found, however, was that a good number of software programs that were available on his bulletin board were not what software developers considered "freeware"—software that developers freely permit Internet users to download and use. Instead, some of these programs were what developers considered "shareware," or commercial software. Even so, it was LaMacchia's contention that people downloading these packages could tweak them, refine them, and ultimately help the software developer produce a more sophisticated product. MIT officials, however, once they heard what LaMacchia was doing on their computers, turned the case over to the FBI. The FBI viewed LaMacchia's bulletin board as a violation of copyright laws and as wire fraud. But is it really?

David LaMacchia never personally transferred the programs. He simply provided information about them on his bulletin board. He didn't really have control over who visited his bulletin board or what actions those visitors took. And, under the law, software pirating is a crime only when there's a profit motive behind it. Copying and distributing software when there's no commercial advantage (i.e., profits) is not a crime! To LaMacchia, it's free speech.

On the other hand, each person who copies a software program on LaMacchia's bulletin board decreases the number of individuals who would legitimately purchase the product by one. His bulletin board, after all, had evolved into a swap shop for copyrighted software programs. Although he personally didn't benefit or make a profit from this action, more than a million dollars' worth of pirated software exchanged hands. That, according LaMacchia's accusers, "made him a computerized wheelman for a million dollar heist."

Questions:

1. Do you believe David LaMacchia has done anything wrong in establishing his bulletin board that resulted in more than a million dollars' worth of software being pirated? Why or why not?
2. Should LaMacchia be held responsible for the actions of the visitors to his bulletin board who actually copied the software? Explain your position.
3. "The information highway is changing too rapidly to be policed or even controlled." Do you agree or disagree with the statement? Defend your position.

Source: "Law and Order on the Information Highway," *ABC News Nightline,* May 2, 1994.

Basic Organization Designs

7

LEARNING OBJECTIVES

What will I be able to do after I finish this chapter?

1. **IDENTIFY** the six elements of organization structure.
2. **DESCRIBE** the advantages and disadvantages of work specialization.
3. **CONTRAST** authority and power.
4. **IDENTIFY** the five different ways by which management can departmentalize.
5. **CONTRAST** mechanistic and organic organizations.
6. **SUMMARIZE** the effect on organization structures of strategy, size, technology, and environment.
7. **CONTRAST** the divisional and functional structures.
8. **EXPLAIN** the strengths of the matrix structure.
9. **DESCRIBE** the boundaryless organization and what elements have contributed to its development.
10. **DESCRIBE** what is meant by the term *organization culture.*

HOW DOES A MANAGER TURN TERROR, confusion, and upheaval into understanding, cooperation, and success? Ask Sister M. Sylvia Egan.

In 1994 Sister Egan was the CEO of St. Francis Regional Medical Center in Wichita, Kansas. St. Francis had enjoyed almost 100 years of continuous growth since its founding.[1] Started in 1889 as a ten-bed hospital, the medical center had grown to an 800-bed facility by the mid-1980s. During that time, it competed very effectively with the three other area hospitals, typically keeping each of its 800 beds occupied. But, in the late 1980s, bed occupancy rates, and hospital revenues along with them, began to go down.

Health care in the United States has been a major topic of interest for health insurers, medical personnel, and politicians alike. At issue is an attempt to reduce escalating health care costs, many of which are associated with hospital stays. The health care environment had drastically changed, and many hospitals were caught in the middle. For example, several decades ago, a new mother enjoyed a relaxed stay in a hospital for nearly a week after giving birth. By 1996, that week had shrunk to just about twenty-four hours.

Hospitals saw bed utilization rates drop significantly. At St. Francis, for instance, in just over four years, there was more than a 20 percent decrease in daily rate (the number of beds filled each day). Funds to buy new equipment or offer additional quality services were shrinking. And that trend was expected to continue. Sister Egan realized that her hospital had to shift its strategic direction to caring for people on an outpatient basis as opposed to its nearly 100-year tradition of "classic" hospital operations. Once that decision had been reached, it was a given that the structure would need to change to facilitate the medical center's new direction.

Sister M. Sylvia Egan, former CEO of St. Francis Regional Medical Center, met with her managers to receive updates on the department's operations. Before restructuring, the department heads would not have been as directly involved with the CEO but would have communicated through several layers of management.

Sister Egan launched a two-year process of evaluating and implementing her new organization. Her goal was to "lead the Medical Center through challenging health care evolutions to a successful corporate restructuring so that St. Francis [could] continue to provide quality services." She began by eliminating all policies and dismantling the departmental structure. She didn't want to be constrained by the past or by the status quo. Sister Egan initiated the reorganizing process at the top. She reduced the number of departments reporting to her from six to three and structured each department around service areas. These service areas would encompass closely related service groups. For example, one area, Women and Children, included such service groups as maternal public education, in-patient pediatrics, labor and delivery, and the nursery. The impetus for this decision was to make the service areas more efficient and effective in providing quality medical services than the old departments had been.

Sister Sylvia viewed these changes as a "rebirth" of the hospital rather than as a slashing. But when restructuring occurs, some people are displaced. Sister Egan did not want to base personnel decisions on long-term relationships. Instead, she and the three vice presidents of the three service areas defined the management jobs that were needed on the basis of the strategic direction of the hospital. Once these new jobs had been defined, current management employees were informed, were told of the skills needed, and were invited to apply for any positions for which they felt qualified. The only catch was that there were some 200 fewer slots on the new organization chart. Obviously, that change had the potential for creating morale problems.

To support morale, Sister Egan launched concurrently a cultural change. She recognized that communications would be the key. People who were going to be laid off had to be told as quickly as possible. Although these would be trying times, affected employees had to be prepared for the separation. The survivors, too, needed to know what was going on. They needed to know who they would report to and what authority they had. As a result of the reorganizing, employees at all levels in the organization were empowered to make decisions that affected their work. And, to keep communication channels as current as possible, Sister Egan moved the three vice presidents out of "executive row" and into open office spaces in the service areas they led.

In the end, Sister Sylvia Egan successfully reorganized her hospital. Decisions were being made more efficiently than ever before, and patient-response time had been reduced. St. Francis was competing more effectively with the other area hospitals, had stopped the decline in its bed utilization rate, had increased patient satisfaction, and had improved its financial picture. On October 1, 1995, St. Francis Ministry Corporation and CSJ Health System united to form Via Christi Health System.

Yoichi Morishita, president of Matsushita—the world's largest consumer electronics company—has embarked on a major organization design effort in an attempt to improve white-collar productivity and simplify the organization. He has transferred 6,000 administrators to production units, centralized research and development under his direct control, and decentralized to division chiefs everything else—including personnel matters, product development, and financial control.

The St. Francis Medical Center example demonstrates the importance of having the right structure in an organization. In this chapter, we will present the foundations of organization structure. We will define the concept and its key components, introduce organization design options, consider contingency variables that determine when certain design options work better than others, and explore the concept of organization culture.

Once certain organizational members have made decisions regarding corporate strategies, they must develop an effective structure that will best facilitate the attainment of those goals. Recall from Chapter 1 that we defined *organizing* as the function of management that creates the organization's structure. When managers develop or change the organization's structure, we say they are engaging in **organization design.** This process involves making decisions about how specialized jobs should be allocated, the rules to guide employees' behaviors, and at what level decisions are to be made. Organization design decisions are typically made by senior managers. Occasionally, perhaps, they might seek input from midlevel managers, but lower-level managers and operatives rarely have an opportunity for giving input. Nonetheless, it still is important to understand the process. Why? Because each of us works in some type of organization structure, and we need to know why we are "grouped" as we are. In addition, given the changing environment and the need for organizations to rapidly adapt, we should begin our understanding of what "tomorrow's" structures may look like.

organization design
A process in which managers develop or change their organization's structure.

As you read this chapter, recognize that the organization design material presented throughout will apply to any type of organization—whether it's a business enterprise interested in making profits for its owners or a not-for-profit organization that provides service to specialized customers (such as St. Francis Medical Center or your college) or to the community at large (such as the U.S. Postal Service or your local sanitation department).

The Elements of Structure

The basic concepts of organization design were formulated by management writers in the early years of this century. These theorists offered a set of principles for managers to follow in organization design. More than six decades have passed since most of those principles were originally proposed. Given the passing of that much time and all the changes that have taken place in our society, you might think that they would be pretty worthless today. Surprisingly, they're not. For the most part, these principles still provide valuable insights into designing effective and efficient organizations. Of course, we have also gained a great deal of knowledge over the years as to their limitations. In the following sections, we will discuss the six elements of structure: work specialization, chain of command, span of control, authority and responsibility, centralization versus decentralization, and departmentalization.

What Is Work Specialization?

Work specialization has been around for centuries in industrialized countries. In fact, back in the 1700s when economist Adam Smith published his book *Wealth of Nations,* he advocated that jobs should be divided into smaller parts. In **work specialization,** a job is broken down into a number of steps and each step is completed by a separate individual. In essence, individuals specialize in doing part of an activity rather than the entire activity. Installing only the mother boards and hard-disk drives in a computer assembly line is an example of work specialization. So, too, are the specific tasks crew members perform each time they make french fries at McDonald's.

work specialization
A component of organization structure that involves having each discrete step of a job done by a different individual rather than having one individual do the whole job.

Work specialization makes efficient use of the diversity of skills that workers hold. In most organizations, some tasks require highly developed skills; others can be performed by the those who have lower skill levels. If all workers were engaged in all the steps of, say, a manufacturing process, all would have to have the skills necessary to perform both the most demanding and the least demanding jobs. The result would be that, except when performing the most highly skilled or highly sophisticated tasks, employees would be working below their skill level. In addition, skilled workers are paid more than unskilled workers, and, because wages tend to reflect the highest level of skill, all workers would be being paid at highly skilled rates to do easy tasks—an inefficient use of resources. That is why you rarely find a cardiac surgeon "closing up" a patient after surgery. Persons not as skilled in open heart surgery or those learning the skill are usually the ones who stitch and staple the patient after the surgeon has performed bypass surgery.

Work specialization makes efficient use of the diversity of skills that workers hold.

Early proponents of work specialization believed that it could lead to infinitely increasing productivity. At the turn of the twentieth century and earlier, that generalization was reasonable. Because specialization was not widely practiced, its introduction almost always generated higher productivity. But a good thing can be carried too far. There is a point at which the human diseconomies from division of labor—which surface as boredom, fatigue, stress, low productivity, poor quality, increased absenteeism, and high turnover—exceed the economic advantages (see Exhibit 7-1).

By the 1960s, that point had been reached in a number of jobs. In such cases, productivity could be increased by enlarging, rather than narrowing, the scope of job activities.[2] For instance, successful efforts to increase productivity included giving employees a variety of activities to do, allowing them to do a whole and complete piece of work, and putting them together into teams. Those are some of the primary features of the job characteristics model (Chapter 6). Each of those ideas, of course, runs counter to the work specialization concept. Yet, overall, work specialization is alive and well in most organizations today. We have to recognize the economies it provides in certain types of jobs, but we also have to recognize its limitations.

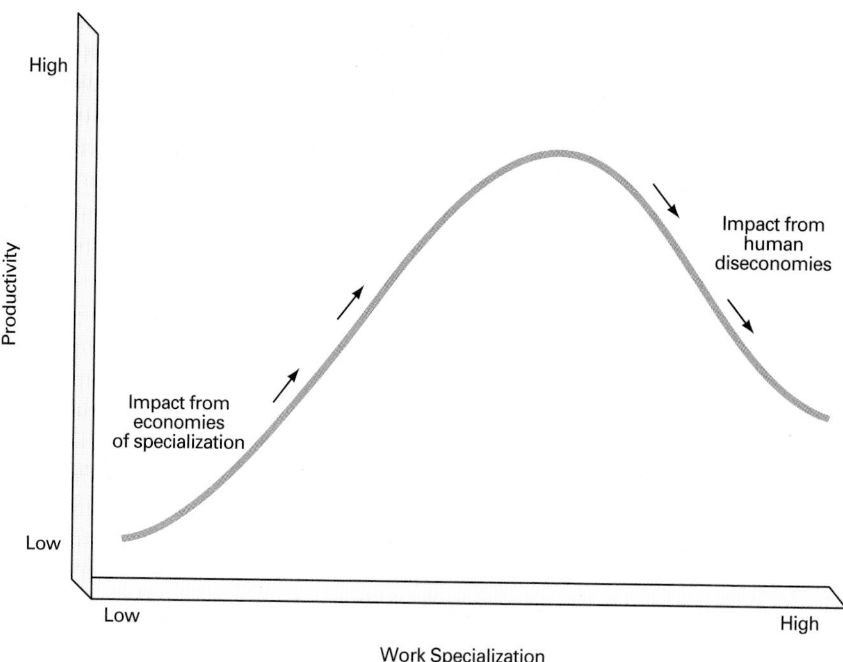

Exhibit 7-1
Economies and Diseconomies of Work Specialization

What Is the Chain of Command?

chain of command
The management principle that no person should report to more than one boss.

The early management writers argued that an employee should have one and only one superior to whom he or she is directly responsible. An employee who had to report to two or more bosses might have to cope with conflicting demands or priorities.[3] In those rare instances when the **chain of command** principle had to be violated, early management writers' viewpoint always explicitly designated that there be a clear separation of activities and a supervisor responsible for each.

The chain of command concept was logical when organizations were comparatively simple. Under many circumstances it is still sound advice—even some contemporary organizations adhere to it. Yet there are instances, which we will introduce later in this chapter, when strict adherence to the chain of command creates a degree of inflexibility that hinders an organization's performance.[4]

What Is the Span of Control?

span of control
The number of employees a manager can direct efficiently and effectively.

How many employees can a manager efficiently and effectively direct? This question of **span of control** received a great deal of attention from early management writers. Although there was no consensus on a specific number, the early writers favored small spans—typically no more than six—in order to maintain close control.[5] However, several writers did acknowledge level in the organization as a contingency variable. They argued that as a manager rises in an organization, he or she has to deal with a greater number of ill-structured problems, so top managers need a smaller span than do middle managers, and middle managers require a smaller span than do supervisors. Over the last decade, however, we are seeing some change in thinking about effective spans of control.

Many organizations are increasing their spans of control. The span for managers at such companies as General Electric and Reynolds Metals has expanded to ten or twelve employees—twice the number of fifteen years ago.[6] The span of control is increasingly being determined by looking at contingency variables.[7] It is obvious that the more training and experience employees have, the less direct supervision they need. Managers who have well-trained and experienced employees can function with a wider span. Other contingency variables that will determine the appropriate span include similarity of employee tasks, the complexity of those tasks, the physical proximity of employees, the degree to which standardized procedures are in place, the sophistication of the organization's management information system, the strength of the organization's value system, and the preferred managing style of the manager.[8]

Who says that government bureaucracy is unbreakable? Don't tell that to Nora Statkin, the executive director of the Central Intelligence Agency (CIA). She believes that even a "stubbornly resistant" bureaucracy can be reinvented. For this $3 billion, 17,000-member organization, that means changing its structure by centralizing the agency's human resources and career development practices and making CIA employees accountable not only to their immediate boss but also to her and to Congress.

What Are Authority and Responsibility?

Authority refers to the rights inherent in a managerial position to give orders and expect the orders to be obeyed. Authority was a major tenet of the early management writers; it was viewed as the glue that held the organization together. It was to be delegated downward to lower-level managers, giving them certain rights while providing certain prescribed limits within which to operate (see Details on a Management Classic). Each management position has specific inherent rights that incumbents acquire from the position's rank or title. Authority, therefore, is related to one's position within an organization and ignores the personal characteristics of the individual manager. It has nothing directly to do with the individual. The expression "The king is dead; long live the king" illustrates the concept. Whoever is king acquires the rights inherent in the king's position. When a position of authority is vacated, the person who has left the position no longer has any authority. The authority remains with the position and its new incumbent.

When managers delegate authority, they must allocate commensurate **responsibility.** That is, when employees are given rights, they also assume a corresponding obligation to perform. Allocating authority without responsibility creates opportunities for abuse, and no one should be held responsible for something over which he or she has no authority.

Are There Different Types of Authority Relationships? The early management writers distinguished between two forms of authority: line authority and staff authority. **Line authority** entitles a manager to direct the work of an employee. It is the employer-employee authority relationship that extends from the top of the organization to the lowest echelon, according to the chain of command, as shown in Exhibit 7-2. As a link in the chain of command, a manager with line authority has the right to direct the work of employees and to make certain decisions without consulting anyone. Of course, in the chain of command, every manager is also subject to the direction of his or her superior.

authority
The rights inherent in a managerial position to give orders and expect them to be obeyed.

responsibility
An obligation to perform assigned activities.

line authority
The authority that entitles a manager to direct the work of an employee.

Sometimes the term *line* is used to differentiate line managers from staff managers. In this context, *line* emphasizes managers whose organizational function contributes directly to the achievement of organizational objectives. In a manufacturing firm, line managers are typically in the production and sales functions, whereas managers in human resources and payroll are considered staff managers. These staff managers have staff authority. But whether a manager's function is classified as line or staff depends on the organization's objectives. For example, at Staff-Builders, a supplier of temporary employees, interviewers have a line function. Similarly, at the payroll firm of ADP, payroll is a line function.

As organizations get larger and more complex, line managers find that they do not have the time, expertise, or resources to get their jobs done effectively. In response,

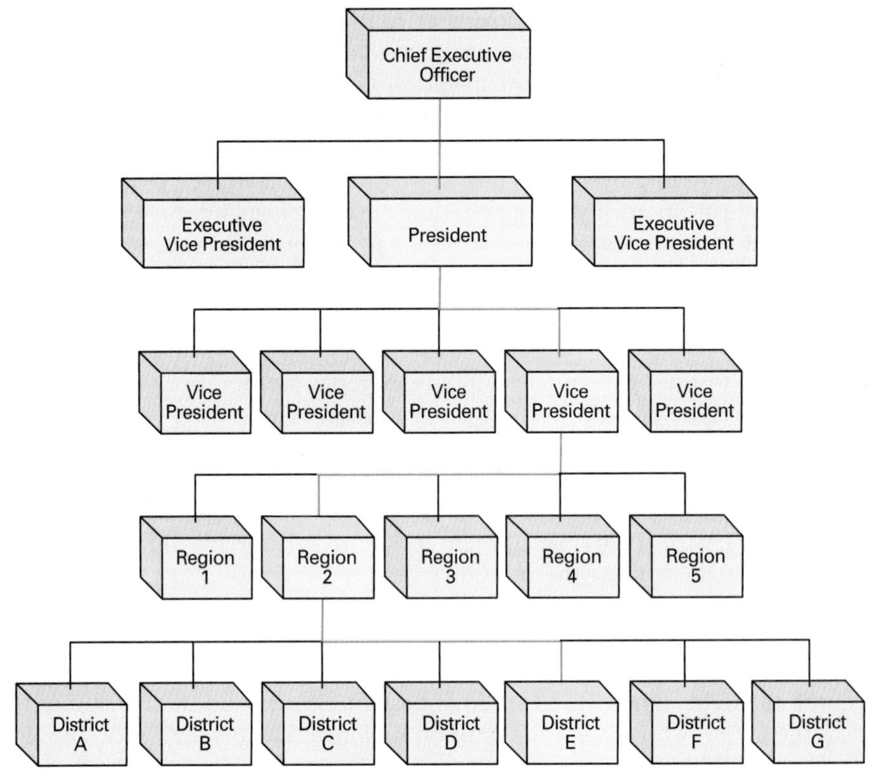

Exhibit 7-2
Chain of Command

Details on a Management Classic

STANLEY MILGRAM AND FOLLOWING ORDERS

Stanley Milgram, a social psychologist at Yale University, wondered how far individuals would go in following orders.[9] If subjects were placed in the role of a teacher in a learning experiment and told by the experimenter to administer a shock to a learner each time that learner made a mistake, would the subjects follow the commands of the experimenter? Would their willingness to comply decrease as the intensity of the shock was increased?

To answer those questions, Milgram hired a set of subjects. Each was led to believe that the experiment was to investigate the effect of punishment on memory. Their job was to act as teachers and administer punishment whenever the learner made a mistake on a learning test. Punishment in this case was an electric shock. The subject sat in front of a shock generator with thirty levels of shock—beginning at zero and progressing in 15-volt increments to a high of 450 volts. The demarcations of these positions ranged from "slight shock" at 15 volts to "danger: severe shock" at 450 volts. The subjects—who had received a sample shock of 45 volts—were able to see the learner strapped in an electric chair in an adjacent room. Of course, the learner was an actor, and the electric shocks were phony—but the subjects didn't know that.

The subjects were instructed to shock the learner each time he made a mistake. And subsequent mistakes would result in an increase in shock intensity. Throughout the experiment, the subject got verbal feedback from the learner. At 75 volts, the learner began to grunt and moan; at 150 volts, he demanded to be released from the experiment; at 180 volts he cried out that he could no longer stand the pain; and at 300 volts, he insisted he be let out because of a heart condition. After 300 volts, the learner did not respond to further questions.

Most subjects protested and, fearful that they might kill the learner if the increased shocks were to bring on a heart attack, insisted that they could not go on. But the experimenter responded by saying that they had to, that was their job. Most of the subjects dissented. But dissension isn't synonymous with disobedience. Sixty-two percent of the subjects increased the shock level to the maximum of 450 volts. The average level of shock administered by the remaining 38 percent was nearly 370 volts—more than enough to kill even the strongest human!

What can we conclude from Milgram's results? Well, one obvious conclusion is that authority is a potent source of getting people to do things. Subjects in Milgram's experiment administered levels of shock far above what they felt comfortable giving. They did it because they were told they had to, despite the fact that they could have walked out of the room any time they wanted.

they create **staff authority** functions to support, assist, advise, and generally reduce some of the informational burdens they have. The hospital administrator cannot effectively handle the purchasing of all the supplies the hospital needs, so she creates a purchasing department. The purchasing department is a staff department. Of course, the head of the purchasing department has line authority over her subordinate purchasing agents. The hospital administrator might also find that she is overburdened and needs an assistant. In creating the position of assistant to the hospital administrator, she has created a staff position. Exhibit 7-3 illustrates line and staff authority.

staff authority
Positions that have some authority but that are created to support, assist, and advise the holders of line authority.

Exhibit 7-3
Line versus Staff Authority

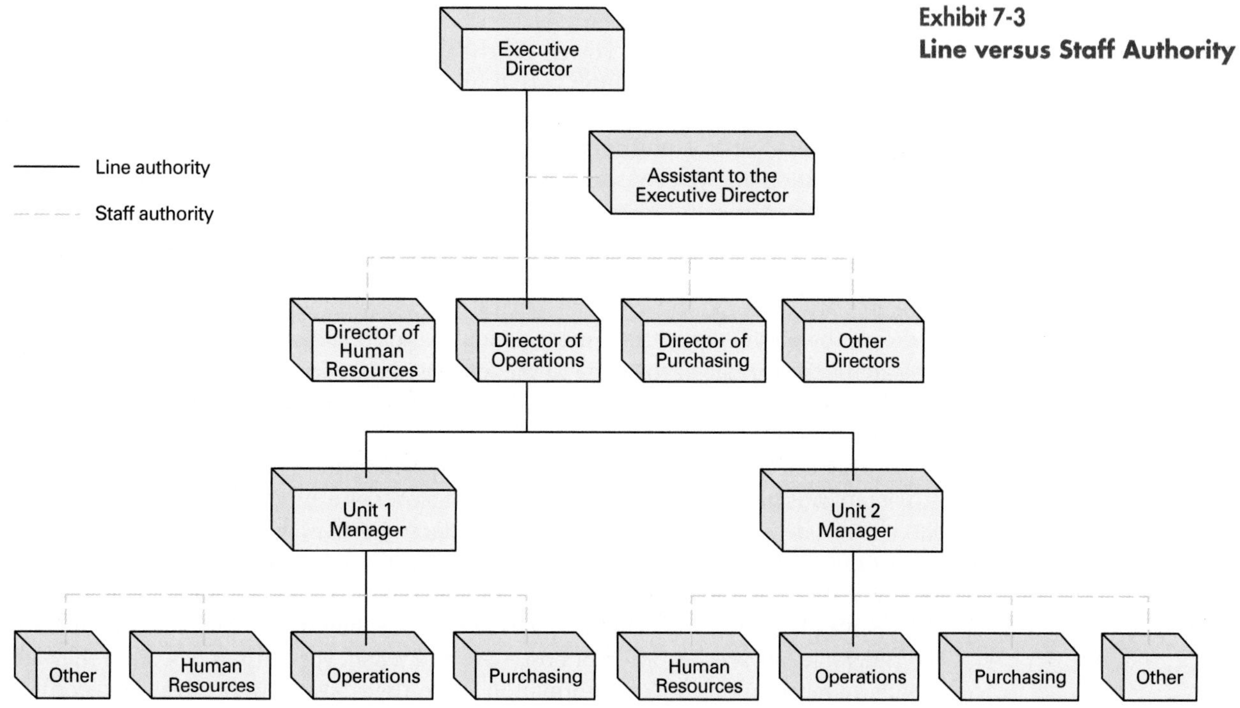

How Does the Contemporary View of Authority and Responsibility Differ from the Historical View? The early management writers were enamored with authority. They actively assumed that the rights inherent in one's formal position in an organization were the sole source of influence. They believed that managers were all-powerful. This might have been true sixty or more years ago. Organizations were simpler. Staff was less important. Managers were only minimally dependent on technical specialists. Under such conditions, influence is the same as authority. And the higher a manager's position in the organization, the more influence he or she had. However, those conditions no longer hold. Researchers and practitioners of management now recognize that you do not have to be a manager to have power, nor is power perfectly correlated with one's level in the organization.

Authority is an important concept in organizations, but an exclusive focus on authority produces a narrow, unrealistic view of influence in organizations. Today, we recognize that authority is but one element in the larger concept of power.[10]

How Do Authority and Power Differ? The terms *authority* and *power* are frequently confused. Authority is a right, the legitimacy of which is based on the authority figure's position in the organization. Authority goes with the job. **Power,** on the other hand, refers to an individual's capacity to influence decisions. Authority is part of the larger concept of power. That is, the formal rights that come with an individual's position in the organization are just one means by which an individual can affect the decision process.

power
An individual's capacity to influence decisions.

Exhibit 7-4 visually depicts the difference between authority and power. The two-dimensional arrangement of boxes in part A portrays authority. The area in which the authority applies is defined by the horizontal dimension. Each horizontal grouping represents a functional area. The influence one holds in the organization is defined by the vertical dimension in the structure. The higher one is in the organization, the greater one's authority.

You do not have to be a manager to have power.

Power, on the other hand, is a three-dimensional concept (the cone in part B of Exhibit 7-4). It includes not only the functional and hierarchical dimensions but also a third dimension called *centrality.* While authority is defined by one's vertical position in the hierarchy, power is made up of both one's vertical position and one's distance from the organization's power core, or center.

Think of the cone in Exhibit 7-4 as being an organization. The center of the cone is the power core. The closer you are to the power core, the more influence you have on decisions. The existence of a power core is, in fact, the only difference between A and B in Exhibit 7-4. The vertical hierarchy dimension in A is merely one's level on the outer edge of the cone. The top of the cone corresponds to the top of the hierarchy, the middle of the cone to the middle of the hierarchy, and so on. Similarly, the functional groups in A become wedges in the cone. Each wedge represents a functional area.

The cone analogy explicitly acknowledges two facts: (1) The higher one moves in an organization (an increase in authority), the closer one moves to the power core; and (2) it is not necessary to have authority in order to wield power because one can move horizontally inward toward the power core without moving up. For instance, have you ever noticed that administrative assistants are "powerful" in a company even though they have little authority? Often, as gatekeepers for their bosses, these assistants have considerable say over whom their bosses see and when. Furthermore, because they are regularly relied upon to pass information on to their bosses, they have some control

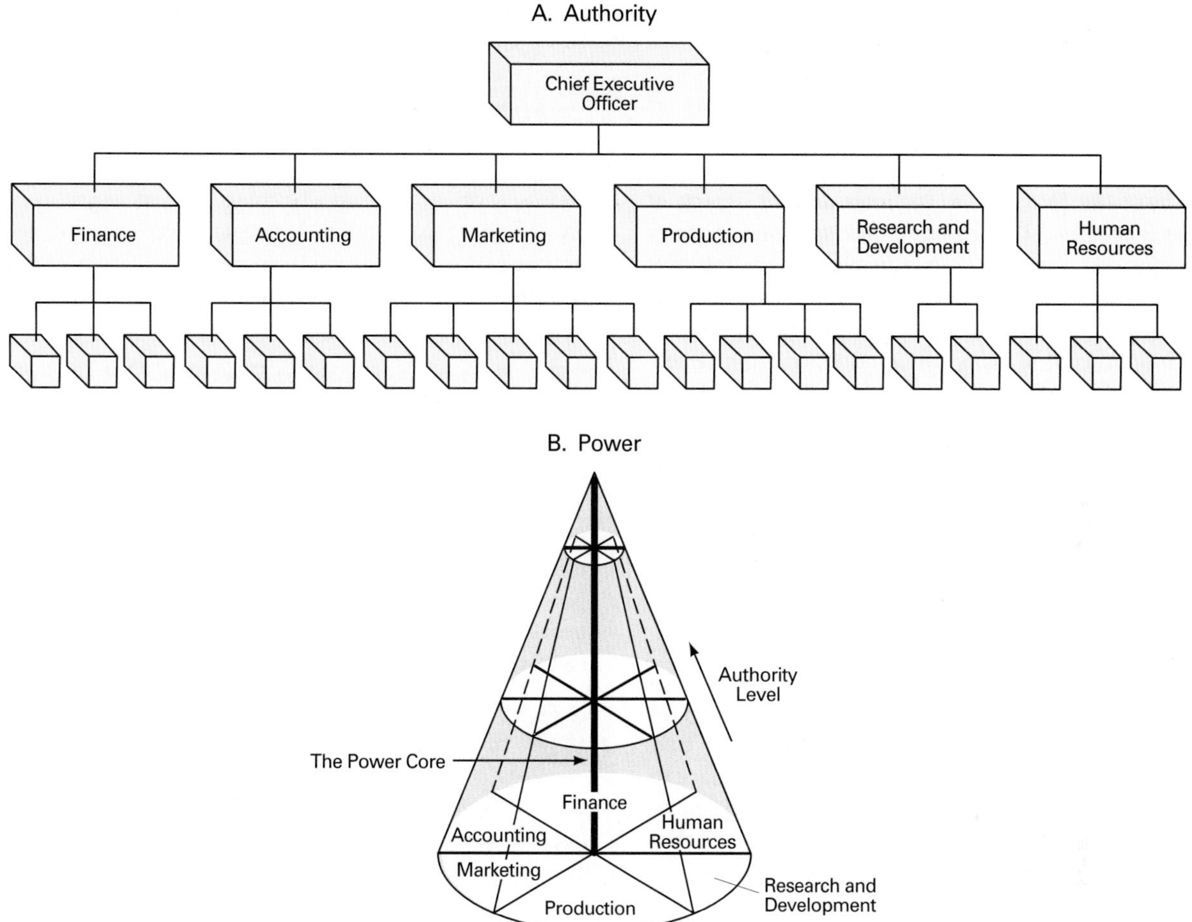

Exhibit 7-4
Authority versus Power

over what their bosses hear. It is not unusual for $95,000 a year middle managers to tread very carefully in order not to upset their boss's $35,000 a year administrative assistant. Why? Because the assistant has power! This individual may be low in the authority hierarchy but close to the power core.

Low-ranking employees who have relatives, friends, or associates in high places might also be close to the power core. So, too, are employees with scarce and important skills. The lowly production engineer with twenty years of experience in a company might be the only one in the firm who knows the inner workings of all the old production machinery. When pieces of this old equipment break down, no one but this engineer understands how to fix them. Suddenly, the engineer's influence is much greater than it would appear from his or her level in the vertical hierarchy. What does this tell us about power? It states that power can come from different areas (see Developing a Management Skill). John French and Bertram Raven have identified five sources, or bases, of power: coercive, reward, legitimate, expert, and referent.[11] We have summarized them in Exhibit 7-5.

Developing a Management Skill
BUILDING A POWER BASE

About the Skill: *One of the more difficult aspects of power is acquiring it. For some individuals, power comes naturally, and, for some, it is a function of the job they hold. But what can others do to develop power? The answer is respect others, build power relationships, develop associations, control important information, gain seniority, and build power in stages.*[12]

Steps in practicing the skill

1. ***Respect others.*** One of the most crucial aspects of developing power is to treat others the way you would like to be treated. That sentence may be a cliché, but it holds a tremendous key for you. If others don't respect you, your power will generally be limited. Sure, they may do the things you ask, but only because of the authority of your position. People need to know that you're genuine—and that means respecting others! In today's world, with the great diversity that exists, you must be sensitive to others' needs. Failure to do so may only lead to problems, most of which can be avoided if you see the good in people and realize that most people try their best and want to do a good job.

2. ***Build power relationships.*** People who possess power often associate with others who also have power. It appears to be a natural phenomenon—birds of a feather do flock together! You need to identify who these people are and model their behavior.[13] The idea is that you want to make yourself visible to "powerful" people and let them observe you in a number of situations.

3. ***Develop associations.*** We learned at an early age that there is strength in numbers. In the "power" world, this tenet also applies. By associating with others, you become part of a group in which all the members' energies are brought together to form one large base of power. Often called coalitions, these groups form to influence some event.

4. ***Control important information.*** Get yourself into a position that gives you access to information other people perceive as important. Access to information is especially critical in a world where people's lives depend so much on information processing. One of the greatest means of developing this power is to continue to learn. Finding new approaches to solve old problems or creating a special process are ways of gaining a level of expertise that can make you indispensable to the organization.

5. ***Gain seniority.*** Seniority is somewhat related to controlling information. Power can be gained by simply having been around for a long time. People will often respect individuals who have lived through the ups and downs of an organization. Their experience gives them a perspective or information that newcomers don't have.

6. ***Build power in stages.*** No one goes from being powerless one moment to being powerful the next. That simply doesn't occur. Power comes in phases. As you build your power, remember, it will start off slowly. You will be given opportunities to demonstrate that you can handle the power. After each test you "pass," you'll more than likely be given more power.

centralization
A function of how much decision-making authority is pushed down to lower levels in an organization; the more centralized an organization is, the higher is the level at which decisions are made.

How Do Centralization and Decentralization Differ?

One of the questions that needs to be answered in the organizing function is At what level are decisions made? **Centralization** is a function of how much decision-making authority is pushed down to lower levels in the organization. Centralization-decentralization, however, is not an either-or concept. Rather, it's a degree phenomenon. By that we mean that no organization is completely centralized or completely decentralized. Few, if any, organizations could effectively function if all their decisions were made by a select few people (centralization) or if all decisions were pushed down

Coercive power	Power based on fear
Reward power	Power based on the ability to distribute something that others value
Legitimate power	Power based on one's position in the formal hierarchy
Expert power	Power based on one's expertise, special skill, or knowledge
Referent power	Power based on identification with a person who has desirable resources or personal traits

Exhibit 7-5
Types of Power

to the lowest levels **(decentralization).** Let's look, then, at how the early management writers viewed centralization, as well as at how it exists today.

decentralization
The pushing down of decision-making authority to the lowest levels of an organization.

Early management writers proposed that centralization in an organization depended on the situation.[14] Their objective was the optimum and efficient use of employees. Traditional organizations were structured in a pyramid, with power and authority concentrated near the top of the organization. Given this structure, historically, centralized decisions were the most prominent. But organizations today have become more complex and are responding to dynamic changes in their environments. As such, many managers believe that decisions need to be made by those individuals closest to the problems faced—regardless of their organizational level. In fact, the trend over the past three decades—at least in U.S. and Canadian organizations—has been movement toward more decentralization in organizations.[15]

Today, managers often choose the amount of centralization or decentralization that will allow them to best implement their decisions and achieve organizational goals. What works in one organization, however, won't necessarily work in another. So managers must determine the amount of decentralization for each organization and work units within it. For instance, at Motorola, while many production decisions are pushed down to lower levels in the organization, or even outside to some suppliers, financial and product distribution decisions remain in the hands of senior management.[16] You may also recall that, in Chapter 2, one of the central themes of our discussion of empowering employees was to give them the "authority" to make decisions on those things that affect their work and to change the way that they think about work.[17] That's the issue of decentralization at work! Notice, however, that it doesn't imply that senior management no longer makes decisions!

Can You Identify the Five Ways to Departmentalize?

Early management writers argued that activities in the organization should be specialized and grouped into departments. Work specialization creates specialists who need coordination. This coordination is facilitated by putting specialists together in departments under the direction of a manager. Creation of these departments is typically based on the work functions being performed, the product or service being offered, the target customer or client, the geographic territory being covered, or the process being used to turn inputs into outputs. No single method of departmentalization was advocated by the early writers. The method or methods used should reflect the grouping that would best contribute to the attainment of the organization's objectives and the goals of individual units.

What Do the Five Departmentalizations Look Like? One of the most popular ways to group activities is by functions performed, or **functional departmentalization.** A manager might organize his or her plant by separating engineering, accounting, information systems, human resources, and purchasing specialists into common departments (see Exhibit 7-6). Functional departmentalization can be used in all

functional departmentalization
The grouping of activities by functions performed.

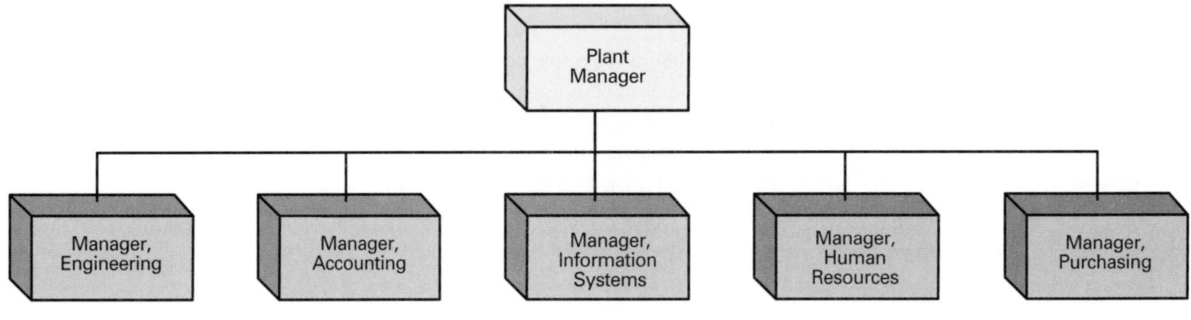

Exhibit 7-6
Functional Departmentalization

types of organizations. Only the functions change to reflect the organization's objectives and activities. A hospital might have departments devoted to research, patient care, accounting, and so forth. A professional indoor soccer franchise might have departments labeled player personnel, ticket sales, and travel and accommodations.

product departmentalization The grouping of activities by product produced.

Exhibit 7-7 illustrates the **product departmentalization** method used at Bombadier Ltd., a Canadian company. Each major product area in the corporation is placed under the authority of a senior manager who is a specialist in, and is responsible for, everything having to do with his or her product line. Another company that uses product departmentalization is L.A. Gear. Its structure is based on its varied product lines, which include women's footwear, men's footwear, and apparel and accessories. If an organization's activities were service-related, rather than product-related—as are those of Bombardier and L.A. Gear—each service would be autonomously grouped. For instance, an accounting firm would have departments for taxes, manage-

Exhibit 7-7
Product Departmentalization

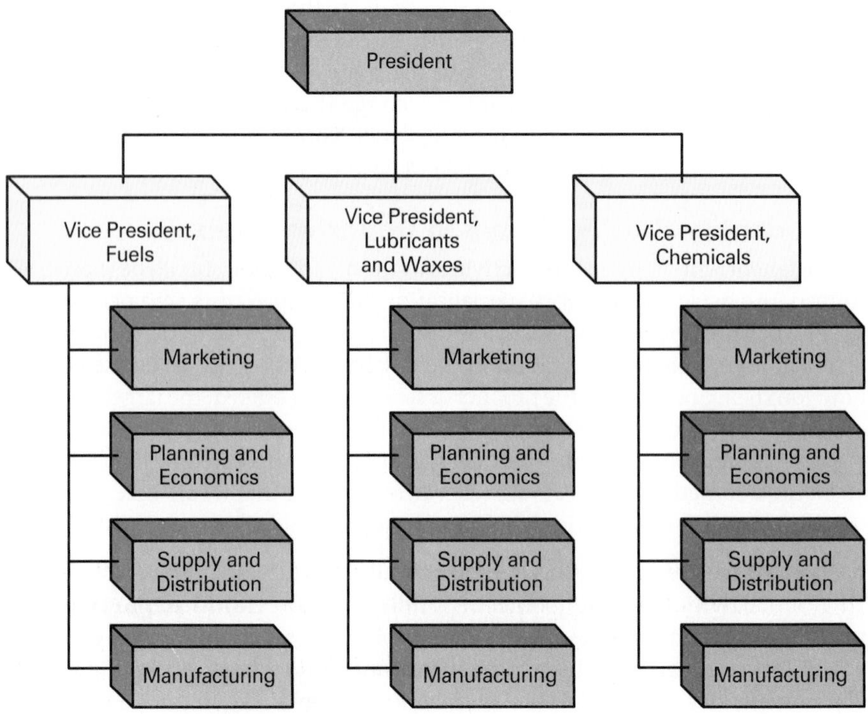

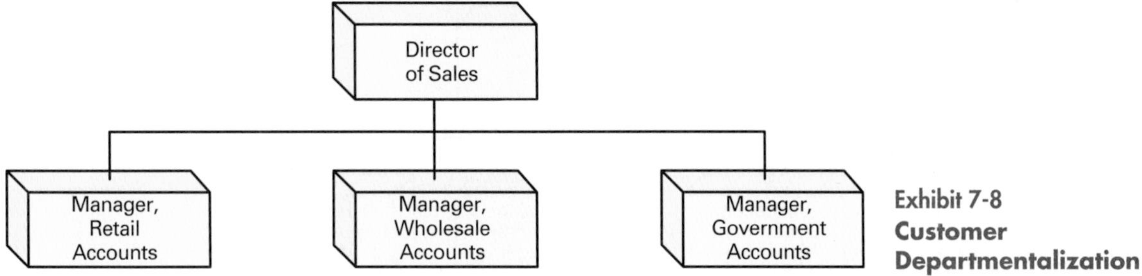

Exhibit 7-8
Customer Departmentalization

ment consulting, auditing, and the like. In such a case, each department offers a common array of services under the direction of a product or service manager.

The particular type of customer the organization seeks to reach can also be used to group employees. The sales activities in an office supply firm, for instance, can be broken down into three departments to serve retail, wholesale, and government customers (see Exhibit 7-8). A large law office can segment its staff on the basis of whether it serves corporate or individual clients. The assumption underlying **customer departmentalization** is that customers in each department have a common set of problems and needs that can best be met by having specialists for each.

customer departmentalization The grouping of activities by common customers.

geographic departmentalization The grouping of activities by territory.

Another way to departmentalize is on the basis of geography or territory—**geographic departmentalization.** The sales function might have western, southern, midwestern, and eastern regions (see Exhibit 7-9). A large school district might have six high schools to provide for each of the major geographic territories within the district. If an organization's customers are scattered over a large geographic area, this form of departmentalization can be valuable. For instance, the organization structure used by Coca-Cola in the mid-1990s reflects the company's operations in two broad geographic areas—the North American business sector and the international business sector (which includes the Pacific Rim region, the European Community Group, Northeast Europe and Africa Group, and Latin America).

Tom Warner, president of Warner Corporation—a plumbing and heating ventilation and air conditioning firm in the Washington, D.C., metropolitan area—knew something had to be done to "spark" his business. Hampered by severe competition in the area, Tom has reorganized his technicians by customers served. Called area technical directors, Warner employees are assigned to zip codes in the area and provide an array of services to their clientele.

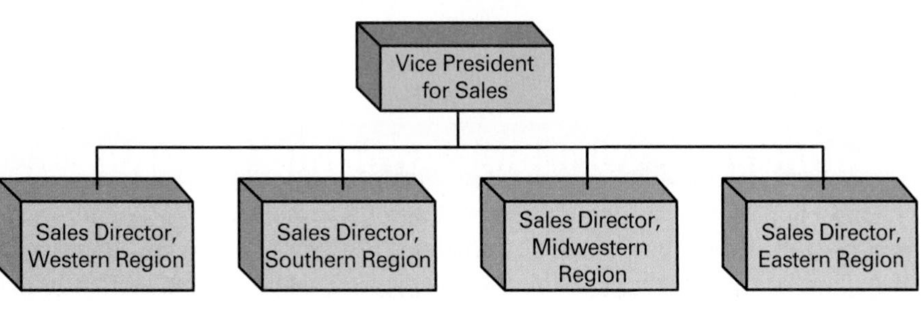

Exhibit 7-9
Geographic Departmentalization

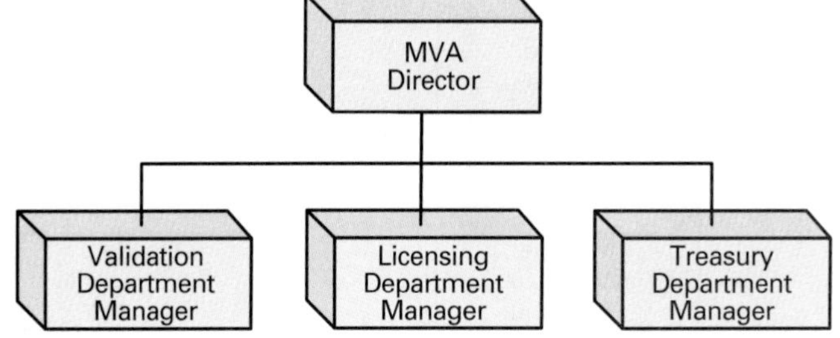

Exhibit 7-10
Process Departmentalization

process departmentalization
The grouping of activities by work or customer flow.

The final form of departmentalization is called **process departmentalization,** which groups activities on the basis of work or customer flow. Exhibit 7-10 represents an example of process departmentalization by depicting the various departments in a motor vehicle department. If you have ever been to a state motor vehicle office to get a driver's license, you probably went through several departments before receiving your license. In some states, applicants must go through three steps, each handled by a separate department: (1) validation, by the motor vehicles division; (2) processing, by the licensing department; and (3) payment collection, by the treasury department.

How Does the Contemporary View of Departmentalization Differ from the Historical View? Most large organizations continue to use most or all of the departmental groups suggested by the early management writers. Black & Decker, for instance, organizes each of its divisions along functional lines, its manufacturing units around processes, its sales around geographic regions, and its sales regions around customer groupings. But a recent trend needs to be mentioned. That is, rigid departmentalization is being complemented by the use of teams that cross over traditional departmental lines.

Today's competitive environment has refocused the attention of management to its customers. To better monitor the needs of customers and to be able to respond to changes in those needs, many organizations have given greater emphasis to customer departmentalization. Xerox, for example, has eliminated its corporate marketing staff and has placed marketing specialists out in the field.[18] This arrangement allows the company to better identify its customers and to respond faster to their requirements.

We are also seeing a great deal more use of teams today as a device for accomplishing organizational objectives. A list of some of the companies using cross-departmental teams includes Chrysler, Digital Equipment, Brazilian manufacturer Semco, and Rubbermaid. As tasks have become more complex and diverse skills are needed to accomplish those tasks, management has increasingly introduced the use of teams and task forces. We will look at the issue of teams in Chapter 11.

If we combine the basic organizational structural elements, we arrive at what most of the early writers believed to be the ideal structural design: the mechanistic, or bureaucratic, organization. Today we recognize that there is no single "ideal" organization structure for all situations (see Understanding Yourself).

Contingency Variables Affecting Structure

The most appropriate structure to use will depend on contingency factors. In this section, we will address two generic organization structure models and then look at the more popular contingency variables—strategy, size, technology, and environment.

Understanding Yourself

What Kind of Organization Design Do You Want to Work For?

Do you have an idea of what type of organization you would like to work for? Most likely you have given it some thought, but your focus has probably been on the type of job or maybe its location. What about the personality of the organization? How much consideration have you given to the culture you would work best in? For this exercise, first complete the questions below and score them. Then, in your group, compare responses to the following questions: Are there group members who prefer to work in large bureaucratic organizations? Who prefer to work in smaller companies? Discuss with your group members why you feel that type of organization will best suit you. Also, imagine that you work in an organization whose culture is opposite your preference. How might that affect your work? Discuss with your class members.

For each of the following statements, circle the level of agreement or disagreement that you personally feel:

SA = *Strongly agree* **D** = *Disagree*
A = *Agree* **SD** = *Strongly disagree*
U = *Uncertain*

1. I like being part of a team and having my performance assessed in terms of my contribution to the team.	SA	A	U	D	SD
2. No person's needs should be compromised in order for a department to achieve its goals.	SA	A	U	D	SD
3. I prefer a job where my boss leaves me alone.	SA	A	U	D	SD
4. I like the thrill and excitement of taking risks.	SA	A	U	D	SD
5. People shouldn't break rules.	SA	A	U	D	SD
6. Seniority in an organization should be highly rewarded.	SA	A	U	D	SD
7. I respect authority.	SA	A	U	D	SD
8. If a person's job performance is inadequate, it's irrelevant how much effort he or she made.	SA	A	U	D	SD
9. I like things to be predictable.	SA	A	U	D	SD
10. I'd prefer my identity to come from my professional expertise rather than from the organization that employs me.	SA	A	U	D	SD

Scoring: For items 5, 6, 7, and 9, give yourself −2 for each SA, −1 for A, 0 for U, +1 for D, and +2 for SD. For items 1, 2, 3, 4, 8, and 10, reverse the scoring (+2 for SA, +1 for A, and so forth). Add up your total.

What the Assessment Means: Your score will fall somewhere between +20 and −20. The higher your score (positive), the higher your preference for small, innovative, flexible, team-oriented cultures, which are most likely to be found in research units, team-based structures, small businesses, or boundaryless organizations. Negative scores, on the other hand, indicate that you would be more comfortable in a stable, rule-oriented culture. This is synonymous with large companies and government agencies.

How Is a Mechanistic Organization Different from an Organic Organization?

mechanistic organization
A bureaucracy; a structure that is high in specialization, formalization, and centralization.

Exhibit 7-11 describes two organizational forms.[19] The **mechanistic organization** (or bureaucracy) was the natural result of combining the six elements of structure. Adhering to the chain of command principle ensured the existence of a formal hierarchy of authority, with each person controlled and supervised by one superior. Keeping the span of control small at increasingly higher levels in the organization created tall, impersonal structures. As the distance between the top and the bottom of the organization expanded, top management would increasingly impose rules and regulations. Because top managers couldn't control lower-level activities through direct observation and ensure the use of standard practices, they substituted rules and regulations. The early writers' belief in a high degree of division of labor created jobs that were simple, routine, and standardized. Further specialization through the use of departmentalization increased impersonality and the need for multiple layers of management to coordinate the specialized departments.

organic organization
An adhocracy; a structure that is low in specialization, formalization, and centralization.

The **organic organization** (also referred to as an *adhocracy*) is a direct contrast to the mechanistic form. The organic organization is a highly adaptive form that is as loose and flexible as the mechanistic organization is rigid and stable. Rather than having standardized jobs and regulations, the adhocracy's loose structure allows it to change rapidly as needs require. Adhocracies have division of labor, but the jobs people do are not standardized. Employees tend to be professionals who are technically proficient and trained to handle diverse problems. They need very few formal rules and little direct supervision because their training has instilled in them standards of professional conduct. For instance, a petroleum engineer does not need to be given procedures on how to locate oil sources miles offshore. The engineer can solve most problems alone or after conferring with colleagues. Professional standards guide his or her behavior. The organic organization is low in centralization so that the professional can respond quickly to problems and because top management cannot be expected to possess the expertise to make necessary decisions.

The organic organization is a highly adaptive form that is loose and flexible.

When is each of these two models appropriate? Let's look at the contingency variables that affect organization structure.

Exhibit 7-11
Mechanistic versus Organic Organizations

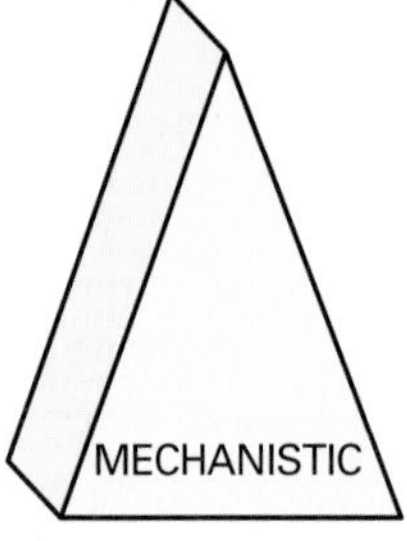

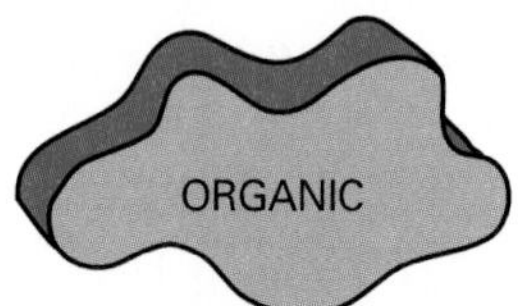

Mechanistic	Organic
□ Rigid hierarchical relationships	□ Collaboration (both vertical and horizontal)
□ Fixed duties	□ Adaptable duties
□ Many rules	□ Few rules
□ Formalized communication channels	□ Informal communication
□ Centralized decision authority	□ Decentralized decision authority
□ Taller structures	□ Flatter structures

How Does Strategy Affect Structure?

An organization's structure is a means to help management achieve its objectives. Since objectives are derived from the organization's overall strategy, it is only logical that strategy and structure should be closely linked. For example, if the organization focuses on providing certain services—say, police protection in a community—its structure will be one that promotes standardized and efficient services. Similarly, if an organization is attempting to employ a growth strategy by entering into global markets, it will need a structure that is flexible, fluid, and readily adaptable to the environment. Accordingly, organizational structure should follow strategy. And, if management makes a significant change in its organization's strategy, it will need to modify structure to accommodate and support that change (see Managers Who Made a Difference).

The first important research on the strategy-structure relationship was Alfred Chandler's study of close to 100 large U.S. companies.[20] After tracing the development of these organizations over a period of fifty years and compiling extensive case histories of companies such as du Pont, General Motors, Standard Oil of New Jersey, and Sears, Chandler concluded that changes in corporate strategy precede and lead to changes in an organization's structure. Specifically, he found that organizations usually begin with a single product or line. The simplicity of the strategy requires only a simple or loose form of structure to execute it. Decisions can be centralized in the hands of a single senior manager, and complexity and formalization will be low. As organizations grow, their strategies become more ambitious and elaborate.

Recent research has generally confirmed the strategy-structure relationship but has used the strategy terminology presented in Chapter 3.[21] For instance, organizations pursuing a differentiation strategy (see Chapter 3) must innovate to survive. Unless they can maintain their uniqueness, they may lose their competitive advantage. An organic organization matches best with this strategy because it is flexible and maximizes adaptability. In contrast, a cost-leadership strategy seeks stability and efficiency. Stability and efficiency help to produce low-cost goods and services. This, then, can best be achieved with a mechanistic organization.

How Does Size Affect Structure?

There is considerable historical evidence that an organization's size significantly affects its structure.[22] For instance, large organizations—those typically employing 2,000 or more employees—tend to have more division of labor, horizontal and vertical differentiation, and rules and regulations than do small organizations. However, the relationship is not linear; the impact of size becomes less important as an organization expands. Why? Essentially, once an organization has around 2,000 employees, it is already fairly mechanistic. An additional 500 employees will not have much impact. On the other hand, adding 500 employees to an organization that has only 300 members is likely to result in a shift toward a more mechanistic structure.

How Does Technology Affect Structure?

Every organization uses some form of technology to convert its inputs into outputs. To attain its objectives, the organization uses equipment, materials, knowledge, and experienced individuals and puts them together into certain types and patterns of activities. For instance, college instructors teach students by a variety of methods: formal lectures, group discussions, case analyses, programmed learning, and so forth. Each of these methods is a type of technology. Over the years, several studies regarding the effect of technology have been conducted.[23] For instance, in one study, British scholar Joan Woodward found that distinct relationships exist between size of pro-

Managers Who Made a Difference

PERCY BARNEVIK OF ABB

Percy Barnevik is the CEO of ABB (Asea Brown Boveri), a $28 billion Zurich-based engineering company. Operating in 140 countries around the world, ABB is a world leader in high-speed trains, robotics, and environmental control.[24]

ABB was formed in 1988 through a merger of Asea, a Swedish engineering group, with Brown Boveri, a Swiss competitor. Being named as CEO of the newly created organization, Percy inherited an organization that had nearly 210,000 employees—some 2,000 being part of the headquarters staff. One of Barnevik's first challenges was to organize this giant to meet its strategic goal of becoming a world-class operation. Here's what he did.

First, Barnevik cut the headquarters staff from 2,000 to 176 people. In doing so, he decentralized decision making down to the operating levels. He then divided the organization into 1,300 separate companies—each focusing on a particular customer and market. And he continues to refine these units; he has sold or consolidated 300 of the less profitable ones. But probably his most innovative idea was to introduce a dual chain of command. Barnevik recognizes that "globalization requires a global organization." ABB has approximately 100 managers who run their operations with a local board of directors. Most of these managers are citizens of the country in which they work. In addition, there are about sixty global managers who are organized into eight segments—in such areas as financial services, transportation, process automation and engineering, electrical equipment, and three electric power businesses of power generation, transportation, and distribution. This structure makes it easier for "local" managers to capitalize on information and other technologies from other countries and transport these "best practices" to other parts of the organization.

Have Percy Barnevik's actions been successful? By most accounts, the answer is Yes. Through reorganization, ABB has improved customer service measures by 50 percent and has reduced cycle times for producing products. ABB has also been recognized by *Financial Times* as the most-admired company in Europe. But Barnevik isn't done. What has occurred to date reflects the dynamic environment of ABB. Tomorrow, however, may require more changes and different directions. As technology improves, it will directly affect his business. Therefore, he's keeping the organization fluid in an effort to remain competitive.

duction runs and the structure of the firm. She also found that the effectiveness of organizations was related to "fit" between technology and structure.[25] Most of these studies, like Woodward's, have focused on the processes or methods that transform inputs into outputs and how they differ by their degree of routineness. For example, mass production of steel, tires, and automobiles or refining petroleum is generally characteristic of routine technology. The more routine the technology, the more standardized the structure can be. Conversely, Rockwell International's development of the Space Shuttle represents a nonroutine technology. Since the technology was more nonroutine, the structure was more organic.[26]

This Hanover, Germany, employee of the Continental Tire company is one of the lucky few who have kept their jobs. With some 12,000 employees laid off over the past three years, the remaining employees have had to change how they work. Once specialized into departments, workers at Continental are now grouped into teams and are working with new technologies that are helping the organization keep its position as the only profitable tire manufacturer in Europe.

How Does Environment Affect Structure?

In Chapter 2, we introduced the organization's environment as a constraint on managerial discretion. Research has demonstrated that environment is also a major influence on structure.[27] Essentially, mechanistic organizations are most effective in stable environments. Organic organizations are best matched with dynamic and uncertain environments.

The evidence on the environment-structure relationship helps to explain why so many managers have restructured their organizations to be lean, fast, and flexible.[28] Global competition, accelerated product innovation by all competitors, and increased demands from customers for higher quality and faster deliveries are examples of dynamic environmental forces. Mechanistic organizations tend to be ill-equipped to respond to rapid environmental change. As a result, we are seeing managers, like Charles Knight at the St. Louis–based household appliance company Emerson Electric, redesigning their organizations in order to make them more organic.[29] Knight has regained market share once lost to low-cost producers in Japan, Brazil, and Korea by giving employees more autonomy to do their jobs and instilling in them a pride of ownership.

Organization Design Applications

What types of organization designs exist in companies such as Toshiba, MVP Athletic Shoes, Liz Claiborne, Hershey Foods, and Sun Life Assurance Company of Canada, Ltd.? Let's look at the various types of organization designs that you might see in contemporary organizations.

What Is a Simple Structure?

Most organizations start as an entrepreneurial venture with a simple structure. This organization design reflects the owner as president, with all employees reporting directly to her.

A **simple structure** is defined more by what it is not than by what it is. It is not an elaborate structure.[30] If you see an organization that appears to have almost no structure, it is probably of the simple variety. By that we mean that work specialization is low, few rules govern the operations, and authority is centralized in a single person—the owner. The simple structure is a "flat" organization; it usually has only two or three vertical levels, a loose body of empowered employees in whom the decision-making authority is centralized.

simple structure
An organization that is low in specialization and formalization but high in centralization.

The simple structure is most widely used in smaller businesses in which the manager and the owner are often the same. The strengths of the simple structure should be obvious. It is fast, flexible, and inexpensive to maintain, and accountability is clear. One major weakness is that it is effective only in small organizations. It becomes increasingly inadequate as an organization grows because its few policies or rules to guide operations and its high centralization result in information overload at the top. As size increases, decision making becomes slower and can eventually come to a standstill as the single executive tries to continue making all the decisions. If the structure is not changed and adapted to its size, the firm is likely to lose momentum and eventually fail. The simple structure's other weakness is that it is risky: Everything depends on one person. If anything happens to the owner-manager, the organization's information and decision-making center is lost.

What Are the Classic Bureaucracies?

Many organizations do not remain simple structures. That decision is often made by choice or because structural contingency factors dictate it. For example, as production or sales increase significantly, companies generally reach a point at which more employees are needed. As the number of employees rises, informal work rules of the simple structure give way to more-formalized rules. Rules and regulations are implemented, departments are created, and levels of management are added to coordinate the activities of departmental people. At this point, a bureaucracy is formed. Two of the most popular bureaucratic design options grew out of the function and product departmentalizations. These are appropriately called the functional and divisional structures, respectively.

functional structure
An organization in which similar and related occupational specialties are grouped together.

Why Do Companies Implement Functional Structures? We introduced functional departmentalization a few pages ago. The **functional structure** merely expands the functional orientation to make it the dominant form for the entire organization. As displayed in Exhibit 7-6 (page 208), management can choose to organize its structure by grouping similar and related occupational specialties together. The strength of the functional structure lies in the advantages that accrue from work specialization. Putting like specialties together results in economies of scale, minimizes duplication of personnel and equipment, and makes employees comfortable and satisfied because it gives them the opportunity to "talk the same language" as their peers. The most obvious weakness of the functional structure, however, is that the organization frequently loses sight of its best interests in the pursuit of functional goals. No one function is totally responsible for end results, so members within individual functions become insulated and have little understanding of what people in other functions are doing.

divisional structure
An organization made up of self-contained units.

What Is the Divisional Structure? The **divisional structure** is an organization design made up of self-contained units or divisions. Hershey Foods, PepsiCo, and Daimler Benz are examples of companies that have implemented such a structure. Building on product departmentalization (see Exhibit 7-7, page 208), each division is generally autonomous, with a division manager responsible for performance and holding complete strategic and operational decision-making authority. In most divisional structures, central headquarters provides support services—such as financial and legal services—to the divisions. Of course, the headquarters also acts as an external overseer to coordinate and control the various divisions. Divisions are, therefore, autonomous within given parameters.

The chief advantage of the divisional structure is that it focuses on results. Division managers have full responsibility for a product or service. The divisional structure also frees the headquarters staff from being concerned with day-to-day operating details so that they can pay attention to long-term and strategic planning. The major disadvantage of the divisional structure is duplication of activities and resources. Each division, for instance, may have a marketing research department. In the absence of autonomous divisions, all of the organization's marketing research might be centralized and done for a fraction of the cost that divisionalization requires. Thus, the divisional form's duplication of functions increases the organization's costs and reduces efficiency.

Can an Organization Design Capture the Advantages of Bureaucracies While Eliminating Their Disadvantages?

The functional structure offers the advantages that accrue from specialization. The divisional structure has a greater focus on results but suffers from duplication of activities and resources. Does any structure combine the advantages of functional specialization with the focus and accountability that product departmentalization provides? The answer is Yes, and it's called the **matrix structure.**[31]

matrix structure
An organization in which specialists from functional departments are assigned to work on one or more projects led by a project manager.

Exhibit 7-12 illustrates the matrix structure of an aerospace firm. Notice that along the top of the figure are the familiar functions of engineering, accounting, human resources, manufacturing, and so forth. Along the vertical dimension, however, the various projects that the aerospace firm is currently working on have been added. Each program is directed by a manager who staffs his or her project with people from the functional departments. The addition of this vertical dimension to the traditional horizontal functional departments, in effect, weaves together elements of function and product departmentalization—hence the term *matrix*.

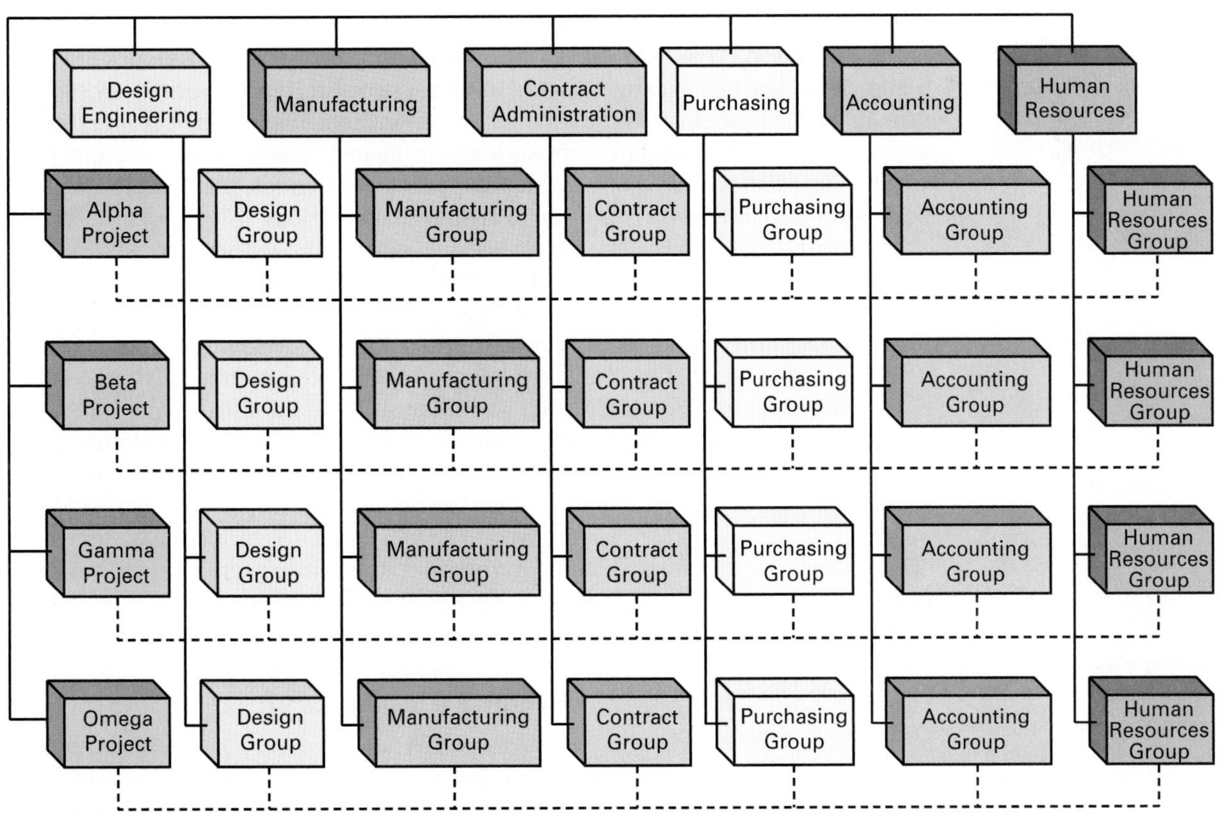

Exhibit 7-12
Sample Matrix Structure

In Chapter 4, we introduced the concept of PERT and project management. In part, much of that discussion was related directly to a matrix structure. How? Project management looks at employing specific resources (functional) on specific work activities (projects or programs). Accordingly, when you work in a project management setting, you are actually working in a form of a matrix.

The unique characteristic of the matrix is that employees in this structure have at least two bosses: their functional departmental manager and their product or project managers—just like those working for ABB, a global equipment corporation. Project managers have authority over the functional members who are part of that manager's project team. But authority is shared between the two managers. Typically, the project manager is given authority over project employees relative to the project's goals, but decisions such as promotions, salary recommendations, and annual reviews remain the functional manager's responsibility. To work effectively, project and functional managers must communicate regularly and coordinate the demands upon their common employees.

The primary strength of the matrix is that it can facilitate coordination of a multiple set of complex and interdependent projects while still retaining the economies that result from keeping functional specialists grouped together.[32] The major disadvantages of the matrix lie in the confusion it creates and its propensity to foster power struggles. When you dispense with the chain of command principle, you significantly increase ambiguity. Confusion can exist over who reports to whom. This confusion and ambiguity, in turn, plant the seeds for power struggles.

What Are Team-Based Structures?

team-based structure
An organization that consists entirely of work groups, or teams.

In a **team-based structure,** the entire organization consists of work groups or teams that perform the organization's work.[33] In such a structure, it goes without saying that team members have the authority to make decisions that affect them, because there is no rigid chain of command in these work arrangements. How can team structures benefit the organization? Let's look at what happened at Thermos, the Schaumburg, Illinois, bottle and lunch box company, to answer that question.

In early 1990, company officials became aware of how Thermos's bureaucracy was slowing up decision making and constraining innovation—especially in creating new products.[34] Thermos's CEO, Monte Peterson, attacked the problem by revamping the corporate structure. He flattened the organization by developing interdisciplinary team-based structures. These teams were made up of employees from such areas as engineering, marketing, manufacturing, and finance. In addition, each team also had members who were external to the company—such as suppliers or customers. The prime directive was "listen to customers, and develop products they want." In doing so, the company would be able to satisfy its customers and its performance could improve. In fact, since the company moved to a team-based design, sales have increased dramatically, and its market share in, for instance, the barbecue grill market, has risen from 2 to 20 percent. We'll look more closely at teams and their inner workings in Chapter 11.

boundaryless organization
An organization that is not defined or limited by boundaries or categories imposed by traditional structures.

Why Is There Movement toward a Boundaryless Organization?

The last organization design application that we will cover is the idea of a boundaryless organization. A **boundaryless organization** is an organization design that is not defined or limited by boundaries or categories imposed by traditional structures.[35]

It blurs the historical boundaries surrounding an organization by increasing its interdependence with its environment.[36] Sometimes called network organizations, learning organizations, barrier-free, modular, or virtual corporations,[37] boundaryless structures cut across all aspects of the organization. Rather than having functional specialties located in departments working on distinctive tasks, these internally boundaryless organizations group employees to accomplish some core processes.[38] A core process is a basic focus of the business, such as Thermos's vacuum technology. Core processes, then, encompass the entire work to be accomplished, from beginning to end, rather than focusing on individualized job tasks. For instance, at Sweden's Karolinska Hospital, surgical teams handle all of a patient's needs—from diagnosis, to surgery, to recovery. Surgeries once involved forty-seven departments. Now these surgical teams are performing 3,000 surgeries each year with fifteen fewer operating rooms available. And patient waiting times for surgery have been cut from six to eight months to just under three weeks.[39]

But boundaryless organizations are not merely flatter organizations. They frequently require an internal revolution.[40] Managers must break down the traditional hierarchies that have existed for many decades. Horizontal organizations require multidisciplinary work teams who have the authority to make the necessary decisions to do the work and be held accountable for measurable outcomes.[41] What factors have contributed to the rise of boundaryless organization designs in today's organizations? Undoubtedly, many of the topics we covered in Chapter 2 have had an effect. Specifically, globalization of markets and competitors has played a major role. An organization's need to respond and adapt to the complex and dynamic environment is best served by boundaryless organizations. Changes in technology have also contributed to this movement. Advances in computer power, "intelligent" software, and telecommunications enable boundaryless organizations to exist. Each of these supports the information network that makes the virtual workplace (see Chapter 6) possible. Finally, a rapidly changing environment compels an organization to rapidly innovate to survive. A boundaryless organization provides the flexibility and fluid structure that facilitates quick movements to capitalize on opportunities.

Boundaryless organizations are not merely flatter organizations. They frequently require an internal revolution.

Organization Culture

We know that every individual has something that psychologists have termed "personality." An individual's personality is made up of a set of relatively permanent and stable traits. When we describe someone as warm, innovative, relaxed, or conservative, we are describing personality traits. An organization, too, has a personality, which we call the organization's culture.

What Is an Organization Culture?

What do we specifically mean by the term **organization culture?** We use the term to refer to a system of shared meaning. Just as tribal cultures have totems and taboos that dictate how each member will act toward fellow members and outsiders, organizations have cultures that govern how their members should behave. In every organization, there are systems or patterns of values, symbols, rituals, myths, and practices that have evolved over time.[42] These shared values

organization culture A system of shared meaning within an organization that determines, in a large degree, how employees act.

- ▶ **1.** *Member identity.* The degree to which employees identify with the organization as a whole rather than with their type of job or field of professional expertise
- ▶ **2.** *Group emphasis.* The degree to which work activities are organized around groups rather than individuals
- ▶ **3.** *People focus.* The degree to which management decisions take into consideration the effect of outcomes on people within the organization
- ▶ **4.** *Unit integration.* The degree to which units within the organization are encouraged to operate in a coordinated or interdependent manner
- ▶ **5.** *Control.* The degree to which rules, regulations, and direct supervision are used to oversee and control employee behavior
- ▶ **6.** *Risk tolerance.* The degree to which employees are encouraged to be aggressive, innovative, and risk-seeking
- ▶ **7.** *Reward criteria.* The degree to which rewards such as salary increases and promotions are allocated on employee performance criteria in contrast to seniority, favoritism, or other nonperformance factors
- ▶ **8.** *Conflict tolerance.* The degree to which employees are encouraged to air conflicts and criticisms openly
- ▶ **9.** *Means-end orientation.* The degree to which management focuses on results or outcomes rather than on the techniques and processes used to achieve those outcomes
- ▶ **10.** *Open-systems focus.* The degree to which the organization monitors and responds to changes in the external environment

Exhibit 7-13
Ten Characteristics of Organization Culture

determine, in large degree, what employees see and how they respond to their world.[43]

How Can Cultures Be Assessed?

Though we currently have no definitive method for measuring an organization's culture, preliminary research suggests that cultures can be analyzed by assessing how an organization rates on ten characteristics.[44] We have listed these characteristics in Exhibit 7-13. These ten characteristics are relatively stable and permanent over time. Just as an individual's personality is stable and permanent—if you were outgoing last month, you're likely to be outgoing next month—so, too, is an organization's culture.

Where Does an Organization's Culture Come from?

An organization's culture usually reflects the vision or mission of the organization's founders. Because the founders have the original idea, they also have biases on how to carry out the idea. They are unconstrained by previous customs or ideologies. The founders establish the early culture by projecting an image of what the organization should be. The small size of most new organizations also helps the founders impose their vision on all organization members. An organization's culture, then, results from the interaction between (1) the founders' biases and assumptions and (2) what the first employees learn subsequently from their own experiences.[45] For example, the founder of IBM, Thomas Watson, established a culture based on "pursuing excellence, providing the best customer service, and respect for employees."[46] Ironically, some seventy years later, in an effort to revitalize the ailing IBM, CEO Louis Gerstner is dismantling that culture and replacing it with such guiding principles as "the marketplace drives

How can culture affect business? Denny's Restaurant has been in the press the past few years, accused of "racist" practices. Its parent company, Flagstar, is attempting to change that image to get customers to return. Flagstar's management is increasing its contracts with minority suppliers and moving minorities into management positions. Furthermore, Flagstar is increasing minority-owned franchises going from one to twenty-seven in just under three years. One of those franchises is owned by Charles Davis. Although past practices at Denny's have affected his business, Davis uses every opportunity to "let the community know that Denny's is in town with a new attitude."

everything we do," and, "think and act with a sense of urgency."[47] At Southwest Airlines, Herb Kelleher reinforces the company's "people culture" by doing things and having in place practices—such as compensation and benefits that are above industry averages—to make employees happy.[48]

How Does Culture Influence Structure?

An organization's culture may have an effect on an organization's structure, depending on how strong, or weak, the culture is. For instance, in organizations that have a strong culture—like that of Barclay PLC, a large British bank characterized as a formal, cold, risk-averse organization—accepting these dominant values creates behavioral consistency. In such a case, the organization's culture actually can substitute for the rules and regulations that formally guide employees. In essence, strong cultures can create predictability, orderliness, and consistency without the need for written documentation. Therefore, the stronger an organization's culture, the less managers need to be concerned with developing formal rules and regulations. Instead, those guides will be internalized in employees when they accept the organization's culture. If, on the other hand, an organization's culture is weak—there are no dominant shared values—its effect on structure is less clear.

Summary

How will I know if I fulfilled the Learning Objectives found on page 196? You will have fulfilled the Learning Objectives if you understand the following.

1. **Identify the six elements of organization structure.** The six elements of organization structure are: work specialization, chain of command, span of control, authority and responsibility, centralization versus decentralization, and departmentalization.

2. **Describe the advantages and disadvantages of work specialization.** The advantages of work specialization are related to economic efficiencies. It makes efficient use of the diversity of skills that workers hold. Skills are developed through repetition. Less time is wasted than when workers are

generalists. Training is also easier and less costly. The disadvantage of work specialization is that it can result in human diseconomies. Excessive work specialization can cause boredom, fatigue, stress, low productivity, poor quality, increased absence, and high turnover.

3. **Contrast authority and power.** Authority is related to rights inherent in a position. Power describes all means by which an individual can influence decisions, including formal authority. Authority is synonymous with legitimate power. However, a person can have coercive, reward, expert, or referent power without holding a position of authority. Thus, authority is actually a subset of power.
4. **Identify the five different ways by which management can departmentalize.** Managers can departmentalize on the basis of function (work being done), product (product or service being generated), customer (group served), geography (location of operations), or process (work flow). In practice, most large organizations use all five.
5. **Contrast mechanistic and organic organizations.** The mechanistic organization, or bureaucracy, rates high on worker specialization, formal work rules and regulations, and centralized decisions. The organic organization, or adhocracy, scores low on these same three dimensions.
6. **Summarize the effect on organization structures of strategy, size, technology, and environment.** The strategy-determines-structure thesis argues that structure should follow strategy. As strategies move from single product, to vertical integration, to product diversification, structure must move from organic to mechanistic. As size increases, so too do specialization, formalization, and horizontal and vertical differentiation. But size has less of an impact on large organizations than on small ones because once an organization has around 2,000 employees it tends to be fairly mechanistic. All other things equal, the more routine the technology, the more mechanistic the organization should be. The more nonroutine the technology, the more organic the structure should be. Finally, stable environments are better matched with mechanistic organizations, while dynamic environments fit better with organic organizations.
7. **Contrast the divisional and functional structures.** The functional structure groups similar or related occupational specialties together. It takes advantage of specialization and provides economies of scale by allowing people with common skills to work together. The divisional structure is composed of autonomous units or divisions, with managers having full responsibility for a product or service. However, these units are frequently organized as functional structures inside their divisional framework. So divisional structures typically contain functional structures within them—and they are less efficient.
8. **Explain the strengths of the matrix structure.** By assigning specialists from functional departments to work on one or more projects led by project managers, the matrix structure combines functional and product departmentalization. It thus has the advantages of both work specialization and high accountability.
9. **Describe the boundaryless organization and what elements have contributed to its development.** The boundaryless organization is an organization design application in which the structure is not defined by, or limited to, the boundaries imposed by traditional structures. It is a structure that is flexible and adaptable to environmental conditions. The factors contributing to boundaryless organizations include global markets and competition, technology advancements, and the need for rapid innovation.
10. **Describe what is meant by the term *organization culture*.** Organization culture is a system of shared meaning within an organization that determines, in large degree, how employees act.

Review & Discussion Questions

1. Describe what is meant by the term *organization design*.
2. Which do you believe to be more efficient—a wide or a narrow span of control? Support your decision.
3. How are authority and organization structure related? Authority and power?
4. In what ways can management departmentalize? When should one method be considered over the others?
5. "An organization can have no structure." Do you agree or disagree with this statement? Explain.
6. Show how both the functional and matrix structures might create conflict within an organization.

7. Why is the simple structure inadequate in large organizations?
8. Do you think the various types of structures described in this chapter can be appropriate for charitable organizations? Which organization design application would you believe to be most appropriate? Explain.
9. Describe the characteristics of a boundaryless organization structure. How do you think "tomorrow's" employees will accept these characteristics?
10. Classrooms have cultures. Describe your class culture. How does it affect your instructor?

Applying the Concepts

How Is Your School Organized?

Every university or college displays a specific type of organizational structure. That is, if you are a business major, your classes are often "housed" in a department, school, or college of business. But have you ever asked why? Or is it something you just take for granted?

In Chapter 3 you had an opportunity to assess your college's strengths, weaknesses, and comparative advantage and see how this fits into its strategy. Now, in this chapter we have built a case that structure follows strategy. Given your analysis in Chapter 3 (if you have not done so, you may want to turn to page 97 for the strategy part of this exercise), analyze your college's overall structure in terms of formalization, centralization, and complexity. Furthermore, look at the departmentalization that exists. Is your college more organic or mechanistic? Now analyze how well your college's structure fits with its strategy. Do the same thing for your college's size, technology, and environment. That is, assess its size, degree of technological routineness, and environmental uncertainty. Based on these assessments, what kind of structure would you predict your college to have? Does it have this structure now? Compare your findings with other classmates. Are there similarities in how each viewed the college? Differences? What do you believe has attributed to these findings?

Take It to the Net

We invite you to visit the Robbins/De Cenzo page on the Prentice Hall Web site at:

http://www.prenhall.com/robbinsfom

for this chapter's World Wide Web exercise.

You can also visit the Web sites for these companies featured within this chapter:

ADP
http://www.adp.com

Coca-Cola
http://www.cocacola.com

Hershey Foods:
http://www.hersheys.com/~hershey

Rockwell International
http://www.rockwell.com

Rubbermaid
http://www.rubbermaid.com

Testing Your Comprehension • • •

Circle the correct answer, then check yourself on page AK-1.

1. Determining where decisions are made in the organization's hierarchy
   a. defines spatial differentiation
   b. refers to work specialization
   c. defines the degree of centralization
   d. refers to the process of organization design

2. The early management writers proposed
   a. one set of organizational principles for all organizations
   b. the separation of authority and responsibility
   c. an organic structure
   d. a simple structure as the basis for all organizations

3. The idea that jobs should be broken down into the simplest of steps, with one step generally assigned to each individual refers to
   a. span of control
   b. work specialization
   c. chain of command
   d. line authority

4. The MAIN problem to be expected when the chain of command principle is ignored is that
   a. employees have potential trouble coping with conflicting priorities and demands
   b. supervisors cannot keep abreast of what all their subordinates are doing
   c. decision making is slow
   d. there is not enough flexibility

5. Authority is to a specific position as ___________ is to an individual.
   a. decision making
   b. responsibility
   c. span of control
   d. power

6. Which of the following statements is LEAST accurate regarding power?
   a. Functional departments are wedges in the core.
   b. The closer one is to the outer edge of the core, the more power one has.
   c. The organization's hierarchy is directly represented at the edge of the core.
   d. The closer one is to the power core, the more influence one has on decisions.

7. The rights inherent in one's job constitute _______________, while the capacity to influence decisions is _________.
   a. power; authority
   b. power; responsibility
   c. authority; responsibility
   d. authority; power

8. Concerning the span of control, early management writers believed that
   a. stronger managers should have a larger span of control
   b. top managers should have a larger span of control
   c. lower-level managers should have a larger span of control
   d. newer managers should have a larger span of control

9. When the manager of an insurance claims department groups together all construction-claims personnel under one manager, _______________ is being demonstrated.
   a. functional departmentalization
   b. geographic departmentalization
   c. process departmentalization
   d. product departmentalization

10. Which of the following statements is INCONSISTENT with the relationship between strategy and structure?
    a. A change in strategy is followed by a change in structure.
    b. Strategy is a major influence on structure.
    c. A change in structure will result in a change in strategy.
    d. None of the above are inconsistent with the relationship between strategy and structure.

11. Which of the following is LEAST likely to be a disadvantage of the functional structure?
    a. little cross-training among managers
    b. optimization of goals at the department level rather than the organizational level
    c. insulation among various departments that often results in suboptimization of organizational goals
    d. duplication of facilities, people, and information

12. A major advantage of the simple structure is
    a. clear responsibility and accountability
    b. low risk
    c. appropriateness for almost any business
    d. ability to build managers through participative decision making

13. Which of the following statements is INCORRECT regarding divisional structures?
    a. A divisional structure's roots are based in product departmentalization.
    b. A major disadvantage of a divisional structure is its duplication of resources.
    c. A divisional structure manager is required to seek corporate approval for implementing tactical plans.
    d. An advantage of the divisional structure is that it focuses on results.

14. Which of the following is NOT a strength of the matrix structure?
    a. the accountability of the divisional structure
    b. the efficiency from specialization attributable to the functional structure
    c. elimination of the duplication of resources and facilities
    d. minimizes ambiguity in reporting relationships

15. The Massachusetts office of Sun Life Assurance Company has organized its customer representatives into groups of eight employees who are cross-trained to handle all customer's requests. This grouping of employees is best representative of which type of structure?
    a. divisional
    b. team-based
    c. matrix
    d. boundaryless

16. Which of the following statements is TRUE with regard to boundaryless organizations?
    a. Boundaryless organizations are just flatter organizations that attempt to emulate simple structures.
    b. When teams are put in place, managers must find new ways to continue to base employee rewards on individual performance.
    c. Team members will be rewarded for mastering multiple skills.
    d. Supervisory evaluations will be the only evaluations.

17. An organization's culture is
    a. a system of shared norms and beliefs
    b. an important determinant of its external environment
    c. best when top management centralizes decision making
    d. determined by the board of directors

Thinking Critically

Making a Value Judgment: Following Orders

Several years back, a study of business executives revealed that most had obeyed orders that they had found personally objectionable or unethical.[49] Far more thought-provoking was a survey taken among the general public near the end of the Vietnam War. Despite public dismay over the actions of some military personnel during that war, about half of the respondents said that they would have shot civilian men, women, and children in cold blood if they had been ordered to do so by their commanding officer.[50]

More recently, a survey of U.S. managers has revealed that there was a significant difference in the values, attitudes, and beliefs they personally held and what they encountered in the workplace.[51] And this is not simply a U.S. phenomenon. Managers around the world, in such places as the Pacific Rim, Europe, and India, are all facing the same predicaments.

Questions:

1. If you were asked to follow orders that you believed were unconscionable, would you comply? For example, what if your boss asked you to destroy evidence that he or she had been stealing a great deal of money from the organization?
2. What if you merely disagreed with the orders? For instance, what if your boss asked you to bring him or her coffee each morning even though no such task is included in your job description? What would you do?
3. What effect do you feel national culture has on your complying with orders that have been given to you?

Flattening the Structure at Imedia, Inc.

In the 1920s and 1930s, as organizations built successive layers of hierarchy, there was a need to provide coordination. Management writers of that time, for instance, argued that formal, rigid organizational structures would best serve the company. That may have been true sixty or more years ago, when these bureaucratic structures flourished. But by the 1980s, the environment was changing. Global competition, technological advancements, a changing work force, and the like were making bureaucracies inefficient for many businesses. Since the late 1980s, most organizations have restructured themselves to be more customer- and market-oriented and to increase productivity.

If we look at those companies that are growing fastest and are most successful, we see some common characteristics. For example, among the 500 fastest-growing U.S. firms, 51 percent have no senior manager of marketing or human resource management, 32 percent have no chief financial officer, and 67 percent do not rely on an information systems department for their communication needs.[52] Rather, those specialized activities have been pushed down and subsumed by individuals lower in the organization. In management terms, we say that empowering is occurring in these situations. That's precisely what Jo-Anne Dressendofer has done.[53]

Jo-Anne is the president of Imedia, Inc., a Morristown, New Jersey–based marketing firm. Dressendofer always believed in keeping the company simple. When she started the company in 1989, she set herself up as the only manager and had all thirty people report directly to her. This structure, to Jo-Anne, was consistent with the lean-and-mean trend. Her employees, however, didn't see it that way. It was not that any of them disliked reporting directly to the president; they were just fed up with Jo-Anne's making all the decisions. The Imedia staff had to seek her permission to do, in their view, even the most mundane of tasks. This frustration went on for over three years, until several of her staff marched into Dressendofer's office in early 1992 to confront her. Their demand: Either she let go of the tight reins immediately or they would quit on the spot.

Recognizing that she couldn't afford to lose these critical employees without losing a substantial part of her business, Jo-Anne agreed. She immediately implemented a team-management structure, giving employee groups responsibility for many activities and decisions. During the first year following the reorganization, she witnessed some startling changes. Although some employees initially had difficulty in accepting a major role in company decisions, the firm's sales increased over $1 million. That's almost a 50 percent increase in the firm's revenues from the previous year! Employees are more creative, more productive, and happier at work. Of course, so is Jo-Anne Dressendofer!

Questions:

1. How would you characterize the "old" structure of Imedia, Inc.—mechanistic or organic? The "new" one? Give examples to support your choice.

2. Top management usually is involved in making organization design changes. Employees frequently do not have input. Do you believe that Jo-Ann Dressendofer made the design changes because they were appropriate or because of pressure from her employees? Discuss your position.
3. What effect do you believe the organization's culture had on the structure changes? Explain.

Video Case ABCNEWS

Rules, Regulations, and You Say What?

Rules and regulations often help to keep order in an organization and set the parameters in which organizational members operate. In most organizations, for instance, rules and regulations help members plan, organize, control, and make decisions. And, depending on the size of the organization, these same rules and regulations help to coordinate activities—keeping work focused on goal attainment. But, sometimes, rules become unwieldy and end up creating an amazing and inefficient runaround. Let's look at two such situations involving the Environmental Protection Agency (EPA) and the Department of Transportation (DOT).

The concern in the first instance revolved around testing for clean water at a site in Phoenix, Arizona. To do this testing, the EPA places flathead minnows and waterfleas into stormwater drains. These small creatures are then tracked as they float in the stormwater as it makes its way into streams and rivers. If, when the water reaches its destination, the minnows and waterfleas are alive, the water is considered not contaminated. If, however, they die en route, the water is considered to be polluted. Simple enough, right? Well, maybe not!

The problem in Phoenix is that the riverbed being tested is dry. There's absolutely no water, and there hasn't been any for years. Yet the EPA spends about $500,000 annually on this aquatic life test—and no aquatic life exists. The EPA defends its actions on the grounds that they are charged with protecting the groundwater, which will ultimately become drinking water for citizens in the general vicinity. Although this is an important task, the EPA regulations, ironically, don't focus on drinking water—just on protecting aquatic life. So the test they are performing in Phoenix is worthless. Even EPA administrator Carol Browner has to agree.

If you think testing dry riverbeds is inappropriate just look at the rule imposed by the Department of Transportation and the Occupational Safety and Health Administration. These two government agencies require lumber companies to have specially designed gas cans to hold the fuel that is used in chainsaws. These gas containers—which usually hold 5 gallons of gasoline—are required to have "a double roll bar on top, double-walled steel sides, a screw filter on top, and it must be vented." A gas can that meets these regulations costs about $230. And, if the extra costs weren't enough, there are also the maddening results. The filler neck on the government-approved gas can won't fit into the chainsaw, so about half of the gas poured spills out onto the ground. But then, when it contaminates the ground it's not really the DOT's responsibility. That would fall under the jurisdiction of the EPA.

Questions:

1. How would you describe the rules and regulations at such government agencies as the EPA and the DOT?
2. For rules and regulations to be effective, they must be enforced. Yet, at times, they may not be applicable to every situation—like the dry riverbeds in Phoenix. Can an organization have contingencies built into its rules and regulations and still effectively coordinate and control member actions? Explain your position.
3. Build an argument in support of a government agency's requirement that organizations abide by the rules and regulations. Now build an argument against it. Which one of the two arguments do you feel is stronger? Discuss.

Source: "Rules, Regs, and Runaround," *ABC PrimeTime,* June 7, 1995.

Staffing and Human Resource Management

8

LEARNING OBJECTIVES

What will I be able to do after I finish this chapter?

1. **DESCRIBE** the strategic human resource management process.
2. **DISCUSS** the influence of government regulations on human resource decisions.
3. **DIFFERENTIATE** between job descriptions and job specifications.
4. **CONTRAST** recruitment and decruitment options.
5. **EXPLAIN** the importance of validity and reliability in selection.
6. **DESCRIBE** the selection devices that work best with various kinds of jobs.
7. **IDENTIFY** various training methods.
8. **EXPLAIN** the various techniques managers can use in evaluating employee performance.
9. **DESCRIBE** the goals of compensation administration and factors that affect wage structures.
10. **EXPLAIN** what is meant by the terms *sexual harassment*, *family-friendly benefits*, and *layoff-survivor sickness*.

MOST ORGANIZATIONS UNDERSTAND that finding the best employees is an iffy process. The best candidates might not hear about the jobs or might not accept them if offered. You would expect that, with fierce competition for jobs and an ample supply of workers—especially with the prevalence of downsizing in the 1990s—getting a large pool of job applicants would be easy. But that's not the case for many software developers, such as Oracle, Informix, Microsoft, and Sybase.[1] Let's see what one company, Sybase, Inc., has had to do.

Software developers, such as Sybase, Inc., are having difficulty filling job openings. They have had to resort to highly creative means of announcing that they are hiring and are using generous financial inducements to attract and retain qualified employees.

Sybase is an Emeryville, California, database software manufacturer that has to "give away the store" to get people to join the company. One reason is that employment in the software industry has grown nearly 10 percent annually for the past decade—compared with about 2 percent for the general job market. Another is that there are not enough qualified people to fill all the jobs that have been created. What is Sybase doing to overcome these problems? Consider the following.

Sybase has earmarked nearly $40,000 to advertise that they have positions available. These ads run on local television and in a variety of print media. The company also has spent thousands of dollars on designing and distributing posters that advertise how great a place Sybase is to work. In addition, they have hired a bi-plane to frequently fly over competitors' places of business carrying a banner stating that well-paying jobs are available at Sybase. Current employees, too, are being enlisted for help. Any employee who refers a job candidate is eligible to win a prize—such as a sports vehicle. If that person is hired, the referring employee can get up to $10,000 as a finder's fee. Candidates, too, can benefit from just listening to what Sybase representatives have to say. Anyone who goes through an employment interview has his or her name entered into a "home-run" drawing. Applicants are eligible to win a large-screen TV, a barbecue hammock, 44 pounds of charcoal, five cases of beer, and thirty-six Baby Ruth candy bars!

Sybase's tactics to attract and retain quality employees may be seen as gimmicks. But a company has to be aggressive in a seller's job market. So individuals who accept jobs with Sybase get a signing bonus and often even stock options. For instance, in 1991, several executives received approximately $500,000 apiece in stock options for accepting a position. Currently, the company is offering options worth closer to $5 million to similar-level executives.

The quality of an organization is, to a large degree, determined by the quality of people it hires and holds. Success for most organizations depends on finding the right employees with the necessary skills to successfully perform the tasks required to attain the company's strategic goals. Staffing and human resource management decisions and methods are critical to ensuring that the organization hires and keeps the right personnel.

Managers and the Human Resource Management Process

Some of you may be thinking, "Sure, personnel decisions are important. But aren't most of them made by people in the human resources department?" It's true that, in many organizations, a number of the activities grouped under the label **human resource management (HRM)** are done by specialists in human resources. In other cases, HRM activities may even be outsourced. But not all managers may have HRM staff support. Small business managers, for instance, are an obvious example of individuals who frequently must do their own hiring without the assistance of HRM specialists. Even managers in larger organizations are frequently involved in recruiting candidates, reviewing application forms, interviewing applicants, inducting new employees, making decisions about employee training, providing career advice to employees, and evaluating employees' performance. Accordingly, whether or not an organization provides HRM support activities, every manager is involved with human resource decisions in his or her unit.

human resource management (HRM)
The management function that is concerned with getting, training, motivating, and keeping competent employees.

Exhibit 8-1 introduces the key components of an organization's human resource management process. It represents eight activities, or steps (the purple-shaded boxes), that, if properly executed, will staff an organization with competent, high-performing employees who are capable of sustaining their performance level over the long term.

The first three steps represent strategic human resource planning, the adding of staff through recruitment, the reduction in staff through downsizing, and selection. When executed properly, these steps lead to the identification and selection of competent employees. Once you have selected competent people, you need to help them adapt to the organization and to ensure that their job skills and knowledge are kept current. You do this through orientation and training and development. The last steps in the HRM process are designed to identify performance goals, correct performance problems if necessary, and help employees sustain a high level of performance over their entire work life. The activities involved include performance appraisal, compensation and benefits, and safety and health.

Every manager is involved with human resource decisions in his or her unit.

Notice in Exhibit 8-1 that the entire employment process is influenced by the external environment. Many of the factors introduced in Chapter 2 (e.g., globalization, downsizing, diversity) directly affect all management practices. But their impact is probably most severe in the management of human resources, because whatever happens to an organization ultimately influences what happens to its employees. So, before we review the human resource management process, let's briefly examine two critical environmental forces that affect HRM—labor unions and employment discrimination laws.

How Does a Union Constrain Management?

Unions exist in most industrialized nations—such as Sweden, Great Britain, Italy, Germany, Japan, Spain, France, and the United States.[2] A **union** is a group of workers, acting together, seeking to promote and protect their mutual interests through collective bargaining. Although only about 11 percent of the U.S. private-sector work force is unionized,[3] the successes and failures of unions affect all segments of the work force in two important ways. First, because major industries—such as automobile, steel, and electrical manufacturers as well as most branches of transportation—are unionized, unions play a major role in some of the most important sectors of the economy. Sec-

union
A group of workers, acting together, seeking to promote and protect their mutual interests through collective bargaining.

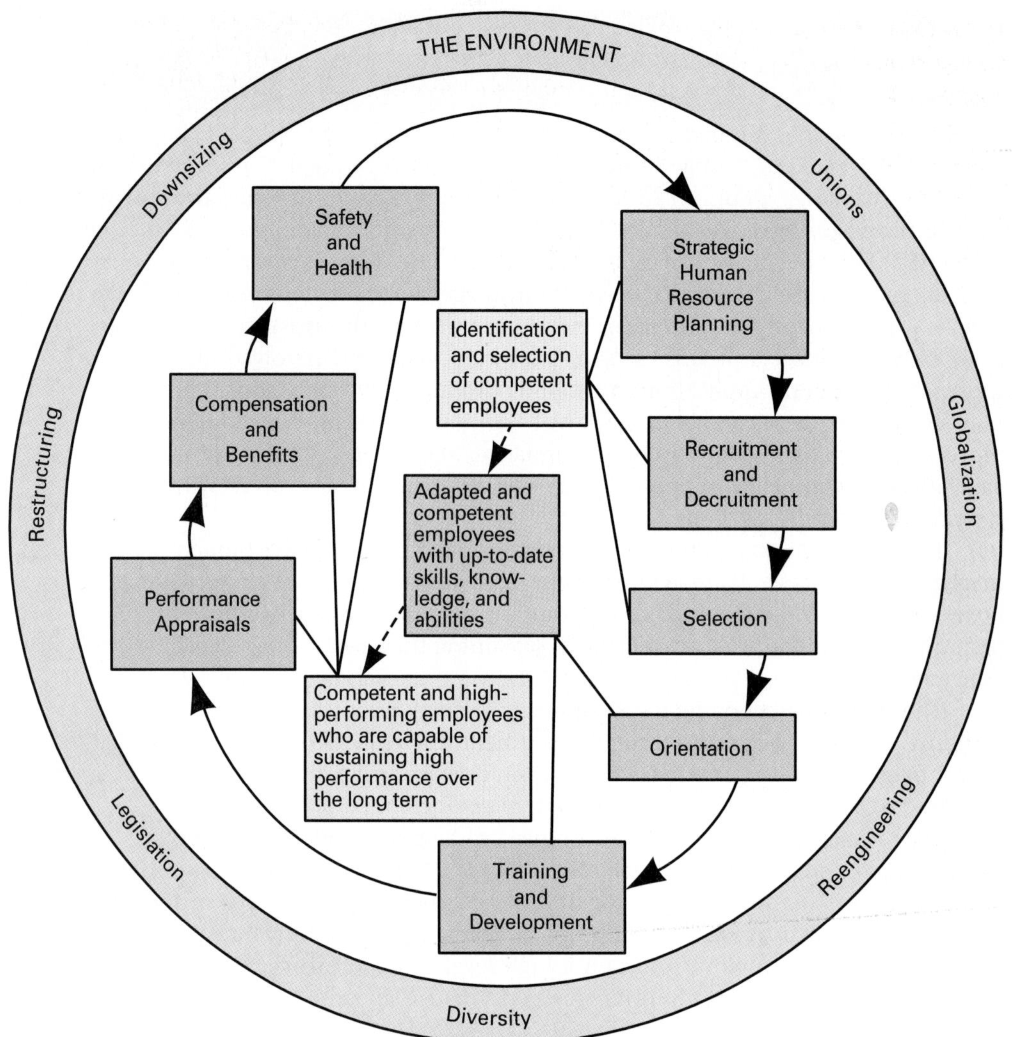

Exhibit 8-1
The Strategic Human Resource Management Process

ond, gains achieved by unions typically spill over into other nonunionized sectors of the economy. So the wages, hours, and working conditions of nonunion employees at a Columbia, Maryland, meatpacking plant may be affected by an agreement reached between the United Auto Workers and General Motors' at GM's Baltimore minivan facility.

When employees are represented by a union, management is required to implement very specific practices spelled out in the *collective bargaining agreement.* These agreements define such things as wages, work hours, criteria for promotions and layoffs, training eligibility, and disciplinary practices. For instance, how employees are compensated, what benefits they get, procedures for determining who works overtime, how workers are disciplined, criteria for attending training programs, and the like are not decided solely by management. Instead, such decisions have already been reached in negotiations. But not everything that happens in the organization is subject to ne-

Labor unions and management, no matter where they are, all have one thing in common. They must work with one another to achieve a collective bargaining agreement that deals with such issues as wages and work-related matters. The union representing workers at OWP Brillen, a German eyeglass maker, has been working with management to find ways to cut production costs rather than cut jobs.

gotiations. Management still has the discretion to run the business. Those things that do not directly affect employee matters, then, are outside the scope of negotiations. These are called *management rights*. For example, management need not negotiate over such items as what products to produce, their selling prices, the size of the work force, sending jobs overseas, or the location of operations.

What Influence Do Laws Have on HRM?

Since the mid-1960s, the federal government has greatly expanded its influence over HRM decisions by enacting a wealth of laws and regulations (see Exhibit 8-2 for examples). As a result of this legislation, employers today must ensure that equal employment opportunities exist for job applicants and current employees. Decisions regarding who will be hired, for example, or which employees will be chosen for a management training program must be made without regard to race, sex, religion, age, color, national origin, or disability. Exceptions can occur only when special circumstances exits. For instance, a police department can deny employment to a police officer applicant who is in a wheelchair. But if that same individual is applying for a desk job, such as police dispatcher, the disability cannot be used as a reason to deny employment. The issues involved, however, are rarely that clear-cut. For example, in the fall of 1995, the federal government took action against the Hooters Restaurant Chain because its management refused to hire male bartenders and waiters on the grounds that its current hiring practices "maintain the restaurants' image."[4] But, Hooters did hire men for management positions and for such jobs as cook and kitchen help.

Trying to balance the "shoulds and should-nots" of complying with these laws often falls under the realm of affirmative action. Many organizations have **affirmative action programs** to ensure that decisions and practices enhance the employment, upgrading, and retention of members from protected groups, such as minorities and females. That is, the organization not only refrains from discrimination but actively seeks to enhance the status of members from protected groups.

affirmative action programs
Programs that ensure that decisions and practices enhance the employment, upgrading, and retention of members of protected groups.

Our conclusion is that managers are not completely free to choose whom they hire, promote, or fire. While these regulations have significantly helped to reduce employment discrimination and unfair employment practices in organizations, they have, at the same time, also reduced management's discretion over human resource decisions.

YEAR	LAW OR REGULATION	DESCRIPTION
1963	Equal Pay Act	Prohibits pay differences based on sex for equal work
1964 (amended in 1972)	Civil Rights Act, Title VII	Prohibits discrimination based on race, color, religion, national origin, or sex
1967 (amended in 1978)	Age Discrimination in Employment Act	Prohibits age discrimination against employees between 40 and 65 years of age
1973	Vocational Rehabilitation Act	Prohibits discrimination on the basis of physical or mental disabilities
1974	Privacy Act	Gives employees the legal right to examine letters of reference concerning them
1978	Pregnancy Discrimination Act, Title VII	Prohibits dismissal because of pregnancy alone and protects job security during maternity leaves
1978	Mandatory Retirement Act	Prohibits the forced retirement of most employees before the age of 70; later amended to eliminate upper limit
1986	Immigration Reform and Control Act	Prohibits unlawful employment of aliens and unfair immigration-related employment practices
1988	Polygraph Protection Act	Limits an employer's ability to use lie detectors
1988	Worker Adjustment and Retraining Notification Act	Requires employers to provide 60 days' notice before a facility closing or mass layoff
1990	Americans with Disabilities Act	Prohibits employers from discriminating against and requires reasonable accommodation of essentially qualified individuals with physical or mental disabilities or the chronically ill
1991	Civil Rights Act	Reaffirms and tightens prohibition of discrimination; permits individuals to sue for punitive damages in cases of intentional discrimination
1993	Family and Medical Leave Act	Permits employees in organizations with 50 or more workers to take up to 12 weeks of unpaid leave each year for family or medical reasons

Exhibit 8-2
Major U.S. Federal Laws and Regulations Related to HRM

Strategic Human Resource Planning

strategic human resource planning (SHRP)
The process by which management ensures that it has the right personnel, who are capable of completing those tasks that will help the organization reach its objectives.

Strategic human resource planning (SHRP) is the process by which management ensures that it has the right number and kinds of people in the right places, and at the right times, who are capable of effectively and efficiently completing those tasks that will help the organization achieve its overall objectives. Strategic human resource planning, then, translates the organization's mission and objectives into a personnel plan that will allow the organization to achieve its goals.[5] SHRP can be condensed into two steps: (1) assessing current human resources and (2) assessing future human resource needs and developing a program to meet future human resource needs.

How Does an Organization Conduct an Employee Assessment?

Management begins by reviewing its current human resource status. This review is typically done by generating a human resource inventory. In an era of sophisticated computer systems, it is not too difficult a task for most organizations to generate a **human resource inventory report.** The input for this report is derived from forms completed by employees. Such reports might list the name, education, training, prior employment, languages spoken, capabilities, and specialized skills of each employee in the organization. This inventory allows management to assess what talents and skills are currently available in the organization.

human resource inventory report
a report listing the name, education, training, prior employer, languages spoken, and the like of each employee in the organization.

Another part of the current assessment is the **job analysis.** Whereas the human resource inventory is concerned with telling management what individual employees can do, job analysis is more fundamental. It is a lengthy process, one in which work flows are analyzed and behaviors that are necessary to perform jobs are identified. For instance, what does an international photographer who works for National Geographic do? What minimal knowledge, skills, and abilities are necessary for the adequate performance of the photographer's job? How do the job requirements for an international photographer compare with those for a domestic photographer, or for a photo librarian? These are questions that job analysis can answer. Ultimately, the purpose of job analysis is to determine the kinds of skills, knowledge, and abilities needed to successfully perform each job. This information is then used to develop, or revise if they exist, job descriptions and job specifications.

job analysis
An assessment of the kinds of skills, knowledge, and abilities needed to successfully perform each job in an organization.

A **job description** is a written statement of what a jobholder does, how it is done, and why it is done. It typically portrays job content, environment, and conditions of employment. The **job specification** states the minimum acceptable qualifications that an incumbent must possess to perform a given job successfully. It identifies the knowledge, skills, and abilities needed to do the job effectively. The job description and specification are important documents when managers begin recruiting and selecting. For instance, the job description can be used to describe the job to potential candidates. The job specification keeps the manager's attention on the list of qualifications necessary for an incumbent to perform a job and assists in determining whether candidates are qualified. Furthermore, hiring individuals on the basis of the information contained in these two documents helps to ensure that the hiring process is not discriminatory.

job description
A written statement of what a jobholder does, how it is done, and why it is done.

job specification
A statement of the minimum acceptable qualifications that an incumbent must possess to perform a given job successfully.

How Are Future Employee Needs Determined?

Future human resource needs are determined by the organization's strategic direction. Demand for human resources (its employees) is a result of demand for the organization's products or services. On the basis of its estimate of total revenue, management can attempt to establish the number and mix of human resources needed to reach that revenue. In some cases, however, the situation may be reversed. Where particular skills are necessary and in scarce supply, the availability of satisfactory human resources determines revenues. This might be the case, for example, at Sybase as it finds it has more business opportunities than it can handle. Its only limiting factor in building revenues is its ability to locate and hire staff with the qualifications necessary to satisfy the firm's clients. In most cases, however, the overall organizational goals and the resulting revenue forecast provide the major input determining the organization's human resource demand requirements.

After it has assessed both current capabilities and future needs, management is able to estimate shortages—both in number and in kind—and to highlight areas in

Strategic human resource planning not only must take into account employee needs in the future, it also must deal with a more difficult subject. Who will replace another—especially top management—when the time arises? The gravity of this question was truly felt when more than thirty executives died with Commerce Secretary Ron Brown when their plane crashed in the Balkans. Organizations that had prepared for replacing their executives were better able to make the transition—especially during a time filled with sorrow.

which the organization is overstaffed. A program can then be developed that matches these estimates with forecasts of future labor supply. So strategic human resource planning provides not only information to guide current staffing needs but also to project future employee needs and availability.

Recruitment and Selection

recruitment
The process of locating, identifying, and attracting capable applicants.

decruitment
Techniques for reducing the labor supply within an organization.

Once managers know their current SHRP status—whether they are understaffed or overstaffed—they can begin to do something about it. If one or more vacancies exist, they can use the information gathered through job analysis to guide them in **recruitment**—that is, the process of locating, identifying, and attracting capable applicants.[6] On the other hand, if strategic human resource planning indicates a surplus, management will want to reduce the labor supply within the organization. This activity initiates downsizing or layoff activities—sometimes referred to as **decruitment.**[7]

Where Does a Manager Look to Recruit Candidates?

Candidates can be found by using several sources—including the World Wide Web. Exhibit 8-3 offers some guidance. The source that is used should reflect the local labor market, the type or level of position, and the size of the organization.

Are Certain Recruiting Sources Better Than Others? Do certain recruiting sources produce superior candidates? The answer is Yes. The majority of studies have found that employee referrals produce the best candidates.[8] The explanation for this finding is intuitively logical. First, applicants referred by current employees are prescreened by those employees. Because the recommenders know both the job and the person being recommended, they tend to refer applicants who are well qualified for the job. Second, because current employees often feel that their reputation in the organization is at stake with a referral, they tend to refer others only when they are reasonably confident that the referral won't make them look bad. But this finding should not be interpreted to mean that management should always opt for the employee-referred candidate. Employee referrals may not increase the diversity and mix of employees.

Employee referrals may not increase the diversity and mix of employees.

SOURCE	ADVANTAGES	DISADVANTAGES
Internal searches	Low cost; build employee morale; candidates are familiar with organization	Limited supply; may not increase proportion of protected group employees
Advertisements	Wide distribution can be targeted to specific groups	Generate many unqualified candidates
Employee referrals	Knowledge about the organization provided by current employees; can generate strong candidates because a good referral reflects on the recommender	May not increase the diversity and mix of employees
Public employment agencies	Free or nominal cost	Candidates tend to be lower skilled, although some skilled employees available
Private employment agencies	Wide contacts; careful screening; short-term guarantees often given	High cost
School placement	Large, centralized body of candidates	Limited to entry-level positions
Temporary help services	Fill temporary needs	Expensive
Employee leasing and independent contractors	Fill temporary needs, but usually for more specific, longer-term projects	Little commitment to organization other than current project

Exhibit 8-3
Traditional Recruiting Sources

How Does a Manager Handle Decruitment? In the past decade, most large U.S. corporations, as well as many government agencies and small businesses, have been forced to shrink the size of their work force or restructure their skill composition.[9] Decruitment is becoming an increasingly relevant means of meeting the demands of a dynamic environment.

What are a manager's decruitment options? Obviously, people can be fired. But other choices may be more beneficial to the organization.[10] Exhibit 8-4 summarizes a manager's major decruitment options. But keep in mind, regardless of the decruitment method chosen, employees will suffer. We will discuss this phenomenon for employees—both victims and survivors—later in this chapter.

Is There a Basic Premise to Selecting Job Candidates?

Once the recruiting effort has developed a pool of candidates, the next step in the employment process is to identify who is "best" qualified for the job. In essence, then, the **selection process** is a prediction exercise. It seeks to predict which applicants will be successful if hired. "Successful" in this case means performing well on the criteria the organization uses to evaluate its employees. In filling a network administrator position, for example, the selection process should be able to predict which applicants will be able to properly install, debug, and manage the organization's computer network. For a position as a marketing representative, it should predict which applicants will be effective in generating high sales volumes. Consider, for a moment, that any selection decision can result in four possible outcomes. As shown in Exhibit 8-5, two of those outcomes would indicate correct decisions, but two would indicate errors.

selection process
The process of screening job applicants to ensure that the most appropriate candidates are hired.

OPTION	DESCRIPTION
Firing	Permanent involuntary termination
Layoffs	Temporary involuntary termination; may last only a few days or extend to years
Attrition	Not filling openings created by voluntary resignations or normal retirements
Transfers	Moving employees either laterally or downward; usually does not reduce costs but can reduce intraorganizational supply-demand imbalances
Reduced workweeks	Having employees work fewer hours per week, share jobs, or perform their jobs on a part-time basis
Early retirements	Providing incentives to older and more-senior employees for retiring before their normal retirement date
Job sharing	Having employees, typically two part-timers, share one full-time position

Exhibit 8-4
Decruitment Options

A decision is correct (1) when the applicant was predicted to be successful (was accepted) and later proved to be successful on the job or (2) when the applicant was predicted to be unsuccessful (was rejected) and, if hired, would not have been able to do the job. In the former case, we have successfully accepted; in the latter case, we have successfully rejected. Problems occur, however, when we make errors by rejecting candidates who, if hired, would have performed successfully on the job (called reject errors) or by accepting those who subsequently perform poorly (accept errors). These problems are, unfortunately, far from insignificant. A generation ago, reject errors meant only that the costs of selection would be increased because more candidates would have to be screened. Today, selection techniques that result in reject errors can open the organization to charges of employment discrimination, especially if applicants from protected groups are disproportionately rejected. Accept errors, on the other hand, have very obvious costs to the organization, including the cost of training the employee, the costs generated or profits foregone because of the employee's incompetence, and the cost of severance and the subsequent costs of further recruiting and selection screening. The major thrust of any selection activity is therefore to reduce the probability of making reject errors or accept errors while increasing the probability of making correct decisions. We do this by using selection activities that are both reliable and valid.

Exhibit 8-5
Selection Decision Outcomes

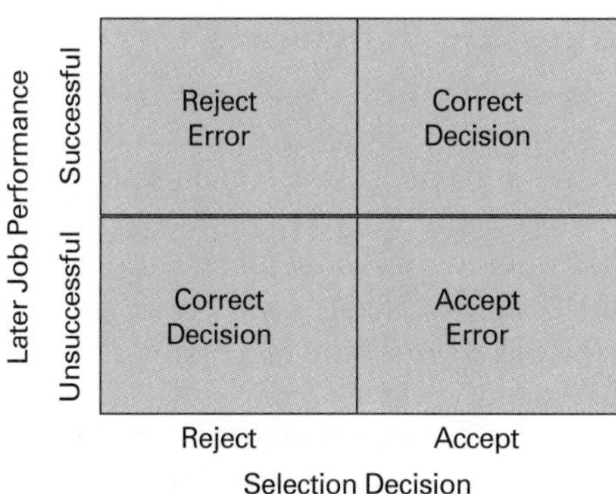

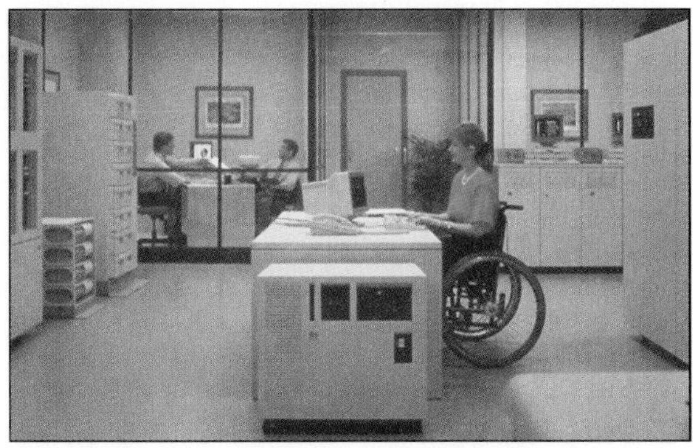

This individual has many fine qualities to offer an organization. Refusing to offer her employment simply because she's wheelchair-bound is discriminatory. In addition, organizations have a legal responsibility to alter work stations and doorways such that this employee's wheelchair can move freely in the workplace.

What Is Reliability? Reliability addresses whether a selection device measures the same thing consistently. For example, if a test is reliable, any single individual's score should remain fairly stable over time, assuming that the characteristics it is measuring are also stable. The importance of reliability should be self-evident. No selection device can be effective if it is low in reliability. Using such a device would be the equivalent of weighing yourself every day on an erratic scale. If the scale is unreliable—randomly fluctuating, say, ten to fifteen pounds every time you step on it—the results will not mean much. To be effective predictors, selection devices must possess an acceptable level of consistency.

reliability
The degree to which a selection device measures the same thing consistently.

What Is Validity? Any selection device that a manager uses—such as application forms, tests, interviews, or physical examinations—must also demonstrate **validity.** That is, there must be a proven relationship between the selection device used and some relevant measure. For example, a few pages ago we introduced a police applicant who was wheelchair-bound. Because of the physical requirements of a police officer's job, someone confined to a wheelchair would be unable to pass the physical endurance tests. In that case, denying employment could be considered valid. But requiring the same physical endurance tests for the dispatching job would not be job-related. Thus, the law prohibits management from using any selection device that cannot be shown to be directly related to successful job performance. And that constraint goes for "entrance" tests, too; management must be able to demonstrate that, once on the job, individuals with high scores on this test outperform individuals with low test scores. Consequently, the burden is on management to verify that any selection device it uses to differentiate applicants is related to job performance.

validity
The proven relationship between a selection device and some relevant criterion.

Are There Selection Devices That Every Manager Should Use?

Managers can use a number of selection devices to reduce accept and reject errors. The best-known devices include an analysis of a candidate's completed application form, written and performance-simulation tests, interviews, background investigations, and, when valid, a physical examination. Let's briefly review each of these devices, giving particular attention to the validity of each in predicting job performance. After we review the devices, we will discuss when each should be used.

What Is the Application Form? Almost all organizations require candidates to complete an application. It may be a form on which a candidate gives only his or her name, address, and telephone number. At the other extreme, it might be a comprehensive personal history profile, detailing the applicants' activities, skills, and accomplishments. Hard and relevant biographical data that can be verified—for example, rank in high school graduating class—have been shown to be valid measures of performance for some jobs.[11] In addition, when application form items have been appropriately weighted to reflect job relatedness, the device has proved to be a valid predictor for such diverse groups as salesclerks, engineers, factory workers, district managers, clerical employees, and technicians.[12] But, typically, only a couple of items on the application prove to be valid predictors, and then only for a specific job. Use of weighted applications for selection purposes is difficult and expensive because the weights have to be validated for each specific job and must be continually reviewed and updated to reflect changes in weights over time.

Do Written Tests Serve a Useful Purpose? Typical written tests include tests of intelligence, aptitude, ability, and interest. Such tests have long been used as selection devices, although their popularity has run in cycles. Written tests were widely used for twenty years after World War II. Beginning in the late 1960s, however, they fell into disfavor. Written tests were frequently characterized as discriminatory, and many organizations could not validate that their written tests were job-related.[13] But, since the late 1980s, written tests have made a comeback.[14] Managers have become increasingly aware that poor hiring decisions are costly and that properly designed tests could reduce the likelihood of making such decisions. In addition, the cost of developing and validating a set of written tests for a specific job has come down markedly.

A review of the evidence finds that tests of intellectual ability, spatial and mechanical ability, perceptual accuracy, and motor ability are moderately valid predictors for many semiskilled and unskilled operative jobs in industrial organizations.[15] And intelligence tests are reasonably good predictors for supervisory positions.[16] However, an enduring criticism of written tests is that intelligence, and other tested characteristics, can be somewhat removed from the actual performance of the job itself. For example, a high score on an intelligence test is not necessarily a good indicator that the applicant will perform well as a computer programmer. This criticism has led to an increased use of performance-simulation tests.

What Are Performance-Simulation Tests? What better way is there to find out whether an applicant for a technical writing position at Siemens can write technical manuals than to have him or her do it? The logic of this question has led to the expanding interest in performance-simulation tests. Undoubtedly, the enthusiasm for these tests lies in the fact that they are based on job analysis data and therefore should more easily meet the requirement of job relatedness than do written tests. **Performance-simulation tests** are made up of actual job behaviors rather than surrogates. The best-known performance-simulation tests are work sampling (a miniature replica of the job) and assessment centers (simulating real problems one may face on the job). The former is suited to routine jobs, the latter to selecting managerial personnel.

performance-simulation tests
Selection devices that are based on actual job behaviors; work sampling and assessment centers.

Is the Interview Effective? The interview, along with the application form, is an almost universal selection device.[17] Few of us have ever gotten a job without one or more interviews. The irony of this fact is that the value of the interview as a selection device has been the subject of considerable debate.[18]

Interviews can be reliable and valid selection tools, but too often they are not. When interviews are structured and well-organized, and when interviewers are held to common questioning, interviews are effective predictors.[19] But those conditions do not characterize many interviews. The typical interview—in which applicants are asked a varying set of essentially random questions in an informal setting—often provides little in the way of valuable information.

All kinds of potential biases can creep into interviews if they are not well structured and standardized. To illustrate, a review of the research leads us to the following conclusions:

- **1.** Prior knowledge about the applicant will bias the interviewer's evaluation.
- **2.** The interviewer tends to hold a stereotype of what represents a "good" applicant.
- **3.** The interviewer tends to favor applicants who share his or her own attitudes.
- **4.** The order in which applicants are interviewed will influence evaluations.
- **5.** The order in which information is elicited during the interview will influence evaluations.
- **6.** Negative information is given unduly high weight.
- **7.** The interviewer may make a decision concerning the applicant's suitability within the first four or five minutes of the interview.
- **8.** The interviewer may forget much of the interview's content within minutes after its conclusion.
- **9.** The interview is most valid in determining an applicant's intelligence, level of motivation, and interpersonal skills.
- **10.** Structured and well-organized interviews are more reliable than unstructed and unorganized ones.[20]

What can managers do to make interviews more valid and reliable? A number of suggestions have been made over the years. We list some in Developing a Management Skill.

What Is a Background Investigation? A **background investigation** includes contacting former employers to confirm the candidate's work record and to obtain an appraisal of the applicant's work performance. It may also include contacting other job-related references, verifying educational accomplishments shown on the application, and checking credit references and criminal records.[21] The premise behind these investigations is that one can predict an individual's future behavior on the basis of what he or she has done in the past.[22]

background investigation
A selection device to confirm a candidate's work record, obtain an appraisal of work performance, verify educational accomplishments, and check credit references and criminal records.

Several studies indicate that verifying "facts" given on the application form pays dividends. A significant percentage of job applicants—upward of 33 percent—exaggerate or misrepresent dates of employment, job titles, past salaries, or reasons for leaving a prior position.[23] Confirmation of hard data on the application with prior employers is therefore a worthwhile endeavor. Companies must assess the liability that potential employees may create and delve into their backgrounds in as much depth as necessary.[24] For example, a daycare center must go to great extremes to assure that potential employees will not pose a risk to the center's children. Failure to do the background check could prove detrimental to the organization if an unfortunate event occurred and the employee committing the act had a history of such behaviors.

Is a Physical Examination Necessary? For jobs with certain physical requirements, the physical examination has some validity. However, this includes a very small number of jobs today. In many cases, the physical examination primarily is done for insurance purposes—especially if a company has an insurance policy that does not provide medical coverage for preexisting conditions.

Great care must be taken to ensure that physical requirements are job related and do not discriminate. Some physical requirements may exclude certain disabled persons, when, in fact, such requirements do not affect job performance. Doing so would

Developing a Management Skill

INTERVIEWING CANDIDATES

About the Skill: *The difficulty in interviewing comes from the realization that interviewing is an art. Developing the art of the interview is to know what to do, and how to do it. Then it is a matter of practice so that one's interviewing skills don't become stale from lack of use.*

Steps in practicing the skill

1. ***Review the job description and job specification.*** Reviewing pertinent information about the job provides valuable information about what you will assess the candidate on. Furthermore, relevant job requirements help to eliminate interview bias.

2. ***Prepare a structured set of questions you want to ask all applicants for the job.*** By having a set of prepared questions, you ensure that the information you wish to elicit is attainable. Furthermore, by asking similar questions, you are able to better compare all candidates' answers against a common base.

3. ***Before meeting a candidate, review his or her application form and résumé.*** Doing so helps you to create a complete picture of the candidate in terms of what is represented on the résumé or application and what the job requires. You will also begin to identify areas to explore in the interview. That is, areas that are not clearly defined on the résumé or application but that are essential for the job will become a focal point in your discussion with the candidate.

4. ***Open the interview by putting the applicant at ease and by providing a brief preview of the topics to be discussed.*** Interviews are stressful for job candidates. By opening with small talk—e.g., the weather—you give the candidate time to adjust to the interview setting. By providing a preview of topics to come, you are giving the candidate an "agenda." This helps the candidate to begin framing what he or she will say in response to your questions.

5. ***Ask your questions and listen carefully to the applicant's answers.*** Select follow-up questions that naturally flow from the answers given. Focus on the responses as they relate to information you need to ensure that the candidate meets your job requirements. Any uncertainty you may still have requires a follow-up question to further probe for the information.

6. ***Close the interview by telling the applicant what is going to happen next.*** Applicants are anxious about the status of your hiring decision. Be up-front with the candidate regarding others who will be interviewed and the remaining steps in the hiring process. If you plan to make a decision in two weeks or so, let the candidate know what you intend to do. In addition, tell the applicant how you will let him or her know about your decision.

7. ***Write your evaluation of the applicant while the interview is still fresh in your mind.*** Don't wait until the end of your day, after interviewing several candidates, to write your analysis of a candidate. Memory can fail you! The sooner you complete your write-up after an interview, the better chance you have for accurately recording what occurred in the interview.

be a violation of the Americans with Disabilities Act! Additionally, even if a candidate has a disability, that still may not be enough to disqualify him or her from the job.

Orientation, Training, and Development

If we have done our recruiting and selecting properly, we should have hired competent individuals who can perform successfully. But successful performance requires more than possession of certain skills. New hires must be acclimated to the organization's culture and be trained to do the job in a manner consistent with the organization's objectives. To achieve these ends, HRM embarks on two processes—orientation and training.

How Do We Introduce New Hires to the Organization?

Once a job candidate has been selected, he or she needs to be introduced to the job and organization. This introduction is called **orientation.** The major objectives of orientation are to reduce the initial anxiety all new employees feel as they begin a new job; to familiarize new employees with the job, the work unit, and the organization as a whole; and to facilitate the outsider-insider transition. Job orientation expands on the information the employee obtained during the recruitment and selection stages. The new employee's specific duties and responsibilities are clarified, as well as how his or her performance will be evaluated. This is also the time to rectify any unrealistic expectations new employees might hold about the job (see Details on a Management Classic). Work-unit orientation familiarizes the employee with the goals of the work unit, makes clear how his or her job contributes to the unit's goals, and includes introduction to his or her coworkers. Organization orientation informs the new employee about the organization's objectives, history, philosophy, procedures, and rules. This information should include relevant personnel policies such as work hours, pay procedures, overtime requirements, and benefits. A tour of the organization's physical facilities is often part of the orientation.

orientation
The introduction of a new employee to the job and the organization.

Management has an obligation to make the integration of the new employee into the organization as smooth and as free of anxiety as possible. Successful orientation, whether formal or informal, results in an outsider-insider transition that makes the new member feel comfortable and fairly well adjusted, lowers the likelihood of poor work performance, and reduces the probability of a surprise resignation by the new employee only a week or two into the job.

What Is Employee Training?

On the whole, planes don't cause airline accidents, people do. Most collisions, crashes, and other mishaps—about 74 percent to be exact—result from errors by the pilot or air traffic controller or inadequate maintenance. Weather and structural failures typically account for the remaining causes of accidents.[25] We cite these statistics to illustrate the importance of training in the airline industry. These maintenance and human errors could be prevented or significantly reduced by better employee training.

Employee training is a learning experience in that it seeks a relatively permanent change in employees such that their ability to perform on the job improves. Thus, training involves changing skills, knowledge, attitudes, or behavior.[26] This may mean changing what employees know, how they work, or their attitudes toward their jobs, coworkers, managers, and the organization. It has been estimated, for instance, that U.S. business firms alone spend $40 billion a year on formal courses and training programs to build workers' skills.[27] Management, of course, is responsible for deciding when employees are in need of training and what form that training should take.

employee training
A learning experience that seeks to improve employees' job performance by changing their skills, knowledge, attitudes, or behavior.

Determining training needs typically involves generating answers to several questions (see Exhibit 8-6). If some of these questions sound familiar, you are paying close attention. It is precisely the type of analysis that has taken place when managers develop an organization structure to achieve their strategic goals—only now the focus is on the people dimension.

U.S. businesses spend $40 billion a year on training programs to build workers' skills.

The leading questions in Exhibit 8-6 suggest the kinds of signals that can warn a manager that training may be necessary. The more obvious ones are related directly to productivity. That is, there may be indications that job performance is declining. These may include actual decreases in production numbers, lower quality, more accidents, and higher scrap or rejection rates. Any of these outcomes might suggest that worker skills need to be fine-tuned. Of course, we are assuming that the employee's performance decline is in no way related to lack of effort. Managers, too, must also recognize that training may be required because of a "future" element. Changes that are being imposed on employees as a result of job design or a technological breakthrough also require training. For example, at XEL Corporation in Aurora, Colorado, company officials wanted to make the organization a premier producer of communications equipment. Unfortunately, many of the XEL employees lacked the necessary

Details on a Management Classic

JOHN P. WANOUS AND THE REALISTIC JOB PREVIEW

Managers who treat the recruiting and hiring of employees as if the applicants must be sold on the job and exposed only to an organization's positive characteristics set themselves up to have a work force that is dissatisfied and prone to high turnover. That is the conclusion of John P. Wanous.[28]

Every job applicant acquires, during the hiring process, a set of expectations about the company and about the job for which he or she is interviewing. When the information an applicant receives is excessively inflated, a number of things happen that have potentially negative effects on the company. First, Wanous found that mismatched applicants would be less likely to withdraw from the search process. Second, he found that, because inflated information builds unrealistic expectations, new employees are likely to become quickly dissatisfied and to prematurely resign. Third, new hires are prone to become disillusioned and less committed to the organization when they face unexpected "harsh" realities of the job. In many cases, Wanous revealed that these individuals feel that they were duped or misled during the hiring process and, therefore, may become problem employees.

To increase job satisfaction among employees and reduce turnover, Wanous advocated providing applicants with a *realistic job preview (RJP)*. An RJP includes both positive and negative information about the job and the company. For example, in addition to the positive comments typically expressed in the interview, the candidate would be told of the downside of joining the company. For instance, he or she might be told that there are limited opportunities to talk to coworkers during work hours, that promotional advancement is slim, or that work hours fluctuate so erratically that employees may be required to work during typically off hours (nights and weekends). Wanous's research, supported by that of others, indicates that applicants who have been given a realistic job preview hold lower and more-realistic job expectations for the jobs they will be performing and are better able to cope with the job and its frustrating elements than are applicants who have been given only inflated information. The result is fewer unexpected resignations by new employees.

For managers, realistic job previews offer a major insight into the HRM process. That is, retaining good people is as important as hiring them in the first place. Presenting only the positive aspects of a job to a job applicant may initially entice him or her to join the organization, but it may be an affiliation that both parties quickly regret.

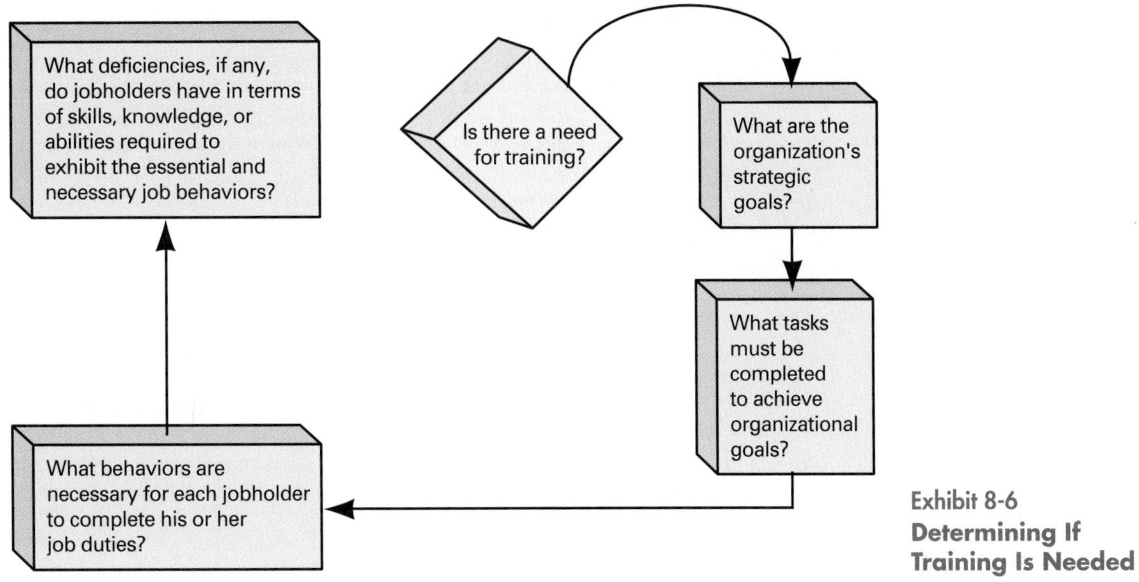

Exhibit 8-6
Determining If Training Is Needed

skills to work with new technologies, or even to accept the autonomy managers wanted to give them.[29] Rather than "change" its entire work force, XEL contracted with a local community college to provide training programs that would correct employee deficiencies. Companies like XEL view training proactively, as opposed to waiting and reacting to unsatisfactory performance conditions that may arise later.

How Are Employees Trained? Most training takes place on the job. The prevalence of on-the-job training can be attributed to the simplicity of such methods and their usually lower cost. However, on-the-job training can disrupt the workplace and result in an increase in errors while learning takes place. Also, some skill training is too complex to learn on the job. In such cases, it should take place outside the work setting.

What Are Some of the Typical Methods Used? Many different types of training methods are available. For the most part, however, we can classify them in two ways: on-the-job or off-the-job. We have summarized the more popular training methods in Exhibit 8-7.

How Can Managers Ensure That Training Is Working? It is relatively easy to offer a new training program. But if the training program is not evaluated, it becomes impossible to truly justify its existence. Any training that is offered by an organization must be cost-effective. That is, managers must be able to show that the benefits gained by the training outweigh the costs associated with it. Only by analyzing the outcomes training may have generated can effectiveness be determined.

Is there a general way in which training programs are typically evaluated? Frequently, the following scenario takes place. Several managers, representatives from the training department, and a group of workers are asked to provide some insight into a recently completed training program. If the comments are generally positive, the program often gets a favorable evaluation. And, on the basis of that evaluation, the program continues—unless, of course, something occurs that causes the program to be changed or eliminated. The reactions of the evaluators, however, are questionable. The participants' opinions are often heavily influenced by factors that have little to do with actual training effectiveness—factors such as difficulty, entertainment value, or

Sample On-the-Job Training Methods	
Job rotation	Lateral transfers allowing employees to work at different jobs. Provides good exposure to a variety of tasks.
Understudy assignments	Working with a seasoned veteran, coach, or mentor. Provides support and encouragement from an experienced worker. In the trades industry, this may also be an apprenticeship.
Sample Off-the-Job Training Methods	
Classroom lectures	Lectures designed to convey specific technical, interpersonal, or problem-solving skills.
Films and videos	Using the media to explicitly demonstrate technical skills that are not easily presented by other training methods.
Simulation exercises	Learning a job by actually performing the work (or its simulation). May include case analyses, experiential exercises, role playing, and group interaction.
Vestibule training	Learning tasks on the same equipment that one actually will use on the job, but in a simulated work environment.

Exhibit 8-7
Typical Training Methods

personality of the instructor. Obviously, those are not the factors we want evaluated. Rather, managers must be certain that employee performance improves. Accordingly, training programs must be evaluated on some performance-based measures such as how well employees perform their jobs after the training or the difference between pre- and posttraining performance.

How Is Development Different from Training?

employee development
A learning experience that seeks to prepare employees for future positions that will require higher-level skills, knowledge, or abilities.

In many organizations, the terms *training* and *development* are used synonymously. In many respects, that may be correct. But employee development is different from training. Whereas employee training focuses on the skills needed to do one's current job, **employee development** is more future-oriented. That is, it deals with preparing employees for future positions that will require higher-level skills, knowledge, or abilities—such as the analytical, human, conceptual, political, and specialized skills we introduced in Chapter 1 that all managers need. Although the methods of "delivering" employee development programs are similar to those used for training methods, they focus more heavily on employees' personal growth.

It is important to consider one critical component of employee development in today's organizations. All employees, no matter what their level, can be developed. Historically, *development* was reserved for managers and people aspiring to be managers. There is no question that development still must include preparing managers, but downsizing, reengineering, and empowering have shown us that nonmanagerial personnel need planning, organizing, leading, and controlling skills, too. For instance, the use of work teams, giving workers the opportunity to participate in decision-making, and placing a greater emphasis on customer service and quality have all led to development's being "pushed" down in the organization. But, like training, development efforts must be evaluated to ensure that the organization is getting its "money's worth."

What Is a Career?

career
The sequence of positions occupied by a person during the course of a lifetime.

The term *career* has a number of meanings. In popular usage, it can mean advancement ("his career is progressing nicely"), a profession ("she has chosen a career in medicine"), or a lifelong sequence of jobs ("his career has included fifteen jobs in six organizations"). For our purposes, we define a **career** as the sequence of positions occupied by a person during the course of a lifetime.[30] By this definition, it is apparent that we all have, or will have, a career. Moreover, the concept is as relevant to transient, unskilled laborers as it is to engineers or physicians.

Individuals—not the organization—are responsible for their careers!

Although career development has been an important topic in management-related courses for the past three decades, we have witnessed some drastic changes over the years. Years ago, career development programs were designed to assist employees in advancing their work lives. Their focus was to provide the information and assessment needed to help employees realize their career goals. Career development was also a way for the organization to attract and retain highly talented personnel. But those concerns are all but disappearing in today's organizations. Instead, downsizing, restructuring, reengineering, and the like have drawn us to one significant conclusion about career development: The individual—not the organization—is responsible for his or her career! Some 3 million employees have learned that the hard way over the past few years.[31] You, therefore, must be prepared to do what is necessary to advance your career (see Understanding Yourself). We address some of these issues and offer some guidelines in Appendix B.

Performance Management

It is important for managers to get their employees to behave in ways that management considers desirable. How do managers ensure that employees are performing as they are supposed to? In organizations, the formal means of assessing the work of employees is through a systematic performance appraisal process.

What Is a Performance Management System?

performance management system A process of establishing performance standards and evaluating performance in order to arrive at objective human resource decisions and to provide documentation to support personnel actions.

A **performance management system** is a process of establishing performance standards and evaluating performance in order to arrive at objective human resource decisions—such as pay increases and training needs—as well as to provide documentation to support any personnel actions. Undoubtedly, performance appraisals are important. But how do you evaluate an employee's performance? That is, what are the specific techniques for appraisal? We have listed them in Exhibit 8-8.[32]

Exhibit 8-8 Performance Appraisal Methods

METHOD	ADVANTAGE	DISADVANTAGE
Written essay	Simple to use	More a measure of evaluator's writing ability than of employee's actual performance
Critical incidents	Rich examples behaviorally based	Time-consuming; lack quantification
Graphic rating scales	Provide quantitative data; less time-consuming than others	Do not provide depth of job behavior assessed
BARS	Focus on specific and measurable job behaviors	Time-consuming; difficult to develop measures
Multiperson	Compares employees with one another	Unwieldy with large number of employees
MBO	Focuses on end goals; results-oriented	Time-consuming

Understanding Yourself

How Do You Define Life Success?

Circle the appropriate number to rate the following forty-two statements according to the scale below:

5 = *Always important*
4 = *Very often important*
3 = *Fairly often important*
2 = *Occasionally important*
1 = *Never important*

1. Getting others to do what I want	5	4	3	2	1
2. Having inner peace and contentment	5	4	3	2	1
3. Having a happy marriage	5	4	3	2	1
4. Having economic security	5	4	3	2	1
5. Being committed to my organization	5	4	3	2	1
6. Being able to give help, assistance, advice, and support to others	5	4	3	2	1
7. Having a job that pays more than peers earn	5	4	3	2	1
8. Being a good parent	5	4	3	2	1
9. Having good job benefits	5	4	3	2	1
10. Having a rewarding family life	5	4	3	2	1
11. Raising children to be independent adults	5	4	3	2	1
12. Having people work for me	5	4	3	2	1
13. Being accepted at work	5	4	3	2	1
14. Enjoying my nonwork activities	5	4	3	2	1
15. Making or doing things that are useful to society	5	4	3	2	1
16. Having high income and the resulting benefits	5	4	3	2	1
17. Having a sense of personal worth	5	4	3	2	1
18. Contributing to society	5	4	3	2	1
19. Having long-term job security	5	4	3	2	1
20. Having children	5	4	3	2	1
21. Getting good performance evaluations	5	4	3	2	1
22. Having opportunities for personal creativity	5	4	3	2	1
23. Being competent	5	4	3	2	1
24. Having public recognition	5	4	3	2	1
25. Having children who are successful emotionally and professionally	5	4	3	2	1
26. Having influence over others	5	4	3	2	1
27. Being happy with my private life	5	4	3	2	1
28. Earning regular salary increases	5	4	3	2	1
29. Having personal satisfaction	5	4	3	2	1

	5	4	3	2	1
30. Improving the well-being of the work force	5	4	3	2	1
31. Having a stable marriage	5	4	3	2	1
32. Having the confidence of my bosses	5	4	3	2	1
33. Having the resources to help others	5	4	3	2	1
34. Being in a high-status occupation	5	4	3	2	1
35. Being able to make a difference in something	5	4	3	2	1
36. Having money to buy or do anything I want	5	4	3	2	1
37. Being satisfied with my job	5	4	3	2	1
38. Having self-respect	5	4	3	2	1
39. Helping others to achieve	5	4	3	2	1
40. Having personal happiness	5	4	3	2	1
41. Being able to provide quality education for my children	5	4	3	2	1
42. Making a contribution to society	5	4	3	2	1

Scoring: This questionnaire taps six dimensions of life success: the achievement of status and wealth, contribution to society, good family relationships, personal fulfillment, professional fulfillment, and security. The questions that pertain to each category are listed beneath the category heading in the table below. Insert the number you circled beside each question. Calculate your scores as follows: Add your scores and divide by the number of questions in each category to determine a mean score on each dimension.

Status/Wealth	Contribution to Society	Family Relationships	Personal Fulfillment
1	6	3	2
7	15	8	14
12	18	10	17
16	22	11	23
24	33	20	27
26	35	25	29
34	39	31	38
36	42	41	40
total ___	total ___	total ___	total ___
mean ___	mean ___	mean ___	mean ___

Professional Fulfillment	Security
5	4
13	9
21	19
32	28
37	30
total ___	total ___
mean ___	mean ___

What the Assessment Means: The dimensions on which you scored the highest are the ones that are most important to you. Those things that are important to you must be considered when choosing a career. For instance, if family relationships are important to you, then you want to work in an organization where you can combine both your personal and professional life. Jobs that do not offer what you want or do not help you achieve your life success can create problems for you.

Continued

You can also compare your scores with the following norms based on surveys of managers.

Dimension	Females (*N* = 439)	Males (*N* = 317)
Status/wealth	3.48	3.65
Social contribution	4.04	4.07
Family relationships	4.44	4.28
Personal fulfillment	4.60	4.43
Professional fulfillment	4.21	4.15
Security	4.30	4.21

The *written essay* requires no complex forms or extensive training to complete. However, a "good" or "bad" appraisal may be determined as much by the evaluator's writing skill as by the employee's actual level of performance. The use of *critical incidents* focuses the evaluator's attention on those critical or key behaviors that separate effective from ineffective job performance. The appraiser writes down anecdotes that describe what the employee did that was especially effective or ineffective. The key here is that only specific behaviors are cited, not vaguely defined personality traits. One of the oldest and most popular methods of appraisal is *graphic rating scales.* This method lists a set of performance factors such as quantity and quality of work, job knowledge, cooperation, loyalty, attendance, honesty, and initiative. The evaluator then goes down the list and rates each factor on an incremental scale. Finally, an approach that has received attention in recent years involves *behaviorally anchored rating scales (BARS).*[33] These scales combine major elements from the critical incident and graphic rating scale approaches: The appraiser rates an employee according to items along a numerical scale, but the items are examples of actual behavior on a given job rather than general descriptions or traits.

Should We Compare People with One Another or Against Some Set Standards? The methods identified above have one thing in common. They require us to evaluate employees on the basis of how well their performance matches established or absolute criteria. *Multiperson comparisons,* on the other hand, compare one person's performance with that of one or more individuals. Thus, it is a relative, not an absolute, measuring device. The three most popular uses of this method are group order ranking, individual ranking, and paired comparison.

The *group order ranking* requires the evaluator to place employees into a particular classification such as "top one-fifth" or "second one-fifth." When this method is used to appraise employees, managers rank all their employees. If a rater has twenty employees, only four can be in the top fifth, and, of course, four must be relegated to the bottom fifth. The *individual ranking* approach requires the evaluator merely to list the employees in order from highest to lowest. Only one can be "best." In an appraisal of thirty employees, the difference between the first and second employee is assumed to be the same as that between the twenty-first and twenty-second. Even though some employees may be closely grouped, there can be no ties. In the paired comparison approach, each employee is compared with every other employee in the comparison group and rated as either the superior or weaker member of the pair. After all paired comparisons are made, each employee is assigned a summary ranking based on the number of superior scores he or she achieved. While this approach ensures that each employee is compared against every other, it can become unwieldy when large numbers of employees are being assessed.

Isn't MBO an Appraisal Approach, Too? We introduced management by objectives during our discussion of planning in Chapter 3. MBO, however, is also a mechanism for appraising performance. In fact, it is the preferred method for assessing managers and professional employees.[34]

With MBO, employees are evaluated by how well they accomplish a specific set of objectives that have been determined to be critical in the successful completion of their jobs. As you'll recall from our discussion in Chapter 3, these objectives need to be tangible, verifiable, and measurable. MBO's popularity among managerial personnel is probably due to its focus on end goals. Managers tend to emphasize such results-oriented outcomes as profit, sales, and costs. This emphasis aligns with MBO's concern with quantitative measures of performance. Because MBO emphasizes ends rather than means, this appraisal method allows managers the discretion to choose the best path for achieving their goals.

What Happens When Performance Falls Short?

So far this discussion has focused on the performance management system. And, although that is designed to help managers ensure a productive work force, one important question needs to be raised. What if an employee is not performing in a satisfactory manner? What can you do?

If, for some reason, an employee is not meeting his or her performance goals, a manager needs to find out why. If it is because the employee is mismatched for the job (a hiring error) or because he or she does not have adequate training, something relatively simple can be done; the manager can either reassign the individual into a job that better matches his or her skills or train the employee in how to do the job more effectively. If the problem is associated not with the employee's abilities but with his or her desire to do the job, it becomes a **discipline** problem. In that case, a manager can rely on employee counseling and if necessary can take disciplinary action. This may include verbal and written warnings, suspensions—and even terminations.

discipline
Actions taken by a manager to enforce an organization's standards and regulations.

employee counseling
A process designed to help employees overcome performance-related problems.

How Can Employee Counseling Help? Employee counseling is a process designed to help employees overcome performance-related problems. Rather than viewing the performance problem from a punitive point of view (discipline), employee counseling attempts to uncover why employees have lost their desire to work productively. More important, it is designed to find ways to "fix" the problem. In many cases, employees don't go from being productive one day to being unproductive the next. Rather, the change happens gradually and may be a function of something that is occurring in someone's personal life. Employee counseling attempts to assist employees in getting help to resolve whatever is bothering them.

The premise behind employee counseling is fairly simple. It is beneficial to both the organization and the employee. Just as it is costly to have someone quit shortly after being hired, it is costly to fire someone. The time spent recruiting and selecting, orienting, training, and developing employees translates into money. If, through some assistance, however, an organization can help employees overcome personal problems and get them back on the job quickly the organization can avoid those costs. That's the intent of employee counseling. But make no mistake about it, employee counseling is not an activity to lessen the effect of an employee's poor performance, nor is it intended to reduce his or her responsibility to change inappropriate work behavior. If the employee can't or won't accept help, then disciplinary actions will be taken.

Compensation and Benefits

You open the newspaper and the following job advertisement grabs your attention. "Wanted—hard-working individual who is willing to work sixty hours a week in a less-than-ideal environment. The job pays no money but gives you the opportunity to say "I've done that.'" Sound intriguing to you? Probably not! In fact, although there are exceptions, most of us work for money. What our jobs pay and what benefits we get fall under the heading of compensation and benefits. Determining what these will be is by no means easy.

How Are Pay Levels Determined?

compensation administration
The process of determining a cost-effective pay structure that will attract and retain competent employees, provide an incentive for them to work hard, and ensure that pay levels will be perceived as fair.

How does management decide who gets paid $6.65 an hour and who receives $325,000 a year? The answer lies in compensation administration. The goals of compensation administration are to design a cost-effective pay structure that will attract and retain competent employees and to provide an incentive for these individuals to exert high energy levels at work. **Compensation administration** also attempts to ensure that whatever pay levels are determined will be perceived as fair by all employees. Fairness means that the established pay levels are adequate and consistent for the demands and requirements of the job. Therefore, the primary determination of pay is the kind of job an employee performs. Different jobs require different kinds and levels of skills, knowledge, and abilities—and these vary in their value to the organization.[35] So, too, do the responsibility and authority held in certain positions. In short, the higher the skills, knowledge, and abilities—and the greater the authority and responsibility—the higher the pay.

Compensation administration attempts to design a cost-effective pay structure that will attract and retain competent employees.

Although skills, abilities, and the like directly affect pay levels, there are other factors that may come into play. Pay levels may be influenced by the kind of business, the environment surrounding the job, geographic location, and employee performance levels and seniority. For example, private-sector jobs typically provide higher rates of pay than comparable positions in public and not-for-profit jobs. Employees who work under hazardous conditions (say bridge builders operating 200 feet in the air), work unusual hours (e.g., the midnight shift), or work in geographic areas where cost of living is higher (e.g., New York City versus Tucson, Arizona) are typically more highly compensated. Likewise, employees who have been with an organization for a long time may have had a salary increase each year.

Irrespective of the factors mentioned above, there is one other factor that is most critical—management's compensation philosophy. Some organizations, for instance, have the philosophy that they don't pay employees any more than they have to. In the absence of a union contract that stipulates wage levels, those organizations only have to pay minimum wage for most of their jobs. On the other hand, some organizations are committed to a compensation philosophy of paying their employees at or above area wage levels in order to emphasize that they want to attract and keep the best pool of talent.

Why Do Organizations Offer Employee Benefits?

employee benefits
Nonfinancial rewards designed to enrich employees' lives.

When an organization designs its overall compensation package, it has to look further than just an hourly wage or annual salary. It has to take into account another element, employee benefits. **Employee benefits** are nonfinancial rewards that are designed to enrich employees' lives. They have grown in importance and variety over the past several decades. Once viewed as "fringes," today's benefit packages reflect great thought in an effort to provide something that each employee values.

The benefits offered by an organization will vary widely in scope. Most organizations are legally required to provide social security and workers' and unemployment compensations, but organizations also provide an array of benefits such as paid time off from work, life and disability insurance, retirement programs, and health insurance. The costs of some of these, such as retirement and health insurance benefits, are often borne by both the employer and the employee.

Safety and Health

Managers at all levels have a legal responsibility to ensure that the workplace is free from unnecessary hazards and that conditions in the organization are not detrimental to employees' physical or mental health. Of course, accidents can, and do, happen, and their severity can be astounding. There are approximately 10,000 reported work-related deaths and 2 million injuries each year in the United States. These occurrences result in more than 90 million days of lost productivity.[36] That's seven times the loss rate that occurs in Japan.[37] Heartless as it sounds, managers must be concerned about safety and health if for no other reason than that unsafe and unhealthy environments cost money and hurt their competitive ability! Thus a manager must accept responsibility to prevent such occurrences from happening.

What Guides Safety and Health Practices?

In 1970, Congress passed the **Occupational Safety and Health Act** to assure that every worker experiences safe and healthful working conditions. The act is enforced by the Occupational Safety and Health Administration (OSHA). This agency inspects workplaces, penalizes employers that don't meet safety and health standards, and provides health and safety consultation to firms.

Occupational Safety and Health Act
A federal law designed to assure that workers experience safe and healthful working conditions.

OSHA places very specific responsibility on managers for documenting employee injuries and illnesses. For instance, each occupational injury and illness that results in death, medical treatment other than minor first-aid, loss of consciousness, restriction of work or motion, or transfer to another job must be recorded on a standardized form within six working days after learning of the injury or illness. In addition, managers are expected to participate in and oversee training of employees to ensure that they understand pertinent OSHA regulations (as well as state laws governing safety and health). Managers may also be required to accompany OSHA officials during inspections of work areas. The intent is to scrutinize the work environment to locate sources of potential hazards—such as loose carpets, oil on walkways, sharp protrusions on equipment at eye level, or blocked fire exits.

How Can a Healthy Work Environment Be Achieved?

Safety issues typically focus on preventing accidents at work. Although that's critical, there is another element that is equally important—maintaining a healthy work environment. If workers cannot function properly at their jobs because of constant headaches, watering eyes, breathing difficulties, or fear of exposure to materials that may cause long-term health problems, their productivity will be affected. Consequently, creating a healthy work environment is not only legally required but is also the right thing to do.

Phil Thompson, president of Industrial Supply Company in Salt Lake City, Utah, implemented a smoking ban in his company a few years ago. Since then, the company's productivity has increased 30 percent, and premiums paid for health insurance for employees have significantly decreased.

Current Issues in Human Resources Management

We'll conclude this chapter by looking at several human resource issues facing today's managers. These are managing work force diversity, sexual harassment, family-friendly benefits, and employee anxiety.

How Can Work Force Diversity Be Managed?

We have discussed the changing makeup of the work force in several places in this book. Let's now consider how work force diversity will affect such basic HRM concerns as recruitment, selection, and orientation.

Improving work force diversity requires managers to widen their recruiting net. For example, the popular practice of relying on current employee referrals as a source of new job applicants tends to result in candidates who have similar characteristics to present employees. So managers have to look for applicants in places where they haven't typically looked before. To increase diversity, managers are increasingly turning to nontraditional recruitment sources. These include women's job networks, over-fifty clubs, urban job banks, disabled people's training centers, ethnic newspapers, and gay-rights organizations. This type of outreach should enable the organization to broaden its pool of applicants.

Once a diverse set of applicants exists, efforts must be made to ensure that the selection process does not discriminate. Moreover, applicants need to be made comfortable with the organization's culture and be made aware of management's desire to accommodate their needs. For instance, at Microsoft Corporation, only a small number of women apply for its technical jobs. However, the company makes every effort to hire a high percentage of female applicants and strives to make sure that these women have a successful experience once they are on the job.[38]

Finally, orientation is often difficult for women and minorities. Many organizations today, such as Lotus and Hewlett-Packard, provide special workshops to raise diversity consciousness among current employees, as well as programs for new employees that focus on diversity issues. The thrust of these efforts is to increase individual understanding of the differences each of us brings to the workplace. For example, at Kraft Cheese's manufacturing plant in Missouri, managers have put together an ambitious diversity program that reflects the increased values the organization has placed on incorporating diverse perspectives. One thing they did was to reward "diversity champions," individual employees who supported and promoted the benefits of diversity. They also added diversity goals to employee evaluations, encouraged nontraditional promotions, sponsored ethnic meal days, and trained over half the plant's employees in diversity issues.[39] A number of companies also have special mentoring programs to deal with the reality that lower-level female and minority managers have few role models with whom to identify.[40]

What Is Sexual Harassment?

Sexual harassment is no longer a hidden or secret subject in organizations. Data indicate that almost all Fortune 500 companies in the United States have had complaints lodged against them by employees, and about one-third have been sued.[41] These cases represented a substantial cost to the companies not only in terms of litigation and settlements; it is estimated that sexual harassment costs a typical Fortune 500 company $6.7 million a year in absenteeism, low productivity, and turnover.[42] And sexual harassment is not just a U.S. phenomenon. It is a worldwide issue.[43] Sexual harassment charges have been filed by employees in such countries as Japan, Australia, the Netherlands, Belgium, New Zealand, Sweden, and Ireland.[44]

Sexual harassment generally encompasses sexually suggestive remarks, unwanted touching and sexual advances, requests for sexual favors, or other verbal and physical conduct of a sexual nature.[45] Sexual harassment can occur between a male and a female or between people of the same gender. A manager must be sensitive to this concern because sexual harassment intimidates employees, interferes with job performance, and exposes the organization to liability. On this last point, the courts have ruled that if the employee who is guilty of sexual harassment is a manager or agent for an organization, then the organization is liable for sexual harassment, regardless of whether the act was authorized or forbidden by the organization or whether the organization knew of the act.

sexual harassment Sexually suggestive remarks, unwanted touching and sexual advances, requests for sexual favors, or other verbal and physical conduct of a sexual nature.

To avoid liability, and to do the right thing, managers must follow the organization's established policy against sexual harassment.[46] These policies should then be reinforced by regular discussion sessions with all employees in which managers communicate the rules and carefully instruct employees that even the slightest sexual overture to another employee will not be tolerated. Studies have shown that the best training on sexual harassment gives participants a chance to talk to each other instead of just making them listen to a lecture or watch a film on the subject.[47]

Rena Weeks was elated when a California jury found her employer guilty of sexual harassment. Given the circumstances and seriousness of the case, the jury awarded Rena $7.1 million for the emotional trauma she suffered as a result of being sexually harassed. And $250,000 of that award is to be paid by the person who harassed Rena.

Can Organizations Be Family-Friendly?

family-friendly benefits Employee benefits, such as flextime, child care, relocation programs, parental leave, and adoption benefits, that are supportive of caring for one's family.

Another major trend affecting managers today is the push for benefits that fall under the category called **family-friendly benefits.** Family-friendly benefits are so named because they are supportive of caring for one's family.[48] These would include such benefits as flextime, child care, part-time employment, relocation programs, summer camp, parental leave, and adoption benefits.[49] Companies such as Hewlett-Packard, IBM, and Prudential Insurance Company currently offer such benefits.[50] At the heart of such programs, however, is increasing child- and elder-care benefits. Today's working parents and people caring for elderly relatives are eagerly seeking ways of having

Managers Who Made a Difference

Christiane Kolbus, Assistant General Manager, Commerzbank

Competitive, aggressive, and career- and goal-oriented. These are all characteristics frequently associated with American workers. But don't say that to Christiane Kolbus. She would disagree! Well, up to a point.[51]

Christiane Kolbus was born and raised in Germany. As a strong-willed, professionally driven woman, she chose to enter the male-dominated world of the banking industry in Germany. Fully aware of the work ahead of her, Christiane was more than confident that she could excel on her job and still have a rewarding family life. Sadly, that didn't happen.

She started as a Commerzbank management trainee in Bremen, Germany, and her career quickly soared. Within several years, she had been promoted to the position of chief of corporate training for the bank. Her job, however, had its trade-offs. On the positive side, it enabled her to become a member of the bank's prestigious executive development program—the one in which all future executives are trained. But also with the job came many fourteen-hour workdays. Furthermore, her position required Christiane to travel more than three months a year. As a result, her family life—especially her marriage—became strained. When the bank transferred her to Leipzig to develop employee training programs for the bank's eastern region, she moved without her husband.

Kolbus began to recognize what her career goals were costing her and what the continued costs could be. For example, she realized that the higher up one went in the organization, the more political one had to be. Even more, she felt that this political arena caused her to be "less honest" in her dealings with others—something she despised. Torn between her values and family and professional lives, Christiane Kolbus decided to give up her position as chief training executive. She also quit the prestigious executive development program. She opted for a more-relaxed position as the training assistant manager of the Saxony-Anhalt region. As she states, "I don't want to fight anymore." Her new position has given her the opportunity to revise her career goal to one that focuses on building a much more satisfying personal life. Making it to the top of the bank carried with it too high a price for Christiane. A price she was no longer willing to accept.

quality child and elder care near their place of work. This concern is especially important in organizations that operate staggered shifts or around the clock.

Family-friendly benefits are also addressing the issue of employees who have children and who can't (and won't) leave their family concerns behind when they go to work. When an organization hires employees, they not only get their special skills, they also get their feelings, personal problems, and family commitments. Although management cannot be sympathetic to every detail of employees' lives, we are seeing that organizations are becoming more considerate in family issues that may be arising (see Managers Who Made a Difference). For instance, summer can be a difficult time for employees because the children are out of school. Companies such as Johnson & Johnson and Stratco—a Leawood, Kansas–based chemical engineering organization—permit children to be brought to work with employees. At Johnson & Johnson, employees' children are then transported to a summer camp; at Stratco, infants are permitted to spend the entire day at the workplace.[52]

Another family concern that arises is the large number of dual-career couples—couples in which both partners have a professional, managerial, or administrative occupation.[53] An organization's human resource management policies need to reflect the special needs this situation creates for couples. For instance, special attention needs to be given to an organization's policies regarding nepotism, relocations, transfers, and conflicts of interest.[54]

Are Contemporary Organizations Anxiety-Producing?

As we discussed in Chapter 2, one of the significant management trends during the 1990s has been organizational downsizing. Because downsizing typically involves shrinking the organization's work force, it is an issue in human resource management that needs to be addressed.

Many organizations have done a fairly good job of helping layoff victims by offering a variety of job-help services, psychological counseling, support groups, severance pay, extended health insurance benefits, and detailed communications. Although some affected individuals react very negatively to being laid off (the worst cases involve returning to the separating organization and committing some form of violence), the assistance offered reveals that the organization does care about its former employees. Unfortunately, very little has been done for those who have been left behind and have the task of keeping the organization going or even of revitalizing it.

It may surprise you to learn that both victims *and* survivors experience feelings of frustration, anxiety, and loss.[55] But layoff victims get to start over with a clean slate and a clear conscience. Survivors don't. As one author suggested, "The terms could be reversed: Those who leave become survivors, and those who stay become victims."[56] A new syndrome seems to be popping up in more and more organizations: **layoff-survivor sickness.** It is a set of attitudes, perceptions, and behaviors of employees who remain after involuntary employee reductions.[57] Symptoms include job insecurity, perceptions of unfairness, guilt, depression, stress from increased workloads, fear of change, loss of loyalty and commitment, reduced effort, and an unwillingness to do anything beyond the required minimum.

layoff-survivor sickness
A set of attitudes, perceptions, and behaviors of employees who remain after involuntary employee reductions; include insecurity, guilt, depression, stress, fear, loss of loyalty, and reduced effort.

To address this survivor syndrome, managers may want to provide opportunities for employees to talk to counselors about their guilt, anger, and anxiety. Group discussions can also provide an opportunity for the "survivors" to vent their feelings. Some organizations have used downsizing efforts as the spark to implement increased employee participation programs such as empowerment and self-managed work teams. In short, to keep morale and productivity high, every attempt should be made to ensure that those individuals who are still working in the organization know that they are a valuable and much-needed resource.

Summary

How will I know if I fulfilled the Learning Objectives found on page 229? You will have fulfilled the Learning Objectives if you understand the following.

1. **Describe the strategic human resource management process.** The human resource management process seeks to staff the organization and to sustain high employee performance through strategic human resource planning, recruitment or decruitment, selection, orientation, training, performance appraisal, compensation and benefits, safety and health, and by dealing with contemporary issues in HRM.
2. **Discuss the influence of government regulations on human resource decisions.** Since the mid-1960s, the U.S. government has greatly expanded its influence over HRM decisions by enacting new laws and regulations. Because of the government's effort to provide equal employment opportunities, management must ensure that key HRM decisions—such as recruitment, selection, training, promotions, and terminations—are made without regard to race, sex, religion, age, color, national origin, or disability. Financial penalties can be imposed on organizations that fail to follow these laws and regulations.
3. **Differentiate between job descriptions and job specifications.** A job description is a written statement of what a jobholder does, how it is done, and why it is done. A job specification states the minimum acceptable qualifications that a potential employee must possess to successfully perform a given job.
4. **Contrast recruitment and decruitment options.** Recruitment seeks to develop a pool of potential job candidates. Typical sources include an internal search, advertisements, employee referrals, employment agencies, school placement centers, and temporary help services. Decruitment reduces the labor supply within an organization through options such as firing, layoffs, attrition, transfers, reduced workweeks, early retirements, and job sharing.
5. **Explain the importance of validity and reliability in selection.** All HRM decisions must be based on factors or criteria that are both reliable and valid. If a selection device is not reliable, then it cannot be assumed to be a consistent measure. If a device is not valid, then no proven relationship exists between it and relevant job criteria.
6. **Describe the selection devices that work best with various kinds of jobs.** Selection devices must match the job in question. Work sampling works best with low-level jobs. Assessment centers work best for managerial positions. The validity of the interview as a selection device increases at progressively higher levels of management.
7. **Identify various training methods.** Employee training can be on-the-job or off-the-job. Popular on-the-job methods include job rotation, understudying, and apprenticeships. The more popular off-the-job methods are classroom lectures, films, and simulation exercises.
8. **Explain the various techniques managers can use in evaluating employee performance.** Managers can use several techniques in evaluating employee performance. These can include comparing employee performance against some set performance standard, comparing employees with one another, or measuring performance on the basis of preset objectives.
9. **Describe the goals of compensation administration and factors that affect wage structures.** Compensation administration attempts to ensure that whatever pay levels are determined will be perceived as fair by all employees. Fairness means that the established levels of pay are adequate and consistent for the demands and requirements of the job. Therefore, the primary determination of pay is the kind of job an employee performs.
10. **Explain what is meant by the terms *sexual harassment, family-friendly benefits,* and *layoff-survivor sickness.*** Sexual harassment encompasses sexually suggestive remarks, unwanted touching and sexual advances, requests for sexual favors, or other verbal and physical conduct of a sexual nature. Family-friendly benefits are benefits offered to employees that are supportive of caring for one's family. These include such benefits as flextime, child care, part-time employment, relocation programs, summer camp, parental leave, and adoption benefits. The layoff-survivor sickness represents a set of attitudes, perceptions, and behaviors of employees who remain after involuntary employee reductions.

Review & Discussion Questions

1. How does HRM affect all managers?
2. Contrast reject errors and accept errors. Which one is most likely to open an employer to charges of discrimination? Why?
3. Should an employer have the right to choose employees without government interference into the hiring process? Explain your position.
4. What are the major problems of the interview as a selection device?
5. What is the relationship between selection, recruitment, and job analysis?
6. Do you think there are moral limits on how far a prospective employer should delve into an applicant's life by means of interviews, tests, and background investigations? Explain your position.
7. How are orientation and employee training alike? How are they different?
8. What constitutes sexual harassment? How can companies minimize the occurrences of sexual harassment in the workplace?
9. Why should managers be concerned with diversity in the workplace? What special HRM issues does diversity raise?
10. "Victims of downsizing are not those employees who were let go. Rather, the victims are the ones who have kept their jobs." Do you agree or disagree with this statement? Defend your position.

Testing Your Comprehension • • • 

Circle the correct answer, then check yourself on page AK-1.

1. Which of the following is LEAST likely to be a reason to adopt an affirmative action program?
   a) the potential cost of defending discrimination lawsuits
   b) because discrimination does still exist, there are many above-average minority persons as potential employees
   c) organizational social responsibility
   d) to comply with federal legislation mandating affirmative action

---

2. As a result of federal legislation since the mid-1960s, employers must ensure that equal employment opportunities exist for
   a) every employee of their organization and all those organizations with which they do interstate business
   b) current employees
   c) current employees and job applicants
   d) job applicants

---

3. Strategic human resource planning is the process by which management
   a) plans for future business needs in terms of land, labor, and capital
   b) develops its restructuring plan
   c) ensures that the organization has the right personnel
   d) allocates resources to product line managers

---

4. The document describing how a job fits into the organization's strategic direction is called
   a) a job description
   b) a job evaluation
   c) a job specification
   d) a job analysis

---

5. A human resource inventory is
   a) a statement of what a current jobholder does, how it is to be done, and the accountabilities of the job
   b) a statement indicating employees' education, capabilities, and specialized skills
   c) a statement of the minimum qualifications required for job candidates to be successful on the job
   d) none of the above

---

6. Where there exists a proven relationship between a selection device and job performance, there is
   a) no discrimination
   b) reliability
   c) validity
   d) selectivity

---

7. Which of the following is NOT a benefit attained from an internal recruiting search?
   a) building employee morale
   b) reducing recruiting costs
   c) reducing orientation time
   d) facilitating affirmative action goals

---

8. Which of the following is MOST CORRECT about the interview as a selection method for hiring a job candidate?
   a) Interviews should be structured before any interview is conducted.
   b) Interviewers should check an applicant's background data before conducting an interview.
   c) Negative information about a job candidate is often discounted or overlooked.
   d) Most interviewers wait until a candidate is leaving the interview before making a decision.

---

9. Which of the following statements BEST reflects the difference between employee training and employee development?
   a) Employee training focuses on job skills needed for future positions. Employee development focuses on skills needed for current jobs.

b) Employee development primarily involves off-the-job training methods. Employee training primarily involves on-the-job training methods.

c) Employee training focuses on skills needed for current jobs. Employee development focuses on skills needed for future positions.

d) Employee development focuses on current employees. Employee training focuses on potential job applicants.

---

10. A performance management system assumes that

a) an employee has the ability to perform the essential elements of the job

b) organizational goals have been set

c) a manager can compare one employee's work with that of another

d) all of the above

---

11. The process designed to help employees overcome performance-related problems is best referred to as

a) performance appraisal

b) employee counseling

c) employee assistance

d) none of the above

---

12. The activities involved in compensation administration center primarily on

a) determining pay structures consistent with competing organizations in the area

b) determining pay levels for jobs in the organization

c) determining pay structures in accordance with federal wage laws

d) determining pay levels for employees in the organization

---

13. Which of the following is NOT considered a legally required employee benefit for most organizations?

a) health insurance

b) social security

c) workers' compensation

d) unemployment insurance

---

14. Sexual harassment

a) involves only physical conduct between male and female organizational members

b) does not interfere with job performance

c) holds the organization liable for the conduct of the manager

d) is relevant only in large organizations

---

15. Which of the following is NOT a suggestion for managers who are establishing an organization's policy on sexual harassment?

a) The organization should educate all employees on sexual harassment.

b) The organization should monitor encounters between its male and female employees.

c) The organization should have a mechanism in place to reinforce its sexual harassment policy.

d) The organization should offer training to employees regarding sexual harassment issues.

---

16. Which of the following statements BEST reflects the concern for addressing the layoff-survivor sickness?

a) Restructuring and downsizing have created events in organizations when job security is no longer guaranteed.

b) Global competition has mandated that companies reengineer in order to become more cost-effective.

c) Restructuring has caused many employees' career goals to be placed on hold.

d) Downsized individuals receive most of management's attention when an organization lays off workers.

Applying the Concepts

Decruitment

Every manager, at some point in his or her career, will be faced with one of the more difficult tasks of managing—laying off employees. No matter how unpleasant this task may be, it may be necessary in order to pave the way for the organization to attain its goals. Assume that you are the manager in the marketing department of a 5,500-member corporation. You have been notified by top management that you must permanently reduce your staff by two individuals.[58] Below are some data about your employees.

Rhonda Barry: *African-American female, age 36. Rhonda has been employed with your company for five years, all in the Marketing Department. Her evaluations over the past three years have been outstanding, above average, and outstanding. Rhonda has an MBA from a top-25 business school. She also has been in the top 10 percent of all sales representatives in terms of total sales. She has been on short-term disability the past few weeks because of the birth of her second child and is expected to return to work in twenty weeks.*

Aaron Brown: *White male, age 46. Aaron has been with you for four months and has eleven years of experience in the company in Research and Development. He has an associate's degree in data processing and bachelor's and master's degrees in market research. Aaron's evaluations over the past three years in R&D have been average, but he did save the company $750,000 on a suggestion he made regarding adapting a product line to a new market niche.*

José Ramiriz: *Hispanic male, age 29. José has been with the company almost four years. His evaluations over the past three years in your department have been outstanding. He is committed to getting the job done and devoting whatever it takes. He has also shown initiative by taking territories that no one else wanted. And he has turned what others believed to be dying areas into successful markets for the company.*

Leslie Alexander: *White female, age 35. Leslie has been with your company five years. Three years ago, Leslie was in an automobile accident while traveling on business to a customer's location. As a result of the accident, she was disabled and is wheelchair-bound. Rumors have it that she is about to receive several million dollars from the insurance company of the driver that hit her. Her performance the last two years has been above average. She has a bachelor's degree in business.*

Steven Hill: *African-American male, age 41. Steve just completed his MBA. He has been with your department the past three years. His evaluations have been good to above-average. Five years ago, Steve won a lawsuit against your company for discriminating against him in a promotion to a supervisory position. Rumors have it that now, with his new degree, Steve is actively pursuing another job outside the company.*

Given these five brief descriptions, make a decision on which two employees will be laid off. Discuss any other options that you feel can be used to meet the requirement of downsizing by two employees—yet not resorting to layoffs. Discuss what you will do to (1) assist the two individuals who have been let go and (2) assist the remaining three employees. Then, in a group of three to five students, seek consensus on the questions posed above. Be prepared to defend your action.

Take It to the Net

We invite you to visit the Robbins/De Cenzo page on the Prentice Hall Web site at:

http://www.prenhall.com/robbinsfom

for this chapter's World Wide Web exercise.

You can also visit the Web sites for these companies featured within this chapter:

Hooters Restaurant Chain
http://www.hooters.com

IBM
http://www.ibm.com

Informix
http://www.informix.com

Kraft Cheese
http://www.kraftfoods.com

Microsoft
http://www.microsoft.com

National Geographic
http://www.nationalgeographic.com

Oracle
http://www.oracle.com

Sybase
http://www.sybase.com

Thinking Critically

Making a Value Judgment: English-Only Rules

As we discussed in Chapter 2, our world of work is rapidly changing. With that change has come an influx of people from all parts of the globe into the jobs in the United States. We suggest that, in order for organizational members to be successful, they must find ways to work in harmony with one another—irrespective of race, religion, gender, nationality, or any other "personal" defining characteristic. In many respects, that means developing, and practicing, a sensitivity toward one another. But management in some organizations—although they state they embrace such ideas—may be paying lip service to the issue. Their sensitivity to individuals from different cultures seems questionable in light of the fact that they require all of their employees to speak English only at the work site. First of all, is that legal? In general, yes. At least that's what the Supreme Court has indicated.

At issue here are several items. On the one hand, employers say they need to have a common language spoken at the work site. They claim it's needed so that they can communicate effectively with all employees—especially when safety matters are at stake. It's also a way for them to know if their employees are making fun of the organization or harassing other workers. Nonetheless, workers in today's organizations do speak different languages. It is estimated that about 32 million U.S. employees speak a language other than English. Consider their need to speak their native language, to communicate effectively with their peers, and their desire to maintain their cultural heritage. To them, being required to speak English only is discriminatory.

Questions:

1. On what grounds should employers require employees to speak English only in the workplace?
2. Would your position change even if speaking English only had nothing to do with employees' jobs and did not create a safety hazard? Discuss.
3. "An adage that applies in a global environment is, 'When in Rome, do as the Romans do.' If people from around the globe want to work in the United States, they had better adjust to the U.S. culture. And that means speaking English." Do you agree or disagree with this statement? Explain your position.

Henry Liang Job Hunts Using the Net

After organizations have established their strategic direction and have designed and implemented a structure that will best assist in reaching company goals, the organization must turn its attention to getting the right people. The jobs that have been identified and their associated skills point to very specific types of employees that are required. But these employees don't just magically appear—nor do they come knocking on the organization's door. Instead, the company must embark on an employment process of finding, hiring, and retaining qualified people.

That process starts when the organization notifies the "public" that openings exist. The organization wants to get its information out in such a way that large numbers of potentially qualified applicants respond. Then, after several interactions with the most promising of these candidates, employees are hired. These candidates will be the ones who best demonstrate the skills, knowledge, and abilities needed to successfully perform the job.

Years ago, this entire process was dominated by paper and face-to-face interactions. Technology, today, is changing that. For individuals like Henry Liang, the job search has gone to the "Net."[59] Many jobs in organizations today are heavily influenced by technology. In fact, technology-related jobs in the United States grew by 320 percent in 1995, and that growth is predicted to continue through the turn of the century.[60] Accordingly, candidates must be able to demonstrate that they have the requisite skills and can offer something to organizations. But explaining that in a letter to an employer often doesn't have the same effect as showing potential employers what you can do. When Henry, a University of Pennsylvania senior, wanted to let employers know he understood technology, he opted for an electronic résumé. By developing a "home page" on the Internet, Liang was able to refer potential employers to his Web page, which he had designed. The electronic résumé, however, was only the beginning. Through the creation of links to other Web pages, applicants like Henry can refer readers to a variety of Web sites that provide substantial data about them. For example, Liang can provide the details about his college, as well as his major course of study; he can show some of his completed works or even graphically highlight other pertinent data about his "fit" with the organization.

Although the use of the Internet for job hunting is still in its infancy, as more and more employers explore this technique, it's sure to gain momentum. For now, though, it's safe to say that a competitive advantage can be gained for highly technical jobs by using the Internet as a means of displaying one's skills. And in the end, as Henry Liang found, the creativity and initiative that the Internet job search requires are what employers really want.

Questions:

1. Describe the HRM implications of job candidates' placing résumés on the World Wide Web.
2. How can electronic résumés help demonstrate that a job candidate possesses technical skills? Would your position be different if you found out that another person had developed the candidate's "home page?" Explain.
3. Describe a selection process using the Internet in which you can determine that a candidate like Henry Liang does possess the technical skill required for a job.

Video Case ABCNEWS

Unequal Opportunity at the CIA

"If you want your career to go somewhere, sleep with me." Those words were allegedly spoken by some experienced male supervisors at the Central Intelligence Agency (CIA). At issue is an "old-boy" network that is running rampant in the agency.

In many high-risk professions—such as the military and police and fire departments—old-boy networks had been the norm. Although these environments often just happened and resulted in a strong brotherhood among its male members, today they have a tendency to create an offensive environment for women members. And, although across the United States significant effort has been expended to challenge and eliminate these networks, there's one organization that hasn't yet addressed the issue. That organization is the CIA. Because some of its efforts involve covert activities, it has been difficult for women to register their complaints and seek help with their employment problems. But women like Lynne Larkin and Sulynn Taylor are challenging this secrecy by going public.

Lynne Larkin, a former CIA case officer, was given a choice. Sleep with her supervisor and have her career go somewhere, or don't and get poor performance ratings and little challenging work to perform. The saddest aspect about this "career choice" is that it had absolutely nothing to do with Lynne's abilities. She was properly trained—like the men—and had good skills. But that apparently didn't matter, for the old-boy network could keep her out of special assignments. In fact, she and several of her colleagues knew that, in some cases, station chiefs simply refused to employ women.

Sulynn Taylor, another former case officer, had yet another perspective. After twenty-eight years in the CIA, she retired in frustration. Through the years, she worked jobs that, had a man held them, would have paid significantly more. She kept finding an invisible barrier that she just couldn't break through. Her career just couldn't advance any further. As she stated, the CIA has a "culture in which women are considered second-class citizens." Furthermore, any male who sympathized with women in the organization—and maybe tried to help them—suffered too. In one case, Taylor's supervisor refused to lower his high evaluation of her work as requested by his boss. Consequently, his career suffered for years because of his unwillingness to inappropriately rate Taylor.

Over the past few years, many of the women working for the CIA have been challenging its culture. Filing suit against the agency, these women attempted to change the atmosphere so that they, too, could get an equal opportunity. In March 1995, lawyers for about 450 female employees and lawyers for the CIA reached a settlement: These women were to divide up $940,000; twenty-five of them were to be promoted, and mechanisms were to be established to monitor CIA personnel practices. Although the settlement is in question—not all of the women involved believe it was fair or that it would have any real effect on the CIA's culture—it was an indication that discrimination practices did exist.

But the story doesn't end there. While changes should be occurring, there's still some feeling among these women that little if anything has changed or ever will. As Lynn Larkin said, "All the people who have stepped forward in the case have already received veiled threats and some very direct threats, as to saying that their career will go nowhere."

Questions:

1. Given that laws exist that are supposed to prevent employment discrimination in today's organizations, can you explain how an organization with a fully functioning HRM department like the CIA can have these events happening?
2. "Covert activities involve dangerous work elements. One mistake and you could be 'eliminated.' As such, to protect women from the potential violence, it's a bona fide occupational qualification to select only men for these jobs." Do you agree or disagree with the statement? Explain your position.
3. What effect on productivity and employee morale do you believe this action by some CIA supervisors is having on case officers like Larkin and Taylor? How would you stop it?

Source: "Women of the CIA Come Forward," *ABC News Nightline,* June 7, 1995.

Managing Change and Innovation

9

LEARNING OBJECTIVES

What will I be able to do after I finish this chapter?

1. **DESCRIBE** what change variables are within a manager's control.
2. **IDENTIFY** external and internal forces for change.
3. **EXPLAIN** how managers can serve as change agents.
4. **CONTRAST** the "calm waters" and "white water rapids" metaphors for change.
5. **EXPLAIN** why people are likely to resist change.
6. **LIST** techniques for reducing resistance to change.
7. **IDENTIFY** what is meant by the term *organization development* and specify four popular OD techniques.
8. **EXPLAIN** the causes and symptoms of stress.
9. **DIFFERENTIATE** between creativity and innovation.
10. **EXPLAIN** how organizations can stimulate innovation.

WILL WRITING CHECKS TO PAY bills be a thing of the past? Will your local branch bank go out of business or drastically change the way it operates? According to Galia Maor, chief executive officer of Bank Leumi Le-Israel, the answer may be Yes! She foresees a world in the not-too-distant future in which "technobanking" will be the norm not just something that a few "techies" prefer. And this observation is from an individual whom many regard as the most influential woman in Israel![1]

Galia Maor is not a novice to either banking or technology. A thirty-year veteran of the banking industry, she averted sanctions on Bank Leumi Le-Israel in the early 1980s when a major scandal nearly led to the collapse of what was then Israel's largest bank. Although the bank survived, it no longer holds the distinction of being number one. Now that Maor is in charge, she wants to recapture the number one rank. Doing so, however, requires a lot of work—and change. For example, Galia is reshaping the bank's foreign operations and moving them away from New York, where the bank lost $300 million in 1994 because of loan defaults. She is taking Leumi into the Far East, where investments in countries such as Japan are generating high profits. But her boldest move to date involves personalized electronic banking.

Maor lives her life around a personal computer. As a business executive and busy mother of three children, she attempts to do all she can on a personal computer—even grocery and clothing shopping. Doing so saves her time, and she can do these things when it's convenient for her. Why then, she wondered, couldn't the same be done in banking? Since asking that question, Maor has never looked back.

Galia Maor is leading the charge for revamping banking practices in Israel. Her efforts to have technobanking the "standard of banking" are being realized. Not only is the bank saving money through electronic banking, customers are enjoying lower fees, too.

She calls her system First Direct, a "home banking from your easy chair program." Leumi customers are able to do all of their banking electronically. They can not only pay bills or transfer funds from one account to another but can also apply for and receive loans. When a loan is approved, the money is electronically transferred to the customer's account.

Will computer banking work on a large-scale basis? Maor thinks so. From Leumi's perspective, it's cheaper for the bank because it can eliminate costly branch offices. But for it to work, it has to be viewed as beneficial to customers. The early results suggest that customers see the benefits: for instance, faster and more-efficient services and a 20 percent reduction in bank service charges.

The problems faced by Galia Maor are not unique in the 1990s. Big companies, small businesses, universities, state and city governments, hospitals, and even the military are being forced to significantly change the way they do things. Although change has always been a part of the manager's job, it has become more so in recent years. We'll describe why in this chapter. We will also discuss ways in which managers can stimulate innovation and increase their organization's adaptability.

What Is Change?

change
An alteration of an organization's environment, structure, technology, or people.

Change is an alteration of an organization's environment, structure, technology, or people. If it weren't for change, the manager's job would be relatively easy. Planning would be without problems because tomorrow would be no different from today. The issue of organization design would be solved. Since the environment would be free from uncertainty, there would be no need to adapt. All organizations would be tightly structured. Similarly, decision making would be dramatically simplified because the outcome of each alternative could be predicted with almost certain accuracy. It would, indeed, simplify the manager's job if, for example, competitors did not introduce new products or services, if customers did not make new demands, if government regulations were never modified, if technology never advanced, or if employees' needs always remained the same.

Change is an organizational reality.

However, change is an organizational reality. Handling change is an integral part of every manager's job. But what can a manager change? The manager's options essentially fall into one of three categories: altering structure, technology, or people (see Exhibit 9-1). We will look at these three areas of change later in this chapter.

Forces for Change

In Chapter 2, we pointed out that there are both external and internal forces that constrain managers. These same forces also bring about the need for change. Let's briefly look at the factors that can create the need for change.

What Are the External Forces Creating a Need for Change?

The external forces that create the need for change come from various sources (see Understanding Yourself). In recent years, the marketplace has affected firms such as Mercedes and Domino's by introducing new competition. Mercedes now has upscale Japanese cars produced by Lexus and Infiniti to compete against, and Domino's must now contend with a host of new competitors such as Pizza Hut and Little Caesar's, which recently have moved into the home-delivery market. Government laws and regulations are a frequent impetus for change. The passage of a major tax revision in 1986, which included the phasing out of interest deductibility except for home mortgages, created instant huge opportunities for firms such as Chase Manhattan and Signet Bank to sell home equity loans. In 1990, the passage of the Americans with Disabilities Act required thousands of businesses to widen doorways, reconfigure restrooms, add ramps, and take other actions to improve accessibility.

Technology also creates the need for change. In the mid-1990s, the World Wide Web has become a multifaceted vehicle for getting information and selling products. And, as we discussed in Chapter 3, recent developments in sophisticated equipment

Exhibit 9-1
Three Categories of Change

Structure		Technology		People
Authority relationships Coordinating mechanisms Job redesign Spans of control	+	Work processes Work methods Equipment	+	Attitudes Expectations Perceptions Behavior

Understanding Yourself

How Ready Are You for Managing in a Turbulent World?

Listed below are some statements a manager made about managing at a large, successful corporation. If your job had these characteristics, how would you react to them? After each statement are five letters, A to E. Circle the letter that best describes how you think you would react according to the following scale:

A = *I would enjoy this very much; it's completely acceptable.*
B = *This would be enjoyable and acceptable most of the time.*
C = *I'd have no reaction to this feature one way or another, or it would be about equally enjoyable and unpleasant.*
D = *This feature would be somewhat unpleasant for me.*
E = *This feature would be very unpleasant for me.*

1. I regularly spend 30 to 40 percent of my time in meetings.	A	B	C	D	E
2. A year and a half ago, my job did not exist, and I have been essentially inventing it as I go along.	A	B	C	D	E
3. The responsibilities I either assume or am assigned consistently exceed the authority I have for discharging them.	A	B	C	D	E
4. At any given moment in my job, I have on the average about a dozen phone calls to be returned.	A	B	C	D	E
5. There seems to be very little relation in my job between the quality of my performance and my actual pay and benefits.	A	B	C	D	E
	A	B	C	D	E
6. About two weeks a year of formal management training is needed in my job just to stay current.	A	B	C	D	E
7. Because we have very effective equal employment opportunity (EEO) in my company and because it is thoroughly multinational, my job consistently brings me into close working contact at a professional level with people of many races, ethnic groups, and nationalities and of both sexes.	A	B	C	D	E
8. There is no objective way to measure my effectiveness.	A	B	C	D	E
9. I report to three different bosses for different aspects of my job, and each has an equal say in my performance appraisal.	A	B	C	D	E
10. On average, about a third of my time is spent dealing with unexpected emergencies that force all scheduled work to be postponed.	A	B	C	D	E
11. When I have to have a meeting of the people who report to me, it takes my secretary most of a day to find a time when we are all available, and even then, I have yet to have a meeting where everyone is present for the entire meeting.	A	B	C	D	E

Continued

12. The college degree I earned in preparation for this type of work is now obsolete, and I probably should go back for another degree. A B C D E
13. My job requires that I absorb 100–200 pages per week of technical materials. A B C D E
14. I am out of town overnight at least one night a week. A B C D E
15. My department is so interdependent with several other departments in the company that all distinctions about which departments are responsible for which tasks are quite arbitrary. A B C D E
16. I will probably get a promotion in about a year to a job in another division that has most of the same characteristics. A B C D E
17. During the period of my employment here, either the entire company or the division I worked in has been reorganized every year or so. A B C D E
18. Although there are several possible promotions I can see ahead of me, I have no real career path in an objective sense. A B C D E
19. Although there are several possible promotions I can see ahead of me, I think I have no realistic chance of getting to the top levels of the company. A B C D E
20. Although I have many ideas about how to make things work better, I have no direct influence on either the business policies or the personnel policies that govern my division. A B C D E
21. My company has recently put in an "assessment center" where I and all other managers will be required to go through an extensive battery of psychological tests to assess our potential. A B C D E
22. My company is a defendant in an antitrust suit, and if the case comes to trial, I will probably have to testify about some decisions that were made a few years ago. A B C D E
23. Advanced computer and other electronic office technologies are continually being introduced into my division, necessitating constant learning on my part. A B C D E
24. The computer terminal and screen I have in my office can be monitored in my bosses' offices without my knowledge. A B C D E

Scoring: Give yourself 4 points for each A, 3 points for each B, 2 points for each C, 1 point for each D, and no points for each E. Compute your total, and divide that score by 24. Round your answer to one decimal place.

What the Assessment Means: Although the results of this assessment are not intended to be more than suggestive, the higher your score, the more comfortable you appear to be with change. The test's author suggests analyzing scores as if they were grade point averages. In this way, a 4.0 average is an A, a 2.0 is a C, and scores below 1.0 flunk. Using replies from nearly 500 MBA students and individuals new to management positions, the range of scores was found to be relatively narrow: between 1.0 and 2.2. The average score was between 1.5 and 1.6—a D+/C− sort of grade!

have created significant economies of scale for many organizations. At Charles Schwab (the discount brokerage firm) new technology has given them the ability to process 20,000 mutual fund trades a day in 1996 compared with just 2,000 only two years earlier.[2] The assembly line in many industries is undergoing dramatic changes as employers replace human labor with technologically advanced mechanical robots, and the fluctuation in labor markets is forcing managers to initiate changes. For instance, the shortage of software developers has required many software firms to redesign jobs and alter their reward and benefit packages.

Economic changes, of course, affect almost all organizations. The dramatic increases in crude oil and gasoline prices in the spring of 1996 forced many U.S. companies that depended on fuel to transport their goods to increase prices, consolidate travel trips, or eliminate some delivery services. Meanwhile, in many parts of Europe, where gasoline prices approach US$4, increasing crude oil prices had very little effect.

What Are the Internal Forces Creating a Need for Change?

In addition to the external forces noted previously, internal forces can also stimulate the need for change. These internal forces tend to originate primarily from the internal operations of the organization or from the impact of external changes.

When management redefines or modifies its strategy, it often introduces a host of changes. For example, when L'Oreal (the cosmetics maker) developed a new strategy of competing more aggressively in mass merchandising markets, the organizational members had to change how the business operated; they reduced production costs to support mass marketing of products and increased research and development emphasis, among other changes.[3] The introduction of new equipment represents another internal force for change. Employees may have their jobs redesigned, need to undergo training to operate the new equipment, or be required to establish new interaction patterns within their formal group. An organization's work force is rarely static. Its composition changes in terms of age, education, gender, nationality, and so forth. In a stable organization where managers have been in their positions for years, there might be a need to restructure jobs in order to retain more-ambitious employees, affording them some upward mobility. The compensation and benefits systems might also need to be reworked to reflect the needs of a diverse work force and market forces in which certain skills are in short in supply. Employee attitudes, such as increased job dissatisfaction, may lead to increased absenteeism, more voluntary resignations, and even strikes. Such events will, in turn, often lead to changes in management policies and practices.

How Can a Manager Serve as a Change Agent?

Changes within an organization need a catalyst. People who act as catalysts and assume the responsibility for managing the change process are called **change agents.**

change agent
A person who initiates and assumes the responsibility for managing a change in an organization.

Any manager can be a change agent (see Managers Who Made a Difference). As we review the topic of change, we assume that it is initiated and carried out by a manager within the organization. However, the change agent can be a nonmanager—for example, an internal staff specialist or outside consultant whose expertise is in change implementation. For major systemwide changes, internal management will often hire outside consultants to provide advice and assistance. Because they are from the outside, they often can offer an objective perspective that insiders usually lack. However, outside consultants may be at a disadvantage because they have an inadequate understanding of the organization's history, culture, operating procedures, and personnel.

Managers Who Made a Difference

Patrick Purcell, Publisher of the *Boston Herald*

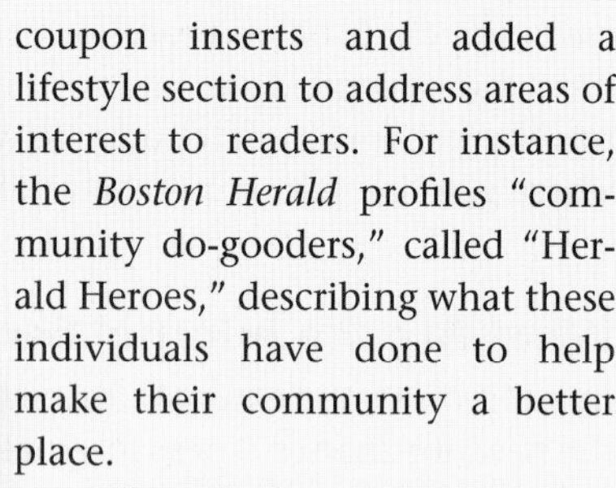

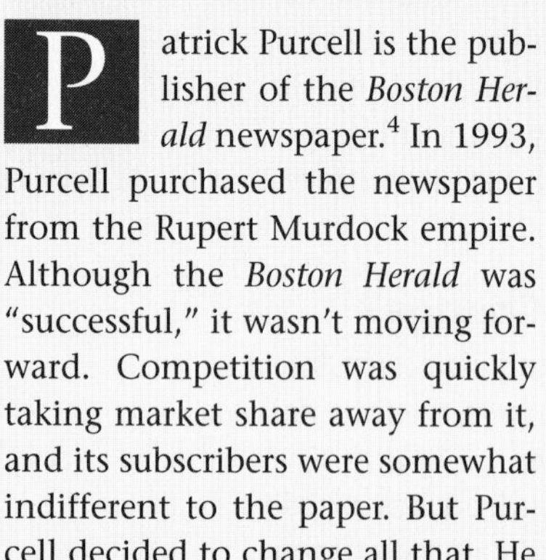

Patrick Purcell is the publisher of the *Boston Herald* newspaper.[4] In 1993, Purcell purchased the newspaper from the Rupert Murdock empire. Although the *Boston Herald* was "successful," it wasn't moving forward. Competition was quickly taking market share away from it, and its subscribers were somewhat indifferent to the paper. But Purcell decided to change all that. He knew that to succeed in the new millennium, an organization—his included—had to "try something new." After all, as Purcell stated, "What did the paper have to lose?" That something new was quickly evident.

One of the fist actions taken was to revamp the Sunday edition of the paper. Many readers had stopped buying the Sunday paper because the inserts—magazines, comics, and so on—were not what they wanted. After consulting with subscribers, Purcell cut several magazines out of the Sunday edition. He greatly improved its weekly TV guide, making it more informative and inclusive of cable channels. He offered his readers more coupon inserts and added a lifestyle section to address areas of interest to readers. For instance, the *Boston Herald* profiles "community do-gooders," called "Herald Heroes," describing what these individuals have done to help make their community a better place.

Purcell also recognized that Boston is a "sports-crazed" town. The town fields all major sports and has a wealth of college team sports in the area. But before he bought the paper, the *Herald* covered local sports very poorly. That changed under Purcell. Sports pages have been greatly expanded.

To Purcell's credit, he recognized that change is necessary in any organization—even for those who sell a product that is often viewed as a commodity. And many of the paper's employees are happy he did. As a result of the changes, the *Herald's* circulation has increased more than 21 percent. Advertising revenues have increased by more than 15 percent. And, in an area where competition is fierce—classified ads—the *Herald* now enjoys 54 percent of the market.

Outside consultants are also prone to initiate more-drastic changes than insiders—which can be either a benefit or a disadvantage—because they do not have to live with the repercussions after the change is implemented. In contrast, internal managers who act as change agents may be more thoughtful (and possibly more cautious) because they must live with the consequences of their actions.

"calm waters" metaphor A description of traditional practices in and theories about organizations that likens the organization to a large ship making a predictable trip across a calm sea and experiencing an occasional storm.

Two Views on the Change Process

We often use two metaphors to clarify the change process.[5] The **"calm waters" metaphor** envisions the organization as a large ship crossing a calm sea. The ship's captain and crew know exactly where they are going because they have made the trip many times before. Change surfaces as the occasional storm, a brief distraction in an otherwise calm and predictable trip. In the **"white water rapids" metaphor,** the organization is seen as a small raft navigating a raging river with uninterrupted white water rapids. Aboard the raft are half-a-dozen people who have never worked together before, who are totally unfamiliar with the river, who are unsure of their eventual destination, and who, as if things weren't bad enough, are traveling in the pitch dark of night. In the white water rapids metaphor, change is a natural state and managing change is a continual process.

"white water rapids" metaphor
A description of the contemporary business environment that likens an organization to a group of strangers on a small raft navigating the uninterrupted white water rapids of an unfamiliar river to an unknown destination in the dark of night.

These two metaphors present very different approaches to understanding and responding to change. Let's take a closer look at each one.

What Is the "Calm Waters" Metaphor?

Until very recently, the "calm waters" metaphor dominated the thinking of practicing managers and academics. The prevailing model for handling change in calm waters is best illustrated in Kurt Lewin's three-step description of the change process[6] (see Exhibit 9-2).

According to Lewin, successful change requires unfreezing the status quo, changing to a new state, and refreezing the new change to make it permanent. The status quo can be considered an equilibrium state. Unfreezing is necessary to move from this equilibrium. It can be achieved in one of three ways:

1. The driving forces, which direct behavior away from the status quo, can be increased.
2. The restraining forces, which hinder movement from the existing equilibrium, can be decreased.
3. The two approaches can be combined.

Once unfreezing has been accomplished, the change itself can be implemented. However, the mere introduction of change does not ensure that it will take hold. The new situation, therefore, needs to be refrozen so that it can be sustained over time. Unless this last step is attended to, there is a strong chance that the change will be short-lived and employees will revert to the previous equilibrium state. The objective of refreezing, then, is to stabilize the new situation by balancing the driving and restraining forces.

Note how Lewin's three-step process treats change as a break in the organization's equilibrium state. The status quo has been disturbed, and change is necessary to establish a new equilibrium state. This view might have been appropriate to the relatively calm environment that most organizations faced in the 1950s, 1960s, and early

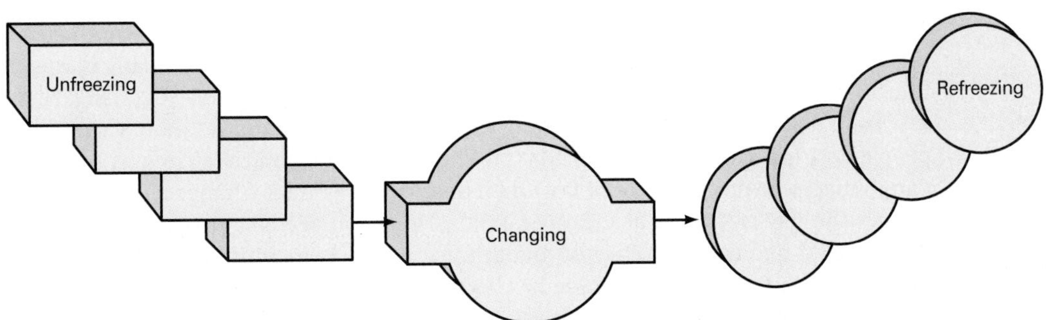

Exhibit 9-2
The Change Process

1970s. But the calm waters metaphor is increasingly obsolete as a way to describe the kind of seas that current managers have to navigate.

What Is the "White Water Rapids" Metaphor?

The "white water" metaphor takes into consideration that environments are both uncertain and dynamic. To get a feeling for what managing change might be like when you have to continually maneuver in uninterrupted rapids, consider attending a college that had the following curriculum: Courses vary in length. Unfortunately, when you sign up, you don't know how long a course will last. It might go for two weeks or thirty weeks. Furthermore, the instructor can end a course any time he or she wants, with no prior warning. If that isn't bad enough, the length of the class changes each time it meets—sometimes it lasts twenty minutes, other times it runs for three hours—and determination of the time of the next class meeting is set by the instructor during the previous class. Oh yes, there's one more thing. The exams are all unannounced, so you have to be ready for a test at any time. To succeed in this college, you would have to be incredibly flexible and be able to respond quickly to every changing condition. Students who were too structured or slow on their feet would not survive.

Change in a dynamic environment is often filled with uncertainty. Just as white water rafters have to continuously maneuver to make it through the rapids at the Payette in Idaho, a manager, too, must be prepared to deal with unexpected issues.

A growing number of managers are coming to accept that their job is much like what a student would face in such a college. The stability and predictability of the calm waters do not exist. Disruptions in the status quo are not occasional and temporary, followed by a return to calm waters. Many of today's managers never get out of the rapids. They face constant change, bordering on chaos. These managers are being forced to play a game they have never played before that is governed by rules that are created as the game progresses.[7]

Is the white water rapids metaphor merely an overstatement? No! Take the case of Harry Quadracci, founder and president of Quad/Graphics, Inc., a commercial printing firm based in Pewaukee, Wisconsin.[8] Founded in 1971, the company is one of the largest and fastest-growing printers in the United States. It prints such magazines as *Time, People,* and *Architectural Digest.* The company now employs more than 3,000 people and has sales in excess of $800 million a year. Quadracci attributes his company's success to its ability to act fast when opportunities arise. Change and growth are among the few constants at Quad/Graphics. He encourages his people to "act now, think later." The company has no budgets because it is moving too fast; its annual growth rate during the past decade has been an astounding 40 percent! As Quadracci points out, when every department looks 30 percent different every six months, budgets aren't much use. Instead of budgets, each of the company's ten divisions is measured against its own previous performance.

Does Every Manager Face a World of Constant and Chaotic Change?

Not every manager faces a world of constant and chaotic change. But the set of managers who don't is dwindling rapidly.

Managers in such businesses as women's fashion apparel and computer software have long confronted a world of white water rapids. These managers used to look with envy at their counterparts in industries such as auto manufacturing, oil exploration, banking, publishing, telecommunications, and air transportation, who historically faced a stable and predictable environment. That might have been true in the 1960s, but it's not a correct statement today!

The quantum change that is required to remain competitive in today's global marketplace cannot be overstated.

Few organizations today can treat change as the occasional disturbance in an otherwise peaceful world. Even those few do so at great risk. Too much is changing too fast for any organization or its managers to be complacent.[9] Most competitive advantages last less than eighteen months. A firm such as People Express—a no-frills, no-reservations airline—was described in business periodicals as the model "new look" firm; it went bankrupt a short time later. As management writer Tom Peters has aptly noted, the old saying "If it ain't broke, don't fix it" no longer applies. In its place, he suggests "If it ain't broke, you just haven't looked hard enough. Fix it anyway."[10] Of course, what Peters is saying is consistent with current reengineering trends. Recall from our discussion of reengineering in Chapter 2 that management needs to rethink all of the activities and processes in its organization. The quantum change that is required to remain competitive in today's global marketplace cannot be overstated.

Organizational Change and Member Resistance

As change agents, managers should be motivated to initiate change because they are concerned with improving their organization's effectiveness. However, change can be a threat to managers. It can be a threat to nonmanagerial personnel as well. Organizations, and people within them, can build up inertia that propels them to resist any change, even if that change might be beneficial (see Details on a Management Classic). In this section, we review why people in organizations resist change and what can be done to lessen that resistance.

Why Do People Resist Change?

It has been said that most people hate any change that doesn't jingle in their pockets. This resistance to change is well documented.[11] But why do people resist change? An individual is likely to resist change for three reasons: uncertainty, concern over personal loss, and the belief that the change is not in the organization's best interest[12] (see Exhibit 9-3 on page 277).

Changes substitute ambiguity and uncertainty for the known. Regardless of how much students may dislike some of the work associated with attending college, at least they know the ropes. They understand what is expected of them. When they leave college and venture out into the world of full-time employment, regardless of how eager they are to get out of college, they will have to trade the known for the unknown. Employees in organizations hold the same dislike for uncertainty. For example, the introduction in manufacturing plants of quality control methods based on sophisticated

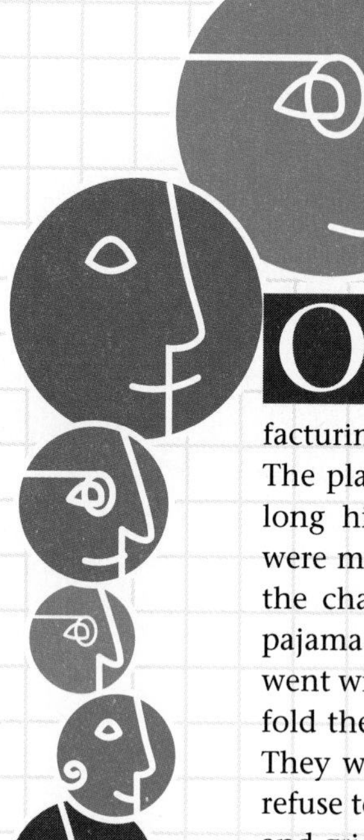

Details on a Management Classic

COCH AND FRENCH: RESISTANCE TO CHANGE

One of the most famous studies on organizational change took place in the late 1940s at a plant of the Harwood Manufacturing Company, where pajamas were made.[13] The plant employed about 500 people and had a long history of disruptions every time changes were made in the way work progressed. Although the changes were typically minor—for example, pajama folders who formerly folded tops that went with prefolded bottoms would be required to fold the bottoms as well—the employees resisted. They would complain bitterly and would openly refuse to make the changes. Production decreased, and grievances, absenteeism, and job turnover increased.

The usual way that Harwood's management made these changes was autocratically. Management would make the decision and then would call a group meeting at which they would announce the changes to employees. The changes would be implemented immediately. Then, as mentioned, the employees would rebel. So Harwood's executives brought in a consultant as a change agent to help with their problem. As an experiment, the consultant arranged for the next change to be conducted in three groups, using three different methods. In the first group, the change was initiated in the usual manner—autocratically. This was the control group. The second group involved employee participation through selective representatives. These representatives, with management, worked out the details of the change, then tried the new methods and trained others in the new procedures. In the third group, there was full participation. All employees shared in the designing of the new methods with management.

The change agent gathered data over a forty-day period; what he found strongly supported the value of participation. In the control group, resistance occurred as before. Seventeen percent of the employees quit during the forty-day period, and grievances and absenteeism increased. However, in the representative and full-participation groups, there were no resignations, only one grievance, and no absenteeism. Moreover, participation was positively related to productivity. In the control group, output actually dropped from an average of sixty units per hour to forty-eight during the experimental period. The participation group generated sixty-eight units per hour, and the total-participation group averaged seventy-three units per hour.

The conclusion of the Coch and French study back in the late 1940s holds a major key for today's organizational change. That is, for permanent change to occur without extensive resistance, employees must be involved. Without employee involvement in those things that directly affect their work, companies run the risk of negating any possible gain a change can bring about or, worse, making the situation more serious than what it was originally.

statistical models means that many quality control inspectors will have to learn these new methods. Some inspectors who have been out of school for some time, or who have weak math and statistics backgrounds, may fear that they will be unable to do so. They may, therefore, develop a negative attitude toward statistical control techniques or behave dysfunctionally if required to use them.

The second cause of resistance is the fear of losing something already possessed. Change threatens the investment one has already made in the status quo. The more

Exhibit 9-3
Why People Resist Change

people have invested in the current system, the more they resist change. Why? They fear the loss of their position, money, authority, friendships, personal convenience, or other benefits that they value. That is why senior employees resist change more than do relatively new employees. Senior employees generally have invested more in the current system and, therefore, have more to lose by adapting to a change.

A final cause of resistance is a person's belief that the change is incompatible with the goals and best interests of the organization. If an employee believes that a new job procedure proposed by a change agent will reduce productivity or product quality, that employee can be expected to resist the change. If the employee expresses his or her resistance positively (clearly expressing it to the change agent, along with substantiation), this form of resistance can be beneficial to the organization.

What Are Some Techniques for Reducing Resistance to Organizational Change?

When management sees resistance to change as dysfunctional, what actions can it take? Several tactics have been suggested for use by managers or other change agents in dealing with resistance to change.[14] These include education and communication, participation, facilitation and support, negotiation, manipulation and co-optation, and coercion. These are summarized below and described in Exhibit 9-4.

Education and communication can help reduce resistance to change by helping employees to see the logic of the change effort.[15] This technique, of course, assumes that much of the resistance lies in misinformation or poor communication. *Participation* involves bringing those individuals directly affected by the proposed change into the decision-making process. Their participation allows these individuals to express their feelings, increase the quality of the process, and increase employee commitment to the final decision. *Facilitation and support* involves helping employees deal with the fear and anxiety associated with the change effort. This help may include employee counseling, therapy, new skills training, or a short paid leave of absence. *Negotiation* involves exchanging something of value for lessening the resistance to the change effort. This resistance technique may be quite useful when the resistance comes from a powerful source. *Manipulation and cooptation* refers to covert attempts to influence others about the change. It may involve twisting or distorting facts to make the change appear more attractive. Finally, *coercion* can be used to deal with resistance to change. Coercion involves the use of direct threats or force against the resisters.

TECHNIQUE	WHEN USED	ADVANTAGE	DISADVANTAGES
Education and communication	When resistance is due to misinformation	Clear up misunderstandings	May not work where mutual trust and credibility are lacking
Participation	When resisters have the expertise to make a contribution	Increases involvement and acceptance	Time-consuming; has potential for a poor solution
Facilitation and support	When resisters are fearful and anxiety-ridden	Can facilitate needed adjustments	Expensive; no guarantee of success
Negotiation	Necessary when resistance comes from a powerful group	Can "buy" commitment	Potentially high cost; opens door for others to apply pressure, too
Manipulation and co-optation	When a powerful group's endorsement is needed	Inexpensive easy way to gain support	Can backfire, causing change agent to lose credibility
Coercion	When a powerful group's endorsement is needed	Inexpensive, easy way to gain support	May be illegal; may undermine change agent's credibility

Exhibit 9-4
Techniques for Reducing Resistance to Change

Making Changes in the Organization

What can a manager change? The manager's options, as we mentioned at the beginning of this chapter, fall into one of three categories: structure, technology, or people. Let's look more closely at each of these three areas.

Changing structure includes any alteration in any authority relationships, coordination mechanisms, degree of centralization, job design, or similar organization structure variables. For instance, in our previous discussions we mentioned that reengineering, restructuring, and empowering result in decentralization, wider spans

Not all change requires a rocket scientist. Some things just appear to be in need of change. For instance, Linda Ahlers, head of hard goods for Target Stores, made a startling discovery. The hammers and screwdrivers with pink handles, designed for a "women's line" of tools, weren't selling. When the color of the handles was changed to reds and blues, tool sales immediately increased more than 10 percent.

of control, reduced work specialization, and cross-functional teams. These structural components give employees the authority and means to implement process improvements. For instance, the creation of work teams that cut across departmental lines allows those people who understand a problem best to solve that problem. In addition, cross-functional work teams encourage cooperative problem solving rather than "us versus them" blame placing.

Changing *technology* encompasses modification in the way work is processed or the methods and equipment used. The primary focus on technological change in TQM is directed at developing flexible processes to support continuous improvement. Employees committed to continuous improvements are constantly looking for things to fix. Thus, work processes must be adaptable to continual change and fine-tuning. Achieving this adaptability requires an extensive commitment to educating and training workers. The organization must provide employees with skills training in problem solving, decision making, negotiation, statistical analysis, and team building.[16] For example, employees need to be able to analyze and act on data. An organization with a continuous process improvement program should provide work teams with quality data such as failure rates, reject rates, and scrap rates. It should provide feedback data on customer satisfaction. It should give the teams the necessary information to create and monitor process control charts. And, of course, the structure should allow the work teams to make continual improvements in the operations on the basis of process control data.

Changes in *people* refers to changes in employee attitudes, expectations, perceptions, or behaviors. The people dimension of change requires a work force committed to the organization's objectives of quality and continuous improvement. Again, this dimension necessitates proper education and training. It also demands a performance evaluation and reward system that supports and encourages continuous improvements. For example, successful programs put quality objectives into bonus plans for executives and incentives for operating employees.[17]

How Do Organizations Implement "Planned" Changes?

One of the fundamental issues behind organization development is its reliance on employee participation.

We know that most change that employees experience in an organization does not happen by chance. Often, management makes a concerted effort to alter some aspect of the organization. Whatever happens—in terms of structure or technology—however, ultimately affects organizational members. The effort to assist organizational members with a planned change is referred to as organization development.

What Is Organization Development?

Organization development (OD) is an activity designed to facilitate long-term organization-wide changes. Its focus is to constructively change the attitudes and values of organizational members so that they can more readily adapt to, and be more effective in achieving, the new directions of the organization.[18] When OD efforts are planned, organization leaders are, in essence, attempting to change the organization's culture.[19] However, one of the fundamental issues behind organization development is its reliance on employee participation in an effort to foster an environment in which open communications and trust exist.[20] Persons involved in OD efforts acknowledge that change can create stress for employees. Therefore, OD attempts to involve organizational members in those things that will affect their jobs and seeks their input about how the change is affecting them.

organization development (OD)
Any activity designed to facilitate planned, long-term organization-wide change that focuses on the attitudes and values of organizational members; essentially an effort to change an organization's culture.

Are There Typical OD Techniques?

Any organizational activity that assists with implementing planned change can be viewed as an OD technique. However, the more popular OD efforts in organizations rely heavily on group interactions and cooperation. These include survey feedback, process consultation, team building, and intergroup development.

survey feedback
A method of assessing employees' attitudes about and perceptions of a change they are encountering by asking specific questions.

Survey feedback efforts are designed to assess employee attitudes about and perceptions of the change they are encountering. Employees are generally asked to respond to a set of specific questions regarding how they view such organizational activities as decision making, leadership, communication effectiveness, and satisfaction with their jobs, coworkers, and management. The data the change agent obtains are used to clarify problems that employees may be facing. As a result of this identification, the change agent can take some action to remedy the problems.

process consultation
The use of consultants from outside an organization to help change agents within the organization assess process events such as work flow, informal intra-unit relationships, and formal communications channels.

In **process consultation,** outside consultants help managers to "perceive, understand, and act upon process events" with which they must deal.[21] These might include, for example, work flow, informal relationships among unit members, and formal communications channels. Consultants give managers insight into what is going on. It is important to recognize that consultants are not there to solve these problems. Rather, they act as coaches to help managers diagnose which interpersonal processes need improvement. If managers, with consultants' help, cannot solve the problem, consultants will often help managers locate experts who have the requisite knowledge.

team building
An activity that helps work groups set goals, develop positive interpersonal relationships, and clarify the role and responsibilities of each team member.

Organizations are made up of individuals working together to achieve some goals. Since organizational members are frequently required to interact with peers, a primary effort of OD is to help them become a team. **Team building** is generally an activity that helps work groups set goals, develop positive interpersonal relationships, and clarify the role and responsibilities of each team member. However, not every one of these activities may be emphasized. There may be no need to address each area because the group may be in agreement and understand what is expected of them. Regardless, team building's primary focus is to increase each group's trust and openness toward one another.

intergroup development
An activity that attempts to make several work groups become more cohesive.

Whereas team building focuses on helping a work group to become more cohesive, **intergroup development** attempts to achieve the same results among different work groups. That is, intergroup development attempts to change attitudes, stereotypes, and perceptions that one group may have for another group. In doing so, better coordination among the various groups can be achieved.

The Aftermath of Organizational Change: Stress

For many employees, change creates stress. A dynamic and uncertain environment characterized by restructurings, downsizings, empowerment, and the like, has created a large number of employees who are overworked and "stressed out."[22] In this section, we will review specifically what is meant by the term *stress,* what causes stress and how to identify it, and what managers can do to reduce anxiety.

stress
A force or influence a person feels when he or she faces opportunities, constraints, or demands that he or she perceives to be both uncertain and important.

What Is Stress?

Stress is a force or influence you feel when you face opportunities, constraints, or demands that you perceive to be both uncertain and important.[23] Stress is a complex issue, so let us look at it more closely. Stress can show itself in both positive and negative ways. Stress is said to be positive when the situation offers someone an opportunity to gain something. For example, stress allows an athlete or entertainer to perform at his or her highest level in critical situations.

However, stress is more often associated with constraints or demands. Constraints are barriers that keep individuals from doing what they desire. If becoming a lawyer is your desire, but you performed poorly on the Law School Admission Test, you may not be accepted into law school. Constraints restrict individuals in ways that take control of a situation out of their hands. Demands, on the other hand, may cause people to give up something they want. If your boss is expecting you to turn in an important project the next morning, and it's not finished yet, the tickets just offered you to attend the championship game of the NBA basketball finals may have to be turned down. Thus, demands preoccupy your time and force you to shift priorities.

The stress associated with an auto accident can be overwhelming. Aside from injuries that can occur, the aftermath of repairing a damaged vehicle can be almost more frustrating than the accident itself. That's because dealing with insurance companies is often confrontational. But at Progressive Corporation, an insurance company based in Cleveland, Ohio, unique practices are trying to reduce the anxiety of dealing with an insurance company. Having someone available around the clock to take "live" claims and acting on claims within twenty-four hours are helping to make this process more "certain" for policyholders.

Constraints and demands can lead to potential stress. When they are coupled with uncertainty of the outcome and importance of the outcome, potential stress becomes actual stress.[24] Performance evaluations are good examples of how stress may manifest itself. If a good performance appraisal can lead to a promotion, greater responsibility, and a higher salary stress may exist. Similarly, if a poor evaluation could keep one from getting those things, or could lead to some disciplinary action, stress, again, thrives. The key, though, is that the outcome is uncertain and important.

Regardless of the situation, a stressful condition exists when there is doubt or uncertainty regarding whether the opportunity will be seized, whether the constraint will be removed, or whether a loss will be avoided. That is, stress will be highest for individuals who think that winning or losing is a certainty. The importance of that outcome is also a critical factor. If winning or losing is unimportant, stress does not exist. As such, if one of your employees feels that keeping a job or earning a promotion is unimportant, he or she will experience little or no stress before a performance review.

Are There Common Causes of Stress?

Stress can be caused by a number of factors called **stressors.** Factors that create stress can be grouped into two major categories—organizational and personal (see Exhibit 9-5). Both directly affect employees and, ultimately, their jobs.

stressor
A factor that causes stress.

An employee's job and the organization's structure are widespread causes of stress. Excessive workloads, as well as downsizing, reengineering, and technological advancements (change) all create stress. Role conflict and ambiguity over job expectations can also create stress.[25] Role conflict imposes contradictory demands on employees—as when an employee is responsible to more than one boss. Role ambiguity creates uncertainty over job requirements—jobs are ill-defined, decision making is centralized, and so on. Job boredom, too, can cause stress. Just how rampant is stress in today's organizations? Various surveys indicate that up to three-fourths of workers in the United States experience high job stress.[26] And stress on the job knows no political boundaries. In Japan, worker stress was identified in 70 percent of the workers

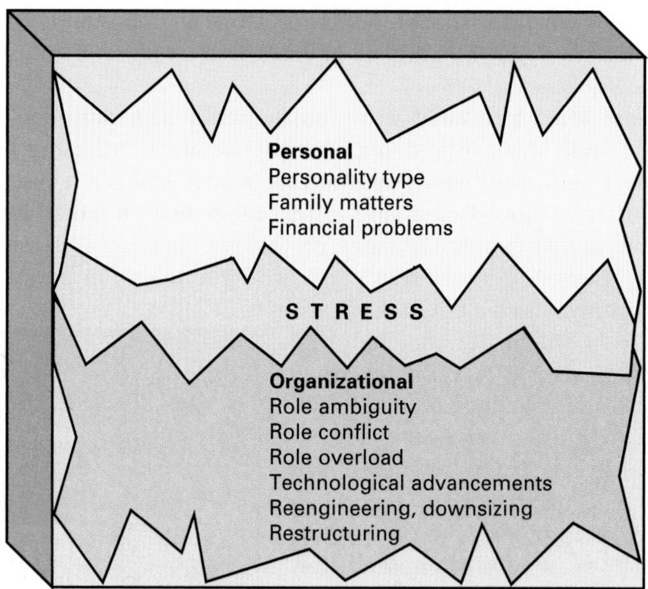

Exhibit 9-5
Major Stressors

karoshi
A Japanese term that refers to a sudden heart attack caused by overworking.

by a Fukoku Life Insurance Company study.[27] In fact, in Japan, there is a concept called ***karoshi,*** which refers to sudden heart attacks caused by overworking. *Karoshi,* experts cite, affects over 10,000 Japanese workers each year.[28]

Personal factors that can create stress include a serious illness, death of a family member, a divorce, and personal financial difficulties.[29] Because employees bring their personal problems to work with them, a full understanding of employee stress requires a manager to be understanding of these personal factors. There is also evidence that employees' personalities have an effect on how susceptible they are to stress. The most commonly used description of these personality types is called the Type A–Type B dichotomy.[30]

Type A personalities
People who have a chronic sense of urgency and an excessive competitive drive.

Type B personalities
People who are relaxed and easy-going and who accept change easily.

Type A personalities are characterized by a chronic sense of urgency and an excessive competitive drive. Type A people often are extremely ambitious, have a strong desire for achievement, and have difficulty accepting and enjoying leisure time. **Type B personalities** are just the opposite. Type B people are more relaxed and easy-going, and they accept change more easily. But Type B personalities are likely to experience many of the same anxiety-related ailments—such as hypertension and heart disease—that Type A personalities experience. For managers, what is important is to recognize that Type A employees are more likely to show symptoms of stress even if organizational and personal stressors are low.

What Are the Symptoms of Stress?

What signs indicate that an employee's stress level might be too high? Stress reveals itself in three general ways: physiological, psychological, and behavioral symptoms.

Most of the early interest in stress focused heavily on health-related, or *physiological,* concerns. This interest was attributed to the realization that high stress levels result in changes in metabolism, increased heart and breathing rates, increased blood pressure, headaches, and increased risk of heart attacks. Because detecting many of these symptoms requires the skills of trained medical personnel, their immediate and direct relevance to managers is negligible.

Of greater importance to managers are psychological and behavioral symptoms of stress. It is these things that can be witnessed in the person. The *psychological* symptoms can be seen as increased tension and anxiety, boredom, and procrastination—all of which can lead to productivity decreases. So too, can the *behavioral* symptoms—changes in eating habits, increased smoking or substance consumption, rapid speech, or sleep disorders. The astute manager, upon witnessing such symptoms, does what he or she can to assist the employee in reducing stress levels.

How Can Stress Be Reduced?

Reducing stress is one thing that presents a dilemma for managers. As mentioned above, some stress in organizations is absolutely necessary. Without it, there's no energy in people. Accordingly, whenever one considers stress reduction, what is at issue is reducing the dysfunctional aspects of stress.

One of the first means of reducing stress is to make sure that employees are properly matched to their jobs and that they understand the extent of their "authority." Furthermore, letting employees know precisely what is expected of them (see the discussion of realistic job previews, Chapter 8) can reduce role conflict and ambiguity. Redesigning jobs can also help ease stressors related to work overload. Employees should also have some input into those things that affect them. Their involvement and participation have been found to lessen stress.[31]

As a manager, you must recognize that no matter what you do to eliminate organizational stressors, some employees will still be stressed out. You simply have little or no control over the personal factors. You also face an ethical issue when it is personal factors that are causing stress. That is, just how far can you intrude on an employee's personal life? To help deal with this issue, many companies have started employee assistance and wellness programs.

Employee assistance programs (EAPs), as they exist today, are extensions of programs that began in companies in the 1940s. Companies such as Du Pont, Standard Oil, and Kodak recognized that some of their employees were experiencing problems with alcohol.[32] To help their employees, these companies implemented special programs on the company's site to educate these workers on the dangers of alcohol and to help them overcome their "addiction." The idea behind these programs, which still holds today, is to get a productive employee back on the job as swiftly as possible. Since their early focus on alcoholic employees, EAPs have gone into new areas. One of the more notable areas is the use of EAPs to help control rising health care costs, especially in the areas of "mental health and substance abuse services."[33] For example, the Campbell's Soup Company EAP program is the first step for individuals seeking psychiatric or substance-abuse help. Campbell's EAP assistance for these individuals was able to cut health care insurance premiums by 28 percent.[34] Similar findings have occurred elsewhere; studies suggest that organizations that have EAPs save up to $5 for every EAP dollar spent.[35] That's a significant return on investment!

employee assistance programs (EAPs)
Programs offered by organizations to help their employees overcome personal and health-related problems.

A **wellness program** is any type of program in an organization that is designed to keep employees healthy. These programs are varied, and may focus on such things as smoking cessation, weight control, stress management, physical fitness, nutrition education, high blood pressure control, and so forth.[36] In return, these programs can help cut employer health costs and lower absenteeism and turnover by preventing health and stress-related problems. For instance, it is estimated that over a

wellness programs
Programs offered by organizations to help their employees prevent health problems.

ten-year period, the Adolph Coors Company saved several million dollars in decreased medical premium payments, reduced sick leave, and increased productivity.[37]

Stimulating Innovation

"Innovate or die!" These harsh words are increasingly becoming the rallying cry of today's managers. In the dynamic world of global competition, organizations must create new products and services and adopt state-of-the-art technology if they are to compete successfully. The standard of innovation to which many organizations strive is that achieved by such companies as du Pont, Eastman Chemical, and the 3M Company.[38] Management at 3M, for example, has developed a reputation for being able to stimulate innovation over a long period of time. One of its stated objectives is that 25 percent of each division's profits are to come from products less than five years old. Toward that end, 3M typically launches more than 200 new products each year. During one recent five-year period, 3M generated better than 30 percent of its $13 billion in revenues from products introduced during the previous five years.[39]

3M generated better than 30 percent of its $13 billion in revenues from products introduced during the previous five years.

What's the secret to 3M's success? What, if anything, can other managers do to make their organizations more innovative? In the following pages, we will try to answer those questions as we discuss the factors behind innovation.

How Are Creativity and Innovation Related?

creativity
The ability to combine ideas in a unique way or to make unusual connections.

innovation
The process of taking a creative idea and turning it into a useful product, service, or method of operation.

In general usage, **creativity** means the ability to combine ideas in a unique way or to make unusual associations between ideas.[40] For example, when Nolan Bushnell thought that combining television and playing games might be of interest to the American public, he turned his idea into a $100 million video invention.[41] An organization that stimulates creativity is one that develops novel approaches to things or unique solutions to problems. **Innovation** is the process of taking a creative idea and turning it into a useful product, service, or method of operation. Northstar Ski Resort in Tahoe, California, for instance, has increased its revenues by more than $2 million annually by having such innovative products as a personalized microchip wristband that allows the wearer to charge "lift tickets, food, ski lessons, on-site child care"—and even to receive electronic messages while skiing.[42] At Novo Nordisk, a biotechnology company in Denmark, scientists found ways of replacing manufactured chemicals by natural substances. For instance, they uncovered "an enzyme found in soil which helps turn starch into soil, and one from a bug which removes protein stains."[43]

The innovative organization is characterized by the ability to channel its creative juices into useful outcomes. When managers talk about changing an organization to make it more creative, they usually mean that they want to stimulate innovation.[44] The 3M Company is aptly described as innovative because it has taken novel ideas and turned them into profitable products such as cellophane tape, Scotch-Guard protective coatings, Post-It notepads, and diapers with elastic waistbands. So, too, is the highly successful microchip manufacturer Intel. It leads all chip manufacturers in miniaturization, and the success of its 386 and 486 chips gives the company a 75 percent share of the microprocessor market for IBM-compatible PCs. With $5 billion a year in sales, Intel's commitment to staying ahead of the competition by introducing a stream of new and more powerful products is supported by annual expenditures of $1.2 billion for its plant and equipment and $800 million for research and development.

Being creative means seeing things from a unique perspective.

What Is Involved in Innovation?

Some people believe that creativity is inborn; others believe that with training, anyone can be creative.[45] It is in this latter view that creativity can be viewed as a fourfold process consisting of perception, incubation, inspiration, and innovation.[46]

Perception involves how you see things. Being creative means seeing things from a unique perspective. That is, an employee may see solutions to a problem that others cannot or will not see at all. Going from perception to reality, however, doesn't occur instantaneously. Instead, ideas go though a process of *incubation*. Sometimes, employees need to "sit" on their ideas. This doesn't mean sitting and doing nothing. Rather, during this incubation period, employees should collect massive data that are stored, retrieved, studied, reshaped, and finally molded into something new. During this period, it is common for years to pass.

Talk about innovation! At Northstar Ski Resort, skiers can access a number of services by wearing a personalized, preprogrammed wristband. When scanned, the wristband can track how far a skier has skied or it can be used to charge such items as food, ski lessons, and even child care.

Think for a moment about a time you struggled for an answer on a test. Although you tried hard to jog your memory, nothing worked. Then suddenly, like a flash of light, the answer popped into your head. You found it! *Inspiration* in the creative process is similar. Inspiration is the moment when all your prior efforts successfully come together.

Although inspiration leads to euphoria, the creative work is not complete. It requires an innovative effort. *Innovation* involves taking that inspiration and turning it into a useful product, service, or way of doing things. Thomas Edison is often credited with saying that "Creativity is 1 percent inspiration and 99 percent perspiration." That 99 percent, or the innovation, involves testing, evaluating, and retesting what the inspiration found (see Developing a Management Skill). It is usually at this stage that an individual involves others more in what he or she had been working on. That involvement is critical because even the greatest invention may be delayed, or lost, if an individual cannot effectively deal with others in communicating and achieving what the creative idea is supposed to do!

How Can a Manager Foster Innovation?

There are three sets of variables that have been found to stimulate innovation. They pertain to the organization's structure, culture, and human resource practices.

How Do Structural Variables Affect Innovation? On the basis of extensive research, we can make three statements regarding the effect of structural variables on innovation.[47] First, organic structures positively influence innovation. Because they are lower in work specialization, have fewer rules, and are more decentralized than mechanistic structures, they facilitate the flexibility, adaptation, and cross-fertilization that make the adoption of innovations easier.[48] Second, easy availability of plentiful resources provides a key building block for innovation. An abundance of resources allows management to afford to purchase innovations, bear the cost of instituting innovations, and absorb failures. Finally, frequent interunit communication helps to break

Developing a Management Skill

Becoming More Creative

About the Skill: *Creativity is a frame of mind. You need to expand your mind's capabilities—to open your mind up to new ideas. Every individual has the ability to be creative. But many people, for a variety of reasons, simply don't try to develop the ability to be creative. In today's organizations, those people can no longer get by. Dynamic environments and managing chaos require that managers look for new and innovative ways to attain their goals, as well as those of the organization.*

Steps in Practicing the Skill[49]

1. ***Think of yourself as creative.*** Although this is a simple suggestion, research shows that if you think you can't be creative, you won't be. Believing in yourself is the first step in becoming more creative.

2. ***Pay attention to your intuition.*** Every individual has a subconscious mind that works well. Sometimes answers come to you when least expected. For example, when you are about to go sleep, your relaxed mind sometimes whispers a solution to a problem you're facing. Listen to that voice. In fact, most creative people keep a notepad near their bed and write down those "great" ideas when they come to them. That way, they don't forget them.

3. ***Move away from your comfort zone.*** Every individual has a comfort zone in which certainty exists. But creativity and the known often do not mix. To be creative, you need to move away from the status quo and focus your mind on something new.

4. ***Engage in activities that put you outside your comfort zone.*** You not only must think differently; you need to do things differently. By engaging in activities that are different, you challenge yourself. Learning to play a musical instrument or learning a foreign language, for example, opens your mind up and allows it to be challenged.

5. ***Seek a change of scenery.*** People are often creatures of habit. Creative people force themselves out of their habits by changing their scenery. That may mean going into a quiet and serene area where you can be alone with your thoughts.

6. ***Find several right answers.*** In the discussion of bounded rationality (Chapter 5), we said that people seek solutions that are good enough. Being creative means continuing to look for other solutions even when you think you have solved the problem. A better, more creative solution just might be found.

7. ***Play your own devil's advocate.*** Challenging yourself to defend your solutions helps you to develop confidence in your creative efforts. Second guessing yourself may also help you to find more-creative solutions.

8. ***Believe in finding a workable solution.*** Like believing in yourself, you also need to believe in your ideas. If you don't think you can find a solution, you probably won't.

9. ***Brainstorm with others.*** Creativity is not an isolated activity. Bouncing ideas off of others creates a synergistic effect.

10. ***Turn creative ideas into action.*** Coming up with ideas is only half of the process. Once the ideas are generated, they must be implemented. Keeping great ideas in your mind, or on papers that no one will read, does little to expand your creative abilities.

down possible barriers to innovation by facilitating interaction across departmental lines.[50] 3M, for instance, is highly decentralized and takes on many of the characteristics of small, organic organizations. The company also has the "deep pockets" needed to support its policy of allowing scientists and engineers to use up to 15 percent of their time on projects of their own choosing. Of course, none of three contributors to innovation can exist unless top management is committed to them.[51]

How Does an Organization's Culture Affect Innovation? Innovative organizations tend to have similar cultures.[52] They encourage experimentation. They reward both successes and failures. They celebrate mistakes. For example, at Sony, employees are encouraged and rewarded for experimenting with new products in the marketplace. Unlike other organizations, Sony "sends a lot of products into the market knowing not all will be successful."[53] Their culture, therefore, promotes this risk-taking behavior. Had it not, the Sony Walkman would probably never have made it into stores! An innovative culture is likely to have the following seven characteristics:

1. *Acceptance of ambiguity.* Too much emphasis on objectivity and specificity constrains creativity.
2. *Tolerance of the impractical.* Individuals who offer impractical, even foolish, answers to what-if questions are not stifled. What seems impractical at first might lead to innovative solutions.
3. *Low external controls.* Rules, regulations, policies, and similar controls are kept to a minimum.
4. *Tolerance of risk.* Employees are encouraged to experiment without fear of consequences should they fail. Mistakes are treated as learning opportunities.
5. *Tolerance of conflict.* Diversity of opinions is encouraged. Harmony and agreement between individuals or units are not assumed to be evidence of high performance.
6. *Focus on ends rather than on means.* Goals are made clear, and individuals are encouraged to consider alternative routes toward their attainment. Focusing on ends suggests that there might be several right answers to any given problem.
7. *Open systems focus.* The organization closely monitors the environment and responds rapidly to changes as they occur.

What Human Resource Variables Affect Innovation? Within the human resources category, we find that innovative organizations actively promote the training and development of their members so that their knowledge remains current, offer their employees high job security to reduce the fear of getting fired for making mistakes, and encourage individuals to become champions of change. Once a new idea is developed, champions of change actively and enthusiastically promote the idea, build support, overcome resistance, and ensure that the innovation is implemented. Recent research finds that champions have common personality characteristics: extremely high self-confidence, persistence, energy, and a tendency to take risks. Champions also display characteristics associated with dynamic leadership. They inspire and energize

Companies like Toyota do more than pay lip service to creativity and innovation. In their "Idea Olympics," company officials encourage employees to test their imagination and develop new products. The 1995 grand prize winner (shown) developed a device that accurately simulates rowing—something that can be useful for people training for competitive boat racing.

others with their vision of the potential of an innovation and through their strong personal conviction in their mission. They are also good at gaining the commitment of others to support their mission. In addition, champions have jobs that provide considerable decision-making discretion. This autonomy helps them introduce and implement innovations.[54]

Summary

How will I know if I fulfilled the Learning Objectives found on page 266? You will have fulfilled the Learning Objectives if you understand the following.

1. **Describe what change variables are within a manager's control.** Managers can change the organization's structure by altering work specialization, rules and regulations, or centralization variables or by redesigning jobs; they can change the organization's technology by altering work processes, methods, and equipment; or they can change people by altering attitudes, expectations, perceptions, or behavior.

2. **Identify external and internal forces for change.** External forces for change include the marketplace, government laws and regulations, technology, labor markets, and economic changes. Internal forces of change include organizational strategy, equipment, the work force, and employee attitudes.

3. **Explain how managers can serve as change agents.** Managers can serve as change agents by becoming the catalyst for change in their units and by managing the change process.

4. **Contrast the "calm waters" and "white water rapids" metaphors for change.** The "calm waters" metaphor views change as a break in the organization's equilibrium state. Organizations are seen as stable and predictable, disturbed by only an occasional crisis. The "white water rapids" metaphor views change as continual and unpredictable. Managers must deal with ongoing and almost chaotic change.

5. **Explain why people are likely to resist change.** People resist change because of the uncertainty it creates, concern for personal loss, and belief that it might not be in the organization's best interest.

6. **List techniques for reducing resistance to change.** Six tactics have been proposed for reducing the resistance to change. They are education and communication, participation, facilitation and support, negotiation, manipulation and cooptation, and coercion.

7. **Identify what is meant by the term *organization development* and specify four popular OD techniques.** Organization development is an organizational activity designed to facilitate long-term organization-wide changes. Its focus is to constructively change the attitudes and values of organizational members so that they can more readily adapt to, and be more effective in achieving, the new directions of the organization. The more popular OD efforts in organizations rely heavily on group interactions and cooperation and include survey feedback, process consultation, team building, and intergroup development.

8. **Explain the causes and symptoms of stress.** Stress is something individuals feel when they face opportunities, constraints, or demands that they perceive to be both uncertain and important. It can be caused by organizational factors, such as work overload, role conflict, and role ambiguity. Personal factors can also contribute to stress: a serious illness, death of a family member, divorce, financial difficulties, or personality type.

9. **Differentiate between creativity and innovation.** Creativity is the ability to combine ideas in a unique way or to make unusual associations between ideas. Innovation is the process of taking creative ideas and turning them into a useful product, service, or method of operation.

10. **Explain how organizations can stimulate innovation.** Organizations that stimulate innovation will have structures that are flexible, easy access to resources, and fluid communication; a culture that is relaxed, supportive of new ideas, and encourages monitoring of the environment; and creative people who are well trained, current in their fields, and secure in their jobs.

Review & Discussion Questions

1. Why is handling change an integral part of every manager's job?
2. Who are change agents? Do you think that a low-level employee could act as a change agent? Explain.
3. Describe Lewin's three-step change process. How is it different from the change process needed in the white water rapids metaphor of change?
4. Why is OD considered to be planned change?
5. Which organization—Kodak or Quad/Graphics—do you believe would have more difficulty changing its culture? Explain your position.
6. How do work overload, role conflict, and role ambiguity contribute to employee stress?
7. What responsibility do managers have to employees who are suffering serious ill effects of stress?
8. How do creativity and innovation differ? Give an example of each.
9. How can an innovative culture make an organization more effective? Could such an innovative culture make an organization less effective? Explain.
10. Can changes occur in an organization without a champion to foster innovation? Explain.

Testing Your Comprehension • • • 

Circle the correct answer, then check yourself on page AK-1.

1. Some of your employees who ride the subway show up for work one hour late every day. Leaving their homes earlier does not work because of construction delays on the subway. You decide to allow these, and other employees, to start work one hour later. Of course, they work an hour later in the afternoon. What type of change did you make?
   a) people-oriented
   b) technological
   c) structural
   d) environmental

2. If an organization used an insider as a change agent, as opposed to an outside consultant,
   a) the change would probably be more conservative
   b) the change would probably be more drastic
   c) the change would probably be more objective
   d) the change would probably be more liberal

3. The "white water rapids" metaphor for change
   a) is of little use to most organizations today
   b) is consistent with dynamic environmental forces
   c) involves unfreezing, changing, and refreezing
   d) encourages individualism

4. A participative approach to overcoming resistance to change works best when
   a) there is close alignment of the goals of all concerned
   b) the source of resistance is misinformation or poor communication
   c) obsolescent skills are a concern of the individuals resisting the change
   d) coercion, manipulation, and co-optation have failed

5. Which of the following is the correct order of change in the "calm waters metaphor"?
   a) unfreezing—changing—refreezing
   b) unfreezing—refreezing—changing
   c) freezing—refreezing—changing
   d) freezing—changing—unfreezing

6. The MOST relevant disadvantage of using outside consultants as change agents is
   a) the cost
   b) internal members do not accept external recommendations
   c) they do not have to live with the repercussions after the change
   d) they cannot offer an objective perspective

7. If resistance to change is caused by misinformation, which of the following tactics would BEST reduce change resistance?
   a) participation
   b) facilitation and support
   c) negotiation
   d) education and communication

8. Which of the following statements about process consultation is NOT true?
   a) A process consultant solves a manager's problems.
   b) A process consultant gives the manager insight into what's going on in the department.
   c) A process consultant assists the manager in acting on process events.
   d) A process consultant helps the manager better understand his or her work unit.

9. For potential stress to become actual stress, which two conditions must exist?
   a) people and organizations
   b) uncertainty and importance
   c) certainty and importance
   d) uncertainty and risk

10. Symptoms of stress characterized by increased turnover, lower productivity, and higher absenteeism are __________ symptoms.
   a) psychological
   b) physiological
   c) behavioral
   d) none of the above

11. Role conflict refers to a situation in which
   a) contradictory demands are placed on employees
   b) jobs are ill defined
   c) decision-making is centralized
   d) job boredom is rampant

12. Which of the following statements is NOT true about stress?
   a) Stress is associated with constraints.
   b) Stress is caused by uncertainty of an outcome.
   c) Stress requires that outcomes must be important.
   d) Stress, when it exists, should be reduced.

13. You simply cannot finish your project on time because of delays in parts delivery. You speak to your boss, who says that you can delay the project consistent with the delay of the parts. Which of the following is probably the BEST explanation of your reaction?
   a) You become stressed because the project is not finished.
   b) You feel that the project is in conflict with your work schedule.
   c) Your boss has eliminated the uncertainty to some extent by allowing you to delay the project.
   d) You recognize that the importance of the project has been diminished by your boss.

14. Which of the following describes the main distinction between employee assistance programs and wellness programs?
   a) Employee assistance programs focus on helping employees prevent problems. Wellness programs focus on helping employees overcome problems.
   b) Employee assistance programs focus on alcoholic employees. Wellness programs focus on substance abusers.
   c) Employee assistance programs return $5 for every $1 invested in them. Wellness programs return only $3 for every $1 invested in them.
   d) Employee assistance programs focus on helping employees overcome their problems. Wellness programs focus on helping employees prevent problems.

15. Innovation refers to
   a) a decision-making technique
   b) the implementation of a creative idea
   c) a type of process consultation
   d) a type of automation

16. A culture conducive to creativity and innovation would probably have a high __________ and a low __________ .
   a) tolerance of risk; division of labor
   b) external control; tolerance of risk
   c) tolerance of conflict; acceptance of ambiguity
   d) tolerance of risk; tolerance of the impractical

Applying the Concepts

The Celestial Aerospace Company

Objectives:

1. To illustrate how forces for change and stability must be managed in organizations.
2. To illustrate the effects of alternative change techniques on the relative strength of forces for change and forces for stability.

The situation:

The marketing division of the Celestial Aerospace Company (CAP) has gone through two major reorganizations in the past three years. Initially, the structure changed from a functional to a matrix form. But the matrix form did not satisfy some functional managers. They complained that the structure confused the authority and responsibility relationships. In reaction to these complaints, the marketing department revised the structure back to the functional form. This new structure maintained market and project teams, which were managed by project managers with a few general staff personnel. But no functional specialists were assigned to these groups. After the change, some problems began to surface. Project managers complained that they could not obtain necessary assistance from functional staffs. It not only took more time to obtain necessary assistance but also created problems in establishing stable relationships with functional staff members. Since these problems affected their services to customers, project managers demanded a change in the organizational structure—probably again toward a matrix structure. Faced with these complaints and demands from project managers, the vice president is pondering yet another reorganization. He has requested an outside consultant (you) to help him in the reorganization plan.

1. Divide into groups of five to seven and take the role of consultants.
2. Each group should identify the forces necessitating the change and the resistance to that change found in the company.
3. Each group should develop a set of strategies for dealing with the resistance to change and for implementing those strategies.
4. Reassemble the class and hear each group's recommendations and explanations.
5. After each group has presented, probing questions should be posed by other "consulting groups" about the presenting group's recommendations.

Take It to the Net

We invite you to visit the Robbins/De Cenzo page on the Prentice Hall Web site at:

http://www.prenhall.com/robbinsfom

for this chapter's World Wide Web exercise.

You can also visit the Web sites for these companies featured within this chapter:

Apple Computer
http://www.apple.com

Bank Leumi Le-Israel
http://www.bll.co.il

Charles Schwab
http://www.schwab.com

Novo Nordisk
http://www/novo.ok/

Signet Bank
http://www.signetbank.com

Thinking Critically

Making a Value Judgment: The OD Intervention

Organization development interventions often produce change results that are viewed as positive. Interventions that rely on participation of organizational members can create openness and trust among coworkers and respect for others. Interventions can also help employees understand that the company wants to promote risk taking and empowerment. "Living" these characteristics can lead to better organizational performance.

However, any change agent involved in an OD effort may impose his or her value system on those involved in the intervention. This is particularly true when the cause for the intervention is coworker mistrust. To deal with this issue, the change agent may bring all affected parties together to openly discuss their perceptions of the dilemma in an effort to resolve any problems that exist. Although many change agents are well versed in OD practices, sometimes they walk a very thin line between success and failure. For personal problems to be resolved in the workplace, participants must disclose very sensitive information. In other words, they must allow their privacy—namely their inner thoughts—to be invaded. Even though every individual in such a setting can refuse to divulge such information, doing so may carry with it negative ramifications. To its fullest extent, this avoidance could result in some adverse career impacts—lower performance appraisals, fewer pay increases—or it could even create career-threatening barriers.

On the other hand, active participation could lead to employees' speaking their minds. But that, too, carries some risks. Saying what one truly believes could result in having that information used against one at a later time. For instance, imagine, in such a setting, that an employee challenges something his or her manager does. This employee fully believes that the manager's behavior is detrimental to the work unit. This individual's "reward" for being open and honest could be purely punitive. Although, at the time, the manager may appear to be receptive to the feedback, he or she may get even later. In either case—participating or not—then, employees could be hurt. Even though the intent was to help overcome coworker mistrust, the end result may be more back stabbing, more hurt feelings, and more distance placed between the understandings of the participants.

Questions:

1. Do you think that coworkers can be *too* open and honest under this type of OD intervention? Explain your position.
2. What can a change agent do to ensure that employees' rights will be protected when the intervention is designed to help rebuild strained coworker relations?
3. Do you believe that change agents have too much power and control in deciding how to gather "sensitive" data to build effective work groups? Discuss.

What Ever Happened to Apple Computer?

Back in 1977, two self-proclaimed "hippies" and a "thirty-something" Intel retiree pooled their brainpower and financial resources and started a computer company. Within a few short years, this creative and innovative company took the computer world by storm. Apple Computer was a significant and leading player in the personal computer industry.[55] Although it has sold more than 22 million Macintosh computers, the company today is likely to be described as a group of chronic underachievers. What happened? Apple computer was unable to adapt to environmental changes surrounding it.

Many individuals believe that Apple's business strategy was never correct—or, at the very least, it was executed poorly. Since its inception, the company seemed to value its independence over everything else. For example, Apple's management would not consider licensing its technology to other businesses even if doing so would have helped it to compete aggressively in the "clone" market. But its apparent quest for independence may have been misunderstood. It appears that company officials actually worked on secret plans with such companies as DEC, Kodak, Sony, Sun Microsystems, Compaq, and IBM in an effort to develop an alliance "to compete against and keep Microsoft from controlling the public's destiny." Apple opted to put its emphasis on IBM, and the two computer giants were well on their way to achieving their goals. But hardware design clashes, coupled with IBM's own troubles, put an end to the talks between them. Sadly, Apple had no contingency plan if an IBM-Apple merger didn't occur. Compounding the problems were product shortages then gluts. Apple's aggressive production, intended to make products available, led to an oversupply, and the company had to "dump" inventory at below-cost prices.

One of the difficulties facing Apple was that it lost focus on its core values. It had been a company that prided itself on bringing innovative products to market, but little new was being developed. For instance, to compete with the faster Intel Pentium chips used in DOS-based systems, Apple's management sought to purchase a promising new microprocessor being developed by Motorola. But that search stopped because the chips were too expensive. Even when Apple did come up with a new product, its quality was questioned. For instance, Apple knew well in advance that Microsoft was planning to release Windows 95. In fact, that software took almost an extra year to come to market. Windows 95 was developed to directly compete with the MacIntosh operating system, but Apple didn't have something new of its own. It simply gave the edge to Microsoft. Furthermore, when Apple released its Powerbook PC, it shipped many with faulty batteries—which caused some of them to burst into flames. The result was a very embarrassing recall of the product. Internally, too, the organization was hurting. Layoffs became a corporate game plan. In fact, even one top marketing executive "reorganized himself out of a job." He left, as did another six vice presidents. And, on Wall Street, stock prices began to tumble. After almost two decades, some drastic changes were in order.

By early 1996, Apple's management was returning to basics—innovative technology. They were putting the final touches on a new operating system that will involve relational data bases. That is, using this operating system, an individual can access a data base and ask, for instance, for all published reports about Apple Computer dated after July 10, 1996, but not by any author whose last name is Dilbert. The company has also developed a "computer/CD-ROM machine/internet terminal" called Pippin. The notable feature of this appliance-computer is that it sits atop, and works through, a television set. Apple is also moving forward with its licensing agreements. To date, three companies are now licensed to sell Mac clones.

Apple is attempting to revitalize itself. But the changes it is making may be too late. Despite what they are doing, they may simply be merged into another company—losing the independence that they once so proudly held onto. What's the reaction of one of Apple's founders (whose interest in the company was bought out years ago)? Steven Jobs believes that "Apple needs to get on with business" and get everything it can from the Macintosh technology. After all, he says, the "PC wars are over—Microsoft won it a long time ago!"

Questions:

1. Do you think Apple Computer could have continued to be a highly profitable and successful company if it had used a conservative, incremental approach to adapt to changes in its environment? Explain.
2. Do you believe that Apple's management can survive and remain independent given the sweeping changes it started making in early 1996? Discuss your rationale.

Video Case ABCNEWS

Houston, We've Got a Problem

Houston, we've got a problem! Unforgettable words spoken by James Lovell, commander of the *Apollo 13* Space Mission.

The *Apollo 13* mission had started uneventfully, like many of the *Apollo* space flights that preceded it. And every flight experienced some minor glitch. For *Apollo 13,* that appeared to come just thirty-eight minutes into the flight, when one of the spacecraft's main engines cut off early. Fortunately, the thrust of the remaining engines still provided ample power to keep the mission on target. Even Lovell, a veteran astronaut, appeared unconcerned about the engine failure when he told his crewmates "almost every flight has something wrong with it, so sit back and relax, and enjoy a nice tranquil flight to the moon." Nothing went wrong for the next two days. But the tranquility abruptly ended when one of the astronauts stirred the space capsule's oxygen tanks, causing an explosion. From that moment on, *Apollo 13*'s mission was anything but ordinary.

The explosion that occurred on the spacecraft sent all concerned parties into a frenzy. Never before in NASA's history had mission control, or astronauts, experienced such an emergency. The command module *Odyssey* was dying. And without it, the astronauts would be unable to return safely to earth. In that split moment, *Apollo 13*'s mission changed. Rather than landing on the moon, the issue became one of getting astronauts Lovell, Haise, and Swigert home alive. To achieve this, many steps had to be taken—actions that NASA had never attempted or anticipated. For the rest of the flight, the astronauts would have to rely on their instincts, trial-and-error suggestions from mission control, and hope. Creativity and ingenuity were needed from all involved to save the lives of the marooned space travelers.

For instance, having shut down *Apollo 13*'s power, the astronauts could no longer power themselves using engine thrust. Instead, they had to rely on the gravitational pull of the earth for energy. That in itself was a major challenge for the astronauts, given that, without power, all guidance and navigational controls were unusable. Using gravity as power meant, however, that the flight had to be lengthened. To do what they wanted, the crew had to circle around the moon and catapult the capsule toward earth. That may not have appeared to be a major concern considering that the original destination was the moon. But the fact that oxygen would be in short supply given the extra time needed to circle the moon and carbon dioxide would be building up to dangerous levels made this action more life-threatening. To deal with the carbon dioxide buildup, for example, engineers at Johnson Space Center jury-rigged a "set of scrubbers, using anything the astronauts could find—cardboard, plastic bags, even their socks."

In the end, *Apollo 13* achieved the unimaginable. The space capsule returned home, safely bringing back its three stranded crew members. Through some of the most "remarkable examples of ingenuity and tenacity," as Gene Kranz, lead flight director, emotionally stated when seeing *Apollo 13* floating down toward the South Pacific landing spot, "We did it."

Questions:

1. "It's primarily when faced with a crisis that creativity and innovation become important." Do you agree or disagree? Discuss.
2. Identify how perception, incubation, inspiration, and innovation existed in the *Apollo 13* example when NASA engineers jury-rigged the carbon dioxide scrubber.

Source: "Apollo 13—The Real Stuff," *ABC News Nightline,* July 14, 1995.

• PART 4 •
Leading

Foundations of Individual and Group Behavior

10

LEARNING OBJECTIVES

What will I be able to do after I finish this chapter?

1. **DEFINE** the focus and goals of organizational behavior.
2. **IDENTIFY** and describe the three components of attitudes.
3. **EXPLAIN** cognitive dissonance.
4. **DESCRIBE** the Myers-Briggs personality type framework and its use in organizations.
5. **DEFINE** perception and describe the factors that can shape or distort perception.
6. **EXPLAIN** how managers can shape employee behavior.
7. **CONTRAST** formal and informal groups.
8. **EXPLAIN** why people join groups.
9. **STATE** how roles and norms influence employees' behavior.
10. **DESCRIBE** how group size affects group behavior.

THE ECONOMIC CLIMATE IN SOME COUNTRIES can best be described as chaotic. And in some of these, strong national cultures discourage taking chances. But some individuals are unwilling to accept that situation. Instead, they have an entrepreneurial spirit and a strong desire to better themselves. Take the case of Alexander Panikin, the head proprietor of the Moscow textile company Paninter.[1]

Growing up in the former Soviet Union proved difficult for Panikin. Jobs were hard to find, and those that were available paid very little in the state-run economy. But Alexander never gave up hope of one day being his own boss. He worked long hours at any odd job he could find—such as theater manager and goods trader—in an effort to save enough money to start his company. In 1989, his dream came true. He established a small sewing business, starting with five employees and six sewing machines.

Panikin had a lot of faith in his ability to be successful. He knew, though, that to be successful he would have to take some risks. He also recognized that his success could not come at the expense of his employees. Because labor is abundant and cheap in Moscow, Alexander could have hired all the employees he wanted at the state wage of US$100 a month. He could have "squeezed" them to work harder by taking advantage of their fears and anxieties and the economic uncertainties following the fall of the former Soviet Union. But Panikin's attitude toward workers was much different. He was uneasy with "traditional" management practices in Russia. He believed that "to manufacture something takes a lot of talent and work," and to get that, you had to make employees believe in you. Panikin treats his employees compassionately and does what he can to create an environment that will entice them to give that extra effort. He also pays his employees twice the state-wage rate!

Alexander Panikin, head of Paninter, a Moscow textile manufacturer, understands something about human behavior. His attitude toward workers and his management actions have created an environment that employees perceive as positive.

Alexander Panikin's actions have not gone unnoticed. Today, he employs more than 1,000 workers who, using state-of-the-art German looms, make more than 1 million pieces of clothes annually. Paninter now has annual revenues in excess of $3 million and is regarded as one of several private companies that are helping Russia revitalize itself. As for Alexander Panikin, his achievements demonstrate that he understands something about human behavior.

Alexander Panikin's story illustrates one way for managers to increase productivity by better understanding their employees. This chapter looks at a number of factors that influence employee and group behavior and their implications for management practice.

Toward Explaining and Predicting Behavior

The material in this and the following four chapters draws heavily on the field of study that has come to be known as organizational behavior. Although it is concerned with the subject of behavior—that is, the actions of people—**organizational behavior (OB)** is concerned specifically with the actions of people at work.

organizational behavior (OB) The study of the actions of people at work.

One of the challenges of understanding organizational behavior is that it addresses some issues that are not obvious. Like an iceberg, a lot of organizational

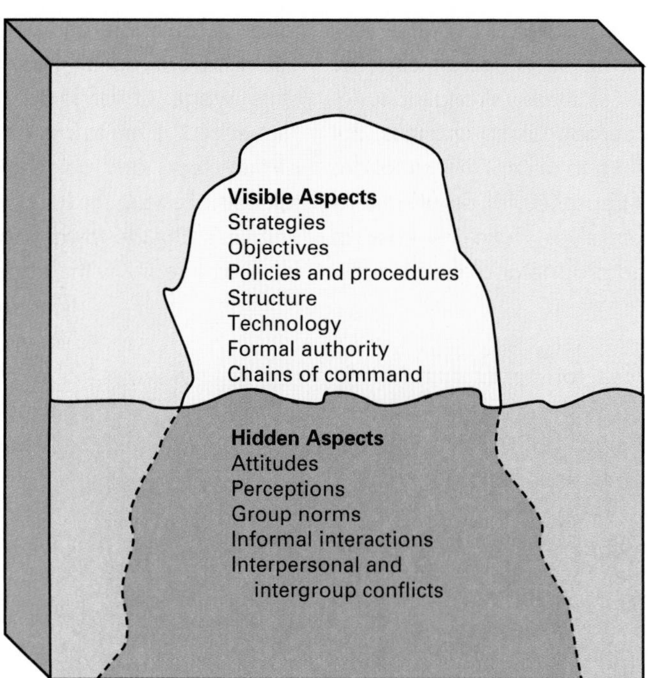

Exhibit 10-1
The Organization as an Iceberg Metaphor

behavior is not visible to the naked eye (see Exhibit 10-1). What we tend to see when we look at organizations are their formal aspects—strategies, objectives, policies and procedures, structure, technology, formal authority, and chains of command. But, just under the surface, there lie informal elements that managers need to understand. As we will show, OB provides managers with considerable insight into these important, but hidden, aspects of the organization.

What Is the Focus of Organizational Behavior?

Organizational behavior focuses primarily on two major areas. First, OB looks at individual behavior. Based predominantly on contributions from psychologists, this area includes such topics as attitudes, personality, perception, learning, and motivation. Second, OB is concerned with group behavior, which includes norms, roles, team building, and conflict. Our knowledge about groups comes basically from the work of sociologists and social psychologists. Unfortunately, the behavior of a group of employees cannot be understood by merely summing up the actions of the individuals, because individuals in groups behave differently from individuals acting alone. You see this characteristic when a street gang in a large city harasses innocent citizens. The gang members, acting individually, might never engage in such behavior. Put them together, and they act differently. Therefore, because employees in an organization are both individuals and members of groups, we need to study them at two levels. In this chapter, we will provide the foundation for understanding individual and group behavior. In the next chapter, we will introduce basic concepts related to special cases of group behavior—when individuals come together as a work team.

What Are the Goals of Organizational Behavior?

The goals of OB are to *explain* and to *predict* behavior. Why do managers need this skill? Simply, in order to manage their employees' behavior. We know that a manager's success depends on getting things done through other people. Toward this goal, the manager needs to be able to explain why employees engage in some behaviors rather than others and to predict how employees will respond to various actions the manager might take.

What employee behaviors are we specifically concerned about explaining and predicting? The emphasis will be on employee productivity, absenteeism, and turnover. In addition, we will look at job satisfaction. Although job satisfaction is an attitude rather than a behavior, it is an outcome about which many managers are concerned.

The goals of OB are to explain *and to* predict *behavior.*

In the following pages, we'll address how an understanding of employee attitudes, personality, perception, and learning can help us to predict and explain employee productivity, absence and turnover rates, and job satisfaction.

Attitudes

Attitudes are valuative statements—either favorable or unfavorable—concerning objects, people, or events. They reflect how an individual feels about something. When a person says, "I like my job," he or she is expressing an attitude about work.

To better understand the concept of attitudes, we should look at an attitude as being made up of three components: cognition, affect, and behavior.[2] The **cognitive component of an attitude** is made up of the beliefs, opinions, knowledge, and information held by a person. For example Sid Wing, president of Datametrics in Woodland Hills, California, believes that only one employee should be "recognized" at a time.[3] This belief illustrates Sid's cognition. The **affective component of an attitude** is the emotional, or feeling, segment of an attitude. This component would be reflected in the statement, "I don't like Eric because he discriminates against minorities." Finally, cognition and affect can lead to behavioral outcomes. The **behavioral component of an attitude** refers to an intention to behave in a certain way toward someone or something. So, to continue our example, I might choose to avoid Eric because of my feelings about him. Looking at attitudes as being made up of three components—cognition, affect, and behavior—helps to show the complexity of attitudes. But for the sake of clarity, keep in mind that the term *attitude* usually refers only to the affective component.

attitudes
Valuative statements concerning objects, people, or events.

cognitive component of an attitude
The beliefs, opinions, knowledge, and information held by a person.

affective component of an attitude
The emotional, or feeling, segment of an attitude.

behavioral component of an attitude
An intention to behave in a certain way toward someone or something.

Naturally, managers are not interested in every attitude an employee might hold. They are specifically interested in job-related attitudes. The three most important, and most studied, of these are job satisfaction, job involvement, and organizational commitment.[4] *Job satisfaction* is an employee's general attitude toward his or her job. When people speak of employee attitudes, more often than not they mean job satisfaction. *Job involvement* is the degree to which an employee identifies with his or her job, actively participates in it, and considers his or her job performance important to his or her self-worth. Finally, *organizational commitment* represents an employee's orientation toward the organization in terms of his or her loyalty to, identification with, and involvement in the organization.

Do an Individual's Attitude and Behavior Need to Be Consistent?

Did you ever notice how people change what they say so that it doesn't contradict what they do? Perhaps a friend of yours had consistently argued that American cars were poorly built and that he'd never own anything but a foreign import. But his parents gave him a late-model American-made car, and suddenly they weren't so bad. Or, when going through sorority rush, a new freshman believes that sororities are good and that pledging a sorority is important. If she fails to make a sorority, however, she may say, "I recognized that sorority life isn't all it's cracked up to be, anyway!"

Research has generally concluded that people seek consistency among their attitudes and between their attitudes and their behavior.[5] This means that individuals try to reconcile differing attitudes and align their attitudes and behavior so that they appear rational and consistent. When there is an inconsistency, individuals will take steps to correct it. They can correct it by altering either the attitudes or the behavior or by developing a rationalization for the discrepancy.

For example, consider a recruiter for Shanghai Jielong Industry Corp. (SJIC). It is her job to visit college campuses, identify qualified job candidates, and sell them on the advantages of SJIC as a place to work. Her attitude and job would be in conflict if she personally believed that the company had poor working conditions and few opportunities for new college graduates. This recruiter could, over time, find her attitudes toward SJIC becoming more positive. She may, in effect, convince herself by continually articulating the merits of working for SJIC. Another alternative would be for the recruiter to remain negative about SJIC and the opportunities within the firm for prospective candidates. However, the recruiter might acknowledge that, although SJIC is an undesirable place to work, her obligation as a professional recruiter is to present the positive side of working for the company. She might, therefore, rationalize that no workplace is perfect and that her job is not to present both sides of the issue but rather to present a rosy picture of the company.

What Is Cognitive Dissonance Theory?

Can we additionally assume from this consistency principle that an individual's behavior can always be predicted if we know his or her attitude on a subject? The answer is, unfortunately, more complex than merely a Yes or a No.

cognitive dissonance Any incompatibility between two or more attitudes or between behavior and attitudes.

Leon Festinger, in the late 1950s, proposed the theory of **cognitive dissonance.**[6] This theory sought to explain the relationship between attitudes and behavior. Dissonance in this case means inconsistency. Cognitive dissonance refers to any incompatibility that an individual might perceive between two or more of his or her attitudes or between his or her behavior and attitudes. Festinger argued that any form of inconsistency is uncomfortable and that individuals will attempt to reduce the dissonance and, hence, the discomfort. Therefore, individuals will seek a stable state where there is a minimum of dissonance.

Of course, no individual can completely avoid dissonance. You know that cheating on your income tax is wrong, but you may "fudge" the numbers a bit every year, and hope you won't be audited. Or you tell your children to brush after every meal, but you might not. So how do people cope? Festinger proposed that the desire to reduce dissonance is determined by the importance of the elements creating the dissonance, the degree of influence the individual believes he or she has over the elements, and the rewards that may be involved in dissonance. Let's look at some examples of cognitive dissonance.

Suppose that the factors creating the dissonance are relatively unimportant. In this case, the pressure to correct the imbalance would be low. However, say that a corporate manager—Shoreh Kaynama—believes strongly that no company should lay off employees. Unfortunately, Kaynama, because of the requirements of her job, is placed in the position of having to make decisions that would trade off her company's strategic direction against her attitudes on layoffs. She knows that, because of restructuring in the company, some jobs may no longer be needed, and the layoffs are in the best

These striking American Airlines workers claim to love their work. How then, can they take this job action against their employer for using nonunion workers? Group pressures from peers and union officials induce them to participate. These workers still have a positive attitude toward their work but engage in the work shutdown to reduce dissonance.

economic interest of her firm. What will she do? Undoubtedly, Shoreh is experiencing a high degree of cognitive dissonance. Because of the importance of the issues in this example, we cannot expect Kaynama to ignore the inconsistency. There are several paths that she can follow to deal with her dilemma. She can change her behavior (lay off employees). Or she can reduce dissonance by concluding that the dissonant behavior is not so important after all ("I've got to make a living, and in my role as a decision maker, I often have to place the good of my company above that of individual organizational members"). A third alternative would be for Shoreh Kaynama to change her attitude ("There is nothing wrong in laying off employees"). Still another choice would be to seek out more consonant elements to outweigh the dissonant ones ("The long-term benefits to the surviving employees from our restructuring more than offset the cost associated with the retrenchment effort").

The degree of influence that individuals like Shoreh Kaynama believe they have over the elements also will have an impact on how they will react to the dissonance. If they perceive the dissonance to be an uncontrollable result—something over which they have no choice—they are less likely to feel a need for an attitude change. If, for example, the dissonance-producing behavior were required as a result of the boss's directive, the pressure to reduce dissonance would be less than if the behavior were performed voluntarily. Dissonance would exist, but it could be rationalized and justified. Rewards also influence the degree to which individuals are motivated to reduce dissonance. High dissonance, when accompanied by high rewards, tends to reduce the tension inherent in the dissonance. The reward acts to reduce dissonance by increasing the consistency side of the individual's balance sheet.

These moderating factors suggest that just because individuals experience dissonance they will not necessarily move directly toward consistency, that is, toward reduction of the dissonance. If the issues underlying the dissonance are of minimal importance, if an individual perceives that the dissonance is externally imposed and is substantially uncontrollable by him or her, or if rewards are significant enough to offset the dissonance, the individual will not be under great tension to reduce the dissonance.

How Can an Understanding of Attitudes Help Managers Be More Effective?

We know that employees can be expected to try to reduce dissonance. Therefore, not surprisingly, there is relatively strong evidence that committed and satisfied employees have low rates of turnover and absenteeism.[7] Because most managers want to minimize the number of resignations and absences—especially among their more productive employees—they should do those things that will generate positive job attitudes. Dissonance can be managed. If employees are required to engage in activities that appear inconsistent to them or that are at odds with their attitudes, managers should remember that pressure to reduce the dissonance is lessened when the employee perceives that the dissonance is externally imposed and uncontrollable. The pressure is also lessened if rewards are significant enough to offset the dissonance.

But let's not confuse satisfied workers with productive workers. We need to be aware of a debate that has lasted almost seven decades. That is, are happy workers more productive? Several research studies in the past have provided important implications for managers.[8] They suggested that making employees satisfied would lead to high productivity. That suggestion, in part, explains why in the 1930s, 1940s, and 1950s, management spent considerable time doing things that would create a "caring" environment. For instance, there were company bowling teams, picnics, and credit unions—all formed to give something to employees and make them happy. But their effect on productivity was questioned.[9] As a result, most researchers perceived that managers, like Alexander Panikin, for instance, would get better results by directing their attention primarily to what would help employees become more productive.[10] Successful job performance should then lead to feelings of accomplishment, increased pay, promotions, and other rewards—all desirable outcomes—which then lead to satisfaction with the job. Recent research, however, is providing renewed support for the original premise that happy workers are productive workers.[11] The difference in this research is that satisfaction and productivity data were gathered for entire organizations—as opposed to individual employees. Organizations that had satisfied employees were more effective than organizations that had less-satisfied employees.

Recent research is providing renewed support that happy workers are productive workers.

Personality

Some people are quiet and passive; others are loud and aggressive. When we describe people in terms such as *quiet, passive, loud, aggressive, ambitious, extroverted, loyal, tense,* or *sociable,* we are categorizing them in terms of personality traits. An individual's **personality** is the combination of the psychological traits we use to classify that person.[12]

personality
A combination of psychological traits that classifies a person.

Can Personality Predict Behavior?

There are literally dozens of personality traits. Many of these personalty characteristics are used to describe an individual's behavior. The more popular of these traits include shyness, aggressiveness, submissiveness, laziness, ambitiousness, loyalty, and timidness. These characteristics, when exhibited consistently in a large number of situations, are called *personality traits.*[13] Through the years, researchers attempted to focus specifically on which traits would lead to identifying sources of one's personality. Two of these efforts have been widely recognized—the Myers-Briggs Type Indicator, and the five-factor model of personality.

What Is the Myers-Briggs Type Indicator? One of the more widely used methods of identifying personalities is the **Myers-Briggs Type Indicator (MBTI).**[14] Building on the works of psychologist Carl Jung, the MBTI uses four dimensions of personality to identify sixteen different personality types—for example, INFJ, ENFJ, and so on—based on the responses to an approximately 100-item questionnaire (see Exhibit 10-2). More than 2 million individuals each year in the United States alone take the MBTI. And

Myers-Briggs Type Indicator (MBTI)
A method of identifying personality types.

		SENSING TYPES S		INTUITIVE TYPES N	
		THINKING T	FEELING F	FEELING F	THINKING T
INTROVERTS I	JUDGING J	**ISTJ** Serious, quiet, earn success by concentration and thoroughness. Practical, orderly, matter-of-fact, logical, realistic, and dependable. Take responsibility.	**ISFJ** Quiet, friendly, responsible, and conscientious, Work devotedly to meet their obligations. Thorough, pains-taking, accurate. Loyal, considerate.	**INFJ** Succeed by perseverance, originality, and desire to do whatever is needed or wanted. Quietly forceful, conscientious, concerned for others. Respected for their firm principles.	**INTJ** Usually have original minds and great drive for their own ideas and purposes. Skeptical, critical, independent, determined, often stubborn.
INTROVERTS I	PERCEIVING P	**ISTP** Cool onlookers—quiet, reserved, and analytical. Usually interested in impersonal principles, how and why mechanical things work. Flashes of original humor.	**ISFP** Retiring, quietly friendly, sensitive, kind, modest about their abilities. Shun disagreements. Loyal followers. Often relaxed about getting things done.	**INFP** Care about learning, ideas, language, and independent projects of their own. Tend to undertake too much, then some-how get it done. Friendly, but often too absorbed.	**INTP** Quiet, reserved, impersonal. Enjoy theoretical or scientific subjects. Usually interested mainly in ideas, little liking for parties or small talk. Sharply defined interests.
EXTROVERTS E	PERCEIVING P	**ESTP** Matter-of-fact, do not worry or hurry, enjoy whatever comes along. May be a bit blunt or insensitive. Best with real things that can be taken apart or put together.	**ESFP** Outgoing, easygoing, accepting, friendly, make things more fun for others by their enjoyment. Like sports and making things. Find remembering facts easier than mastering theories.	**ENFP** Warmly enthusiastic, high-spirited, ingenious, imaginative. Able to do almost anything that interests them. Quick with a solution and to help with a problem.	**ENTP** Quick, ingenious, good at many things. May argue either side of a question for fun. Resourceful in solving challenging problems, but may neglect routine assignments.
EXTROVERTS E	JUDGING J	**ESTJ** Practical, realistic, matter-of-fact, with a natural head for business or mechanics. Not interested in subjects they see no use for. Like to organize and run activities.	**ESFJ** Warm-hearted, talkative, popular, conscientious, born cooperators. Need harmony. Work best with encouragement. Little interest in abstract thinking or technical subjects.	**ENFJ** Responsive and responsible. Generally feel real concern for what others think or want. Sociable, popular. Sensitive to praise and criticism.	**ENTJ** Hearty, frank, decisive, leaders. Usually good in any-thing that requires reasoning and intelligent talk. May sometimes be more positive than their experience in an area warrants.

Exhibit 10-2
The Myers-Briggs Personality Types

Source: Modified and reproduced by special permission of the publisher, Consulting Psychologists Press, Inc., Palo Alto, CA 94303, from *Introduction to Type,* 5e, by Isabel Briggs Meyers. Copyright 1993 by Consulting Psychologists Press, Inc. All rights reserved. Further Reproduction is prohibited without the publisher's written permission.

it's used in such companies as Apple Computer, AT&T, Exxon, 3M, as well as many hospitals, educational institutions, and the U.S. armed forces.[15]

The sixteen personality types are based on the four dimensions noted in Exhibit 10-2. That is, the MBTI dimensions include extraversion versus introversion (EI);

sensing versus intuitive (SN); thinking versus feeling (TF); and judging versus perceiving (JP). The EI dimension measures an individual's orientation toward the inner world of ideas (I) or the external world of the environment (E). The sensing-intuitive dimension indicates an individual's reliance on information gathered from the external world (S) or from the world of ideas (N). Thinking-feeling reflects one's preference to evaluate information in an analytical manner (T) or on the basis of values and beliefs (F). Last, the judging-perceiving index reflects an attitude toward the external world that is either task completion–oriented (J) or information-seeking (P).

Using that information, then, let's describe someone who is identified as an INFP (introvert-intuitive-feeling-perceiving). Under Myers-Briggs, the INFP individual would be someone who is quiet and reserved and generally in deep thought, sees the "big picture," is flexible and adaptable, likes a challenge, looks for complete information before making a decision, and cares for others.[16]

How could the MBTI help managers? Proponents of the instrument believe that it's important to know these personality types because they influence the way people interact and solve problems. For example, if your boss is an intuitor and you are a sensor, you will gather information in different ways. An intuitor prefers gut reactions, whereas a sensor prefers facts. To work well with your boss, you would have to present more than just facts about a situation and discuss how you feel. Also, the MBTI has been used to help managers select employees better matched for certain types of jobs. A marketing position that requires extensive interaction with "outsiders" would be best filled by someone who has extroverted tendencies.

What Is the Big-Five Model of Personality?Although the MBTI is very popular, it suffers from one major criticism. It lacks evidence to support its validity. That same criticism, however, cannot be imposed on the five-factor model of personality—more typically called the **Big-Five model.**[17] The Big Five factors are:

big-five model
Five-factor model of personality that includes extraversion, agreeableness, conscientiousness, emotional stability, and openness to experience.

1. *Extraversion.* A personality dimension that describes the degree to which someone is sociable, talkative, and assertive
2. *Agreeableness.* A personality dimension that describes the degree to which someone is good-natured, cooperative, and trusting
3. *Conscientiousness.* A personality dimension that describes the degree to which someone is responsible, dependable, persistent, and achievement-oriented
4. *Emotional stability.* A personality dimension that describes the degree to which someone is calm, enthusiastic, and secure (positive) or tense, nervous, depressed, and insecure (negative)
5. *Openness to experience.* A personality dimension that describes the degree to which someone is imaginative, artistically sensitive, and intellectual

The Big Five provide more than just a personality framework. Research has shown that important relationships exist between these personality dimensions and job performance.[18] For example, one study reviewed five categories of occupations: *professionals* (e.g., engineers, architects, attorneys), *police, managers, sales,* and *semi-skilled and skilled employees.*[19] Job performance was defined in terms of employee performance ratings, training competency, and personnel data such as salary level. The results of the study showed that conscientiousness predicted job performance for all five occupational groups. Predictions for the other personality dimensions depended on the situation and the occupational group. For example, extraversion predicted performance in managerial and sales positions, in which high social interaction is necessary. Openness to experience was found to be important in predicting training competency.

Ironically, emotional security was not positively related to job performance. Although it would appear logical that calm and secure workers would be better performers, that wasn't the case. Perhaps that result is a function of the likelihood that emotionally stable workers often keep their jobs and emotionally unstable people may not. Given that all those participating in the study were employed, the variance on that dimension would tend to be small.

What personality characteristics does L. Fallasha Erwin, an agent who represents NBA basketball players, have? The Big-Five model states that these characteristics include extraversion, agreeableness, conscientiousness, emotional stability, and openness to experience.

Can Personality Traits Predict Practical Work-Related Behaviors?

Five specific personality traits have proven most powerful in explaining individual behavior in organizations. These are locus of control, Machiavellianism, self-esteem, self-monitoring, and risk propensity.

Who has control over an individual's behavior? Some people, like Vinod Gupta of American Business Information, Inc., believe that they control their own fate.[20] After nearly being fired from his job at Commodore Corporation for having 4,800 Yellow Page directories stored in his office, he opted to take the books home and transfer the information into a massive data base. Although it took him over thirteen years to do so, Vinod created a data base with over 70 million entries, which he sells to marketers around the world. He and his staff of 700 employees, verify, update and add entries to the data base in this $100 million business.

Others see themselves as pawns of fate, believing that what happens to them in their lives is due to luck or chance. The **locus of control** in the first case is internal; people like Gupta believe that they control their destiny. In the second case it is external; these people believe that their lives are controlled by outside forces.[21] A manager might also expect to find that externals blame a poor performance evaluation on their boss's prejudice, their coworkers, or other events outside their control, whereas internals explain the same evaluation in terms of their own actions (see Understanding Yourself).

locus of control
A personality attribute that measures the degree to which people believe that they are masters of their own fate.

The second characteristic is called **Machiavellianism** ("Mach"). It was named after Niccolo Machiavelli, who wrote in the sixteenth century on how to gain and manipulate power. An individual who is high in Machiavellianism—in contrast to someone who is low—is pragmatic, maintains emotional distance, and believes that ends can justify means.[22] "If it works, use it" is consistent with a high Mach perspective. Do high Machs make good employees? That answer depends on the type of job and whether you consider ethical implications in evaluating performance. In jobs that require bargaining skills (such as labor negotiator) or that have substantial rewards for winning (such as a commissioned salesperson), high Machs are productive. In jobs in which ends do not justify the means or that lack absolute standards of performance, it is difficult to predict the performance of high Machs (see Exhibit 10-3).

Machiavellianism
A measure of the degree to which people are pragmatic, maintain emotional distance, and believe that ends can justify means.

People differ in the degree to which they like or dislike themselves. This trait is called **self-esteem.**[23] The research on self-esteem (SE) offers some interesting insights into organizational behavior. For example, self-esteem is directly related to expectations for success. High SEs believe that they possess the ability they need in order to succeed at

self-esteem
An individual's degree of like or dislike for him- or herself.

Understanding Yourself

Who Controls Your Life?

This assessment is designed to help you determine your locus of control. Read each of the following ten statements and indicate (by circling the statement number) whether you agree more with choice A or choice B.

A	B
1. Making a lot of money is largely a matter of getting the right breaks.	*1.* Promotions are earned through hard work and persistence.
2. I have noticed that there is usually a direct connection between how hard I study and the grades I get.	*2.* Many times the reactions of teachers seem haphazard to me.
3. The number of divorces indicates that more and more people are not trying to make their marriages work.	*3.* Marriage is largely a gamble.
4. It is silly to think that one can really change another person's basic attitudes.	*4.* When I am right I can convince others.
5. Getting promoted is really a matter of being a little luckier than the next person.	*5.* In our society a person's future earning power depends upon his or her ability.
6. If one knows how to deal with people, they are really quite easily led.	*6.* I have little influence over the way other people behave.
7. The grades I make are the result of my own efforts; luck has little or nothing to do with it.	*7.* Sometimes I feel that I have little to do with the grades I get.
8. People like me can change the course of world affairs if we make ourselves heard.	*8.* It is only wishful thinking to believe that one can really influence what happens in our society at large.
9. A great deal that happens to me is probably a matter of chance.	*9.* I am the master of my fate.
10. Getting along with people is a skill that must be practiced.	*10.* It is almost impossible to figure out how to please some people.

Scoring: Give yourself one point if you circled the following statements: 1B; 2A; 3A; 4B; 5B; 6A; 7A; 8A; 9B; and 10A. Total your score. Your total score should be 10 or less.

What the Assessment Means: The following scale can be used to help interpret your score.

8–10 points = *High internal locus of control*
6–7 points = *Moderate internal locus of control*
5 points = *Mixed*
3–4 points = *Moderate external locus of control*
1–2 points = *High external locus of control*

Source: Adapted from J. B. Rotter, "External Control and Internal Control," *Psychology Today,* June 1971, p. 42. Copyright 1971 by the American Psychological Association. Adapted with permission.

Exhibit 10-3
Machiavellianism Dilbert Style

Source: Scott Adams © 1994 United Features Syndicate, Inc. Reprinted with permission.

work. Individuals with high SE will take more risks in job selection and are more likely to choose unconventional jobs than are people with low SE.[24]

The most common finding on self-esteem is that low SEs are more susceptible to external influence than are high SEs. Low SEs are dependent on the receipt of positive evaluations from others.[25] As a result, they are more likely to seek approval from others and more prone to conform to the beliefs and behaviors of those they respect than are high SEs. In managerial positions, low SEs will tend to be concerned with pleasing others and, therefore, less likely to take unpopular stands than are high SEs. Not surprisingly, self-esteem has also been found to be related to job satisfaction. A number of studies confirm that high SEs are more satisfied with their jobs than are low SEs.

Another personality trait that has recently received increased attention is called **self-monitoring.**[26] It refers to an individual's ability to adjust his or her behavior to external, situational factors. Individuals high in self-monitoring can show considerable adaptability in adjusting their behavior to external, situational factors. They are highly sensitive to external cues and can behave differently in different situations. High self-monitors are capable of presenting striking contradictions between their public persona and their private selves. Low self-monitors can't alter their behavior. They tend to display their true dispositions and attitudes in every situation; hence, there is high behavioral consistency between who they are and what they do.

self-monitoring
A measure of an individual's ability to adjust his or her behavior to external, situational factors.

The research on self-monitoring is in its infancy, so predictions are hard to make. Preliminary evidence suggests, however, that high self-monitors tend to pay closer attention to the behavior of others and are more capable of conforming than are low self-monitors.[27] We might also hypothesize that high self-monitors will be more successful in managerial positions that require individuals to play multiple, and even contradicting, roles. The high self-monitor is capable of putting on different "faces" for different audiences.[28]

The final personality type influencing worker behavior at work reflects their willingness to take chances—their propensity for risk taking (see Managers Who Made a Difference). This preference to assume or avoid risk has been shown to have an impact

Managers Who Made a Difference

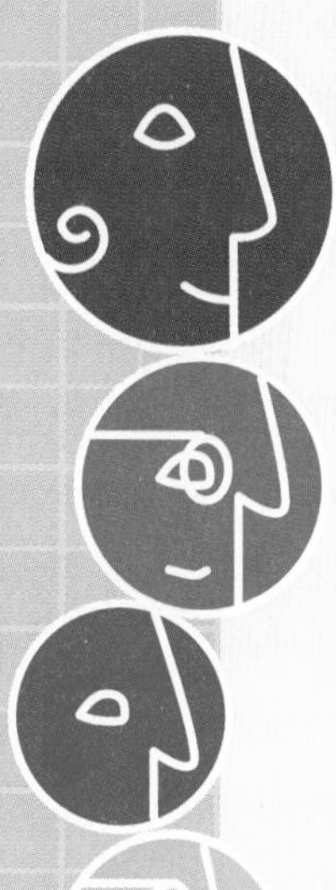

Anne Beiler, Founder of Auntie Anne's Pretzel Chain

What makes a person change his or her attitude toward a chosen career? Is it the dissonance between the ideals one possesses and the reality of making them come true? Is it a matter of chance? Or can it be strong personality traits that take an individual in other directions? For Anne Beiler, founder of Auntie Anne's Pretzel Chain, it's probably a combination of all three.[29]

Anne Beiler grew up in Gap, Pennsylvania, a town with a population of 2,000. Her early childhood was well rooted in the Mennonite traditions of this Amish town. That meant, in part, that family values would be the centerpiece of her life—including working hard on the family farm, marrying young, and raising a family of her own. Those were elements of certainty for Mennonites. And for the first thirty-eight years of her life, those were precisely the things she did. In 1987, however, Beiler—somewhat restless after raising two children and in need of some extra cash—decided to earn an income. She took a job managing a food stand some two hours away from her home. While there, she began to get a feel for the business—recognizing that hand-rolled pretzels were the best food seller. And selling them for 55 cents each proved to be quite profitable for the food stand owner, considering pretzels cost less than 7 cents each to make. Although she had never had a formal business course, Anne realized that selling pretzels could be very lucrative. Nearly a year later—and tiring of the two-hour commute—Anne opened her own pretzel stand in the farmer's market in the heart of Gap.

Anne's goal was to make her pretzel stand a successful business where she and her family could all work together. As in any new business start-up, the early times were difficult. But what she didn't expect was how quickly success would be thrust on her. Several weeks into the operation, business proved to be so good that Anne opened a second stall across town. Several months later, her brother paid Anne $2,500 for her pretzel recipe and the right to use the Auntie Anne's name to start a pretzel shop in the next town. Weeks later, she sold an additional ten franchises to family and friends, generating almost $50,000 in revenues. In 1991, she sold another forty-three—this time to "strangers" who were willing to pay $15,000 for the right to use Anne's pretzel recipe.

Anne Beiler took a chance that paid off in order to have some "control of her life." Today, Auntie Anne's franchises sell for $28,000 each. There are now 348 stores spread out in thirty-five states—pretzel shops that sell ten varieties of pretzels for $1.25 each. And Auntie Anne's annual revenues are nearing the $100 million mark! Yet, even with this much success, Anne's "traditions" haven't changed much. She is still family-oriented, donates more than $150,000 annually to charities, and is underwriting "a local marriage counseling center for the village of Gap." About the only change in her life that says she has made it is her Cadillac El Dorado.

on how long it takes individuals to make a decision and how much information they require before making their choice. For instance, seventy-nine managers worked on a simulated human resource management exercise that required them to make hiring decisions.[30] High-risk-taking managers made more rapid decisions and used less information in making their choices than did the low-risk-taking managers. Interestingly, the decision accuracy was the same for both groups.

Although it is generally correct to conclude that managers in organizations are risk-aversive,[31] there are still individual differences on this dimension.[32] As a result, it makes sense to recognize these differences and even to consider aligning risk-taking propensity with specific job demands. For instance, a high-risk-taking propensity may lead to effective performance for a stock trader in a brokerage firm. This type of job demands rapid decision making. On the other hand, this personality characteristic might prove a major obstacle to accountants performing auditing activities. The latter job might be better filled by someone with a low-risk-taking propensity.

How Do We Match Personalities and Jobs?

Obviously, individual personalities differ. So, too, do jobs. Following this logic, efforts have been made to match the proper personalities with the proper jobs. The best-documented personality–job fit theory has been developed by psychologist John Holland.[33] His theory states that an employee's satisfaction with his or her job, as well as his or her propensity to leave that job, depends on the degree to which the individual's personality matches his or her occupational environment. Holland has identified six basic personality types an organization's employees might possess. Exhibit 10-4 describes each of the six types, their personality characteristics, and examples of congruent occupations.

TYPE	PERSONALITY CHARACTERISTICS	SAMPLE OCCUPATIONS
Realistic. Prefers physical activities that require skill, strength, and coordination	Shy, genuine, persistent, stable, conforming, practical	Mechanic, drill press operator, assembly-line worker, farmer
Investigative. Prefers activities involving thinking, organizing, and understanding	Analytical, original, curious, independent	Biologist, economist, mathematician, reporter
Social. Prefers activities that involve helping and developing others	Sociable, friendly, cooperative, understanding	Social worker, teacher, counselor, clinical psychologist
Conventional. Prefers rule-regulated, orderly, and unambiguous activities	Conforming, efficient, practical, unimaginative, inflexible	Accountant, corporate manager, bank teller, file clerk
Enterprising. Prefers verbal activities where there are opportunities to influence others and attain power	Self-confident, ambitious, energetic, domineering	Lawyer, real estate agent, public relations specialist, small business manager
Artistic. Prefers ambiguous and unsystematic activities that allow creative expression	Imaginative, disorderly, idealistic, emotional, impractical	Painter, musician, writer, interior decorator

Exhibit 10-4
Holland's Typology of Personality and Sample Occupations

Source: Reproduced by special permission of the publisher, Psychological Assessment Resources, Inc., *Making Vocational Choices,*

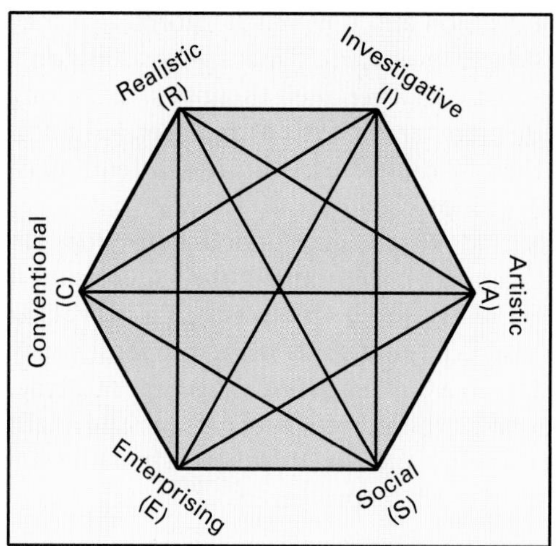

Exhibit 10-5
Relationships among Occupational Personality Types

Source: Reproduced by special permission of the publisher, Psychological Assessment Resources, Inc., *Making Vocational Choices,* copyright 1973, 1985 by Psychological Assessment Resources, Inc. All rights reserved.

Holland's research strongly supports the hexagonal diagram in Exhibit 10-5.[34] This exhibit shows that the closer two fields or orientations are in the hexagon, the more compatible they are. Adjacent categories are quite similar, while those opposite are highly dissimilar.

What does all this mean? The theory argues that satisfaction is highest and turnover lowest when personality and occupation are in agreement. Social individuals should be in social jobs, conventional people in conventional jobs, and so forth. A realistic person in a realistic job is in a more congruent situation than is a realistic person in an investigative job. A realistic person in a social job is in the most incongruent situation possible. The key points of this model are that (1) there do appear to be intrinsic differences in personality among individuals; (2) there are different types of jobs; and (3) people in job environments congruent with their personality types should be more satisfied and less likely to resign voluntarily than should people in incongruent jobs.

How Can an Understanding of Personality Help Managers Be More Effective?

The major value of a manager's understanding personality differences probably lies in selection. Managers are likely to have higher-performing and more-satisfied employees if consideration is given to matching personality types with compatible jobs. In addition, there may be other benefits. By recognizing that people approach problem solving, decision making, and job interactions differently, a manager can better understand why, for instance, an employee is uncomfortable with making quick decisions or why an employee insists on gathering as much information as possible before addressing a problem. Or, for instance, managers can expect that individuals with an external locus of control may be less satisfied with their jobs than internals and also that they may be less willing to accept responsibility for their actions.

Do Personality Attributes Differ across National Cultures?

There certainly are no common personality types for a given country. You can, for instance, find high risk takers and low risk takers in almost any culture. Yet a country's culture should influence the dominant personality characteristics of its population. We can see this influence by looking at the locus of control.

In Chapter 2, we introduced you to the issues of national cultures. One aspect of that discussion was that national cultures differ in terms of the degree to which people believe they control their environment. North Americans, for example, believe that they can dominate their environment, whereas other societies, such as Middle Eastern countries, believe that life is essentially preordained. Notice the close parallel to internal and external locus of control. We should expect a larger proportion of internals in the United States and Canadian work forces than in the work forces of Saudi Arabia or Iran.

As we have described throughout this section, personality traits influence employees' behavior. For global managers, understanding how personality traits differ takes on added significance when looking at it from the perspective of national culture.

Perception

Perception is a process by which individuals organize and interpret their sensory impressions in order to give meaning to their environment. Research on perception consistently demonstrates that individuals may look at the same thing yet perceive it differently. One manager, for instance, can interpret the fact that her assistant regularly takes several days to make important decisions as evidence that the assistant is slow, disorganized, and afraid to make decisions. Another manager, with the same assistant, might interpret the same action as evidence that the assistant is thoughtful, thorough, and deliberate. The first manager would probably evaluate her assistant negatively, while the second manager would probably evaluate the person positively. The point is that none of us actually sees reality. We interpret what we see and call it reality. And, of course, as the preceding example illustrates, we act according to our perceptions.

perception
The process of organizing and interpreting sensory impressions in order to give meaning to the environment.

What Influences Perception?

How do we explain the fact that Bob, a marketing supervisor for a large commercial petroleum products organization, age forty-five, noticed Naomi's nose ring during her employment interview and Sean, a human resources recruiter, age twenty-two, didn't? A number of factors operate to shape and sometimes distort perception. These factors can reside in the perceiver; in the object, or target, being perceived; or in the context of the situation in which the perception is made.

When an individual looks at a target and attempts to interpret what he or she sees, that individual's personal characteristics will heavily influence the interpretation.[35] These personal characteristics include attitudes, personality, motives, interests, past experiences, and expectations.

The characteristics of the target being observed can also affect what is perceived. Loud people are more likely than quiet people to be noticed in a group. So, too, are extremely attractive or unattractive individuals. Because targets are not looked at in isolation, the relationship of a target to its background also influences perception (see Exhibit 10-6 for an example), as does our tendency to group close things and similar things together.

The context in which we see objects or events is also important. The time at which an object or event is seen can influence attention, as can location, light, heat, and any number of other situational factors.

Manual Villar, chairman of C&P Homes in Manila, the Philippines, perceived different targets than many of his peers. For instance, while other home builders were building larger and more expensive homes in the Pacific Rim region, he was doing the opposite—building smaller and cheaper homes. As a result of high birth rates in the region and a move to cities, demand for his homes have soared. That demand has translated into a billion dollar company.

How Do Managers Judge Employees?

Much of the research on perception is directed at inanimate objects. Managers, though, are more concerned with human beings. So our discussion of perception should focus on person perception. Our perceptions of people differ from our perceptions of such inanimate objects as computers, robots, or buildings because we make inferences about the actions of people that we don't make about inanimate objects. Nonliving objects have no beliefs, motives, or intentions. People do. The result is that when we observe people, we attempt to develop explanations of why they behave in certain ways. Our perception and judgment of a person's actions, therefore, will be significantly influenced by the assumptions we make about the person's internal state. Many of these assumptions have led researchers to the development of attribution theory.

What Is Attribution Theory? Attribution theory has been proposed to develop explanations of how we judge people differently depending on what meaning we attribute to a given behavior.[36] Basically, the theory suggests that when we observe an individual's behavior, we attempt to determine whether it was internally or externally caused. Internally caused behaviors are those that are believed to be under the personal control of the individual. Externally caused behavior results from outside causes; that is, the person is seen as having been forced into the behavior by the situation. That determination, however, depends on three factors: distinctiveness, consensus, and consistency.

attribution theory
A theory used to develop explanations of how we judge people differently depending on the meaning we attribute to a given behavior.

Distinctiveness refers to whether an individual displays a behavior in many situations or whether it is particular to one situation. Is the employee who arrived late to work today also the source of complaints by coworkers for being a "goof-off"? What we want to know is whether this behavior is unusual. If it is, the observer is likely to give the behavior an external attribution. If this action is not unique, it will probably be judged as internal.

If everyone who is faced with a similar situation responds in the same way, we can say the behavior shows *consensus*. Our tardy employee's behavior would meet this criterion if all employees who took the same route to work were also late. From an attribution perspective, if consensus is high you would be expected to give an external attribution to the employee's tardiness, whereas if other employees who took the same route made it to work on time, your conclusion for the reason would be internal.

Finally, a manager looks for *consistency* in an employee's actions. Does the individual engage in the behaviors regularly and consistently? Does the employee respond

Exhibit 10-6
Perceptual Challenges

Here are two classic perceptual challenges. Look at both images. What do you see? In image 1, is it two faces or a vase—or both? In image 2, can you see the word that's spelled out?

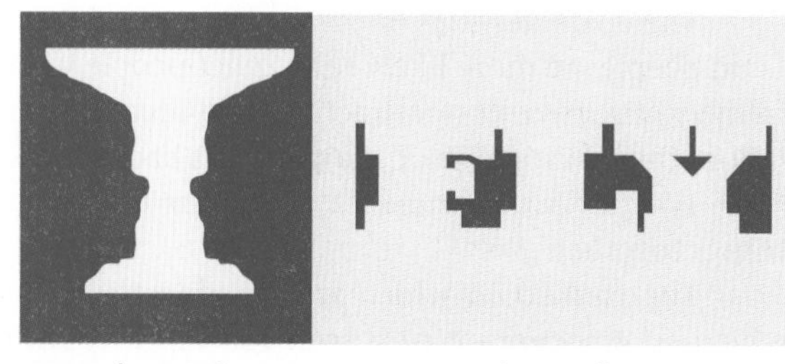

Image 1 Image 2

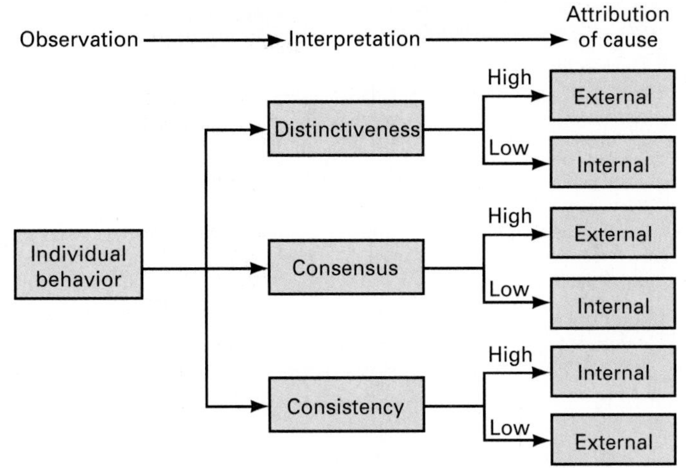

Exhibit 10-7
The Process of Attribution Theory

the same way over time? Coming in ten minutes late for work is not perceived in the same way if, for one employee, it represents an unusual case (she hasn't been late for several months), while for another it is part of a routine pattern (he is regularly late two or three times a week). The more consistent the behavior, the more the observer is inclined to attribute it to internal causes.

Exhibit 10-7 summarizes the key elements in attribution theory. It would tell us, for instance, that if an employee—let's call him Mr. Ryland—generally performs at about the same level on other related tasks as he does on his current task (low distinctiveness), if other employees frequently perform differently—better or worse—than Mr. Ryland does on that current task (low consensus), and if Mr. Ryland's performance on this current task is consistent over time (high consistency), his manager or anyone else who is judging Mr. Ryland's work is likely to hold him primarily responsible for his task performance (internal attribution).

Can Attributions Be Distorted? One of the more interesting findings drawn from attribution theory is that there are errors or biases that distort attributions. For instance, there is substantial evidence to support that when we make judgments about the behavior of other people, we have a tendency to underestimate the influence of external factors and overestimate the influence of internal or personal factors.[37] This is called the **fundamental attribution error** and can explain why a sales manager may be prone to attribute the poor performance of her sales agents to laziness rather than to the innovative product line introduced by a competitor. There is also a tendency for individuals to attribute their own successes to internal factors such as ability or effort while putting the blame for failure on external factors such as luck. This is called the **self-serving bias** and suggests that feedback provided to employees in performance reviews will be predictably distorted by recipients depending on whether it is positive or negative.

fundamental attribution error
The tendency to underestimate the influence of external factors and overestimate the influence of internal or personal factors when making judgments about the behavior of others.

self-serving bias
The tendency for individuals to attribute their own successes to internal factors while putting the blame for failures on external factors.

What Shortcuts Do Managers Use in Judging Others?

Managers use a number of shortcuts to judge others. Perceiving and interpreting what others do is burdensome. As a result, individuals develop techniques for making the task more manageable. These techniques are frequently valuable; they allow us to make accurate perceptions rapidly and provide valid data for making predictions. However, they are not foolproof. They can and do get us into trouble. An understanding of these shortcuts can be helpful toward recognizing when they can result in significant distortions (see Exhibit 10-8).

SHORTCUT	WHAT IT IS	DISTORTION
Selectivity	People assimilate certain bits and pieces of what they observe depending on their interests, background, experience, and attitudes	"Speed reading"others may result in an inaccurate picture of others
Assumed similarity	People assume that others are like them	May fail to take into account individual differences, resulting in incorrect similarities
Stereotyping	People judge others on the basis of their perception of a group to which the others belong	May result in distorted judgments because many stereotypes have no factual foundation
Halo effect	People form an impression of others on the basis of a single trait	Fails to take into account the "total" picture of what an individual has done
Self-fulfilling prophecy	People perceive others in a certain way, and, in turn, those others behave in ways that are consistent with the perception	May result in getting the behavior expected, not the true behavior of individuals

Exhibit 10-8
Distortions in Shortcut Methods in Judging Others

Individuals cannot assimilate all they observe, so they engage in *selectivity.* They take in bits and pieces. These bits and pieces are not chosen randomly; rather, they are selectively chosen depending on the interests, background, experience, and attitudes of the observer. Selective perception allows us to "speed read" others but not without the risk of drawing an inaccurate picture.

It is easy to judge others if we assume that they are similar to us. In *assumed similarity,* or the "like-me" effect, the observer's perception of others is influenced more by the observer's own characteristics than by those of the person observed. For example, if you want challenge and responsibility in your job, you will assume that others want the same. People who assume that others are like them can, of course, be right. But most of the time they're wrong.

When we judge someone on the basis of our perception of a group to which he or she belongs, we are using the shortcut called *stereotyping.* "Most women won't relocate for a promotion" and "older workers are less productive employees" are examples of stereotyping. From a perceptual standpoint, if someone holds such stereotypes, that is what he or she will perceive—whether or not it's accurate. When stereotypes have no foundation in fact, they distort judgments.

When we form a general impression about an individual on the basis of a single characteristic such as intelligence, sociability, or appearance, we are being influenced by the *halo effect.* This effect frequently occurs, for instance, when students evaluate their classroom instructor. Students may isolate a single trait such as enthusiasm and allow their entire evaluation to be tainted by their perception of this one trait. An instructor might be quiet, assured, knowledgeable, and highly qualified, but if his style lacks zeal, he or she may be rated lower on a number of other characteristics.

A final shortcut in judging others that we'll discuss involves a manager's expectations of employees. It is called a *self-fulfilling prophecy* (or the pygmalion effect).[38] The self-fulfilling prophecy involves how a manager perceives others, and how they, in turn, behave in ways that are consistent with the manager's expectations. For example, if a manager expects outstanding performance from his employees, they are not likely to disappoint him. They will work (or be perceived to work) up to the manager's expectations. On the other hand, if this same manager believes that he is supervising a group of underachievers, his employees will respond accordingly. As a result, the manager's expectations will become a reality as the employees work so as to meet his low expectations.

How Can an Understanding of Perceptions Help Managers Be More Effective?

Managers need to recognize that their employees react to perceptions not to reality. So whether a manager's appraisal of an employee is *actually* objective and unbiased, or whether the organization's wage levels are *actually* among the highest in the industry, is less relevant than what employees *perceive* them to be. If employees perceive appraisals to be biased or wage levels as low, they will behave as if those conditions actually exist. Employees organize and interpret what they see, creating the potential for perceptual distortion.

The message to managers should be clear. Pay close attention to how employees perceive both their jobs and management practices. Remember, the valuable employee who quits because of an *inaccurate perception* is just as great a loss to an organization as the valuable employee who quits for a *valid reason.*

Learning

The last individual-behavior concept we will introduce in this chapter is learning. It is included for the obvious reason that almost all complex behavior is learned. If we want to explain and predict behavior, we need to understand how people learn. What is learning? A psychologist's definition is considerably broader than the layperson's view that "it's what we did when we went to school." In actuality, each of us is continuously "going to school." Learning occurs all the time. We continually learn from our experiences. A workable definition of **learning** is, therefore, any relatively permanent change in behavior that occurs as a result of experience.

learning
Any relatively permanent change in behavior that occurs as a result of experience.

How do we learn? Two popular theories have been offered to explain the process by which we acquire patterns of behavior. These are operant conditioning and social learning theory.

What Is Operant Conditioning?

Operant conditioning argues that behavior is a function of its consequences. People learn to behave to get something they want or to avoid something they don't want. Operant behavior means voluntary or learned behavior in contrast to reflexive or unlearned behavior. The tendency to repeat such behavior is influenced by the reinforcement or lack of reinforcement brought about by the consequences of the behavior. Reinforcement, therefore, strengthens a behavior and increases the likelihood that it will be repeated.

operant conditioning
A behavioral theory that argues that voluntary, or learned, behavior is a function of its consequences.

Building on earlier work in the field, the late Harvard psychologist B. F. Skinner's research has extensively expanded our knowledge of operant conditioning.[39] Even his staunchest critics, who represent a sizable group, admit that his operant concepts work.

Behavior is assumed to be determined from without—that is, learned—rather than from within—reflexive, or unlearned. Skinner argued that creating pleasing consequences to follow a specific form of behavior will increase the frequency of that behavior. People will most likely engage in desired behaviors if they are positively reinforced for doing so. Rewards, for example, are most effective if they immediately follow the desired response. In addition, behavior that is not rewarded, or is punished, is less likely to be repeated.

You see illustrations of operant conditioning everywhere. For example, any situation in which it is either explicitly stated or implicitly suggested that reinforcements are contingent on some action on your part involves the use of operant learning. Your instructor says that if you want a high grade in the course you must supply correct answers on the test. A real estate agent wanting to earn a sizable income finds that high income is contingent on generating many home listings and sales in his or her territory. Of course, the linkage can also work to teach the individual to engage in behaviors that work against the best interests of the organization. Assume that your boss tells you that if you will work overtime during the next three-week busy season, you will be compensated for it at the next performance appraisal. However, when performance appraisal time comes, you are given no positive reinforcement for your overtime work. The next time your boss asks you to work overtime, what will you do? You may decline! Your behavior can be explained by operant conditioning: If a behavior fails to be positively reinforced, the probability that the behavior will be repeated declines.

People will most likely engage in desired behaviors if they are positively reinforced for doing so.

What Is Social Learning Theory?

Individuals can also learn by observing what happens to other people and just by being told about something, as well as by direct experiences. So, for example, much of what we have learned comes from watching models—parents, teachers, peers, television and movie performers, bosses, and so forth. This view that we can learn through both observation and direct experience has been called **social learning theory.**[40]

social learning theory The theory that people can learn through observation and direct experience.

Social learning theory is an extension of operant conditioning—that is, it assumes that behavior is a function of consequences—but it also acknowledges the existence of observational learning and the importance of perception in learning. People respond to how they perceive and define consequences, not to the objective consequences themselves.

A German expert instructor, called a Meister, uses social learning theory to help this apprentice learn. This process bases learning on both observation and direct, hands-on, experience.

The influence of models is central to the social learning viewpoint. Four processes have been found to determine the influence that a model will have on an individual:

▶ **1.** *Attentional processes.* People learn from a model only when they recognize and pay attention to its critical features. We tend to be most influenced by repeatedly available models that we think are attractive, important, or similar to us.

▶ **2.** *Retention processes.* A model's influence will depend on how well the individual remembers the model's action, even after the model is no longer readily available.

3. *Motor reproduction processes.* After a person has seen a new behavior by observing the model, the watching must be converted to doing. This process then demonstrates that the individual can perform the modeled activities.
4. *Reinforcement processes.* Individuals will be motivated to exhibit the modeled behavior if positive incentives or rewards are provided. Behaviors that are reinforced will be given more attention, learned better, and performed more often than will behaviors that are not reinforced.

How Can Managers Shape Behavior?

Because learning takes place on the job as well as before it, managers will be concerned with how they can teach employees to behave in ways that most benefit the organization. Thus, managers will often attempt to mold individuals by guiding their learning in graduated steps. This process is called **shaping behavior** (see Developing a Management Skill).

shaping behavior Systematically reinforcing each successive step that moves an individual closer to a desired behavior.

Consider the situation in which an employee's behavior is significantly different from that sought by management. If management reinforced the individual only when he or she showed desirable responses, there might be very little reinforcement

Developing a Management Skill

SHAPING BEHAVIOR

About the Skill: *In today's dynamic work environments, learning is a continual process. But this learning needn't be done in isolation or without any guidance. Rather, most employees need to be shown what is expected of them on the job. As a manager, you must teach your employees the behaviors that are most critical to their, and the organization's, success.*

Steps in Practicing the Skill

1. ***Identify the critical behaviors that have a significant impact on an employee's performance.*** Not everything employees do on the job is equally important in terms of performance outcomes. A few critical behaviors may, in fact, account for the majority of one's performance. It is these high-impact behaviors that need identifying.

2. ***Establish a baseline of performance.*** This is obtained by determining the number of times the identified behaviors occur under the employee's present job conditions.

3. ***Analyze contributing factors to performance and their consequences.*** A number of factors, such as the norms of a group, may be contributing to the baseline performance. Identify these factors and their effect on performance.

4. ***Develop a "shaping" strategy.*** The change that may occur will entail changing some element of performance—structure, processes, technology, groups, or the task. The purpose of the strategy is to strengthen the desirable behaviors and weaken the undesirable ones.

5. ***Apply the appropriate strategy.*** Once the strategy has been developed, it needs to be implemented. In this step, the intervention occurs.

6. ***Measure the change that has occurred.*** The intervention should produce desired results in performance behaviors. Evaluate the number of times the identified behaviors now occur. Compare these with the baseline evaluation in step 2.

7. ***Reinforce desired behaviors.*** If the intervention has been successful and the new behaviors are producing the desired results, maintain these behaviors through reinforcement mechanisms.

taking place. In such a case, shaping offers a logical approach toward achieving the desired behavior.

We shape behavior by systematically reinforcing each successive step that moves the individual closer to the desired response. If an employee who has chronically been thirty minutes late for work comes in only twenty minutes late, we can reinforce this improvement. Reinforcement would increase as responses more closely approximated the desired behavior.

There are four ways in which to shape behavior: through positive reinforcement, negative reinforcement, punishment, or extinction. When a response is followed with something pleasant, such as when a manager praises an employee for a job well done, it is called *positive reinforcement.* Rewarding a response with the termination or withdrawal of something unpleasant is called *negative reinforcement.* Managers who habitually criticize their employees for taking extended coffee breaks are using negative reinforcement. The only way these employees can stop the criticism is to shorten their breaks. *Punishment* penalizes undesirable behavior. Suspending an employee for two days without pay for showing up drunk is an example of punishment. Eliminating any reinforcement that is maintaining a behavior is called *extinction.* When a behavior isn't reinforced, gradually it disappears. In meetings, managers who wish to discourage employees from continually asking distracting or irrelevant questions can eliminate that behavior by ignoring those employees when they raise their hands to speak. Soon, the behavior will be diminished.

Both positive and negative reinforcement result in learning. They strengthen a desired response and increase the probability of repetition. Both punishment and extinction also result in learning; however, they weaken behavior and tend to decrease its subsequent frequency.

How Can an Understanding of Learning Help Managers Be More Effective?

Managers can undoubtedly benefit from understanding the learning process. Because employees must continually learn on the job, the only issue is whether managers are going to let employee learning occur randomly or whether they are going to manage learning through the rewards they allocate and the examples they set. If marginal employees are rewarded with pay raises and promotions, they will have little reason to change their behavior. If managers want a certain type of behavior but reward a different type of behavior, it shouldn't surprise them to find that employees are learning to engage in the other type of behavior. Similarly, managers should expect that employees will look to them as models. Managers who are constantly late to work, or who take two hours for lunch, or who help themselves to company office supplies for personal use should expect employees to read the message they are sending and model their behavior accordingly.

Foundations of Group Behavior

The behavior of individuals in groups is not the same as the sum total of all the individuals' behavior. Individuals act differently in groups than they do when they are alone. Therefore, if we want to understand organizational behavior more fully, we need to study groups.

What Is a Group?

A **group** is defined as two or more interacting and interdependent individuals who come together to achieve particular objectives. Groups can be either formal or informal. Formal groups are work groups established by the organization and have designated work assignments and established tasks. In formal groups, the behaviors in which one should engage are stipulated by and directed toward organizational goals.

In contrast, informal groups are of a social nature. These groups are natural formations that appear in the work environment in response to the need for social contact. Informal groups tend to form around friendships and common interests.

group
Two or more interacting and interdependent individuals who come together to achieve particular objectives.

Why Do People Join Groups?

There is no single reason why individuals join groups. Because most people belong to a number of groups, it's obvious that different groups provide different benefits to their members. Most people join a group out of needs for security, status, self-esteem, affiliation, power, or goal achievement (see Exhibit 10-9).

Security reflects a strength in numbers. By joining a group, individuals can reduce the insecurity of "standing alone." The group helps the individual to feel stronger, have fewer self-doubts, and be more resistant to threats. *Status* indicates a prestige that comes from belonging to a particular group. Inclusion in a group that others view as important provides recognition and status for its members. *Self-esteem* conveys people's feelings of self-worth. That is, in addition to conveying status to those outside the group, membership can also raise feelings of self-esteem—being accepted into a highly valued group.

Affiliation with groups can fulfill one's social needs. People enjoy the regular interaction that comes with group membership. For many people, on-the-job interactions are their primary means of fulfilling their need for affiliation. For almost all people, work groups significantly contribute to fulfilling their need for friendships and social relations. One of the appealing aspects of groups is that they represent *power*. What often cannot be achieved individually becomes possible through group action. Of course, this power might not be sought only to make demands on others. It might be desired merely as a countermeasure. To protect themselves from unreasonable demands by management, individuals may align with others. Informal groups additionally provide opportunities for individuals to exercise power over others. For

Exhibit 10-9
Reasons Why People Join Groups

REASON	PERCEIVED BENEFIT
Security	Gaining strength in numbers; reducing the insecurity of standing alone
Status	Achieving some level of prestige from belonging to a particular group
Self-esteem	Enhancing one's feeling of self-worth—especially membership in a highly valued group
Affiliation	Satisfying one's social needs through social interaction
Power	Achieving something through a group action not possible individually; protecting group members from unreasonable demands of others
Goal achievement	Providing an opportunity to accomplish a particular task when it takes more than one person's talents, knowledge, or power to complete the job

Employees at Wickfield, Inc., in Milwaukee, Wisconsin, participate on the company's softball team. This informal group activity meets members' needs for affiliation. And when the team wins, it also enhances the group's status and self-esteem.

individuals who desire to influence others, groups can offer power without a formal position of authority in the organization. As a group leader, you might be able to make requests of group members and obtain compliance without any of the responsibilities that traditionally go with formal managerial positions. For people with a high power need, groups can be a vehicle for fulfillment. Finally, people may join a group for *goal achievement.* There are times when it takes more than one person to accomplish a particular task; there is a need to pool talents, knowledge, or power in order to get a job completed. In such instances, management will rely on the use of a formal group.

What Are the Basic Concepts for Understanding Group Behaviors?

The basic foundation for understanding group behavior includes roles, norms and conformity, status systems, and group cohesiveness. Let's take a closer look at each of those concepts.

What Are Roles? We introduced the concept of roles in Chapter 1 when we discussed what managers do. Of course, managers are not the only individuals in an organization who have roles. The concept of roles applies to all employees in organizations and to their life outside the organization as well.

role
A set of expected behavior patterns attributed to someone who occupies a given position in a social unit.

A **role** refers to a set of expected behavior patterns attributed to someone who occupies a given position in a social unit. Individuals play multiple roles, adjusting their roles to the group to which they belong at the time. In an organization, employees attempt to determine what behaviors are expected of them. They read their job descriptions, get suggestions from their boss, and watch what their coworkers do. An individual who is confronted by divergent role expectations experiences role conflict. Employees in organizations often face such role conflicts. The credit manager expects her credit analysts to process a minimum of thirty applications a week, but the work group pressures members to restrict output to twenty applications a week so that everyone has work to do and no one gets laid off. A young college instructor's colleagues want him to give out very few high grades in order to maintain the department's "tough standards" reputation, whereas students want him to give out lots of high grades to enhance their grade point averages. To the degree that the instructor sincerely seeks to satisfy the expectations of both his colleagues and his students, he faces role conflict.

How Do Norms and Conformity Affect Group Behavior? All groups have established **norms,** or acceptable standards that are shared by the group's members. Norms dictate things such as output levels, absenteeism rates, promptness or tardiness, and the amount of socializing allowed on the job.

norms
Acceptable standards shared by a group's members.

Norms, for example, dictate the "dress code" among customer service representatives at one cellular phone company. Most workers who have little face-to-face customer contact come to work dressed very casually. However, on occasion, a newly hired employee will come to work the first few days dressed up in a suit. Those who do are often teased and pressured until their dress conforms to the group's standard.

Although each group will have its own unique set of norms, there are common classes of norms that appear in most organizations. These focus on effort and performance, dress, and loyalty. Probably the most widespread norms are related to levels of effort and performance. Work groups typically provide their members with very explicit cues on how hard to work, what level of output to have, when to look busy, when it's acceptable to goof off, and the like. These norms are extremely powerful in affecting an individual employee's performance. They are so powerful that performance predictions that are based solely on an employee's ability and level of personal motivation often prove to be wrong.

Some organizations have formal dress codes. However, even in their absence, norms frequently develop to dictate the kind of clothing that should be worn to work. College seniors, interviewing for their first postgraduate job, pick up this norm quickly. Every spring, on college campuses throughout the country, the students who are interviewing for jobs can usually be spotted; they are the ones walking around in the dark gray or blue pinstriped suits. They are enacting the dress norms that they have learned are expected in professional positions. Of course, what connotes acceptable dress in one organization may be very different from the norms in another.

Few managers appreciate employees who ridicule the organization. Similarly, professional employees and those in the executive ranks recognize that most employers view persons who actively look for another job unfavorably. People who are unhappy know that they should keep their job searches secret. These examples demonstrate that loyalty norms are widespread in organizations. This concern for demonstrating loyalty, by the way, often explains why ambitious aspirants to top management positions in an organization willingly take work home at night, come in on weekends, and accept transfers to cities where they would otherwise not prefer to live.

Because individuals desire acceptance by the groups to which they belong, they are susceptible to conformity pressures. The impact that group pressures for conformity can have on an individual member's judgment and attitudes was demonstrated in the now-classic studies by Solomon Asch[41] (see Details on a Management Classic). Asch's results suggest that there are group norms that press us toward conformity. We desire to be one of the group and avoid being visibly different. We can generalize this finding further to say that when an individual's opinion of objective data differs significantly from that of others in the group, he or she feels extensive pressure to align his or her opinion to conform with those of the others (see also groupthink, p. 151).

What Is Status, and Why Is It Important? Status is a prestige grading, position, or rank within a group. As far back as scientists have been able to trace human groupings, they have found status hierarchies: tribal chiefs and their followers, nobles and peasants, the Haves and the Have-nots. Status systems are an important factor in understanding behavior. Status is a significant motivator and has behavioral consequences when individuals see a disparity between what they perceive their status to be and what others perceive it to be.

status
A prestige grading, position, or rank within a group.

Status may be informally conferred by characteristics such as education, age, skill, or experience. Anything can have status value if others in the group admire it. Of course, just because status is informal does not mean that it is unimportant or that there is disagreement on who has it or who does not. Members of groups have no

Details on a Management Classic

Solomon Asch and Group Conformity

Does one's desire to be accepted as part of a group leave him or her susceptible to conforming to the group's norms? Will the group place strong enough pressure to change a member's attitude and behavior? In the research by Solomon Asch, the answer appears to be Yes.

Asch's study involved groups of seven or eight people who sat in a classroom and were asked to compare two cards held by an investigator.[42] One card had one line; the other had three lines of varying length. As shown in Exhibit 10-10, one of the lines on the three-line card was identical to the line on the one-line card. Also, as shown in Exhibit 10-10, the difference in line length was quite obvious; under ordinary conditions, subjects made less than 1 percent errors. The object was to announce aloud which of the three lines matched the single line. But what happens if all the members in the group begin to give incorrect answers? Will the pressures to conform cause the unsuspecting subject (USS) to alter his or her answers to align with those of the others? That was what Asch wanted to know. He arranged the group so that only the USS was unaware that the experiment was "fixed." The seating was prearranged so that the USS was the last to announce his or her decision.

The experiment began with two sets of matching exercises. All the subjects gave the right answers. On the third set, however, the first subject gave an obviously wrong answer—for example, saying *C* in Exhibit 10-10. The next subject gave the same wrong answer, and so did the others, until it got to the unsuspecting subject. He knew that *B* was the same as *X*, but everyone had said *C*. The decision confronting the USS was this: Do you publicly state a perception that differs from the preannounced position of the others? Or do you give an answer that you strongly believe is incorrect in order to have your response agree with the other group members? Asch's subjects conformed in about 35 percent of many experiments and many trials. That is, the subjects gave answers that they knew were wrong but that were consistent with the replies of other group members.

For managers, the Asch study provides considerable insight into group behaviors. The tendency, as Asch showed, is for individual members to go along with the "pack." To diminish the negative aspects of conformity, managers should create a climate of openness in which employees are free to discuss problems without fear of retaliation.

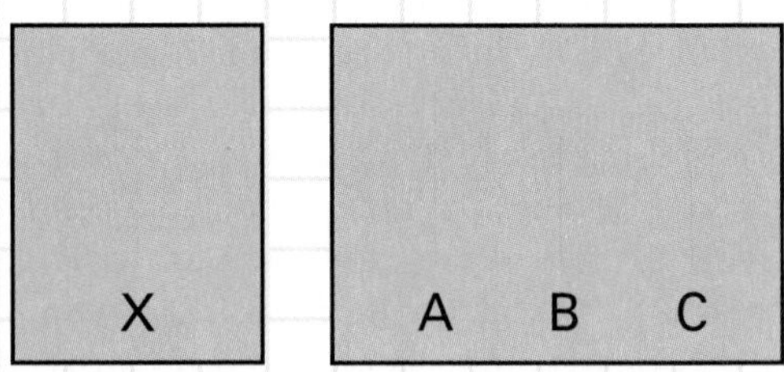

Exhibit 10-10
Examples of Cards Used in Asch Study

problem placing people into status categories, and they usually agree closely about who is high, low, and in the middle.

It is important for employees to believe that the organization's formal status system is *congruent*. That is, there should be equity between the perceived ranking of an individual and the status "symbols" he or she is given by the organization. For instance, incongruence may occur when a supervisor is earning less than his or her employees or when a desirable office is occupied by a lower-ranking individual. Employees may view such cases as a disruption to the general pattern of order and consistency in the organization.

Does Group Size Affect Group Behavior? The size of a group has an effect on the group's behavior. However, specifically what that effect is depends on what criteria you are looking at.[43]

The evidence indicates, for instance, that small groups are faster at completing tasks than are larger ones. However, if the group is engaged in problem solving, large groups consistently get better marks than their smaller counterparts. Translating these results into specific numbers is a bit more hazardous, but we can offer some parameters. Large groups—with a dozen or more members—are good for gaining diverse input. Thus, if the goal of the group is to find facts, larger groups should be more effective. On the other hand, smaller groups are better at doing something productive with those facts. Groups of approximately five to seven members tend to be more effective for taking action.

One of the more disturbing findings related to group size is that, as groups get incrementally larger, the contribution of individual members often tends to lessen.[44] That is, although the total productivity of a group of four is generally greater than that of a group of three, the individual productivity of each group member declines as the group expands. Thus, a group of four will tend to produce at a level less than four times the average individual performance. The best explanation for this reduction of effort in groups is that dispersion of responsibility encourages individuals to slack off; this behavior is referred to as **social loafing.** When the results of the group cannot be attributed to any single person, the relationship between an individual's input and the group's output is clouded. In such situations, individuals may be tempted to become "free riders" and coast on the group's efforts. In other words, there will be a reduction in efficiency when individuals think that their contributions cannot be measured. The obvious conclusion from this finding is that when managers use work teams they should also provide means by which individual efforts can be identified.

Large groups are good for gaining diverse input; smaller groups are better for taking action.

social loafing
The tendency of an individual in a group to decrease his or her effort because responsibility and individual achievement cannot be measured.

Are Cohesive Groups More Effective? Intuitively, it makes sense that groups in which there is a lot of internal disagreement and lack of cooperation are less effective in completing their tasks than are groups in which individuals generally agree, cooperate, and like each other. Research on this position has focused on **group cohesiveness,** or the degree to which members are attracted to one another and share the group's goals. The more the members are attracted to one another and the more the group's goals align with their individual goals, the greater the group's cohesiveness.

group cohesiveness
The degree to which members of a group are attracted to each other and share goals.

Research has generally shown that highly cohesive groups are more effective than are those with less cohesiveness,[45] but the relationship between cohesiveness and effectiveness is more complex. A key moderating variable is the degree to which the group's attitude aligns with its formal goals or those of the larger organization of which it is a part.[46] The more cohesive a group is, the more its members will follow its goals. If these goals are favorable (for instance, high output, quality work, cooperation with individuals outside the group), a cohesive group is more productive than a less cohesive group. But if cohesiveness is high and attitudes are unfavorable, productivity decreases. If cohesiveness is low and goals are supported, productivity increases but not as much as when both cohesiveness and support are high. When cohesiveness is low and goals are not supported, cohesiveness has no significant effect upon productivity. These conclusions are summarized in Exhibit 10-11.

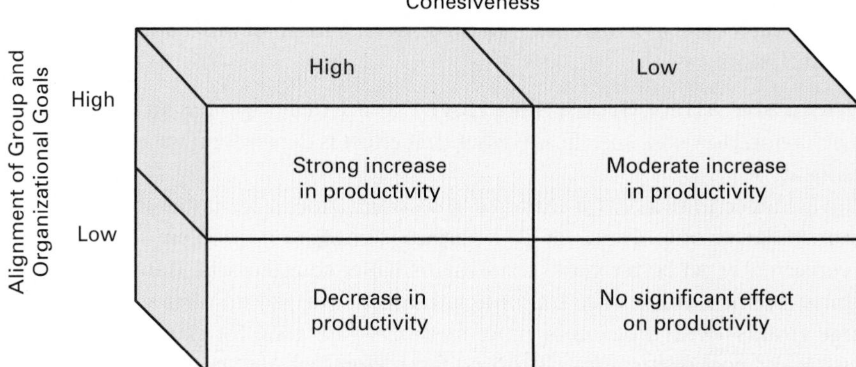

Exhibit 10-11
The Relationship between Group Cohesiveness and Productivity

Summary

How will I know if I fulfilled the Learning Objectives found on page 296? You will have fulfilled the Learning Objectives if you understand the following.

1. **Define the focus and goals of organizational behavior.** The field of organizational behavior is concerned with the actions of people—managers and operatives alike—in organizations. By focusing on individual- and group-level concepts, OB seeks to explain and predict behavior. Because they get things done through other people, managers will be more effective leaders if they have an understanding of behavior.
2. **Identify and describe the three components of attitudes.** Attitudes are made up of three components. The cognitive component involves the beliefs, opinions, knowledge, or information held by the person. The affective component is the emotional, or feeling, segment of the individual. And the behavioral component of an attitude is one's intention to behave in a certain manner toward someone or something.
3. **Explain cognitive dissonance.** Cognitive dissonance, proposed by Leon Festinger in the late 1950s, explains the relationship between attitudes and behavior. Cognitive dissonance refers to any incompatibility that an individual might perceive between two or more attitudes or between behavior and attitudes.
4. **Describe the Myers-Briggs personality type framework and its use in organizations.** The Myers-Briggs Type Indicator (MBTI) is a personality assessment test that asks individuals how they usually act or feel in different situations. The way the individual responds to the questions is combined into one of sixteen different personality types. The MBTI can help managers understand and predict employees' behaviors.
5. **Define perception and describe the factors that can shape or distort perception.** Perception is the process of organizing and interpreting sensory impressions in order to give meaning to the environment. Several factors operate to shape and sometimes distort perceptions. These factors can reside in the perceiver, in the target being perceived, or in the context of the situation in which the perception is being made.
6. **Explain how managers can shape employee behavior.** Managers can shape or mold employee behavior by systematically reinforcing each successive step that moves the employee closer to the response desired by the manager.
7. **Contrast formal and informal groups.** Formal groups are defined by the organization's structure, with designated work assignments establishing tasks. Informal groups are social alliances that are neither structured nor organizationally determined.
8. **Explain why people join groups.** People join groups because of their needs for security, status, self-esteem, affiliation, power, and goal achievement.
9. **State how roles and norms influence employees' behavior.** A role refers to a set of behavior patterns expected of someone occupying a given position in a social unit. At any given time, em-

ployees adjust their role behaviors to the group of which they are a part. Norms are standards shared by group members. They informally convey to employees which behaviors are acceptable and which are unacceptable.

10. **Describe how group size affects group behavior.** Group size affects group behavior in a number of ways. Smaller groups are faster at completing tasks than larger ones. However, larger groups are better for fact finding.

Review & Discussion Questions

1. How is an organization like an iceberg? Use the iceberg metaphor to describe the field of organizational behavior.
2. What role does role consistency play in one's attitude?
3. Clarify how individuals reconcile inconsistencies between attitudes and behaviors.
4. What behavioral predictions might you make if you knew that an employee had (a) an external locus of control? (b) a low Mach score? (c) low self-esteem? (d) high self-monitoring tendencies?
5. Discuss how a manager might use personality traits to improve employee selection.
6. Name five different shortcuts used in judging others. What effect does each have on perception?
7. What is social learning theory? What are its implications for managing people at work?
8. "Informal groups in an organization can be detrimental to management." Do you agree or disagree with that statement? Explain your position.
9. Discuss the implications drawn from Asch's conformity studies.
10. What is the most effective size of a group?

Testing Your Comprehension • • • 

Circle the correct answer, then check yourself on page AK-1.

1. The hidden aspects of organizations refers to
   a) the strategies and objectives, which are useless to most employees
   b) the attitudes, perceptions, and group dynamics
   c) the behaviors that are restricted by authoritarian managers
   d) any illegal activities of some department of an organization

2. OB essentially seeks to ____________ and ____________ behavior.
   a) explain; manage
   b) predict; manipulate
   c) predict; manage
   d) explain; predict

3. The cognitive component of an attitude refers to
   a) the intention to behave a certain way
   b) the emotional feeling associated with an attitude
   c) the factors such as opinions, beliefs, and knowledge
   d) the desires, wishes, and dreams of employees

4. Which of the following statements is TRUE regarding the satisfaction–productivity controversy?
   a) There is a strong positive relationship that satisfied employees are more productive employees.
   b) The satisfaction–productivity relationship is stronger when an employee's behavior is constrained by outside forces.
   c) Successful job performance always leads to those things that satisfy employees.
   d) None of the above.

5. Individuals who believe that they are basically in the hands of fate and their lives are generally beyond their control have
   a) an internal locus of control
   b) an external locus of control
   c) high risk-taking propensity
   d) Machiavellian characteristics

6. The Myers-Briggs Type Indicator (MBTI) does NOT include which of the following as one of its four dimensions?
   a) style of making decisions
   b) preference for gathering data
   c) locus of control
   d) social interactions

7. A personality dimension that describes the degree to which someone is imaginative, artistically sensitive, and intellectual is referred to as
   a) agreeableness
   b) conscientiousness
   c) emotional stability
   d) openness to experience

8. A major contribution of Holland's personality–job fit theory is the idea that
   a) congruency between personality traits and occupations should improve job satisfaction
   b) changing jobs to fit one's personality increases productivity
   c) personality must adapt to different jobs
   d) ability to assert will enhances job satisfaction

9. The halo effect is
   a) an attempt to identify good behaviors by managers
   b) judging someone on the basis of a single personality trait
   c) judging someone on the basis of the group to which the person belongs
   d) a model to predict group behavior

10. The fact that several people can see the same crime being committed and yet give different descriptions of the suspect is due to
   a) the halo effect
   b) assumed similarity
   c) perception
   d) stereotyping

11. "Behavior is a function of its consequences" demonstrates
   a) operant conditioning
   b) the halo effect
   c) assumed similarity
   d) modeling

12. A new employee can't recall how a job that was demonstrated yesterday was done. The employee is experiencing
   a) one of the drawbacks of classical conditioning
   b) a breakdown in the motor reproduction process of the social learning theory
   c) one of the drawbacks of operant conditioning
   d) a breakdown in the retention process of the social learning theory

13. Formal groups differ from informal groups in that formal groups
   a) have a leader
   b) have a purpose
   c) are organizationally sanctioned
   d) are often friendship groups

14. Joining a group that others view as important and influential refers to what kind of motivation?
   a) affiliation
   b) status
   c) self-esteem
   d) power

15. A prestigious ranking within a group is
   a) a role
   b) a norm-conformity pattern
   c) status hierarchy
   d) indicative of cohesive groups

16. Large groups are generally superior when
   a) speed of decision making is desired
   b) more diversity is sought
   c) performing productively with predetermined facts
   d) flexibility is necessary

17. As groups get larger
   a) average performance declines
   b) total performance declines
   c) individual effort increases
   d) speed increases

18. The degree to which group members are attracted to one another and share the group's goals is
   a) a norm
   b) a role
   c) status
   d) cohesiveness

Applying the Concepts

Salary Increase Request[47]

Objectives:

1. To illustrate how perceptions can influence decisions.
2. To illustrate the effects of shortcuts used in evaluating others.

The situation:

Your instructor will give you a scenario involving an employee's salary increase request. You are to read it and make a recommendation (either favorable or unfavorable) about the raise.

Procedure:

1. Divide into groups of five to seven and take the role of a manager making the salary increase decision.
2. Each group should identify their perceptions about the employee's work habits and so on in support of its decision.
3. Reassemble the class and hear each group's recommendations and explanations.

Take It to the Net

We invite you to visit the Robbins/De Cenzo page on the Prentice Hall Web site at:

http://www.prenhall.com/robbinsfom

for this chapter's World Wide Web exercise.

You can also visit the Web sites for these companies and agencies featured within this chapter:

3M
http://www.3m.com

American Business Information Inc.
http://www.abii.com

AT&T
http://www.att.com

Datametrics
http://www.dtsc.com

Exxon
http://www.exxon.com

U.S. Air Force
http://www.af.mil

U.S. Army
http://www.army.mil

U.S. Marines
http://www.usmc.mil

U.S. Navy
http://www.navy.com

Thinking Critically

Making a Value Judgment: Must Attitudes and Behaviors Align?

You work for a large international organization that manufactures and sells computer components. In your position as a recruiter, you have been given the primary responsibility to hire individuals to fill open entry-level positions in your company. Your organization has found that hiring recent college graduates for these entry-level manufacturing and marketing positions works well for them. They get an opportunity to hire individuals who have the latest knowledge in their fields, and they get them at a discounted price.

Your job requires you to travel extensively. In fact, over the past several years, you have averaged visiting thirty-five colleges during a semester. Your performance evaluation rests primarily on one factor—how many people you have hired. Your goal is to fill the vacancies that exist in the organization.

Over the past several months you have noticed a surge in open positions. These are not new positions but replacements for employees who have quit. A little investigating on your part indicates that, after about five years with the organization, employees hired into entry-level positions quit. It appears that there is no upward mobility for them and that they tend to get burned out by being asked to work at times up to twelve hours a day, six days a week. Furthermore, you know that employee benefits—especially vacation and sick leave—for entry-level employees is not competitive with benefits offered by other firms of your size. There is little doubt in your mind why they quit. On the other hand, almost everyone who has quit has gone on to a bigger, better job—with more responsibility and greater pay. To get the most productivity out of these employees, your company invested heavily in their training. Almost everyone in these positions receives over forty hours of specialized training each year. They came to the job well skilled, and, after a period of time, developed into top-quality employees. Nevertheless, your organization, although spending a lot of money training these employees, isn't interested in advancing them in the organization. Rather, management prefers to start the cycle over again. Top management believes it is better to hire new people than to pay higher salaries that seniority and experience demand. Although philosophically you don't totally agree with management's treatment of these employees, you recognize that the company is giving many of these individuals a great start in their career.

Questions:

1. Would you disclose to college recruits during an interview that the jobs they are being considered for are dead-end jobs in the organization? Why or why not?
2. Would your response to question 1 change if you were evaluated not only on how many people you hire but also on how long they stay with the organization? Explain your position.

The Entrepreneurial Spirit of Japanese Women

In many discussions about comparing work life in Japan with that in the United States, one factor is frequently mentioned. Workers in Japan often enjoy the luxury of having a job for life, at least historically. That is, once a Japanese citizen is hired by an organization, he or she can be somewhat sure of having that job until retirement. On face value, that may appear to be an important work benefit. Compared with what is occurring in U.S. organizations with respect to downsizing, reengineering, and the like, the security of a job for life is appealing. It sounds almost too good to be true. Of course, it comes with some strings attached.

When the economy is in recession, Japanese employers, like those in the United States, cannot afford to keep all working. Some layoffs occur. The difference is that, in Japan, those layoffs are targeted toward a particular group. In their attempt to save management positions, Japanese company officials decimate their clerical staffs.[48] Considering that 99 percent of all clerical workers are women, when layoffs occur, women are the hardest hit. Women are treated as second-class employees. If a recession doesn't result in their being laid off or fired, getting married or having a child surely will!

What can Japanese women do? Should they accept the culture of their society and live with the employment cycles they experience? Should they revolt against the "man's" world and fight for their rightful place in the organization? For many, such suggestions are impossible. The fight would be too great, and they would be up against a societal culture that is hundreds of years old. Instead, they have opted for another device—starting their own businesses. By the mid-1990s, in fact, five of every six new business start-ups in Japan were women-owned businesses. And, of those that started in the early 1990s, most have been exceptionally successful and are now the envy of many of the men who laughed at them years ago.

Questions:

1. Using locus of control, Machiavellianism, self-esteem, and risk propensity, discuss how each is present in the Japanese women who start their own businesses.
2. Identify how men's cognitive, affective, and behavioral components of attitudes are evident in the case toward women in Japan.
3. Are attitudes different in the United States that prevent women from being treated as expendable workers in U.S. organizations? Explain your position.

Video Case ABCNEWS

Attitudes about Age

Do you remember from the discussion of human resource management that a U.S. federal law considers anyone forty years of age or more to be an "older worker"? That puts an awful lot of Americans in the category of workers to whom laws against age discrimination apply. Yet, as more and more companies continue to downsize and millions of middle-aged workers are desperately looking for work, examples of age discrimination are happening every day in every profession across the United States. Statistics show that it takes older job seekers 64 percent longer to find work than younger ones. Even though age discrimination is illegal, it appears to be such an ingrained part of our culture that we may not even recognize if and when we're doing it.

Think about what your perception is of older workers. Would you say they're sick more often, they can't work as hard, and they don't stay with a company as long as younger workers do? Well, if that is what you think, you're wrong! A study by Days Inn Corporation, which deliberately recruits older workers, found that older workers stay with the company longer, take fewer sick days, and are just as productive as younger workers. In fact, the president of Days Inn says that older workers are actually less expensive than the average worker.

How do these attitudes we may subconsciously have about older workers affect the way we behave? We find that these attitudes often have subtle influences on the way we perceive older people. For instance, in job interviews, differences can be seen in the treatment of younger and older applicants. In twenty-four staged interviews with pairs of women applicants—one older and one younger—the younger women were accommodated more by the interviewer. The older women were subtly discouraged. In fact, in one-third of these staged interviews, a startling difference in the way older and younger job applicants were treated could be seen. In another staged interview situation, a man was made up to look younger one time and older another. A brokerage firm offered his "younger" self a job even though this "person" had less job experience and didn't follow up on the interview with a letter or a phone call. Although the interviewers didn't appear to purposely discriminate (after all, it is illegal) against the older job applicants, differences could still be seen in the way they acted and in the questions they asked. Attitudes that we have about elderly people in general, and older workers in particular, appear to influence the way we react and act.

Questions:

1. Describe the three components of an attitude—cognitive, affective, and behavioral—in relation to the attitudes often held about older workers as shown in this video clip.
2. What role do you think perception plays in the way we subtly behave toward older people?
3. Is stereotyping part of the problem with attitudes about age? Explain.

Source: "Age and Attitudes," *ABC News PrimeTime,* June 9, 1994.

Understanding Work Teams

11

LEARNING OBJECTIVES

What will I be able to do after I finish this chapter?

1. **EXPLAIN** the growing popularity of work teams in organizations.
2. **DESCRIBE** the five stages of team development.
3. **CONTRAST** work groups with work teams.
4. **IDENTIFY** four common types of work teams.
5. **LIST** the characteristics of high-performing work teams.
6. **IDENTIFY** how managers can build trust among team members.
7. **DISCUSS** how organizations can create team players.
8. **EXPLAIN** how managers can keep teams from becoming stagnant.
9. **DESCRIBE** the current legal climate surrounding the use of teams in unionized settings.
10. **EXPLAIN** the role of teams in TQM.

IMPERIAL OIL'S REFINERY IN DARTMOUTH, NOVA Scotia, is small by North American standards. It has a capacity of 86,000 barrels of oil a day. In terms of oil production, in the early 1990s, it ranked among the lowest 25 percent of the 115 refineries in North America. Its energy, maintenance, and people costs were well out of line with industry standards. Imperial Oil's management considered closing down the refinery, but Ken Ball, the refinery manager, had other ideas. He presented a plan to the head office that was accepted with the understanding that he had approximately one year to make it work or the shutdown would proceed.[1]

Ball's analysis of the situation showed that the main problem at Imperial rested with the people rather than with the technology or equipment. Over time, the refinery had spawned little empires that insulated themselves from one another. Job descriptions were important; people tended to do what their job descriptions said, and little else. There was almost no crossing of functional boundaries. For instance, it was difficult to get a pipefitter to help a mechanic without the approval of up to four levels of management. The boundaries between units made cooperative effort costly as well as very time- and energy-consuming.

As a result of his findings, Ken Ball created four main business teams to tackle the problem. Each business team—consisting of forty to fifty people—was responsible for a large segment of the refinery's operations. Each team member worked under the management of a team leader. Ball also disbanded the refinery's joint industrial council, which had managed the relationships between management and workers. In its place, a system in which workers' concerns were handled one on one with team leaders was instituted.

Where once seniority had been the major criterion for promotion or protection from layoff, an individual's performance now became the deciding factor. Ball also cut the work force from 330 employees to 235. Some employees' initial reactions to the changes were negative, as evidenced by two attempts to unionize. But in both cases the majority of employees voted to remain nonunion.

Was Ken Ball's team concept successful for Imperial Oil? For the most part Yes. Communication in the organization is much better. Rigid departmental communication flows have been broken. And employees are now willing to work outside their job description. For instance, there were once thirty workers on the docks; now there are twelve. When a tanker docks, other workers and team leaders who have been cross-trained are summoned to help. And they respond! These same teams have also developed innovative ways to solve problems. For example, several brainstorming sessions resulted in developing a better way to use the on-line quality-monitoring system.

Ken Ball turned to teams to save his refinery. Through teams, he was able to turn around a company that was one of the lowest producers in the industry to one that's now in the top 20 percent.

But the surest sign of success is that upper management at the refinery are no longer considering shutting Imperial down. Why would they? Ball's teams cut organizational costs by 30 percent in just under twelve months. Today, Imperial Oil's Dartmouth refinery is among the top 20 percent of North American refineries.

The management of many organizations today believe, like Ken Ball, that the use of teams will allow them to produce better products, faster, and at lower costs. Using a teamwork approach can reinvigorate productivity and better position an organization to deal with a rapidly changing environment.

The Popularity of Teams

More than two decades ago, when companies such as Toyota, General Foods, and Volvo introduced teams, they made news because no one else was doing it. Today, it's just the opposite; it is the organization that does not use some form of team that is noteworthy. Pick up almost any business publication and you will read how teams have become an essential part of the way work is done in companies such as Honeywell, General Electric, Saab, John Deere, Australian Airlines, Honda, Florida Power and Light, Shiseido, Boeing, and Federal Express.

How do we explain the current popularity of teams? The evidence suggests that teams typically outperform individuals when the tasks being done require multiple skills, judgment, and experience.[2] At Honeywell, for example, work teams have helped the "defense-avionics" plant to improve on-time delivery to 99 percent—up from 40 percent just six years ago when it didn't have teams.[3]

As organizations restructure themselves to compete more effectively and efficiently, they are turning to teams as a way to better utilize employee talents. Management has found that teams are more flexible and responsive to a changing environment than traditional departments or other forms of permanent work groupings. Teams also can be quickly assembled, deployed, refocused, and disbanded.

Teams have become an essential part of the way business is being done.

Finally, teams may offer more than just increased efficiency and enhanced performance for the organization. They can serve as a source of job satisfaction.[4] Because team members are frequently empowered to handle many of the things that directly affect their work, teams serve as an effective means for management to enhance employee involvement, increase employee morale, and promote work force diversity.[5]

These employees are part of a special Boeing team responsible for helping other teams involved in the production of the new 777 jet. The benefits that teams can offer organizations do not happen automatically. It takes time for team members to "gel." And sometimes, they need some help from others.

What Are the Stages of Team Development?

Team development is a dynamic process. Most teams find themselves in a continual state of change. But even though teams probably never reach stability, there's a general pattern that describes how most teams evolve. The five stages of team development, shown in Exhibit 11-1, are forming, storming, norming, performing, and adjourning.[6]

The first stage, **forming,** is characterized by a great deal of uncertainty about the group's purpose, structure, and leadership. Members are "testing the waters" to determine what types of behaviors are acceptable. This stage is complete when members have begun to think of themselves as part of a team.

forming
The first stage of work team development, characterized by uncertainty about purpose, structure, and leadership.

The **storming** stage is one of intragroup conflict. Members accept the existence of the team, but there is resistance to the control that the group imposes on individuality. Further, there is conflict over who will control the team. When stage II is complete, there will be relatively clear leadership within the team.

storming
The second stage of work team development, characterized by intragroup conflict.

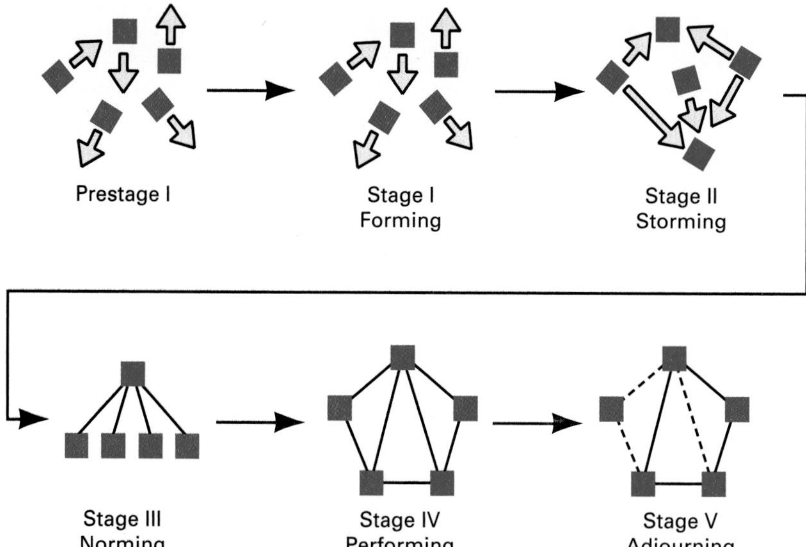

Exhibit 11-1
Stages of Team Development

norming
The third stage of work team development, in which close relationships develop and members begin to demonstrate cohesiveness.

performing
The fourth stage of work team development, in which structure is fully functional and accepted by team members; the last stage in the development of permanent work teams.

adjourning
The fifth and final stage of the development of temporary work teams, in which the team prepares for its disbandment.

The third stage is one in which close relationships develop and members begin to demonstrate cohesiveness. There is now a stronger sense of team identity and camaraderie. This **norming** stage is complete when the team structure solidifies and members have assimilated a common set of expectations of what defines appropriate work behavior. The fourth stage is **performing.** The structure is fully functional and accepted by team members. Their energy has moved from getting to know and understand each other to performing the necessary tasks. For permanent teams, performing is the last stage of their development. For temporary teams—those that have a limited task to perform—there is an **adjourning** stage. In this stage, the team prepares for its disbandment. A high level of task performance is no longer the members' top priority. Instead, their attention is directed toward wrapping-up activities.

Recognizing that teams progress through these stages, an obvious question one can pose is: Do they become more effective as they progress through each stage? Some researchers argue that the effectiveness of work units does increase at advanced stages, but it's not that simple.[7] Although that assumption may be generally true, what makes a team effective is complex. Under some conditions, high levels of conflict are conducive to high levels of group performance.[8] We might expect, then, to find situations in which teams in stage II outperform those in stages III or IV. Similarly, teams do not always proceed clearly from one stage to the next. Sometimes, in fact, several stages are going on simultaneously—as when teams are storming and performing at the same time. Therefore, one should not always assume that all teams precisely follow this developmental process or that stage IV is always most preferable. Instead, it is better to think of these stages as a general framework. It should remind you that teams are dynamic entities and can help you better understand what issues may surface in a team's life.

Aren't Work Groups and Work Teams the Same?

At this point, you may be asking yourself where this discussion is going. Aren't teams really groups of people? And don't they come together in the same way any grouping of individuals does? If you're asking those questions, you are making a logical connec-

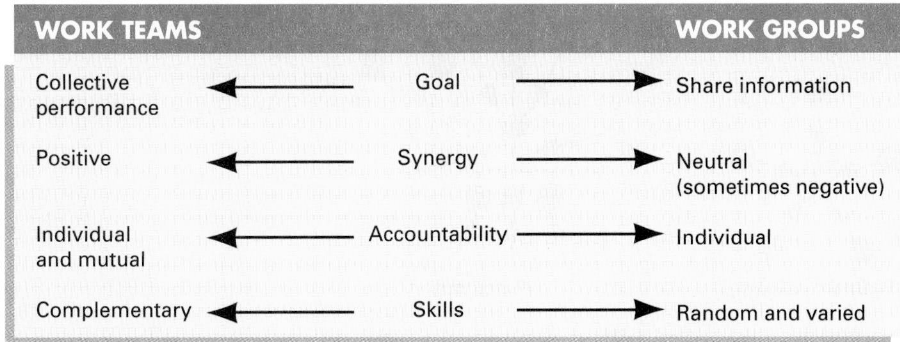

Exhibit 11-2
Comparing Work Teams and Work Groups

tion. But groups and teams are not the same thing. In this section, we will define and clarify the difference between a work group and a work team.[9]

In the last chapter, we defined a *group* as two or more individuals who have come together to achieve certain objectives. A **work group** is a group that interacts primarily to share information and to make decisions that will help each group member perform within his or her area of responsibility. Work groups have no need or opportunity to engage in collective work that requires joint effort. Consequently, their performance is merely the summation of all the group members' individual contributions. There is no positive synergy that would create an overall level of performance greater than the "sum of the inputs."

work group
A group that interacts primarily to share information and to make decisions that will help each group member perform within his or her area of responsibility.

A **work team,** on the other hand, generates positive synergy through a coordinated effort. Their individual efforts result in a level of performance that is greater than the sum of those individual inputs. Exhibit 11-2 highlights the main differences between work groups and work teams.

work team
A group that engages in collective work that requires joint effort and generates a positive synergy.

These descriptions should help to clarify why so many organizations have restructured work processes around teams. Management is looking for that positive synergy that will allow the organization to increase performance. The extensive use of teams creates the potential for an organization to generate greater outputs with no increase in (or even fewer) inputs. For example, at Electrosource, an Austin, Texas, battery maker, productivity doubled within twelve months after work teams were formed. And that happened even while employment was cut from 300 to 80 employees.[10]

Notice, however, that such increases are simply "potential." Nothing inherently magical in the creation of work teams guarantees that this positive synergy, and its accompanying productivity, will occur. Accordingly, merely calling a group a team doesn't automatically increase its performance.[11] As we will show later in this chapter, successful or high-performing work teams have certain common characteristics. If management hopes to gain increases in organizational performance—like those at Electrosource—it will need to ensure that its teams possess those characteristics.

A work team generates positive synergy through a coordinated effort.

Types of Work Teams

Work teams can be classified on the basis of their objective. The four most common forms of teams we are likely to find in an organization are functional teams, problem-solving teams, self-managed teams, and cross-functional teams (see Exhibit 11-3).

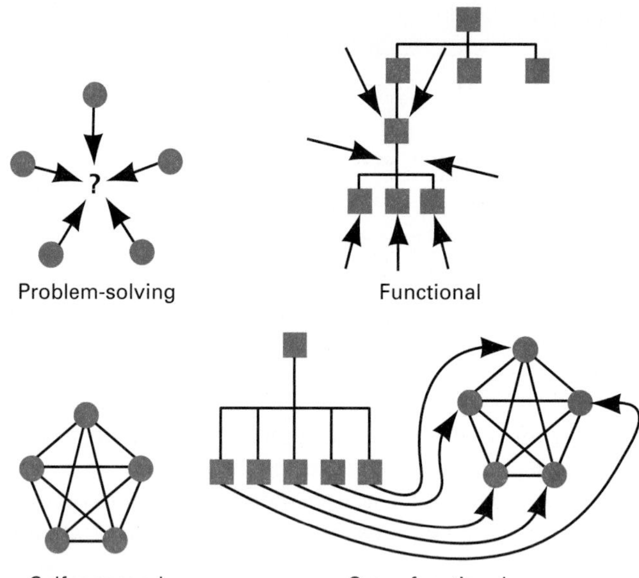

Exhibit 11-3
Types of Work Teams

What Is a Functional Team?

functional team
A work team composed of a manager and the employees in his or her unit; involved in efforts to improve work activities or to solve specific problems within the particular functional unit.

Functional teams are composed of a manager and the employees in his or her unit. Within this functional team, issues such as authority, decision making, leadership, and interactions are relatively simple and clear. Functional teams are often involved in efforts to improve work activities or to solve specific problems within that particular functional unit. For example, at the California headquarters of Birkenstock Footprint Sandals, employees in sales, credit, production, warehousing, and other functional areas now work in independent teams to complete tasks and solve customer problems.[12]

problem-solving teams
Teams typically composed of five to twelve hourly employees from the same department who meet each week to discuss ways of improving quality, efficiency, and the work environment.

quality circles
Work teams composed of eight to ten employees and supervisors who share an area of responsibility and who meet regularly to discuss quality problems, investigate the causes of the problems, recommend solutions, and take corrective actions but who have no authority.

How Does a Problem-Solving Team Operate?

If we look back almost twenty years ago, teams were just beginning to grow in popularity. And the form they took was strikingly similar. These teams typically were composed of five to twelve hourly employees from the same department who met for a few hours each week to discuss ways of improving quality, efficiency, and the work environment.[13] We call these **problem-solving teams.**

In problem-solving teams, members share ideas or offer suggestions on how work processes and methods can be improved (see Managers Who Made a Difference). One of the most widely practiced applications of problem-solving teams witnessed during the 1980s were **quality circles.** These are work teams of eight to ten employees and supervisors who share an area of responsibility. They meet regularly to discuss their quality problems, investigate causes of the problems, recommend solutions, and take corrective actions. They assume responsibility for solving quality problems, and they generate and evaluate their own feedback. Rarely, however, are these teams given the authority to unilaterally implement any of their suggestions. Instead, they make a recommendation to management, who usually makes the final decision about the implementation of recommended solutions. An example of a quality circle

Managers Who Made a Difference

MEI-LIN CHENG, HEWLETT-PACKARD

Read about any successful experience with teams in organizations, and somewhere you will find some mention of Hewlett-Packard. But not everything this giant of a company does is cutting-edge. In fact, some of their processes bordered on the verge of extinction. At least that's what Mei-Lin Cheng found.[14]

One of the difficulties causing some concern at Hewlett-Packard was the realization that when a customer order was placed, it took almost twenty-six days for the order to be filled. Part of the problem stemmed from the fact that this high-tech company still used some seventy computers—many were decades old—to drive its information system. This situation simply wasn't acceptable to upper management. They asked Mei-Lin to reengineer the process and fix the problem!

Fixing a problem like this one in any organization is, at best, difficult. But Mei-Lin believed that she would have a fighting chance only if top management gave her free rein to change anything she felt necessary and allowed her to establish a problem-solving team. Top management appeared somewhat perplexed—and intrigued—by her request, especially when Cheng offered to have a new system operating in about nine months and said that if she didn't succeed, she and her employees could have their funding cut off immediately. In other words, Mei-Lin put her job, as well as some thirty-five others, on the line.

When Mei-Lin formed her team of thirty-five members—including two individuals from outside companies—she started with one simple rule. Her team would have no supervisors, no hierarchies, no titles, no job descriptions, no plans, and no step-by-step milestones. There would be just a conceptual design to develop a data base that would cover customer orders, credit checks, shipping, and inventory control. She knew this approach would create chaos—but out of that chaos she felt great things would come. She believed that such an arrangement would give team members personal ownership, increase their commitment, and make their work more meaningful. Besides, the chaos would allow the team to tackle this complex problem and develop a complex solution.

Did Mei-Lin succeed? Obviously she did, or she would not be featured in this spot. Seriously though, her team made remarkable progress. After extensive training to get everyone up to speed in terms of team skills, the team worked ardently for the next eight months. And with one month to spare, the team reached its goal. Now, instead of taking twenty-six days to get parts to customers, it takes eight. In addition, the timed saved has helped Hewlett-Packard reduce its inventories by more than 20 percent.

was when Honda Motor Company recognized that the costs of producing the Honda Civic were increasing. As a result, management put together a team to investigate the reasons for the increases and to make recommendations about how the car could be built more cheaply.[15] After eighteen months of work, the team made recommendations that, after being implemented, reduced the price of the Honda Civic by more than 3 percent.

What Is a Self-Managed Work Team?

self-managed work team
A formal group of employees who operate without a manager and are responsible for a complete work process or segment that delivers a product or service to an external or internal customer.

Another type of team commonly being used in organizations is the self-directed, or self-managed team. A **self-managed work team** is a formal group of employees who operate without a manager and are responsible for a complete work process or segment that delivers a product or service to an external or internal customer.[16] Typically this kind of team has control over its work pace, determination of work assignments, when breaks are taken, and inspection of its work. Fully self-managed work teams even select their own members and have the members evaluate each other's performance. As a result, supervisory positions take on decreased importance and may even be eliminated. For example, at L-S Electrogalvanizing Company in Cleveland, Ohio, the entire plant is run by self-managed teams. They do their own hiring and scheduling, rotate jobs on their own, establish production targets, set pay scales that are linked to skills, and fire coworkers whenever necessary.[17] Xerox, General Motors, Coors Brewing, Tokyo String Quartet, U.S. Navy Seals, Stanadyne Automotive Corporation, Massachusetts General Hospital, Hewlett-Packard, and Textron are just a few of the many organizations that have implemented self-managed work teams.[18]

How Do Cross-Functional Teams Operate?

cross-functional work team
A team composed of employees from about the same hierarchical level but from different work areas in an organization who are brought together to accomplish a particular task.

The last type of team we will identify is the **cross-functional work team.** This type of team consists of employees from about the same hierarchical level but from different work areas in the organization. They are brought together to accomplish a particular task.[19]

Many organizations have used cross-functional teams for years. For example, in the 1960s IBM created a large team—made up of employees from across departments in the company—to develop the highly successful System 360. But the popularity of cross-functional work teams exploded in the late 1980s. All the major automobile manufacturers—including Toyota, Chrysler, Nissan, General Motors, Ford, Honda, and BMW—have turned to this form of team in order to coordinate complex projects. For example, Chrysler has used cross-functional teams to get such popular models as the subcompact Neon, the full-size Ram pickup, and the sporty Viper to market. And with cross-functional teams, Chrysler is getting closer to the industry leader, Toyota, in terms of the time it takes to assemble a car and in terms of quality.[20]

Cross-functional teams are also an effective way to allow employees from diverse areas within an organization to exchange information, develop new ideas, solve problems, and coordinate complex tasks. But cross-functional teams can be difficult to manage.[21] The early stages of development (e.g., storming) are very often time-consuming, as members learn to work with diversity and complexity. This difficulty with diversity, however, has the ability to be turned into an advantage. For example, remember our discussion of group decision making in Chapter 5. One of the tenets of that process was that groups provided more-complete information and were more creative than individuals. The diversity that exists on a work team can help identify creative or unique solutions. Furthermore, the lack of a common

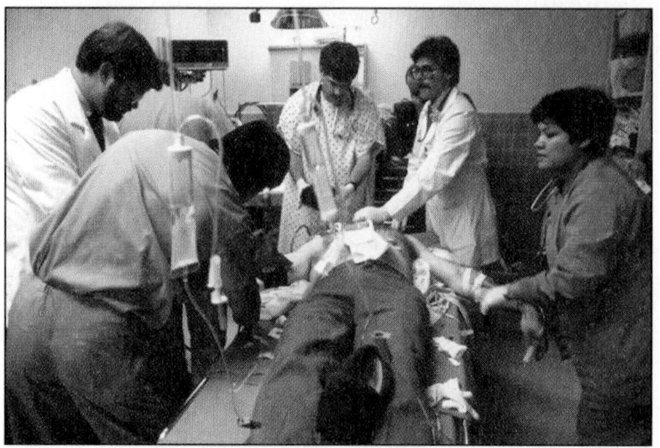

This cross-functional work team at the Massachusetts General Hospital emergency-trauma unit brings together specialties from different parts of the hospital to deal with life-or-death situations.

perspective due to diversity usually means that diverse team members will spend more time discussing relevant issues—which decreases the likelihood that a weak solution will be selected. However, keep in mind that the positive contribution that diversity makes to teams probably will decline over time. As team members become more familiar with one another, they become a more cohesive group. But the positive aspect of this decline is that a "team bond" is built. And this can do more than anything else to overcome the initial difficulties that arise when diverse members work with one another. Hence, it takes time to build trust and teamwork. Later in this chapter we will present ways managers can help facilitate and build trust among team members.

Characteristics of High-Performance Work Teams

Teams are not automatic productivity enhancers. We know that they can also be disappointments for management. What common characteristics, then, do effective teams have? Research provides some insight into the primary characteristics associated with high-performance work teams.[22] Let's take a look at these characteristics as summarized in Exhibit 11-4.

High-performance work teams have both a *clear understanding of the goal* to be achieved and a belief that the goal embodies a worthwhile or important result. Moreover, the importance of these goals encourages individuals to redirect energy away from personal concerns and toward team goals. In high-performing work teams, members are committed to the team's goals, know what they are expected to accomplish, and understand how they will work together to achieve those goals. Effective teams are composed of competent individuals. They have the *relevant* technical *skills* and abilities to achieve

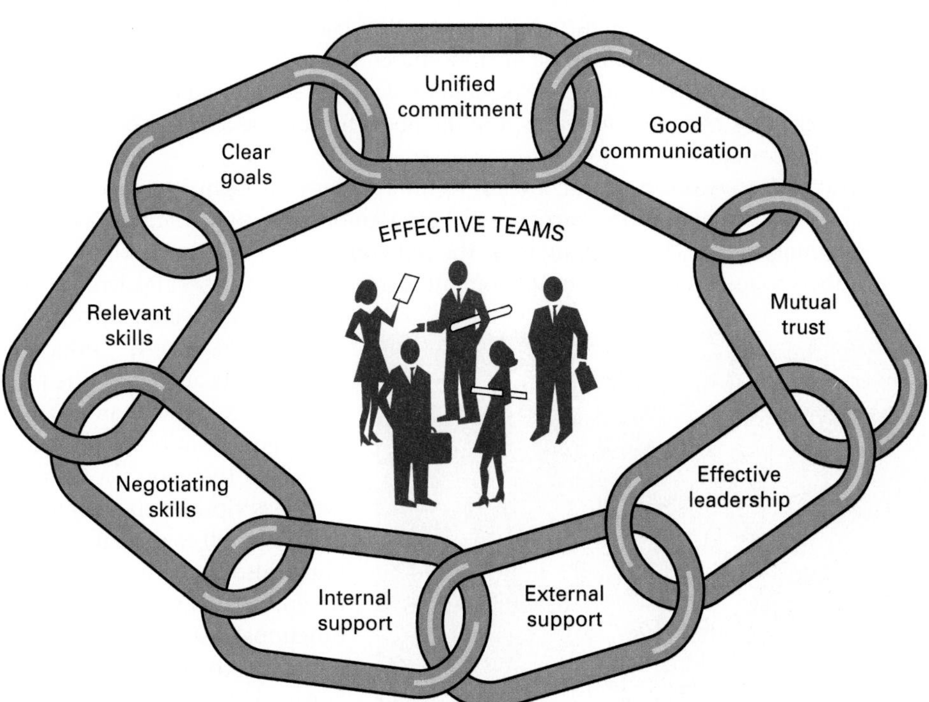

Exhibit 11-4
Characteristics of High-Performing Work Teams

the desired goals and the personal characteristics required to achieve excellence while working well with others. These same individuals are also capable of readjusting their work skills—called *job-morphing*—to fit the needs of the team.[23] It's important not to overlook the personal characteristics. Not everyone who is technically competent has the skills to work well as a team member. High-performing teams have members who possess both technical and interpersonal skills.

Effective teams are characterized by high *mutual trust* among members. That is, members believe in the integrity, character, and ability of one another. But, as you probably know from personal relationships, trust is fragile. It takes a long time to build and can easily be destroyed. The climate of trust within a group tends to be strongly influenced by the organization's culture and the actions of management. Organizations that value openness, honesty, and collaborative processes and that also encourage employee involvement and autonomy are likely to create trusting cultures (see Developing a Management Skill).

Members of an effective team exhibit intense loyalty and dedication to the team. They are willing to do anything that has to be done to help their team succeed. We call this loyalty and dedication *unified commitment*. Studies of successful teams have found that members identify with their teams.[24] Members redefine themselves to include membership in the team as an important aspect of the self. Unified commitment, then, is characterized by dedication to the team's goals and a willingness to expend extraordinary amounts of energy to achieve them.

Not surprisingly, effective teams are characterized by *good communication*. Members are able to convey messages between each other in a form that is readily and clearly understood. This includes nonverbal as well as spoken messages. Good communication is also characterized by a healthy dose of feedback from team members and management.[25] This helps to guide team members and to correct misunderstandings. Like two individuals who have been together for many years, members on high-performing teams are able to quickly and efficiently share ideas and feelings.

When jobs are designed around individuals, job descriptions, rules and procedures, and other types of formalized documentation clarify employee roles. Effective teams, on the other hand, tend to be flexible and continually making adjustments, so team members must possess adequate *negotiating skills*. Because problems and relationships are regularly changing in teams, the members have to be able to confront and reconcile differences.

Effective leaders can motivate a team to follow them through the most difficult situations. How? Leaders help clarify goals. They demonstrate that change is possible by overcoming inertia. And they increase the self-confidence of team members, helping members to realize their potential more fully. Importantly, the best leaders are not necessarily directive or controlling. Increasingly, effective team leaders are taking the role of coach and facilitator. They help guide and support the team, but they don't control it. This description obviously applies to self-managed teams, but it also increasingly applies to problem-solving and cross-functional teams in which the members themselves are empowered. For some traditional

These workers at Fiat understand the meaning of job-morphing. In order to increase their productivity, workers are trained in several skills and assigned to "multiskilled" work units. Doing so helps them be more productive and gives them job security.

Developing a Management Skill

BUILDING TRUST AMONG TEAM MEMBERS

About the Skill: *Managers and team leaders have a significant effect on a team's trust climate. As a result, managers and team leaders need to build trust between themselves and team members. The following steps summarize ways you can build trust.*[26]

Steps in Practicing the Skill

1. ***Demonstrate that you are working for others' interests as well as for your own.*** All of us are concerned with our own self-interests. But if others see you using them, your job, or the organization for your personal goals to the exclusion of the team, your credibility will be undermined.

2. ***Be a team player.*** Support your work team through both words and actions. Defend the team and team members when they are attacked by outsiders. This action goes a long way to demonstrate your loyalty to the team.

3. ***Practice openness.*** Mistrust comes as much from what people do not know as from what they do know. Openness leads to confidence and trust. Therefore, keep team members informed, explain your decisions, be candid about problems, and pay attention to equity perceptions in reward distributions.

4. ***Speak your feelings.*** Managers and leaders who convey only hard facts come across as cold and distant. When you share your feelings, others see you as real—and human. Speaking your feelings can let team members know who you are, and it may help increase their respect for you.

5. ***Show consistency in the basic values that guide your decisions.*** Mistrust also comes from not knowing what to expect. Take the time to think about your values and beliefs. Then let them consistently guide your decisions. When you know your central purpose, your actions will follow accordingly and you will project a consistency that earns trust.

6. ***Keep confidences.*** You trust those who you can confide in and rely on. So if people tell you something in confidence, they need to feel assured that you won't discuss it with others or betray that confidence. If team members perceive you as someone who leaks personal confidences or someone who can't be depended on, you won't be perceived as trustworthy.

7. ***Demonstrate competence.*** Develop the admiration and respect of team members by demonstrating technical and professional ability and good business sense. Pay particular attention to developing and displaying your communication, team-building, and other interpersonal skills.

managers, changing their role from boss to facilitator—from giving orders to working for the team—is a difficult transition. Although most managers relish the new-found shared authority or come to understand its advantages through leadership training, some hard-nosed dictatorial managers are just ill-suited to the team concept and must be transferred or replaced.

The final condition necessary to making an effective team is a *supportive climate*. Internally, the team should be provided with a sound infrastructure. This includes proper training, an understandable measurement system with which team members can evaluate their overall performance, an incentive program that recognizes and rewards team activities, and a supportive human resource system. The infrastructure should support members and reinforce behaviors that lead to high levels of performance. Externally, management should provide the team with the resources needed to get the job done.

Turning Individuals into Team Players

So far, we have made a strong case for the value and growing popularity of work teams. But not every worker is inherently a team player[27] (see Understanding Yourself). Some individuals prefer to be recognized for their individual achievements. In some organizations, too, work environments are such that only the "strong" survive. Creating teams in such an environment may meet some resistance. Finally, as we introduced in Chapter 2, countries differ in terms of how they rate on individualism and collectivism. Teams fit well with countries that score high on collectivism. But what if an organization wants to introduce teams into a highly individualistic society (like that of the United States)? As one writer appropriately stated regarding teams in the United States, "Americans don't grow up learning how to function in teams. In school they don't get a team report card, or learn the names of the team of sailors who traveled with Columbus to America."[28] This limitation apparently would be true of Canadians, British, Australians, and others from highly individualistic societies.

What Are the Management Challenges of Creating Team Players?

The points raised previously are meant to dramatize that one substantial barrier to using work teams is the individual resistance that may exist. Employees' success, when they are part of teams, is no longer defined in terms of individual performance. Instead, it's a function of how well the team as a whole performed. To perform well as team members, individuals must be able to communicate openly and honestly with one another; to confront differences and resolve conflicts; and to place lower priority on personal goals for the good of the team. For many employees, these are difficult—and sometimes impossible—things to do!

The challenge of creating team players will be greatest where (1) the national culture is highly individualistic and (2) the teams are being introduced into an established organization that has historically valued individual achievement. This describes, for instance, what faced managers at AT&T, Ford, Motorola, and other large U.S. companies. These firms prospered by hiring and rewarding corporate stars, and they bred a competitive work climate that encouraged individual achievement and recognition. Employees in these types of organizations can experience "culture shock" caused by a sudden shift to the importance of teamwork.[29] For example, one employee in a large organization who had been well rewarded for working independently for more than twenty years found himself having serious difficulty working as a team player. This difficulty was reflected in his performance evaluation—the first negative evaluation of his career.[30]

In contrast, the challenge for management is less demanding when teams are introduced where employees have strong collectivism values—such as in Japan or Mexico. The challenge of forming teams will also be less in new organizations that use teams as their initial form of structuring work. Saturn Corporation, for instance, is an American organization. Although owned by General Motors, the company was designed around teams from its start. Everyone at Saturn was initially hired with the knowledge that they would be working in teams. And the ability to be a good team player was a hiring prerequisite.

To perform well as team members, individuals must be able to communicate openly and honestly with one another.

Understanding Yourself

Is a Team for You?

Think for a moment about a team you were recently a member of or are currently working with. Maybe it's a sports team, a group working together on a class project, or people who you share some common interest with. Use this experience to answer the following twenty questions. Rate each question on a scale of 1 to 5. The ratings are as follows:

1 = *Mostly agree*
2 = *Sometimes agree*
3 = *Maybe*
4 = *Sometimes disagree*
5 = *Mostly disagree*

1. I prefer to remain a member of this group.	1	2	3	4	5
2. I dislike some of my team members.	1	2	3	4	5
3. I enjoy frequently meeting with my team members.	1	2	3	4	5
4. I care what happens to any one of my team members.	1	2	3	4	5
5. My team often does not involve me in making decisions.	1	2	3	4	5
6. Given an opportunity, I'd change teams.	1	2	3	4	5
7. I don't like meeting so often with my team members.	1	2	3	4	5
8. I wish my team's work would end soon so I can go on to other things.	1	2	3	4	5
9. I am satisfied with the overall performance of my team.	1	2	3	4	5
10. I think I'd work better with people from some other team.	1	2	3	4	5
11. I am included in all decisions that affect my team.	1	2	3	4	5
12. There's a feeling of unity among me and my team members.	1	2	3	4	5
13. My team is not as interesting as others.	1	2	3	4	5
14. I am part of my team's activities.	1	2	3	4	5
15. My team wouldn't care if I stopped showing up.	1	2	3	4	5
16. I'd be upset if my team asked me to leave.	1	2	3	4	5
17. There's little love lost between my team and me.	1	2	3	4	5
18. I want to work with my team so we can excel.	1	2	3	4	5
19. My personal goals are more import ant to me than are my team's goals.	1	2	3	4	5
20. I'll frequently make up an excuse in order to miss a team meeting.	1	2	3	4	5

Scoring: For items 2, 5, 6, 7, 8, 10, 13, 15, 17, 19, and 20, total your circled scores. Place that number on line A. For items 1, 3, 4, 9, 11, 12, 14, 16, and 18, subtract your circled

Continued

score from six. For example, if, in question 1, you circled the value 2 (Sometimes agree), your score for this question is 4 (6 − 2 = 4). Total all adjusted scores, and place them on line B. Add the numbers on lines A and B to get your "Team Aptitude."

Line A: ______________
\+
Line B: ______________
=
Total ______________

What the Assessment Means: There are a total of 100 points possible in this assessment. In general, the higher your total score, the better your potential to work well with a team. Scores and their interpretations can be given as follows:

80 to 100 points = *True team player*
60 to 79 points = *Team supporter*
46 to 59 points = *Can take or leave teams*
25 to 45 points = *Tolerant of some team activity*
24 points or fewer = *Work by yourself*

Whatever your response, you need to recognize a few facts. It's alright to prefer to work by yourself. But if you do, you need to make sure that you prepare for jobs that allow you to work alone. For example, computer programmers and surgeons, although they interact often with others, are primarily solely responsible for their work activities. However, in this changing world of work, you can expect to find more and more opportunities requiring team efforts. Accordingly, those scoring below 60 points should reflect on what they can do to improve their willingness to work in teams.

Source: Adapted from N. J. Evans and P. A. Jarvis, "The Group Attitude Scale: A Measure of Attraction to Groups," *Small Group Behavior,* May 1986, pp. 203–16. Used with permission.

How Can a Manager Shape Team Behavior?

There are several options available for managers who are trying to turn individuals into team players. The three most popular ways include proper selection, employee training, and rewarding the appropriate team behaviors. Let's look at each of these.

What Role Does Selection Play? Some individuals already possess the interpersonal skills to be effective team players. When hiring team members, in addition to checking on the technical skills required to successfully perform the job, the organization should ensure that applicants can fulfill their team roles (see Details on a Management Classic).

As we have mentioned before, some individuals have been socialized around individual contributions. Consequently, some job applicants lack team skills. So too, might some current employees who are restructuring into teams. When faced with such candidates, a manager can do several things. First, and most obvious, if team skills are woefully lacking, don't hire that candidate. If successful performance requires team interaction, rejecting such a candidate is appropriate. On the other hand, a candidate who has some basic team skills but needs more refinement can be hired on a probationary basis and be required to undergo training to "shape" him or her into a team player. If the skills aren't learned, or practiced, the individual may have to be separated from the company for failing to achieve the skills necessary for performing successfully on the job.

Details on a Management Classic

TEAM ROLES

High-performing work teams properly match people to various roles. One stream of research by Charles Margerison and Dick McCann has identified nine potential roles that work team members often can "play." These nine roles are the creator-innovator, explorer-promoter, assessor-developer, thruster-organizer, concluder-producer, controller-inspector, upholder-maintainer, reporter-adviser, and linker.[31] Let's briefly review each team role.

Creator-innovators are people who are usually imaginative and good at initiating ideas or concepts. They are typically very independent and prefer to work at their own pace in their own way—and very often on their own time. *Explorer-promoters* like to take new ideas and champion their cause. These individuals are good at picking up ideas from the creator-innovator and finding the resources to promote those ideas. However, they often lack the patience and control skills to ensure that the ideas are followed through in detail. *Assessor-developers* have strong analytical skills. They're at their best when given several different options to evaluate and analyze before a decision is made. *Thruster-organizers* like to set up operating procedures to turn ideas into reality and get things done. They set goals, establish plans, organize people, and establish systems to ensure that deadlines are met. And, somewhat like thruster-organizers, *concluder-producers* are concerned with results. Only their role focuses on insisting that deadlines are kept and ensuring that all commitments are followed through. Concluder-producers take pride in producing a regular output to a standard.

Controller-inspectors are individuals with a high concern for establishing and enforcing rules and policies. They are good at examining details and making sure that inaccuracies are avoided. They want to check all the facts and figures to make sure they're complete. *Upholder-maintainers* hold strong convictions about the way things should be done. They will defend the team and fight its battles with outsiders while, at the same time, strongly supporting fellow team members. Accordingly, these individuals provide team stability. *Reporter-advisers* are good listeners and don't tend to press their point of view on others. They tend to favor getting more information before making decisions. As such, they perform an important role in encouraging the team to seek additional information before making decisions and discouraging the team from making hasty decisions.

The last role—the *linkers*—overlaps the others. This role can be "played" by any of the previous eight roles. Linkers try to understand all views. They are coordinators and integrators. They dislike extremism and try to build cooperation among all team members. They also recognize the various contributions that other team members make and try to integrate people and activities despite differences that might exist.

If forced to, most individuals can perform in any of these roles. However, most have two or three they strongly prefer. Managers need to understand the strengths that each individual can bring to a team, select team members on the basis of an appropriate mix of individual strengths, and allocate work assignments that fit with each member's preferred style. By matching individual preferences with team role demand, managers increase the likelihood that the team members will work well together. Both Margerison and McCann argue that unsuccessful teams have an unbalanced portfolio of individual talents with too much energy being expended in one area and not enough in other areas.

Can We Train Individuals to Be Team Players? The well in a team involves a set of behaviors. As we introduced in the last chapter, new behaviors can be learned. Even a large portion of people who were raised on the importance of individual accomplishment can be trained to become team players. Training specialists can conduct exercises that allow employees to experience the satisfaction that teamwork can provide. The workshops offered usually cover such topics as team problem solving, communications, negotiations, conflict resolution, and coaching skills. It's not unusual, too, for these individuals to be exposed to the five stages of team development we discussed earlier. At Bell Atlantic, for example, trainers focus on how a team goes through various stages before it gels. And employees are reminded of the importance of patience, because teams take longer to do some things—such as make decisions—than do employees acting alone.[32] Emerson Electric's Specialty Motor Division in Missouri has achieved remarkable success in getting its 650-member work force to not only accept but to welcome team training.[33] Outside consultants provide a learning environment in which workers can gain practical skills for working in teams. And, after less than one year, employees have enthusiastically accepted the value of teamwork.

What Role Do Rewards Play in Shaping Team Players? The organization's reward system needs to encourage cooperative efforts rather than competitive ones. For instance, Lockheed Martin's Space Launch Systems has organized its 1,400 employees into teams. Rewards are structured to return a percentage increase in the bottom line to the team members on the basis of achievement of the team's performance goals.

Promotions, pay raises, and other forms of recognition should be given to employees for how effective they are as a collaborative team member. This doesn't mean that individual contribution is ignored, but rather that it is balanced with selfless contributions to the team. Examples of behaviors that should be rewarded include training new colleagues, sharing information with teammates, helping resolve team conflicts, and mastering new skills in which it's deficient. Last, managers cannot forget the inherent rewards that employees can receive from teamwork. Work teams provide camaraderie. It's exciting and satisfying to be an integral part of a successful team. The opportunity to engage in personal development and to help teammates grow can be a very satisfying and rewarding experience for employees.

It's exciting and satisfying to be an integral part of a successful team.

How Can a Manager Reinvigorate a Mature Team?

Just because a team is performing well at any given point in time is no assurance that it will continue to do so.[34] Effective teams can become stagnant. Initial enthusiasm can give way to apathy. Time can diminish the positive value from diverse perspectives as cohesiveness increases. In terms of the five-stage development model, teams don't automatically stay at the "performing" stage. Familiarity and team success can lead to contentment and complacency. And, as that happens, the team may become less open to novel ideas and innovative solutions. Mature teams, also, are particularly prone to suffer from groupthink (see Chapter 5), as team members begin to believe they can read everyone's mind and assume that they know what the others are thinking. Consequently, team members become reluctant to express their thoughts and less likely to challenge one another.

Another source of problems for mature teams is that their early successes are often due to having taken on easy tasks. It's normal for new teams to begin by taking on those issues and problems they can most easily handle. But as time passes, the easy problems are solved and the team has to begin to tackle the more difficult issues. At this point, the team has frequently established its processes and routines. And team

1. Prepare members to deal with the problems of maturity.
2. Offer refresher training.
3. Offer advanced training.
4. Encourage teams to treat their development as a constant learning experience.

Exhibit 11-5
How to Reinvigorate Mature Work Teams

members are often reluctant to change the workable system they have developed. When that happens, problems arise. Internal team processes no longer work smoothly. Communication bogs down. And conflict increases because problems are less likely to have obvious solutions. All in all, team performance may dramatically drop.

What can a manager do to reinvigorate mature teams—especially ones that are encountering the problems described above? We offer four suggestions (see Exhibit 11-5). *Prepare team members to deal with the problems of team maturity.* Remind team members that they are not unique. All successful teams eventually have to address maturity issues. They shouldn't feel let down or lose their confidence in the team concept when the initial excitement subsides and conflicts begin to surface. *Offer refresher training.* When teams get into ruts, it may help to provide them with refresher training in communication, conflict resolution, team processes, and similar skills. This training can help team members regain their confidence and trust in each other. *Offer advanced training.* The skills that worked well with easy problems may be insufficient for some of the more difficult problems the team is addressing. Mature teams can often benefit from advanced training to help members develop stronger problem-solving, interpersonal, and technical skills. *Encourage teams to treat their development as a constant learning experience.* Just as organizations use total quality management, teams should approach their own development as part of a search for continuous improvement. Teams should look for ways to improve, to confront member fears and frustrations, and to use conflict as a learning opportunity.

Contemporary Team Issues

As we close this chapter, we will address two issues related to managing teams. These are labor law and total quality management.

Are Teams Legal in Labor-Management Relations?

Historically, the relationship between labor and management was built on conflict. The interests of management and labor were seen as being basically at odds, and each treated the other as the opposition. But times have changed somewhat. Management has become increasingly aware that successful efforts to increase productivity, improve quality, and lower costs require employee involvement and commitment. Similarly, some labor unions have come to recognize that they can help their members more by cooperating with management than by fighting with them.

Unfortunately, current U.S. labor laws, passed in the era of mistrust and antagonism between labor and management, have become barriers to their becoming cooperative partners. As a case in point, the National Labor Relations Act was passed in 1935 to encourage collective bargaining and to balance workers' power against that of management.[35] That legislation also sought to eliminate a then-widespread practice: Firms would set up company unions for the sole purpose of undermining the efforts of outside

Exhibit 11-6
When a Team Might Be Illegal in a Unionized Setting

Source: Based on A. Berstein, "Making Teamwork Work—And Appeasing Uncle Sam," *Business Week*, January 25, 1993, p. 101.

An affirmative response to any one of the following questions may mean that having a team violates national labor law.

1. Does management dominate the teams by controlling their formation, setting their goals, or deciding how they operate?
2. Does the team address issues affecting other, nonteam, employees?
3. Does the team deal with traditional bargaining issues such as wages and working conditions?
4. Does the team deal with any supervisors, managers, or executives on any issue?

unions to organize their employees. So the law prohibits employers from creating or supporting a "labor organization." Ironically, labor laws—such as the National Labor Relations Act—are now working against cooperation between management and labor. Specifically, they are making it difficult for companies to establish employee work teams.[36]

Although this issue is the subject of Congressional debate,[37] the current legal environment does not prohibit labor and management teams in the United States. Rather, to comply with the law, management is required to give its work teams independence. That is, when work teams become dominated by management, they are likely to be interpreted as groups that perform some functions of labor unions but are controlled by management. What kinds of actions would indicate that a team is *not* dominated by management? Some examples might include choosing team members through secret ballot elections, giving teams wide latitude in deciding what issues to deal with, permitting teams to meet apart from management, and specifying that work teams are not susceptible to dissolution by management whim. The key theme that labor laws appear to be conveying is that, where work teams are introduced, they must have the power to make decisions and act independently of management. Exhibit 11-6 suggests some key questions that might indicate that having a team violates national labor law.

Why Are Teams Central to Total Quality Management?

One of the central characteristics of total quality management is the use of teams. Why teams? The essence of TQM is process improvement, and employee participation is the linchpin of process improvement. In other words, TQM requires management to encourage employees to share ideas and to act on what the employees suggest. As one author put it, "None of the various TQM processes and techniques will catch on and be applied except in work teams. All such techniques and processes require high levels of communication and contact, response, adaption, and coordination and sequenc-

This Honda team focused its energies in cutting costs and improving the production process of the Honda Civic. Through their efforts, Honda was able to offer its Civic model at a 3 percent price reduction over the previous year's model price.

ing. They require, in short, the environment that can be supplied only by superior work teams."[38]

Teams provide the natural vehicle for employees to share ideas and implement improvements. As stated by Gil Mosard, a TQM specialist at McDonnell-Douglas: "When your measurement system tells you your process is out of control, you need teamwork for structured problem-solving. Not everyone needs to know how to do all kinds of fancy control charts for performance tracking, but everybody does need to know where their process stands so they can judge if it is improving."[39] Examples from Ford Motor Company and Amana Refrigeration, Inc. illustrate how teams are being used in TQM programs.[40]

Ford began its TQM efforts in the early 1980s, with teams as the primary organizing mechanism. "Because this business is so complex, you can't make an impact on it without using a team approach," noted one Ford manager. In designing their quality problem-solving teams, Ford's management identified five goals. The teams should (1) be small enough to be efficient and effective, (2) be properly trained in the skills their members will need, (3) be allocated enough time to work on the problems they plan to address, (4) be given the authority to resolve the problems and implement corrective action, and (5) have a designated "champion" whose job it is to help the team get around roadblocks that arise.

At Amana, teams made up of people from different levels within the company are used to deal with quality problems that cut across various functional areas. Each of the various teams has a unique area of problem-solving responsibility. For instance, one handles in-plant products, another deals with items that arise outside the production facility, and still another focuses specifically on supplier problems. Amana claims that the use of these teams has improved vertical and horizontal communication within the company and substantially reduced both the number of units that don't meet company specifications and the number of service problems in the field.

Summary

How will I know if I fulfilled the Learning Objectives found on page 331? You will have fulfilled the Learning Objectives if you understand the following.

1. **Explain the growing popularity of work teams in organizations.** Teams have become increasingly popular in organizations because they typically outperform individuals when the tasks being done require multiple skills, judgment, and experience. Teams are also more flexible and responsive to a changing environment. Teams may also serve as an effective means for management to enhance employee involvement, increase employee morale, and promote work force diversity.
2. **Describe the five stages of team development.** The five stages of team development are forming, storming, norming, performing, and adjourning. In forming, people join the team and define the team's purpose, structure, and leadership. Storming is a stage of intragroup conflict over control issues. During the norming stage, close relationships develop and the team demonstrates cohesiveness. Performing is the stage at which the team is doing the task at hand. Finally, adjourning is the stage when teams with a limited task to perform prepare to be disbanded.
3. **Contrast work groups with work teams.** A work group is a group that interacts primarily to share information and to make decisions to help each group member perform within his or her area of responsibility. Work groups have no need nor opportunity to engage in collective work that requires joint effort. Consequently, their performance is merely the summation of all the group members' individual contributions. There is no positive synergy that would create an overall level of performance greater than the "sum of the inputs." A work team, on the other hand, generates positive synergy through a coordinated effort. Their individual efforts result in a level of

performance that is greater than the sum of those individual inputs.

4. **Identify four common types of work teams.** The four most popular types of teams are functional teams (composed of a manager and the employees in his or her unit); problem-solving teams (typically composed of five to twelve hourly employees from the same department who meet for a few hours each week to discuss ways of improving quality, efficiency, and the work environment); self-managed teams (a formal group of employees who operate without a manager and are responsible for a complete work process or segment that delivers a product or service to an external or internal customer); and cross-functional teams (consisting of employees from about the same hierarchial level, but from different work areas in the organization, brought together to accomplish a particular task).
5. **List the characteristics of high-performing work teams.** High-performing work teams are characterized by clear goals, members with relevant skills, mutual trust among members, unified commitment, good communication, adequate negotiating skills, and effective leadership.
6. **Identify how managers can build trust among team members.** Managers can help to build trust among team members by (1) demonstrating that they are working for others' interests as well as for their own, (2) being a team player, (3) practicing openness, (4) speaking their feelings, (5) showing consistency in the basic values that guide their decisions, (6) keeping confidences, and (7) demonstrating competence.
7. **Discuss how organizations can create team players.** Organizations can create team players by selecting individuals with the interpersonal skills to be effective team players, providing training to develop teamwork skills, and rewarding individuals for cooperative efforts.
8. **Explain how managers can keep teams from becoming stagnant.** As teams mature, they can become complacent. To keep this from occurring, managers need to support mature teams with advice, guidance, and training if these teams are to continue to improve.
9. **Describe the current legal climate surrounding the use of teams in unionized settings.** The current legal environment doesn't necessarily outlaw teams in the United States. What it does is require management to give its work teams independence. That is, when work teams become dominated by management, they are likely to be interpreted as groups that perform some functions of labor unions but are controlled by management. This latter action is a violation of current labor laws.
10. **Explain the role of teams in TQM.** Teams provide a natural vehicle for employees to share ideas and to implement improvements as part of the TQM process. Teams are particularly effective for resolving complex problems.

Review & Discussion Questions

1. How do you explain the rapidly increasing popularity of work teams in the countries, such as the United States and Canada, whose national cultures place a high value on individualism?
2. What problems might surface on teams during each of the five stages of team development?
3. "All work teams are work groups, but not all work groups are work teams." Do you agree or disagree with the statement? Discuss.
4. Contrast self-managed work teams with cross-functional work teams.
5. What is a problem-solving team?
6. Would you prefer to work alone or as part of a team? Why?
7. Why is trust so important to developing high-performing work teams?
8. When might individuals, acting independently, outperform teams in an organization?
9. Contrast the pros and cons of having diverse work teams.
10. How are federal labor laws undermining efforts to implement teams in unionized settings?

Testing Your Comprehension • • • 

Circle the correct answer, then check yourself on page AK-1.

1. Which of the following statements is NOT a reason teams are more popular in organizations today?
   a) Teams may outperform individual workers when the tasks being done require multiple skills, judgment, and experience.
   b) Teams may serve as a means of enhancing collectivism in a national culture.
   c) Teams are more flexible and responsive to a changing environment.
   d) Teams may serve as an effective means for management to promote work force diversity.

2. A ______________ interacts primarily to share information and to make decisions to help each member to perform within his or her area of responsibility.
   a) work team
   b) cohesive group
   c) work group
   d) none of the above

3. Which stage of team development is complete when members have begun to think of themselves as part of a team?
   a) performing
   b) norming
   c) storming
   d) forming

4. Chris is part of a work team that is a formal group that has no manager and is responsible for a complete work process. Chris is part of which type of work team?
   a) functional
   b) self-managed
   c) problem-solving
   d) none of the above

5. Which type of work team consists of employees from about the same hierarchical level but from different work areas in the organization?
   a) functional
   b) self-managed
   c) problem-solving
   d) none of the above

6. Which of the following is a primary characteristic of high-performing work teams?
   a) good communication among team members
   b) broad work goals set by management
   c) cooperation with customers
   d) responsibility for task completion

7. Willingness to do what has to be done for the team to succeed is called
   a) clear goals
   b) appropriate leadership
   c) unified commitment
   d) internal support

8. High-performance work teams gain a clearer understanding when managers
   a) create a clear purpose
   b) provide resources
   c) build mutual trust
   d) change the team's membership

9. For teams to be effective,
   a) all team members must like each other
   b) team members must resolve petty differences from the start
   c) team members cannot disagree
   d) team members must put aside differences in light of goals

Continued

10. Benefits of work teams generally do NOT include
   a) faster decisions
   b) lower costs
   c) improved performance
   d) improved morale

11. Quality circles
   a) identify problems
   b) determine their own membership
   c) investigate the causes of problems
   d) make final decisions regarding recommended solutions

12. Which of the following is NOT a result of using work teams?
   a) lower absenteeism
   b) improved morale
   c) increased productivity
   d) increased centralization

13. Which of the following is identified as a way to build trust among team members?
   a) demonstrate competence
   b) demonstrate conservative communication
   c) demonstrate creativity
   d) demonstrate flexibility

14. Readjusting work skills to fit the needs of the team is called
   a) career development
   b) job-morphing
   c) skills training
   d) none of the above

15. The challenge of creating team players will be LOWEST in which of the following?
   a) where the national culture is highly individualistic
   b) where teams are introduced into an established organization that has historically valued individual achievement
   c) where the national culture is highly collective
   d) all of the above

16. Which of the following is NOT recommended as a means for a manager to shape individuals into team players?
   a) hiring primarily individuals who come from collective societies
   b) selecting individuals who have the necessary skills to work well with teams
   c) rewarding employees for working collectively
   d) training team members to develop team-related skills

17. Which of the following statements is correct regarding the current state of labor laws affecting teams in the United States?
   a) The current legal environment outlaws most teams in the United States.
   b) Work teams are legal if they can be dissolved by management at any time.
   c) Work teams are legal when they have the power to make decisions and act independently of management.
   d) Work teams are legal when they are controlled by management.

18. Teams are the essence of TQM because they
   a) serve as functional work groups
   b) serve as a means of reducing groupthink
   c) limit employee participation
   d) encourage employees to share ideas and act on what they suggest

Applying the Concepts

Designing Effective Teams

1. Break into teams of four or five.
2. Each person in the team is to share a *positive* experience he or she has had while participating on a team.
3. After step 2 has been completed, each person on the team is to share a *negative* experience he or she has had while participating on a team.
4. Team members should now analyze the shared responses.
   a. What common characteristics, if any, did you see when team members described a positive experience? A negative experience?
   b. What implications can your team draw from these shared experiences for the design of teams? For making teams more effective?

Take It to the Net

We invite you to visit the Robbins/De Cenzo page on the Prentice Hall Web site at:

http://www.prenhall.com/robbinsfom

for this chapter's World Wide Web exercise.

You can also visit the Web sites for these companies and agencies featured within this chapter:

Birkenstock Footprint Sandals
http://www.southwind.net/iv/aircapbirkl

Saab
http://www.saabusa.com

Saturn Corporation
http://www.saturncars.com/index.html

Square D
http://www.industry.net/squared

U.S. Navy Seals
ftp://ftp.netcom.com/pub/od/odin/seal/seals.html

Volvo
http://www.volvo.se/

Thinking Critically

Making a Value Judgment: Must Employees Work on a Team?

After earning her bachelor's degree in business administration from the University of Illinois, Caitlin Barnes took a job with Cable News Network (CNN) in its Paris, France, bureau. She was assigned to the business group in the news division. Her job was to provide producers and newspeople with research material for their on-air stories. She would be given certain leads, and it was her sole responsibility to do the research and make the data available. Caitlin took the job knowing it wasn't exactly how she wanted to spend her whole professional career. But she thought the job would be interesting and would give her an opportunity to travel throughout the world.

After several years at CNN, Caitlin decided to return to the U.S. and earn a master's degree. She applied, and was accepted at Duke's business school. Her time studying at Duke was demanding but exciting. She flourished in the "competitive" environment of the program. She thoroughly enjoyed the opportunity to analyze complex cases and argue the merits of her conclusions with classmates. Two years later, Caitlin graduated in the top 10 percent of her class.

During her last semester at Duke, Caitlin interviewed with a number of companies. Despite having several attractive offers from health-related organizations, she wanted to work in a high-tech company doing market research. When Motorola made her an offer, she happily accepted.

After about four months on the job, Caitlin was told she was being assigned to a cross-functional team that would look at ways the company could reduce inventory costs. This cross-functional team was to be a permanent structure and would include individuals from cost accounting, production, supplier relations, and marketing. Caitlin was not happy about her new assignment; she felt that she was not a team player. In fact, she even bragged at times about being a loner. Although she knew she could work well with others, she didn't like the "added" time it took to get things done. She preferred to just jump in and do things without discussing them. And, although she prided herself on being an outstanding performer, she didn't like the idea of having her performance dependent on the actions of others. As she said, "I know I won't shirk my responsibilities, but I can't be so sure of the others."

Questions:

1. Do you think that Caitlin's boss should have allowed her to decide for herself whether she would join the team? Discuss.
2. Do you think that everyone should be expected to be a team player, given the trends that we're seeing as we near the twenty-first century?
3. Is it ethical for a manager to require an employee to do his or her job as part of a team? Explain your position.

Teams at Published Image, Inc.

Some people might say that Eric Gershman, president and founder of Published Image, is a little off his rocker. Why? Because his career goal is eliminating his job. That's the statement he made when he organized his small Boston company into four self-managed teams.[41]

Published Image Inc. produces newsletters and other publications for shareholders of mutual fund companies. Revenues during 1993 hit $4 million with a profit margin of 20 percent. Gershman notes, with some pride, that most of the profit margin gain came during the fourth quarter after he implemented the teams. And the company expects to hit revenues of $6 million during 1994. Yet, prior to the radical reorganization, the situation was serious enough that the company was on the brink of failure. Employee turnover was high (around 50 percent a year), product quality was pathetic (customers complained about numerous factual errors in the publications), and the company was losing a third of its clients every year. That's when Gershman decided he had to do something drastic.

And he did. The old company was "blown up" and in its place now are four largely autonomous work teams, each with its own clients who are serviced by staff from sales, editorial, and production. The teams set their own work schedules, prepare their own budgets, and receive bonuses based on their team's performance. Each team member specializes in a skill, but can perform any function to meet daily deadlines. This type of job sharing broadens each team member's perspective and improves planning.

Managers are now called *coaches,* and they offer advice and assistance rather than give orders. Managers also rate the teams for timeliness and accuracy. A monthly score of 90 or higher on these performance measures qualifies team members to biannual bonuses, which can equal up to 15 percent of an employee's base pay.

So, even though some people might think he's a little crazy for trying to "lose" his job, Eric Gershman feels he has found a way to better manage his company's growth.

Questions:

1. What did teams do for Published Image Inc. that the previous structure couldn't?
2. What problems should Eric be prepared for as a result of the changes he's made?

Video Case ABCNEWS

Square D Assembly-Line Teams

Teams and teamwork are increasingly being used in numerous organizations worldwide. Square D is a major U.S. manufacturer of electrical equipment that has chosen to use employee teams. At its Lexington, Kentucky, plant, teams were introduced in 1988 to help improve quality, speed customer orders, and increase productivity. What has been their experience with this approach?

Every day begins with a team meeting. The 800 employees are divided into twenty- to thirty-person self-managed teams. Each team operates like its own little factory within the factory. Team members control their own work and can make decisions without having to check with management first. The employee teams are fully responsible for their own products, from start to finish. One employee describes what a team member's role is like: "Now, if I see something that I'm not satisfied with, I stop the line. Used to be, you didn't. Whatever your boss told you, you did it. But if I don't like it, I'll stop the line."

The decision by Square D managers to introduce teams wasn't made lightly. Management realized that employees would need training in order to effectively convert from a system in which workers did narrow, specialized tasks on an assembly line and never saw the finished product they were working on, to being on a team that was fully responsible for its own products from start to finish. Part of that training has included exercises to help employees learn how to work as part of a team, learn to solve problems, learn how to handle new technology, and learn how to service customers better. The Lexington plant continues to spend 4 percent of its payroll on employee training.

Has the switch to employee teams worked? The results at Lexington are impressive. Employees no longer have to wait for maintenance personnel when equipment breaks down. They have been trained in maintenance and can fix their own machines. Employees exhibit pride in their work and greater commitment to doing a good job. And management is pleased with the 75 percent reduction in the product reject rate and the ability to process customer orders in an average of three days versus six weeks under the old system.

Questions:

1. Why do you think employees need to be trained to work effectively on teams?
2. What characteristics of effective teams can you see in this Square D example?
3. Not all efforts to introduce teams are successful. Is there anything in the Square D example to suggest why this program is doing so well?

Source: "Assembly-Line Teams Are Better Trained and More Efficient," *ABC News World News Tonight,* February 24, 1993.

Motivating and Rewarding Employees

12

LEARNING OBJECTIVES

What will I be able to do after I finish this chapter?

1. **DESCRIBE** the motivation process.
2. **DEFINE** needs.
3. **EXPLAIN** the hierarchy of needs theory.
4. **DIFFERENTIATE** Theory X from Theory Y.
5. **EXPLAIN** the motivational implications of the motivation-hygiene theory.
6. **IDENTIFY** the characteristics that high achievers seek in a job.
7. **DESCRIBE** the motivational implications of equity theory.
8. **EXPLAIN** the key relationships in expectancy theory.
9. **DESCRIBE** the effect of work force diversity on motivational practices.
10. **IDENTIFY** the motivational effects of employee stock ownership plans.

HAVE YOU EVER HEARD OF THE FormPac Corporation? Probably not. But it's a good bet you've used one of their products. For instance, the paint tray at your local Home Depot was probably made by FormPac. So were many of the containers that hold your favorite soda. The company, based in Sandusky, Ohio, is a major supplier of custom plastic products.[1] What's interesting about FormPac is that it has been rejuvenated over the past several years. And much of the credit for the change goes to its employees. Of course, FormPac's president, William Duff, played an important role, too!

William Duff (on right), FormPac's president, and Kent Johnson, plant manager, are excited about what they see in their employees. Since a pay-for-performance bonus was implemented, the employees have helped the organization increase profits by more than 25 percent. In return, employees have received a bonus of almost 10 percent of their base salary. FormPac's bonus program is paying dividends for both the organization and the employees.

Duff has always believed that employees should be rewarded for having a productive year. When the company exceeded its production and profit goals, Duff shared the profits with his employees. But his bonus program was ill-defined. No employee knew precisely what entered into the bonus "equation," nor did any have a clue of how much bonus each might get. In the past, Duff had simply made those determinations. But in 1994, things started to sour. After FormPac lost a major account and was heavily debt-ridden from building a new plant, no bonuses were given. Understandably, employees were puzzled. Some were even angry enough to become publicly vocal—claiming that Duff had the money for bonuses but was pocketing it all himself! That simply was not correct. And Duff recognized why some of the employees were reacting this way—they had no information about how bonuses were awarded.

So Duff changed the way things were done. He spelled out in understandable terms a precise formula for individual bonuses for annual performance. The primary components of the formula were based on the company's financial statements: specifically, profits and monthly sales. Each month, Duff would post in the cafeteria where the company stood on those two variables. These data enabled employees to compare their past work with the projected targets set by the company. In this manner, employees were able to see whether they were ahead of, even with, or below the targets. In addition, posted next to the productivity trend data was a formula of how profits would be divided among the employees. Sixty percent of that amount would be divided among all employees, with the remaining 40 percent being split between hourly workers and management personnel. While this "formula" provided the amount of money available in the pay-for-performance bonus pool, the specific amount any one employee would receive was based on a formula that factors in their wages and seniority. This, as Duff puts it, was to reward "loyalty and commitment, too."

FormPac's new variable pay-for-performance bonus plan has been an unqualified success. Employees have been earning bonuses in the range of 10 percent, while the company has enjoyed a 25 percent increase in profitability. In addition, FormPac's productivity has increased by more than 20 percent. As for the employees who are making this happen, they no longer view William Duff in that negative light. They now understand how the bonus system works and Duff's role in it.

As William Duff learned, compensation plans can play a key role in affecting employee motivation. In this chapter, we will provide some insight into how to maximize employee motivation. Let's begin by defining *motivation.*

Motivation and Individual Needs

Some employees regularly spend a lot of time talking with friends at work in order to satisfy their social needs. There is a high level of effort, but it's being unproductively directed.

To understand what motivation is, let us begin by pointing out what motivation isn't. Why? Because many people incorrectly view motivation as a personal trait—that is, they think that some have it and others don't. In practice, this attitude would characterize the manager who labels a certain employee as unmotivated. Our knowledge of motivation, though, tells us that people can't be labeled in this way. What we know is that motivation is the result of the interaction between the individual and the situation. Certainly, individuals differ in motivational drive, but an individual's motivation varies from situation to situation. As we analyze the concept of motivation, keep in mind that level of motivation varies both between individuals and within individuals at different times.

motivation
The willingness to exert high levels of effort to reach organizational goals, conditioned by the effort's ability to satisfy some individual need.

We'll define **motivation** as the willingness to exert high levels of effort to reach organizational goals, conditioned by the effort's ability to satisfy some individual need. Although general motivation refers to effort toward any goal, here it will refer to organizational goals because our focus is on work-related behavior. The three key elements in our definition are effort, organizational goals, and needs.

The effort element is a measure of intensity. When someone is motivated, he or she tries hard. But high levels of effort are unlikely to lead to favorable job performance outcomes unless the effort is channeled in a direction that benefits the organization.[2] Therefore, we must consider the quality of the effort as well as its intensity. Effort that is directed toward, and consistent with, the organization's goals is the kind of effort that we should be seeking. Finally, we will treat motivation as a need-satisfying process. This is depicted in Exhibit 12-1.

need
An internal state that makes certain outcomes appear attractive.

A **need,** in our terminology, means some internal state that makes certain outcomes appear attractive. An unsatisfied need creates tension that stimulates drives within an individual. These drives generate a search behavior to find particular goals that, if attained, will satisfy the need and reduce the tension.

We can say that motivated employees are in a state of tension. To relieve this tension, they exert effort. The greater the tension, the higher the effort level. If this effort successfully leads to the satisfaction of the need, it reduces tension. Since we are interested in work behavior, this tension-reduction effort must also be directed toward organizational goals. Therefore, inherent in our definition of motivation is the require-

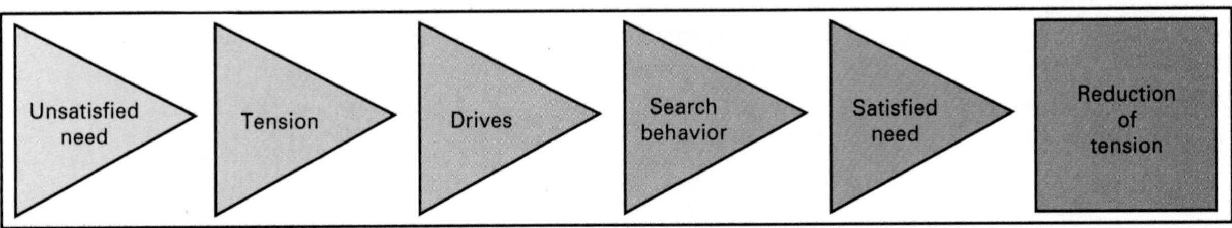

Exhibit 12-1
The Motivation Process

ment that the individual's needs be compatible and consistent with the organization's goals. When they aren't, individuals may exert high levels of effort that run counter to the interests of the organization. Incidentally, this situation is not so unusual. Some employees regularly spend a lot of time talking with friends at work in order to satisfy their social needs. There is a high level of effort, but it's being unproductively directed.

Early Theories of Motivation

The 1950s were a fruitful time for the development of motivation concepts. Three specific theories were formulated during this period that, although heavily attacked and now considered questionably valid, are probably still the best-known explanations for employee motivation. These are the hierarchy of needs theory, Theories X and Y, and the motivation-hygiene theory. Although more-valid explanations of motivation have been developed, you should know these theories for at least two reasons: (1) They represent the foundation from which contemporary theories grew; and (2) practicing managers regularly use these theories and their terminology in explaining employee motivation.

What Is Maslow's Hierarchy of Needs Theory?

The best-known theory of motivation is probably psychologist Abraham Maslow's **hierarchy of needs theory.**[3] He stated that within every human being there exists a hierarchy of five needs:

hierarchy of needs theory
Maslow's theory states that there is a hierarchy of five human needs: physiological, safety, social, esteem, and self-actualization; as each need becomes satisfied, the next need becomes dominant.

1. *Physiological needs.* Food, drink, shelter, sexual satisfaction, and other bodily requirements
2. *Safety needs.* Security and protection from physical and emotional harm
3. *Social needs.* Affection, belongingness, acceptance, and friendship
4. *Esteem needs.* Internal esteem factors such as self-respect, autonomy, and achievement and external esteem factors such as status, recognition, and attention
5. *Self-actualization needs.* Growth, achieving one's potential, and self-fulfillment; the drive to become what one is capable of becoming.

As each need is substantially satisfied, the next need becomes dominant. In terms of Exhibit 12-2, the individual moves up the hierarchy. From a motivation viewpoint, the theory says that, although no need is ever fully gratified, a substantially

Is there support for Maslow's hierarchy of needs theory of motivation in business today? That depends on who you talk to. Empirical research efforts have been unable to support the theory, but people like Dave Jensen, president of Search Masters International, a biotechnology executive search firm in Sedona, Arizona, believes in it. Through his business dealings, he has been able to identify several traits of the "self-actualized" employee. To Jensen, this individual is one who is financially secure, has other basic needs met, is motivated by making a contribution to an organization, has a sense of purpose, and is independent, altruistic, and spontaneous.

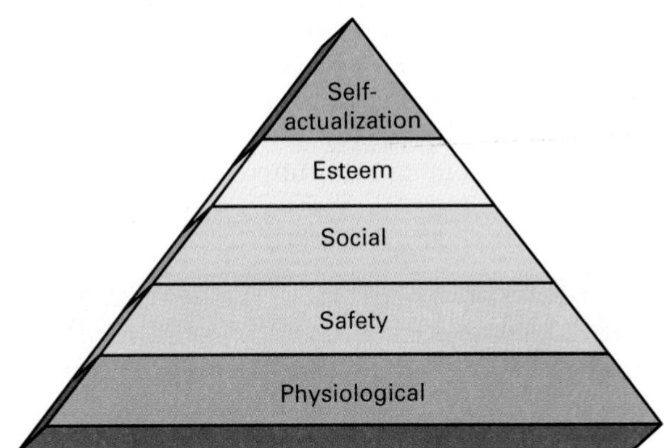

Exhibit 12-2
Maslow's Hierarchy of Needs

satisfied need no longer motivates. If you want to motivate someone, according to Maslow, you need to understand where that person is in the hierarchy and focus on satisfying needs at or above that level (see Understanding Yourself).

Maslow's need theory has received wide recognition, particularly among practicing managers.[4] Its popularity can be attributed to the theory's intuitive logic and ease of understanding. Unfortunately, however, research does not generally validate the theory. Maslow provided no empirical substantiation for his theory, and several studies that sought to validate it found no support.[5]

Theory X
McGregor's term for the assumption that employees dislike work, are lazy, seek to avoid responsibility, and must be coerced to perform.

Theory Y
McGregor's term for the assumption that employees are creative, seek responsibility, and can exercise self-direction.

What Is McGregor's Theory X and Theory Y?

Douglas McGregor proposed two distinct views of the nature of human beings: a basically negative view, labeled **Theory X,** and a basically positive view, labeled **Theory Y.**[6] After viewing the way managers dealt with employees, McGregor concluded that a manager's view of human nature is based on a group of assumptions, either positive or negative (see Exhibit 12-3), and that the manager molds his or her behavior toward employees according to these suppositions.

Exhibit 12-3
Theory X and Theory Y Premises

Theory X: A manager who views employees from a Theory X (negative) perspective believes:

- **1.** Employees inherently dislike work and, whenever possible, will attempt to avoid it
- **2.** Because employees dislike work, they must be coerced, controlled, or threatened with punishment to achieve desired goals
- **3.** Employees will shirk responsibilities and seek formal direction whenever possible
- **4.** Most workers place security above all other factors associated with work and will display little ambition

Theory Y: A manager who views employees from a Theory Y (positive) perspective believes:

- **1.** Employees can view work as being as natural as rest or play
- **2.** Men and women will exercise self-direction and self-control if they are committed to the objectives
- **3.** The average person can learn to accept, even seek, responsibility
- **4.** The ability to make good decisions is widely dispersed throughout the population and is not necessarily the sole province of managers

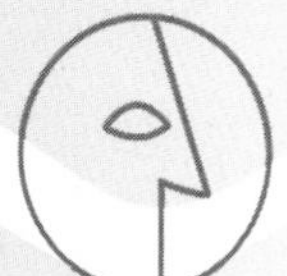

Understanding Yourself

What Needs Are Most Important to You?

Rank your responses for each of the following questions. The response that is most important or truest for you should receive a 5; the next should receive a 4; the next a 3; the next a 2; and the least important or least true should receive a 1. In the example below, for instance, the person prefers a mixture of social and solitary work and least likes working entirely alone.

Example: The Work I Like Best Involves:

5 **A** *Working alone.*
1 **B** *A mixture of time spent with people and time spent alone.*
4 **C** *Giving speeches.*
2 **D** *Discussion with others.*
3 **E** *Working outdoors.*

1. Overall, the most important thing to me about a job is whether or not:
   - *A* The pay is sufficient to meet my needs.
   - *B* It provides the opportunity for fellowship and good human relations.
   - *C* It is a secure job with good employee benefits.
   - *D* It allows me freedom and the chance to express myself.
   - *E* There is opportunity for advancement based on my achievements.
2. If I were to quit a job, it would probably be because:
   - *A* It was a dangerous job, such as working with inadequate equipment or poor safety procedures.
   - *B* Continued employment was questionable because of uncertainties in business conditions or funding sources.
   - *C* It was a job people looked down on.
   - *D* It was a one-person job, allowing little opportunity for discussion and interaction with others.
   - *E* The work lacked personal meaning to me.
3. For me, the most important regards in working are those that:
   - *A* Come from the work itself—important and challenging assignments.
   - *B* Satisfy the basic reasons why people work—good pay, a good home, and other economic needs.
   - *C* Are provided by fringe benefits—such as hospitalization insurance, time off for vacations, security for retirement, etc.
   - *D* Reflect my ability—such as being recognized for the work I do and knowing I am one of the best in my company or profession.
   - *E* Come from the human aspects of working—that is, the opportunity to make friends and to be a valued member of a team.
4. My morale would suffer most in a job in which:
   - *A* The future was unpredictable.
   - *B* Other employees received recognition, when I didn't, for doing the same quality of work.

Continued

C My coworkers were unfriendly or held grudges.

D I felt stifled and unable to grow.

E The job environment was poor—no air conditioning, inconvenient parking, insufficient space and lighting, primitive toilet facilities.

5. In deciding whether or not to accept a promotion, I would be most concerned with whether:

A The job was a source of pride and would be viewed with respect by others.

B Taking the job would constitute a gamble on my part, and I could lose more than I gained.

C The economic rewards would be favorable.

D I would like the new people I would be working with and whether we would get along.

E I would be able to explore new areas and do more creative work.

6. The kind of job that brings out my best is one in which:

A There is a family spirit among employees and we all share good times.

B The working conditions—equipment, materials, and basic surroundings—are physically safe.

C Management is understanding and there is little chance of losing my job.

D I can see the returns on my work from the standpoint of personal values.

E There is recognition for my achievement.

7. I would consider changing jobs if my present position:

A Did not offer security and fringe benefits.

B Did not provide a chance to learn and grow.

C Did not provide recognition for my performance.

D Did not allow close personal contacts.

E Did not provide economic rewards.

8. The job situation that would cause the most stress to me is:

A Having a serious disagreement with my coworkers.

B Working in an unsafe environment.

C Having an unpredictable supervisor.

D Not being able to express myself.

E Not being appreciated for the quality of my work.

9. I would accept a new position if:

A The position would be a test of my potential.

B The new job would offer better pay and physical surroundings.

C The new job would be secure and offer long-term fringe benefits.

D The position would be respected by others in my organization.

E Good relationships with coworkers and business associates were probable.

10. I would work overtime if:

A The work were challenging.

B I needed the extra income.

C My coworkers were also working overtime.

D I had to do it to keep my job.

E The company recognized my contribution.

Scoring: Place the values you gave A, B, C, D, and E for each question in the spaces provided in the scoring key below. Notice that the letters are not always in the same place. After placing all your values, add up each column and determine a total score for each of the motivation levels.

Scoring Key:

Question 1	A	C	B	E	D
Question 2	A	B	D	C	E
Question 3	B	C	E	D	A
Question 4	E	A	C	B	D
Question 5	C	B	D	A	E
Question 6	B	C	A	E	D
Question 7	E	A	D	C	B
Question 8	B	C	A	E	D
Question 9	B	C	E	D	A
Question 10	B	D	C	E	A
TOTAL SCORE					
	1	2	3	4	5
	MOTIVATION LEVELS				

What the Assessment Means: The five motivation levels correspond to the categories identified in Abraham Maslow's hierarchy of needs theory. The first level "1" corresponds to the physiological needs (food, shelter, water, etc.). Level 2, safety needs; level 3 social needs; level 4, esteem needs, and level 5, self-actualization needs. The levels that received the highest scores are the most important needs identified by you in your work. On the other hand, the lowest scores show that those needs have been relatively well satisfied or that they have been de-emphasized by you at this time.

Source: G. Manning and K. Curtis, *Human Behavior: Why People Do What They Do* (Cincinnati: Vista Systems/South-Western Publishing, 1988), pp. 17–20. With permission.

What does McGregor's analysis imply about motivation? The answer is best expressed in the framework presented by Maslow. Theory X assumes that physiological and safety needs dominate the individual. Theory Y assumes that social and esteem needs are dominant. McGregor himself held to the belief that the assumptions of Theory Y were more valid than those of Theory X. Therefore, he proposed that participation in decision making, responsible and challenging jobs, and good group relations would maximize work effort.

Unfortunately, there is no evidence to confirm that either set of assumptions is valid or that accepting Theory Y assumptions and altering one's actions accordingly will make one's employees more motivated. In the real world, there are examples of effective managers who make Theory X assumptions. For instance, Bob McCurry, vice president of Toyota's U.S. marketing operations, essentially follows Theory X. He drives his staff hard and uses a "crack-the-whip" style. Yet he has been extremely successful at increasing Toyota's market share in a highly competitive environment.

What Is Herzberg's Motivation-Hygiene Theory?

motivation-hygiene theory
Herzberg's theory that intrinsic factors are related to job satisfaction and extrinsic factors are related to job dissatisfaction.

The **motivation-hygiene theory** was proposed by psychologist Frederick Herzberg.[7] Believing that an individual's relation to his or her work is a basic one and that his or her attitude toward work can very well determine success or failure, Herzberg investigated the question What do people want from their jobs? He asked people to describe in detail situations in which they felt exceptionally good or bad about their jobs. Their responses were then tabulated and categorized. Exhibit 12-4 represents Herzberg's findings.

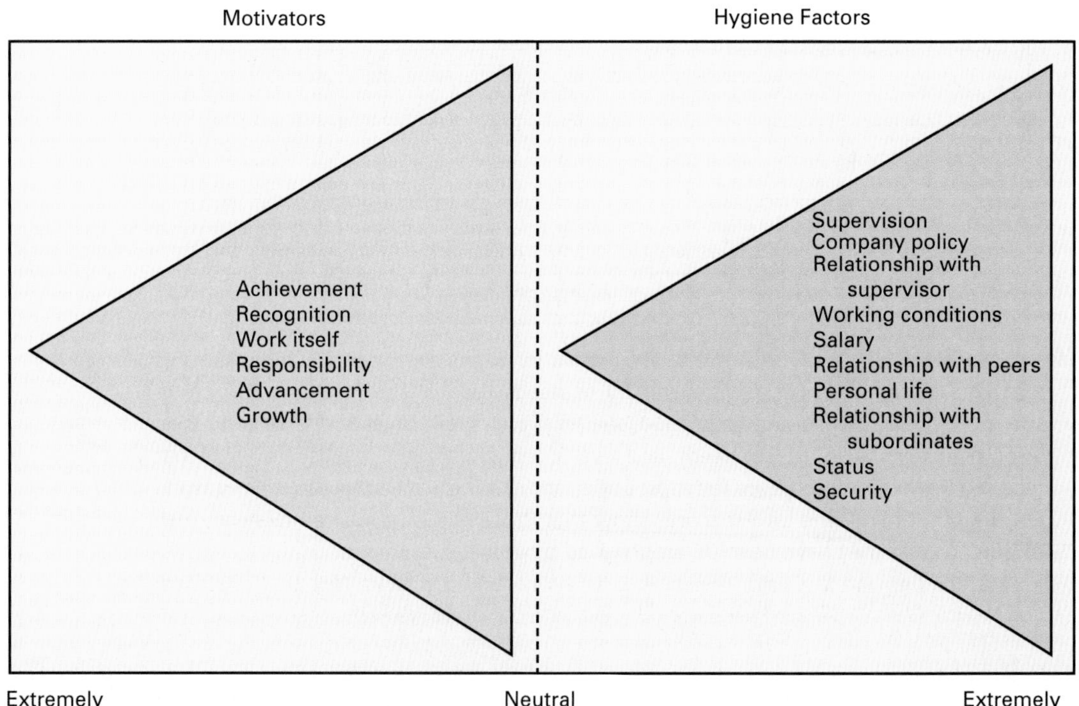

Exhibit 12-4
Herzberg's Motivation-Hygiene Theory

Pat Johnson, deli manager at Publix Super Markets, Inc., understands the difference between hygiene and motivating factors. Although the organization has a number of programs designed to "motivate" employees, its management is being accused of large-scale sex-discrimination. That is, women cannot break into the better-paying, higher-status management jobs. Because of the company's failure to address this hygiene factor, Publix's 50,000 female employees have filed a class action suit against the company and have become dissatisfied with the organization.

From analyzing the responses, Herzberg concluded that the replies people gave when they felt good about their jobs were significantly different from the replies they gave when they felt bad. As seen in Exhibit 12-4, certain characteristics were consistently related to job satisfaction (factors on the left side of the figure) and others to job dissatisfaction (the right side of the figure). Intrinsic factors such as achievement, recognition, and responsibility were related to job satisfaction. When the people questioned felt good about their work, they tended to attribute these characteristics to themselves. On the other hand, when they were dissatisfied, they tended to cite extrinsic factors such as company policy and administration, supervision, interpersonal relationships, and working conditions.

The data suggest, said Herzberg, that the opposite of satisfaction is not dissatisfaction, as was traditionally believed. Removing dissatisfying characteristics from a job does not necessarily make the job satisfying. As illustrated in Exhibit 12-5, Herzberg proposed that his findings indicate the existence of a dual continuum: The opposite of "satisfaction" is "no satisfaction," and the opposite of "dissatisfaction" is "no dissatisfaction."

According to Herzberg, the factors that lead to job satisfaction are separate and distinct from those that lead to job dissatisfaction. Therefore, managers who seek to eliminate factors that create job dissatisfaction can bring about peace but not necessarily motivation. They are placating their work force rather than motivating it. Because they don't motivate employees, the factors that eliminate job dissatisfaction were characterized by

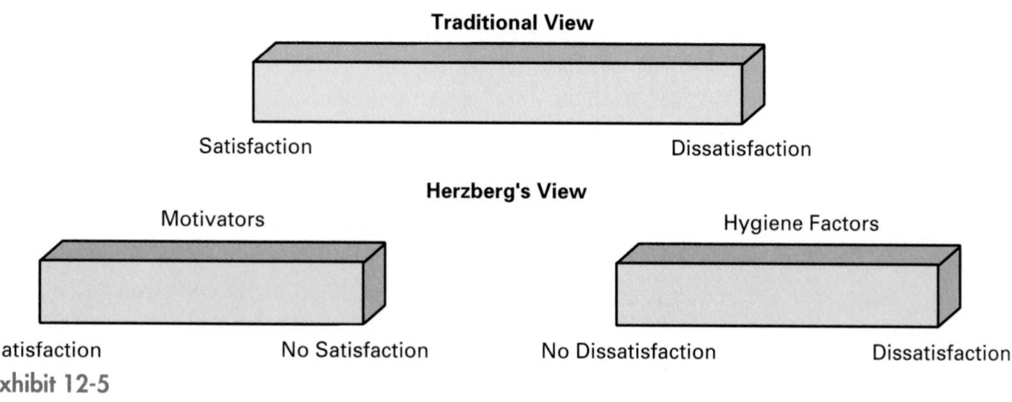

Exhibit 12-5
Contrasting Views of Satisfaction-Dissatisfaction

hygiene factors
Herzberg's term for factors, such as working conditions and salary, that, when adequate, may eliminate job dissatisfaction but do not necessarily increase job satisfaction.

motivators
Herzberg's term for factors, such as recognition and growth, that increase job satisfaction.

Herzberg as **hygiene factors.** When these factors are adequate, people will not be dissatisfied; but neither will they be satisfied. To motivate people on their jobs, Herzberg suggested emphasizing **motivators,** those factors that increase job satisfaction.

The motivation-hygiene theory is not without its detractors. The criticisms of the theory include the methodology Herzberg used to collect data and his failure to account for situational variables.[8] Regardless of any criticism, Herzberg's theory has been widely popularized, and few managers are unfamiliar with his recommendations. Much of the enthusiasm for job enrichment, cited in Chapter 6, can be attributed to Herzberg's findings and recommendations.

Contemporary Theories of Motivation

Although the previous theories are well known, they unfortunately have not held up well under close examination. However, all is not lost. Some contemporary theories have one thing in common: Each has a reasonable degree of valid supporting documentation. The following theories represent the current "state-of-the-art" explanations of employee motivation.

three-needs theory
McClelland's theory that the needs for achievement, power, and affiliation are major motives in work.

need for achievement *(nAch)*
The drive to excel, to achieve in relation to a set of standards, and to strive to succeed.

need for power *(nPow)*
The need to make others behave in a way that they would not have behaved otherwise.

need for affiliation *(nAff)*
The desire for friendly and close interpersonal relationships.

What Is McClelland's Three-Needs Theory?

David McClelland and others have proposed the **three-needs theory,** which maintains that there are three major relevant motives or needs in work situations:

1. **Need for achievement *(nAch).*** The drive to excel, to achieve in relation to a set of standards, to strive to succeed
2. **Need for power *(nPow).*** The need to make others behave in a way that they would not have behaved otherwise
3. **Need for affiliation *(nAff).*** The desire for friendly and close interpersonal relationships.[9]

Some people have a compelling drive to succeed, but they are striving for personal achievement rather than for the rewards of success per se *(nAch)*. They have a desire to do something better or more efficiently than it has been done before. This drive is the need for achievement. From research concerning the achievement need, McClelland found that high achievers differentiate themselves from others by their desire to do things better.[10] They seek situations in which they can attain personal responsibility for finding solutions to problems, in which they can receive rapid and unambiguous feedback on their performance in order to tell whether they are improving or not, and in which they can set moderately challenging goals (see Details on a Management Classic). High achievers are not gamblers; they dislike succeeding by chance. They prefer the challenge of working at a problem and accepting the personal responsibility for success or failure rather than leaving the outcome to chance or the actions of others. An important point is that they avoid what they perceive to be very easy or very difficult tasks.

High achievers are not gamblers; they dislike succeeding by chance. They prefer the challenge of working at a problem and accepting the personal responsibility for success or failure rather than leaving the outcome to chance or the actions of others.

The need for power *(nPow)* is the desire to have impact and to be influential. Individuals high in nPow enjoy being "in charge," strive for influence over others, and prefer to be in competitive and status-oriented situations. The third need isolated by McClelland is affiliation *(nAff)*, which is the desire to be liked and accepted by others. This

What characteristics best describe Nina Liu, a kindergarten and first-grade teacher? Research tells us that as a high achiever, Nina is not a gambler; she dislikes succeeding by chance. She prefers the challenge of encouraging her students to learn and accepting the personal responsibility for making this happen.

need has received the least attention by researchers. Individuals with high nAff strive for friendships, prefer cooperative situations rather than competitive ones, and desire relationships involving a high degree of mutual understanding.

How Do Inputs and Outcomes Influence Motivation?

Employees don't work in a vacuum. They make comparisons. If someone offered you $60,000 a year on your first job upon graduation from college, you would probably grab the offer and report to work enthusiastic and certainly satisfied with your pay. How would you react if you found out a month or so into the job that a coworker—another recent graduate, your age, with comparable grades from a comparable college—was getting $70,000 a year? You probably would be upset! Even though, in absolute terms, $60,000 is a lot of money for a new graduate to make (and you know it!), that suddenly would not be the issue. The issue would now center on relative rewards and what you believe is fair. There is considerable evidence that employees make comparisons of their job inputs and outcomes relative to others and that inequities influence the degree of effort that employees exert.[11]

equity theory
Adams's theory that employees perceive what they get from a job situation (outcomes) in relation to what they put into it (inputs) and then compare their inputs-outcomes ratio with the inputs-outcomes ratios of relevant others.

Developed by J. Stacey Adams, **equity theory** says that employees perceive what they get from a job situation (outcomes) in relation to what they put into it (inputs) and then compare their inputs-outcomes ratio with the inputs-outcomes ratios of relevant others. This relation is shown in Exhibit 12-6. If they perceive their ratio to be equal to those of the relevant others with whom they compare themselves, a state of equity exists. They perceive that their situation is fair—that justice prevails. If the ratios are unequal, inequity exists; that is, they view themselves as underrewarded or overrewarded. When inequities occur, employees attempt to correct them.

Exhibit 12-6
Equity Theory Relationships

PERCEIVED RATIO COMPARISON*	EMPLOYEE'S ASSESSMENT
$\frac{\text{Outcomes A}}{\text{Inputs A}} < \frac{\text{Outcomes B}}{\text{Inputs B}}$	Inequity (underrewarded)
$\frac{\text{Outcomes A}}{\text{Inputs A}} = \frac{\text{Outcomes B}}{\text{Inputs B}}$	Equity
$\frac{\text{Outcomes A}}{\text{Inputs A}} > \frac{\text{Outcomes B}}{\text{Inputs B}}$	Inequity (overrewarded)

*Person A is the employee, and Person B is a relevant other or referrent.

Details on a Management Classic

David McClelland and the Three-Needs Theory

David McClelland's work in helping to understand motivation in organizational settings focused on aspects of personality characteristics. Much of his research centered on achievement, power, and affiliation orientations. Of the three needs, McClelland found that some people have a compelling drive to succeed for personal achievement rather than for the rewards of success per se. The questions then are How do you find out if someone is, for instance, a high achiever, and What effect can that person's need for achievement have on an organization?

In his research, McClelland would give individuals a projective test in which subjects responded to a set of pictures. Each picture was briefly shown to a subject, who then wrote a story based on the picture. The responses generated were then classified by McClelland as focusing on a need for achievement, power, or affiliation. Those who had a high need for achievement, however, shared some similar attributes.

High achievers perform best when they perceive their probability of success as being 0.5—that is, when they estimate they have a 50–50 chance of success. They dislike gambling when the odds are high because they get no achievement satisfaction from happenstance success. Similarly, they dislike low odds (high probability of success) because then there is no challenge to their skills. They like to set goals that require stretching themselves a little. When there is an approximately equal chance of success or failure, there is optimum opportunity to experience feelings of successful accomplishment and satisfaction in their efforts.

On the basis of an extensive amount of research, some reasonably well-supported predictions can be made between the relationship of the achievement need and job performance. Though less research has been done on power and affiliation needs, there are consistent findings in those areas too. First, individuals with a high need to achieve prefer job situations with personal responsibility, feedback, and an intermediate degree of risk. When these characteristics are prevalent, high achievers are strongly motivated. The evidence consistently demonstrates, for instance, that high achievers are successful in entrepreneurial activities such as running their own business, managing a self-contained unit within a large organization, and many sales positions.[12] Second, a high need to achieve does not necessarily lead to being a good manager, especially in large organizations. A high nAch salesperson at Hitachi Ltd. does not necessarily make a good sales manager, and good managers in large organizations such as General Electric, Glaxo Wellcome, or Unilever do not necessarily have a high need to achieve.[13] Third, the needs for affiliation and power are closely related to managerial success.[14] The best managers are high in the need for power and low in the need for affiliation. Last, employees can be trained successfully to stimulate their achievement need.[15] If a job calls for a high achiever, management can select a person with a high nAch or develop its own candidate through achievement training.

The **referent** with whom employees choose to compare themselves is an important variable in equity theory.[16] The three referent categories have been classified as "other," "system," and "self." The *other* category includes other individuals with similar jobs in the same organization and also includes friends, neighbors, or professional associates. On the basis of information they receive through word of mouth, newspapers, and magazine articles on issues such as executive salaries or a recent union contract, employees compare their pay with that of others.

referent
In equity theory, the other persons, the systems, or the personal experiences against which individuals compare themselves to assess equity.

The *system* category considers organizational pay policies and procedures and the administration of that system. It considers organizationwide pay policies, both implied and explicit. Patterns by the organization in terms of allocation of pay are major determinants in this category.

The *self* category refers to inputs-outcomes ratios that are unique to the individual. It reflects past personal experiences and contacts. This category is influenced by criteria such as past jobs or family commitments.

The choice of a particular set of referents is related to the information available about referents as well as to their perceived relevance. On the basis of equity theory, when employees perceive an inequity, they might (1) distort either their own or others' inputs or outcomes, (2) behave in some way to induce others to change their inputs or outcomes, (3) behave in some way to change their own inputs or outcomes, (4) choose a different comparison referent, and/or (5) quit their job.

Equity theory recognizes that individuals are concerned not only with the absolute rewards they receive for their efforts but also with the relationship of those rewards to what others receive. They make judgments concerning the relationship between their inputs and outcomes and the inputs and outcomes of others. On the basis of one's inputs, such as effort, experience, education, and competence, one compares outcomes such as salary levels, raises, recognition, and other factors. When people perceive an imbalance in their inputs-outcomes ratio relative to those of others, they experience tension. This tension provides the basis for motivation as people strive for what they perceive as equity and fairness.

The theory establishes the four propositions relating to inequitable pay. These propositions, listed in Exhibit 12-7, have generally proven to be correct.[17] A review of the research consistently confirms the equity thesis: Employee motivation is influenced significantly by relative rewards as well as by absolute rewards. Whenever employees perceive inequity, they will act to correct the situation.[18] The result might be lower or higher productivity, improved or reduced quality of output, increased absenteeism, or voluntary resignation.

Equity theory recognizes that individuals are concerned not only with the absolute rewards they receive for their efforts but also with the relationship of these rewards to what others receive.

From the discussion above, however, we should not conclude that equity theory is without problems. The theory leaves some key issues still unclear.[19] For instance, how do employees define inputs and outcomes? How do they combine and weigh their inputs and outcomes to arrive at totals? When and how do the factors change over time? Regardless of these problems, equity theory has an impressive amount of research support and offers us some important insights into employee motivation.

expectancy theory
Vroom's theory that an individual tends to act in a certain way in the expectation that the act will be followed by a given outcome and according to the attractiveness of that outcome.

Why Is Expectancy Theory Considered a Comprehensive Theory of Motivation?

Currently the most comprehensive explanation of motivation is Victor Vroom's **expectancy theory.**[20] Though it has its critics,[21] most of the research evidence is supportive of the theory.[22]

- **1. Given payment by time, overrewarded employees will produce more than equitably paid employees.** Hourly and salaried employees will generate a high quantity or quality of production in order to increase the input side of the ratio and bring about equity.
- **2. Given payment by quantity of production, overrewarded employees will produce fewer but higher-quality units than equitably paid employees.** Individuals paid on a piece-rate basis will increase their effort to achieve equity, which can result in greater quality or quantity. However, increases in quantity will only increase inequity, since every unit produced results in further overpayment. Therefore, effort is directed toward increasing quality rather than quantity.
- **3. Given payment by time, underrewarded employees will produce less or poorer-quality output.** Effort will be decreased, which will bring about lower productivity or poorer-quality output than equitably paid subjects.
- **4. Given payment by quantity of production, underrewarded employees will produce a large number of low-quality units in comparison with equitably paid employees.** Employees on piece-rate pay plans can bring about equity because trading off quality of output for quantity will result in an increase in rewards with little or no increase in contributions.

Exhibit 12-7
Equity Theory Propositions

Expectancy theory states that an individual tends to act in a certain way on the basis of the expectation that the act will be followed by a given outcome and the attractiveness of that outcome to the individual. It includes three variables or relationships:

- **1.** *Effort-performance linkage.* The probability perceived by the individual that exerting a given amount of effort will lead to performance
- **2.** *Performance-reward linkage.* The degree to which the individual believes that performing at a particular level will lead to the attainment of a desired outcome
- **3.** *Attractiveness.* The importance that the individual places on the potential outcome or reward that can be achieved on the job. This considers the goals and needs of the individual.[23]

Although this might sound complex, it really is not that difficult to visualize. It can be summed up in the following questions: How hard do I have to work to achieve a certain level of performance, and can I actually achieve that level? What reward will performing at that level get me? How attractive is this reward to me, and does it help achieve my goals? Whether one has the desire to produce at any given time depends on one's particular goals and one's perception of the relative worth of performance as a path to the attainment of those goals.

How Does Expectancy Theory Work? Exhibit 12-8 shows a very simple version of expectancy theory that expresses its major contentions. The strength of a person's motivation to perform (effort) depends on how strongly that individual believes that he or she can achieve what is being attempted. If this goal is achieved (performance), will he or she be adequately rewarded by the organization? If so, will the reward satisfy his or her individual goals? Let us consider the four steps inherent in the theory and then attempt to apply it.

First, what perceived outcomes does the job offer the employee? Outcomes may be positive: pay, security, companionship, trust, employee benefits, a chance to use talent or skills, or congenial relationships. On the other hand, employees may view the

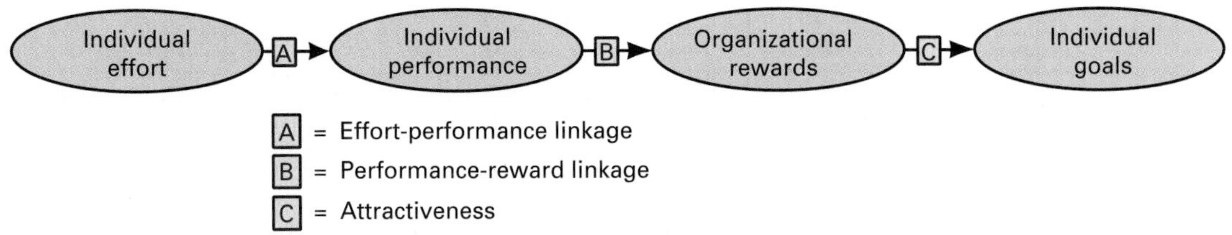

Exhibit 12-8
Simplified Expectancy Theory

outcomes as negative: fatigue, boredom, frustration, anxiety, harsh supervision, or threat of dismissal. Reality is not relevant here: The critical issue is what the individual employee perceives the outcome to be, regardless of whether his or her perceptions are accurate.

Second, how attractive do employees consider these outcomes to be? Are they valued positively, negatively, or neutrally? This obviously is an internal issue and considers the individual's personal attitudes, personality, and needs. The individual who finds a particular outcome attractive—that is, values it positively—would rather attain it than not attain it. Others may find it negative and therefore prefer not attaining it to attaining it. Still others may be neutral.

Third, what kind of behavior must the employee exhibit to achieve these outcomes? The outcomes are not likely to have any effect on an individual employee's performance unless the employee knows, clearly and unambiguously, what he or she must do to achieve them. For example, what is "doing well" in terms of performance appraisal? What criteria will be used to judge the employee's performance?

Fourth and last, how does the employee view his or her chances of doing what is asked? After the employee has considered his or her own competencies and ability to control those variables that will determine success, what probability does he or she place on successful attainment?[24]

How Can Expectancy Theory Be Applied? Let's use a classroom analogy as an illustration of how one can use expectancy theory to explain motivation.

Most students prefer an instructor who tells them what is expected of them in the course. They want to know what the assignments and examinations will be like, when they are due or to be taken, and how much weight each carries in the final term grade. They also like to think that the amount of effort they exert in attending classes, taking notes, and studying will be reasonably related to the grade they will make in the course. Let's assume that you, as a student, feel this way. Consider that five weeks into a class you are really enjoying (we'll call it MNGT 301), an examination is given back to you. You studied hard for this examination, and you have consistently made A's and B's on examinations in other courses in which you have expended similar effort. The reason you work so hard is to make top grades, which you believe are important for getting a good job upon graduation. Also, you are not sure, but you might want to go on to graduate school. Again, you think grades are important for getting into a good graduate school.

Well, the results of that first examination are in. The class average was 76. Ten percent of the class scored an 88 or higher and got an A. Your grade was 54; the minimum passing mark was 60. You're mad. You're frustrated. Even more, you're perplexed. How could you possibly have done so poorly on the examination when you usually score in the top range in other classes by preparing as you did for this one?

Several interesting things are immediately evident in your behavior. Suddenly, you may no longer be driven to attend MNGT 301 classes regularly. You may find several reasons why you don't want to study for the course either. When you do attend classes, you may find yourself daydreaming—the result is an empty notebook instead of several pages of notes. One would probably be correct in describing you as "lacking in motivation" in MNGT 301. Why did your motivation level change? You know and we know, but let's explain it in expectancy terms.

If we use Exhibit 12-8 to understand this situation, we might say the following: Studying for MNGT 301 (effort) is conditioned by the resulting correct answers on the examination (performance), which will produce a high grade (reward), which will lead, in turn, to the security, prestige, and other benefits that accrue from obtaining a good job (individual goal).

These employees of the Fantastic Foods Company, based in Petaluma, California, recognize that their employer makes every attempt to link their rewards to their work effort. By performing their duties, employees are able to achieve rewards they value, which in turn, makes them even more productive. One of Fantastic Foods' secrets is to let these employees know what is expected of them, hold them accountable for completing their tasks, and let them evaluate their own work. This freedom and the learning environment have not only enabled employees to build their self-esteem but also have energized them to exert high levels of effort.

The attractiveness of the outcome, which in this case is a good grade, is high. But what about the performance-reward linkage? Do you feel that the grade you received truly reflects your knowledge of the material? In other words, did the test fairly measure what you know? If the answer is Yes, then this linkage is strong. If the answer is No, then at least part of the reason for your reduced motivational level is your belief that the test was not a fair measure of your performance. If the test was an essay type, maybe you believe that the instructor's grading method was poor. Was too much weight placed on a question that you thought was trivial? Maybe the instructor does not like you and was biased in grading your paper. These are examples of perceptions that influence the performance-reward linkage and your level of motivation.

Another possible demotivating force may be the effort-performance relationship. If, after you took the examination, you believe that you could not have passed it regardless of the amount of preparation you had done, then your desire to study may drop. Possibly, the instructor wrote the examination under the assumption that you had a considerably broader background in the subject matter. Maybe the course had several prerequisites that you did not know about, or possibly you had the prerequisites but took them several years ago. The result is the same: You place a low value on your effort leading to answering the examination questions correctly; hence, your motivational level decreases, and you lessen your effort.

Can we relate this classroom analogy to a work setting? In other words, what does expectancy theory say that can help us motivate our employees? To answer that question, let's summarize some of the issues surrounding the theory. First, expectancy theory emphasizes payoffs, or rewards. As a result, managers have to believe that the rewards they offer will align with what the employee wants. As such, it is a theory based on self-interest, wherein each individual seeks to maximize his or her expected satisfaction.[25] Second, expectancy theory stresses that managers understand why employees view certain outcomes as attractive or unattractive. They will want to reward individuals with those things they value positively. Third, the expectancy theory emphasizes expected behaviors. Do individuals know what is expected of them and how they will be appraised? Unless employees see this connection between performance and rewards, organizational goals may not be met. Finally, the theory is concerned with perceptions. What is realistic is irrelevant. An individual's own perceptions of performance, reward, and goal-satisfaction outcomes will determine his or her level of effort, not the objective outcomes themselves. Accordingly, there must be continuous feedback to align perceptions with reality.

How Can We Integrate the Contemporary Theories of Motivation?

There is a tendency to view the motivation theories in this chapter independently. Doing so is a mistake. Many of the ideas underlying the theories are complementary, and your understanding of how to motivate people is maximized when you see how the theories fit together.[26]

Exhibit 12-9 presents a model that integrates much of what we know about motivation. Its basic foundation is the simplified expectancy model shown in Exhibit 12-8. Let's work through Exhibit 12-9, beginning at the left.

The individual effort box has an arrow leading into it. This arrow flows out of the individual's goals. This goals-effort loop is meant to remind us that goals direct behavior. Expectancy theory predicts that an employee will exert a high level of effort if he or she perceives that there is a strong relationship between effort and performance, performance and rewards, and rewards and satisfaction of personal goals. Each of these relationships, in turn, is influenced by certain factors. For effort to lead to good performance,

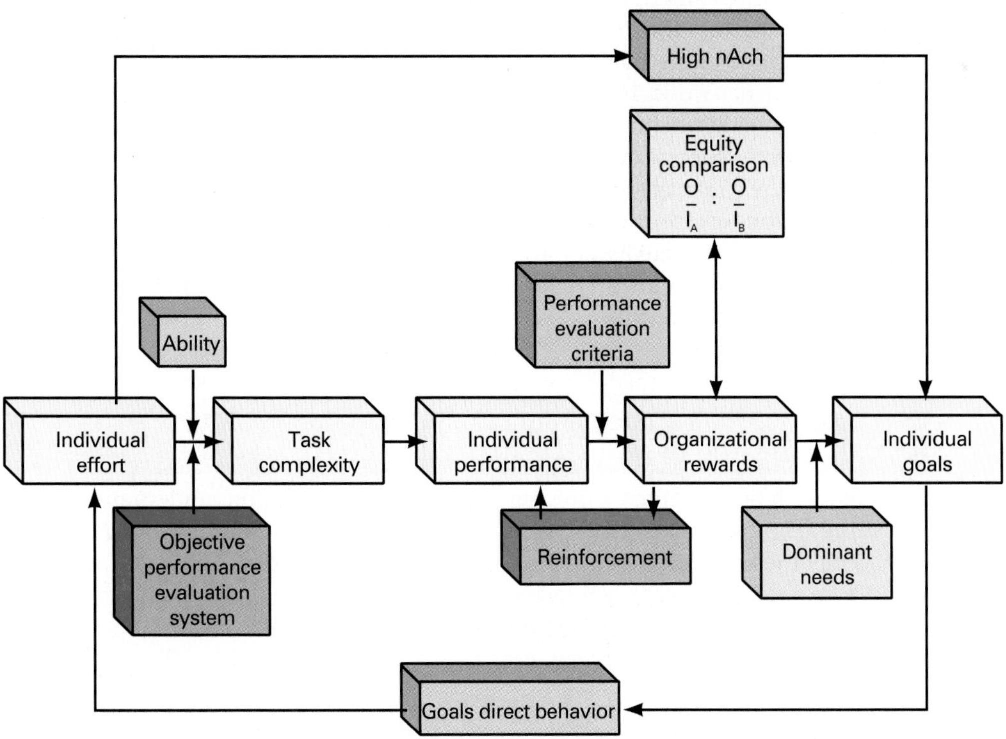

Exhibit 12-9
Integrating Theories of Motivation

the individual must have the requisite ability to perform, and the performance-evaluation system that measures the individual's performance must be perceived as being fair and objective. The performance-reward relationship will be strong if the individual perceives that it is performance (rather than seniority, personal favorites, or other criteria) that is rewarded. Thus, if management has designed a reward system that is seen by employees as "paying off" for good performance, the rewards will reinforce and encourage continued good performance. The final link in expectancy theory is the rewards-goals relationship. Need theories would come into play at this point. Motivation would be high to the degree that the rewards an individual received for his or her high performance satisfied the dominant needs consistent with his or her individual goals.

A closer look at Exhibit 12-9 will also reveal that the model considers the need for achievement, equity, and the job characteristics model (the JCM was discussed in Chapter 6) theories. The high achiever is not motivated by the organization's assessment of his or her performance or organizational rewards, hence the jump from effort to individual goals for those with a high nAch. Remember that high achievers are internally driven as long as the jobs they are doing provide them with personal responsibility, feedback, and moderate risks. They are not concerned with the effort-performance, performance-rewards, or rewards-goal linkages. Rewards also play the key part in equity theory. Individuals will compare the rewards (outcomes) they receive from the inputs they make with the inputs-outcomes ratio of relevant others ($O/I_A:O/I_B$), and inequities may influence the effort expended.

Finally, we can see the JCM in this exhibit. Task characteristics (job design) influence job motivation at two places. First, jobs that score high in motivating potential are likely to lead to higher actual job performance since the employee's motivation is stimulated by the job itself. So jobs that are high in complexity (that is, have motivating potential) increase the linkage between effort and performance. Second, jobs that score high in motivating potential also increase an employee's control over key elements in his or her work. Therefore, jobs that offer autonomy, feedback, and similar complex task characteristics help to satisfy the individual goals of those employees who desire greater control over their work.[27]

If you were a manager concerned with motivating your employees, what specific recommendations could you draw from this integration? Although there is no simple, all-encompassing set of guidelines, we offer the following suggestions, which draw on the essence of what these theories have taught us about motivating employees (see Developing a Management Skill).

Contemporary Issues in Motivation

Although we have presented a number of theories of motivation, understanding and predicting employee motivation continues to be one of the most popular areas in management research. Many of the current studies of employee motivation are influenced by several significant workplace issues. These include motivating a diversified work force, pay-for-performance programs, employee stock option programs, and motivating minimum-wage employees. Let's take a closer look at each of these issues.

What Is the Key to Motivating a Diverse Work Force?

To maximize motivation among today's diversified work force, management needs to think in terms of *flexibility*.[28] For instance, studies tell us that men place considerably more importance on having autonomy in their jobs than do women. In contrast, the

Developing a Management Skill
MOTIVATING EMPLOYEES

About the Skill: *There is no simple, all-encompassing set of motivational guidelines, but the following suggestions draw on the essence of what we know about motivating employees.*[29]

Steps in practicing the skill

1. ***Recognize individual differences.*** Almost every contemporary motivation theory recognizes that employees are not homogeneous. They have different needs. They also differ in terms of attitudes, personality, and other important individual variables.

2. ***Match people to jobs.*** There is a great deal of evidence showing the motivational benefits of carefully matching people to jobs. People who lack the necessary skills to perform successfully will be disadvantaged.

3. ***Use goals.*** You should ensure that employees have hard, specific goals and feedback on how well they are doing in pursuit of those goals. In many cases, these goals should be participatively set.

4. ***Ensure that goals are perceived as attainable.*** Regardless of whether goals are actually attainable, employees who see goals as unattainable will reduce their effort. Be sure, therefore, that employees feel confident that increased efforts can lead to achieving performance goals.

5. ***Individualize rewards.*** Because employees have different needs, what acts as a reinforcer for one may not for another. Use your knowledge of employee differences to individualize the rewards over which you have control. Some of the more obvious rewards that you can allocate include pay, promotions, autonomy, and the opportunity to participate in goal setting and decision making.

6. ***Link rewards to performance.*** You need to make rewards contingent on performance. Rewarding factors other than performance will only reinforce those other factors. Key rewards such as pay increases and promotions should be given for the attainment of employees' specific goals.

7. ***Check the system for equity.*** Employees should perceive that rewards or outcomes are equal to the inputs given. On a simplistic level, experience, ability, effort, and other obvious inputs should explain differences in pay, responsibility, and other obvious outcomes.

8. ***Don't ignore money.*** It's easy to get so caught up in setting goals, creating interesting jobs, and providing opportunities for participation that you forget that money is a major reason why most people work. Thus, the allocation of performance-based wage increases, piecework bonuses, employee stock ownership plans, and other pay incentives are important in determining employee motivation.

opportunity to learn, convenient work hours, and good interpersonal relations are more important to women than to men.[30] Managers need to recognize that what motivates a single mother with two dependent children who is working full-time to support her family may be very different from the needs of a young, single, part-time worker or the older employee who is working to supplement his or her pension income. Employees have different personal needs and goals that they're hoping to satisfy through their job. The offer of various types of rewards to meet their diverse needs can be highly motivating for employees.[31] We have seen some of these before. For instance, family-friendly benefits and flexible work schedules (see Chapter 6) are a response to the varied needs of a diverse work force.[32]

To maximize motivation among today's diversified work force, management needs to think in terms of flexibility.

Motivating a diverse work force also means that managers must be flexible by being aware of *cultural* differences. The theories of motivation we have been studying were developed largely by U.S. psychologists and were validated by studying American workers. Therefore, these theories need to be modified for different cultures.[33]

For instance, the self-interest concept is consistent with capitalism and the extremely high value placed on individualism in countries such as the United States. Because almost all the motivation theories presented in this chapter are based on the self-interest motive, they should be applicable to employees in such countries as Great Britain and Australia, where capitalism and individualism are highly valued. In more-collectivist nations—such as Venezuela, Singapore, Japan, and Mexico—the link to the organization is the individual's loyalty to the organization or society, rather than his or her self-interest. Employees in collectivist cultures should be more receptive to team-based job design, group goals, and group-performance evaluations. Reliance on the fear of being fired in such cultures is likely to be less effective, even if the laws in those countries allow managers to fire employees.

The need-for-achievement concept provides another example of a motivation theory with a U.S. bias. The view that a high need for achievement acts as an internal motivator presupposes the existence of two cultural characteristics: a willingness to accept a moderate degree of risk and a concern with performance. These characteristics would exclude countries with high uncertainty avoidance scores and high quality-of-life ratings. The remaining countries are exclusively Anglo-American countries such as New Zealand, South Africa, Ireland, the United States, and Canada.

Results, however, of several recent studies among employees in countries other than the United States indicate that some aspects of motivation theory are transferable.[34] For instance, motivational techniques presented earlier in this chapter were shown to be effective in changing performance-related behaviors of Russian textile mill workers. However, we should not assume that motivation concepts are universally applicable. Managers must change their motivational techniques to fit their culture.[35] The technique used by a large department store in Xian, China—recognizing and embarrassing the worst sales clerks by giving them awards—may be effective in China,[36] but doing something that humiliates employees isn't likely to work in North America or Western Europe.

Should Employees Be Paid for Performance or Time on the Job?

What's in it for me? That's a question every person consciously or unconsciously asks before engaging in any form of behavior. Our knowledge of motivation tells us that people do what they do to satisfy some need. Before they do anything, therefore, they look for a payoff or reward. Although there may be many different rewards offered by organizations, most of us are concerned with earning an amount of money that allows us to satisfy our needs and wants. Because pay is an important variable in motivation as one type of reward, we need to look at how we can use pay to motivate high levels of employee performance. This concern explains the intent and logic behind pay-for-performance programs.

pay-for-performance programs
Compensation plans, such as piece-rate plans, profit sharing, and the like, that pay employees on the basis of some performance measure.

Pay-for-performance programs, like the one used at FormPac, are compensation plans that pay employees on the basis of some performance measure.[37] Piece-rate plans, gainsharing, wage incentive plans, profit sharing, and lump sum bonuses are examples of pay-for-performance programs.[38] What differentiates these forms of pay from the more traditional compensation plans is that instead of paying an employee for *time* on the job, pay is adjusted to reflect some *performance* measures. These performance measures might include such things as individual productivity, team or work group productivity, departmental productivity, or the overall organization's profits for a given period.[39]

Performance-based compensation is probably most compatible with expectancy theory. That is, employees should perceive a strong relationship between their performance and the rewards they receive if motivation is to be maximized. If rewards are allocated solely on nonperformance factors—such as seniority, job title, or across-the-board cost-of-living raises—then employees are likely to reduce their efforts.[40]

Rewarding employees for certain performance measures can take on various meanings. Employees at Southwest Airlines, for example, are evaluated in part for how they foster a fun atmosphere for customers. Here, this Southwest flight attendant surprises a passenger to "liven things up" before the plane's departure.

Pay-for-performance programs are gaining in popularity in organizations. One survey of 2,000 companies found that almost 70 percent of firms surveyed were practicing some form of pay-for-performance for salaried employees.[41] The growing popularity can be explained in terms of both motivation and cost control. From a motivation perspective, making some or all of a worker's pay conditional on performance measures focuses his or her attention and effort on that measure, then reinforces the continuation of that effort with rewards. However, if the employee, team, or the organization's performance declines, so too does the reward.[42] Thus, there is an incentive to keep efforts and motivation strong. For instance, employees at Hallmark Cards, Inc., in Kansas City, have up to 10 percent of their pay at risk. Depending on their productivity on such performance measures as customer satisfaction, retail sales, and profits, employees can turn that 10 percent into rewards as high as 25 percent.[43] However, failure to reach the performance measures can result in the forfeiture of the 10 percent of salary placed at risk. Companies such as Saturn, Steelcase, TRW, Hewlett-Packard, du Pont, and Ameri-Tech use similar formulas, in which employee compensation is composed of base and reward pay.[44] On the cost-savings side, performance-based bonuses and other incentive rewards avoid the fixed expense of permanent—and often annual—salary increases. The bonuses do not accrue to base salary—which means that the amount is not compounded in future years. As a result, they save the company money!

A recent extension of the pay-for-performance concept is called **competency-based compensation.** A competency-based compensation program pays and rewards employees on the basis of the skills, knowledge, or behaviors employees possess.[45] These competencies may include such behaviors and skills as leadership, problem solving, decision making, or strategic planning. Pay levels are established on the basis of the degree to which these competencies exist. Pay increases in a competency-based system are awarded for growth in personal competencies as well as for the contributions one makes to the overall organization.[46] Accordingly, an employee's rewards are tied directly to how capable he or she is of contributing to the achievement of the organization's goals and objectives.

competency-based compensation
A program that pays and rewards employees on the basis of skills, knowledge, or behaviors they possess.

How Can Employee Stock Ownership Plans Affect Motivation?

Many companies are using employee stock ownership plans for improving and motivating employee performance. An **employee stock ownership plan (ESOP)** is a compensation program in which employees become part owners of the organization

employee stock ownership plan (ESOP)
A compensation program in which employees become part owners of the organization by receiving stock as a performance incentive.

by receiving stock as a performance incentive. More than 10 million employees in such companies as United Airlines, British Petroleum, Avis, NationsBank, Pfizer, Owens Corning, Weirton Steel, and Starbucks participate in ESOPs.[47] Also, many ESOPs allow employees to purchase additional stocks at attractive, below-market prices. Under an ESOP, employees often are motivated to give more effort because it makes them owners who will share in any gains and losses. The fruits of their labors are no longer just going into the pockets of some unknown owners—the employees are the owners!

Do ESOPs positively affect productivity and employee satisfaction? The answer appears to be Yes! The research on ESOPs indicates that they increase employee satisfaction and frequently result in higher performance.[48] For instance, one study compared forty-five ESOP companies against 238 companies that did not have ESOPs. The ESOP firms outperformed the non-ESOP organizations in terms of both employment and sales growth.[49] Other studies showed that productivity in organizations with ESOPs does increase, but the impact is greater the longer the ESOP has been in existence.[50] So organizations should not expect immediate increases in employee motivation and productivity if an ESOP is implemented. But, over time, employee productivity and satisfaction should go up. Other studies also show that ESOPs work better in smaller, private firms where "worker-input issues are easier to handle."[51]

Although ESOPs have the potential to increase employee satisfaction and work motivation, employees need to psychologically experience ownership in order to realize that potential (see Managers Who Made a Difference).[52] What this means is that in addition to merely having a financial stake in the organization, employees need to be regularly informed on the status of the business to have the opportunity to exercise influence over the operation. When these conditions are met, "employees will be more satisfied with their jobs, more satisfied with their organizational identification, motivated to come to work, and motivated to perform well while at work."[53]

Can Managers Motivate Minimum-Wage Employees?

Imagine for a moment that your first managerial job after graduating from college involves overseeing a group made up of minimum-wage employees. Offering more pay to these employees for high levels of performance is out of the question. Your company just can't afford it. What are your motivational options at this point?[54] One of the toughest motivational challenges facing many managers today is how to achieve high performance levels among minimum-wage workers.

One trap many managers fall into is thinking that employees are motivated only by money. Although money is important as a motivator, it's not the only "reward" that people seek and that managers can use. In motivating minimum-wage employees, managers should look at other types of rewards that help motivate employees. What are some other types of rewards that managers can use? Many companies use employee recognition programs such as employee of the month, quarterly employee-performance award ceremonies, or other celebrations of employee accomplishment.[55] For instance, at many fast-food restaurants such as McDonald's and Wendy's, you'll often see plaques hanging in prominent places that feature the "Crew Member of the Month." These types of programs serve the purpose of highlighting employees whose work performance has been of the type and level the organization wants to encourage. Many managers also recognize the power of praise. When praise is used, you need

Managers Who Made a Difference

STEVEN FORTH, EXECUTIVE DIRECTOR, FACT INTERNATIONAL, INC.

In 1990, Steven Forth returned to Vancouver, British Columbia, after spending a decade abroad. His time overseas was spent working a variety of odd jobs in the publishing field—specializing in "international rights for Japanese publishing companies."[56] You would think that his experience would have been helpful in starting his career when he returned to Vancouver. But all he got was advice from prospective employers—"with all that experience, become a tour guide." That's advice that Forth simply ignored.

Instead, in 1992, he started his own company, Fact International, Inc. This organization specializes in providing customized software for companies in East Asia. Its main market niche is in translating software programs developed elsewhere in the world—for example, in the United States—into useful forms residents in East Asia can use. The company has been growing at 80 to 100 percent a year—a rate that Forth, himself, agrees is too fast. Nonetheless, the $2 million in sales in 1995 were welcomed by all. And this growth is being achieved with fewer than twenty-five employees—individuals from such countries as Poland, Greece, Turkey, China, Japan, and Canada.

The irony behind Fact International's success is that none of the company's employees earn more than $50,000 (Canadian). In fact, most are in the $25–$35,000 range. You would think that many of these skilled employees would leave Fact. Even Forth, who makes less than $50,000, refuses to accept offers from larger software companies to sell his business—and become an instant millionaire. Why? Forth and his employees believe in what they are doing. They know that, one day, their efforts will pay off handsomely. Forth gives each employee a stake in the business; therefore, employees are not just workers, but partners in the organization. And they are hoping their "sweat equity" invested today will someday offer them a major reward. At their current rate of growth and target to take the company to $100 million in sales within a decade, they may just get that reward.

to be sure that these "pats on the back" are sincere and done for the right reasons; otherwise, employees can see such actions as manipulative. But we know from the motivation theories presented earlier that rewards are only part of the motivation equation. We can look to job design and expectancy theories for additional insights. In service industries such as travel and hospitality, retail sales, child care, and maintenance, where pay for front-line employees generally doesn't get much above the minimum-wage level, successful companies are empowering these front-line employees with more authority to address customers' problems. If we use the JCM to examine this change, we can see that this type of job redesign provides enhanced motivating potential because employees now experience increased skill variety, task identity, task significance, autonomy, and feedback. For instance, Marriott International is redesigning almost every job in its hotels to place more workers in contact with more guests more of the time.[57] These employees are now able to take care of customer complaints and requests that formerly were referred to a supervisor or another department. In addition, employees have at least part of their pay tied to customer satisfaction, so there is a clear link between level of performance and reward (a key linkage from expectancy theory). So, even though motivating minimum-wage employees may be more of a challenge, we can still use what we know about employee motivation to help us come up with some answers.

Summary

How will I know if I fulfilled the Learning Objectives found on page 356? You will have fulfilled the Learning Objectives if you understand the following.

1. **Describe the motivation process.** Motivation is the willingness to exert high levels of effort toward organizational goals, conditioned by the effort's ability to satisfy some individual need. The motivation process begins with an unsatisfied need, which creates tension and drives an individual to search for goals that, if attained, will satisfy the need and reduce the tension.
2. **Define needs.** A need is some internal state that makes certain outcomes appear attractive.
3. **Explain the hierarchy of needs theory.** The hierarchy of needs theory states that there are five needs—physiological, safety, social, esteem, and self-actualization—that individuals attempt to satisfy in a steplike progression. A substantially satisfied need no longer motivates.
4. **Differentiate Theory X from Theory Y.** Theory X is basically a negative view of human nature, assuming that employees dislike work, are lazy, seek to avoid responsibility, and must be coerced to perform. Theory Y is basically positive, assuming that employees are creative, seek responsibility, and can exercise self-direction.
5. **Explain the motivational implications of the motivation-hygiene theory.** The motivation-hygiene theory states that not all job factors can motivate employees. The presence or absence of certain job characteristics, or hygiene factors, can only placate employees and not lead to satisfaction or motivation. Factors that people find intrinsically rewarding, such as achievement, recognition, responsibility, and growth, act as motivators and produce job satisfaction.
6. **Identify the characteristics that high achievers seek in a job.** High achievers prefer jobs that offer personal responsibility, feedback, and moderate risks.
7. **Describe the motivational implications of equity theory.** In equity theory, individuals compare their job's inputs-outcomes ratio with those of relevant others. If they perceive that they are underrewarded, their work motivation declines. When individuals perceive that they are overrewarded, they often are motivated to work harder in order to justify their pay.
8. **Explain the key relationships in expectancy theory.** The expectancy theory states that an individual tends to act in a certain way based on the expectation that the act will be followed by a given outcome and on the attractiveness of that outcome to the individual. Its prime components are the relationships between effort and performance, performance and rewards, and rewards and individual goals.
9. **Describe the effect of work force diversity on motivational practices.** Maximizing motivation in contemporary organizations requires that managers be flexible in their practices. They must recognize that employees have different personal needs and goals that they are attempting to satisfy through work. Managers must also recognize that cultural differences may play a role, too. As such, various types of rewards must be developed to meet and motivate these diverse needs.
10. **Identify the motivational effects of employee stock ownership plans.** The primary motivational effect of ESOPs stems from the fact that employees become part owners of the organization by receiving stock as a performance incentive. As a result, their efforts no longer go directly into the pockets of an unknown owner. Instead, because they are the owners, their efforts directly affect their rewards.

Review & Discussion Questions

1. How do needs affect motivation?
2. What role would money play in (a) the hierarchy of needs theory, (b) motivation-hygiene theory, (c) equity theory, (d) expectancy theory, and (e) motivating employees with a high *nAch*?
3. Contrast lower-order and higher-order needs in Maslow's needs hierarchy.
4. If you accept Theory Y assumptions, how would you be likely to motivate employees?
5. Describe the three needs in the three-needs theory.
6. Would an individual with a high *nAch* be a good candidate for a management position? Explain.
7. What are some of the possible consequences of employees' perceiving an inequity between their inputs and outcomes and those of others?
8. What difficulties do you think work force diversity causes for managers who are trying to use equity theory?
9. What are some advantages of using pay-for-performance to motivate employee performance? Are there drawbacks? Explain.
10. What can you do to motivate a minimum-wage employee? Which of these suggestions do you think is best? Why?

Applying the Concepts

How Can You Motivate Others?

This exercise is designed to help increase your awareness of how and why you motivate others and to help focus on the needs of those you are attempting to motivate.

Step 1: *Break into groups of five to seven people. Each group member is to individually respond to the following:*

Situation 1: *You are the owner and president of a fifty-employee organization. Your goal is to motivate all fifty employees to their highest effort level.*

Task 1: *On a separate piece of paper, list the factors you would use to motivate your employees. Avoid general statements such as "give them a raise." Rather, be as specific as possible.*

Task 2: *Rank order (from highest to lowest) all the factors listed in task 1 above.*

Situation 2: *Consider now that you are one of the fifty employees who has been given insight as to what motivates you.*

Task 3: *As an employee, list those factors that would most effectively motivate you. Again, be as specific as possible.*

Task 4: *Rank order (from highest to lowest) all the factors listed in task 3.*

Step 2: *Each member should share his or her prioritized lists (the lists from tasks 2 and 4) with the other members of the group.*

Step 3: *After each member has presented his or her lists, the group should respond to the following questions:*

1. Are each individual's lists (task 2 and task 4) similar or dissimilar? What do the differences or similarities suggest to you?
2. What have you learned about how and why to motivate others, and how can you apply these data?

Step 4: *Each group should appoint a spokesperson to present its answers from step 3 to the class.*

Source: Adapted from B. E. Smith, "Why Don't They Respond: A Motivational Experience," *Organizational Behavior Teaching Review,* 10, No. 2 (1985–86), pp. 98–100.

Testing Your Comprehension • • • 

Circle the correct answer, then check yourself on page AK-1.

1. A state within an individual that results in an outcome's appearing attractive is called
   a) a reward
   b) a hygiene factor
   c) perception
   d) a need

2. Which of the following BEST describes a highly motivated employee?
   a) an employee who spends company time raising funds for the Red Cross
   b) an employee who is working hard at increasing his or her department's profits
   c) an employee who just received his or her annual cost-of-living raise
   d) an employee who puts out only as much effort as necessary

3. Unsatisfied needs create
   a) tension
   b) aggravation
   c) frustration
   d) aggression

4. The motto "Let each become all he or she is capable of being," BEST illustrates
   a) the expectancy theory of motivation
   b) the relationship between needs and tension
   c) self-actualization needs
   d) Theory Y

5. According to Maslow, when does a need stop motivating?
   a) when it is substantially satisfied
   b) never
   c) when the person returns to a lower-level need
   d) when the situation changes

6. The Theory Y manager would
   a) monitor and continually prompt his or her employees to keep them working
   b) use threats and punishment to ensure performance
   c) obtain more desirable results with subordinates who had a predominately external locus of control
   d) delegate and use participative management techniques more than a Theory X manager would

7. Factors that eliminate dissatisfaction are
   a) motivators
   b) hygiene factors
   c) referents
   d) eliminators

8. When an individual is characterized by a need to constantly do better, to accomplish rather difficult goals, and to succeed, he or she has
   a) a high nAch
   b) an external locus of control
   c) an unfulfilled need for hygiene factors
   d) a high nAff

9. According to the equity theory, individuals are constantly perceiving the
   a) cost-benefit ratio
   b) efficiency-effectiveness trade-off
   c) quantity-quality trade-off
   d) inputs-outcomes ratio

10. If a salaried employee is overpaid, one would expect from the equity theory assumptions that
   a) quantity will increase and quality will decrease
   b) quantity and quality will decrease
   c) quantity and quality will increase
   d) quantity will decrease and quality will increase

11. The "self," "other," and "system" are categories of
   a) motivation
   b) hygiene factor
   c) McClelland's three-needs theories
   d) referents

12. The degree to which an individual believes that working at a particular level will generate a desired outcome is defined by the expectancy theory as
   a) attractiveness
   b) performance-reward linkage
   c) effort-performance linkage
   d) value or valence

13. Which of the following concepts is INCONSISTENT with the expectancy theory of motivation?
   a) self-interest
   b) relative worth of rewards
   c) knowledge of performance criteria
   d) one's inputs and outputs compared with another's

14. Motivation theories
   a) are universal
   b) are specific to the United States
   c) need to be modified for different cultures
   d) rarely work today

15. The key to motivating today's diversified work force lies in
   a) creativity
   b) goal setting
   c) support
   d) flexibility

16. Which of the following would NOT be considered a pay-for-performance program?
   a) cost-of-living plan
   b) piece-rate plan
   c) gainsharing plan
   d) profit sharing plan

17. A compensation program that pays and rewards employees on the basis of the skills, knowledge, or behaviors employees possess is called a ________ plan.
   a) pay-for-performance
   b) gainsharing
   c) competency-based
   d) none of the above

18. Which of the following statements about motivating minimum-wage employees is FALSE?
   a) One of the toughest motivation challenges a manager faces is how to motivate minimum-wage workers.
   b) Minimum-wage employees are motivated only by money.
   c) Employee recognition programs can encourage high performance.
   d) Job redesign can enhance the motivating potential of minimum-wage employees.

Take It to the Net

We invite you to visit the Robbins/De Cenzo page on the Prentice Hall Web site at:

http://www.prenhall.com/robbinsfom

for this chapter's World Wide Web exercise.

You can also visit the Web sites for these companies featured within this chapter:

Ameri-Tech
http://www.ameritech.com

Hallmark Cards
http://www.hallmark.com

Marriott International
http://www.marriott.com

McDonald's
http://www.mcdonalds.com

Steelcase
http://www.steelcase.com

Wendy's
http://www.wendys.com

Thinking Critically

Making a Value Judgment: Rewarding Appropriate Behavior

You have just been hired as a sales representative at the SeaCruise Travel Agency in Canton, Ohio. In this job, customers call to arrange travel plans. You look up airline flights, times, and fares on your computer and help your customers make travel reservations that work best for them. You also know that customers often want assistance in reserving rental cars or finding suitable hotel accommodations.

Most car rental agencies and hotels frequently run contests for the sales representative who reserves the most cars for a particular firm or books the most clients for a specific hotel chain. The rewards for doing so are very attractive, too. For instance, one car rental firm offers to place your name in a monthly drawing to win $2,500 if you book just twenty reservations. Book a hundred in the same amount of time, and you will be eligible for a $10,000 prize. And, if you book 200 clients, you will receive an all-expenses-paid, four-day Caribbean vacation for two. So the incentives are attractive enough for you to "steer" customers toward those companies even though it might not be the best or the cheapest for them. Your supervisor doesn't discourage your participation in these programs. In fact, the programs are viewed as a bonus for your hard work.

Questions:

1. Do you believe that there is anything wrong with doing business with those car rental and hotel firms that offer "kickbacks" to you? Explain.
2. What ethical issues do you see in this case for (a) you, (b) your employer, (c) your customers?
3. How could your organization design a performance reward system that would encourage you to high levels of "bookings" while at the same time not compromise good ethical practices?

Motivating Employees at Roppe Corporation

Do you think that production workers should be given substantial freedom to work as they wish—so long as they meet their goals? In essence, you would be empowering all employees, giving them the flexibility in their schedules to do their work, eliminating the traditional "clock punching" practice. Do you think workers would take advantage of the situation? Would management lose control? Management at the Roppe Corporation, based in Fostoria, Ohio, believe that the answer to both questions is No.[58]

The Roppe Corporation produces rubber products (baseboards, stair treads, floor tiles, etc.). The company was generating annual sales in the $50 million range. Although this was "adequate" in management's view, they knew that the company could do better. In fact, although sales growth appeared imminent with the upswing in the building economy in the mid- to late 1990s, production employees were producing at only 75 percent of standard. That's because employees felt that if they produced more to meet the quota, management would merely increase the standard. As a result, the employees, after hitting the 75 percent range, just stopped working. So management tried an experiment. Employees were offered the following proposition. Production goals would be increased by 10 percent. And when employees met the new standard, their hourly pay would also increase by 10 percent. Furthermore, although the standard would be set according to what time studies showed could be produced in eight hours of work, if the employees met the daily goals more quickly, they could go home—and still get eight hours of pay at the 10 percent increased level.

In less than one week, management noticed a dramatic change. Employees increased their productivity (and the quality of the products) to meet the new standard. For example, the old standard for rubber baseboards was 26,000 feet per day per line. Typically, workers made approximately 21,500 feet. Yet, under this new plan, the goal was increased to 29,000 feet per day per line. And the workers produced every inch of it! That's a 35 percent increase over what they had been producing the week before! What's more, they did it in under seven hours and left for the day. Since the program was implemented, employees police themselves. Sabotage of machinery has disappeared. The machines don't suddenly break down after reaching 75 percent of standard. Supervisors also don't have to monitor the length of workers' breaks or lunch periods. And overtime for maintenance workers has significantly decreased. In fact, routine, preventive maintenance can often be performed between shifts now—especially when the employees leave early.

Questions:

1. Describe the employees' behavior before and after the company "empowered" them in terms of (a) hierarchy of needs, (b) motivation hygiene theory, (c) equity theory, and (d) expectancy theory.
2. Do you believe that practices such as the ones used at Roppe Corporation can be used successfully at other companies? Why or why not? Do special conditions have to exist for such a system to work? Explain.

Video Case ABCNEWS

Pedaling Your Way to Fame

Three weeks of constant pain and punishment that demands extreme levels of courage, endurance, and motivation. This is how participants in the Tour de France describe what they go through. It's called the greatest bicycle race in the world. It's a race in which every participant must be incredibly strong, have a significant amount of courage, and possess a phenomenal endurance level.

The cyclists who race in the Tour belong to teams sponsored by commercial companies. These teams exist, however, to help their "star" win the race. Usually only one or two members of a team are capable of winning. The other riders are there to help them. They push the leaders to pick up the pace and support each other to keep going. Not surprisingly, the winner of the Tour traditionally donates the $400,000 prize to his or her teammates. However, the winner doesn't go home empty-handed! Corporate sponsors pay their star athletes million-dollar salaries, and a winner of the Tour stands to earn millions more in commercial endorsements.

What sets the Tour de France apart as one of the greatest sporting spectacles in the world and as a test of individual motivation and endurance? First of all, there's the speed. These bicyclists, on two thin weak wheels, can reach speeds of more than 60 miles an hour. One racer says that's the ultimate thrill—going fast. But there's also the danger of a crash. The uncertainty and potential danger associated with speed and equipment failure provide participants with the thrill of "living on the edge." However, what really sets the Tour apart is its almost inhuman test of endurance. For three weeks, the Tour rolls and rolls, on through cities and small villages. The riders push themselves to the limit, and sometimes beyond, through a race course that covers a total of 2,500 miles, pedaling up to 150 miles each day, six hours a day, until they reach the finish line in Paris. Some describe the experience as like running a marathon, then getting up and having to run it again the next day, and the next, and the next. It takes enormous levels of athletic skill and stamina, as well as mental discipline and experience. It also takes knowing yourself very well. Successful racers must know their bodies, their state of mind, and what they can and cannot do. It's a challenge that those who participate in the race gladly take.

Questions:

1. In this situation, what role does the team play in motivating extraordinary levels of performance from individuals? What implications can you see for managing?
2. Use expectancy theory to explain an individual's motivation to compete in the Tour de France.
3. On what level of Maslow's hierarchy of needs do you think participants in the Tour de France would be? Discuss.

Source: "Test of Courage—Tour de France," *ABC News Nightline*, July 21, 1994.

Leadership and Supervision

13

LEARNING OBJECTIVES

What will I be able to do after I finish this chapter?

1. **DEFINE** the term *leader* and explain the difference between managers and leaders.
2. **SUMMARIZE** the conclusions of trait theories of leadership.
3. **DESCRIBE** the Fiedler contingency model.
4. **SUMMARIZE** the path-goal model of leadership.
5. **EXPLAIN** situational leadership.
6. **IDENTIFY** the qualities that characterize charismatic leaders.
7. **DESCRIBE** how credibility and trust affect leadership.
8. **EXPLAIN** gender and cultural differences in leadership.
9. **DISCUSS** when formal leadership may not be that important.
10. **DESCRIBE** the unique characteristics of being a first-line supervisor.

NEARLY SIXTY YEARS AGO, WANG Seng Liang had a dream. He wanted to build a large textile business in his homeland that would rank him among the top Chinese industrialists in the nation. But the communist takeover of Shanghai in 1949 shattered that dream. Although he lost his business, Wang didn't lose his desire. In 1960, he moved to Hong Kong, where he founded Johnson Electric Holdings, Ltd. This company's primary focus would be to produce tiny electric motors for "motorized" toys.[1]

For well over two decades, Wang Seng Liang built his business—his way. He fostered an environment in which nepotism and secrecy abounded. The business was profitable, but its profits came at the expense of his employees. For instance, Wang typically purchased the cheapest furniture he could and kept the company's electric bills down by dimming the lights on the shop floor. Although many of the employees didn't vocally complain about this treatment, they did so in terms of productivity and quality. As a result, the organization stagnated. Wang's "traditional" managerial style had taken its toll on the organization. And, as younger employees accepted jobs with the company, they began to complain about the company's leadership. Finally recognizing that he was a major impediment to his firm, Wang turned the business over to his son, Patrick Wang Shui Chung.

Patrick was representative of the "new-age" professional in China. Educated at Purdue University in the United States, he recognized that significant changes had to be made in the organization for it to survive. He knew that to be successful, he had to create an environment in which employees felt important. To achieve that goal, Patrick began to revitalize the organization. He began by letting every employee know what the organization's primary goals were. He wanted to have an organization capable of responding quickly to its customers—modeled after organizations such as Black & Decker, Mercedes-Benz, and Krupp. He also wanted all employees of the organization to be on the cutting edge of technology and marketing trends. To achieve those goals, Chung eliminated cross-functional barriers by dismantling departments. In their place, he created thirty work teams. Each team was responsible for producing and selling

Patrick Wang Shui Chung is one of the new leaders in China. Managing director of Johnson Electric Holdings, Ltd., in Shanghai, he has turned around a stagnating organization by building trust with his employees. His leadership abilities and style are helping the organization to come closer to being the world's number one small-motor producer.

Johnson products to a specific segment in the market, such as power tools, automotive, and kitchen appliances. Chung also designed office space to include what he called interactive centers—glass-partitioned office space in the center of work areas that were to be used by teams when they needed to set goals, solve problems, or make decisions. These open work areas were Patrick's way of conveying to employees that the traditional management practices of his father were being "shelved."

Patrick Wang Shui Chung had set aggressive goals. And, to achieve them, he sought to build trust between himself and organizational members. He began offering every employee leadership training. Inviting consultants to Hong Kong from the U.S.-based Outward Bound program, Patrick used this training as a means of bringing together engineers and managers from Johnson's sites in Asian, European, and North American countries and to get them to think of themselves as "one." And Patrick traveled to the United States each year to attend refresher courses on effective leadership offered at Harvard University.

Have Patrick's efforts paid off? It appears they have. Johnson Electric is experiencing double-digit growth in sales and has revenues nearing $300 million annually. The company's motors are now used in a variety of products, from hair dryers to car windshield wipers. And its design centers in the United States, Europe, and Asia are able to turn their ideas into products in just under a few weeks—something that was unthinkable a few years ago. But probably the best success indicator for Patrick is the fact that he has created a culture built on credibility and trust in which professionals can do their jobs. Because of that, Johnson Electric may soon overtake the number one spot in the small-motor market by surpassing Japan's Mabuchi Motor Company.

Patrick Wang Shui Chung reminds us of the importance of leadership. It's the leaders in organizations who make things happen. But if leadership is so important, it's only natural to ask: Are leaders born or made? What differentiates leaders from nonleaders? What can you do if you want to be seen as a leader? In this chapter we will try to answer such questions.

Managers versus Leaders

Let's begin by clarifying the distinction between *managers* and *leaders*. Writers frequently use the two terms synonymously. However, they aren't necessarily the same.

Managers are appointed. They have legitimate power that allows them to reward and punish. Their ability to influence is based on the formal authority inherent in their positions. In contrast, leaders may either be appointed or emerge from within a group. Leaders can influence others to perform beyond the actions dictated by formal authority.[2]

Should all managers be leaders? Conversely, should all leaders be managers? Because no one yet has been able to demonstrate through research or logical argument that leadership ability is a handicap to a manager, we can state that all managers should ideally be leaders. However, not all leaders necessarily have capabilities in other managerial functions, and thus not all should hold managerial positions. The fact that an individual can influence others does not tell whether he or she can also plan, organize, and control. Given (if only ideally) that all managers should be leaders, we will pursue the subject from a managerial perspective. Therefore, **leaders** in this chapter mean those who are able to influence others—and who possess managerial authority.

Not all leaders are managers, nor are all managers leaders.

leaders
People who are able to influence others and who possess managerial authority.

Trait Theories of Leadership

Ask the average person on the street what comes to mind when he or she thinks of leadership. You're likely to get a list of qualities such as intelligence, charisma, decisiveness, enthusiasm, strength, bravery, integrity, and self-confidence. These responses represent, in essence, **trait theories of leadership.** The search for traits or characteristics that differentiate leaders from nonleaders, though done in a more sophisticated manner than our on-the-street survey, dominated the early research efforts in the study of leadership.

trait theories of leadership
Theories that isolate characteristics that differentiate leaders from nonleaders.

Is it possible to isolate one or more traits in individuals who are generally acknowledged to be leaders—for instance, Ted Turner, Margaret Thatcher, Nelson Mandela, or Patrick Wang Shui Chung—that nonleaders do not possess? We may agree that these individuals meet our definition of a leader, but they represent individuals with

What traits characterize leaders like Mattel's CEO Jill Barad? Research has identified six: drive, the desire to lead, honesty and integrity, self-confidence, intelligence, and job-relevant knowledge.

utterly different characteristics. If the concept of traits were to prove valid, all leaders would have to possess specific characteristics.

Research efforts at isolating these traits resulted in a number of dead ends. Attempts failed to identify a set of traits that would always differentiate leaders from followers and effective leaders from ineffective leaders. Perhaps it was a bit optimistic to believe that a set of consistent and unique personality traits could apply across the board to all effective leaders, whether they were in charge of the Chicago Bulls, Chubu Electric Power, Cedars-Sinai Hospital, Volvo, Bombardier, United Way, or Outback Steakhouse.

However, attempts to identify traits consistently associated with leadership have been more successful. Six traits on which leaders are seen to differ from nonleaders include drive, the desire to lead, honesty and integrity, self-confidence, intelligence, and job-relevant knowledge.[3] These traits are briefly described in Exhibit 13-1.

Yet traits alone are not sufficient for explaining leadership. Explanations based solely on traits ignore situational factors. Possessing the appropriate traits only makes it more likely that an individual will be an effective leader. He or she still has to take the right actions. And what is right in one situation is not necessarily right for a different situation. So, while there has been some resurgent interest in traits during the past decade, a major movement away from trait theories began as early as the 1940s. Leadership research from the late 1940s through the mid-1960s emphasized the preferred behavioral styles that leaders demonstrated.

Exhibit 13-1
Six Traits That Differentiate Leaders from Nonleaders

Source: S. A. Kirkpatrick and E. A. Locke, "Leadership: Do Traits Really Matter?," *Academy of Management Executive,* May 1991, pp. 48–60.

1. **Drive.** Leaders exhibit a high effort level. They have a relatively high desire for achievement, they're ambitious, they have a lot of energy, they're tirelessly persistent in their activities, and they show initiative.
2. **Desire to lead.** Leaders have a strong desire to influence and lead others. They demonstrate the willingness to take responsibility.
3. **Honesty and integrity.** Leaders build trusting relationships between themselves and followers by being truthful or nondeceitful and by showing high consistency between word and deed.
4. **Self-confidence.** Followers look to leaders for an absence of self-doubt. Leaders, therefore, need to show self-confidence in order to convince followers of the rightness of goals and decisions.
5. **Intelligence.** Leaders need to be intelligent enough to gather, synthesize, and interpret large amounts of information and to be able to create visions, solve problems, and make correct decisions.
6. **Job-relevant knowledge.** Effective leaders have a high degree of knowledge about the company, industry, and technical matters. In-depth knowledge allows leaders to make well-informed decisions and to understand the implications of those decisions.

Behavioral Theories of Leadership

The inability to explain leadership solely from traits led researchers to look at the behavior that specific leaders exhibited. Researchers wondered whether there was something unique in the behavior of effective leaders. For example, do leaders tend to be more democratic than autocratic?

It was hoped that the **behavioral theories** approach would not only provide more definitive answers about the nature of leadership but, if successful, would also have practical implications quite different from those of the trait approach. If trait research had been successful, it would have provided a basis for selecting the "right" people to assume formal positions in organizations requiring leadership. In contrast, if behavioral studies were to turn up critical behavioral determinants of leadership, we could train people to be leaders.[4]

behavioral theories of leadership
Theories that isolate behaviors that differentiate effective leaders from ineffective leaders.

A number of studies looked at behavioral styles. We shall briefly review three of the most popular studies: Kurt Lewin's studies at the University of Iowa, the Ohio State group, and the University of Michigan studies. Then we shall see how the concepts that those studies developed could be used to create a grid for looking at and appraising leadership styles.

Are There Identifiable Leadership Behaviors?

One of the first studies of leadership behavior was done by Kurt Lewin and his associates at the University of Iowa.[5] In their studies, the researchers explored three leadership behaviors, or styles: autocratic, democratic, and laissez-faire. An **autocratic style** describes a leader who typically tends to centralize authority, dictate work methods, make unilateral decisions, and limit employee participation. The **democratic style** of leadership describes a leader who tends to involve employees in decision making, delegates authority, encourages participation in deciding work methods and goals, and uses feedback as an opportunity to coach employees. The democratic style can be further classified in two ways: consultative and participative. A *democratic-consultative leader* seeks input and hears the concerns and issues of employees but makes the final decision him- or herself. In this capacity, the democratic-consultative leader is using the input as an information-seeking exercise. A *democratic-participative leader* often allows employees to have a "say" in what's decided. Here, decisions are made truly by the group, with the leader serving as one input to that group. Finally, the **laissez-faire** leader generally gives his or her employees complete freedom to make decisions and to complete their work in whatever way they see fit. The behaviors a laissez-faire leader might exhibit include providing necessary materials and answering questions.

autocratic style
The term used to describe a leader who centralizes authority, dictates work methods, makes unilateral decisions, and limits employee participation.

democratic style
The term used to describe a leader who involves employees in decision making, delegates authority, encourages participation in deciding work methods and goals, and uses feedback to coach employees.

laissez-faire
The term used to describe a leader who gives employees complete freedom to make decisions and to decide on work methods.

Lewin and his associates wondered which one of the three leadership styles was most effective. On the basis of their studies involving leaders from boys' clubs, they concluded that the laissez-faire style was ineffective on every performance criterion when compared with both democratic and autocratic styles. Quantity of work done was equal in groups with democratic and autocratic leaders, but work quality and group satisfaction were higher in democratic groups. The results suggest that a democratic leadership style could contribute to both good quantity and high quality of work (see Understanding Yourself).

Later studies of autocratic and democratic styles of leadership showed mixed results. For example, democratic leadership styles sometimes produced higher performance levels than autocratic styles, but at other times they produced group performance that was lower than, or equal to, that of autocratic styles. Nonetheless, more consistent results were found when a measure of employee satisfaction was used.

Understanding Yourself

Your Preferred Leadership Style

The following items describe aspects of leadership behavior. Respond to each item according to the way you would be most likely to act if you were the leader of a work group. Circle whether you would be likely to behave in the described way always (A), frequently (F), occasionally (O), seldom (S), or never (N).

If I were the leader of a work group . . .

A F O S N *1.* I would most likely act as the spokesperson of the group.
A F O S N *2.* I would encourage overtime work.
A F O S N *3.* I would allow members complete freedom in their work.
A F O S N *4.* I would encourage the use of uniform procedures.
A F O S N *5.* I would permit the members to use their own judgment in solving problems.
A F O S N *6.* I would stress being ahead of competing groups.
A F O S N *7.* I would speak as a representative of the group.
A F O S N *8.* I would needle members for greater effort.
A F O S N *9.* I would try out my ideas in the group.
A F O S N *10.* I would let the members do their work the way they think best.
A F O S N *11.* I would be working hard for a promotion.
A F O S N *12.* I would be able to tolerate postponement and uncertainty.
A F O S N *13.* I would speak for the group when visitors were present.
A F O S N *14.* I would keep the work moving at a rapid pace.
A F O S N *15.* I would turn the members loose on a job and let them go to it.
A F O S N *16.* I would settle conflicts when they occur in the group.
A F O S N *17.* I would get swamped by details.
A F O S N *18.* I would represent the group at outside meetings.
A F O S N *19.* I would be reluctant to allow the members any freedom of action.
A F O S N *20.* I would decide what would be done and how it would be done.
A F O S N *21.* I would push for increased production.
A F O S N *22.* I would let some members have authority that I could keep.
A F O S N *23.* Things would usually turn out as I predict.
A F O S N *24.* I would allow the group a high degree of initiative.
A F O S N *25.* I would assign group members to particular tasks.
A F O S N *26.* I would be willing to make changes.
A F O S N *27.* I would ask the members to work harder.
A F O S N *28.* I would trust the group members to exercise good judgment.
A F O S N *29.* I would schedule the work to be done.
A F O S N *30.* I would refuse to explain my actions.
A F O S N *31.* I would persuade others that my ideas are to their advantage.
A F O S N *32.* I would permit the group to set its own pace.
A F O S N *33.* I would urge the group to beat its previous record.

A F O S N *34.* I would act without consulting the group.

A F O S N *35.* I would ask that group members follow standard rules and regulations.

Scoring: The scoring for this assessment may appear complex, but it isn't if you carefully follow these instructions. Circle statement numbers 8, 12, 17, 18, 19, 30, 34, and 35. If you checked *S* (seldom) or *N* (never) for any of those eight statements, place a 1 in the left margin next to the circled number. For the 27 statements not circled above, place a 1 in the left margin next to the statement number for each that you responded *A* (always) or *F* (frequently). You now have 1s to the left of many of the 35 statements. Circle the 1s you have written in front of the following statements: 3, 5, 8, 10, 15, 18, 19, 22, 24, 26, 28, 30, 32, 34, and 35. Count the number of circled 1s you have and place that number in Box A. Count the number of 1s that are not circled for the remaining statements. Place that number in Box B.

What the Assessment Means: Using the diagram below, place a mark on the people-centered scale that corresponds to your score in Box A. Likewise, using your score in Box B, place a mark on the task-centered scale. Draw a straight line connecting those two marks. The point at which this line intersects the leadership behavior scale indicates your leadership behavior.

Task-Centered	Leadership Behavior	People-Centered
20		20
	Laissez-faire	
15		15
10	Participative	10
5		5
	Autocratic	
0		0

Source: Adapted from J. W. Pfeiffer and J. E. Jones, eds., *A Handbook of Structural Experiences for Human Relations Training,* vol. 1 (San Diego: University Associates, 1974). © 1974 by the American Educational Research Assn. With permission.

Group members' satisfaction levels were generally higher under a democratic leader than under an autocratic one.[6] Did this mean that managers should always exhibit a democratic style of leadership? Two researchers, Robert Tannenbaum and Warren Schmidt, attempted to provide that answer.[7]

Tannenbaum and Schmidt developed a continuum of leader behaviors (see Exhibit 13-2). As you can see from the continuum, a range of leadership behaviors, all the way from boss-centered (autocratic) on the left side of the model to employee-centered (democratic) on the right side of the model, is possible. In deciding which leader behavior from the continuum to use, Tannenbaum and Schmidt proposed that managers look at forces within themselves (such as comfort level with the chosen leadership style), forces within the employees (such as readiness to assume responsibility), and forces within the situation (such as time pressures). They suggested that managers

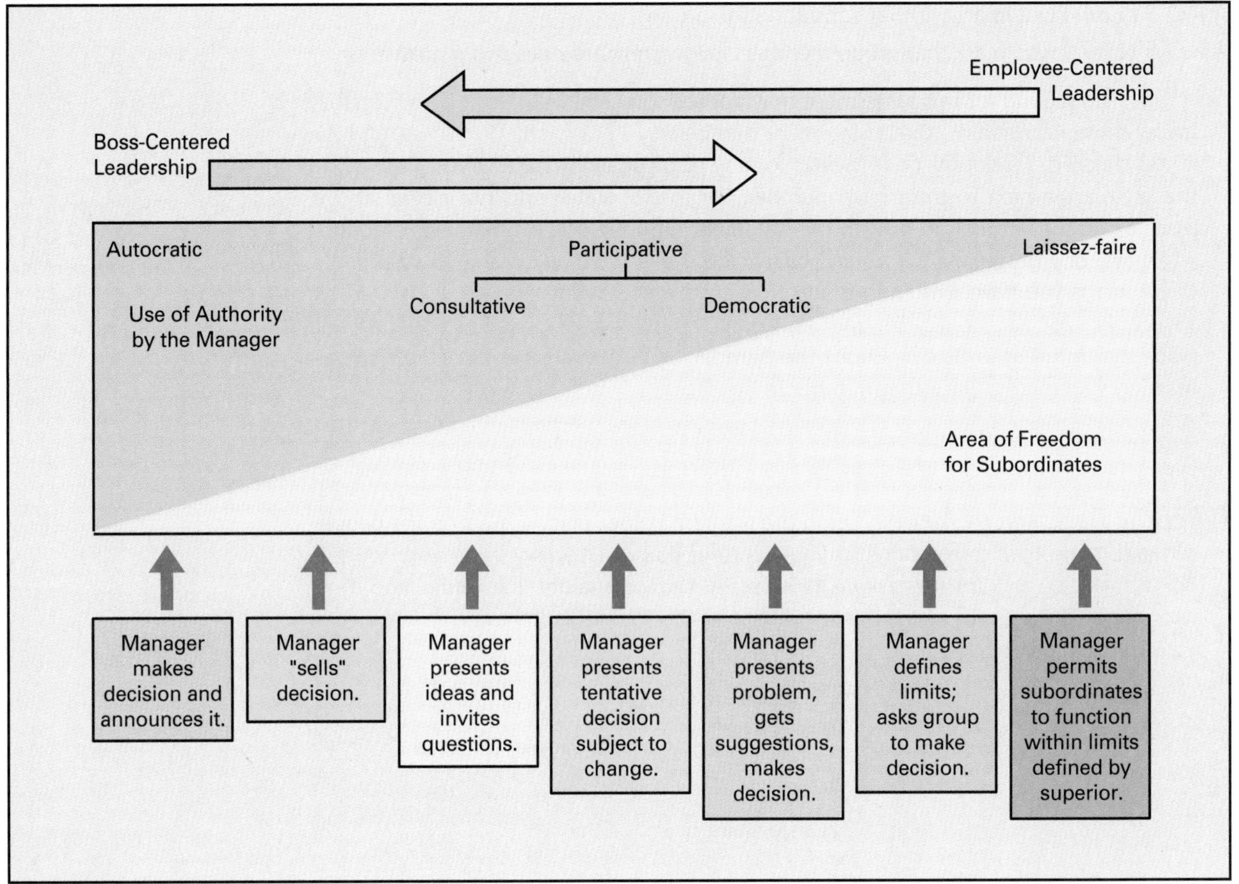

Exhibit 13-2
Continuum of Leader Behavior

Source: Reprinted by permission of the *Harvard Business Review.* An Exhibit adapted from "How to Choose a Leadership Pattern," by R. Tannenbaum and W. Schmidt (May–June 1973). Copyright © 1973 by the President and Fellows of Harvard College. All rights reserved.

should move toward more employee-centered styles in the long run because of the positive influence such behavior would have on increasing employee motivation, decision quality, teamwork, morale, and employee development.

This dual nature of leader behaviors—that is, focusing on the work to be done or focusing on the employees—is also a key characteristic of the Ohio State and University of Michigan studies.

What Was the Importance of the Ohio State Studies?

The most comprehensive and replicated of the behavioral theories resulted from research that began at Ohio State University in the late 1940s.[8] These studies sought to identify independent dimensions of leader behavior. Beginning with over 1,000 dimensions, they eventually narrowed the list down to two categories that accounted for most of the leadership behavior described by employees. They called these two dimensions initiating structure and consideration.

initiating structure
The extent to which a leader defines and structures his or her role and the roles of employees to attain goals.

Initiating structure refers to the extent to which a leader is likely to define and structure his or her role and those of employees in the search for goal attainment.

It includes behavior that attempts to organize work, work relationships, and goals. For example, the leader who is characterized as high in initiating structure assigns group members to particular tasks, expects workers to maintain definite standards of performance, and emphasizes the meeting of deadlines.

Consideration is defined as the extent to which a leader has job relationships characterized by mutual trust and respect for employees' ideas and feelings. A leader who is high in consideration helps employees with personal problems, is friendly and approachable, and treats all employees as equals. He or she shows concern for his or her followers' comfort, well-being, status, and satisfaction.

consideration
The extent to which a leader has job relationships characterized by mutual trust, respect for employees' ideas, and regard for their feelings.

Extensive research based on these definitions found that a leader who is high in initiating structure and consideration (a "high-high" leader) achieved high employee performance and satisfaction more frequently than one who rated low on either consideration, initiating structure, or both. However, the high-high style did not always yield positive results. For example, leader behavior characterized as high on initiating structure led to greater rates of grievances, absenteeism, and turnover and lower levels of job satisfaction for workers performing routine tasks. Other studies found that high consideration was negatively related to performance ratings of the leader by his or her manager. In conclusion, the Ohio State studies suggested that the high-high style generally produced positive outcomes, but enough exceptions were found to indicate that situational factors needed to be integrated into the theory.

Are Army leadership styles changing with the times? Previously, drill instructors were typically high in initiating structure. They gave orders and structured recruits' activities from sunrise to bedtime. They emphasized accomplishing tasks, accepting authority, and obeying orders. The "new" Army still focuses on those goals, but it is also taking into account consideration factors—such as sensitivity training.

What Were the Leadership Dimensions of the University of Michigan Studies?

Leadership studies undertaken at the University of Michigan's Survey Research Center, at about the same time as those being done at Ohio State, had similar research objectives: to locate behavioral characteristics of leaders that were related to performance effectiveness. The Michigan group also came up with two dimensions of leadership behavior, which they labeled employee-oriented and production-oriented.[9] Leaders who were **employee-oriented** were described as emphasizing interpersonal relations; they took a personal interest in the needs of their employees and accepted individual differences among members. The **production-oriented** leaders, in contrast, tended to emphasize the technical or task aspects of the job, were concerned mainly with accomplishing their group's tasks, and regarded group members as a means to that end.

employee-oriented
The term used to describe a leader who emphasizes interpersonal relations, takes a personal interest in the needs of employees, and accepts individual differences.

production-oriented
The term used to describe a leader who emphasizes the technical or task aspects of a job, is concerned mainly with accomplishing tasks, and regards group members as a means to accomplishing goals.

The conclusions of the Michigan researchers strongly favored leaders who were employee-oriented. Employee-oriented leaders were associated with higher group productivity and higher job satisfaction. Production-oriented leaders were associated with lower group productivity and lower worker satisfaction.

What Is the Managerial Grid?

managerial grid
A two-dimensional view of leadership style that is based on concern for people versus concern for production.

The **managerial grid** is a two-dimensional view of leadership style developed by Robert Blake and Jane Mouton.[10] They proposed a managerial grid based on the styles of "concern for people" and "concern for production," which essentially represent the Ohio State dimensions of consideration and initiating structure and the Michigan dimensions of employee orientation and production orientation.

The grid, depicted in Exhibit 13-3, has nine possible positions along each axis, creating eighty-one different positions into which a leader's style may fall. The grid does not show the results produced but rather the dominating factors in a leader's thinking in regard to getting results. That is, although there are eighty-one positions on the grid, the five key positions identified by Blake and Mouton focus on the four corners of the grid and a middle-ground area (see Exhibit 13-3).

From their findings, Blake and Mouton concluded that managers perform best using a 9,9 style. Unfortunately, the grid offers no answers to the question of what makes an effective leader but only a framework for conceptualizing leadership style. In fact, there is little substantive evidence to support the conclusion that a 9,9 style is most effective in all situations.[11]

What Did the Behavioral Theories Teach Us about Leadership?

We have described the most popular and important attempts to explain leadership in terms of behavior. There were also other efforts,[12] but they faced the same problem that confronted the early behavioral researchers: They had very little success in identifying consistent relationships between patterns of leadership behavior and successful performance. General statements could not be made because results would vary over different ranges of circumstances. What was missing was consideration of the situa-

Exhibit 13-3
The Managerial Grid

Source: Reprinted by permission of *Harvard Business Review.* An exhibit from "Breakthrough in Organization Development" by R. R. Blake, J. S. Mouton, L. B. Barnes, and L. E. Greiner, November–December 1964, p. 136. Copyright © 1964 by the President and Fellows of Harvard College; all rights reserved.

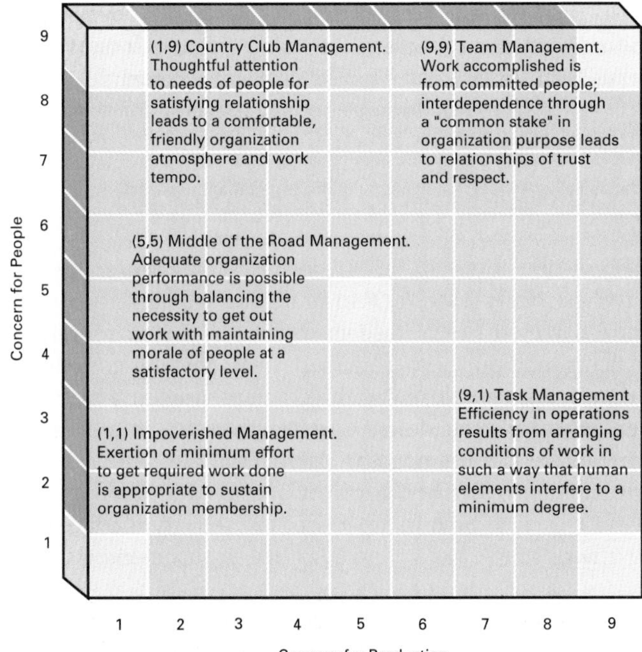

tional factors that influence success or failure. For example, would Mother Teresa have been a great leader of the poor at the turn of the century? Would Ralph Nader have risen to lead a consumer activist group had he been born in 1834 rather than in 1934 or in Costa Rica rather than in Connecticut? It seems quite unlikely, yet the behavioral approaches we have described could not clarify such situational factors. These uncertainties about applying certain leadership styles in *all* situations led researchers to try to better understand the effect of the situation on effective leadership styles.

Contingency Theories of Leadership

It became increasingly clear to those studying the leadership phenomenon that predicting leadership success involved something more complex than isolating a few traits or preferable behaviors. The failure to obtain consistent results led to a new focus on situational influences. The relationship between leadership style and effectiveness suggested that under condition *a,* style *X* would be appropriate, whereas style *Y* would be more suitable for condition *b,* and style *Z* for condition *c.* But what were the conditions *a, b, c,* and so forth? It was one thing to say that leadership effectiveness depended on the situation and another to be able to isolate situational conditions.

Several approaches to isolating key situational variables have proved more successful than others and, as a result, have gained wider recognition. We shall consider four: the Fiedler model, path-goal theory, the leader-participation model, and Hersey and Blanchard's situational theory.

What Is the Fiedler Model?

The first comprehensive contingency model for leadership was developed by Fred Fiedler.[13] The **Fiedler contingency model** proposes that effective group performance depends upon the proper match between the leader's style of interacting with his or her employees and the degree to which the situation gives control and influence to the leader. Fiedler developed **the least-preferred coworker (LPC) questionnaire,** which claims to measure whether a person is task- or relationship-oriented. Further, he isolated three situational criteria that he believes can be manipulated to create the proper match with the behavioral orientation of the leader. In a sense, the Fiedler model is an outgrowth of trait theory, since the LPC questionnaire is a simple psychological test. However, Fiedler goes significantly beyond trait and behavioral approaches by isolating situations, relating an individual's personality to the situation, and then predicting leadership effectiveness as a function of the two.

Fiedler contingency model
The theory that effective group performance depends on the proper match between the leader's style of interacting with employees and the degree to which the situation gives control and influence to the leader.

least-preferred coworker (LPC) questionnaire
A questionnaire that measures whether a person is task- or relationship-oriented.

Fiedler believes that a key factor in leadership success is an individual's basic leadership style. Thus, he first tries to find out what that basic style is. Fiedler created the LPC questionnaire for that purpose. As shown in Exhibit 13-4, it contains sixteen pairs of contrasting adjectives. Respondents are asked to think of all the coworkers they have ever had and to describe the one person they least enjoyed working with by rating him or her on a scale of 1 to 8 for each of the sixteen sets of adjectives. Fiedler believes that, on the basis of the respondents' answers to this LPC questionnaire, you can determine most people's basic leadership style.

If the least-preferred coworker is described in relatively positive terms (a high LPC score), then the respondent is primarily interested in good personal relations with this coworker. That is, if you describe the person you are least able to work with in favorable terms, Fiedler would label you relationship-oriented. In contrast, if you see the least-preferred coworker in relatively unfavorable terms (a low LPC score), you are

Pleasant	8	7	6	5	4	3	2	1	Unpleasant
Friendly	8	7	6	5	4	3	2	1	Unfriendly
Rejecting	1	2	3	4	5	6	7	8	Accepting
Helpful	8	7	6	5	4	3	2	1	Frustrating
Unenthusiastic	1	2	3	4	5	6	7	8	Enthusiastic
Tense	1	2	3	4	5	6	7	8	Relaxed
Distant	1	2	3	4	5	6	7	8	Close
Cold	1	2	3	4	5	6	7	8	Warm
Cooperative	8	7	6	5	4	3	2	1	Uncooperative
Supportive	8	7	6	5	4	3	2	1	Hostile
Boring	1	2	3	4	5	6	7	8	Interesting
Quarrelsome	1	2	3	4	5	6	7	8	Harmonious
Self-assured	8	7	6	5	4	3	2	1	Hesitant
Efficient	8	7	6	5	4	3	2	1	Inefficient
Gloomy	1	2	3	4	5	6	7	8	Cheerful
Open	8	7	6	5	4	3	2	1	Guarded

Exhibit 13-4
Fiedler's LPC Scale

Source: From F. E. Fiedler and M. M. Chemers, *Leadership and Effective Management* (Glenview, Ill.: Scott, Foresman & Co., 1974). Reprinted by permission of authors.

primarily interested in productivity and thus would be labeled task-oriented. Using the LPC instrument, Fiedler is able to place most respondents into either of these two leadership styles (see Details on a Management Classic).

Once an individual's basic leadership style has been assessed through the LPC, it is necessary to evaluate the circumstances and match the leader with the situation. Fiedler has identified three contingency dimensions that, he argues, define the key situational factors for determining leadership effectiveness. These are leader-member relations (the degree of confidence, trust, and respect employees have in their leader); task structure (the degree to which the job assignments are structured or unstructured); and position power (the degree of influence a leader has over power variables such as hiring, firing, discipline, promotions, and salary increases). These situational dimensions are then evaluated. Leader-member relations are either good or poor, task structure either high or low, and position power either strong or weak. Altogether, by mixing the three contingency variables, there are potentially eight different situations or categories in which a leader could find him- or herself.

It's important to note that Fiedler assumes that an individual's leadership style is fixed. This means that if a situation requires a task-oriented leader and the person in that leadership position is relationship-oriented, either the situation has to be modified or the leader has to be removed and replaced if optimum effectiveness is to be

Details on a Management Classic

FRED FIEDLER AND THE FIEDLER CONTINGENCY MODEL OF LEADERSHIP

The Fiedler contingency model of leadership proposes matching an individual's LPC (least-preferred coworker) score and an assessment of the three contingency variables to achieve maximum leadership effectiveness. In his studies of over 1,200 groups, in which he compared relationship- versus task-oriented leadership styles in each of the eight situational categories, Fiedler concluded that task-oriented leaders tend to perform best in situations that are either very favorable or very unfavorable to them (see Exhibit 13-5). Fiedler would predict that, when faced with a category I, II, III, VII, or VIII situation, task-oriented leaders would perform well. Relationship-oriented leaders, however, perform best in moderately favorable situations—categories IV through VI.

Remember that, according to Fiedler, an individual's leadership style is fixed. Therefore, there are really only two ways in which to improve leader effectiveness. First, you can change the leader to fit the situation. For example, if a group situation rates as highly unfavorable to the leader but is currently led by a relationship-oriented manager, the group's performance could be improved by replacing that manager with one who is task-oriented. The second alternative would be to change the situation to fit the leader. That could be done by restructuring tasks or increasing or decreasing the power that the leader has to control factors such as salary increases, promotions, and disciplinary actions.

As a whole, reviews of the major studies undertaken to test the overall validity of the Fiedler

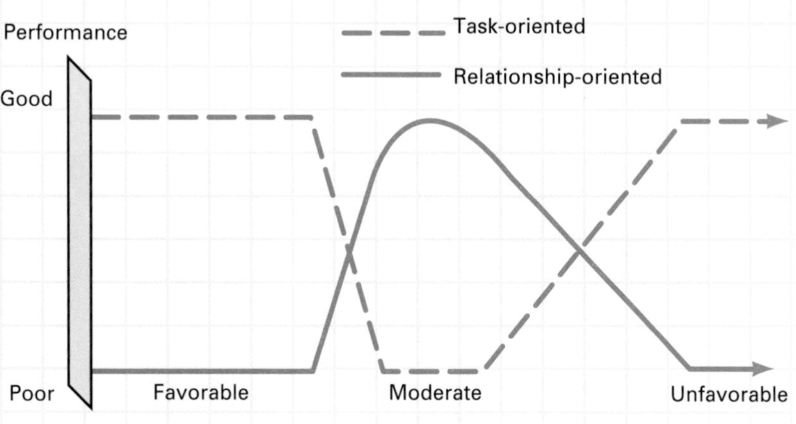

Category	I	II	III	IV	V	VI	VII	VIII
Leader-member relations	Good	Good	Good	Good	Poor	Poor	Poor	Poor
Task structure	High	High	Low	Low	High	High	Low	Low
Position power	Strong	Weak	Strong	Weak	Strong	Weak	Strong	Weak

Exhibit 13-5
The Findings of the Fiedler Model

Continued

Fred Fiedler and the Fiedler Contingency Model of Leadership Continued

model show there is considerable evidence to support it.[14] But there are problems with the LPC and the practical use of the model that need to be addressed.[15] Nonetheless, Fiedler has made an important contribution toward understanding leadership effectiveness. His work continues to be a dominant input in the development of contingency explanations of leadership effectiveness.

achieved. Fiedler argues that leadership style is innate—you can't change your style to fit changing situations!

How Does Path-Goal Theory Operate?

path-goal theory
The theory that it is a leader's job to assist followers in attaining their goals and to provide the necessary direction and support.

Currently, one of the most respected approaches to leadership is **path-goal theory.** Developed by Robert House, path-goal theory is a contingency model of leadership that extracts key elements from the Ohio State leadership research and the expectancy theory of motivation (see Chapter 12).[16]

The essence of the theory is that it is the leader's job to assist his or her followers in attaining their goals and to provide the necessary direction and support to ensure that their goals are compatible with the overall objectives of the group or organization. The term *path-goal* is derived from the belief that effective leaders clarify the path to help their followers get from where they are to the achievement of their work goals and make the journey along the path easier by reducing roadblocks and pitfalls.

According to path-goal theory, a leader's behavior is acceptable to employees to the degree that they view it as an immediate source of satisfaction or as a means of future satisfaction. A leader's behavior is motivational to the degree that it (1) makes employee need-satisfaction contingent on effective performance and (2) provides the coaching, guidance, support, and rewards that are necessary for effective performance. To test these statements, House identified four leadership behaviors. The *directive* leader lets

Phil Jackson, the highly successful head coach of the Chicago Bulls basketball team, generally confirms Fiedler's belief that a person's leadership style is fixed. Jackson's leader-member relations seem unwavering. He regularly works with many "hi-ego" players in a calm and collective way—even having a separate "heart-to-heart" room where he and players can speak freely and calmly to one another without interference from others. Actions such as this have helped him earn the respect and trust of his players.

employees know what is expected of them, schedules work to be done, and gives specific guidance as to how to accomplish tasks. This type of leadership closely parallels the Ohio State dimension of initiating structure. The *supportive* leader is friendly and shows concern for the needs of employees. This type of leadership is essentially synonymous with the Ohio State dimension of consideration. The *participative* leader (à la Lewin's democratic-consultative style) consults with employees and uses their suggestions before making a decision. The *achievement-oriented* leader sets challenging goals and expects employees to perform at their highest level. In contrast to Fiedler's view of a leader's behavior, House assumes that leaders are flexible. Path-goal theory implies that the same leader can display any or all of these leadership styles depending on the situation.[17]

A leader's job is to assist his or her followers in attaining their goals.

As Exhibit 13-6 illustrates, path-goal theory proposes two classes of situational or contingency variables that moderate the leadership behavior–outcome relationship—those in the environment that are outside the control of the employee (task structure, the formal authority system, and the work group) and those that are part of the personal characteristics of the employee (locus of control, experience, and perceived ability). Environmental factors determine the type of leader behavior required as a complement if employee outcomes are to be maximized, while personal characteristics of the employee determine how the environment and leader behavior are interpreted. The theory proposes that leader behavior will be ineffective when it is redundant with sources of environmental structure or incongruent with subordinate characteristics.

Research to validate path-goal predictions is generally encouraging, although not every study found positive support.[18] However, the majority of the evidence supports the logic underlying the theory. That is, employee performance and satisfaction are likely to be positively influenced when the leader compensates for shortcomings with the employee or the work setting. But if the leader spends time explaining tasks when those tasks are already clear or the employee has the ability and experience to

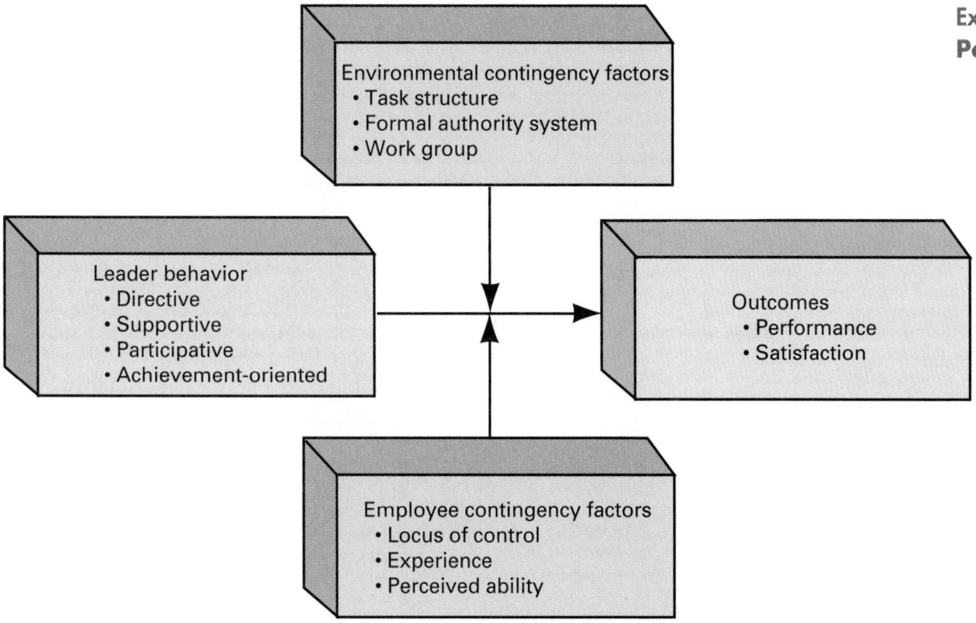

Exhibit 13-6
Path-Goal Theory

handle them without interference, the employee is likely to see such directive behavior as redundant or even insulting.

What Is the Leader-Participation Model?

leader-participation model
A leadership theory that provides a sequential set of rules for determining the form and amount of participation a leader should exercise in decision making according to different types of situations.

Back in 1973, Victor Vroom and Phillip Yetton developed a **leader-participation model** that related leadership behavior and participation to decision making.[19] Recognizing that task structures have varying demands for routine and nonroutine activities, these researchers argued that leader behavior must adjust to reflect the task structure. Vroom and Yetton's model was normative. That is, it provided a sequential set of rules that should be followed in determining the form and amount of participation in decision making, as determined by different types of situations. The model was a decision tree incorporating seven contingencies (whose relevance could be identified by making yes-or-no choices) and five alternative leadership styles.

More recent work by Vroom and Arthur Jago has resulted in a revision of that model.[20] The new model retains the same five alternative leadership styles but expands the contingency variables to twelve—from the leader's making the decision completely by him- or herself to sharing the problem with the group and developing a consensus decision. These are listed in Exhibit 13-7.

Research testing the original leader-participation model was very encouraging.[21] But, unfortunately, the model is far too complex for the typical manager to use regularly. In fact, Vroom and Jago have developed a computer program to guide managers through all the decision branches in the revised model. Although we obviously cannot do justice to this model's sophistication in this discussion, the model has provided us

Exhibit 13-7
Contingency Variables in the Revised Leader-Participation Model

Source: V. H. Vroom and A. G. Jago, *The New Leadership: Managing Participation in Organizations* (Englewood Cliffs, N.J.: Prentice Hall, 1988), pp. 111–12. With permission.

QR:	Quality Requirement:	How important is the technical quality of this decision?
CR:	Commitment Requirement:	How important is employee commitment to the decision?
LI:	Leader Information:	Do you have sufficient information to make a high-quality decision?
ST:	Problem Structure:	Is the problem well-structured?
CP:	Commitment Probability:	If you were to make this decision by yourself, is it reasonably certain that your employees would be committed to the decision?
GC:	Goal Congruence:	Do employees share the organizational goals to be attained in solving this problem?
CO:	Employee Conflict:	Is conflict among employees over preferred solutions likely?
SI:	Employee Information:	Do employees have sufficient information to make a high-quality decision?
TC:	Time Constraint:	Does a critically severe time constraint limit your ability to involve employees?
GD:	Geographical Dispersion:	Are the costs involved in bringing together geographically dispersed employees prohibitive?
MT:	Motivation Time:	How important is it to you to minimize the time it takes to make the decision?
MD:	Motivation-Development:	How important is it to you to maximize the opportunities for employee development?

with some solid, empirically supported insights into key contingency variables related to leadership effectiveness. Moreover, the leader-participation model confirms that leadership research should be directed at the situation rather than at the person. That is, it probably makes more sense to talk about autocratic and participative situations rather than autocratic and participative leaders. As did House in his path-goal theory, Vroom, Yetton, and Jago argue against the notion that leader behavior is inflexible. The leader-participation model assumes that the leader can adapt his or her style to different situations.[22]

How Does Situational Leadership Operate?

Another model of leadership that has received considerable attention by practicing managers was proposed several years ago by Paul Hersey and Kenneth Blanchard. Called **situational leadership,** it shows how a leader should adjust his or her leadership style to reflect what followers want.[23] This model has been applied in such varied organizations as Caterpillar, IBM, Mobil Oil, Xerox, BankAmerica, and the U.S. Armed Forces.[24] Although the theory hasn't undergone extensive evaluation to test its validity, we include it here because of its wide acceptance and strong intuitive appeal.

situational leadership
A model of leadership behavior that reflects how a leader should adjust his or her leadership style in accordance with the readiness of followers.

Situational leadership is a contingency theory that focuses on the followers. The emphasis on the followers in determining leadership effectiveness reflects the reality that it is they who accept or reject a leader. Regardless of what the leader does, effectiveness depends on the action of the followers. This important dimension has been overlooked or underemphasized in most leadership theories. Successful leadership is achieved by selecting the right leadership style, which Hersey and Blanchard argue is contingent on the follower's level of readiness. **Readiness** reflects how able and willing a follower is to complete a task. Hersey and Blanchard have identified four stages of follower readiness:

readiness
The situational leadership model term for a follower's ability and willingness to perform.

- **R1.** A follower is both unable and unwilling to do a job.
- **R2.** A follower is unable to do the job but willing to perform the necessary tasks.
- **R3.** A follower is able to do the job but unwilling to be told by a leader what to do.
- **R4.** A follower is both able and willing to do the job.

A point should be made here concerning willingness. As defined, for example, in R1, a follower is unwilling to do something. This is not the same unwillingness that you would associate with being insubordinate. Rather, it is an unwillingness because someone is not confident or competent enough to do a job.

Situational leadership uses the same two dimensions that Fiedler identified: task and relationship behaviors. However, Hersey and Blanchard go a step further by considering each as either high or low and then combining them into four specific leadership styles:

- *Telling* (high task–low relationship). The leader defines roles and tells employees what, how, when, and where to do various tasks.
- *Selling* (high task–high relationship). The leader provides both directive and supportive behaviors.
- *Participating* (low task–high relationship). The leader and follower share in decision making; the main role of the leader is facilitating and communicating.
- *Delegating* (low task–low relationship). The leader provides little direction or support.

Exhibit 13-8 integrates the various components into the situational leadership model. As followers reach high levels of readiness, the leader responds not only by continuing to decrease control over activities but also by continuing to decrease

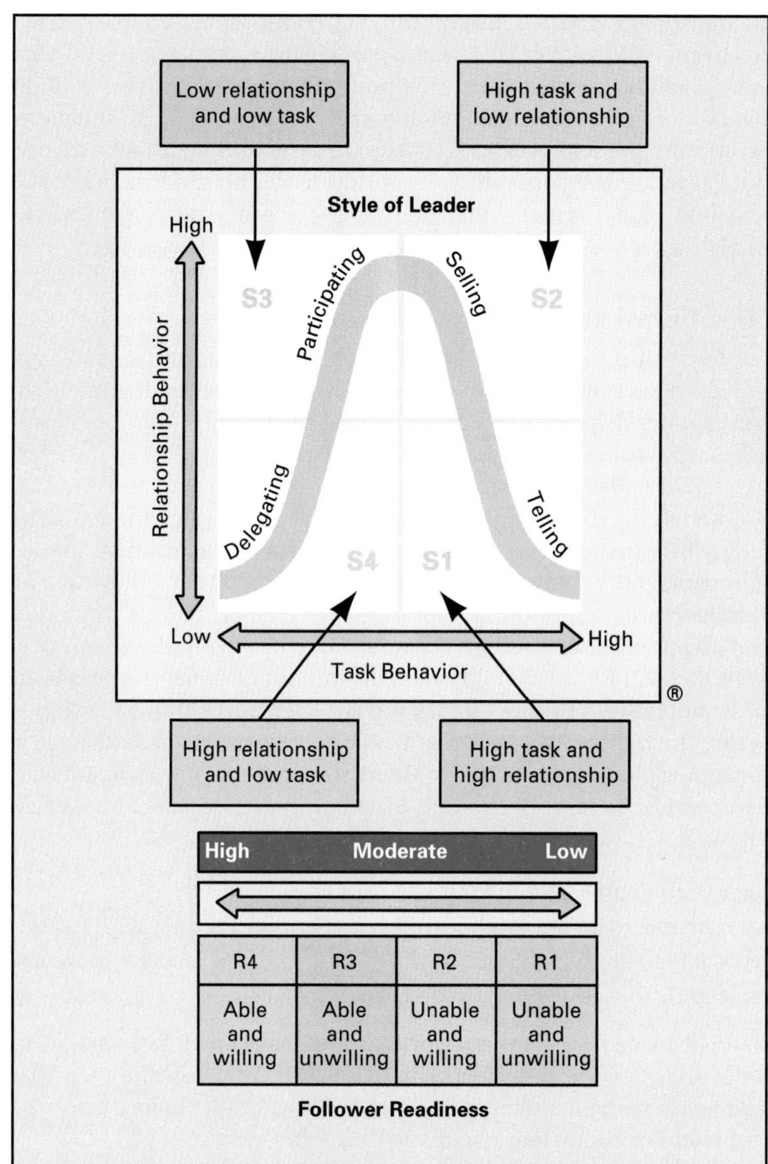

Exhibit 13-8
Hersey and Blanchard's Situational Leadership Model

Source: Reprinted with permission from the Center for Leadership Studies. Situational Leadership® is a registered trademark of the Center for Leadership Studies, Escondido, California. All rights reserved.

relationship behavior. At stage R1, for instance (where low levels of readiness dominate), followers need clear and specific directions, as would be provided by a high task–low relationship leader. At R2, both high-task and high-relationship behavior are needed. The high-task behavior compensates for the follower's lack of ability, and the high-relationship behavior tries to get the follower psychologically to "buy into" the leader's desire. R3 creates motivational problems that are best solved by a supportive, nondirective, participative style (high-relationship–low task leader). Finally, at stage R4, the leader doesn't have to do much because followers are both willing and able to take responsibility. The leader's role is often reduced to dealing with the exceptions.

You might have noticed the close similarity between Hersey and Blanchard's four leadership styles and the four "corners" of Blake and Mouton's *managerial grid.* The "telling" style corresponds to the 9,1 leader; "selling" to the 9,9 style; "participating" to the 1,9 style, and "delegating" is the same as the 1,1 leader style. Is situational leadership merely the managerial grid reconfigured to replace the 9,9 category (one style for all occasions) with the recommendation that the "right" style be aligned with the readiness of the followers? Hersey and Blanchard say No![25] They argue that the managerial grid emphasizes *concern* for production and *concern* for people; those are attitudinal dimensions of leadership. In contrast, the situational leadership model emphasizes task and relationship *behavior.* Despite Hersey and Blanchard's claim, this is a small difference. The situational leadership theory is probably better understood by being considered as a fairly direct adaptation of the grid framework to reflect four stages of follower readiness.

Finally, comes the crucial question: Is there evidence to support situational leadership theory? The evidence is mixed,[26] so any enthusiastic endorsement of the situational leadership theory as the best contingency theory of leadership at this time should be made with caution.

Emerging Approaches to Leadership

We will conclude our review of leadership theories by presenting two emerging approaches to the subject: charismatic leadership and transactional versus transformational leadership. If there is one theme that underlies these approaches, it is that they take a more practical view of leadership than previous theories have (with the exception of trait theories, of course). That is, both approaches look again at leadership from the way the average "person on the street" does.

What Is Charismatic Leadership Theory?

In Chapter 10, we discussed attribution theory in relation to perception. **Charismatic leadership theory** is an extension of that theory. It says that followers make attributions of heroic or extraordinary leadership abilities when they observe certain behaviors.[27] Studies on charismatic leadership have, for the most part, been directed at identifying those behaviors that differentiate charismatic leaders—the Jesse Jacksons and Oprah Winfreys of the world—from their noncharismatic counterparts.[28]

charismatic leadership theory
The theory that followers make attributions of heroic or extraordinary leadership abilities when they observe certain behaviors.

Several authors have attempted to identify personal characteristics of the charismatic leader. Robert House (of path-goal fame) has identified three: extremely high confidence, dominance, and strong convictions in his or her beliefs.[29] Warren Bennis, after studying ninety of the most effective and successful leaders in the United States,

What leadership traits does Jean Monty, CEO of Northern Telecom, Ltd., in Ontario, Canada, possess that helped him take the organization from a $1.03 billion loss to $473 million profits in just under two years? Warren Bennis would state that they include Monty's compelling vision, consistency in his actions, and ability to communicate his vision to employees and to capitalize on his personal strengths.

Exhibit 13-9
Key Characteristics of Charismatic Leaders

Source: Based on J. A. Conger and R. N. Kanungo, "Behavioral Dimensions of Charismatic Leadership," in J. A. Conger and R. N. Kanungo, *Charismatic Leadership* (San Francisco: Jossey-Bass, 1988), p. 91.

1. **Self-confidence.** Charismatic leaders have complete confidence in their judgment and ability.
2. **Vision.** hey have an idealized goal that proposes a future better than the status quo. The greater the disparity between this idealized goal and the status quo, the more likely that followers will attribute extraordinary vision to the leader.
3. **Ability to articulate the vision.** They are able to clarify and state the vision in terms that are understandable to others. This articulation demonstrates an understanding of the followers' needs and, hence, acts as a motivating force.
4. **Strong convictions about the vision.** Charismatic leaders are perceived as being strongly committed and willing to take on high personal risk, incur high costs, and engage in self-sacrifice to achieve their vision.
5. **Behavior that is out of the ordinary.** They engage in behavior that is perceived as being novel, unconventional, and counter to norms. When successful, these behaviors evoke surprise and admiration in followers.
6. **Appearance as a change agent.** Charismatic leaders are perceived as agents of radical change rather than as caretakers of the status quo.
7. **Environmental sensitivity.** They are able to make realistic assessments of the environmental constraints and resources needed to bring about change.

found that they had four common competencies: They had a compelling vision or sense of purpose; they could communicate that vision in clear terms that their followers could readily identify with; they demonstrated consistency and focus in the pursuit of their vision; and they knew their own strengths and capitalized on them.[30] The most comprehensive analysis, however, has been completed by Jay Conger and Rabindra Kanungo at McGill University.[31] Some of their conclusions are that charismatic leaders have an idealized goal that they want to achieve and a strong personal commitment to that goal, are perceived as unconventional, are assertive and self-confident, and are perceived as agents of radical change rather than as managers of the status quo. Exhibit 13-9 summarizes the key characteristics that appear to differentiate charismatic leaders from noncharismatic ones.

What can we say about the charismatic leader's effect on his or her followers? There is an increasing body of research that shows impressive correlations between charismatic leadership and high performance and satisfaction among followers.[32] Compared with people working for noncharismatic leaders, people working for charismatic leaders are motivated to exert extra work effort and, because they like their leader, express greater satisfaction.[33] But charismatic leadership may not always be needed to achieve high levels of employee performance. It may be most appropriate when the follower's task has an ideological component.[34] This aspect may explain why charismatic leaders most often surface in politics, religion, or a business firm that is introducing a radically new product or facing a life-threatening crisis. Such conditions tend to involve ideological issues. Second, charismatic leaders may be ideal for pulling an organization through a crisis but become a liability to an organization once the crisis and the need for dramatic change subside.[35] Why? Because the charismatic leader's overwhelming self-confidence often becomes a problem. He or she is unable to listen to others, becomes uncomfortable when challenged by assertive employees, and begins to hold an unjustifiable belief in his or her "rightness" on issues.

How Do Transactional Leaders Differ from Transformational Leaders?

The second section of research we will touch on is the continuing interest in differentiating transformational leaders from transactional leaders.[36] As you will see, because transformational leaders are also charismatic, there is some overlap between this topic and our discussion on charismatic leadership.

Most of the leadership theories presented in this chapter—for instance, the Ohio State studies, Fiedler's model, path-goal theory, the leader-participation model, and Hersey and Blanchard's situational leadership model—address the issue of **transactional leaders.** These leaders guide or motivate their followers in the direction of established goals by clarifying role and task requirements. But there is another type of leader who inspires followers to transcend their own self-interests for the good of the organization and is capable of having a profound and extraordinary effect on his or her followers. These are **transformational leaders** and include such individuals as Herb Kelleher of Southwest Airlines, Orit Gadiesh of Bain & Company, Peter Neff of Rhone-Poulenc, and Jim Clark of Netscape.[37] They pay attention to the concerns and developmental needs of individual followers; they change followers' awareness of issues by helping those followers to look at old problems in new ways; and they are able to excite, arouse, and inspire followers to put out extra effort to achieve group goals.

transactional leaders Leaders who guide or motivate their followers toward established goals by clarifying role and task requirements.

transformational leaders Leaders who inspire followers to transcend their own self-interests for the good of the organization and are capable of having a profound and extraordinary effect on followers.

Transactional and transformational leadership should not be viewed as opposing approaches to getting things done.[38] Transformational leadership is built on transactional leadership. Transformational leadership produces levels of employee effort and performance that go beyond what would occur with a transactional approach alone.[39] Moreover, transformational leadership is more than charisma. "The purely charismatic [leader] may want followers to adopt the charismatic's world view and go no further; the transformational leader will attempt to instill in followers the ability to question not only established views but eventually those established by the leader."[40]

What is it that indicates that Orit Gadiesh, CEO of Bain & Company, is a charismatic leader? Research tells us that she pays attention to the concerns and developmental needs of individual employees; helps her employees to look at old problems in new ways; and excites, arouses, and inspires employees to put out extra effort to achieve group goals.

The evidence supporting the superiority of transformational leadership over the transactional variety is overwhelmingly impressive. For instance, a number of studies with U.S., Canadian, and German military officers found, at every level, that transformational leaders were evaluated as being more effective than their transactional counterparts.[41] Managers at Federal Express who were rated by their followers as exhibiting transformational leadership were evaluated by their immediate supervisors as the highest performers and most promotable.[42] In summary, the overall evidence indicates that transformational, as compared with transactional, leadership is more strongly correlated with lower turnover rates, higher productivity, and higher employee satisfaction.[43]

Contemporary Leadership Roles

Let's turn to important issues that every effective leader in the 1990s and beyond is, and will continue to be, concerned about. Specifically, how do leaders build credibility and trust with their employees? And how can they become more empowering leaders?

Do Credibility and Trust Really Matter?

Willie Williams, Chief of Police for the City of Los Angeles, has been widely criticized within his organization for his lack of leadership.[44] Although police officers acknowledge the challenges that Williams faced coming into his job as an outsider—previously he was Chief of Police in Philadelphia—and his success at reducing crime, they claim that he has lost their trust. "He lied, and that's unforgivable," said one police officer. The main issue in question is whether Williams and his wife accepted free room and gratuities while staying in Las Vegas. He first denied the charge, then changed his story. As another officer put it, "I don't care if he got freebies or not. That's not the issue. The issue is he lied about it!" What lesson is there in the Willie Williams story? The primary issue is that followers want leaders who are credible and whom they can trust. But what do these terms—*credibility* and *trust*—really mean?

What Are Credibility and Trust? The dominant component of *credibility* is honesty. Surveys have found that honesty is consistently singled out as the number one characteristic of admired leaders.[45] "Honesty is absolutely essential to leadership. If people are going to follow someone willingly, whether it be into battle or into the boardroom, they first want to assure themselves that the person is worthy of their trust."[46] In addition to honesty, credible leaders have been found to be competent and inspiring.[47] That is, they are capable and able to effectively communicate their confidence and enthusiasm. So followers judge a leader's **credibility** in terms of his or her honesty, competence, and ability to inspire.

credibility
A characteristic attributed to a leader in terms of honesty, competence, and ability to inspire.

Trust is so closely entangled with the concept of credibility that the two terms are frequently used interchangeably. For instance, the authors of the definitive work on credibility state that "The credibility check can reliably be simplified to just one question: Do I trust this person."[48]

trust
The belief in the integrity, character, and ability of a leader.

We define **trust** as the belief in the integrity, character, and ability of a leader. Followers who trust a leader are willing to be vulnerable to the leader's actions because they are confident that their rights and interests will not be abused.[49] Recent evidence has identified five dimensions that underlie the concept of trust (see Exhibit 13-10): *integrity, competence, consistency, loyalty,* and *openness*.[50] Consistent with the work on credibility, the evidence indicates that integrity and competence are the most critical characteristics that an individual looks for in determining another's trustworthiness. Integrity seems to be rated highest because "without a perception of other's 'moral character' and 'basic honesty,' other dimensions of trust were meaningless."[51]

Why Are Credibility and Trust Important? The top rating of honesty as an identifying characteristic of admired leaders indicates the importance of credibility and trust to leadership effectiveness.[52] They probably have always been important, but

▶	Integrity	Honesty and truthfulness
▶	Competence	Technical and interpersonal knowledge and skills
▶	Consistency	Reliability, predictability, and good judgment
▶	Loyalty	Willingness to protect and save face for a person
▶	Openness	Willingness to share ideas and information freely

Exhibit 13-10
Five Dimensions of Trust

Source: Based on P. L. Schindler and C. C. Thomas, "The Structure of Interpersonal Trust in the Workplace," *Psychological Reports,* October 1993, pp. 563–73.

recent changes in the workplace have ignited heated interest in and concern with leaders' building trust.

The trend toward empowering individuals and creating self-managed work teams has reduced or removed many of the traditional control mechanisms used to monitor employees.[53] For instance, employees are increasingly free to schedule their own work, evaluate their own performance, and even make their own team hiring decisions. Therefore, trust becomes critical. Employees have to trust management to treat them fairly, and management has to trust employees to conscientiously fulfill their responsibilities. And the trend toward expanding nonauthority relationships within and between organizations widens the need for interpersonal trust.[54] Managers are increasingly having to lead others who are not in their direct line of authority—members of cross-functional teams, individuals who work for suppliers, customers, and people who represent other organizations through such arrangements as corporate partnerships. These situations do not allow leaders to fall back on their formal positions to exact compliance. Many of the relationships, in fact, are dynamic. So the ability to quickly develop trust may be crucial to the success of the relationship.

There is evidence to support the value of credibility and trust.[55] One study, for instance, divided 186 managers into high and low credibility groups on the basis of scores on a credibility questionnaire. Comparisons between the two groups found that employees who perceived their managers as having high credibility felt significantly more positive about their work and organization than did those who perceived their managers as low on credibility. In another study, individuals who reported that their manager was honest, competent, and inspiring were significantly more likely to feel a strong sense of teamwork and commitment to their organization than were those who reported their managers as less honest, competent, and inspiring.

How can leaders build trust? We have listed several suggestions in Developing a Management Skill.

How Can One Lead through Empowerment?

Several times in different sections of this text, we have stated that managers are increasingly leading by empowering their employees. Millions of individual employees and teams of employees are making key operating decisions that directly affect their work. They are developing budgets, scheduling workloads, controlling inventories, solving quality problems, evaluating their own performance, and so on—activities that until very recently were viewed exclusively as part of the manager's job.

The increased use of empowerment is being driven by two forces. First is the need for quick decisions by those people who are most knowledgeable about the issues. That requires moving decisions to lower levels. If organizations are to successfully compete in

Developing a Management Skill
BUILDING TRUST

About the Skill: *Given the importance trust plays in the leadership equation, today's leaders should actively seek to build trust with their followers. Here are some suggestions for achieving that goal.*[56]

Steps in Practicing the Skill

1. ***Practice openness.*** Mistrust comes as much from what people don't know as from what they do know. Openness leads to confidence and trust. So keep people informed, make clear the criteria on how decisions are made, explain the rationale for your decisions, be candid about problems, and fully disclose relevant information.

2. ***Be fair.*** Before making decisions or taking actions, consider how others will perceive them in terms of objectivity and fairness. Give credit where credit is due, be objective and impartial in performance appraisals, and pay attention to equity perceptions in reward distributions.

3. ***Speak your feelings.*** Leaders who convey only hard facts come across as cold and distant. When you share your feelings, others will see you as real and human. They will know who you are and their respect for you will increase.

4. ***Tell the truth.*** If honesty is critical to credibility, you must be perceived as someone who tells the truth. Followers are more tolerant of learning something they "don't want to hear" than of finding out that their leader lied to them.

5. ***Be consistent.*** People want predictability. Mistrust comes from not knowing what to expect. Take the time to think about your values and beliefs. Then let them consistently guide your decisions. When you know your central purpose, your actions will follow accordingly, and you will project a consistency that earns trust.

6. ***Fulfill your promises.*** Trust requires that people believe that you are dependable. So you need to ensure that you keep your word. Promises made must be promises kept.

7. ***Maintain confidences.*** You trust those who you believe to be discrete and who you can rely on. If people make themselves vulnerable by telling you something in confidence, they need to feel assured that you won't discuss it with others or betray that confidence. If people perceive you as someone who leaks personal confidences or someone who can't be depended on, you won't be perceived as trustworthy.

8. ***Demonstrate confidence.*** Develop the admiration and respect of others by demonstrating technical and professional ability. Pay particular attention to developing and displaying your communication, negotiating, and other interpersonal skills.

a dynamic global village, they have to be able to make decisions and implement changes quickly. Second is the reality that the downsizing and restructuring of organizations through the mid-1990s left many managers with considerably larger spans of control than they had earlier. In order to cope with the demands of an increased "work" load, managers have to empower their people. As a result, managers are sharing power and responsibility with their employees.[57] Their role is to show trust, provide vision, remove performance-blocking barriers, offer encouragement, motivate, and coach employees.[58] Companies such as General Electric, Scandinavian Airline Systems, Harley-Davidson, and Conrail encourage this "leading through empowerment," and many of them include it in their efforts to implement total quality management.[59]

Does this wholesale support of shared leadership appear strange in light of the attention we have given earlier to contingency theories of leadership? If it doesn't, it should. Why? Because empowerment proponents are essentially advocating a noncontingent approach to leadership. They claim that empowerment will work anywhere. If that is true, then directive, task-oriented, autocratic leadership is out.

The problem with this kind of thinking is that the current empowerment movement ignores the extent to which leadership can be shared and the conditions facilitating successful shared leadership. Because of factors such as downsizing—which results in the need for higher employee skills—commitment of organizations to continuous training, implementation of continuous improvement programs, and introduction of self-managed teams, the need for shared leadership is increasing. But it is not increasing in all situations. Blanket acceptance of empowerment, or of any approach to leadership, is inconsistent with the best and most current evidence we have on leadership.

Contemporary Leadership Issues

As you may have deduced from the preceding discussions on the various theories, models, and roles of leadership, the concept of "effective leadership" is continually being refined as researchers continue to study leadership in organizations. Let's take a closer look at some of the contemporary issues in leadership: gender and leadership, leadership and national culture, and questioning the relevancy of leadership.

Do Men and Women Lead Differently?

Are there differences in leadership styles based on gender? Are men more effective leaders, or does that honor belong to women? Even asking those questions is certain to evoke emotions on both sides of the debate. But before we attempt to respond, let's lay out one important fact. Although we want to know if women and men lead differently, the fact is that the two sexes are more alike than different in how they lead.[60] Much of this similarity is based on the fact that leaders, regardless of gender, perform similar activities in influencing others. That's their job, and the two sexes do it equally well. The same is true of, for instance, nurses. Although the stereotypical nurse is a woman, men are equally effective, and successful, in this career. But there are noted differences.

The most common difference lies in leadership styles. Women tend to use a more democratic style. They encourage participation of their followers and are willing to share their positional power with others. In addition, women tend to influence others best through their "charisma, expertise, contacts, and their interpersonal skills.[61] Men, on the other hand, tend to typically use a task-centered leadership style—such as directing activities and relying on their positional power to control the organization's activities." But surprisingly, even this difference is blurred. All things considered, when a woman leads in a traditionally male-dominated job (such as that of a police officer), she tends to lead in a manner that is more task-centered (see Managers Who Made a Difference).[62]

Further compounding this issue are the changing roles of leaders in today's organizations. With an increased emphasis on teams, employee involvement, and interpersonal skills, democratic leadership styles are more in demand. Leaders need to be more sensitive to their followers' needs, be more open in their communications, and build more-trusting relationships. Ironically, many of these are behaviors that women have typically grown up developing.

How Does National Culture Affect Leadership?

One general conclusion that surfaces from the leadership literature is that effective leaders do not use any single style. They adjust their style to the situation. Although not mentioned specifically in any of the theories we have presented, national culture

Managers Who Made a Difference

Linda Wachner, CEO, Warnaco and Authentic Fitness

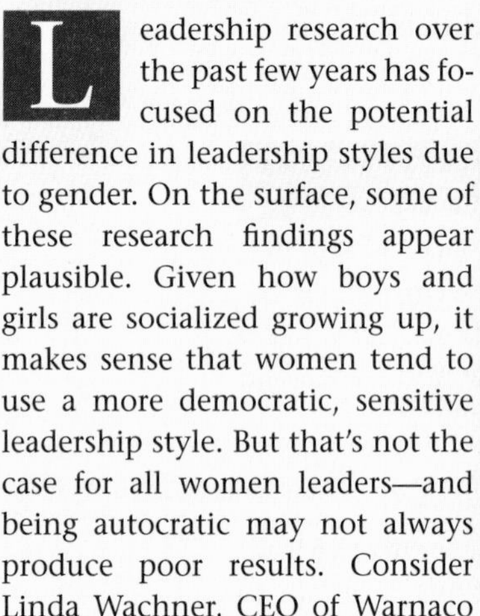

Leadership research over the past few years has focused on the potential difference in leadership styles due to gender. On the surface, some of these research findings appear plausible. Given how boys and girls are socialized growing up, it makes sense that women tend to use a more democratic, sensitive leadership style. But that's not the case for all women leaders—and being autocratic may not always produce poor results. Consider Linda Wachner, CEO of Warnaco and Authentic Fitness, makers of sports and intimate apparel (e.g., Christian Dior, Chaps, Olga, and Speedo).[63]

Linda Wachner is recognized as the first woman to become a Fortune 500 CEO. Yet her position in an organization is not really the focus of stories on her. Rather, they view Wachner from a less flattering title she has earned: "The "Queen of Impatience." Wachner is known for being smart and a good manager who rewards performance, but she is also characterized as a screaming, combative, ruthless taskmaster who always gets her way. She is known for humiliating employees in front of their peers. Simply, she doesn't take any lip from anyone. And she dismisses attacks on how she treats organizational members by one simple motto: "You can't run a company efficiently with a 'bunch of babies.' If you don't like it, leave. This is not a prison."[64]

Consider some of the things Wachner has asked employees to do—and how she has kept the upper hand. One top-level manager was anxiously awaiting spending some time with his family over a Thanksgiving break. Wachner, however, had other thoughts. She telephoned this manager more than thirty times from Thursday morning to Saturday night about work-related matters. And the calls may have continued if the manager hadn't quit his job Sunday morning. In another event, Linda summoned a senior executive from an out-of-town location to headquarters for a meeting. Spending some time with the individual, Wachner notified the executive that she would need to see him again shortly—so please go into the lobby and wait for her. Three days passed before Linda called him into her office. When the meeting did take place, it lasted fewer than two minutes. At its conclusion, Wachner sent him back to his home office. As for advice to other senior managers, she lives by two simple words. Be tough. She advises them from the beginning to show employees they are serious. How? By firing a few employees to set an example!

Wachner also has a compassionate side. She is sensitive to employees who have become ill or have other special needs. She is more than willing to help—so long as the employee has been producing. And those loyal to the company get loyalty in return.

Wachner's formula has worked for her and her companies. She has more than doubled the stock prices of Warnaco in the past few years, increasing equity in the company by more than $140 million during her tenure as CEO. For many of the stockholders, that's translating into a 43 percent return on investment each year.

is clearly an important situational variable in determining which leadership style will be most effective.

National culture affects leadership by way of the followers. Leaders cannot choose their styles at will. Instead, they are constrained by the cultural conditions their employees have come to expect.[65] For example, an autocratic leadership style is compatible with high power distance cultures such as Arab, Far Eastern, and Latin American countries. Power distance rankings should also be good indicators of employee willingness to accept participative leadership. Participation is likely to be most effective in low power distance cultures such as those in Norway, Finland, Denmark, and Sweden.

As we leave this section, remember that most leadership theories we have discussed were developed by North Americans, using North American subjects; and the United States, Canada, and Scandinavian countries all rate below average on power distance. This realization may help explain why our theories tend to favor a more participative and empowering style of leadership. Accordingly, a leader needs to consider national culture as yet another contingency variable in determining the most effective leadership style.

Is Leadership Always Important?

In keeping with the contingency spirit, we conclude this section by offering this notion: The belief that some leadership style will always be effective regardless of the situation may not be true. Leadership may not always be important. Data from numerous studies demonstrate that, in many situations, any behaviors a leader exhibits are irrelevant. Certain individual, job, and organizational variables can act as "substitutes for leadership," negating the influence of the leader.[66]

For instance, characteristics of employees such as experience, training, "professional" orientation, or need for independence can neutralize the effect of leadership. These characteristics can replace the need for a leader's support or ability to create structure and reduce task ambiguity. Similarly, jobs that are inherently unambiguous and routine or that are intrinsically satisfying may place fewer demands on the leadership variable. Finally, such organizational characteristics as explicit formalized goals, rigid rules and procedures, or cohesive work groups can act in the place of formal leadership.

The belief that some leadership style will always be effective regardless of the situation may not be true.

Supervision: A Special Case of Leadership

Supervision is often conveniently lumped together with all levels in the managerial hierarchy, yet lumping them together camouflages the fact that supervisors are uniquely different from all other managers. This difference, together with the growing recognition that the job of supervisor is undergoing rapid change, justifies a separate discussion. The following discussion highlights those factors that make the supervisory position a special case of leadership and show how the supervisor's role suffers from ambiguous interpretations.

Why Are Supervisors Considered First-Level Managers?

The term *supervision* is often used to refer to the activity of directing the immediate activities of employees. In such a context, it can occur at all levels. However, we use a narrower perspective. We consider **supervision** to be a first-level management task and supervisors as first-level managers. That is, counting from the bottom of the

supervision
A first-level management task of directing the activities of operatives.

traditional pyramid-shaped organization, they represent the first, or lowest, level in the management hierarchy.

As first-level managers, supervisors must, by definition, occupy the primary level of management charged with the responsibility of directing the work of nonmanagerial employees. It is true, of course, that all managers may direct activities of their staff, but the primary responsibility of these managers is to direct the activities of other managers. Therefore, it is primarily supervisors who are directly responsible for the daily activities of operative employees.

What Is Unique about Being a Supervisor?

We have already noted one of the unique characteristics of supervisors—they do not direct activities of other managers. In addition, there are specific distinctive characteristics that create problems peculiar to first-level managers. These arise from the supervisor's heavy reliance on technical expertise, having to communicate to both managers and operative employees, coping with role conflict, coping with constrained authority, and being management's representative to operative employees (see Exhibit 13-11).

How Is the Supervisor's Role Different?

Interpretations of the supervisor's role in an organization have been very inconsistent. The position has been described as everything from the "critical link" in an organization to a "necessary evil." A synthesis of five such descriptions of the supervisor's role is shown in Exhibit 13-12.[67]

Exhibit 13-11
Unique Characteristics of Being a Supervisor

1. **Heavy reliance on technical expertise.** Supervisors are required to know the job they supervise. Unlike other managers who are heavily oriented toward planning and controlling, supervisors spend a large portion of their time leading and overseeing the activities of operative employees.
2. **Communicating to both managers and operative employees.** Communication is a problem at all levels in the organization. However, it is particularly a problem for supervisors. Middle- and top-level managers converse with managers both above and below them, in many cases with people who share their educational backgrounds, experiences, and needs. On the other hand, supervisors are required to communicate with two distinct groups—managers and workers. Therefore, they must be able to blend the experiences, expectations, and needs of these divergent groups.
3. **Coping with role conflict.** Supervisors are neither fish nor fowl. They're not operatives, and, although they are officially classified as management, they often are not accepted by other managers. A supervisor may be assumed to be like any other manager, but his or her activities, status, and security are quite different.
4. **Coping with constrained authority.** Sixty years ago, supervisors had complete authority. In the production area, for example, the foreman was the biggest, meanest, and toughest. His word was law. Today, however, key personnel decisions are now determined by the conditions of the labor-management collective bargaining agreement or have been centralized in HRM departments.
5. **Management's representative.** The final problem unique to supervisors is that, to the operatives, they are *the organization*. Rules, policies, procedures, and other dictates from above are implemented at the supervisory level. So when operatives think of management, their main point of reference is their supervisors.

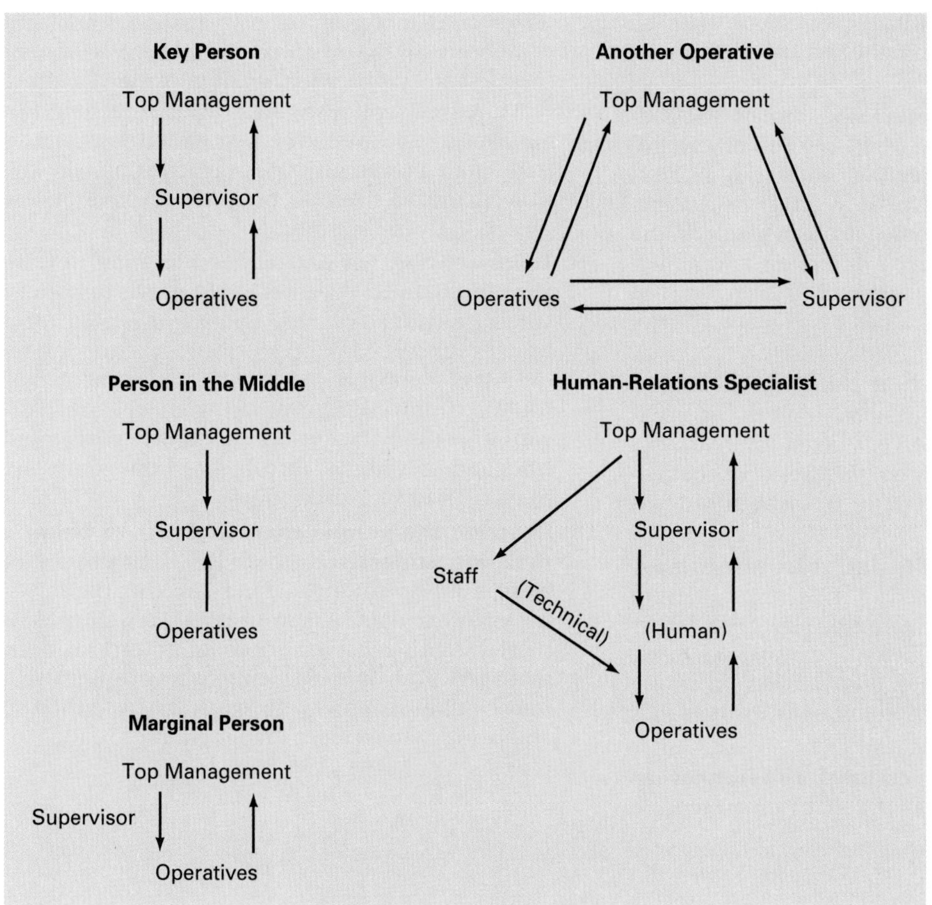

Exhibit 13-12
Different Views of the Supervisor's Role

Source: Adapted from K. Davis, *Human Behavior at Work: Organizational Behavior,* 6th ed. (New York: McGraw-Hill, 1981), p. 142. With permission.

Summary

How will I know if I fulfilled the Learning Objectives found on page 387?
You will have fulfilled the Learning Objectives if you understand the following.

1. **Define the term *leader* and explain the difference between managers and leaders.** A leader is an individual who is able to influence others. Managers are appointed. They have legitimate power that allows them to reward and punish. Their ability to influence is founded upon the formal authority inherent in their positions. In contrast, leaders may either be appointed or emerge from within a group. Leaders can influence others to perform beyond the actions dictated by formal authority.
2. **Summarize the conclusions of trait theories of leadership.** Six traits have been found on which leaders differ from nonleaders—drive, the desire to lead, honesty and integrity, self-confidence, intelligence, and job-relevant knowledge. Yet possession of these traits is no guarantee of leadership because they ignore situational factors.
3. **Describe the Fiedler contingency model.** Fiedler's contingency model identifies three situational variables: leader-member relations, task structure, and position power. In situations that are highly favorable or highly unfavorable, task-oriented leaders tend to perform best. In moderately favorable or unfavorable situations, relations-oriented leaders are preferred.
4. **Summarize the path-goal model of leadership.** The path-goal model proposes two classes of contingency variables—those in the environment and those that are part of the personal characteristics of the subordinate. Leaders select a specific type of behavior—directive, supportive, participative, or

achievement-oriented—that is congruent with the demands of the environment and the characteristics of the subordinate.

5. **Explain situational leadership.** Situational leadership theory, developed by Hersey and Blanchard, proposes that there are four leadership styles—telling, selling, participating, and delegating. Which style a leader chooses to use depends on the followers' readiness—their willingness and ability to do the job. As followers reach higher levels of readiness, the leader responds by reducing control and involvement.
6. **Identify the qualities that characterize charismatic leaders.** Charismatic leaders are self-confident, possess a vision of a better future, have a strong belief in that vision, engage in unconventional behaviors, and are perceived as agents of radical change.
7. **Describe how credibility and trust affect leadership.** Credibility and trust influence leadership effectiveness. If followers do not view their leader as being honest, competent, consistent, loyal, open, and inspiring, they may not have a strong sense of teamwork—or commitment to their jobs or the organization.
8. **Explain gender and cultural differences in leadership.** Research shows that women tend to adopt a democratic or participative leadership style. Men, on the other hand, are likely to use a directive, autocratic leadership style. National culture of employees will also affect leadership style. An autocratic style would be best suited for cultures with high power distance. Participation, on the other hand, is likely to be most effective in low power distance countries.
9. **Discuss when formal leadership may not be that important.** Leaders might not be important when individual variables replace the need for a leader's support or ability to create structure and reduce task ambiguity; when jobs are unambiguous, routine, or intrinsically satisfying; or when such organizational characteristics as explicit goals, rigid rules and procedures, or cohesive work groups act in place of formal leadership.
10. **Describe the unique characteristics of being a first-line supervisor.** Unique characteristics of being a supervisor include not directing the activities of other managers; a heavy reliance on technical expertise; having to communicate to both managers and operative employees; coping with role conflict; coping with constrained authority; and being management's representative to the employees.

Review & Discussion Questions

1. "All managers should be leaders, but not all leaders should be managers." Do you agree or disagree with that statement? Support your position.
2. Discuss the strengths and weaknesses of the trait theory of leadership.
3. What is the managerial grid? Contrast its approach to leadership with that of the Ohio State and Michigan groups.
4. How is a least-preferred coworker determined? What is the importance of one's LPC for the Fiedler theory of leadership?
5. What are the contingencies in the path-goal theory of leadership?
6. What similarities, if any, can you find among Fiedler's model, path-goal theory, and Hersey and Blanchard's situational leadership?
7. "Charismatic leadership is always appropriate in organizations." Do you agree or disagree? Support your position.
8. How do trust and credibility affect leadership? Are they less important under an autocratic than under a democratic leadership style? Discuss.
9. Can we say that either a masculine or a feminine leadership style is better? Why or why not? Support your position.
10. Why is the job of first-line supervisor considered a unique management position?

Testing Your Comprehension • • • 

Circle the correct answer, then check yourself on page AK-2.

1. Which of the following BEST describes a leader?
   a) Being a leader means also being a manager.
   b) A leader always emerges from within the group.
   c) Leaders are appointed into their positions.
   d) Leaders can influence others beyond the formal authority of their position.

2. Theories of leadership that isolate characteristics that differentiate leaders from nonleaders are called
   a) behavioral theories of leadership
   b) trait theories of leadership
   c) contingency theories of leadership
   d) situational theories of leadership

3. Which of the following is LEAST accurate about the Ohio State studies?
   a) "High-high" leaders generally had superior subordinate performance.
   b) High initiating structure is positively related to grievances.
   c) High consideration is positively related to managers' favorable performance evaluations.
   d) "High-high" styles sometimes had negative leadership results.

4. The University of Michigan researchers concluded that
   a) production-oriented leaders were associated with lower employee satisfaction
   b) production-oriented leaders were associated with higher productivity
   c) employee-oriented leaders had lower productivity
   d) employee-oriented leaders had higher productivity

5. The managerial grid was an attempt by Blake and Mouton to
   a) discredit the University of Michigan and Ohio State University studies
   b) explain leadership success using a decision tree
   c) describe leadership style using dimensions similar to the University of Michigan and Ohio State studies
   d) predict managerial success using a production versus a people orientation

6. Which of the following statements is MOST correct?
   a) It has been proved conclusively that physical stature and leadership are positively related.
   b) Behavior theories of leadership research findings are confusing and do not allow for significant generalizations.
   c) The trait view of leadership is accepted by Fiedler.
   d) The Ohio State researchers originally began with a contingency model.

7. If a leader describes his or her least-preferred coworker in relatively unfavorable terms, according to Fiedler,
   a) the leader would be classified as task-oriented
   b) the leader would be classified as relationship-oriented
   c) the leader would be classified as authoritarian
   d) none of the above

8. In which of the following situations would the path-goal model suggest a consideration style of leadership?
   a) when employees have an external locus of control
   b) when employees have low skill levels
   c) when employees work in an organizational culture characterized as authoritarian
   d) when employees have well-structured tasks

Continued

9. According to the leader-participation model of leadership, when goal congruence between the employees and the organization is low,
   a) an autocratic style of leadership is more appropriate
   b) a group style of leadership is more appropriate
   c) a consultative style of leadership is more appropriate
   d) a democratic style of leadership is more appropriate

10. A leader who looks beyond his or her own self-interest and instead places the goals of the organization first, is called a ______________ leader.
    a) transactional c) transformational
    b) authoritarian d) situational

11. Which of the following is NOT true for a charismatic leader?
    a) A charismatic leader is usually participative and is willing to listen to the opinions of employees.
    b) A charismatic leader might not always be needed to achieve high levels of employee performance.
    c) It is not unusual for a charismatic leader to pull an organization though a crisis but to perform poorly after the crisis subsides.
    d) It is more important to have a charismatic leader when the followers' tasks have an ideological component.

12. Which of the following Hersey and Blanchard leadership styles is concerned with facilitating and communicating?
    a) telling c) delegating
    b) participating d) selling

13. A follower who is unable to do the job but willing to perform the necessary tasks would be in which level of readiness in Hersey and Blanchard's situational leadership model?
    a) R4 c) R2 b) R3 d) R1

14. Which of the following characteristics is NOT a dimension of trust?
    a) respectability c) competency
    b) integrity d) consistency

15. Which of the following statements about gender differences in leadership is CORRECT?
    a) There are no differences in leadership based on gender.
    b) Women leaders have a tendency to lead using a directive leadership style.
    c) Men have a tendency to use a leadership style that encourages participation of their followers.
    d) None of the above statements is about gender differences is correct.

16. If the leader of a team suddenly leaves the team, and the team continues to function effectively, which of the following statements is probably the MOST true?
    a) The team never needed the leader.
    b) The leader did such a good job that the team could operate effectively without her.
    c) The leader may or may not have been irrelevant
    d) The team no longer has a leader.

17. What is the main difference between first-line supervisors and other managers?
    a) First-line supervisors are concerned with local issues; managers are concerned with global issues.
    b) First-line supervisors oversee operative employees.
    c) First-line supervisors are not considered "real" managers.
    d) There is no difference between first-line supervisors and other managers.

Applying the Concepts

The Pre-Post Leadership Assessment

Objective: *To compare characteristics intuitively related to leadership with leadership characteristics found in leadership theory.*

Time: *Part I takes approximately ten minutes. Part II takes about twenty-five minutes.*

Procedure: *Part I is to be completed before reading Chapter 13. Identify three people (e.g., friends, relatives, previous boss, public figures, etc.) whom you consider to be outstanding leaders. For each individual, list why you feel he or she is a good leader. Compare your lists of the three individuals. Which traits, if any, are common to all three? Part II is to be completed after the lecture on the material in Chapter 13. Your instructor will lead the class in a discussion of leadership characteristics based on your lists developed in Part I. Students will call out what they identified, and your instructor will write the traits on the chalkboard. When all students have shared their lists, class discussion will focus on the following:*

1. What characteristics consistently appeared on students' lists?
2. Were these characteristics more trait-oriented or behavior-oriented?
3. Under what situations were these characteristics useful?
4. What, if anything, does this exercise suggest about leadership attributes?

Take It to the Net

We invite you to visit the Robbins/De Cenzo page on the Prentice Hall Web site at:

http://www.prenhall.com/robbinsfom

for this chapter's World Wide Web exercise.

You can also visit the Web sites for these companies featured within this chapter:

Bain & Company
http://www.rec.bain.com

Chicago Bulls
http://www.nba.com/bulls/

Netscape
http://www.home.netscape.com

Outward Bound
http://www.outwardbound.org/index.html

Rhone-Poulenc
http://www.rhone-poulenc.com

United Way
http://www.unitedway.org

Thinking Critically

Making a Value Judgment: Creating Charisma

In 1997, no list of charismatic business leaders would have been complete without the names of Bill Gates (Microsoft), Charlotte Beers (Ogilvy & Mather Worldwide), Larry Bossidy (AlliedSignal), and Herb Kelleher (Southwest Airlines).[68] They personified the contemporary idea of charisma in the corporate world. But are these individuals authentically charismatic figures or self-created images?

Most charismatic leaders employ a public relations firm or have public relations specialists on their staff to shape and hone their image. For instance, Bill Gates, cofounder and CEO of Microsoft, has promoted the vision of the aggressive, take-charge executive who is determined to see every software program put in every personal computer. Charlotte Beers, CEO of Ogilvy & Mather Worldwide, relishes her reputation for being humorous and charming—traits that helped her turn around her advertising company. And Ted Turner has worked hard to project his "to hell with tradition" image in the popular press.

One view of these individuals is that they are authentically charismatic leaders whose actions and achievements have caught the fancy of the media. This view assumes that these leaders couldn't hide their charismatic qualities. It was just a matter of time before they were found out and gained the public's eye. Another view—certainly a more cynical one—proposes that these people consciously created an image that they wanted to project and then purposely went about doing things that would draw attention to, and confirm, that image. They may not be inherently charismatic individuals but rather highly astute manipulators of symbols, circumstances, and the media. In support of this latter position, one can identify leaders such as Geoff Bible of Philip Morris or John Bryan of Sara Lee, who are widely viewed as charismatic in their firms and industries but are relatively unknown in the popular press.

Questions:

1. Do you think that charismatic leadership is an inherent quality within a person or a purposely and carefully molded image?
2. Assuming that one's charisma is "molded," do you believe it's ethical to create this charismatic image?

Barrie Ingels at Toronto Mutual, Inc.

Barrie Ingels is twenty-two years old and will be receiving her B.S. degree in mathematics from Concordia University in Montreal at the end of this semester. She has spent the past two summers working for Toronto Mutual, Inc. (TM), filling in on a number of different jobs while employees took their vacations. She has received and accepted an offer to join TM as a project leader in the policy renewal department on a permanent basis upon graduation.

Toronto Mutual is a large insurance company. The headquarters office alone, where Barrie will work, has 5,000 employees. The company believes strongly in the personal development of its employees. This belief translates into a philosophy, flowing down from senior officials, of trust and respect for all TM employees.

The job Barrie will be assuming requires her to work with and direct the activities of eighteen policy renewal representatives. Their job responsibilities are to ensure that renewal notices are sent on current policies, to tabulate any changes in premiums from a standardized table, and to advise the sales division if a policy is to be canceled as a result of nonresponse to renewal notices.

Barrie's group is composed of individuals ranging from nineteen to sixty-two years of age. The median age is thirty-four. The salary range for policy renewal representatives is from $2,370 to $2,950 per month (in U.S. dollars). Barrie will be replacing a long-time TM employee, Petra Finch. Petra is retiring after thirty-seven years with TM, the last eleven spent as a policy renewal team leader. Because Barrie spent a few weeks in Petra's group last summer, she is familiar with Petra's leadership style and knows most of the group members. She anticipates no problems from any of her soon-to-be employees, except possibly for Rasheed Pitulla. Rasheed is well into his forties, has been a policy renewal representative for over sixteen years, and, as one of the senior members of the team, carries a lot of weight with group members. Rasheed did not apply for the team leader's job that Barrie got. He simply didn't want the formal responsibility of being a team leader. He felt that the job duties might interfere with his primary outside interest—coaching his son's soccer team. Nonetheless, Barrie has concluded that her job could prove very difficult without Rasheed's support.

Barrie is determined to get her "leadership" career off on the right foot. As a result, she has been doing a lot of thinking about the qualities of an effective leader.

Questions:

1. What critical factors will affect Barrie's success as a leader? Do you think that those factors would be the same if success were defined as group satisfaction rather than as group productivity?
2. Do you think that Barrie can choose a leadership style? If you do, describe the style that you think would be most effective for her. If you think she can't choose a leadership style, explain your reasons.
3. What suggestions might you make to Barrie to help her win the support of Rasheed Pitulla? What factors may be important in determining which leadership style she should use with Rasheed?

Video Case ABCNEWS

An Unusual Leader

You've probably never heard of Matthew Coon Come. Yet he's proving to be a real leader in the growing fight against Hydro Quebec, the large utility company in Quebec, Canada, that provides much of the power that supplies the eastern seaboard. Many of us may just stand by, merely complaining about the technological developments that are changing the environment. But Matthew Coon Come wasn't content to just stand by; he had something to do. After all, he had to protect the land that he and his people have lived on for the past 5,000 years.

As the Chief of the 12,000-member Cree tribe, Coon Come has taken it upon himself to "protect" his peoples—those alive today and the thousands of ancestors who preceded them. Some might think that leading a tribe of Indians in the wilderness of Quebec isn't sound preparation for fighting a giant company. But don't miscalculate the Chief's abilities. Matthew was born in a tent on the frozen tundra; his mother had gone into labor while out dog sledding. He was raised in the tradition of the Cree Indians, which, for most, meant learning to hunt and fish for survival. Yet, unlike many of his ancestors, Matthew's family also recognized the importance of a formal education. Matthew graduated from college and ultimately law school. There he learned new skills that he could use when he returned to the Cree tribe as its Chief. One of those skills was leadership—the ability to influence others.

How has he used this skill in his fight with Hydro Quebec? He has been able to show others that the flooding done to build hydroelectric power plants has already caused the deaths of 10,000 caribou. Furthermore, the rotting of vegetables now covered with water in the dams is producing a toxin called methyl-mercury. That toxin has been consumed by fish that eat the vegetation and now is being passed on to those who catch and eat the fish. As a result, the Cree Indians have been told that they can't eat the fish in certain areas for at least the next twenty years.

Although one individual's fight can generate results, Coon Come recognized that to battle this "foe" properly would require the assistance of others. To his credit, he has enlisted the help of others whom he has influenced, including environmental activists in both Canada and the United States, especially the State of New York. He was instrumental in getting New York State officials to cancel "a multibillion-dollar deal to buy electricity" from Hydro Quebec when their new plant opened.

Questions:

1. Do you think that Matthew Coon Come is a leader? Why or why not?
2. How could charismatic leadership explain Coon Come's success with his efforts to curtail Hydro Quebec's efforts to build additional hydroelectric plants?
3. What role do current social and political attitudes play in the emergence of leaders? Discuss this topic in relation to Matthew Coon Come.

Source: "Person of the Week—Matthew Coon Come," *ABC World News Tonight,* April 22, 1994.

Communication and Interpersonal Skills

14

LEARNING OBJECTIVES

What will I be able to do after I finish this chapter?

1. **DEFINE** communication and explain why it is important to managers.
2. **DESCRIBE** the communication process.
3. **LIST** techniques for overcoming communication barriers.
4. **IDENTIFY** behaviors related to effective active listening.
5. **EXPLAIN** what behaviors are necessary for providing effective feedback.
6. **DESCRIBE** the contingency factors influencing delegation.
7. **IDENTIFY** behaviors related to effective delegating.
8. **DESCRIBE** the steps in analyzing and resolving conflict.
9. **EXPLAIN** why a manager might stimulate conflict.
10. **CONTRAST** distributive and integrative bargaining.

TOM COLESBERRY'S DESIRE TO OPERATE A successful company leads him to emphasize sound organizational communication policies. Tom is in charge of the 1,200-member Ruiz Foods Products, the Dinuba, California, Mexican food company.[1] Since the early 1990s, Tom has held regular lunch meetings with employees. Each month, he spends an afternoon dining with twenty-four employees to have a frank discussion about the company. During these meetings, Tom provides a statement of the "current state of affairs" for the company then turns the meeting over to his employees for their questions, concerns, and suggestions. Tom wants to hear about the company from the proverbial "horse's mouth." Why? His experience is that information received from employees directly involved in the day-to-day activities provides him the best and most accurate feedback.

For most people, Tom's actions don't appear to be that out of the ordinary. After all, isn't it these employees who should know best what is happening with the production end of the business and any problems they may be encountering? Certainly, but there's more involved for Colesberry. Many of his employees' first language is Spanish, and they can't speak English! Undoubtedly, this language barrier has been a major concern for him. But not insurmountable. For example, Tom's lunch meetings are presented in both English and Spanish (as are all company policies and memos). To make sure that his message is getting through, he has bilingual staff members present in meetings to help those who are encountering language difficulties.

Tom Colesberry, president of Ruiz Foods in Dinuba, California, knows that to run a successful company you need to communicate effectively with employees. Communicating with Ruiz employees posed some problems, however. Some employees didn't speak English. Now, bilingual communications are the norm. And as a result, Ruiz Foods has experienced an increase in productivity.

Tom Colesberry continues to adjust his company's communication practices to reflect his diverse employee group. His company began offering language classes for all employees to help them develop a second language.

Tom is seeing his communication programs pay off handsomely. For instance, some non-English speaking employees conveyed to Tom during his lunch meetings that the company's distribution methods in Hispanic neighborhoods had problems. They explained those problems in detail, and Tom acted on them immediately.

As a result of effective organizational communications, profits at Ruiz Foods have continued to increase, and the company has created more than 600 new jobs over the past few years.

The case of Tom Colesberry illustrates an important point: Effective communication is fundamentally linked to successful performance.[2] In this chapter, we will present basic concepts in interpersonal communication. We will explain the communication process, methods of communicating, barriers to effective communication, and ways to overcome those barriers. In addition, we will review several communication-based interpersonal skills—active listening, providing feedback, delegating, managing conflict, and negotiating—that managers must be proficient in to manage effectively in today's organizations.

Understanding Communication

The importance of effective communication for managers cannot be overemphasized for one specific reason: Everything a manager does involves communicating. Not *some* things, but *everything!* A manager can't make a decision without information. That information has to be communicated. Once a decision is made, communication must again take place. Otherwise, no one will know that a decision has been made. The best idea, the most creative suggestion, or the finest plan cannot take form without communication. Managers therefore need effective communication skills. We are not suggesting, of course, that good communication skills alone make a successful manager. We can say, however, that ineffective communication skills can lead to a continuous stream of problems for the manager.

Everything a manager does involves communicating.

What Is Communication?

Communication involves the transfer of meaning. If no information or ideas have been conveyed, communication has not taken place. The speaker who is not heard or the writer who is not read does not communicate. The philosophical question, "If a tree falls in a forest and no one hears it, does it make any noise?" must, in a communicative context, be answered negatively.

However, for communication to be successful, the meaning must be not only imparted but also understood. A letter addressed to us but written in Farsi (a language of which we are totally ignorant) cannot be considered a communication until we have it translated. **Communication,** then, is the transferring and understanding of meaning. Perfect communication, if such a thing were possible, would exist when a transmitted thought or idea was perceived by the receiver exactly as it was envisioned by the sender.

communication
The transferring and understanding of meaning.

Another point to keep in mind is that good communication is often erroneously defined by the communicator as agreement instead of clarity of understanding.[3] If someone disagrees with us, we may assume that the person just didn't fully understand our position. In other words, we may define good communication as having someone accept our views. But I can understand very clearly what you mean and not agree with what you say. In fact, when observers conclude that a lack of communication must exist because a conflict has continued for a prolonged time, a close examination often reveals that there is plenty of effective communication going on. Each fully understands the other's position. The problem is one of equating effective communication with agreement.

A final point before we move on: Our attention in this chapter will be on **interpersonal communication:** communication between two or more people in which the parties are treated as individuals rather than as objects. Organization-wide communication—which encompasses topics such as the flow of organizational communication, communication networks, and the development of management information systems—will be covered in our discussion of information control systems in Chapter 16.

interpersonal communication
Communication between two or more people in which the parties are treated as individuals rather than as objects.

How Does the Communication Process Work?

Before communication can take place, a purpose, expressed as a **message** to be conveyed, must exist. It passes between a sender (the source) and a receiver. The message is converted to symbolic form (called **encoding**) and passed by way of some medium **(channel)** to the receiver, who translates the sender's message (called **decoding**). The result is the transfer of meaning from one person to another.[4]

message
A purpose to be conveyed.

encoding
The conversion of a message into some symbolic form.

channel
The medium by which a message travels.

decoding
A receiver's translation of a sender's message.

Exhibit 14-1 depicts the communication process. This model is made up of seven stages: (1) the communication source (the sender), (2) the message, (3) encoding, (4) the channel, (5) decoding, (6) the receiver, and (7) feedback. In addition, the entire process

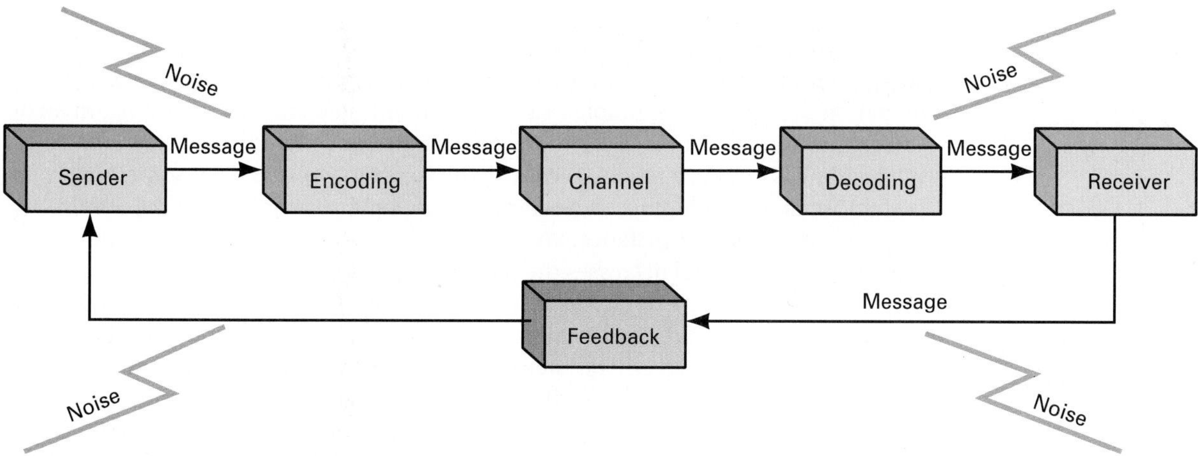

Exhibit 14-1
The Communication Process

is susceptible to **noise**—that is, disturbances that interfere with the transmission of the message (depicted in Exhibit 14-1 as lightning bolts). Typical examples of noise include illegible print, telephone static, inattention by the receiver, or the background sounds of machinery on the production floor. Remember that anything that interferes with understanding—whether internal (such as the low speaking voice of the speaker/sender) or external (such as the loud voices of coworkers talking at an adjoining desk)—represents noise. Noise can create distortion at any point in the communication process. Because the impact of external noise on communication effectiveness is self-evident, let's look at some potential internal sources of distortion in the communication process.

noise
Disturbances that interfere with the transmission of a message.

The main purpose of communications is to get the message across the way it is intended. International symbols, such as this one, which means "no bicycles permitted," transfer meaning and understanding, and effective communication occurs.

A sender initiates a message by encoding a thought. Four conditions affect the encoded message: skills, attitudes, knowledge, and the social-cultural system. For instance, if textbook authors are without the requisite skills, their message will not reach students in the form desired. Our success in communicating to you depends on our writing skills. One's total communicative success also includes speaking, reading, listening, and reasoning skills. As we discussed in Chapter 10, our attitudes influence our behavior. We hold preformed ideas on numerous topics, and these ideas affect our communications. Furthermore, we are restricted in our communicative activity by the extent of our knowledge of a particular topic. We cannot communicate what we do not know, and, should our knowledge be too extensive, it is possible that our receiver will not understand our message. Clearly, the amount of knowledge we have about a subject affects the message we seek to transfer. Finally, just as our attitudes influence our behavior, so does our position in the social-cultural system in which we exist. Our beliefs and values (all part of our culture) act to influence us as communication sources.

The message itself can cause distortion in the communication process, regardless of the supporting apparatus used to convey it. Our message is the actual physical product encoded by the source. "When we speak, the speech is the message. When we write, the writing is the message. When we paint, the picture is the message. When we gesture, the movements of our arms, the expressions on our face are the message."[5] Our message is affected by the code or group of symbols we use to transfer meaning, the content of the message itself, and the decisions that the source makes in selecting and arranging both codes and content. Each of these three segments can act to distort the message.

The channel is the medium through which the message travels. It is selected by the sender. Common channels are air for the spoken word and paper and electronic means for the written word. If you decide to convey to a friend something that happened to you during the day in a face-to-face conversation, you're using spoken words and gestures to transmit your message. But you have choices. A specific message—an invitation to a party, for example—can be communicated orally or in writing. In an organization, certain channels are more appropriate for certain messages. Obviously, if the building is on fire, a memo to convey the fact is inappropriate! If something is important, such as an employee's performance appraisal, a manager might want to use multiple channels—for instance, an oral review followed by a summary letter. Using more than one channel decreases the potential for distortion.

The receiver is the individual to whom the message is directed. But before the message can be received, the symbols in it must be translated into a form that can be understood by the receiver. This step is the decoding of the message. Just as the encoder was limited by his or her skills, attitudes, knowledge, and social-cultural system, so is the receiver. Just as the source must be skillful in writing or speaking, the receiver must be skillful in reading or listening, and both must be able to reason. A person's level of knowledge influences his or her ability to receive, just as it does his or her ability to send. Moreover, the receiver's preformed attitudes and cultural background can distort the message being transferred.

The final link in the communicative process is a feedback loop. Feedback returns the message to the sender and provides a check on whether understanding has been achieved.[6]

What Is Oral Communication?

People communicate with each other most often by talking, or oral communication. In organizations, "oral communication skill is used to send messages 64 percent of the time."[7] Popular forms of oral communication include speeches, formal one-on-one and group discussions, informal discussions, and the rumor mill or grapevine.

The advantages of oral communication are quick transmission and quick feedback. A verbal message can be conveyed and a response received in a minimum amount of time. If the receiver is unsure of the message, rapid feedback allows the sender to detect the uncertainty and to correct it.

The major disadvantage of oral communication surfaces whenever a message has to be passed through a number of people. The more people involved, the greater the potential for distortion. Each person interprets the message in his or her own way. The message's content, when it reaches its destination, is often very different from the original. In an organization where decisions and other communiqués are verbally passed up and down the authority hierarchy, considerable opportunity exists for messages to become distorted.

What Is the Grapevine? Human nature has given most of us a unique personality trait. That is, we have an interest in knowing about things going on around us. This same trait at times also makes us want to share what we know with others. In fact, in this two-way process, good information passes between us fairly fast—bad information, even faster.[8]

The grapevine motto: good information passes between people fairly fast—bad information, even faster.

Here's an example of how this process works. The quarterback on your high school's football team twisted his ankle in a game Friday night. When they saw him hobbling off the field, the coach and the player's parents decided it was best for him to be taken for x-rays immediately. Two hours later, he was home resting, in a cast up to his calf—the result of a broken ankle. At Saturday night's homecoming dance, the air was filled with talk about what had happened. Some good friends of the player who had visited him earlier reported that he had, indeed, broken his ankle and would be in a cast for up to eight weeks. Some even suggested that his football career might be over, for if his ankle didn't heal properly, he would need surgery to place screws in the bone to hold it together. By Monday morning, when school announcements were made, the news that his ankle was broken was already old! Welcome to the grapevine!

The **grapevine** is the unofficial way that communications take place in an organization. It is neither authorized nor supported by the organization. Rather, information is spread by word of mouth—and even through electronic means today. The basis of the grapevine is to get information out to organizational members as quickly as possible.

grapevine
An unofficial channel of communication.

Is the Grapevine Accurate? The biggest question raised about grapevines, however, focuses on the accuracy of the rumors. Research on this topic has been somewhat mixed. In an organization characterized by openness the grapevine may be extremely accurate. In others, in an authoritative culture, the rumor mill may not be accurate. But even then, although the information flowing is inaccurate, it still contains some element of truth. Remember the football player? The need for screws in the ankle was pure conjecture—but the fact that something was wrong was right on target. Likewise, rumors about major layoffs, plant closings, and the like, may be filled with inaccurate information regarding who will be affected or when it may occur. Nonetheless, the fact that something is about to happen is probably on target. Because people cannot be prevented from talking, many managers recognize that instead of trying to stop the grapevine, they can use it to their advantage.

Are Written Communications More Effective Than Oral Ones?

Written communications include memos, letters, e-mail, organizational periodicals, bulletin boards, or any other device that transmits written words or symbols. Why would a sender choose to use written communications? Because they are tangible, verifiable, and more permanent than the oral variety. Typically, both sender and receiver have a record of the communication. The message can be stored for an indefinite period of time. If there are questions about the content of the message, it is physically available for later reference. This feature is particularly important for complex or lengthy communications. For example, the marketing plan for a new product is likely to contain a number of tasks spread out over several months. By putting it in writing, those who have to initiate the plan can readily refer to the document over the life of the plan. A final benefit of written communication comes from the process itself. Except in rare instances, such as when presenting a formal speech, more care is taken with the written word than with the oral word. Having to put something in writing forces a person to think more carefully about what he or she wants to convey. Therefore, written communications are more likely to be well thought out, logical, and clear.

Of course, written messages have their drawbacks. Writing may be more precise, but it also consumes a great deal more time. You could convey far more information to your college instructor in a one-hour oral exam than in a one-hour written exam. In fact, you could probably say the same thing in ten to fifteen minutes that takes you an hour to write. The other major disadvantage is feedback, or rather lack of it. Oral communications allow the receivers to respond rapidly to what they think they hear. However, written communications do not have a built-in feedback mechanism. The result is that sending a memo is no assurance that it will be received; if it is received, there is no guarantee that the recipient will interpret it as the sender meant. The latter point is also relevant in oral communiqués, except that it's easier in such cases merely to ask the receiver to summarize what you have said. An accurate summary presents feedback evidence that the message has been received and understood.

How Do Nonverbal Cues Affect Communications?

Some of the most meaningful communications are neither spoken nor written. These are nonverbal communications. A loud siren or a red light at an intersection tells you something without words. A college instructor doesn't need words to know that students are bored; their eyes get glassy or they begin to read the school newspaper during class. Similarly, when papers start to rustle and notebooks begin to close, the message is clear: Class time is about over. The size of a person's office and desk or the clothes a person wears also convey messages to others. However, the best-known areas of nonverbal communication are body language and verbal intonation (see Managers Who Made a Difference).

body language
Nonverbal communication cues such as facial expressions, gestures, and other body movements.

verbal intonation
An emphasis given to words or phrases that conveys meaning.

Body language refers to gestures, facial configurations, and other movements of the body.[9] A snarled face, for example, says something different from a smile. Hand motions, facial expressions, and other gestures can communicate emotions or temperaments such as aggression, fear, shyness, arrogance, joy, and anger. **Verbal intonation** refers to the emphasis someone gives to words or phrases. To illustrate how intonations can change the meaning of a message, consider the student who asks the instructor a question. The instructor replies, "What do you mean by that?" The student's reaction will vary, depending on the tone of the instructor's response. A soft, smooth tone creates a different meaning from one that is abrasive and puts a strong emphasis on the last word. Most of us would view the first intonation as coming from someone who sincerely sought clarification, whereas the second suggests that the person is aggressive or defensive.

The fact that every oral communication also has a nonverbal message cannot be overemphasized. Why? Because the nonverbal component is likely to carry the greatest impact. One researcher found that 55 percent of an oral message is derived from facial expression and physical posture, 38 percent from verbal intonation, and only 7 percent from the actual words used.[10] Most of us know that animals respond to how we say something rather than to what we say. Apparently, people aren't much different.

Is the Wave of Communication's Future in Electronic Media?

e-mail
A means of instantaneously transmitting written messages on computers that are linked together with the appropriate software.

Today we rely on a number of sophisticated electronic devices to carry our interpersonal communications. In addition to the more common ones—the telephone and public address system—we have closed-circuit television, voice-activated computers, cellular phones, pagers, and **e-mail.** For example, e-mail allows us to instantaneously transmit written messages on computers that are linked together with the appropriate software. Today, it's one of the most widely used methods for organizational members to communicate. Messages sit at the receiver's terminal to be read at the receiver's convenience. E-mail is fast and cheap and can be used to send the same message to dozens of people at the same time. Currently, more than 23 million workers use e-mail daily—with that number expected to reach nearly 100 million workers by the year 2000.[11]

What Barriers Exist to Effective Communication?

In our discussion of the communication process, we noted the consistent potential for distortion. What causes such distortions? In addition to the general distortions identified in the communication process, there are other barriers to effective communication. These are presented below and are summarized in Exhibit 14-2.

Managers Who Made a Difference

Karen Vesper, Vice President of Doorway Rug Service

What do AT&T, IBM, and Doorway Rug Service, Inc., of Buffalo, New York, have in common? These organizations are teaching many of their employees—especially those in marketing and sales—to make decisions on the basis of nonverbal communication cues. For Karen Vesper, vice president of Doorway, focusing on nonverbal communications has become an important part of her interpersonal dealings.[12]

Several years ago, Karen became interested in how body movements and mannerisms truly reflect what an individual is "saying." Continually reading in this area of study, Vesper has been able to make decisions about potential employees and potential customers by "reading" them. For example, Vesper believes that body language can give a person a competitive advantage. It can make the difference between "closing the sale," or in Doorway's case, hiring new employees. For example, during interviews, Vesper pays constant attention to the job candidate's eye movements and mannerisms. Vesper believes that she can correctly predict if the job candidate will be an aggressive salesperson—while simultaneously being personable and friendly. How does she do this? By looking at their eyes and how they present themselves. In one case, a hiring decision came down to two people. Candidate 1 was animated and made constant eye contact. Candidate 2 never looked Karen in the eye, leaned back in his chair, and crossed both his legs and arms. Candidate 1 demonstrated communication skills that Vesper found more aligned with successful performance in her organization.

Karen Vesper is convinced that nonverbal communications can play a significant role in helping her organization achieve its annual sales goals. Personally, she has found that it has helped her "qualify" customers. For instance, even though a potential customer says Yes, crossed arms and legs emphatically state No! Understanding this, she is in a better position to probe further into the possible objections the customer has. What she has found is that, in many cases, she is able to steer the conversation in a direction that ultimately leads to successfully closing a sale. And that, to Karen, is a major competitive advantage.

Has Vesper's system worked? Karen Vesper says it has. Although she doesn't have hard numbers to substantiate her claim, since paying more attention to nonverbal cues—and training her salespeople to do the same—Doorway's business has grown. So too, have company profits!

Filtering is the deliberate manipulation of information to make it appear more favorable to the receiver. For example, when a manager tells his or her boss what the boss wants to hear, the manager is filtering information. The extent of filtering tends to be a function of the height of the structure and the organizational culture. The more vertical levels there are in an organization's hierarchy, the more opportunities there are for filtering. The organizational culture encourages or discourages filtering by the type of behavior it emphasizes through rewards. The more rewards emphasize style and appearance, the more managers are motivated to alter communications in their favor.

filtering
The deliberate manipulation of information to make it appear more favorable to the receiver.

Filtering	The deliberate manipulation of information to make it appear more favorable to the receiver.
Selective Perception	Receiving communications on the basis of what one selectively sees and hears depending on his or her needs, motivation, experience, background, and other personal characteristics.
Emotions	Messages will often be interpreted differently depending on how happy or sad one is when the message is being communicated.
Language	Words have different meanings to different people. Receivers will use their definition of words communicated, which may be different from what the sender intended.
Nonverbal Cues	Body language or intonation that sends the receiver another message. When the two are not aligned, communication is distorted.

Exhibit 14-2
Barriers to Effective Communication

The second barrier can be identified as selective perception. We have mentioned selective perception several times throughout this book. The receiver in the communication process selectively sees and hears communications depending on his or her needs, motivation, experience, background, and other personal characteristics. The receiver also projects his or her interests and expectations into communications in decoding them. The employment interviewer who expects a female job candidate to put family before career is likely to see that priority in female candidates, regardless of whether the candidates feel that way. As we said in Chapter 10, we don't see reality; instead, we interpret what we see and call it reality.

Another obstruction in communications comes from people's emotions. How the receiver feels when a message is received influences how he or she interprets it. Extreme emotions such as jubilation or depression are most likely to hinder effective communication. In such instances, we often disregard our rational and objective thinking processes and substitute emotional judgments.

Owens Corning wants employees to fully understand what the company's stock option plan means. To help achieve this goal, and to avoid any possibility of misunderstandings or the appearance of filtering, the company uses a game called "Sharing the Wealth," which teaches employees how a business operates, the types of decisions that need to be made, and the problems that may be encountered. In this way, when employees get their "stock-option bonus" at year-end, they appreciate what went into the decision of determining how much the bonus would be.

Words, too, mean different things to different people. Age, education, cultural and even technological background are four of the more obvious variables that influence the language a person uses and the definitions he or she gives to words.[13] The language of a "network developer" is clearly different from that of the typical high school–educated factory worker. The latter, in fact, may have trouble understanding much of the developer's terms, such as *morphing, server, java,* and *cyberspeak.*[14] In an organization, employees usually come from diverse backgrounds. And this diversity may mean that you will work with people who don't speak your language. But even if they did, our use of that language is far from uniform. A knowledge of how each of us modifies the language would minimize communication difficulties. The problem is that members in an organization usually don't know how others with whom they interact have modified the language. Senders tend to assume that their words and terms will be appropriately interpreted by the receiver. This assumption, of course, is often incorrect and creates communication difficulties.

Finally, barriers to effective communications can come from nonverbal cues. Earlier, we noted that nonverbal communication is an important way in which people convey messages to others. But nonverbal communication is almost always accompanied by oral communication. As long as the two are in agreement, they act to reinforce each other.

How Can Managers Overcome Communication Barriers?

Given these barriers to communication, what can managers do to overcome them? The following suggestions should help make communication more effective (see also Exhibit 14-3).

Why Use Feedback? Many communication problems can be directly attributed to misunderstandings and inaccuracies.[15] These problems are less likely to occur if the manager uses the feedback loop in the communication process. This feedback can be verbal or nonverbal.

If a manager asks a receiver, "Did you understand what I said?" the response represents feedback. Also, feedback should include more than yes and no answers.[16] The manager can ask a set of questions about a message in order to determine whether the message was received as intended. Better yet, the manager can ask the receiver to restate the message in his or her own words. If the manager then hears what was intended, understanding and accuracy should be enhanced. Feedback also includes subtler methods than the direct asking of questions or the summarizing of messages. General comments can give a manager a sense of the receiver's reaction to a message. In addition, performance appraisals, salary reviews, and promotions represent important forms of feedback.

Of course, feedback does not have to be conveyed in words. Actions may speak louder than words. The sales manager who sends out a directive to his or her staff describing a new monthly sales report that all sales personnel will need to complete receives feedback if some of the salespeople fail to turn in the new report. This feedback suggests that the sales manager needs to clarify the initial directive. Similarly, when you give a speech to a group of people, you watch their eyes and look for other nonverbal clues to tell you whether they are getting your message.

Why Should Simplified Language Be Used? Because language can be a barrier, managers should choose words and structure their messages in ways that will make those messages clear and understandable to the receiver (see Exhibit 14-4). The manager should consider the audience to whom the message is directed so that the language will be tailored to the receivers. Remember, effective communication is

Use Feedback	Check the accuracy of what has been communicated—or what you think you heard.
Simplify Language	Use words that the intended audience understands.
Listen Actively	Listen for the full meaning of the message without making premature judgments or interpretations—or thinking about what you are going to say in response.
Constrain Emotions	Recognize when your emotions are running high. When they are, don't communicate until you have calmed down.
Watch Nonverbal Cues	Be aware that your actions speak louder than your words. Keep the two consistent.

Exhibit 14-3
Overcoming Barriers to Effective Communication

Exhibit 14-4
Using Simple Language?

Source: Scott Adams, copyright 1992, United Features Syndicate, Inc. Used with permission.

achieved when a message is both received and understood. Understanding is improved by simplifying the language used in relation to the audience intended. This means, for example, that a hospital administrator should always try to communicate in clear, easily understood terms and that the language used in messages to the surgical staff should be purposely different from that used with office employees. Jargon can facilitate understanding when it is used within a group of those who know what it means, but it can cause innumerable problems when used outside that group.

Why Must We Listen Actively? When someone talks, we hear. But too often we don't listen. Listening is an active search for meaning, whereas hearing is passive. In listening, two people are thinking—the receiver and the sender.

Many of us are poor listeners. Why? Because listening is difficult, and it's usually more satisfying to be the talker. Listening, in fact, is often more tiring than talking. It demands intellectual effort. Unlike hearing, **active listening** demands total concentration. The average person speaks at a rate of about 150 words per minute, whereas we have the capacity to hear and process at the rate of nearly 1,000 words per minute.[17] The difference obviously leaves idle time for the brain and opportunities for the mind to wander.

active listening
Listening for full meaning without making premature judgments or interpretations.

Active listening is enhanced by developing empathy with the sender—that is, by placing yourself in the sender's position. Because senders differ in attitudes, interests, needs, and expectations, empathy makes it easier to understand the actual content of a message. An empathic listener reserves judgment on the message's content and carefully listens to what is being said. The goal is to improve one's ability to receive the full meaning of a communication without having it distorted by premature judgments or interpretations. We'll return to active listening as an interpersonal skill shortly.

Why Must We Constrain Emotions? It would be naive to assume that managers always communicate in a fully rational manner. We know that emotions can severely cloud and distort the transference of meaning. A manager who is emotionally upset over an issue is likely to misconstrue incoming messages and fail to express his or her outgoing messages clearly and accurately. What can the manager do? The simplest answer is to stop communicating until he or she has regained composure.

Why the Emphasis on Nonverbal Cues? If actions speak louder than words, then it's important to watch your actions to make sure that they align with and reinforce the words that go along with them. We noted that nonverbal messages carry a great deal of weight. Given this fact, the effective communicator watches his or her nonverbal cues to ensure that they too convey the desired message.

Diversity Insights into the Communication Process

Do men and women communicate in the same way? The answer is No! And the differences between men and women may lead to significant misunderstandings and misperceptions.[18]

Research by Deborah Tannen regarding how men and women communicate has uncovered some interesting insights. She found that when men talk, they do so to emphasize status and independence; whereas women talk to create connections and intimacy. For instance, men frequently complain that women talk on and on about their problems. Women, however, criticize men for not listening. What's happening is that when a man hears a woman talking about a problem, he frequently asserts his desire for independence and control by providing solutions. Many women, in contrast, view conversing about a problem as a means of promoting closeness. The woman presents the problem to gain support and connection—not to get the man's advice.

Effective communication between the sexes is important to all organizations for meeting organizational goals. But how can we manage the diverse differences in communication style? To keep gender differences from becoming persistent barriers to effective communication requires acceptance, understanding, and a commitment to communicate adaptively with each other. Both men and women need to acknowledge that there are differences in communication styles, that one style isn't better than the other, and that it takes real effort to "talk" with each other successfully.

When men talk, they emphasize status and independence. Women talk to create connections and intimacy.

Beyond differences in gender communication styles, it's important to recognize that interpersonal communication isn't conducted in the same way around the world.[19] For example, compare countries that place a high value on individualism (such as the United States) with countries where the emphasis is on collectivism (such as Japan).[20]

Owing to the emphasis on the individual in countries such as the United States, communication patterns there are individual-oriented and rather clearly spelled out. For instance, U.S. managers rely heavily on memoranda, announcements, position papers, and other formal forms of communication to stake out their positions in intraorganizational negotiations. Supervisors in the United States often hoard secret information in an attempt to promote their own advancement and as a way of inducing their employees to accept decisions and plans. For their own protection, lower-level employees also engage in this practice.

In collectivist countries such as Japan, there is more interaction for its own sake and a more informal manner of interpersonal contact. The Japanese manager, in contrast to U.S. managers, will engage in extensive verbal consultation over an issue first and only later will draw up a formal document to outline the agreement that was made. Face-to-face communication is encouraged. In addition, open communication is an inherent part of the Japanese work setting. Work spaces are open and crowded

Communications in a global village can pose problems. Not only are languages different, but nonverbal communications can be too. To minimize such problems, these China International Capital Corporation executives often resort to bilingual secretaries to serve as interpreters when visited by an executive from Western cultures.

with individuals at different levels in the work hierarchy. U.S. organizations emphasize authority, hierarchy, and formal lines of communication.

Developing Interpersonal Skills

Would it surprise you to know that more managers are probably fired because of poor interpersonal skills than for a lack of technical ability on the job?[21] A survey of 191 top executives at six Fortune 500 companies found that, according to these executives, the single biggest reason for failure was poor interpersonal skills.[22] The Center for Creative Leadership in North Carolina estimates that half of all managers and 30 percent of all senior managers have some type of difficulty with people. And results of a survey of senior managers in Canada's top 100 corporations showed that 32 percent of the respondents rated interpersonal skills as a top priority in hiring decisions.[23]

If you need any further evidence of the importance of interpersonal skills, we would point to a comprehensive study of people who hire students with undergraduate business degrees and depend on these hires to fill future management vacancies. The study found that the area in which the graduates were most deficient was in leadership and interpersonal skills.[24] Of course, these overall findings are consistent with our view of the manager's job. Because managers ultimately get things done through others, competencies in leadership, communication, and other interpersonal skills are a prerequisite to managerial effectiveness. Therefore, the rest of this chapter will focus on key interpersonal skills that every manager needs to develop.[25]

The biggest reason managers fail in their jobs is due to poor interpersonal skills.

Why Are Active Listening Skills Important?

The ability to be an effective listener is too often taken for granted. We often confuse hearing with listening. Hearing is merely picking up sound vibrations. Listening is making sense of what we hear. Listening requires paying attention, interpreting, and remembering sound stimuli.

What Is the Difference between Active and Passive Listening?

Effective listening is active rather than passive. In passive listening, you are like a tape recorder. You absorb and remember the words spoken. If the speaker provides you with a clear message and makes his or her delivery interesting enough to keep your attention, you'll probably hear most of what the speaker is trying to communicate. But active listening requires you to "get inside" the speaker's mind so you can understand the communication from his or her point of view. As you will see, active listening is hard work.[26] You have to concentrate, and you have to want to fully understand what a speaker is saying. Students who use active listening techniques for an entire fifty-minute lecture are as tired as their instructor when the lecture is over because they have put as much energy into listening as the instructor put into speaking.

There are four essential requirements for listening: (1) intensity, (2) empathy, (3) acceptance, and (4) a willingness to take responsibility for completeness.[27] As noted previously, the human brain is capable of handling a speaking rate that is about six times as fast that of the average speaker. That leaves a lot of time for daydreaming. The active listener concentrates intensely on what the speaker is saying and tunes out the thousands of miscellaneous thoughts (about money, sex, vacation, parties, exams, and so on) that create distractions. What do active listeners do with their idle brain time? They summarize and integrate what has been said. They put each new bit of information into the context of what preceded it!

Empathy requires you to put yourself into the speaker's shoes. You try to understand what the speaker wants to communicate rather than what you want to hear. Notice that empathy demands both knowledge of the speaker and flexibility on your part. You need to suspend your own thoughts and feelings and adjust what you see and feel to your speaker's world. In that way, you increase the likelihood that you'll interpret the message in the way the speaker intended.

An active listener demonstrates acceptance. He or she listens objectively without judging content. This is no easy task. It's natural to be distracted by the content of what a speaker says, especially when we disagree with it. When we hear something we disagree with, we have a tendency to begin formulating our mental arguments to counter what is being said. Of course, in doing so we miss the rest of the message. The challenge for the active listener is to absorb what's being said and to withhold judgment on content until the speaker is finished.

The final ingredient of active listening is taking responsibility for completeness. That is, the listener does whatever is necessary to get the full intended meaning from the speaker's communication. Two widely used active listening techniques to achieve this end are listening for feeling as well as for content and asking questions to ensure understanding.

Just how, though, can you develop effective listening skills? The literature on active listening emphasizes eight specific behaviors (see Developing a Management Skill).[28] As you review these behaviors, ask yourself whether they describe your listening practices. If you're not currently using these techniques, there's no better time than right now to begin developing them.

Why Are Feedback Skills Important?

Ask a manager about the feedback he or she gives to employees, and you're likely to get a qualified answer. If the feedback is positive, it's likely to be given promptly and enthusiastically. Negative feedback is often treated very differently. Like most of us, managers don't particularly enjoy communicating bad news. They fear offending or having to deal with the receiver's defensiveness. The result is that negative feedback is often avoided, delayed, or substantially distorted.[29] The purposes of this section are to show you the importance of providing both positive and negative feedback and to identify specific techniques to help make your feedback more effective.

What Is the Difference between Positive and Negative Feedback? We said that managers treat positive and negative feedback differently. So, too, do receivers. You need to understand this fact and adjust your feedback style accordingly.

Developing a Management Skill

LEARNING TO ACTIVELY LISTEN

About the Skill: *Active listening requires you to concentrate on what is being said. It's more than just hearing the words. It involves a concerted effort to understand and interpret the speaker's message.*

Steps in Practicing the Skill

1. ***Make eye contact.*** How do you feel when somebody doesn't look at you when you're speaking? If you're like most people, you're likely to interpret this behavior as aloofness or disinterest. Making eye contact with the speaker focuses your attention, reduces the likelihood that you will become distracted, and encourages the speaker.

2. ***Exhibit affirmative nods and appropriate facial expressions.*** The effective listener shows interest in what is being said through nonverbal signals. Affirmative nods and appropriate facial expressions, when added to good eye contact, convey to the speaker that you're listening.

3. ***Avoid distracting actions or gestures that suggest boredom.*** The other side of showing interest is avoiding actions that suggest that your mind is somewhere else. When listening, don't look at your watch, shuffle papers, play with your pencil, or engage in similar distractions. They make the speaker feel that you're bored or disinterested or indicate that you aren't fully attentive.

4. ***Ask questions.*** The critical listener analyzes what he or she hears and asks questions. This behavior provides clarification, ensures understanding, and assures the speaker that you're listening.

5. ***Paraphrase using your own words.*** The effective listener uses phrases such as: "What I hear you saying is . . ." or "Do you mean . . .?" Paraphrasing is an excellent control device to check on whether you're listening carefully and to verify that what you heard is accurate.

6. ***Avoid interrupting the speaker.*** Let the speaker complete his or her thought before you try to respond. Don't try to second guess where the speaker's thoughts are going. When the speaker is finished, you'll know it.

7. ***Don't overtalk.*** Most of us would rather speak our own ideas than listen to what someone else says. Talking might be more fun and silence might be uncomfortable, but you can't talk and listen at the same time. The good listener recognizes this fact and doesn't overtalk.

8. ***Make smooth transitions between the roles of speaker and listener.*** The effective listener makes transitions smoothly from speaker to listener and back to speaker. From a listening perspective this means concentrating on what a speaker has to say and practicing not thinking about what you're going to say as soon as you get your chance.

Positive feedback is more readily and accurately perceived than negative feedback. Furthermore, whereas positive feedback is almost always accepted, negative feedback often meets resistance.[30] Why? The logical answer appears to be that people want to hear good news and block out the rest. Positive feedback fits what most people wish to hear and already believe about themselves.

Does this mean, then, that you should avoid giving negative feedback? No! What it means is that you need to be aware of potential resistance and learn to use negative feedback in situations in which it's most likely to be accepted.[31] What are those situations? Research indicates that negative feedback is most likely to be accepted when it comes from a credible source or if it's objective in form. Subjective impressions carry weight only then they come from a person with high status and credibility.[32] This suggests that negative feedback that is supported by hard data—numbers, specific examples, and the like—is more likely to be accepted. Negative feedback that is subjective can be a meaningful tool for experienced managers, particularly those in upper levels of the organization who have built the trust and earned the respect of their employees. From less-experienced managers, those in the lower ranks of the organization, and those whose reputations have not yet been established, negative feedback that is subjective in nature is not likely to be well received.

How Do You Give Effective Feedback?

There are six specific suggestions that we can make to help you become more effective in providing feedback. We will discuss them below and summarize them in Exhibit 14-5.

Focus on specific behaviors. Feedback should be specific rather than general.[33] Avoid statements such as "You have a bad attitude" or "I'm really impressed with the good job you did." They are vague, and, although they provide information, they do not tell the receiver enough to correct the "bad attitude" or on what basis you concluded that a "good job" has been done so the person knows what behaviors to repeat.

Keep feedback impersonal. Feedback, particularly the negative kind, should be descriptive rather than judgmental or evaluative.[34] No matter how upset you are, keep the feedback focused on job-related behaviors and never criticize someone personally because of an inappropriate action. Telling people they are incompetent, lazy, or the like is almost always counterproductive. It provokes such an emotional reaction that the performance deviation itself is apt to be overlooked. When you are criticizing, remember that you are censuring job-related behavior, not the person. You might be tempted to tell someone he or she is rude and insensitive (which might just be true); however, that is hardly impersonal. It's better to say something more specific like, "You've interrupted me three times with questions that weren't urgent when you knew I was talking long distance to a customer in Brazil."

Keep feedback goal-oriented. Feedback should not be given primarily to "dump" or "unload" on another person.[35] If you have to say something negative, make sure it is directed toward the receiver's goals. Ask yourself whom the feedback is supposed to help. If the answer is essentially you—"I've got something I just want to get off my chest"—bite your tongue and hold the comment. Such feedback undermines your credibility and lessens the meaning and influence of future feedback sessions.

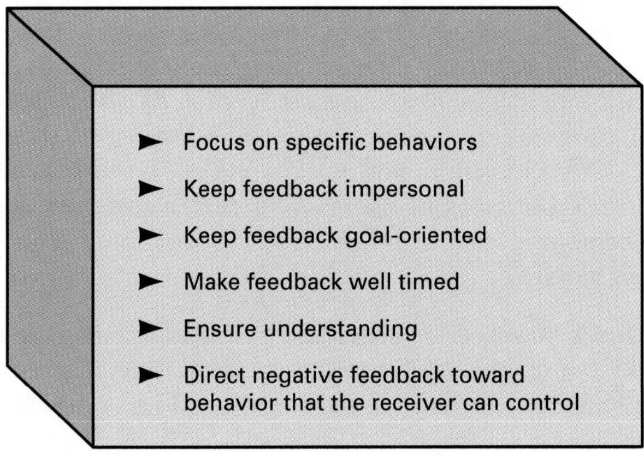

Exhibit 14-5
Suggestions for Effective Feedback

Make feedback well timed. Feedback is most meaningful to a receiver when there is a very short interval between his or her behavior and the receipt of feedback about that behavior.[36] For example, a new employee who makes a mistake is more likely to respond to his or her manager's suggestions for improving right after the mistake or at the end of the work day rather than during a performance review session six months from now. If you have to spend time recreating a situation and refreshing someone's memory of it, the feedback you are providing is likely to be ineffective.[37] Moreover, if you are particularly concerned with changing behavior, delays in providing timely feedback on the undesirable actions lessen the likelihood that the feedback will be effective in bringing about the desired change.[38] Of course, making feedback prompt merely for promptness' sake can backfire if you have insufficient information or if you are emotionally upset. In such instances, "well timed" could mean "somewhat delayed."

Ensure understanding. Is your feedback concise and complete enough that the receiver clearly and fully understands your communication? Remember that every successful communication requires both transference and understanding of meaning. If feedback is to be effective, you need to ensure that the receiver understands it.[39] Consistent with our discussion of listening techniques, you should have the receiver rephrase the content of your message to find out whether he or she fully captured the meaning you intended.

Direct negative feedback toward behavior that the receiver can control. There is little value in reminding a person of some shortcoming over which he or she has no control. Negative feedback should be directed toward behavior the receiver can do something about.[40] For instance, to criticize an employee who's late for work because she forgot to set her alarm clock is valid. To criticize her for being late for work when the subway she takes to work every day had a power failure, stranding her for ninety minutes, is pointless. There is nothing she could have done to correct what happened—short of finding a different means of traveling to work, which may be unrealistic.

In addition, when negative feedback is given concerning something that the receiver can control, it might be a good idea to indicate specifically what can be done to improve the situation. Such suggestions take some of the sting out of the criticism and offer guidance to receivers who understand the problem but don't know how to resolve it.

What Are Delegation Skills?

We have made this point before: Managers get things done through other people. This description recognizes that there are limits to any manager's time and knowledge. Effective managers need to understand the value of delegating and know how to do it.[41]

delegation
The assignment of authority to another person to carry out specific activities.

Delegation is the assignment of authority to another person to carry out specific activities. It allows an employee to make decisions—that is, it is a shift of decision-making authority from one organizational level to another, lower, one (see Exhibit 14-6).[42] Delegation, however, should not be confused with participation. In participative decision making, there is a sharing of authority. With delegation, employees make decisions on their own. That's why delegation is such a vital component of empowering workers!

Don't Managers Abdicate Their Responsibility When They Delegate? When done properly, delegation is not abdication. The key word here is *properly.* If you, as a manager, dump tasks on an employee without clarifying the exact job to be

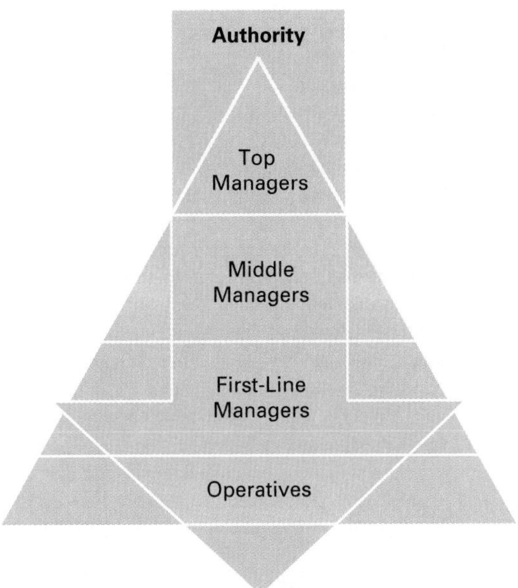

Exhibit 14-6
Effective Delegation

Effective delegation pushes authority down vertically through the ranks of an organization.

done, the range of the employee's discretion, the expected level of performance, the time frame in which the tasks are to be completed, and similar concerns, you are abdicating responsibility and inviting trouble.[43] Don't fall into the trap of assuming that, to avoid the appearance of abdicating, you should minimize delegation. Unfortunately, that is how many new and inexperienced managers interpret the situation. Lacking confidence in their employees or fearful that they will be criticized for their employees' mistakes, these managers try to do everything themselves.

It might very well be true that you are capable of doing tasks better, faster, or with fewer mistakes. The catch is that your time and energy are scarce resources. It is not possible for you to do everything yourself. You need to learn to delegate if you are going to be effective in your job.[44] This fact suggests two important points. First, you should expect and accept some mistakes by your employees. Mistakes are part of delegation. They are often good learning experiences for employees, as long as their costs are not excessive. Second, to ensure that the costs of mistakes don't exceed the value of the learning, you need to put adequate controls in place. As we will discuss shortly, delegation without feedback controls that let you know where there are potentially serious problems is a form of abdication.

How much authority should a manager delegate? Should he or she keep authority centralized, delegating only the minimal amount to complete the delegated duties? What contingency factors should be considered in determining the degree to which authority is delegated? Exhibit 14-7 presents the most widely cited contingency factors to provide some guidance in making those determinations.

How Do You Delegate Effectively? Assuming that the information above indicates that delegation is in order, how do you delegate? A number of actions have been suggested that differentiate the effective from the ineffective delegator.[45]

The size of the organization. The larger the organization, the greater the number of decisions that have to be made. Because top managers in an organization have only so much time and can obtain only so much information, in larger organizations they become increasingly dependent on the decision making of lower-level managers. Therefore, managers in large organizations resort to increased delegation.

The importance of the duty or decision. The more important a duty or decision (as expressed in terms of cost and impact on the future of an organization), the less likely it is to be delegated. For instance, a department head may be delegated authority to make expenditures up to $7,500, and division heads and vice presidents up to $50,000 and $125,000, respectively.

Task complexity. The more complex the task, the more difficult it is for top management to possess current and sufficient technical information to make effective decisions. Complex tasks require greater expertise, and decisions about them should be delegated to the people who have the necessary technical knowledge.

Organizational culture. If management has confidence and trust in employees, the culture will support a greater degree of delegation. However, if top management does not have confidence in the abilities of lower-level managers, it will delegate authority only when absolutely necessary. In such instances, as little authority as possible is delegated.

Qualities of employees. A final contingency consideration is the qualities of employees. Delegation requires employees with the skills, abilities, and motivation to accept authority and act on it. If these are lacking, top management will be reluctant to relinquish authority.

Exhibit 14-7
Contingency Factors in Delegation

Clarify the assignment. The place to begin is to determine what is to be delegated and to whom. You need to identify the person who is most capable of doing the task and then determine whether he or she has the time and motivation to do the job.

Assuming that you have a willing employee, it is your responsibility to provide clear information on what is being delegated, the results you expect, and any time or performance expectations you hold. Unless there is an overriding need to adhere to specific methods, you should delegate only the results. That is, get agreement on what is to be done and the results expected, but let the employee decide by which means the work is to be completed. By focusing on goals and allowing the employee the freedom to use her or her own judgment as to how those goals are to be achieved, you increase trust between you and the employee, improve the employee's motivation, and enhance accountability for results.

Specify employees' range of discretion. Every act of delegation comes with constraints. You are delegating authority to act, but not unlimited authority. What you are delegating is the authority to act on certain issues within certain parameters. You need to specify what those parameters are so that employees know, in no uncertain terms, the range of their discretion. When those parameters have been successfully communicated, both you and employees will have the same idea of the limits to the latter's authority and how far they can go without further approval.

Allow employees to participate. One of the best ways to decide how much authority will be necessary to accomplish a task is to allow employees who will be held accountable for the tasks to participate in that decision. Be aware, however, that participation can present its own set of potential problems as a result of employees' self-interest and biases in evaluating their own abilities. Some employees might be personally motivated to expand their authority beyond what they need and beyond what they are capable of handling. Allowing such people too much participation in deciding what tasks they should take on and how much authority they must have to complete those tasks can undermine the effectiveness of the delegation process.

Inform others that delegation has occurred. Delegation should not take place in a vacuum. No only do you and your employees need to know specifically what has been delegated and how much authority has been granted, anyone else who is likely to be affected by the delegation act needs to be informed. This includes people outside the organization as well as inside it. Essentially, you need to convey what has been delegated (the task and amount of authority) and to whom. Failure to inform others makes conflict likely and decreases the chances that your employees will be able to accomplish the delegated act efficiently.

Establish feedback channels. To delegate without instituting feedback controls is inviting problems. There is always the possibility that employees will misuse the discretion they have been given. The establishment of controls to monitor employees' progress increases the likelihood that important problems will be identified early and that the task will be completed on time and to the desired specification.

Ideally, controls should be determined at the time of initial assignment. Agree on a specific time for completion of the task and then set progress dates when the employees will report back on how well they are doing and on any major problems that have surfaced. These controls can be supplemented with periodic spot checks to ensure that authority guidelines are not being abused, organization policies are being followed, proper procedures are being met, and the like.

Too much of a good thing can be dysfunctional. If the controls are too constraining, employees will be deprived of the opportunity to build self-confidence. As a result, much of the motivational aspect of delegation may be lost. A well-designed control system, which we will elaborate on in more detail in the next chapter, permits your employees to make small mistakes but quickly alerts you when big mistakes are imminent.

Conflict Management Skills

The ability to manage conflict is undoubtedly one of the most important skills a manager needs to possess. A study of middle- and top-level executives by the American Management Association revealed that the average manager spends approximately 20 percent of his or her time dealing with conflict.[46] The importance of conflict management is reinforced by a survey of what topics practicing managers consider most important in management development programs; conflict management was rated as being more important than decision making, leadership, or communication skills.[47] In further support of our claim are the findings of one researcher who studied a group of managers and looked at twenty-five skill and person-

Being successful as a manager depends on knowing how to manage conflict. Resolving differences between employees who are likely to have diverse backgrounds (gender, age, culture) is not an easy task. But it can be done!

conflict
Perceived incompatible differences resulting in interference or opposition.

traditional view of conflict
The view that all conflict is bad and must be avoided.

human relations view of conflict
The view that conflict is natural and inevitable and has the potential to be a positive force.

interactionist view of conflict
The view that some conflict is necessary for an organization to perform effectively.

ality factors to determine which, if any, were related to managerial success (defined in terms of ratings by one's boss, salary increases, and promotions).[48] Of the twenty-five measures, only one—the ability to handle conflict—was positively related to managerial success.

What Is Conflict Management? When we use the term **conflict,** we are referring to perceived incompatible differences resulting in some form of interference or opposition. Whether the differences are real or not is irrelevant. If people perceive that differences exist, then a conflict state exists. In addition, our definition includes the extremes, from subtle, indirect, and highly controlled forms of interference to overt acts such as strikes, riots, and wars.

Over the years, three differing views have evolved toward conflict in organizations[49] (see Exhibit 14-8). One argues that conflict must be avoided, that it indicates a malfunctioning within the organization. We call this the **traditional view of conflict.** A second, the **human relations view of conflict,** argues that conflict is a natural and inevitable outcome in any organization and that it need not be evil but, rather, has the potential to be a positive force in contributing to an organization's performance. The third and most recent perspective proposes not only that conflict can be a positive force in an organization but also that some conflict is absolutely necessary for an organization or units within an organization to perform effectively. We label this third approach the **interactionist view of conflict.**

Exhibit 14-8
Three Views of Conflict

Traditional view	The early approach assumed that conflict was bad and would always have a negative impact on an organization. Conflict became synonymous with violence, destruction, and irrationality. Because conflict was harmful, it was to be avoided. Management had a responsibility to rid the organization of conflict. This traditional view dominated management literature during the late nineteenth century and continued until the mid-1940s.
Human relations view	The human relations position argued that conflict was a natural and inevitable occurrence in all organizations. Because conflict was inevitable, the human relations approach advocated acceptance of conflict. This approach rationalized the existence of conflict; conflict cannot be eliminated, and there are times when it may even benefit the organization. The human relations view dominated conflict thinking from the late 1940s through the mid-1970s.
Interactionist view	The current theoretical perspective on conflict is the interactionist approach. While the human relations approach accepts conflict, the interactionist approach encourages conflict on the grounds that a harmonious, peaceful, tranquil, and cooperative organization is prone to become static, apathetic, and nonresponsive to needs for change and innovation. The major contribution of the interactionist approach, therefore, is that it encourages managers to maintain an ongoing minimum level of conflict—enough to keep units viable, self-critical, and creative.

Can Conflict Be Positive and Negative? The interactionist view does not propose that all conflicts are good. Rather, some conflicts support the goals of the organization; these are **functional conflicts** of a constructive form. Other conflicts prevent an organization from achieving its goals; these are **dysfunctional conflicts** of a destructive form.

functional conflicts Conflicts that support an organization's goals.

dysfunctional conflicts Conflicts that prevent an organization from achieving its goals.

Of course, it is one thing to argue that conflict can be valuable, but how does a manager tell whether a conflict is functional or dysfunctional? Unfortunately, the demarcation is neither clear nor precise. No one level of conflict can be adopted as acceptable or unacceptable under all conditions. The type and level of conflict that promote a healthy and positive involvement toward one department's goals may, in another department or in the same department at another time, be highly dysfunctional. Functionality or dysfunctionality, therefore, is a matter of judgment. Exhibit 14-9 illustrates the challenge facing managers. They want to create an environment within their organization or organizational unit in which conflict is healthy but not allowed to run to pathological extremes. Neither too little nor too much conflict is desirable. Managers should stimulate conflict to gain the full benefits of its functional properties, yet reduce its level when it becomes a disruptive force. Because we have yet to devise a sophisticated measuring instrument for assessing whether a given conflict

Exhibit 14-9
Conflict and Organizational Performance

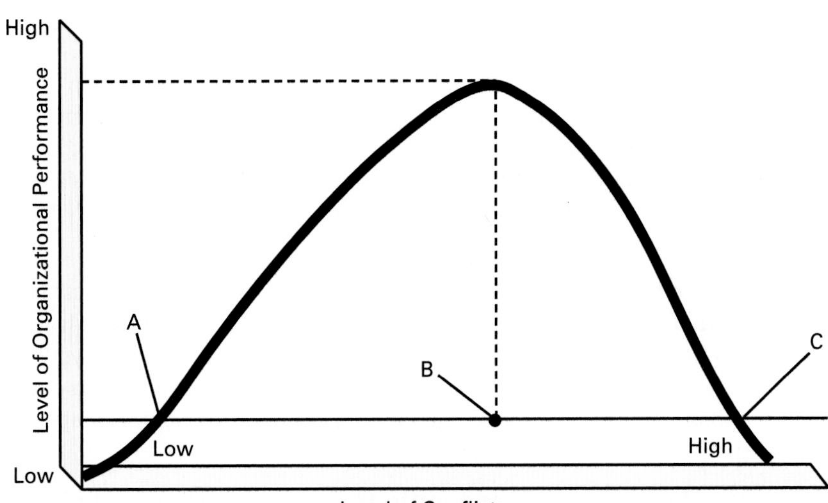

Situation	Level of Conflict	Type of Conflict	Organization's Internal Characteristics	Level of Organizational Performance
A	Low or none	Dys-functional	Apathetic Stagnant Unresponsive to change Lack of new ideas	Low
B	Optimal	Functional	Viable Self-critical Innovative	High
C	High	Dys-functional	Disruptive Chaotic Uncooperative	Low

level is functional or dysfunctional, it remains for managers to make intelligent judgments concerning whether conflict levels in their units are optimal, too high, or too low.

If conflict is dysfunctional, what can a manager do? In the following sections, we will review conflict-resolution skills. Essentially, you need to know your basic conflict-handling style, as well as those of the conflicting parties, to understand the situation that has created the conflict and to be aware of your options.

What Is Your Underlying Conflict-Handling Style? Although most of us have the ability to vary our conflict response according to the situation, each of us has a preferred style for handling conflicts (see Understanding Yourself).[50] You might be able to change your preferred style to suit the context in which a certain conflict exists; however, your basic style tells you how you are most likely to behave and the conflict-handling approaches on which you most often rely.

Which Conflicts Do You Handle? Not every conflict justifies your attention. Some might not be worth the effort; others might be unmanageable. Not every conflict is worth your time and effort to resolve. Avoidance might appear to be a "cop-out," but it can sometimes be the most appropriate response. You can improve your overall management effectiveness, and your conflict-management skills in particular, by avoiding trivial conflicts. Choose your battles judiciously, saving your efforts for the ones that count.

Regardless of our desires, reality tells us that some conflicts are unmanageable.[51] When antagonisms are deeply rooted, when one or both parties wish to prolong a conflict, or when emotions run so high that constructive interaction is impossible, your efforts to manage the conflict are unlikely to meet with much success. Don't be lured into the naive belief that a good manager can resolve every conflict effectively. Some aren't worth the effort. Some are outside your realm of influence. Still others may be functional and, as such, are best left alone.

Who Are the Conflict Players? If you choose to manage a conflict situation, it is important that you take the time to get to know the players. Who is involved in the conflict? What interests does each party represent? What are each player's values, personality, feelings, and resources? Your chances of success in managing a conflict will be greatly enhanced if you can view the conflict situation through the eyes of the conflicting parties.

What Are the Sources of the Conflict? Conflicts don't pop out of thin air. They have causes. Because your approach to resolving a conflict is likely to be determined largely by its causes, you need to determine the source of the conflict. Research indicates that, although conflicts have varying causes, they can generally be separated into three categories: communication differences, structural differences, and personal differences.[52]

Communication differences are disagreements arising from semantic difficulties, misunderstandings, and noise in the communication channels. People are often quick to assume that most conflicts are caused by lack of communication, but, as one author has noted, there is usually plenty of communication going on in most conflicts.[53] As we pointed out at the beginning of this chapter, the mistake many people make is equating good communication with having others agree with their views. What might at first look like an interpersonal conflict based on poor communication is usually found, upon closer analysis, to be a disagreement caused by different role requirements, unit goals, personalities, value systems, or similar factors. As a source of conflict for managers, poor communication probably gets more attention than it deserves.

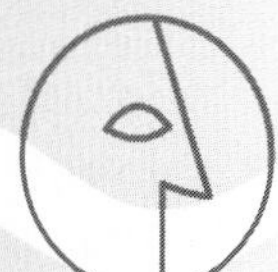

Understanding Yourself

Conflict-Handling Style Questionnaire

Indicate how often you do the following—by circling U (usually), S (sometimes), or R (rarely)—when you differ with someone.

1. I explore our differences, not backing down, but not imposing my view either.	U	S	R
2. I disagree openly, then invite more discussion about our differences.	U	S	R
3. I look for a mutually satisfactory solution.	U	S	R
4. Rather than let the other person make a decision without my input, I make sure I am heard and also that I hear the other out.	U	S	R
5. I agree to a middle ground rather than look for a completely satisfying solution.	U	S	R
6. I admit I am half wrong rather than explore our differences.	U	S	R
7. I have a reputation for meeting a person halfway.	U	S	R
8. I expect to get out about half of what I really want to say.	U	S	R
9. I give in totally rather than try to change another's opinion.	U	S	R
10. I put aside any controversial aspects of an issue.	U	S	R
11. I agree early on, rather than argue about a point.	U	S	R
12. I give in as soon as the other party gets emotional about an issue.	U	S	R
13. I try to win the other person over.	U	S	R
14. I work to come out victorious, no matter what.	U	S	R
15. I never back away from a good argument.	U	S	R
16. I would rather win than end up compromising.	U	S	R

Scoring: Total your choices as follows. Give yourself 5 points for Usually, 3 points for Sometimes, and 1 point for Rarely. Then total your score for each set of statements grouped as follows:

Set A: Items 13–16 Set B: Items 9–12
Set C: Items 5–8 Set D: Items 1–4

What the Assessment Means: Treat each set separately. A score of 17 or above on any set is considered high; scores of 12–16 are moderately high; scores of 8–11 are moderately low; and scores of 7 or less are considered low. Sets A, B, C, and D represent different conflict-resolution strategies.

A = *Forcing: I win, you lose*
B = *Accommodation: I lose, you win*
C = *Compromise: Both you and I win some and lose some*
D = *Collaboration: Both you and I win*

Everyone has a basic underlying conflict-handling style. Your highest scores on this exercise indicate the strategies you rely on most.

Source: From T. J. Von Der Embse, *Supervision: Managerial Skills for a New Era*. Copyright © 1987 by Macmillan Publishing Co. with permission.

As we discussed in Chapter 7, organizations are horizontally and vertically differentiated. This structural differentiation creates problems of integration. The frequent result is conflicts. Individuals disagree over goals, decision alternatives, performance criteria, and resource allocations. These conflicts are not due to poor communication or personal animosities. Rather, they are rooted in the structure of the organization itself.

The third conflict source is personal differences. Conflicts can evolve out of individual idiosyncrasies and personal value systems. The chemistry between some people makes it hard for them to work together. Factors such as background, education, experience, and training mold each individual into a unique personality with a particular set of values. The result is people who may be perceived by others as abrasive, untrustworthy, or strange. These personal differences can create conflict.

What Tools Can You Use to Reduce Conflict?

Managers essentially can draw upon five conflict-resolution options to reduce conflict when it is too high: avoidance, accommodation, forcing, compromise, and collaboration.[54] Each has particular strengths and weaknesses, and no one option is ideal for every situation. Exhibit 14-10 describes when each is best used. You should consider each a "tool" in your conflict-management "tool chest." While you might be better at using some tools than others, the skilled manager knows what each tool can do and when each is likely to be most effective (see Details on a Management Classic).

How Does a Manager Stimulate Conflict? What about the other side of conflict management—situations that require managers to stimulate conflict? The notion of stimulating conflict is often difficult to accept. For almost all of us the term *conflict* has a negative connotation, and the idea of purposely creating conflict seems to be the antithesis of good management. Few of us personally enjoy being in conflict situations. Yet the evidence demonstrates that there are situations in which an increase in conflict is constructive.[55] Although there is no clear demarcation between functional and dysfunctional conflict and there is no definitive method for assessing the need for more

Exhibit 14-10
Conflict Management: What Works Best and When

STRATEGY	BEST USED WHEN:
Avoidance	Conflict is trivial, when emotions are running high and time is needed to cool them down, or when the potential disruption from an assertive action outweighs the benefits of resolution
Accommodation	The issue under dispute isn't that important to you or when you want to build up credits for later issues
Forcing	You need a quick resolution on important issues that require unpopular actions to be taken and when commitment by others to your solution is not critical
Compromise	Conflicting parties are about equal in power, when it is desirable to achieve a temporary solution to a complex issue, or when time pressures demand an expedient solution
Collaboration	Time pressures are minimal, when all parties seriously want a win-win solution, and when the issue is too important to be compromised

Details on a Management Classic

Kenneth W. Thomas and Conflict-Handling Techniques

Conflict in any organization is inevitable. Whenever you put people together and arrange them into some type of structure (formal or informal) there is a good probability that some individuals will perceive that others have negatively affected, or are about to negatively affect, something that they care about. How then do we react to deal with the conflict? The research of Kenneth W. Thomas has given us some insight.

Thomas recognized that in these conflict-laden situations, one must first determine the intention of the other party. That is, one has to speculate about the other person's purpose for causing the conflict in order to respond to that behavior. Thomas concluded that one's response will depend on his or her cooperativeness or assertiveness. Cooperativeness is the degree to which an individual attempts to rectify the conflict by satisfying the other person's concerns. Assertiveness is the degree to which an individual will attempt to rectify the conflict to satisfy his or her own concerns. Placing assertiveness on the *Y* axis of a graph and cooperativeness on the *X* axis (and ranging both from low to high), Thomas was able to identify four distinct conflict-handling techniques—plus one middle-of-the-road combination. These were competing (where one is assertive but uncooperative), collaborating (assertive and cooperative), avoiding (unassertive and uncooperative), accommodating (unassertive but cooperative), and compromising (midrange on both assertiveness and cooperativeness). The question raised, then, is Where should these be used?

Thomas recognized that one conflict-resolution method is not appropriate in all situations.[56] Rather, the situation itself must dictate the technique. For instance, competition is most appropriate when a quick decisive action is vital or against people who take advantage of noncompetitive behaviors. Collaboration is appropriate when one is attempting to merge insights from different people, and avoidance works well when the potential for disruption outweighs the benefits of resolving the conflict. Accommodation can assist in issues that are more important to others than to you or when harmony and stability are important to you. Finally, compromise works well in achieving temporary settlements to complex issues or reaching a solution when time constraints dictate.

Thomas's work provided us with general guidelines for dealing with conflict. Although we know that people do change their intentions because of how they currently see the issue, or in an emotional reaction to the other individual, it appears that people do prefer one of the five techniques more often than the other four. Subsequent research supports that a person's intentions can also be predicted rather well from a combination of intellectual and personality characteristics. Thus, it may be appropriate to view individuals from their preferred style and react accordingly. That is, when confronting a conflict situation, recognize that some people want to win it all at any cost, some want to find an optimum solution, some want to run away, others want to be obliging, and still others want to "split the difference."

conflict, an affirmative answer to one or more of the following questions may suggest a need for conflict stimulation.[57]

1. Are you surrounded by "yes people"?
2. Are employees afraid to admit ignorance and uncertainties to you?
3. Is there so much concentration by decision makers on reaching a compromise that they lose sight of values, long-term objectives, or the organization's welfare?
4. Do managers believe that it is in their best interest to maintain the impression of peace and cooperation in their unit, regardless of the price?
5. Is there an excessive concern by decision makers for not hurting the feelings of others?
6. Do managers believe that popularity is more important for obtaining organizational rewards than competence and high performance?
7. Are managers unduly enamored of obtaining consensus for their decisions?
8. Do employees show unusually high resistance to change?
9. Is there a lack of new ideas?
10. Is there an unusually low level of employee turnover?

We know a lot more about resolving conflict than about stimulating it. That's only natural, because human beings have been concerned with the subject of conflict reduction for hundreds, maybe thousands, of years. The dearth of ideas on conflict-stimulation techniques reflects the very recent interest in the subject. The following are some preliminary suggestions that managers might want to use.[58]

The initial step in stimulating functional conflict is for managers to convey to employees the message, supported by actions, that conflict has its legitimate place. This step may require changing the culture of the organization. Individuals who challenge the status quo, suggest innovative ideas, offer divergent opinions, and demonstrate original thinking need to be rewarded visibly with promotions, salary increases, and other positive reinforcers.

As far back as Franklin Roosevelt's administration, and probably before, the White House consistently has used communication to stimulate conflict. Senior officials "plant" possible decisions with the media through the infamous "reliable source" route. For example, the name of a prominent judge is "leaked" as a possible Supreme Court appointment. If the candidate survives the public scrutiny, his or her appointment will be announced by the president. However, if the candidate is found lacking by the press, media, and public, the president's press secretary or other high-level official will make a formal statement such as, "At no time was this candidate under consideration." Regardless of party affiliation, occupants of the White House have regularly used the reliable source as a conflict-stimulation technique. It is all the more popular because of its handy escape mechanism. If the conflict level gets too high, the source can be denied and eliminated.

Ambiguous or threatening messages also encourage conflict. Information that a plant might close, that a department is likely to be eliminated, or that a layoff is imminent can reduce apathy, stimulate new ideas, and force reevaluation—all are positive outcomes that result from increased conflict.

Another widely used method for shaking up a stagnant unit or organization is to bring in outsiders—either by hiring from outside or by internal transfer—whose backgrounds, values, attitudes, or managerial styles differ from those of present members. Many large corporations have used this technique during the last decade in filling vacancies on their boards of directors. Women, minority group members, consumer activists, and others whose backgrounds and interests differ significantly from those of the rest of the board have been purposely selected to add a fresh perspective.

We also know that structural variables are a source of conflict. It is therefore only logical that managers look to structure as a conflict-stimulation device. Centralizing decisions, realigning work groups, increasing formalization, and increasing interdependencies between units are all structural devices that disrupt the status quo and act to increase conflict levels.

Finally, one can appoint a **devil's advocate.** A devil's advocate is a person who purposely presents arguments that run counter to those proposed by the majority or against current practices. He or she plays the role of the critic, even to the point of arguing against positions with which he or she actually agrees. A devil's advocate acts as a check against groupthink and practices that have no better justification than "that's the way we've always done it around here." When thoughtfully listened to, the advocate can improve the quality of group decision making. On the other hand, others in the group often view advocates as time wasters, and their appointment is almost certain to delay any decision process.

devil's advocate
A person who purposely presents arguments that run counter to those proposed by the majority or against current practices.

What Are Negotiation Skills?

We know that lawyers and auto salespeople spend a significant amount of time on their jobs negotiating. But so, too, do managers. They have to negotiate salaries for incoming employees, cut deals with their bosses, work out differences with their peers, and resolve conflicts with employees. For our purposes, we will define **negotiation** as a process in which two or more parties who have different preferences must make a joint decision and come to an agreement. To achieve this goal, both parties typically use a bargaining strategy.

negotiation
A process in which two or more parties who have different preferences must make a joint decision and come to an agreement.

How Do Bargaining Strategies Differ? There are two general approaches to negotiation—distributive bargaining and integrative bargaining.[59] Let's see what is involved in each.

You see a used car advertised for sale in the newspaper. It appears to be just what you've been looking for. You go out to see the car. It's great and you want it. The owner tells you the asking price. You don't want to pay that much. The two of you then negotiate over the price. The negotiating process you are engaging in is called **distributive bargaining.** Its most identifying feature is that it operates under zero-sum

distributive bargaining
Negotiation under zero-sum conditions, in which any gain made by one party involves a loss to the other party.

Who is one of the best distributive bargaining negotiators? Bill Richardson, Democratic congressman from New Mexico. He has negotiated with some of the most difficult negotiators in the world—Saddam Hussein, Fidel Castro, and General Abacha of Nigeria. What's his trick? Richardson is a good listener, he prepares for the negotiations, and he gets to know what his "adversaries" want.

conditions. That is, any gain you make is at the expense of the other person, and vice versa. Every dollar you can get the seller to cut from the price of the used car is a dollar you save. Conversely, every dollar more he or she can get from you comes at your expense. Thus, the essence of distributive bargaining is negotiating over who gets what share of a fixed pie. Probably the most widely cited example of distributive bargaining is in labor-management negotiations over wages and benefits. Typically, labor's representatives come to the bargaining table determined to get as much as they can from management. Because every cent more that labor negotiates increases management's costs, each party bargains aggressively and often treats the other as an opponent who must be defeated. In distributive bargaining, each party has a target point that defines what he or she would like to achieve. Each also has a resistance point that marks the lowest outcome that's acceptable (see Exhibit 14-11). The area between their resistance points is the settlement range. As long as there is some overlap in their aspiration ranges, there exists a settlement area in which each one's aspirations can be met.

When engaged in distributive bargaining, your tactics should focus on trying to get your opponent to agree to your specific target point or to get as close to it as possible. Examples of such tactics are persuading your opponent of the impossibility of getting to his or her target point and the advisability of accepting a settlement near yours; arguing that your target is fair, while your opponent's isn't; and attempting to get your opponent to feel emotionally generous toward you and thus accept an outcome close to your target point.

A sales representative for a women's sportswear manufacturer has just closed a $15,000 order from a small clothing retailer. The sales rep calls in the order to her firm's credit department. She is told that the firm can't approve credit to this customer because of a past slow-pay record. The next day, the sales rep and the firm's credit manager meet to discuss the problem. The sales rep doesn't want to lose the business. Neither does the credit manager, but he also doesn't want to get stuck with an uncollectible debt. The two openly review their options. After considerable discussion, they agree on a solution that meets both their needs. The credit manager will approve the sale, but the clothing store's owner will provide a bank guarantee that will assure payment if the bill isn't paid within sixty days.

integrative bargaining Negotiation in which there is at least one settlement that involves no loss to either party.

The sales-credit negotiation is an example of **integrative bargaining.** In contrast to distributive bargaining, integrative problem solving operates under the assumption that there is at least one settlement that can create a win-win solution. In general, integrative bargaining is preferable to distributive bargaining. Why? Because the former builds long-term relationships and facilitates working together in the fu-

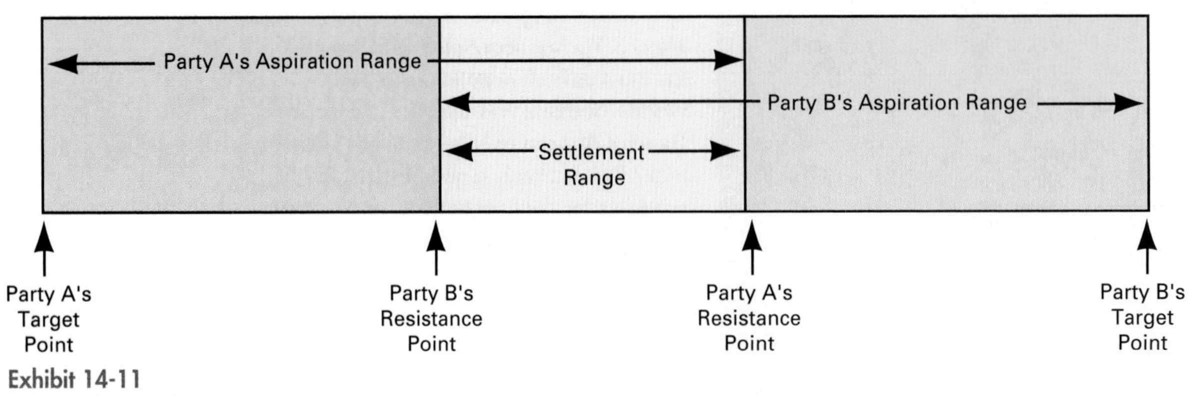

Exhibit 14-11
Determining the Bargaining Zone

ture. It bonds negotiators and allows each to leave the bargaining table feeling that he or she has achieved a victory. Distributive bargaining, on the other hand, leaves one party a loser. It tends to build animosities and deepen divisions between people who have to work together on an ongoing basis.

Why, then, don't we see more integrative bargaining in organizations? The answer lies in the conditions necessary for this type of negotiation to succeed. These conditions include openness with information and frankness between parties, a sensitivity by each party to the other's needs, the ability to trust one another, and a willingness by both parties to maintain flexibility.[60] Because many organizational cultures and intra-organizational relationships are not characterized by openness, trust, and flexibility, it isn't surprising that negotiations often take on a win-at-any-cost dynamic. With that in mind, let's look at some suggestions for negotiating successfully.

How Do You Develop Effective Negotiation Skills? The essence of effective negotiation can be summarized in the following six recommendations.[61]

Research your opponent. Acquire as much information as you can about your opponent's interests and goals.[62] What people must he or she appease? What is his or her strategy? This information will help you to better understand your opponent's behavior, to predict his or her responses to your offers, and to frame solutions in terms of his or her interests.

Begin with a positive overture. Research shows that concessions tend to be reciprocated and lead to agreements. As a result, begin bargaining with a positive overture—perhaps a small concession—and then reciprocate your opponent's concessions.

Address problems, not personalities. Concentrate on the negotiation issues, not on the personal characteristics of your opponent. When negotiations get tough, avoid the tendency to attack your opponent. It is your opponent's ideas or position that you disagree with, not him or her personally. Separate the people from the problem, and don't personalize differences.

Pay little attention to initial offers. Treat an initial offer as merely a point of departure. Everyone has to have an initial position, and initial positions tend to be extreme and idealistic. Treat them as such.

Emphasize win-win solutions. If conditions are supportive, look for an integrative solution. Frame options in terms of your opponent's interests and look for solutions that can allow your opponent, as well as yourself, to declare a victory.

Be open to accepting third-party assistance. When stalemates are reached, consider the use of a neutral third party—a mediator, an arbitrator, or a conciliator. Mediators can help parties come to an agreement, but they don't impose a settlement. Arbitrators hear both sides of the dispute, then impose a solution. Conciliators are more informal and act as a communication conduit, passing information between the parties, interpreting messages, and clarifying misunderstandings.

Summary

How will I know if I fulfilled the Learning Objectives found on page 422? You will have fulfilled the Learning Objectives if you understand the following.

1. **Define communication and explain why it is important to managers.** Communication is the transference and understanding of meaning. It is important because everything a manager does—making decisions, planning, leading, and all other activities—requires that information be communicated.
2. **Describe the communication process.** The communication process begins with a communication sender (a source) who has a message to convey. The message is converted to symbolic form (encoding) and passed by way of a channel to the receiver, who decodes the message. To ensure accuracy, the receiver should provide the sender with feedback as a check on whether understanding has been achieved.
3. **List techniques for overcoming communication barriers.** Some techniques for overcoming communication barriers include using feedback, simplifying language, listening actively, constraining emotions, and watching nonverbal cues.
4. **Identify behaviors related to effective active listening.** Behaviors related to effective active listening are making eye contact, exhibiting affirmative nods and appropriate facial expressions, avoiding distracting actions or gestures, asking questions, paraphrasing, avoiding interruption of the speaker, not overtalking, and making smooth transitions between the roles of speaker and listener.
5. **Explain what behaviors are necessary for providing effective feedback.** Necessary behaviors related to providing effective feedback include focusing on specific behaviors; keeping feedback impersonal, goal-oriented, and well timed; ensuring understanding; and directing negative feedback toward behavior that the recipient can control.
6. **Describe the contingency factors influencing delegation.** Contingency factors guide managers in determining the degree to which authority should be delegated. These factors include the size of the organization (larger organizations are associated with increased delegation), the importance of the duty or decision (the more important a duty or decision is, the less likely it is to be delegated), task complexity (the more complex the task is, the more likely it is that decisions about the task will be delegated), organizational culture (confidence and trust in subordinates are associated with delegation), and qualities of subordinates (delegation requires subordinates with the skills, abilities, and motivation to accept authority and act on it).
7. **Identify behaviors related to effective delegating.** Behaviors related to effective delegating are clarifying the assignment, specifying the subordinate's range of discretion, allowing the subordinate to participate, informing others that delegation has occurred, and establishing feedback controls.
8. **Describe the steps in analyzing and resolving conflict.** The steps to be followed in analyzing and resolving conflict situations begin by finding out your underlying conflict-handling style. Then select only conflicts that are worth the effort and that can be managed. Third, evaluate the conflict players. Fourth, assess the source of the conflict. Finally, choose the conflict-resolution option that best reflects your style and the situation.
9. **Explain why a manager might stimulate conflict.** A manager might want to stimulate conflict if his or her unit suffers from apathy, stagnation, a lack of new ideas, or unresponsiveness to change. A manager can stimulate conflict by changing the organization's culture, through the use of communications, by bringing in outsiders, by restructuring the organization, or by appointing a devil's advocate.
10. **Contrast distributive and integrative bargaining.** Distributive bargaining creates a win-lose situation because the object of negotiation is treated as fixed in amount. Integrative bargaining treats available resources as variable and hence creates the potential for win-win solutions.

Review & Discussion Questions

1. "Ineffective communication is the fault of the sender." Do you agree or disagree with this statement? Support your position.
2. Why isn't effective communication synonymous with agreement?
3. Which type of communication method do you prefer to use at work when sending a message to someone else? Why? Is it the same preference when messages are being sent to you? Explain.
4. Why are effective interpersonal skills so important to a manager's success?
5. Using what you have learned about active listening in this chapter, would you describe yourself as a good listener? Are there any areas in which you are deficient? If so, how could you improve your listening skills?
6. What is conflict?
7. Contrast the traditional, human relations, and interactionist views of conflict. Which of the three views do you think most managers have? Do you think this view is appropriate?
8. What are the five primary conflict-resolution techniques?
9. What can a manager do if he or she wants to be a more effective negotiator?
10. Assume that you found an apartment that you wanted to rent and the ad had said: "$550/month negotiable." What could you do to improve the likelihood that you would negotiate the lowest possible price?

Applying the Concepts

Active Listening

Purpose: *To reinforce that good listening skills are necessary for managers and that as communicators we can motivate listeners to actively listen.*

Time Required: *Approximately thirty minutes.*

Procedure: *Most of us, if we would admit it, are at times pretty poor listeners. This is probably because active listening is very demanding. This exercise is specifically designed to dramatize how difficult it is to listen actively and to accurately interpret what is being said. It also points out how emotions can distort communication.*

Your instructor will read you a story and ask you some follow-up questions. You will need a clean piece of paper and a pencil.

Take It to the Net

We invite you to visit the Robbins/De Cenzo page on the Prentice Hall Web site at:

http://www.prenhall.com/robbinsfom

for this chapter's World Wide Web exercise.

You can also visit the Web sites for these companies featured within this chapter:

AT&T
http://www.att.com

IBM
http://www.ibm.com

Testing Your Comprehension • • • 

Circle the correct answer, then check yourself on page AK-2.

1. Good communication does NOT require
   a) transference
   b) agreement
   c) understanding
   d) meaning

2. The encoding step in the communication process
   a) is not necessary for verbal communications
   b) enables the sender to keep the message from everyone except the intended receiver
   c) involves converting the message into some type of symbol
   d) follows the transmission of the message to the receiver

3. Before communication in any form occurs, which of the following is required?
   a) a sender
   b) a receiver
   c) a message
   d) a purpose

4. Which of the following is an advantage of oral communication?
   a) permanent record of the communication
   b) accurate when passing through many people
   c) chance for timely feedback
   d) more likely to be well thought out

5. The GREATEST value of feedback is that it
   a) improves communication by reducing the chance of misunderstandings
   b) allows for further discussions between the sender and receiver
   c) is not necessary in written communication because the message is tangible and verifiable
   d) forces the sender to think twice about what is communicated

6. A major disadvantage to written communication is
   a) only the recipient of the communication gets a written record
   b) lack of thought and precision
   c) the double meanings often accompanying written communication
   d) the minor role feedback plays in the process

7. Intentional distortion of information to enhance its appearance is
   a) more likely to occur in simple organizational structures
   b) called shaping communication
   c) consistent with cultures that reward performance
   d) called filtering

8. Communication is distorted when
   a) body language and verbal intonations are used
   b) e-mail, which lacks feedback opportunities, is used
   c) body language and intonation are not aligned
   d) the information is complex

9. Which of the following is NOT true regarding paraphrasing in active listening?
   a) Paraphrasing distorts efforts required for effective active listening.
   b) Paraphrasing is a control device that a listener uses to be sure he or he is listening carefully.
   c) Paraphrasing is a feedback mechanism.
   d) none of the above

10. What should active listeners do with idle brain time?
    a) summarize and integrate what has been said
    b) organize their schedules for the next few hours

c) plan how to ask questions of the speaker
d) rest and prepare to receive future communication

11. According to the interactionist view of conflict
a) very low levels of conflict indicate the optimal state
b) managers may need to stimulate dysfunctional conflict
c) some conflict keeps the group critical of itself
d) managers may need to stifle dysfunctional conflict

12. Which of the following LEAST suggests the need for a manager to stimulate conflict?
a) when a manager is surrounded by "yes people"
b) when employees in a department lack specific expertise
c) when the work environment is peaceful and cooperative
d) when creativity and innovation are lacking

13. Which of the following conflict-handling orientations represents a desire to maximize the joint outcomes of the two parties involved in the conflict?
a) avoidance
b) collaboration
c) accommodation
d) compromise

14. To achieve a compromise approach, one needs to
a) avoid overt disagreement
b) value openness and trust
c) dominate the other conflicting party
d) give up something of value

15. A person who purposely presents arguments that run counter to those proposed by the majority or against current practices is called
a) a conflict stimulator
b) a devil's advocate
c) an external consultant
d) all of the above

16. Delegation occurs when
a) a manager abdicates some of his or her responsibility to employees in the unit
b) a manager filters information in an attempt to stimulate conflict
c) a manager shifts some of his or her authority to another person to perform a specific task
d) a manager asks an employee to do him or her a personal favor

17. The process in which two or more parties who have different preferences must make a joint decision and come to an agreement is called
a) delegation
b) empowerment
c) conflict handling
d) none of the above

18. The difference between distributive and integrative bargaining is that
a) distributive bargaining creates a win-lose outcome; integrative bargaining creates a win-win outcome
b) distributive bargaining is preferred to integrative in organizations
c) distributive bargaining builds long-term relationships and facilitates working together; integrative bargaining does not
d) integrative bargaining leaves one party a loser; distributive bargaining helps people work together on an ongoing basis

Thinking Critically

Making a Value Judgment: Purposefully Distorting Information

The issue of withholding information was introduced in Chapter 1. Since then, you've had several different dilemmas in other chapters to ponder and ample time to think about the issue of keeping quiet or stretching the truth. Because this is such a broad concern and so closely intertwined with interpersonal communication, this might be a good time to once again think about ethical dilemmas that managers face relating to the intentional distortion of information. Read through the following two incidents.

Incident 1:

> You've just seen your division's sales report for last month. Sales are down considerably. Your boss, who works 2,000 miles away in another city, is unlikely to see last month's sales figures. You're optimistic that sales will pick up this month and next so that your overall quarterly numbers will be right on target. You also know that your boss is the type of person who hates to hear bad news. You're having a phone conversation today with your boss. He happens to ask in passing, how last month's sales went. What do you tell him?

Incident 2:

> An employee asks you about a rumor she's heard that your department and all its employees will be transferred from New York to Dallas. You know the rumor to be true, but you'd rather not let the information out just yet. You're fearful that it could hurt departmental morale and lead to premature resignations. What do you say to your employee?

These two incidents illustrate dilemmas that managers face relating to evading the truth, distorting facts, or lying to others. And here's something else that makes the situation even more problematic: It might not always be in a manager's best interest or those of his or her unit to provide full and complete information. Keeping communications fuzzy can cut down on questions, permit faster decision making, minimize objections, reduce opposition, make it easier to deny one's earlier statements, preserve the freedom to change one's mind, permit one to say no diplomatically, help to avoid confrontation and anxiety, and provide other benefits that work to the advantage of the manager.

Questions:

1. Is it unethical to purposely distort communications to get a favorable outcome?
2. Is distortion of information acceptable but lying about it not?
3. What about "little white lies" that really don't hurt anybody? Are these ethical?
4. What guidelines could you suggest for managers who want guidance in deciding whether distorting information is ethical or unethical?

Communication Barriers at Avianca

At 7:40 P.M. on January 25, 1990, Avianca Flight 52 was cruising at 37,000 feet above the southern New Jersey coast.[63] The aircraft had enough fuel to last nearly two hours—a healthy cushion, considering the plane was less than half an hour from touchdown at New York's Kennedy Airport. Then a series of delays began. First, at 8:00, the air traffic controllers at Kennedy told the pilots on Flight 52 that they would have to circle in a holding pattern because of heavy traffic. At 8:45, the Avianca copilot advised Kennedy that they were "running low on fuel." The controller at Kennedy acknowledged the message, but the plane was not cleared to land until 9:24. In the interim, the Avianca crew relayed no information to Kennedy that an emergency was imminent, yet the cockpit crew spoke worriedly among themselves about their dwindling fuel supplies.

Flight 52's first attempt to land at 9:24 was aborted. The plane had come in too low, and poor visibility made a safe landing uncertain. When the Kennedy controllers gave Flight 52's pilot new instructions for a second attempt, the crew again mentioned that they were running low on fuel, but the pilot told the controllers that the newly assigned flight path was OK. At 9:32, two of Flight 52's engines lost power. A minute later, the other two cut off. The plane, out of fuel, crashed on Long Island at 9:34. All seventy-three people on board were killed.

When investigators reviewed the cockpit tapes and talked with the controllers involved, they learned that a communication breakdown had caused this tragedy. A closer look at the events of that evening help to explain why a simple message was neither clearly transmitted nor adequately received. First, the pilots kept saying they were "running low on fuel." Traffic controllers told investigators that it is fairly common for pilots to use this phrase. In times of delay, controllers assume that everyone has a fuel problem. However, had the pilots uttered the words "fuel emergency," the controllers would have been obligated to direct the jet ahead of all others and clear it to land as soon as possible. As one controller put it, if a pilot "declares an emergency, all rules go out the window and we get the guy to the airport as quickly as possible." Unfortunately, the pilots of Flight 52 never used the word emergency, so the people at Kennedy never understood the true nature of the pilots' problem.

Second, the vocal tone of the pilots on Flight 52 didn't convey the severity or urgency of the fuel problem to the air traffic controllers. Many of these controllers are trained to pick up subtle tones in a pilot's voice in such situations. Although the crew of Flight 52 expressed considerable concern among themselves about the fuel problem, their voice tones in communicating to Kennedy were cool and professional. Finally, the culture and traditions of pilots and airport authorities may have made the pilot of Flight 52 reluctant to declare an emergency. A pilot's expertise and pride can be at stake in such a situation. Declaration of a formal emergency requires the pilot to complete a wealth of paperwork. Moreover, if a pilot has been found to be negligent in calculating how much fuel was needed for a flight, the Federal Aviation Administration can suspend his or her license. These negative reinforcers strongly discourage pilots from calling an emergency.

Questions:

1. Analyze the communications between pilots on Flight 52 and the traffic controllers at Kennedy Airport using the seven-step model presented in this chapter.
2. How could active-listening skills have prevented this crash? Cite specific examples.
3. Avianca is a Columbian airline. A large number of flights into major world airports are foreign carriers. How is it possible for air traffic controllers to be as generally effective as they are given that pilots and controllers may speak different languages?

Video Case ABCNEWS

The Right to Know

Effective communications requires that information between two or more individuals be transferred and understood. For this to happen, all barriers to communications must be eliminated so that the message can "get through." But we know that, at times, individuals purposely distort information or withhold a critical piece of information altogether. That's because they've decided that doing so is in their best interest or that it's no one else's business to know. Understandably, these barriers may be erected. But should they be allowed to exist when they may affect your health? That's one of the questions raised at Mercy Catholic Medical Center in Philadelphia.

The issue at Mercy focuses on one of the hospital's orthopedic surgeons—and his failure to provide complete information to his patients. This individual is HIV-positive. In the last six and one-half years, he has performed more than 1,600 operations. Many of those operations were "some of the most intricate surgeries there are, including repairing bones, joints, muscles, and nerves." Once the hospital administrator at Mercy found out about the doctor's medical condition, he immediately suspended the surgeon's surgical privileges and notified the surgeon's patients of the doctor's HIV status.

The administrator felt that this action was necessary to protect patients. He believed that they had a right to know about their exposure and a right to choose another doctor if they wished. The hospital's position was that the doctor's surgical privileges would be reinstated if he agreed to a compromise. That was, the hospital administrator wanted the surgeon to notify his patients of his medical condition and leave it up to each patient to decide whether he or she wanted to proceed using this doctor's services. Without such a requirement, some 70,000 health care workers and about 8,000 doctors in the United States who are HIV-positive will probably never reveal their conditions to their patients.

The doctor, on the other hand, saw things differently. He felt betrayed by the hospital where he had successfully worked for years. To him, the hospital's actions were the result of a financially based legal decision. He knew he was a skilled orthopedic surgeon, and what medical problems he had were nobody's business but his own. And he felt that as long as he could perform his job properly, his personal situation shouldn't concern others. Although HIV-positive, the doctor also believes that it's not possible "for a glove to break, or for him to cut or nick himself while his hands are inside a patient's body." Even the Centers for Disease Control and Prevention places the risk of such an accident and of patients' being infected to be less than the "risk associated with dying from anesthesia, contracting hepatitis B, or dying in an auto accident." Furthermore, the surgeon firmly believes that patients don't "have the right to know everything there is to know about him, or every other physician or medical worker who takes care of them. They only have the right to know things which are relevant in terms of relevant risks."

Questions:

1. How much information do you expect from your doctors regarding their health status? Do you expect them to disclose their medical history—similar to the medical history they expect from you? Discuss.
2. Do hospital administrators have a social responsibility to notify patients that one of their doctors may have an infectious disease, even if the notification violates the doctor's privacy? Explain your position.

Source: "Right to Know," *ABC PrimeTime,* May 26, 1994.

• PART 5 •
Controlling

Foundations of Control

15

LEARNING OBJECTIVES

What will I be able to do after I finish this chapter?

1. **DEFINE** control.
2. **DESCRIBE** three approaches to control.
3. **EXPLAIN** why control is important.
4. **DESCRIBE** the control process.
5. **DISTINGUISH** between the three types of control.
6. **DESCRIBE** the qualities of an effective control system.
7. **IDENTIFY** the contingency factors in the control process.
8. **EXPLAIN** how controls can become dysfunctional.
9. **DESCRIBE** how national differences influence the control process.
10. **IDENTIFY** the ethical dilemmas in employee monitoring.

WHAT DO QUEEN ELIZABETH, Prince Charles, and Swaine, Adney, and Brigg (S.A.B.) have in common? Each is highly regarded as a symbol of aristocracy in England. For S.A.B., this recognition stems from its production of leather goods, such as riding gear and buggy whips, and umbrellas. In fact, S.A.B.'s products proudly display a "lion propping up a large gold crest, the equivalent of knighthood for inanimate objects."[1] By all accounts, it's a symbol of "royal success."[2]

S.A.B. has been a tradition for nearly 250 years in England. Founded in the 1750s, it had been a family-owned business started by the Adney family. Back then, the company primarily focused on serving the monarchy—providing kings and queens, princes and princesses with top-quality products. For most of S.A.B.'s existence, the company was on top of the world—exceptionally successful and profitable. It had an elite address on Piccadilly Street and catered to a distinguished clientele. In fact, its customer list read like a *Who's Who* in the world—with nearly every head of state of industrialized nations and the British aristocracy proudly displaying some S.A.B. product. The kings and queens of England were so proud of the S.A.B. tradition that they continued to rent the property on Piccadilly Street for a small fraction of its true market value. Unfortunately, the good times didn't last forever.

S.A.B. managers assumed that the growth they were experiencing in the 1980s would be sustainable indefinitely. So they expanded their facilities—building new factories and consolidating all manufacturing operations under one "roof." S.A.B. executives also significantly expanded their firm's retail space—even opening a site in San Francisco to process mail orders coming from the United States. But with this expansion came increased costs. The most notable of these was leaving the Piccadilly Street location (and its low rent) for a facility a few blocks away—at a cost nearly 100 times their previous expense!

Do controls really matter? Can they truly make a difference in an organization? Just ask John de Bruyne, president of S.A.B., a British firm specializing in high-quality leather goods. Taking over a company in 1994 that was losing millions, de Bruyne was able to implement a variety of controls. As a result, in just eighteen months, he has helped the firm post profits exceeding 2 million pounds.

The late 1980s ushered in significant changes that brought the decade of growth to an unexpected halt. The British pound weakened against the dollar, virtually halving S.A.B.'s revenues in their mail-order business. Furthermore, consumers were beginning to change their taste and preferences for purchased goods. Luxury items—which is most of what S.A.B. produces—were no longer in demand. The events of the late 1980s led S.A.B. to the brink of financial disaster as annual losses began exceeding 3 million pounds. In 1990 the Adney family, which had controlled S.A.B. for 240 years, sold out its interest to other investors, leaving England's pride and joy to be run by an impersonal corporation. For the next four years, S.A.B. languished. Then John de Bruyne bought the firm.

What de Bruyne found when he took over the helm of S.A.B. in June 1994 was nothing short of chaos. Few if any control mechanisms were in place. No one really knew what was going on or how well plans were being met. He concluded that it was somewhat doubtful that standards were being set at all. De Bruyne knew he had to make some major changes if S.A.B. were to survive.

One of the first things de Bruyne did was to focus on the firm's core business—making upscale leather goods—to recapture the firm's competitive advantage. He also reduced costs by cutting employees and moving the main production facility to one that had much lower rent. He implemented production controls that would help increase output while simultaneously increasing the quality of each item produced. De Bruyne also implemented procedures to address current customer concerns and he established plans and monitoring systems for capturing new business in locations such as Paris, New York, Moscow, and Hamburg.

What John de Bruyne has done for S.A.B. has been nothing short of remarkable. In just over a year, he has turned the firm completely around. In 1995, the company earned more than 2 million pounds in profit. That was more than a 5 million pound turnaround in eighteen months!

The S.A.B. example illustrates what can happen when an organization's controls are weak and how effective controls can be instrumental in improving an organization's performance. As we will show in this chapter, effective management requires a well-designed control system.

What Is Control?

Control can be defined as the process of monitoring activities to ensure that they are being accomplished as planned and of correcting any significant deviations. All managers should be involved in the control function even if their units are performing as planned. Managers cannot really know whether their units are performing properly until they have evaluated what activities have been done and have compared the actual performance with the desired standard.[3] An effective control system ensures that activities are completed in ways that lead to the attainment of the organization's goals. The criterion that determines the effectiveness of a control system is how well it facilitates goal achievement. The more it helps managers achieve their organization's goals, the better the control system.[4]

control
The process of monitoring activities to ensure that they are being accomplished as planned and of correcting any significant deviations.

Managers cannot really know whether their units are performing properly until they have evaluated what activities have been done and have compared the actual performance with the desired standard.

When we introduced organizations in Chapter 1, we stated that every organization attempts to effectively and efficiently reach its goals. Does that imply, however, that the control systems organizations use are identical? In other words, would Toshiba, Bayer, France Telecom, and Sears Roebuck all have the same type of control system? Probably not. Although similarities may exist, there are generally three different approaches to designing control systems. These are market, bureaucratic, and clan controls.[5] They are described below and summarized in Exhibit 15-1.

Market control is an approach to control that emphasizes the use of external market mechanisms. Controls are built around such criteria as price competition or market share. Organizations using a market control approach are usually organizations that have clearly specified and distinct products and services and considerable competition. Under these conditions, the various divisions of the organization are typically turned into profit centers and evaluated by the percentage of total corporate profits each generates. For instance, at Matsushita, each of the various divisions—which produce such products as videos, home appliances, and industrial equipment—is evaluated according to the profits it contributes to the company's total profits. Using these measures, managers make decisions about future resource allocations, strategic changes, and other work activities that may need attention.

market control
An approach to control that emphasizes the use of external market mechanisms such as price competition and market share.

A second approach to control systems is called bureaucratic control. **Bureaucratic control** is a control approach that emphasizes authority and relies on administrative rules, regulations, procedures, and policies. This type of control depends on standardization of activities, well-defined job descriptions to direct employee work

bureaucratic control
An approach to control that emphasizes authority and relies on administrative rules, regulations, procedures, and policies.

TYPE OF CONTROL	ESTABLISHES STANDARDS FROM:	IS USED IN ORGANIZATIONS:
Market	Price competition	Where products or services are clearly specified
	Relative market share	That face considerable competition
Bureaucratic	Rules, policies, standardization of activities, well-defined job descriptions Budgets	That emphasize authority Rely on hierarchial mechanisms
Clan	Shared values, norms, traditions, rituals, and beliefs Organizational culture	Where teams are common Where technology changes rapidly

Exhibit 15-1
Characteristics of Three Approaches to Control Systems

behavior, and other administrative mechanisms—such as budgets—to ensure that organizational members exhibit appropriate work behaviors and meet established performance standards. At British Petroleum, managers of various divisions are allowed considerable autonomy and freedom to run their units as they see fit. Yet they are expected to stick closely to their budgets and stay within corporate guidelines. And managers at AlliedSignal have taken the control system one step further. They have imposed it on their suppliers in an attempt to control AlliedSignal's production costs.[6]

clan control
An approach to control in which employee behaviors are regulated by the shared values, norms, traditions, rituals, beliefs, and other aspects of the organization's culture.

Clan control refers to an approach to designing control systems in which employee behaviors are regulated by the shared values, norms, traditions, rituals, beliefs, and other aspects of the organization's culture. In contrast to bureaucratic control, in which control is based on strict hierarchial mechanisms, clan control depends on the individual and the group (the clan) to identify appropriate and expected work-related behaviors and performance measures. Clan control is typically found in organizations in which teams are widely used and technologies are changing often. For instance, organizational members at Microsoft are aware of the expectations regarding appropriate work behavior and performance goals. Their culture—fostered by the company's founder, Bill Gates—conveys to employees what's really important in the organization. They are guided and controlled by the clan's culture rather than prescribed administrative controls.

It is important to recognize that most organizations do not totally rely on just one of these three approaches to design an appropriate control system. Instead, an organization typically chooses to emphasize either bureaucratic or clan control and then

What kind of control system is AlliedSignal using in its dealings with Baja Oriente of Ensenada, Mexico? It is using bureaucratic control, demanding a 6 percent cost reduction from Baja. Bureaucratic control is helping AlliedSignal control costs. For Baja Oriente, meeting AlliedSignal's requirement has resulted in a twelve-fold increase in business.

add some market control measures. The key, however, in any of the approaches is to design an appropriate control system that helps the organization effectively and efficiently reach its goals.

The Importance of Control

Planning can be done, an organization structure can be created to efficiently facilitate the achievement of objectives, and employees can be directed and motivated. Still, there is no assurance that activities are going as planned and that the goals managers are seeking are, in fact, being attained. Control is important, therefore, because it is the final link in the functional chain of management. However, the value of the control function lies predominantly in its relation to planning and delegating activities.

In Chapter 3, we described objectives as the foundation of planning. Objectives give specific direction to managers. However, just stating objectives or having employees accept your objectives is no guarantee that the necessary actions have been accomplished. The effective manager needs to follow up to ensure that the actions that others are supposed to take and the objectives they are supposed to achieve are, in fact, being taken and goals achieved.

The Control Process

The **control process** consists of three separate and distinct steps: (1) measuring actual performance, (2) comparing actual performance against a standard, and (3) taking managerial action to correct deviations or inadequate standards (see Exhibit 15-2). Before we consider each step in detail, you should be aware that the control process assumes that standards of performance already exist. They are created in the planning function. If managers use some variation of mutual goal setting, then the objectives they set are, by definition, tangible, verifiable, and measurable. In such instances, those objectives are the standards against which progress is measured and compared. If "goal setting" is not practiced, then standards are the specific performance indicators that management uses. Our point is that these standards are developed in the planning function; planning must precede control.

control process
The process of measuring actual performance, comparing actual performance against a standard, and taking managerial action to correct deviations or inadequate standards.

What Is Measuring?

To determine what actual performance is, a manager must acquire information about it. The first step in control, then, is measuring. Let's consider how we measure and what we measure.

How Do Managers Measure? Four common sources of information frequently used by managers to measure actual performance are personal observation, statistical reports, oral reports, and written reports. Each has particular strengths and weaknesses; however, a combination of them increases both the number of input sources and the probability of receiving reliable information.

Personal observation provides firsthand, intimate knowledge of the actual activity—information that is not filtered through others. It permits intensive coverage because minor as well as major performance activities can be observed, and it provides opportunities for the manager to "read between the lines." Management-by-walking-around can pick up omissions, facial expressions, and tones of voice that may

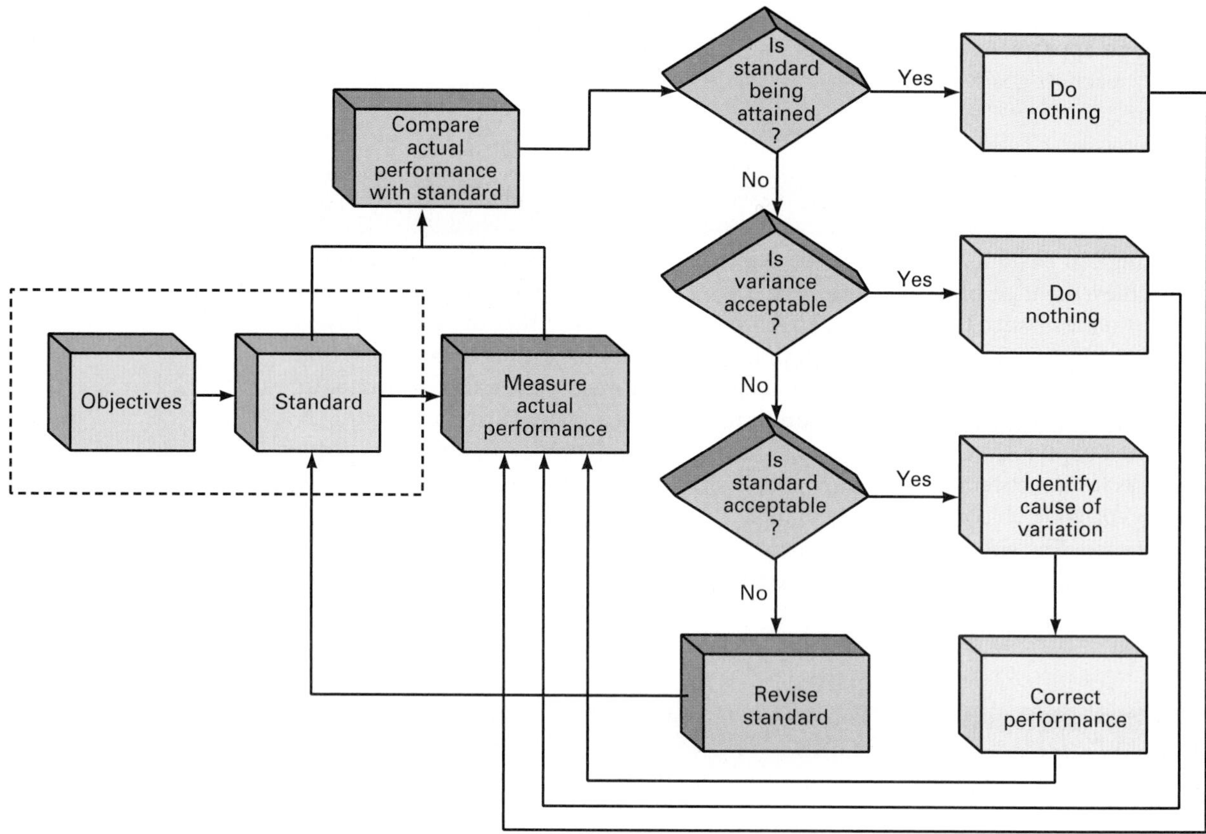

Exhibit 15-2
The Control Process

be missed by other sources. Unfortunately, in a time when quantitative information suggests objectivity, personal observation is often considered an inferior information source. It is subject to perceptual biases; what one manager sees, another might not. Personal observation also consumes a good deal of time. Finally, this method suffers from obtrusiveness. Employees might interpret a manager's overt observation as a sign of a lack of confidence in them or of mistrust.

The current wide use of computers in organizations, such as we described at S.A.B. and Greyhound (see Chapter 6), has made managers rely increasingly on statistical reports for measuring actual performance.[7] Statistical reports, however, are not limited to computer outputs. They can also be presented as graphs, bar charts, or numerical displays of any form that managers can use for assessing performance. Although statistical information is easy to visualize and effective for showing relationships, it provides limited information about an activity. Statistics report on only a few key areas and may often ignore other important factors.

Information can also be acquired through oral reports—that is, through conferences, meetings, one-to-one conversations, or telephone calls. The advantages and disadvantages of this method of measuring performance are similar to those of personal observation. Although the information is filtered, it is fast, allows for feedback, and permits language expression and tone of voice, as well as words themselves, to convey meaning. Historically, one of the major drawbacks of oral reports was the problem of documenting information for later references. However, our technological capabilities have progressed in the last couple of decades to the point where oral reports can be efficiently taped and become as permanent as if they were written.

Actual performance may also be measured by written reports. Like statistical reports, they are slower yet more formal than first- or secondhand oral measures. This formality also often gives them greater comprehensiveness and conciseness than is found in oral reports. In addition, written reports are usually easy to catalog and reference.

Given the varied advantages and disadvantages of each of these four measurement techniques, comprehensive control efforts by managers should use all four.

Craig Lentzsch, CEO of Greyhound, uses a variety of controls to ensure that his business is operating effectively and moving toward attainment of its goals. These include growth in passenger revenues, in market share, and in profitability. They also include talking with managers and customers about the "state of the company's" operations.

What Do Managers Measure? *What* we measure is probably more critical to the control process than *how* we measure. The selection of the wrong criteria can result in serious dysfunctional consequences. Besides, what we measure determines, to a great extent, what people in the organization will attempt to excel at.[8] For example, assume that your instructor has assigned a twenty-page term paper for this course. But, in the grade computation section of the syllabus, you notice that the term paper is not scored. In fact, when you ask your professor if that omission is a mistake, she says No, the term paper is for your own enlightenment and has no grade consequence for the course; grades are solely a function of how well you perform on the three exams in the course. We predict that you would, not surprisingly, exert most, if not all, of your effort toward doing well on the three exams.

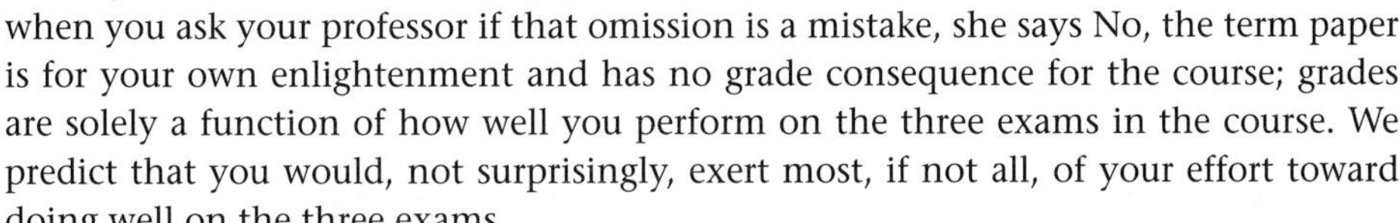
What *we measure is probably more critical to the control process than* how *we measure. The selection of the wrong criteria can result in serious dysfunctional consequences.*

For the most part, controls are directed at one of several areas: information, operations, finances (we'll explore those areas in more detail in the next chapter), or people (see Chapter 8). Some control criteria, however, are applicable to any management situation. For instance, because all managers, by definition, direct the activities of others, criteria such as employee satisfaction or turnover and absenteeism rates can be measured. Most managers have budgets for their area of responsibility set in monetary units (dollars, pounds, francs, lire, and so on). Keeping costs within budget is therefore a fairly common control measure.[9] However, any comprehensive control system needs to recognize the diversity of activities among managers. A production manager in a manufacturing plant might use measures of the quantity of units produced per day, units produced per labor-hour, scrap per unit of output, or percent of rejects returned by customers. The manager of an administrative unit in a government agency might use number of document pages produced per day, number of orders processed per hour, or average time required to process service calls. Marketing managers often use measures such as percent of market captured, average dollar value per sale, or number of customer visits per salesperson.[10]

The performance of some activities is difficult to measure in quantifiable terms. It is more difficult, for instance, for an administrator to measure the performance of a research chemist or an elementary school teacher than of a person who sells life insurance. But most activities can be broken down into objective segments that allow for measurement. The manager needs to determine what value a person, department, or unit contributes to the organization and then convert the contribution into standards.

Most jobs and activities can be expressed in tangible and measurable terms. When a performance indicator cannot be stated in quantifiable terms, managers should look for and use subjective measures. Certainly, subjective measures have significant limitations. Still, they are better than having no standards at all and ignoring the control function. If an activity is important, the excuse that it is difficult to measure is inadequate. In such cases, managers should use subjective performance criteria. Of course, any analysis or decisions made on the basis of subjective criteria should recognize the limitations of the data.

range of variation The acceptable parameters of variance between actual performance and the standard.

How Do Managers Determine Discrepancies between Actual Performance and Planned Goals? The comparing step determines the degree of discrepancy between actual performance and the standard. Some variation in performance can be expected in all activities; it is therefore critical to determine the acceptable **range of variation** (see Exhibit 15-3). Deviations in excess of this range become significant and receive the manager's attention. In the comparison stage, managers are particularly concerned with the size and direction of the variation. An example should help make this clearer.

Steve Morgan is the sales manager for Mid-Western Distributors. The firm distributes imported beers in several states in the Midwest. Steve prepares a report during the first week of each month that describes sales for the previous month, classified by brand name. Exhibit 15-4 displays both the standard and actual sales figures (in hundreds of cases) for the month of July.

Should Steve be concerned about the July performance? Sales were a bit higher than he had originally targeted, but does that mean that there were no significant deviations? Even though overall performance was generally quite favorable, several brands might deserve the sales manager's attention. However, the number of brands that deserve attention depends on what Steve believes to be significant. How much variation should Steve allow before he takes corrective action?

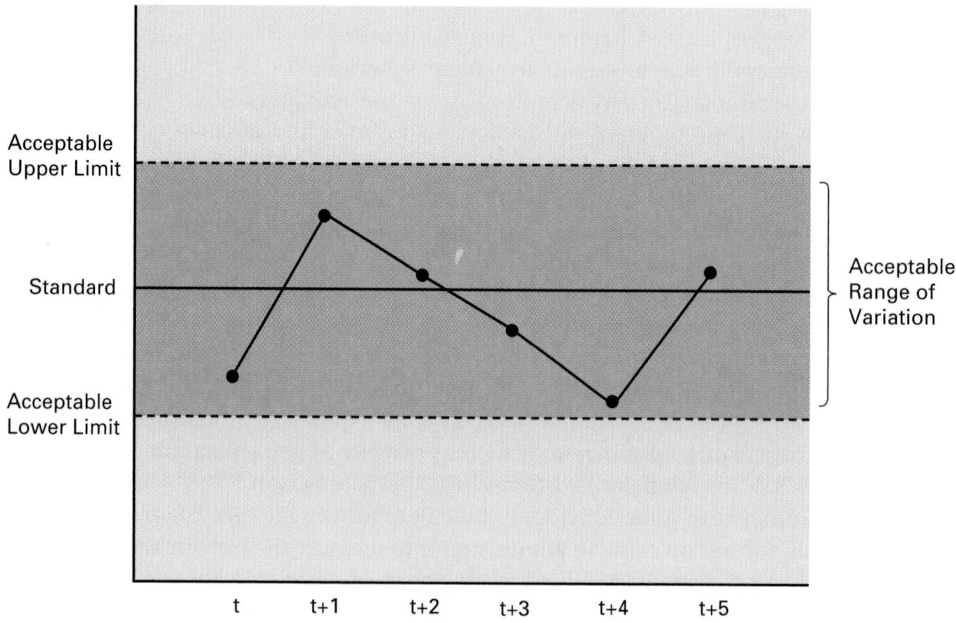

Exhibit 15-3
Defining an Acceptable Range of Variation

BRAND	STANDARD	ACTUAL	OVER (UNDER)
Heineken	1,075	913	(162)
Molson	630	634	4
Beck's	800	912	112
Moosehead	620	622	2
Labatt's	540	672	132
Corona	160	140	(20)
Amstel Light	225	220	(5)
Dos Equis	80	65	(15)
Tecate	170	286	116
Total cases	4,300	4,464	164

Exhibit 15-4
Mid-Western Distributors' Sales Performance for July (hundreds of cases)

The deviation on several brands is very small and undoubtedly not worthy of special attention. These include Molson, Moosehead, and Amstel Light. Are the shortages for Corona and Dos Equis brands significant? That's a judgment Steve must make. Heineken sales were 15 percent below Steve's goal. This brand needs attention. Steve should look for a cause. In this case, Steve attributed the loss to aggressive advertising and promotion programs by the big domestic producers, Anheuser-Busch and Miller. Because Heineken is the number one–selling import, it is most vulnerable to the promotion clout of the big domestic producers. If the decline in Heineken is more than a temporary slump, Steve will need to reduce his orders with the brewery and lower his inventory stock.

An error in understating sales can be as troublesome as an overstatement. For instance, is the surprising popularity of Tecate a one-month aberration, or is this brand increasing its market share? Our Mid-Western example illustrates that both overvariance and undervariance require managerial attention.

What Managerial Action Can Be Taken?

The third and final step in the control process is taking managerial action. Managers can choose among three courses of action: They can do nothing; they can correct the actual performance; or they can revise the standard. Because "doing nothing" is fairly self-explanatory, let's look more closely at the latter two.

If the source of the variation has been deficient performance, the manager will want to take corrective action. Examples of such corrective action might include changes in strategy, structure, compensation practices, or training programs; the redesign of jobs; or the replacement of personnel.

A manager who decides to correct actual performance has to make another decision: Should he or she take immediate or basic corrective action? **Immediate corrective action** corrects problems at once and gets performance back on track. **Basic corrective action** asks how and why performance has deviated and then proceeds to correct the source of deviation. It is not unusual for managers to rationalize that they do not have the time to take basic corrective action and therefore must be content to perpetually "put out fires" with immediate corrective action. Effective managers, however, analyze deviations and, when the benefits justify it, take the time to permanently correct significant variances between standard and actual performance.

immediate corrective action
Correcting a problem at once to get performance back on track.

basic corrective action
Determining how and why performance has deviated and then correcting the source of deviation.

To return to our example of Mid-Western Distributors, Steve Morgan might take basic corrective action on the negative variance for Heineken. He might increase promotion efforts, increase the advertisement budget for this brand, or reduce future

Torben Andersen is vice president of technology for Danish-based shipbuilders Odense Steel Shipyards. Through the use of sophisticated information systems, Andersen is able to provide timely feedback to workers who design automated systems. This feedback helps workers to take any corrective measures necessary to ensure that quality is attainable and the most efficient means of achieving it are used.

orders with the manufacturer. The action he takes will depend on his assessment of each brand's potential effectiveness.

It is also possible that the variance was a result of an unrealistic standard—that is, the goal may have been too high or too low. In such cases it's the standard that needs corrective attention, not the performance. In our example, the sales manager might need to raise the standard for Tecate to reflect its increasing popularity, much as, in sports, athletes adjust their performance goals upward during a season if they achieve their season goal early.

The more troublesome problem is the revising of a performance standard downward. If an employee or unit falls significantly short of reaching its target, the natural response is for the employee or unit to shift the blame for the variance to the standard. For instance, students who make a low grade on a test often attack the grade cutoff points as too high. Rather than accept the fact that their performance was inadequate, students argue that the standards were unreasonable. Similarly, salespeople who fail to meet their monthly quota may attribute the failure to an unrealistic quota. It may be true that standards are too high, resulting in a significant variance and acting to demotivate those employees being assessed against it. But keep in mind that if employees or managers don't meet the standard, the first thing they are likely to attack is the standard itself. If you believe that the standard is realistic, hold your ground. Explain your position, reaffirm to the employee or manager that you expect future performance to improve, and then take the necessary corrective action to turn that expectation into reality.

Types of Control

Management can implement controls before an activity commences, while the activity is going on, or after the activity has been completed. The first type is called feedforward control, the second is concurrent control, and the last is feedback control (see Exhibit 15-5).

Exhibit 15-5
Types of Control

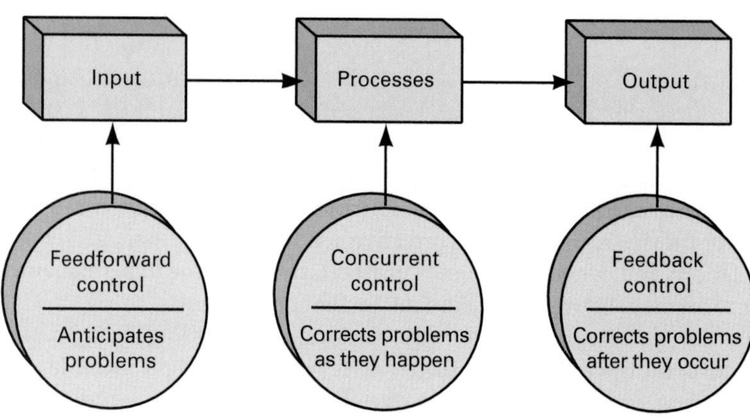

What Is Feedforward Control?

The most desirable type of control—**feedforward control**—prevents anticipated problems. It is called feedforward control because it takes place in advance of the actual activity. It is future-directed.[11] For instance, managers at Lockheed Martin may hire additional personnel as soon as the government announces that the firm has won a major defense contract. The hiring of personnel ahead of time prevents potential delays. The key to feedforward control, therefore, is taking managerial action before a problem occurs.

feedforward control Control that prevents anticipated problems.

Feedforward controls are desirable because they allow management to prevent problems rather than having to cure them later (see Managers Who Made a Difference). Unfortunately, these controls require timely and accurate information that is often difficult to develop. As a result, managers frequently have to use one of the other two types of control.

Managers Who Made a Difference

PAUL CLOUGH OF IMPERIAL PARKING

What kind of control does a business that "rents" parking lots need? A count of cars entering and leaving and some honest employees who can accurately handle money? Absolutely. But there's more than you think. And Paul Clough, president and chairman of Imperial Parking, Ltd. (Impark), is changing the face of the parking business. To do so, he is using some very interesting control techniques![12]

Impark, a Toronto-based organization, has 200,000 parking spaces in 1,270 lots in forty-seven cities in North America. Among their sites are parking lots in Milwaukee, Minneapolis, and Toronto.

There's money to be made renting parking spaces, but it doesn't come easily. By and large, profits are possible chiefly when there exist tight controls and sophisticated management systems. That's one of Clough's recipes for success. For instance, prepurchased parking decals have bar codes that are scanned by hand-held computers. When the drivers enter their parking slots, their parking habits and movements are tracked. Those who typically leave the lots frequently during the day have their cars parked in readily accessible slots. That system helps with efficiency and with customer service. Furthermore, the bar coding helps to track those accounts that are about to expire. When permits are up for renewal, customers receive advanced notice. The letters also double as invoices for Impark. Customers who want to renew their parking privileges simply return the notice with a check for the required amount. This system alone has done wonders for Impark's cash flow. It no longer finds itself having previously registered parkers parking for free.

This same system has also helped Clough's employees determine which parkers no longer have privileges to park in one of Impark's lots. And if a second notice, or some friendly encouragement from attendants that their reserved space will no longer be held, fails to achieve the desired goal, the cars are towed. Drastic yes! But this practice enables Impark to efficiently manage its spaces.

Not everything Impark does involves reserved parking. They also have spaces that are

Paul Clough of Imperial Parking Continued

rented hourly—the old-fashioned metered parking. Yet, Impark's meters are anything but old-fashioned. Their meters are actually minicomputers—devices that not only accept money for parking but also record a lot of data. They serve as a control system that generates feedback vital to the firm. For instance, by simply dialing any meter, managers can obtain such data as volume and revenue levels or whether the meter is functioning properly.

Do all of these controls serve a vital purpose for Clough? Pose that question to him, and you'll get an emphatic nod. Each of these control mechanisms translates into one thing for the organization—profits. They have helped Impark achieve a gross margin of 11 percent on sales. And Clough is convinced that with them, profits will only rise. Determining that, however, will require more information—which Paul is putting controls in place to capture.

When Is Concurrent Control Used?

concurrent control
Control that takes place while an activity is in progress.

Concurrent control, as its name implies, takes place while an activity is in progress. When control is enacted while the work is being performed, management can correct problems before they become too costly.

The best-known form of concurrent control is direct supervision. When a manager directly oversees the actions of an employee, the manager can concurrently monitor the employee's actions and correct problems as they occur. Although there is obviously some delay between the activity and the manager's corrective response, the delay is minimal. Technical equipment can be designed to include concurrent controls. Most computers, for instance, are programmed to provide operators with immediate response if an error is made. If you input the wrong command, the program's concurrent controls reject your command and may even tell you why it is wrong.

Why Is Feedback Control So Popular?

feedback control
Control action that is taken to correct a problem that has already occurred.

The most popular type of control relies on feedback. The control takes place after the action. The control report that Steve Morgan used for assessing beer sales is an example of a **feedback control.**

The major drawback of this type of control is that by the time the manager has the information the damage has already been done. It's analogous to closing the barn door after the horse has been stolen. But for many activities, feedback is the only viable type of control available. We should note that feedback has two advantages over feedforward and concurrent control.[13] First, feedback provides managers with meaningful information on how effective their planning effort was. Feedback that indicates little variance between standard and actual performance is evidence that planning was generally on target. If the deviation is great, a manager can use that information when formulating new plans to make them more effective. Second, feedback control can enhance employee motivation. People want information on how well they have performed. Feedback control provides that information (see Developing a Management Skill.)

Qualities of an Effective Control System

Effective control systems tend to have certain qualities in common.[14] The importance of these qualities varies with the situation, but we can generalize that the following characteristics should make a control system effective.

1. *Accuracy.* A control system that generates inaccurate information can result in management's failing to take action when it should or responding to a problem that doesn't exist. An accurate control system is reliable and produces valid data.
2. *Timeliness.* Controls should call management's attention to variations in time to prevent serious infringement on a unit's performance. The best information has little value if it is dated. Therefore, an effective control system must provide timely information.
3. *Economy.* A control system must be economically reasonable to operate. Any system of control has to justify the benefits that it gives in relation to the costs it incurs. To minimize costs, management should try to impose the least amount of control that is necessary to produce the desired results.
4. *Flexibility.* Effective controls must be flexible enough to adjust to adverse change or to take advantage of new opportunities. Few organizations face environments so stable that there is no need for flexibility. Even highly mechanistic structures require controls that can be adjusted as times and conditions change.
5. *Understandability.* Controls that cannot be understood have no value. It is sometimes necessary, therefore, to substitute less complex controls for sophisticated devices. A control system that is difficult to understand can cause unnecessary mistakes, frustrate employees, and eventually be ignored.
6. *Reasonable criteria.* Control standards must be reasonable and attainable. If they are too high or unreasonable, they no longer motivate. Because most employees don't want to risk being labeled incompetent by accusing superiors of asking too much, employees may resort to unethical or illegal shortcuts. Controls should, therefore, enforce standards that challenge and stretch people to reach higher performance levels without being demotivating or encouraging deception.
7. *Strategic placement.* Management can't control everything that goes on in an organization. Even if it could, the benefits couldn't justify the costs. As a result, managers should place controls on those factors that are strategic to the organization's performance. Controls should cover the critical activities, operations, and events within the organization.[15] That is, they should focus on places where variations from standard are most likely to occur or where a variation would do the greatest harm. In a department where labor costs are $80,000 a month and postage costs are $50 a month, a 5 percent overrun in the former is more critical than a 20 percent overrun in the latter. Hence, we should establish controls for labor and a critical dollar allocation, whereas postage expenses would not appear to be critical.
8. *Emphasis on the exception.* Because managers can't control all activities, they should place their strategic control devices where those devices can call attention only to the exceptions. An exception system ensures that a manager is not overwhelmed by information on variations from standard. For instance, if management policy gives supervisors the authority to give annual raises up to $500 a month, approve individual expenses up to $1,500, and make capital expenditures up to $10,000, then only deviations above those amounts require approval from higher levels of management. These checkpoints become controls that are part of the authority constraints and free higher levels of management from reviewing routine expenditures.
9. *Multiple criteria.* Managers and employees alike will seek to "look good" on the criteria that are controlled. If management controls by using a single measure such as unit profit, effort will be focused only on looking good on that stan-

dard. Multiple measures of performance decrease this narrow focus. Multiple criteria have a dual positive effect. Because they are more difficult to manipulate than a single measure, they can discourage efforts to merely look good. In addition, because performance can rarely be objectively evaluated from a single indicator, multiple criteria make possible more accurate assessments of performance.

▶ **10.** *Corrective action.* An effective control system not only indicates when a significant deviation from standard occurs but also suggests what action should be taken to correct the deviation. That is, it ought to both point out the problem and specify the solution. This form of control is frequently accomplished by establishing if-then guidelines; for instance, if unit revenues drop more than 5 percent, then unit costs should be reduced by a similar amount.

Contingency Factors of Control

Although the generalizations above about effective control systems provide guidelines, their validity is influenced by situational factors. These include size of the organization, one's position in the organization's hierarchy, degree of decentralization, organizational culture, and importance of an activity (see Exhibit 15-6, p. 474).

Control systems should vary to reflect the size of the organization. A small business relies on informal and more-personal control devices. Concurrent control through direct supervision is probably most cost effective. As organizations increase in size, direct supervision is likely to be supported by an expanding formal system. Very large organizations will typically have highly formalized and impersonal feedforward and feedback controls.

The higher one moves in the organization's hierarchy, the greater the need for a multiple set of control criteria, tailored to the unit's goals. This reflects the increased ambiguity in measuring performance as a person moves up the hierarchy.[16] Conversely, lower-level jobs have clearer definitions of performance, which allow for a narrower interpretation of job performance.

The greater the degree of decentralization, the more managers will need feedback on the performance of subordinate decision makers. Since managers who delegate authority are ultimately responsible for the actions of those to whom it is delegated, managers will want proper assurances that their employees' decisions are both effective and efficient.

The organizational culture may be one of trust, autonomy, and openness or one of fear and reprisal. In the former, we can expect to find informal self-control and, in the latter, externally imposed and formal control systems to ensure that performance is within standards. As with leadership styles, motivation techniques, organizational structuring, conflict-management techniques, and the extent to which organizational members participate in decision making, the type and extent of controls should be consistent with the organization's culture.

Finally, the importance of an activity influences whether, and how, it will be controlled. If control is costly and the repercussions from error small, the control system is not likely to be elaborate. However, if an error can be highly damaging to the organization, extensive controls are likely to be implemented—even if the cost is high.

Developing a Management Skill

PROVIDING PERFORMANCE FEEDBACK

About the Skill: *In the last chapter, we introduced several suggestions for providing feedback to others. One of the more critical feedback sessions will occur when you, as a manager, are using feedback control to address performance issues.*

Steps in practicing the skill

1. ***Schedule the feedback session in advance and be prepared.*** One of the biggest mistakes you can make is to treat feedback control lightly. Simply calling in an employee and giving feedback that is not well organized serves little purpose for you and your employee. For feedback to be effective, you must plan ahead. Identify the issues you wish to address and have specific examples that you can cite to reinforce what you are saying. Furthermore, set aside the time for the employee. Make sure that what you do is done in private and can be completed without interruptions. That may mean closing your office door (if you have one), holding phone calls, and the like.

2. ***Put the employee at ease.*** Regardless of how you feel about the feedback, you must create a supportive climate for the employee. Recognize that giving and getting this feedback can be an emotional event—even when the feedback is positive. By putting your employee at ease, you begin to establish a supportive environment in which understanding can take place.

3. ***Make sure the employee knows the purpose of this feedback session.*** What is the purpose of the meeting? That's something any employee will be wondering. Clarifying what you are going to do sets the appropriate stage for what is to come.

4. ***Focus on specific rather than general work behaviors.*** Feedback should be specific rather than general. General statements are vague and provide little useful information—especially if you are attempting to "correct" a problem.

5. ***Keep comments impersonal and job-related.*** Feedback should be descriptive rather than judgmental or evaluative, especially when you are giving negative feedback. No matter how upset you are, keep the feedback job-related and never criticize someone personally because of an inappropriate action. You are censuring job-related behavior, not the person!

6. ***Support feedback with hard data.*** Tell your employee how you came to your "conclusion" on his or her performance. Hard data, which you assimilated in step 1, helps your employees to identify with specific behaviors. Identify the "things" that were done correctly and reinforce them. And, if you need to be critical, state the basis of your conclusion that a "good job" was not completed.

7. ***If the feedback is negative, direct the negative feedback toward work-related behavior that the employee controls.*** Negative feedback should be directed toward work-related behavior that the employee can do something about. Indicate what he or she can do to improve the situation. This practice helps take the sting out of the criticism and offers guidance to an individual who understands the problem but doesn't know how to resolve it.

8. ***Let the employee speak.*** Get the employee's perceptions of what you are saying, especially if you are addressing a problem. Of course, you're not looking for excuses. But you need to be empathetic to the employee. Get his or her side. Maybe there's something that has contributed to the issue. Letting the employee speak involves your employee and just might add information you were unaware of.

9. ***Ensure that the employee has a clear and full understanding of the feedback.*** Feedback must be concise and complete enough so that your employee clearly and fully understands what you have said. Consistent with active listening techniques, have your employee rephrase the content of your feedback to check whether it fully captures your meaning.

10. ***Detail a future plan of action.*** Performing doesn't stop simply because feedback occurred. Good performance must be reinforced, and new performance goals set. However, when there are performance deficiencies, time must be devoted to helping your employee develop a detailed, step-by-step plan to correct the situation. This plan includes what has to be done, when, and how you will monitor the activities. Offer whatever assistance you can to help the employee. But it must be made clear that it is the employee, not you, who has to make the corrections.

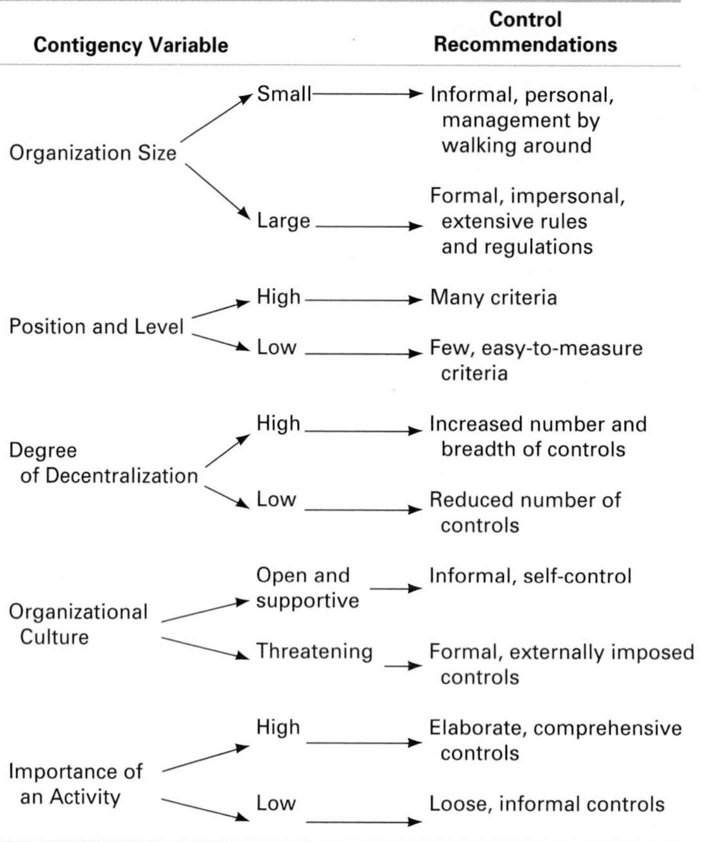

Exhibit 15-6
Contingency Factors in the Design of Control Systems

Adjusting Controls for National Differences

The concepts of control we have been discussing to this point are appropriate for an organization whose units aren't geographically distant or culturally distinct. But what about organizations that operate in a few or many locations worldwide? Would control systems be different, and what should managers know about adjusting controls for national differences?[17]

Methods of controlling employee behavior and operations can be quite different in foreign countries. In fact, the differences we see in organizational control systems of multinational corporations are primarily in the measurement and corrective action steps of the control process.

Managers of foreign operations of multinational corporations tend not to be closely controlled by the head office, if for no other reason than that distance precludes direct controls. The head office of a multinational must rely on extensive formal reports to maintain control. But collecting data that are comparable between countries introduces problems for multinationals. A company's factory in Bombay might produce products similar to those produced by its factory in France. The Bombay factory, however, might be much more labor-intensive than its counterpart in France (to take advantage of low labor costs in India).[18] If headquarters' executives

How does this French manager from Peugeot change control practices when dealing with employees in the Bombay, India, plant? According to research, control systems will change to reflect national differences. In this more labor-intensive Bombay plant, more direct supervision, as well as other "people" controls, will be required.

were to control costs by, for example, calculating labor costs per unit or output per worker, the figures would not be comparable. Therefore, distance creates a tendency to formalize controls, and technological differences often make control data incomparable.

Technology's impact on control is most evident in comparing technologically advanced nations with more-primitive countries. Organizations in technologically advanced nations such as the United States, Japan, Canada, Great Britain, Germany, and Australia use indirect control devices—particularly computer-related reports and analyses—in addition to standardized rules and direct supervision to ensure that activities are going as planned.[19] In less-advanced countries, direct supervision and highly centralized decision making are the basic means of control. Constraints on managerial corrective action may also affect managers in foreign countries. For example, laws in some countries do not allow management the options of closing plants, laying off personnel, taking money out of the country, or bringing in a new management team from outside the country.

The Dysfunctional Side of Controls

Larry Boff called the Dallas Fire Department's emergency number to get immediate help for his stepmother, who was having trouble breathing.[20] The nurse-dispatcher, Billie Myrick, spent fifteen minutes arguing with Boff because he wouldn't bring his stepmother to the phone. He told Myrick that his stepmother was in the bedroom and couldn't speak. Myrick insisted that she was required to talk to the person in question so she could determine if the situation was a true emergency. Boff insisted that his stepmother was unable to speak on the phone and pleaded with Myrick to send an ambulance. Myrick continually responded that she could not send an ambulance until she spoke to Boff's stepmother. After getting nowhere for fifteen minutes, Boff hung up the phone. His stepmother was dead.

Three managers at a big General Motors truck plant in Flint, Michigan, installed a secret control box in a supervisor's office to override the control panel that governed the speed of the assembly line.[21] The device allowed the managers to speed up the assembly line—a serious violation of GM's contract with the United Auto Workers. When caught, the managers explained that, while they knew that what they had done was wrong, the pressure from higher-ups to meet unrealistic production goals was so great that they felt the secret control panel was the only way they could meet their targets. As described by one manager, senior GM executives would say, "I don't care how you do it—just do it."

Did you ever notice that the people who work in the college registrar's office often don't seem to care much about students' problems? They become so fixated on ensuring that every rule is followed that they lose sight of the fact that their job is to serve students not to hassle them!

These examples illustrate what can happen when controls are inflexible or control standards are unreasonable. Employees may lose sight of the organization's overall goals.[22] Instead of the organization running the controls, sometimes the controls run the organization (see Understanding Yourself). Because any control system has imperfections, problems occur when individuals or organizational units attempt to look good exclusively on control measures. The result is dysfunctional because the organization's ability to meet its goals may suffer. More often than not, this dysfunctionality is caused by incomplete measures of performance. If the control system evaluates only the quantity of output, people will ignore quality. Similarly, if the system measures activities rather than results, people will spend their time attempting to look good on the activity measures.

Instead of the organization running the controls, sometimes the controls run the organization.

To avoid being reprimanded by managers because of the control system, people can engage in behaviors that are designed solely to influence the information system's data output during a given control period. Rather than actually performing well, employees can manipulate measures to give the appearance that they are performing well. Evidence indicates that the manipulation of control data is not a random phenomenon. It depends on the importance of an activity. Organizationally important activities are likely to make a difference in a person's rewards; therefore, there is a great incentive to look good on those particular measures.[23] When rewards are at stake, individuals tend to manipulate data to appear in a favorable light by, for instance, distorting actual figures, emphasizing successes, and suppressing evidence of failures. On the other hand, only random errors occur when the distribution of rewards is unaffected.[24]

Our conclusion is that controls have both an upside and a downside. Failure to design flexibility into a control system can create problems more severe than those the controls were implemented to prevent.

Ethical Issues of Control

Even though we know how important control is in an organization and the significant role it plays in the management process, ethical issues can and do arise as managers design efficient and effective control systems. Technological advances in computer hardware and software, for example, have made the process of controlling much easier. But these advantages have also brought with them difficult questions regarding what managers have the right to know about employees and how far they can go in controlling employee behavior both on and off the job. Special attention needs to be given to the topic of employee monitoring.

In Chapter 6, we introduced technology and how it is changing our organizations. Many of these improvements are allowing organizations to become more pro-

Understanding Yourself

How Willing Are You to Give Up Control?

Rate each of the following eighteen statements by circling your choice from 1 to 5, where 5 represents strongly agree, 4 represents agree somewhat, 3 is neither agree nor disagree, 2 represents disagree somewhat, and 1 represents strongly disagree.

	Statement					
1.	I'd delegate more, but the jobs I delegate never seem to get done the way I want them to be done.	5	4	3	2	1
2.	I don't feel I have the time to delegate properly.	5	4	3	2	1
3.	I carefully check on subordinates' work without letting them know I'm doing it so that I can correct their mistakes if necessary before they cause too many problems.	5	4	3	2	1
4.	I delegate the whole job, giving the subordinate the opportunity to complete it without any of my involvement. Then I review the result.	5	4	3	2	1
5.	When I have given clear instructions and the task isn't done right, I get upset.	5	4	3	2	1
6.	I feel that the staff lacks the commitment that I have, so any task I delegate won't get done as well as I'd do it.	5	4	3	2	1
7.	I'd delegate more, but I feel that I can do the task better than the person I might delegate it to.	5	4	3	2	1
8.	I'd delegate more, but if the individual I delegate the task to does an incompetent job, I'll be severely criticized.	5	4	3	2	1
9.	If I were to delegate a task, my job wouldn't be nearly as much fun.	5	4	3	2	1
10.	When I delegate a task, I often find that the outcome is such that I end up doing the task over again myself.	5	4	3	2	1
11.	I have not really found that delegation saves any time.	5	4	3	2	1
12.	I delegate a task clearly and concisely, explaining exactly how it should be accomplished.	5	4	3	2	1
13.	I can't delegate as much as I'd like to because my employees lack the necessary experience.	5	4	3	2	1
14.	I feel that when I delegate I lose control.	5	4	3	2	1
15.	I would delegate more but I'm pretty much a perfectionist.	5	4	3	2	1
16.	I work longer hours than I should.	5	4	3	2	1
17.	I can give employees the routine tasks, but I feel that I must do nonroutine tasks myself.	5	4	3	2	1
18.	My own boss expects me to keep very close to all details of my job.	5	4	3	2	1

Scoring: Total your score by adding the circled numbers for the eighteen statements.

What the Assessment Means: How much control you are willing to give up or share is directly related to how willing you are to delegate your "authority" to others. Depending on your total score, the following interpretations can be made:

72–90 points = *ineffective delegation*
54–71 points = *delegation habits need substantial improvement*
36–53 points = *delegation habits are positive, but more improvement needed*
18–35 points = *superior delegation*

Source: Reprinted by permission from *Management Review,* May 1982.

ductive; to help members work smarter, not harder; and to bring efficiencies into the organization that weren't possible just a decade ago.[25] But technological advancements have also provided employers a means of sophisticated employee monitoring. Although most of this monitoring is designed to enhance worker productivity, it could, and has been, a source of concern over worker privacy.[26]

Just how far can an employer go in monitoring employees? The law gives employers a lot of latitude. They can legally read your e-mail or computer files or film you while on company premises!

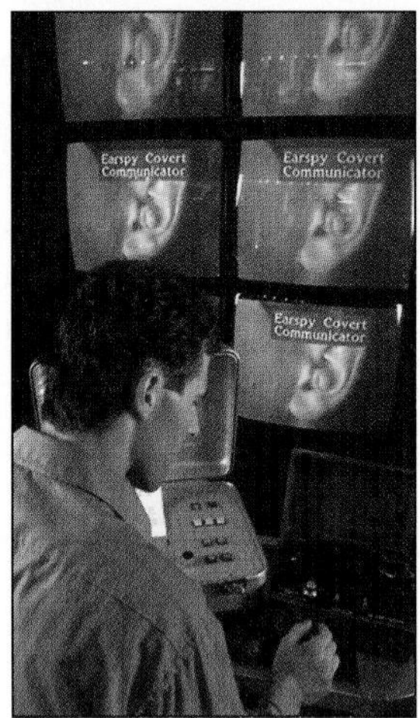

Consider the following. If you work, do you have the right to privacy at your workplace? What can your employer find out about you and your work? You might be surprised by the answers! Employers can, among other things: read your e-mail (even confidential messages), tap your work telephone, monitor your activities by computer, and monitor you in the employee restroom. A recent poll found that employees' concern about workplace privacy is at an all-time high; more than half of the respondents said that they were very concerned about the threat to their privacy at work.[27] Employers, however, see things differently. To them, monitoring is a means of ensuring that workers are being productive. When it comes to reading your e-mail or reviewing computer files, employers argue that there is nothing wrong—after all, it's their equipment.

What about off the job? Just how much control should an organization have over the private lives of its employees away from the job? Where should an employer's rules and controls end? Does your employer have the right to dictate what you do on your own free time and in your own home? Could, in essence, he or she keep you from engaging in riding a motorcycle, skydiving, smoking, drinking alcohol, or eating junk food? Again, the answers may surprise you. What's more, employer involvement in employee's off-work lives has been going on for decades. For instance, in the early 1900s, Ford Motor company would send social workers to employees' homes to determine whether their off-the-job habits and finances were deserving of year-end bonuses. Other firms made sure employees regularly attended church services. Today, many organizations, in their quest to control safety and health insurance costs, are once again delving into their employees' private lives. Let's look at some examples.

Does your employer have the right to dictate what you do on your own free time and in your own home?

Employees at Butterworth Hospital in Grand Rapids, Michigan, get an extra $25 in each biweekly paycheck for living "right." Employees who don't live right are fined $25.[28] Living right at Butterworth means that one refrains from smoking and engages in some exercise program. Employees at Ford Meter Box Company in Wabash, Indiana, are in a slightly different situation. Don't smoke, or you'll be fired. One employee who took a routine urine test for substance abuse was terminated because her test revealed traces of nicotine in her system.[29] And Best Lock Corporation in Indiana terminated an employee who violated the firm's no-drinking policy when he was observed having one alcohol-based drink at a weekend bachelor party.[30]

Although these examples of controlling employees' behaviors on and off the job may appear unjust or unfair, nothing in our legal system prevents employers from engaging in these practices. Rather, the law is based on the premise that "if employees don't like the rules, they have the option of quitting." But legally right doesn't make something ethically right. Where do you think managers should draw the line in monitoring employee behavior?

Summary

How will I know if I fulfilled the Learning Objectives found on page 459? You will have fulfilled the Learning Objectives if you understand the following.

1. **Define control.** Control is the process of monitoring activities to ensure that they are being accomplished as planned and correcting any significant deviations.
2. **Describe three approaches to control.** Three approaches to control are market control, bureaucratic control, and clan control. Market control is an approach that emphasizes the use of external marketing mechanisms such as price competition and relative market share to establish standards used in the control system. Bureaucratic control emphasizes organizational authority and relies on administrative rules, regulations, procedures, and policies. Under clan control, employee behaviors are regulated by the shared values, norms, traditions, rituals, beliefs, and other aspects of organizational culture.
3. **Explain why control is important.** Control is important because it monitors whether objectives are being accomplished as planned and delegated authority is being abused.
4. **Describe the control process.** In the control process, management must first have standards of performance derived from the objectives it formed in the planning stage. Management must then measure actual performance and compare that performance against the standards. If a variance exists between standards and performance, management must either adjust performance, adjust the standards, or do nothing, according to the situation.
5. **Distinguish between the three types of control.** There are three types of control: Feedforward control is future-directed and prevents anticipated problems; concurrent control takes place while an activity is in progress; feedback control takes place after the activity.
6. **Describe the qualities of an effective control system.** An effective control system is accurate, timely, economical, flexible, and understandable. It uses reasonable criteria, has strategic placement, emphasizes the exception, uses multiple criteria, and suggests corrective action.
7. **Identify the contingency factors in the control process.** The contingency factors in control systems include the size of the organization, the manager's level in the organization's hierarchy, the degree of decentralization, the organization's culture, and the importance of the activity.
8. **Explain how controls can become dysfunctional.** Controls can be dysfunctional when they redirect behavior away from an organization's goals. This dysfunction can occur as a result of inflexibility or unreasonable standards. In addition, when rewards are at stake, individuals are likely to manipulate data so that their performance will be perceived positively.
9. **Describe how national differences influence the control process.** Methods of controlling employee behavior and operations can be quite different when there are geographic or cultural differences. As a result, control systems focus primarily on measurement and corrective action steps of the control process.
10. **Identify the ethical dilemmas in employee monitoring.** The ethical dilemmas in employee monitoring revolve around the rights of employees versus the rights of employers. Employees are concerned with protecting their workplace privacy and intrusion into their personal lives. Employers, in contrast, are primarily concerned with enhancing productivity and controlling safety and health costs.

Review & Discussion Questions

1. What is the role of control in management?
2. How are planning and control linked? Is the control function linked to the organizing and leading functions of management? Explain.
3. In Chapter 9 we discussed the white water rapids view of change. Do you think it's possible to establish and maintain effective standards and controls in this type of atmosphere?
4. Why is what is measured in the control process probably more critical to the control process than how it is measured?

5. Name four methods managers can use to acquire information about actual organizational performance.

6. Contrast immediate and basic corrective action.

7. What are the advantages and disadvantages of feedforward control?

8. Why is feedback control the most popular type of control?

9. What can management do to reduce the dysfunctionality of controls?

10. "Organizations have the right to monitor employees—both on and off the job." Do you agree or disagree? Explain your position.

Applying the Concepts

The Paper Plane Corporation

Purposes:

1. To integrate the management functions.

2. To apply planning and control concepts specifically to improve organizational performance.

Required Knowledge: *Planning, organizing, and controlling concepts.*

Time Required: *Approximately one hour.*

Procedure: *Any number of groups of six participants each are used in this exercise. These groups may be directed simultaneously in the same room. Each person should have assembly instructions (Exhibit 15-7) and a summary sheet, plus ample stacks of paper (8½ by 11 inches). The physical setting should be a room that is large enough that individual groups of six can work without interference from other groups. A working space should be provided for each group.*

The participants are doing an exercise in production methodology. Each group must work independently of the other groups. Each group will choose a manager and an inspector, and the remaining participants will be employees. The objective is to make paper airplanes in the most profitable manner possible. The facilitator will give the signal to start. This is a ten-minute, timed event involving competition among the groups. After the first round, each group should report its production and profits to the entire group. Each group reports the manner in which it planned, organized, and controlled for the production of the paper airplanes. This same procedure is followed for as many rounds as there is time.

Your group is the complete work force for Paper Plane Corporation. Established in 1943, Paper Plane has led the market in paper plane production. Currently under new management, the company is contracting to make aircraft for the U.S. Air Force. You must establish a plan and organization to produce these aircraft. You must make your contract with the Air Force under the following conditions:

1. The Air Force will pay $20,000 per airplane.
2. The aircraft must pass a strict inspection.
3. A penalty of $25,000 per airplane will be subtracted for failure to meet the production requirements (bid planes not made or defective planes).
4. Labor and other overhead will be computed at $300,000.
5. Cost of materials will be $3,000 per bid plane. If you bid for ten but make only eight, you must pay the cost of materials for those you failed to make or that did not pass inspection.

Instructions for aircraft assembly

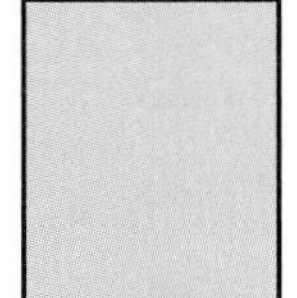

Step 1: Take a sheet of paper and fold it in half, then open it back up.

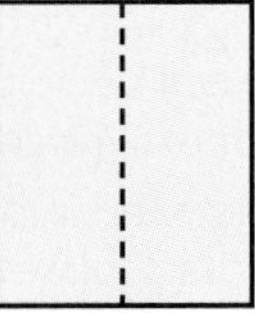

Step 4: Fold in half.

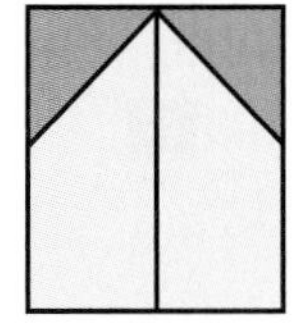

Step 2: Fold upper corners toward the middle.

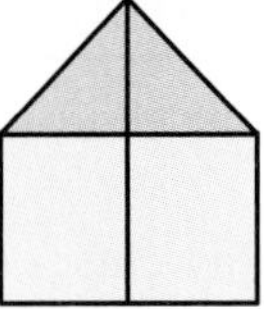

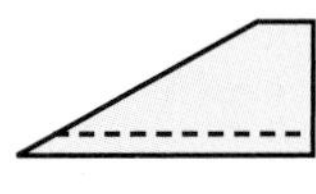

Step 5: Fold both wings down.

Step 6: Fold tail fins up.

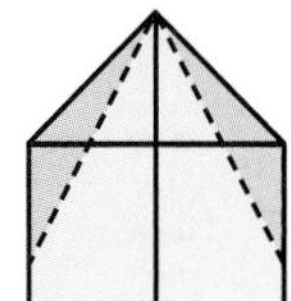

Step 3: Fold the corners to the middle again.

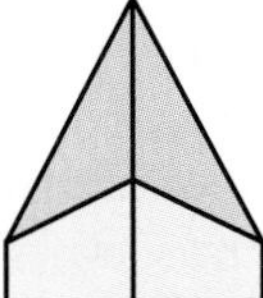

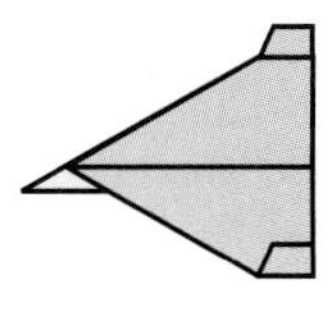

Completed aircraft

ROUND 1

Bid: [number of planes] × \$20,000 per plane	=	________
Result: [number of planes] × \$20,000 per plane	=	________
Less:		
overhead	=	\$300,000
[number of bid planes] × \$3,000 cost of raw materials	=	________
[number of unmade or defective planes] × \$25,000 penalty	=	________
Profit [result − (overhead + raw materials + penalty)]:	=	________

ROUND 2

Bid: [number of planes] × \$20,000 per plane	=	________
Result: [number of planes] × \$20,000 per plane	=	________
Less:		
overhead	=	\$300,000
[number of bid planes] × \$3,000 cost of raw materials	=	________
[number of unmade or defective planes] × \$25,000 penalty	=	________
Profit [result − (overhead + raw materials + penalty)]:	=	________

ROUND 3

Bid: [number of planes] × \$20,000 per plane	=	________
Result: [number of planes] × \$20,000 per plane	=	________
Less:		
overhead	=	\$300,000
[number of bid planes] × \$3,000 cost of raw materials	=	________
[number of unmade or defective planes] × \$25,000 penalty	=	________
Profit [result − (overhead + raw materials + penalty)]:	=	________

Exhibit 15-7
Paper Plan Data Sheet

Source: Based on an exercise in J. H. Donnelly Jr., J. L. Gibson, and J. M. Ivancevich, *Fundamentals of Management,* 8th ed. (Burr Ridge, Ill: Irwin, 1992), pp. 285–89. With permission.

Testing Your Comprehension • • • 

Circle the correct answer, then check yourself on page AK-2.

1. Which of the following would be indicative of a POOR control system?
   a) a frequent goal conflict that leads to suboptimization of goals
   b) the discovery that results are significantly below plans
   c) a change in structure recommended by the control system to improve an inefficient process
   d) the establishment of and adherence to goals prior to controlling

---

2. The ultimate criterion of control is the extent that activities are completed in ways that lead to
   a) cost effectiveness
   b) cost efficiencies
   c) more profits
   d) goal attainment

---

3. The type of control system that focuses on such criteria as organizational values, beliefs, and traditions is
   a) market control
   b) bureaucratic control
   c) organizational control
   d) clan control

---

4. Which of the following is NOT a reason for the importance of control?
   a) It allows managers to delegate.
   b) It helps establish hierarchical relationships.
   c) It ensures that the organization is moving toward established goals.
   d) It is related to planning.

---

5. The MOST important distinguishing fact of personal observation as a measurement method is that
   a) it works for individuals as well as groups
   b) it can be done on a daily basis so the time involved is minimal
   c) firsthand information is not subject to others' biases and filtering
   d) it adds a necessary degree of objectivity

---

6. A disadvantage of personal observation as a method for measuring performance is
   a) the time involved
   b) the level of coverage of performance activities is limited
   c) others' biases
   d) infrequency

---

7. Once actual results have been measured, the next step in the control process is
   a) determination of goals consistent with organizational objectives
   b) taking action to correct unfavorable variations from the plan
   c) comparisons between the plan and results
   d) checking measurements against established legal standards

---

8. If a manager's response to a key employee's repeated absence is to perform that subordinate's job for the day, the manager is
   a) performing immediate corrective action
   b) performing basic corrective action
   c) demonstrating delegation
   d) illustrating the role of an effective manager

---

9. When would it be appropriate for a manager to do nothing when a variance is detected in actual performance compared against a standard?
   a) when people may take offense to efforts to change their behavior
   b) when the variance is not significant
   c) when the standard is obviously incorrect
   d) it is never appropriate for a manger to "do nothing"

10. The MAJOR problem with feedforward controls is that they
   a) are costly to implement
   b) are time-consuming to implement
   c) indicate a problem only after it has occurred
   d) require information that is often difficult or impossible to obtain

11. Which of the following statements is MOST accurate?
   a) The type of control most widely used is feedback control.
   b) The best-known form of feedforward control is direct supervision.
   c) Feedback controls are designed to detect problems before they occur.
   d) Feedforward controls have the greatest impact on motivation.

12. The BIGGEST problem with feedback controls is that
   a) they are of little use as a motivational tool
   b) it is difficult, if not impossible, to obtain the necessary information
   c) when significant deviations are detected, the damage has already been done
   d) they do not provide the type of information needed to judge the accuracy of the planning process

13. The BEST-KNOWN form of concurrent control is
   a) internal selection
   b) direct supervision
   c) feedback
   d) decentralization

14. Reviewing reports is a form of
   a) consecutive control
   b) concurrent control
   c) feedback control
   d) feedforward control

15. Controls should be placed
   a) where they are cost-effective
   b) on all activities
   c) where there are problem areas
   d) on the single most important factor

16. Because management cannot control all activities, controls should be placed on __________ activities.
   a) risky
   b) risk-free
   c) critical
   d) complex

17. Informal controls are recommended when
   a) decentralization is high
   b) organizational culture is threatening
   c) organizational size is large
   d) importance of an activity is low

18. National differences affect control systems because
   a) most countries prohibit management from laying off employees
   b) technology is more prevalent in some countries than in others
   c) labor intensity varies among different countries
   d) all of the above

Take It to the Net

We invite you to visit the Robbins/De Cenzo page on the Prentice Hall Web site at:

http://www.prenhall.com/robbinsfom

for this chapter's World Wide Web exercise.

You can also visit the Web sites for these companies featured within this chapter:

France Telecom
http://www.francetelecom.fr

Greyhound
http://www.greyhound.com

Matsushita
http://www.matsushita.com

Frito-Lay
http://www.fritolay.com

Lockheed Martin
http://www.lmce.com

Toshiba
http://www.toshiba.com

Thinking Critically

Making a Value Judgment: Control Systems and an Invasion of Privacy

When do management's efforts to control the actions of its employees become an invasion of privacy? Consider the following.[31]

You have been a loyal employee of a large hotel chain. You just found out that you and a friend have been secretly videotaped while in the men's room in the hotel lobby. Although you were discussing a private matter (in addition to using the lavatory) you feel as if the hotel doesn't trust you.

If you work for Gateway 2000 in telephone sales, your phone conversations may be monitored. The company uses this monitoring to determine how well you are doing and to identify where you may have areas for improvement. It could also be used to substantiate that you are not doing your job properly—and could lead to your dismissal.

At Olivetti, all employees are given a "smart badge." These identification devices permit you access to various parts of the company. But they can also be used to track your whereabouts. On one hand, knowing where you are assists in forwarding urgent messages to you. On the other, no matter where you are, Olivetti managers can track your location.

Are any of the practices described above an invasion of privacy? This question actually touches on a larger issue: When does management overstep the bounds of decency and privacy by silently (even covertly) scrutinizing the behavior of its employees?

Questions:

1. When does management's need for more information about employee performance cross over the line and interfere with a worker's right to privacy?
2. Should organizations be permitted to monitor employee behavior off the job? Build an argument for and one against such practices.

Control Measures at Frito-Lay

All day long, each working day of the week, salespeople at Frito-Lay (a division of PepsiCo) punch information into their hand-held computers.[32] At the end of each workday, these salespeople "download" the collected information into minicomputers at local sales offices or through modems in their homes. The downloaded data are then relayed to corporate headquarters in Dallas, Texas. The company's CEO will have a complete report within twenty-four hours. Information on 100 Frito-Lay product lines in 400,000 stores is available on his computer screen in easy-to-read, color-coded charts: Red means a sales drop, yellow a slowdown, and green an advance. This system allows problems to be quickly identified and corrected.

Frito-Lay's control system helped the company solve a recent problem in San Antonio and Houston. Sales were slumping in area supermarkets. The CEO turned on his computer, called up data for south Texas, and quickly isolated the cause. A regional competitor had introduced El Galindo, a white-corn tortilla chip. The chip was getting good word-of-mouth advertising, and store managers were giving it more shelf space than Frito's traditional Tostitos tortilla chips. Using this information, the CEO sprang into action. He immediately directed his product development team to produce a white-corn version of Tostitos. Within three months his new product was on the shelves, and his company successfully won back lost market share.

This control mechanism at Frito-Lay is relatively new. Before its installation, the CEO would have needed at least three months just to pinpoint the problem. But this new system gathers data daily from supermarkets, scans it for important clues about local trends, and warns executives about problems and opportunities in all of Frito-Lay's markets. As the chairman of PepsiCo International Foods (who is the Frito-Lay CEO's boss) noted before the company installed the new system, "If I asked how we did in Kansas City on July Fourth weekend, I'd get five partial responses three weeks later." Now he can get that information in a day and act on it immediately.

Questions:

1. Describe the type of control (market, bureaucratic, or clan) that Frito-Lay is using. Why do you think they have chosen that type of control system?
2. Identify instances in the case where Frito-Lay is using feedforward and feedback controls.
3. Describe how controls at Frito-Lay are helping the company enhance organizational performance.

Video Case — ABCNEWS

The Watchful Eye of Big Brother

Can you imagine being watched at work by your employer? That's right, some organizations have been spying on their employees, even when they're not at work. Sheraton Hotels and K-Mart are doing it. How far does a company's control over employees' go? Is there a line between corporate control and personal freedom?

Franklin Etienne and Brad Fair were among dozens of Sheraton employees secretly videotaped at work. On its face value, taping employees at work doesn't appear to be a big deal. What makes this case interesting is that they were taped at times that they were not supposed to be doing their jobs. For instance, Brad was taped undressing in the employees' locker room. Franklin was "caught" reading a book during his scheduled break. Sheraton officials defend their actions by indicating that secret videotaping of employees has resulted in their nabbing one drug-dealing employee. Yet, Etienne, a Haitian immigrant, can't reconcile this action by his employer and the "freedom" people in the United States are supposed to enjoy.

In another case, Lew Hubble had a more troubling episode. He learned that two coworkers whom he befriended were actually private investigators hired by K-Mart to compile reports on employees. They would get their information by going to local bars with employees, visiting them at their homes, and the like. Of primary concern to Hubble was the realization that these investigators reported data that had little or nothing to do with the employees' jobs. For example, one such report indicated that an employee had fathered another employee's child. K-Mart wouldn't address their actions publicly but defended their use of private investigators by saying that they were hired to help break up an "inside" theft ring. That may be prudent for the company, but as one employee noted, "What takes place in that warehouse they have a right to know. They do not have a right to know what goes on in my bedroom, or in my living room."

What's happening at Sheraton and K-Mart are not isolated incidents. One government estimate indicates that at least 6 million American workers are spied on at work each year. This spying includes monitoring phone calls, videotaping work areas, reviewing computer entries, and monitoring e-mail. Ironically, there is little that employees can do to stop management from spying on them—on or off company premises. Although there is a federal law that prohibits employers from listening to workers' personal phone calls, there is almost no other protection from prying eyes on the job!

Questions:

1. When does spying on employees cross the line from effective management controls to invasion of privacy? Support your position.
2. Do you think that organizations like K-Mart or Sheraton have a responsibility to notify employees that they will be monitoring their activities on and off the job to eliminate employees who may be involved in illegal activities? Discuss.
3. Do you think that organizations benefit from "stopping" illegal activities by spying on employees in their organizations even though these actions might decrease employee morale, trust, and commitment?

Source: "Employers Spying on Employees," *ABC World News Tonight,* March 28, 1994.

Control Tools and Techniques

16

LEARNING OBJECTIVES

What will I be able to do after I finish this chapter?

1. **EXPLAIN** the purpose of a management information system (MIS).
2. **DIFFERENTIATE** between data and information.
3. **DESCRIBE** how an MIS affects decision making.
4. **EXPLAIN** the role of information systems in control.
5. **DEFINE** the role of the transformation process in operations management.
6. **EXPLAIN** the relationship between cost centers, direct costs, and indirect costs.
6. **IDENTIFY** three approaches to maintenance control.
8. **CONTRAST** continuous improvement programs and quality control.
9. **DISTINGUISH** between external and internal audits.
10. **EXPLAIN** how cost-benefit analysis can improve financial control.

MOUNT SINAI HOSPITAL IN TORONTO needs a constant flow of medical supplies.[1] It buys about 600 different medical and surgical items from more than sixty vendors. Deliveries to the hospital are almost constant during business hours, and, at times, several vendors arrive at once. Traffic congestion at the delivery doors often makes it nearly impossible for the hospital, located in a crowded downtown area, to have deliveries made as they are needed. The solution? Mount Sinai administrators overstocked all needed items of supplies and equipment into inventory. But what a costly system this was!

Staffing a department to handle supplies—ordering them, paying for them, maintaining inventory control, tracking items, and shipping them to various hospital departments—cost Mount Sinai about $5 million (Canadian) annually. Furthermore, medical and surgical supplies added another $6 million to the budget. Under the hospital's system of buying, inventorying, and transferring supplies to various departments, some items in the hospital would be handled as many as twenty times before reaching their final destination. Costs were getting out of hand. The system was simply inefficient. So Robert Cullen, director of materials management, implemented a better control system.

One of the first things Cullen did was to find a single source for medical and surgical supplies—Livingston Healthcare Services of Oakville, Ontario. Buying in "bulk" meant savings in purchases. But Livingston represented more than just bulk buying. They have systems in place that enhance the efficiency of purchasing and inventorying. Livingston takes orders from a client hospital's departments rather than from a central office. They fill the orders and deliver them directly to the hospital—prepackaged for the ordering unit. This system was made possible by computer technology. For example, all items used by the hospital are bar-coded. A unit clerk scans daily the inventory being used at each work station. At predetermined times during the day, a computer transmits the unit data to a master computer in Cullen's department as well as to Livingston's operation. Then, all orders received by Livingston during the day are packed and delivered that evening to the hospital—boxed and addressed specifically for the requesting unit. Meanwhile, a master copy of the entire delivery is transmitted to Cullen so that he can keep track of all hospital purchases.

Robert Cullen, director of materials management at Toronto's Mount Sinai Hospital incurred high costs in handling its medical and surgical supplies inventory. However, by implementing new control systems, Cullen has helped reduce inventory costs by more than $200,000. And hospital units receive their needed supplies more quickly than they did in the past.

As a result of this system, Mount Sinai's in-stock inventory is much smaller. In addition, if a department finds itself running out of a certain item, the system can tell the department where similar items can be found in the hospital. And, should a critical item not be available, Livingston has a special arrangement to deliver that item to Mount Sinai in under an hour.

Since Cullen has installed the new control system, the hospital has saved more than $200,000 annually. These savings are attributed to fewer sources, more purchasing power, and eliminating more than 5,000 square feet previously used for stocking inventory. Considering that the hospital pays nearly $150 per square foot, that alone amounts to a $750,000 savings. Together, that's nearly a million dollars a year from an efficient inventory system!

In this chapter, we take a closer look at control tools and techniques. Specifically, we address three primary areas that require effective controls: information, operations, and finances.

With the greater importance placed on efficiency, effectiveness, and productivity, managers must develop well-designed operating systems and tight controls to compete in a global economy.

Today's organizations are information-processing "machines."[2] With new technologies available, managers like Robert Cullen need to understand how to best use the information they provide and to ensure that organizational activities are proceeding as planned.[3] With the greater importance placed on efficiency, effectiveness, and productivity, managers must develop well-designed operating systems and tight controls to compete in a global economy. Finally, managers need to monitor the financial side of the organization to ensure that budgets and costs are kept in line.

Information Control Systems

How does management control the rapid, ongoing information about all the major activities in the organization? And how are the techniques for controlling and using this information changing the way managers manage? In this section, we will address those two issues.

What Is a Management Information System (MIS)?

management information system (MIS) A system used to provide management with needed information on a regular basis.

Although there is no universally agreed-upon definition for a **management information system (MIS),** we will define the term as a system used to provide management with needed information on a regular basis.[4] In theory, this system can be manual or computer-based, although all current discussions, including ours, focus on computer-supported applications (see Developing a Management Skill).

The term *system* in MIS implies order, arrangement, and purpose. Further, an MIS focuses specifically on providing management with information, not merely data. These two points are important and require elaboration.

data Raw, unanalyzed facts.

information Analyzed and processed data.

A library provides a good analogy. Although it can contain millions of volumes, a library doesn't do users much good if they can't find what they want quickly. That's why libraries spend a lot of time cataloging their collections and ensuring that volumes are returned to their proper locations. Organizations today are like well-stocked libraries. There is no lack of data. There is, however, a lack of ability to process that data so that the right information is available to the right person when he or she needs it.[5] A library is almost useless if it has the book you want, but either you can't find it or the library takes a week to retrieve it from storage. An MIS, on the other hand, has organized data in some meaningful way and can access the information in a reasonable amount of time. **Data** are raw, unanalyzed facts, such as numbers, names, or quantities. But as data, these facts are relatively useless to managers.[6] When data are analyzed and processed, they become **information.** For example, Robert Cullen collected data on the hospital's inventory and control practices and turned those data into usable information. Other companies, too, are capturing the value of information. For instance, one of American Express Company's most valuable assets is the half-billion bytes of data it has on how its customers have used their 35 million green, gold, platinum, and Optima cards to charge more than $350 billion in the past five years.[7] However, until these data are organized in some meaningful way, they are useless. An MIS collects data and turns them into relevant information for managers to use. Exhibit 16-1 (page 492) summarizes these observations.

Developing a Management Skill
DESIGNING THE MIS

About the Skill: *Just as there is no universal definition of a management information system, there is no universally agreed-on approach to designing the system. However, the following steps represent the key elements in effectively putting an MIS together.*[8]

Steps in Practicing the Skill

1. ***Analyze the decision system.*** The decisions that managers make should drive the design of an MIS. Therefore, the first step is to identify all the management decisions for which information is needed. This analysis should encompass all the functions within the organization and every management level from first-line supervisors to the CEO.

2. ***Analyze information requirements.*** Once the decisions are isolated, you need to know the exact information required to effectively make those decisions. Because information needs differ according to managerial functions, the MIS has to be designed to meet these varying needs.

3. ***Aggregate the decisions.*** After each area and manager's needs have been identified, those that have the same or overlapping information requirements should be located. Identifying these redundancies enables management to create a system that contains the least amount of duplication and that groups together similar decisions under a single manager.

4. ***Design information processing.*** In this step, internal technical specialists or outside consultants are typically used to develop the actual system for collecting, storing, transmitting, and retrieving information. A detailed flowchart of the desired information system will be drawn up, and hardware and software requirements will be determined.

5. ***Implement the system.*** After all the preliminaries have been accomplished, it's time to implement the system. Implementation involves testing the system before it is "turned over" to users and training them in the system's use. The system must also be "secured" so that unauthorized use is prevented.

6. ***Regularly evaluate the system.*** The information that a manager needed last year may not be the same information that's needed today. MIS should be viewed as an ongoing process. If it's to be valuable to managers over time, it must be evaluated periodically and modified to adapt to the changing needs of its users.

Why Are Client/Servers Replacing Centralized Systems?

A few short years ago, managers could avoid computers by claiming, "I don't have to know how to use computers. I can hire people to do that for me." Those days, understandably, are long gone![9] Today's managers use information to control the various organizational areas efficiently and effectively (see Managers Who Made a Difference). Much of this information is stored in computer servers, which are smaller database systems stored on a variety of computers. This information is then generally accessible to the clients (usually the managers) from the monitor on their desks. Without this information, they would find it difficult to perform most of the activities we discussed in the last chapter. For example, in measuring actual performance, managers need information about what has occurred within their area of responsibility. In the comparing stage of control, they need information regarding what the standards and acceptable ranges of variation are. And for managers to take some action, they need information to develop an appropriate course of action. As you can see, information plays a vital role in the controlling function of management. This fact, coupled with the technology available today (see Chapter 6), has fostered the decentralization

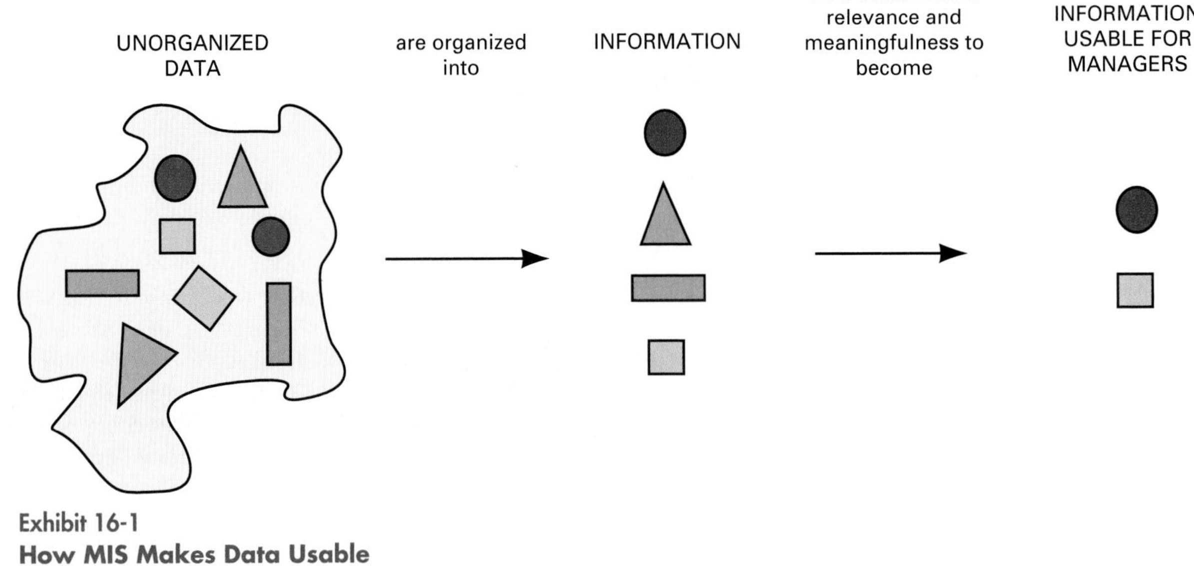

Exhibit 16-1
How MIS Makes Data Usable

of information control. Managers are now becoming end-users—the clients being served!

end-user
The person who uses information and assumes responsibility for its control.

When a manager becomes an **end-user,** he or she takes responsibility for information control.[10] It is no longer delegated to some other department or staff assistant. As end-users, managers have to become knowledgeable about their own needs and the systems that are available to meet those needs, and they have to accept responsibility for their systems' failures. Accordingly, if they don't have the information they want, there is no one to blame but themselves. Managers have come to realize that they now have a better information base from which to make timely decisions and improve managerial control.

This FedEx employee accesses the company's management information system. Since going paperless, this Memphis, Tennessee, office handles all the engineering support for the organization. Because all aircraft data are on the MIS, planned maintenance can easily be scheduled almost anywhere in the world. Their MIS has helped streamline FedEx so that they can meet their goal of "positively, absolutely getting the package there by tomorrow!"

How Can MIS Enhance Planning?

As we discussed in Chapter 3, managers seek to develop organization-wide strategies that will give them an advantage over their competition. We talked about gaining a competitive advantage through strategies such as being the cost leader in a given market or carefully differentiating your product from that of the competition. In recent years, managers at a number of organizations have realized that information systems can be used as a tool to give their firms a competitive advantage.[11] Wal-Mart stores, for example, capitalized on information technology to become the world's largest retailer.[12] A satellite communications system allows it to track inventory and handle accounting and payments. It can also electronically place orders with suppliers. And 1,500 of its vendors can access Wal-Mart's point-of-sale terminals to track sales of their products and resupply a Wal-Mart store before merchandise runs out. Another 3,800

Managers Who Made a Difference

Mark Katz, Chief Architect of MIS, Levi Strauss North America

Rethink, redesign, retool—three words to live by for Mark Katz, chief architect of MIS for Levi Strauss & Co. In 1990, Levi Strauss & Co. began developing and implementing a more modern management information system for the company. It's the company's goal to have meaningful information available to managers quickly in order to sustain a competitive advantage.[13] But the task hasn't been an easy one.

Years ago, companies like Levi Strauss & Co. relied on large data-processing departments for their information needs. These departments issued payrolls, processed batch orders, and created printouts for company managers who needed them to provide input for making decisions. In this type of system, computer programmers spent endless hours writing millions of lines of code and tested and retested the system.

By the late 1980s, however, these systems began to change. Technology was making it possible for managers to acquire information themselves faster and more easily. Excited about the opportunity of being on the ground floor of rapid change, Levi Strauss & Co. began the process of "rewiring the central nervous system of the company." The company broke from the centralized data-processing center as its source of information. Instead, the goal was to have this information available to any manager from his or her personal computer. Achieving this goal meant that databases and systems designed specifically for decision support had to be separated from those performing core business functions. This loose coupling permitted management to have free access to the decision-support data bases without impacting the transaction systems performing core business functions. But there was a trade-off—one that centered on having data that were "good enough" and still needing support from MIS staff.

As a result Levi Strauss & Co. is entering yet another stage in management information. The company's business data are now being made available to thousands of desktops worldwide. The "good enough" data are getting better by becoming visible throughout the company. Through a combination of new technology, coaching, and training efforts, Levi Strauss & Co. has been able to move far beyond the limitations inherent in its systems 20 years ago. Katz has been able to keep the system operating properly by constantly rethinking, redesigning, and retooling it as necessary!

vendors get daily sales data directly from Wal-Mart stores. This system has been a major factor in making Wal-Mart the low-cost operator in its industry.

Once an information system has been put in place and management gains a leg up on its competition, the trick—as with any competitive advantage—is to sustain that advantage. K-Mart, for instance, has recently invested in an information system that seeks to duplicate the one at Wal-Mart. Similarly, Federal Express was able to deliver packages faster and with more-detailed tracking than could its competition for many years because it was the first to computerize the process completely.[14]

But as UPS, the U.S. Postal Service, and other competitors introduced comparable systems, Federal Express's on-time delivery advantage based on its MIS all but disappeared. So, although MIS can provide a competitive edge, that edge is not permanent. The system must be regularly modified and updated if it is to give an organization a sustained advantage.

What Effect Does MIS Have on Decision Making?

We know that managers rely on information to make decisions. Because a sophisticated MIS significantly alters the quantity and quality of information, as well as the speed with which it can be obtained, an effective MIS will improve management's decision-making capability.[15]

The effect will be seen in establishing the need for a decision, in the development and evaluation of alternatives, and in the final selection of the best alternative. On-line, real-time systems allow managers to identify problems almost as they occur.[16] Gone are the long delays between the appearance of a serious discrepancy and a manager's ability to find out about it. Easy access to large data bases allows managers to look things up or get to the facts without either going to other people or digging through piles of paper. This capability reduces a manager's dependence on other people for data and makes fact gathering far more efficient. Today's manager can identify alternatives quickly, evaluate those alternatives, pose a series of what-if questions based on financial data, and, finally, select the best alternative on the basis of answers to those questions. For instance, Taco Bell's CEO, John Martin, is a fanatic about collecting customer information. His company updates from any of Taco Bell's 3,000 stores in just fifteen minutes. With this information, Martin can make decisions about product mix, marketing, employee training, or whatever else might be critical at that moment.[17]

Easy access to large data bases allows managers to look things up or get to the facts without either going to other people or digging through piles of paper.

How Does MIS Affect an Organization's Structure?

Sophisticated information systems are reshaping organizations. For instance, traditional departmental boundaries will be less confining as networks cut across departments, divisions, geographic locations, and levels in the organization. But the most evident change is probably that MISs are making organizations flatter and more organic.[18] A computer-based MIS lessens the need to depend on direct supervision and staff reports as control mechanisms. A manager can monitor what's occurring on the shop floor or in the accounts payable department by simply pushing a few keys on his or her desk terminal.

Managers can now handle more employees. Why? Because computer control substitutes for personal supervision. As a result, there are wider spans of control and fewer levels in the organization. The need for staff support is also reduced with an MIS. By being an end-user, a manager can obtain information directly. Thus, large staff support groups, which traditionally compiled, tabulated, and analyzed data, become redundant.[19] Both forces—wider spans and reduced staff—lead to flatter organizations.

One of the more interesting phenomena created by sophisticated information systems is that they have allowed management to make organizations more organic without any loss in control.[20] Management can lessen rules and regulations and become more decentralized—thus making their organizations more organic—without giving up control. How? MIS substitutes computer control for rules and decision discretion. Computer technology rapidly informs top managers of the consequences of any decision and allows them to take corrective action if the consequences are not to their liking. Thus, there's the appearance of decentralization without any commensurate loss of control.

What Effect Does MIS Have on Power?

We have made the statement before regarding information—information is power. Anything that changes the access to scarce and important information is going to change power relationships in organizations.

An MIS changes the status hierarchy in an organization. Middle managers have less status because they carry less clout. They no longer serve as the vital link between employees and first-line supervisors and key decision makers in the organization. Similarly, staff units have less prestige because senior managers no longer have to depend on them for evaluating operations or giving advice.

Centralized computer departments, which were extremely influential units during the 1970s, have had their role modified and their power reduced.[21] In today's organizations, these units are information support centers that no longer have exclusive control over access to data bases.

All combined, probably the most important effect that computer-based control systems have had on the power structure has been to tighten the reins of top management. In years past, top management regularly depended on lower-level managers to feed information upward. Because information was filtered and "enhanced," top-level managers knew only what their direct reporters wanted them to know. Now these same managers have the "power of information" at their fingertips because they have direct access to the data.

Does MIS Change Communication Patterns in Organizations?

Improvements in information technology are significantly changing the way communication takes place in organizations.[22] Traditional discussions of organizational communication focused on upward and downward communication. The primary flow of formal communication was vertical. The MIS, however, permits more lateral and diagonal communication on a formal basis.

Employees using internal networks can get their work done more efficiently by jumping levels in the organization and avoiding the obstacles involved in "going through channels." The direct accessing of data, rather than the traditional sequential passing of data up and down the hierarchy, also decreases the historical problem of distortion and filtering of information.[23] The breaking down of sequential communication patterns allows managers to formally monitor information across the organization that previously was limited to informal channels such as the grapevine.

MISs also eliminate the need for many communications that previously had to be done face to face. Managers can now get timely, accurate information without being at the site of the action. However, some caution is in order here. Face-to-face communication will not become extinct—nor should it! Rather, such communication will have a different purpose. That is, face-to-face communication will be more important for its symbolic significance. For example, managers will use face-to-face communication when visiting company offices and getting down to the shop floor to talk with employees. This interaction will give managers the opportunity to hear about problems and issues employees face. In doing so, it will appear that managers are exhibiting the coaching behaviors expected of them, and they will be viewed as more caring of their employees. The reason it is symbolic, though, is

Scott McNealy had a dream. As CEO of Sun Microsystems, Inc., he wanted an information system that would be the envy of his peers. After nearly eight years in development, Sun, today, operates its multibillion-dollar company off its management information system. This system provides up-to-date information to some 22,000 work stations. And, as a result of this increased communication flow, the company has witnessed many benefits—including increasing inventory turnover nearly 300 percent and cutting in half the time it takes to collect monies after customer purchases have been made.

that these actions are no longer necessary. They contribute little to any objective measure of enhanced communications, but they are perceived as important by employees.

What Effect Does MIS Have on Controlling?

Inherent in the control function is a manager's need to assess how the work is being performed and compare that performance with the plan. MIS makes it possible to obtain more complete and accurate information in the measuring phase of controlling. Furthermore, the sophistication of the system may also permit managers to focus precisely on what they want to know. For example, suppose a manager at Bridgestone wants to confirm that the P205X70X17 radial tire production is on schedule to fill a Nissan Motors order and that it is shipped by 4:00 P.M. that day. By entering the MIS system and directing the inquiry to the computer that controls the tire-production run, she can obtain the specific information she needs. Accordingly, MIS assists managers in obtaining timely information about workers' quantity of output, the quality level of output, and other performance data. And, because the data are directly assessed, many of the potential distortions that may arise when information is obtained "through channels" are avoided.

But accurate, timely, and complete information is only half of the issue here. With controlling, when a significant variance is determined, managers must take some action. By obtaining the precise information one seeks, and having it faster, a manager can correct a problem sooner. Thus, MIS enables managers to be more efficient and more effective in the controlling function.

Operations Control

This section focuses on the importance of efficiency and productivity in the operations side of the organization. Effective control systems allow organizations to produce higher-quality products and services at prices that meet or beat those of their rivals.

What Is the Transformation Process?

All organizations produce goods or services through a means called the **transformation process.** Exhibit 16-2 portrays, in a very simplified fashion, the fact that every organization has an operations system that creates value by transforming inputs into outputs. The system takes inputs—people, capital, equipment, materials—and transforms them into desired finished goods and services.

transformation process
The process through which an organization creates value by turning inputs (people, capital, equipment, materials) into outputs (goods or services).

You might be asking yourself at this time a profound question. Sure, the transformation process is readily applicable to the manufacturing organizations (organizations that produce physical goods such as steel, automobiles, textiles, and farm machinery), but will it apply to service organizations that now dominate work in the United States, Canada, Australia, and Western Europe? A **service organization** is one that produces nonphysical outputs such as educational, medical, or transportation services that are intangible, can't be stored in inventory, and incorporate the customer in the actual production process. For example, is there a transformation process operating at your college or university? The answer is Yes, and here's why. University administrators bring together instructors, books, journals, multimedia materials, computer labs, and similar resources to transform "unenlightened" students into educated and skilled individuals. Our conclusion: The transformation process is as relevant to service organizations as it is to those in manufacturing. This relevance is also supported by the fact that state and local governments are increasingly emphasizing the transformation process.[24] The study and application of this transformation process to organizations is called **operations management.**

service organization
An organization that produces nonphysical outputs such as educational, medical, or transportation services.

operations management
The study and application of the transformation process to organizations.

Because an organization's survival may very well rest on how successful operations management is, managers need to develop control techniques to monitor their productive processes. We will focus on four primary operations subsystems: cost controls, inventories, maintenance, and quality controls.

How Can Managers Control Costs?

U.S. managers have often treated cost control as an occasional crusade that is initiated and controlled by the accounting staff.[25] Accountants establish cost standards per unit, and if deviations occur, management looks for the cause. Have material prices increased? Is labor being used efficiently? Do employees need additional training? Cost control, nonetheless, needs to play a central part in the design of an operating system, and it needs to be a continuing concern of every manager.

cost-center approach
A cost-control approach in which managers are held responsible for the cost performance of their units.

Many organizations have adopted the **cost-center approach** to controlling costs. Work areas, departments, or plants are identified as distinct cost centers, and their managers are held responsible for the cost performance of their units. Any unit's total costs are made up of two types of costs: direct and indirect. **Direct costs** are costs incurred in proportion to the output of a particular good or service. Labor and

direct costs
Costs incurred in proportion to the output of a particular good or service.

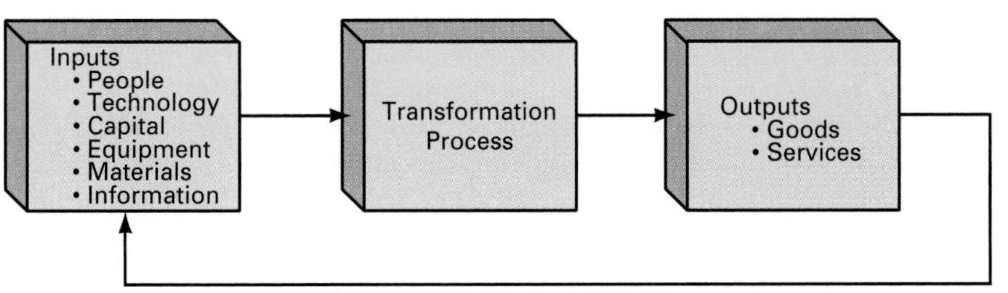

Exhibit 16-2
The Transformation Process

Marilyn Marks, CEO of Dorsey Trailers, keeps close tabs on the financial reports in her company. By doing so, she has helped the firm grow from $93 million in 1991 in sales to more than $200 million four years later.

indirect costs
Costs that are largely unaffected by changes in output.

materials typically fall into this category. On the other hand, **indirect costs** are largely unaffected by changes in output. Insurance expenses and the salaries of staff personnel are examples of typical indirect costs. This direct-indirect distinction is important. Cost-center managers are held responsible for all direct costs in their units, but indirect costs are not necessarily within their control. However, because all costs are controllable at some level in the organization, top managers should identify where the control lies and hold lower managers accountable for costs that are under their control.[26]

How Can Managers Minimize Purchasing Costs?

It has been said that human beings are what they eat. Metaphorically, the same applies to organizations. Their processes and outputs depend on the inputs they "eat." It is difficult to make quality products out of inferior inputs. Gas station operators depend on a regular and dependable inflow of certain octane-rated gasolines from their suppliers in order to meet their customers' demands. If the gas isn't there, they can't sell it. If the gasoline is below the specified octane rating, customers may be dissatisfied and take their business somewhere else. Management must therefore monitor the delivery, performance, quality, quantity, and price of inputs from suppliers. Purchasing control seeks to ensure availability, acceptable quality, continued reliable sources, and, at the same time, reduced costs.

What can managers do to facilitate control of inputs? They need to gather information on the dates and conditions in which supplies arrive. They need to gather data about the quality of supplies and the compatibility of those supplies with operations processes. Finally, they need to obtain data on supplier price performance. Are the prices of the delivered goods the same as those quoted when the order was placed? This information can be used to rate suppliers, identify problem suppliers, and guide management in choosing future suppliers. Trends can be detected. Suppliers can be evaluated, for instance, on responsiveness, service, reliability, and competitiveness.

Why Should an Organization Build Close Links with Suppliers? A rapidly growing trend in business is turning suppliers into partners.[27] Instead of using ten or twelve vendors and forcing them to compete against each other to gain the organization's business, managers like Robert Cullen are using three or fewer vendors and working closely with them to improve efficiency and quality.

Motorola, for instance, sends its design-and-manufacturing engineers to suppliers to help with any problems.[28] Other firms now routinely send inspection teams to rate suppliers' operations. They are assessing these suppliers' production and delivery techniques, statistical process controls that identify causes of defects, and ability to handle data electronically. North American companies and many from around the world are doing what has long been a tradition in Japan—that is, they are developing long-term relationships with suppliers (see Understanding Yourself). As collaborators and partners, rather than adversaries, firms are finding that they can achieve better quality of inputs, fewer defects, and lower costs. Furthermore, when problems arise with suppliers, open communication channels facilitate quick resolutions.

What Is the Economic Order Quantity Model? One of the best-known techniques for mathematically deriving the optimum quantity for a purchase order is the **economic order quantity (EOQ) model** (see Exhibit 16-3). The EOQ model seeks to balance four costs involved in ordering and carrying inventory: the *purchase costs* (purchase price plus delivery charges less discounts); the *ordering costs* (paperwork, follow-up, inspection when the item arrives, and other processing costs); *carrying costs* (money tied up in inventory, storage, insurance, taxes, and so forth); and *stockout costs* (profits foregone from orders lost, the cost of reestablishing goodwill, and additional expenses incurred to expedite late shipments). When these four costs are known, the model identifies the optimal order size for each purchase (see Details on a Management Classic).

economic order quantity (EOQ) model
A technique for balancing purchase, ordering, carrying, and stockout costs to derive the optimum quantity for a purchase order.

What Are Inventory Ordering Systems? In many checkbooks, after you use up about 80 percent of the checks, you find a reorder form included among the few that remain; it reminds you that it's time to reorder. This is an example of a **fixed-point reordering system.** At some preestablished point in the operations process, the system is designed to "flag" the fact that the inventory needs to be replenished. The flag is triggered when the inventory reaches a certain point, or the safety stock level (see Exhibit 16-4).

fixed-point reordering system
A system that "flags" the fact that inventory needs to be replenished when it reaches a certain level.

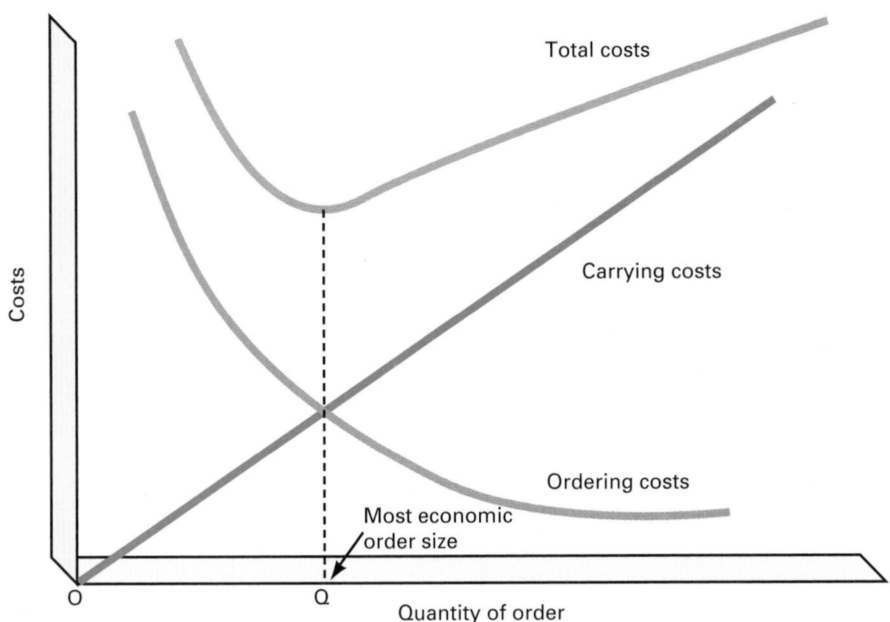

Exhibit 16-3
Determining the Most Economic Order Quantity

Understanding Yourself

How Much Do You Really Know about Japanese Management Practices?

Throughout this book, we have referenced management practices used in Japan and compared them with practices in organizations in other parts of the world. Although many North American practices are widely copied, it appears that, when it comes to the popular press, Japanese management systems get the nod. How much do you really understand about how Japanese management operates? Take the following "test" and find out.

1. In the typical large Japanese company, approximately how many employee suggestions for improvement of operations would there be in a single year?
   - *a.* 1000
   - *b.* 10,000
   - *c.* 100,000
   - *d.* 1,000,000
   - *e.* 10,000,000
2. Compared with the United States, Japan has about ____________ industrial robots in operation.
   - *a.* half as many
   - *b.* the same number of
   - *c.* twice as many
   - *d.* five times as many
   - *e.* ten times as many
3. The term kaizen refers to
   - *a.* an inventory control system
   - *b.* continuous improvement
   - *c.* highest quality
   - *d.* a decision-making process
   - *e.* ethnocentric policies
4. The term kanban refers to
   - *a.* an inventory system
   - *b.* continuous improvement
   - *c.* highest quality
   - *d.* a decision-making process
   - *e.* ethnocentric policies
5. Which specific group is most discriminated against in Japanese companies?
   - *a.* younger workers
   - *b.* all workers with children
   - *c.* elderly workers
   - *d.* female workers
   - *e.* Japanese companies don't discriminate against any groups

6. A fishbone diagram is most relevant for
   a. determining causes of problems
   b. implementing cost controls
   c. use in scrap reduction planning
   d. use in process planning
   e. use in facilities layout planning

7. The typical career path in a Japanese manufacturing company emphasizes
   a. financial experience
   b. manufacturing experience
   c. marketing experience
   d. any specialization
   e. generalization

8. A new hire in a Japanese company would typically expect to receive his or her first promotion in
   a. six months
   b. one year
   c. two years
   d. five years
   e. ten years

9. Which of the following best describes Japanese decision making?
   a. The manager makes the decision and then tells his or her employees.
   b. The manager makes the decision and then gets input from all employees affected by the decision before implementing it.
   c. The manager asks for input from all affected employees before making the decision.
   d. The manager and his or her employees share in making the decision equally.
   e. The manager delegates the decision completely to his or her employees.

10. Which of the following statements is true about the Japanese government's role in business?
   a. It pursues a laissez-faire policy.
   b. It owns most of the major industries.
   c. It provides subsidies and incentives to certain firms.
   d. The key executives in most Japanese corporations are political appointees.
   e. It regularly appropriates the assets of companies that make too much profit.

Scoring: Check your responses against those listed below:

1. d	2. e	3. b	4. a	5. d
6. a	7. e	8. e	9. b	10. c

What the Assessment Means: Treat this assessment like any test you've taken. Eight or more correct responses indicates that you have a considerable knowledge of Japanese manufacturing and business practices. Six or seven correct indicates some "average" knowledge of these practices. Fewer than six correct responses suggests that you might benefit considerably by reading about Japanese practices.

Source: A similar version of this assessment appeared in S. P. Robbins and M. Coulter, Management, 5th ed. (Upper Saddle River, N.J.: Prentice Hall, 1996), pp. 718–20.

Details on a Management Classic

Using the Economic Order Quantity Model

The objective of the economic order quantity (EOQ) model is to minimize the total costs associated with the carrying and ordering costs. As the amount ordered gets larger, average inventory increases and so do carrying costs. For example, if annual demand for an inventory item is 26,000 units, and a firm orders 500 each time, the firm will place 52 (26,000/500) orders per year. This gives the organization an average inventory of 250 (500/2) units. If the order quantity is increased to 2000 units, there will be fewer orders (13 [26,000/2,000]) placed. However, average inventory on hand will increase to 1,000 (2,000/2) units. Thus, as holding costs go up, ordering costs go down, and vice versa. The most economic order quantity is reached at the lowest point on the total cost curve. That's the point at which ordering costs equal carrying costs—or the economic order quantity (see point Q in Exhibit 16-3).

To compute this optimal order quantity, you need the following data: forecasted demand for the item during the period *(D)*; the cost of placing each order *(OC)*; the value or purchase price of the item *(V)*; and the carrying cost (expressed as a percentage) of maintaining the total inventory *(CC)*. Given these data, the formula for EOQ is as follows:

$$EOQ = \sqrt{\frac{2 \times D \times OC}{V \times CC}}$$

Let's work an example of determining the EOQ.

Take for example Baines Electronics, a retailer of high-quality sound and video equipment. The owner of Baines—Susan Baines—wishes to determine the company's economic order quantities of high-quality sound and video equipment. The item in question is a Sony compact radio cassette recorder. Susan forecasts sales of 4,000 units a year. She believes that the cost for the sound system should be $50. Estimated costs of placing an order for these systems are $35 per order and annual insurance, taxes, and other carrying costs at 20 percent of the recorder's value. Using the EOQ formula, and the preceding information, Susan can calculate the EOQ as follows:

$$EOQ = \sqrt{\frac{2 \times 4{,}000 \times 35}{50 \times 0.2}}$$

$$EOQ = \sqrt{28{,}000}$$

$$EOQ = 167.33, \text{ or } 168 \text{ units}$$

The inventory model suggests to Susan that it's most economic to order in quantities or lots of approximately 168 recorders. Stated differently, Baines should order about 24 (4,000/168) times a year. However, what would happen if the supplier offers Baines a 5 percent discount on purchases if Susan buys in minimum quantities of 250 units? Should Susan now purchase in quantities of 168 or 250? Without the discount, and ordering 168 each time, Susan's annual costs for these recorders would be as follows:

Purchase cost:	$50 × 4,000	= $200,000
Carrying cost (average number of inventory units × value of item × percentage):	168/2 × $50 × 0.2	= 840
Ordering cost (number of orders × cost to place order):	24 × $35	= 840
Total cost:		$201,680

Using the Economic Order Quantity Model Continued

With the 5 percent discount for ordering 250 units, the item cost ($50 − [$50 × 0.05]) would be $47.50. The annual inventory costs would be as follows:

Purchase cost:	$47.50	× 4,000	= $190,000
Carrying cost:	250/2	× 47.5 × 0.2 =	1,187.50
Ordering cost:	16 (4,000/250)	× $35 =	560
Total cost:			= $191,747.50

These calculations suggest to Susan that she should take advantage of the 5 percent discount. Even though she now has to stock larger quantities, the annual savings amounts to nearly $10,000. A word of caution, however, needs to be added. The EOQ model assumes that demand and lead times are known and constant. If these conditions can't be met, the model shouldn't be used. For example, it generally shouldn't be used for manufactured component inventory because the components are taken out of stock all at once or in lumps or odd lots rather than at a constant rate. Does this mean that the EOQ model is useless when demand is variable? No. The model can still be of some use in demonstrating trade-offs in costs and the need to control lot sizes. However, there are more sophisticated lot-sizing models for handling demand and special situations. The mathematics for them go far beyond the scope of this text!

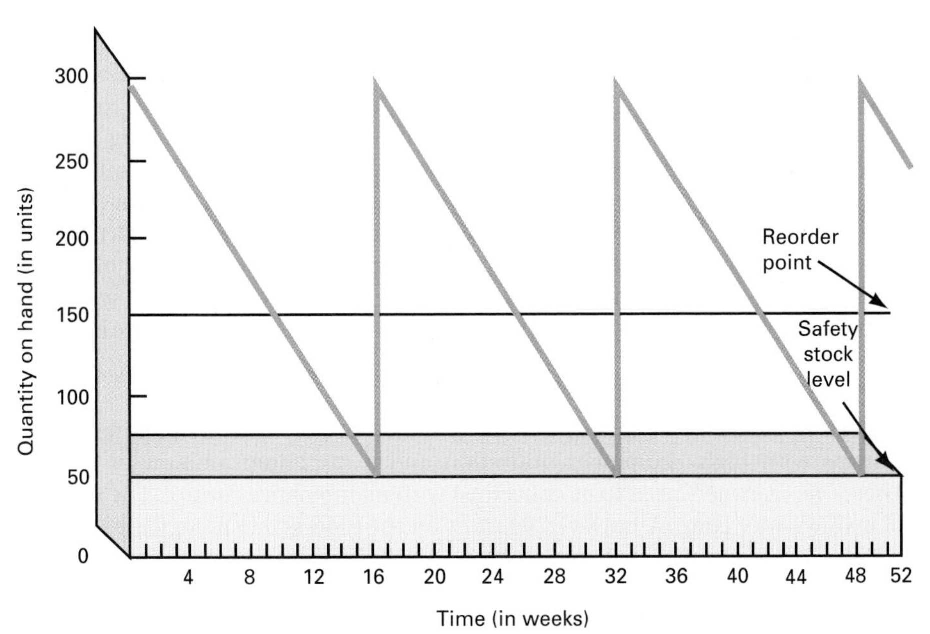

Exhibit 16-4
Inventory Cycle with Safety Stock

These workers at 7-Eleven Japan prepare boxed meals for sale to customers. What's unusual about this practice is that the store chain makes these meals in a central location three times daily—at which time they are delivered to each of 7-Eleven's 6,163 stores in Japan. They arrive "just in time" for the hungry meal crowd that visits the stores throughout the day.

fixed-interval reordering system
A system that uses time as the determining factor for reviewing and reordering inventory items.

Another common inventory system is the **fixed-interval reordering system.** The fixed-interval system uses time as the determining factor for inventory control. At a predetermined time—say, once a week or every ninety days—the inventory is counted, and an order is placed for the number of items necessary to bring the inventory back to the desired level. The desired level is established so that if demand and ordering lead time are average, consumption will draw the inventory down to zero (or some safety lead time can be added) just as the next order arrives. This system may have some transportation economies and quantity discount economies over the fixed-point system. For example, it may allow us to consolidate orders from one supplier if we review all the items we purchase from this source at the same time. This consolidation is not possible in the fixed-point reordering system.

What Is a Just-in-Time Inventory Practice? We introduced you to *just-in-time inventory (JIT)* practices in Chapter 6 as we explored ways of enhancing the production process. We raise the practice here again because it's arguably the fastest-growing control technique for minimizing inventory costs. With JIT, inventory items arrive when they are needed in the production process instead of being stored in stock. The ultimate goal of JIT is to have only enough inventory on hand to complete the day's work—thereby reducing a company's inventory, and its associated costs, to zero.

JIT attempts to eliminate raw material inventories by coordinating production and supply deliveries precisely. When the system works as designed, it results in a number of positive benefits for an organization.[29] These include reduced inventories, reduced setup time, better work flow, shorter manufacturing time, less space consumption, and even higher quality. Of course, suppliers who can be depended on to deliver quality materials on time must be found, because there is no slack in the system to absorb defective materials or delays in shipment given that no inventories are held.

What Is Maintenance Control?

Delivering goods or services in an efficient and effective manner requires operating systems with high equipment utilization and a minimum amount of downtime. Therefore, managers need to be concerned with maintenance control. The importance of maintenance control, however, depends on the process technology used. For example, if a standardized assembly-line process breaks down, it can affect hundreds of employees. On an automobile or dishwasher assembly line, it's not unusual for a serious breakdown on one machine to bring an entire plant to a halt. In contrast, most systems using more general-purpose and redundant processes have less interdependency between activities; therefore, a machine breakdown is likely to have less of an impact. Nevertheless, an equipment breakdown—like an inventory stockout—may mean higher costs, delayed deliveries, or lost sales.

There are three approaches to maintenance control.[30] **Preventive maintenance** is performed before a breakdown occurs. **Remedial maintenance** is a complete overhaul, replacement, or repair of the equipment when it breaks down. **Conditional maintenance** refers to overhaul or repair in response to an inspection and measurement of the equipment's state. When British Airways tears down its planes' engines every 1,000 hours, it is engaging in preventive maintenance. When it inspects the planes' tires every twenty-four hours and changes them when conditions warrant it, it is performing conditional maintenance. Finally, if British Airways' operations policy is to repair lavatory equipment on board its planes only after the equipment breaks down, then it is using remedial maintenance practices. The British Airways example points out that the type of maintenance control depends on the costs of a breakdown. The greater the cost in terms of money, time, liability, or increased loss of goodwill, the greater the benefits from preventive maintenance.

preventive maintenance Maintenance that is performed before a breakdown occurs.

remedial maintenance Maintenance that calls for the overhaul, replacement, or repair of equipment when it breaks down.

conditional maintenance Maintenance that calls for overhaul or repair in response to an inspection and measurement of equipment's state.

Maintenance control should also be considered in the design of equipment. If downtime is highly inconvenient or costly, reliability can be increased by designing redundancy into the equipment. Nuclear power plants, for example, have elaborate backup systems built in. Similarly, equipment can be designed to facilitate fast or low-cost maintenance. Equipment that has fewer parts has fewer things to go wrong. High-failure items can also be placed in locations that are easily accessible or in independent modular units that can be quickly removed and replaced. Cable television operators, for instance, follow these guidelines. Breakdowns infuriate customers, so when they occur management wants to be able to correct them quickly—and preferably through computer control at the cable company's operations center. And when problems are the result of equipment failure in customers' homes, speed is facilitated by centralizing equipment in easy-access locations and making extensive use of modular units. If a piece of equipment fails, the whole module of which it is a part can be pulled or replaced in just a few minutes. Cable service is resumed rapidly, and the pulled modular unit can be taken to the shop and repaired without time pressures.

Are Continuous Improvement and Quality Control the Same Thing?

We have discussed continuous improvement throughout this book, describing it as a comprehensive, customer-focused program to continuously improve the quality of the organization's processes, products, and services. Whereas continuous improvement programs emphasize actions to prevent mistakes, quality control emphasizes identifying mistakes that may have already occurred.

So what do we mean by **quality control?** It refers to monitoring quality—weight, strength, consistency, color, taste, reliability, finish, or any one of myriad characteristics—to ensure that it meets some preestablished standard. Quality control will probably be needed at one or more points, beginning with the receipt of inputs. It will continue with work in process and all steps up to the final product. Assessments at intermediate stages of the transformation process typically are part of quality control. Early detection of a defective part or process can save the cost of further work on the item.

quality control Ensuring that what is produced meets some preestablished standard.

In imposing quality control, managers should begin by asking whether they expect to examine 100 percent of the items or whether a sample can be used. The inspection of each item makes sense if the cost of continuous evaluation is very low or if the consequences of a statistical error are very high (as in the manufacture of a drug used in open-heart surgery). Statistical samples are usually less costly, and sometimes they are the only viable option. For example, if the quality test destroys the product—as happens with bombs or flashbulbs—then sampling has to be utilized. There are two categories of statistical quality control procedures: acceptance sampling and process control. **Acceptance sampling** refers to the evaluation of purchased or manufactured materials or products that already exist. A sample is taken; then the decision to accept or reject the whole lot is based on a calculation of sample risk error. **Process control** refers to sampling items during the transformation process to see whether the transformation process itself is under control. For example, a process control procedure at Snapple would be able to detect if a bottling machine was out of adjustment if it was filling 16-ounce bottles with only 14 ounces of iced tea. Statistical tests would also be used in process control to determine if the variations were outside the range of acceptable quality level. Since most production processes aren't perfectly adjusted and have some innate variations, these tests would indicate serious problems within the production process itself. And quality problems that should be addressed can be seen to immediately.

acceptance sampling
A quality control procedure in which a sample is taken and a decision to accept or reject a whole lot is based on a calculation of sample risk error.

process control
A quality control procedure in which items are sampled during the transformation process to see whether the process itself is under control.

A final consideration in quality control is related to whether the test is done by examining attributes or variables. The inspection and classification of items as acceptable or unacceptable is called **attribute sampling.** An inspector compares the items against some standard and rates their quality as acceptable or not acceptable. In contrast, **variable sampling** involves taking a measurement to determine how much an item varies from the standard. It involves a range rather than a dichotomy. Management typically identifies the standard and an acceptable deviation. Any sample that measures within the range is accepted, and those outside are rejected. For instance, managers at Nippon Steel might test several steel bars to see whether the average breaking strength is between 120 and 140 pounds per square inch. If it's not, the cause can be investigated and corrective action taken.

attribute sampling
A quality control technique that classifies items as acceptable or unacceptable on the basis of comparison to a standard.

variable sampling
A quality control technique in which a measurement is taken to determine how much an item varies from the standard.

Before we leave the issue of quality control, there is an important issue before us. That is, who is really responsible for increasing the quality of our goods and services produced? We know that quality is a function of both operations and people variables. Of course, management needs to focus on both.

A lot of our discussion above has focused on the "operations" side of the equation. Management must ensure that it has a productive transformation process. From the people side, techniques we have discussed in previous chapters should be considered. Empowerment, management by objectives, team-based work groups, and equitable pay systems are examples of people-oriented approaches toward quality enhancement. But much of the people side of the equation focuses on operative employees—those actually performing the work. The late management consultant and quality expert W. Edwards Deming, however, shifted that primary responsibility to managers. Exhibit 16-5 outlines Deming's fourteen points for improving quality. A close look at Exhibit 16-5 reveals Deming's understanding of the interplay between people and operations. High quality cannot come solely from good "people management." Rather, the truly effective organization will maximize quality and ultimately productivity by successfully integrating people into the overall operations system.

Who is really responsible for increasing the quality of our goods and services produced?

- ▶ **1.** Plan for the long-term future, not for next month or next year.
- ▶ **2.** Never be complacent concerning the quality of your product.
- ▶ **3.** Establish statistical control over your production processes and require your suppliers to do so as well.
- ▶ **4.** Deal with the fewest number of suppliers—the best ones, of course.
- ▶ **5.** Find out whether your problems are confined to particular parts of the production process or stem from the overall process itself.
- ▶ **6.** Train workers for the job that you are asking them to perform.
- ▶ **7.** Raise the quality of your line supervisors.
- ▶ **8.** Drive out fear.
- ▶ **9.** Encourage departments to work closely together rather than to concentrate on departmental or divisional distinctions.
- ▶ **10.** Do not be sucked into adopting strictly numerical goals, including the widely popular formula of "zero defect."
- ▶ **11.** Require your workers to do quality work, not just to be at their stations from 9 to 5.
- ▶ **12.** Train your employees to understand statistical methods.
- ▶ **13.** Train your employees in new skills as the need arises.
- ▶ **14.** Make top managers responsible for implementing these principles.

Exhibit 16-5
Deming's Fourteen Points for Improving Quality

Source: W. E. Deming, "Improvement of Quality and Productivity through Action by Management," *National Productivity Review,* Winter 1981–82, pp. 12–22. With permission. Copyright 1981 by Executive Enterprises, Inc., 22 West 21st St., New York, N.Y. 10010-6904. All rights reserved.

Financial Controls

In Chapter 4, we introduced budgets as both a planning and control device. Now, we turn to financial analyses that serve as feedback controls. We know that investors and stock analysts make regular use of an organization's financial documents to assess its worth. These same documents can be analyzed by managers as internal controls, which include ratio analyses, audits, cost-benefit analysis, and activity-based accounting.

What Are the More Popular Ratio Analyses?

Managers often want to examine their organization's balance and income statements to analyze key ratios: that is, comparing two significant figures from the financial statements and expressing them as a percentage or ratio. This practice allows managers to compare current financial performance with that of previous periods and against other organizations in the same industry. Some of the more useful ratios evaluate liquidity, leverage, operations, and profitability. These are summarized below and shown in Exhibit 16-6.

What Are Liquidity Ratios? Liquidity is a measure of the organization's ability to convert assets into cash in order that debts can be met. The most popular liquidity ratios are the current ratio and the acid test ratio.

The **current ratio** is defined as the organization's current assets divided by its current liabilities. Although there is no magic number that is considered safe, the accountant's rule of thumb for the current ratio is 2:1. A significantly higher ratio usually suggests that management is not getting the best return on its assets. A ratio at or below 1:1 indicates potential difficulty in meeting short-term obligations (accounts payable, interest payments, salaries, taxes, and so forth).

current ratio
An organization's current assets divided by its current liabilities.

The **acid test** ratio is the same as the current ratio except that current assets are reduced by the dollar value of inventory held. When inventories turn slowly, or are difficult to sell, the acid test ratio may more accurately represent the organization's

acid test
An organization's current assets, minus inventories, divided by its current liabilities.

OBJECTIVE	RATIO	CALCULATION	MEANING
Liquidity test	Current ratio	Current assets / Current liabilities	Tests the organization's ability to meet short-term obligations
	Acid test	Current assets less inventories / Current liabilities	Tests liquidity more accurately when inventories turn over slowly or are difficult to sell
Leverage test	Debt-to-assets	Total debt / Total assets	The higher the ratio, the more leveraged the organization
	Times-interest-earned	Profits before interest and taxes / Total interest charges	Measures how far profits can decline before the organization is unable to meet its interest expenses
Operations test	Inventory turnover	Revenues / Inventory	The higher the ratio, the more efficiently inventory assets are being used
	Total asset turnover	Revenues / Total assets	The fewer assets used to achieve a given level of sales, the more efficiently management is using the organization's total assets
Profitability	Profit margin-on-revenues	Net profit after taxes / Total revenues	Identifies the profits that various products are generating
	Return-on-investment	Net profit after taxes / Total assets	Measures the efficiency of assets to generate profits

Exhibit 16-6
Popular Financial Controls

true liquidity. That is, a high current ratio that is heavily based on an inventory that is difficult to sell overstates the organization's true liquidity. Accordingly, accountants typically consider an acid test ratio of 1:1 to be reasonable.

debt-to-assets ratio
Total debt divided by total assets.

times-interest-earned ratio
Profits before interest and taxes divided by total interest charges.

inventory turnover ratio
Revenue divided by inventory.

total assets turnover ratio
Revenue divided by total assets.

What Are Leverage Ratios? *Leverage* refers to the use of borrowed funds to operate and expand an organization. The advantage of leverage occurs when funds can be used to earn a rate of return well above the cost of those funds. For instance, if management can borrow money at 6 percent and can earn 10 percent on it internally, it makes good sense to borrow. But there are risks to overleveraging. The interest on the debt can be a drain on the organization's cash resources and can, at the extreme, drive an organization into bankruptcy. The objective, therefore, is to use debt wisely. Leverage ratios such as **debt-to-assets ratio** (computed by dividing total debt by total assets) or the **times-interest-earned ratio** (computed as profits before interest and taxes divided by total interest charges) can help managers control debt levels.

What Are Operating Ratios? Operating ratios describe how efficiently management is using the organization's resources. Probably the most popular operating ratios are inventory turnover and total assets turnover.

The **inventory turnover ratio** is defined as revenue divided by inventory. The higher the ratio, the more efficiently inventory assets are being used. Revenue divided by total assets represents an organization's **total assets turnover ratio.** It measures the level of assets needed to generate the organization's revenue. The fewer assets used to achieve a given level of revenue, the more efficiently management is using the organization's total assets.

What Are Profitability Ratios? Profit-making organizations want to measure their effectiveness and efficiency. Profitability ratios serve such a purpose. The better known of these are profit-margin-on-revenues and return-on-investment ratios.

Managers of organizations that have a variety of products want to put their efforts into those products that are most profitable. The **profit-margin-on-revenues ratio,** computed as net profit after taxes divided by total revenues, is a measure of profits per dollar revenues.

profit-margin-on-revenues ratio
Net profit after taxes divided by total revenues.

One of the most widely used measures of a business firm's profitability is the **return-on-investment ratio.** It's calculated by multiplying (revenues/investments) times (profit/revenues). This percentage recognizes that absolute profits must be placed in the context of assets required to generate those profits.

return-on-investment ratio
[Revenues divided by investments] multiplied by [profit divided by revenues].

What Are Audits?

An **audit** is a formal verification of an organization's accounts, records, operating activities, or performance. It is essentially designed to check an organization's control mechanisms. Audits can generally be characterized as either external or internal.

audit
A formal verification of an organization's accounts, records, operating activities, or performance.

What Is the Difference between External and Internal Audits? An external audit is a verification of an organization's financial statements by an outside and independent accounting firm. The organization creates its own financial statements using its own accountants. The external auditor's job then is to review the various accounts on the financial statements with respect to their accuracy and conformity with generally accepted accounting practices.

The **internal audit,** as its name implies, is done by an organization's own financial or accounting staff. It encompasses verifying the financial statements, just as the external audit does, but additionally includes an evaluation of the organization's operations, procedures, and policies, plus any recommendations for improvement.

internal audit
An audit done by an organization's own financial or accounting staff.

How Can Internal Audits Be Useful as a Managerial Control Tool? Internal audits go beyond verifying financial statements. They seek to uncover inefficiencies in the organization's processes and suggest actions for their corrections. Specifically, managers can use internal audits to identify problems and to ensure that organizational activities are progressing as planned. For example, in our discussion of PERT networks in Chapter 4, we discussed the need to place controls on critical activities. Internal audits, in a like fashion, key into similar activities to ensure that the processes are operating as needed. These preventive measures, then, can be implemented before a major "breakdown" is experienced.

What Role Does Cost-Benefit Analysis Play in Control?

Some organizational activities do not lend themselves to objective financial evaluation techniques. Rather, they compare costs against objectives and use the result to prioritize and evaluate activities. When managers perform this activity, we say they are conducting a **cost-benefit analysis.** Cost-benefit analysis is useful when the amount of costs is known, but the standard against which those costs must be compared is ambiguous or difficult to measure. This is particularly the case, for example, when evaluating the effectiveness of such programs as defense projects, welfare programs, or educational systems. Cost-benefit expresses all the relevant benefits that accrue from an activity in the common denominator of money, so that they can be added together and their costs

cost-benefit analysis
Evaluating an activity when costs are known but the standard against which those costs must be compared is ambiguous or difficult to measure.

Are these mini-cellular phones that are given to concierges at Tokyo's Westin Hotel cost-effective? Using a cost-benefit analysis could help answer that question. Hotel management believes that having hotel workers readily in touch with base units—and not having to carry cumbersome walkie-talkies—enables employees to get information more quickly, which can enhance customer service.

subtracted. This approach helps managers to determine if funds spent by their organizations on a number of activities are achieving benefits in excess of the amount spent.

Cost-benefit analysis is probably more applicable and effective as an informal measuring concept than as a formal control technique, because it is difficult to objectively quantify subjective qualitative factors. Thus, cost-benefit gives no final answer about whether a program or activity is "justified" or "good" or whether it should be expanded or contracted. Rather, it merely suggests how well an activity is operating when viewed in a specific manner.

What Is Activity-Based Accounting?

activity-based accounting (ABC) An accounting procedure whereby costs for producing a good or service are allocated on the basis of the activities performed and resources used.

Activity-based accounting (ABC) is an accounting procedure whereby costs for producing a good or service are allocated on the basis of the "activities performed and resources employed."[31] That is, the purpose of ABC is to reflect production costs accurately. It is gaining an increasingly wide following in all types of organizations—whether they are for or not-for-profit operations. For instance, consider the operating room costs at a regional hospital associated with two medical procedures—tonsillectomy and heart transplant surgeries. Indeed, the latter operation is the more serious one. But what should the heart transplant operating room cost be in relation to that of the tonsillectomy? If hospital records show that a tonsillectomy is a one-hour operation and a heart transplant is an eight-hour procedure, should the operating room charge be eight times as much for the heart procedure? Probably not. Why? Because eight times may actually understate the actual costs, given that the heart transplant requires much more medical equipment be used. For example, a heart and lung machine, which keeps the patient breathing and blood circulating during the heart transplant, is not used in tonsillectomies. So, too, will there be extra costs associated with more medical apparatus and supplies. Therefore, a simple "eight-times" pricing mechanism may not reflect the true costs.

The concept of ABC is relatively simple. It allocates costs solely on the basis of usage!

The concept of ABC is relatively simple. Allocate costs solely on the basis of usage! Instead of spreading costs evenly or on a percentage basis to jobs, as more-traditional accounting methods do, ABC focuses on the specific costs incurred in the production of a good or service and charges them directly to the task. Thus, the tonsillectomy patient won't be charged a flat rate that overstates the costs of the operation. In this manner, organizations, like hospitals, are better able to set accurate prices, which ultimately could lead to the development of a competitive advantage.

Summary

How will I know if I fulfilled the Learning Objectives found on page 486? You will have fulfilled the Learning Objectives if you understand the following.

1. **Explain the purpose of a management information system (MIS).** The purpose of an MIS is to provide managers with accurate and current information for decision making and control.
2. **Differentiate between data and information.** Data are raw, unanalyzed facts. Information is data that have been organized into a usable form.
3. **Describe how an MIS affects decision making.** An MIS significantly alters the speed, quantity, and quality of information from which managers will make a decision. With an MIS, managers can identify problems more quickly, gather appropriate facts more efficiently, test alternatives through what-if questions, and select the best alternative on the basis of answers to those questions.
4. **Explain the role of information systems in control.** An MIS makes it possible to obtain more complete and accurate information in the measuring phase of controlling. It also permits managers to focus precisely on what they want to know.
5. **Define the role of the transformation process in operations management.** Operations management takes inputs, including people and materials, and then acts on them by transforming them into finished goods and services. This applies in service organizations as well as in manufacturing firms.
6. **Explain the relationship between cost centers, direct costs, and indirect costs.** A cost center is a unit in which managers are held responsible for all associated costs. The costs incurred are direct (costs incurred in proportion to the output of a particular good or service) or indirect (costs that are largely unaffected by changes in output). In a cost center, managers are generally held responsible for all direct costs but not for the indirect costs that are not within their control.
7. **Identify three approaches to maintenance control.** The three types of maintenance control are preventive, remedial, and conditional. Preventive maintenance is performed before a breakdown occurs. Remedial maintenance is performed when the equipment breaks down. Conditional maintenance is a response to an inspection.
8. **Contrast continuous improvement programs and quality control.** Continuous improvement programs emphasize actions that an organization can take to prevent mistakes from happening. Quality control emphasizes identifying mistakes that may have already occurred in the production of goods and services.
9. **Distinguish between external and internal audits.** An external audit is a verification of an organization's financial statements by an outside and independent accounting firm. An internal audit is performed by an organization's own financial staff. It also verifies financial data but additionally includes an evaluation of the organization's operations, procedures, and policies.
10. **Explain how cost-benefit analysis can improve financial control.** A cost-benefit analysis is a tool for evaluating the benefits from activities whose benefits are ambiguous or subjective. It expresses all relevant benefits of an activity in the common term of money so they can be added together and their costs subtracted.

Review & Discussion Questions

1. How can an MIS assist a manager in the control function?
2. In what ways is information a unique resource for organizations? Give examples.
3. How can an MIS create a flatter organization while simultaneously giving managers more control over the organization's operations?
4. Does the use of MIS empower all employees, all managers, or only a select few individuals in the organization? Discuss.
5. How has MIS changed power bases in organizations?
6. Describe how the transformation process is as applicable to a service organization as it is to a manufacturing one.

7. Contrast acceptance sampling and process control.
8. Which is more critical for success in organizations—continuous improvement or quality control? Support your position.
9. What are the more popular financial ratios, and how are they calculated?
10. "Cost-benefit analysis is better than no analysis at all. If the data are subjective and do not lend themselves to objective analyses, cost-benefit provides at least a 'good enough' response." Do you agree or disagree with the statement? Explain.

Testing Your Comprehension • • • 

Circle the correct answer, then check yourself on page AK-2.

1. Which of the following is MOST accurate regarding MIS?
   a) It is used sporadically by management.
   b) It usually results in a narrow span of control.
   c) It renders data into information.
   d) It must be computer-based.

2. Increased use of MIS will change the role of managers by
   a) reducing their workload
   b) making managers more dependent on the organization's computer department
   c) increasing the importance of midmanagers at the expense of first-line supervisors
   d) enhancing the effective decision-making capability of managers

3. Most operations managers have considerable influence over
   a) direct costs
   b) indirect costs
   c) fixed costs
   d) overhead costs

4. Reordering goods at some preestablished point in the operations process is reflective of
   a) distribution requirements planning
   b) a fixed-point reorder system
   c) a fixed-interval reordering system
   d) the ABC system

5. When sales are recorded in a computer and the system is preprogrammed to originate a purchase order when a minimal level remains, the system is called
   a) MIS
   b) ABC
   c) fixed-point
   d) fixed-interval

6. Which of the following is NOT required as an assumption of the EOQ model?
   a) All relevant costs are known.
   b) Demand is predictable.
   c) Lead time is known and constant.
   d) The number of employees that need to be scheduled is known.

7. A JIT inventory system is MOST appropriate when
   a) a highly flexible production schedule exists
   b) suppliers are dispersed geographically
   c) reliable transportation and physical distribution systems exist between supplier and buyer
   d) a dynamic distribution system exists

8. A large interstate motor carrier company that rebuilds a diesel engine after it failed a compression test is using
   a) preventive maintenance
   b) conditional maintenance
   c) remedial maintenance
   d) systems maintenance

9. When Budget Rent-a-Car establishes a policy for oil changes for its fleet at 5,000 miles, it is practicing
   a) remedial maintenance
   b) conditional maintenance
   c) preventive maintenance
   d) backup systems maintenance

10. Sampling items during the transformation process to see if the transformation process is under control is called
    a) acceptance sampling
    b) variable sampling
    c) attribute sampling
    d) process control

Continued

11. An examination of some number of materials or products to determine if a lot should be accepted or rejected on the basis of the calculation of sample risk error is called
    a) acceptance sampling
    b) variable sampling
    c) attribute sampling
    d) process control

12. A quality control technique in which items are accepted or rejected on the basis of some measurement is called
    a) acceptance sampling
    b) variable sampling
    c) attribute sampling
    d) process control

13. Formal verification of an organization's accounts, records, operating activities, or performance is
    a) an acid test
    b) a ratio
    c) an audit
    d) a comparison

14. The acid test ratio is
    a) the same as the current ratio
    b) the current ratio plus inventories, divided by its current liabilities
    c) debt-to-assets minus current liabilities
    d) current assets, minus inventories, divided by current liabilities

For questions 15–18 use the following information taken from a company's balance sheet and income statement (all 000s omitted):

Current assets	=	$ 6,267
Net profits, after taxes	=	4,646
Total assets	=	107,223
Current liabilities	=	3,006
Total sales	=	171,211
Inventories	=	7,387

15. The company's current ratio is
    a) 2.085
    b) 0.037
    c) 1.349
    d) 0.848

16. The return-on-investment for the company is
    a) 0.027
    b) 1.546
    c) 0.058
    d) 0.043

17. In a report to the company's CEO, the inventory turnover is reported as
    a) 27.319
    b) 2.085
    c) 1.596
    d) 0.043

18. The company's total asset turnover is
    a) 27.319
    b) 23.177
    c) 14.515
    d) 36.851

Applying the Concepts

Financial Controls

The purpose of this exercise is to provide you with an opportunity to calculate financial ratios given typical financial statements of companies. Using the information from Exhibit 16-7, individually calculate the following: current ratio, acid test ratio, debt-to-assets ratio, times-interest-earned ratio, inventory turnover ratio,

BALANCE SHEET

Assets	**Wollenburg Media Inc.** (000s omitted)	**CMT Research International** (000s omitted)
Current Assets		
Cash	4,123	71,000
Market Securities (short-term investments)	4,236	-0-
Receivables, net	6,331	137,000
Inventories	5,840	202,000
Prepaid Expenses	3,830	16,000
Total Current Assets	24,360	426,000
Net Property, etc.	35,330	159,000
Investments (long-term)	23,346	10,005
Other Assets	10,493	19,460
Total Assets	93,529	614,465
Liabilities and Stockholder Equity		
Current Liabilities		
Notes Payable	1,244	16,438
Accounts Payable	13,851	159,219
Other Liabilities	5,822	30,343
Total Current Liabilities	20,917	206,000
Long-Term Debt	22,195	119,000
Capital Lease Obligations	24,296	20,548
Deferred Income	2,211	9,917
Stockholder Equity	23,910	259,000
Total Liabilities and Equity	93,529	614,465
Income Statement	(000s omitted)	(000s omitted)
Total Revenue	148,889	462,000
Cost of Products Sold	(114,335)	(229,000)
Administrative Costs	(23,475)	(136,000)
Total Costs	(137,810)	(365,000)
Earnings from Operations	11,079	97,000
Interest Expense	(5,771)	(21,000)
Earnings before Taxes	5,308	76,000
Income Taxes	(1,713)	(30,000)
Net Income (Earnings)	3,595	46,000

Exhibit 16-7
Financial Data

Source: Adapted from C. T. Horngren and W. T. Harrison Jr., *Accounting* (Englewood Cliffs, N.J.: Prentice Hall, 1989), pp. 762–77. Used with permission.

total assets turnover ratio, profit-margin-on-revenues ratio, and return-on-investment ratio. You may want to refer to pages 505–7 in this chapter for information about and the formulas used in calculating these ratios.

When you have completed your calculations, get into groups of four to five individuals. Compare your ratios. If differences exist, recalculate them until all group members have the same number. Then, with your group, determine what these ratios mean. For example, if you were deciding to invest in one of the two companies listed in the financial statements, which one would you choose? Why? When all groups have made these determinations, your professor will ask each group to share its results and their support for their decision.

Take It to the Net

We invite you to visit the Robbins/De Cenzo page on the Prentice Hall Web site at:

http://www.prenhall.com/robbinsfom

for this chapter's World Wide Web exercise.

You can also visit the Web sites for these companies and agencies featured within this chapter:

American Express Company
http://www.americanexpress.com

Comp-U-Card International (CUC)
http://www.cuc.com

McAfee
http://www.mcafee.com

Snapple
http://www.snapple.com

U.S. Postal Service
http://www.usps.gov

UPS (United Parcel Service)
http://www.ups.com

Thinking Critically

Making a Value Judgment: Is Sharing Software Okay?

Duplicating software programs for friends and coworkers has become a widespread practice. It has been estimated that, worldwide, software companies (which include such firms as Microsoft, Lotus, and McAfee) lose almost $12 billion annually to software pirates.[32] Yet almost all of these duplicated programs are protected by copyright laws around the world. And being caught for pirating software subjects the offender to fines of up to $100,000 and five years in jail. How, then, has making illegal copies become such a common and accepted practice in people's homes as well as at their place of employment?

Part of the answer revolves around the issue that software isn't like some other intellectual property. Intellectual property is something that's developed by someone and is attributable directly to thinking processes. Software is different from a book in that anyone can easily copy it—and an exact replication is achievable. Another reason is related to cultural differences. A lot of piracy occurs in places such as Brazil, Malaysia, Hong Kong, Pakistan, Mexico, and Singapore, where copyright laws don't apply and sharing rather than protecting creative work is the norm. But don't think that software piracy is just an overseas phenomenon. It has been estimated that in the United States about 40 percent of all software used is pirated,[33] cheating software developers of approximately $1.5 billion. In the United States, employees and managers who pirate software defend their behavior by giving such answers as: "Everybody does it!" "I won't get caught!" "The law isn't enforced!" "No one really loses!" or "Our departmental budget isn't large enough to handle buying dozens of copies of the same program!"

Ask the same employees who copy software if it is acceptable to steal a book from the library or a tape from a video store. Most are quick to condemn such practices. But it seems as if they don't see copying as stealing. Some think that there's nothing wrong with checking out a video, making a copy, and returning it—despite the copyright statement and the Interpol (the international policing agency) warning at the beginning of the tape that specifically states that the act of copying that tape is in violation of the law. Still, if they copy it, they can return the original to the store—no harm done.

Questions:

1. Do you believe that reproducing copyrighted software is ever an acceptable practice? Explain your position.
2. Is it wrong for employees of a corporation to do it but permissible for struggling college students who may be unable to afford their own individual copies of expensive educational software programs?
3. As a manager, what guidelines could you establish to direct your employees' behaviors regarding copying software?

MIS at Comp-U-Card

Just how far can an inspired entrepreneur go in the information age? Can today's technology allow a company to stock no inventory, yet sell everything? Walter Forbes, CEO at Comp-U-Card International (CUC) thinks so.[34] In fact, he has built a $1 billion business around what he calls his "virtual-reality inventory."

CUC is a shopping service company located in Stamford, Connecticut. The company's mission is a relatively simple one—to provide appropriate information to customers about products they want when they want them. Forbes realized several years ago that customers' shopping habits were changing. Today's shoppers have busy lives, and associated time constraints are reflected in their buying habits. Many purchase goods from mail-order catalogs, while others tune in to cable television programs such as the *Home Shoppers Club*. But one missing element, according to Forbes, was that these customers still want to make informed purchasing decisions. For instance, in the past, informed decisions meant researching product information in such magazines as *Consumer Reports*. In many cases, this research required a special trip to the local library. Today's average shopper can't afford the "luxury" of gathering the pertinent data. Therein lies CUC's niche.

CUC maintains an information data base on some 250,000 products encompassing 1,700 brands—from cars and air conditioners to computers and sophisticated electronic equipment. Customers can contact CUC either over the Internet or through its 800 number. By connecting with a CUC customer representative, individuals can obtain immediate information on any item they desire, complete with details on how the product compares with others on the market. Thus, a customer can get "the information necessary to comparison shop" and make an informed decision.

Helpful information, however, was not enough for Forbes. He also wanted to make it easier for CUC's subscribers to order their products. That is, after customers have had an opportunity to gather all their requisite data, they can immediately place their order. CUC, in cooperation with suppliers, can then have the item delivered. CUC becomes a one-stop information and shopping source for the consumer, and that consumer never has to leave his or her living room.

Questions:

1. Describe the transformation process at Comp-U-Card. What inputs does it use and what outputs does it create?
2. How do you think Comp-U-Card's operations affect customer decision making? Cite specific examples.
3. Do you think that virtual inventory systems could be applicable to organizations such as General Motors or Mount Sinai Hospital? How do you anticipate they would work? Explain your position.

Video Case ABCNEWS

Flexible Manufacturing and Ford's Truly Global Car

It's claimed that Henry Ford once said, "Give the customer any color of car he wants . . . as long as it's black." Henry would surely be gratified at what his namesake car company is doing today as a global competitor in the automotive industry. In order to increase its efficiency and effectiveness in an ever-increasing intensely competitive global marketplace, Ford is adopting a manufacturing and marketing strategy that helped make McDonald's Corporation an amazing international success. Just what is that strategy? Well, it's pretty simple—sell one basic product all over the world and keep product quality high and consistent.

Although manufacturing an automobile isn't quite as simple as making a hamburger, fries, and milkshake, Ford's managers think they can make their truly global car a reality and a financial success. This basic car with a few minor local variations will be sold in seventy countries around the world. Now consumers in Stockholm, in Minneapolis, and in Singapore will have available all kinds of individualized and customized choices in the same basic car. Ford's chairman, British-born Alex Trotman, is the driving force behind this vision. He explains that it's a step Ford had to take if it wanted to be the leading automobile company of the next century and if it wanted to be as competitive as any corporation in the world. The production of this new global Ford automobile will be the company's most radical shift since Henry Ford launched the world's first assembly line. And what a change it will be!

For instance, at the company's assembly line in Ghent, Belgium, the metal to make the car is bent more to give the car the sharper-edged European look that consumers there crave. The gearbox also can be adjusted by computer to provide the tighter, sportier shifting action that the Europeans like. In the Kansas City plant, the car's suspension can be adjusted to provide the smoother ride that Americans prefer. A third facility in Mexico that's still to come on line will also produce this new global car and have the capability to adapt features to consumers' demands in that part of the world. Geographic distances and borders won't mean a thing anymore. As one of the project's engineering team leaders states, "We can make a change on this part, transfer it back to Germany. An engineer can work on it in Germany and transfer it back to us. This can all happen in a matter of minutes." These new global links enable the company to pick and choose the least expensive suppliers from anywhere in the world; the steering wheel might be made in the United States, the car's electrical circuitry might come from France, and the rubber trim on the seats might be made in Spain.

Ford hopes to save $2 to $3 billion a year with its global reorganization and pursuit of a global automobile. But its new approach also has risks. Ford's managers are betting that the company can be more efficient and effective by consolidating its operations into one global bureaucracy. However, other large multinational corporations are betting that a more decentralized approach based on specific geographic regions or countries will be more efficient and effective. And there's also the risk that national preferences for a car's features might be more important than Ford anticipates. Yet Ford's top management thinks that its future success is linked to the concept of a truly global automobile and remains strongly committed to pursuing this vision.

Questions:

1. How would the type of flexible manufacturing system as proposed by Ford to produce its global automobile be efficient? How would it be effective?
2. What problems might Ford's managers encounter as they try to implement this type of flexible manufacturing system? How would you address those problems?
3. Do you think McDonald's Corporation was an appropriate choice for benchmarking in this situation? Why or why not?

Source: "Ford's Global Automobile Strategy," *ABC News World News Tonight,* September 15, 1994.

Appendix A

The Historical Roots of Contemporary Management Practices

The purpose of this appendix is twofold. First, it illustrates that things that may appear new and innovative in the practice of management. Second, it can help you better understand current management practices. This appendix will introduce you to the origins of many contemporary management concepts and demonstrate how they have evolved to reflect the changing needs of organizations and society as a whole.

The Premodern Era

Organized activities and management have existed for thousands of years. The Egyptian Pyramids and the Great Wall of China are current evidence that projects of tremendous scope, employing tens of thousands of people, were undertaken well before modern times. The Pyramids are a particularly interesting example. The construction of a single Pyramid occupied over 100,000 people for twenty years.[1] Who told each worker what he or she was supposed to do? Who ensured that there would be enough stones at the site to keep workers busy? The answer to questions such as these is management. Regardless of what managers were called at the time, someone had to plan what was to be done, organize people and materials to do it, and provide direction for the workers.

When you hear the name Michelangelo, what comes to your mind? *Renaissance artist? Genius?* How about *manager?* Recent evidence tells us that the traditional image of Michelangelo—the lonely genius trapped between agony and ecstasy, isolated on his back on a scaffold, single-handedly painting the ceiling of the Sistine Chapel—is a myth.[2] Some 475 years ago, Michelangelo was actually running a medium-sized business. Thirteen people helped him paint the Sistine ceiling; about 20 helped carve the marble tombs in the Medici Chapel in Florentine, and he supervised a crew of at least 200 to build the Laurentian Library in Florence. Michelangelo personally selected his workers, trained them, and assigned them to one or more teams, and he kept detailed employment records. For example, he recorded the names, days worked, and wages of every employee, every week. Meanwhile, Michelangelo played the role of the troubleshooting manager. He would daily dart in and out of the various work areas under his supervision, check on workers' progress, and handle any problems that arose.

These examples from the past demonstrate that organized activities and managers have been with us since before the Renaissance period. However, it has been only in the past several hundred years, particularly in the last century, that management has undergone systematic investigation, acquired a common body of knowledge, and become a formal discipline of study.

What Was Adam Smith's Contribution to the Field of Management?

Adam Smith's name is typically cited in economics courses for his contributions to classical economic doctrine, but his discussion in *The Wealth of Nations,* published in 1776, included a brilliant argument on the economic advantages that organizations and society would reap from the **division of labor.**[3] He used the pin-manufacturing industry for his examples. Smith noted that ten individuals, each doing a specialized

division of labor
The breakdown of jobs into narrow, repetitive tasks.

task, could produce about 48,000 pins a day among them. However, if each were working separately and independently, those ten workers would be lucky to make 200—or even ten—pins in one day.

Smith concluded that division of labor increased productivity by increasing each worker's skill and dexterity, by saving time that is commonly lost in changing tasks, and by the creation of labor-saving inventions and machinery. The wide popularity today of job specialization—in service jobs such as teaching and medicine as well as on assembly lines in automobile plants—is undoubtedly due to the economic advantages cited over 200 years ago by Adam Smith.

How Did the Industrial Revolution Influence Management Practices?

Industrial Revolution The advent of machine power, mass production, and efficient transportation begun in the late eighteenth century in Great Britain.

Possibly the most important pre-twentieth-century influence on management was the **Industrial Revolution.** Begun in the late eighteenth century in Great Britain, the Revolution had crossed the Atlantic to America by the end of the Civil War. Machine power was rapidly being substituted for human power. Using machines, in turn, made it economical to manufacture goods in factories.

The advent of machine power, mass production, the reduced transportation costs that followed the rapid expansion of the railroads, and almost no governmental regulation also fostered the development of big organizations. John D. Rockefeller was putting together the Standard Oil monopoly, Andrew Carnegie was gaining control of two-thirds of the steel industry, and similar entrepreneurs were creating other large businesses that would require formalized management practices. The need for a formal theory to guide managers in running their organizations had arrived. However, it was not until the early 1900s that the first major step toward developing such a theory was taken.

Classical Contributions

classical approach The term used to describe the scientific management theorists and the general administrative theorists.

The roots of modern management lie with a group of practitioners and writers who sought to create rational principles that would make organizations more efficient. Because they set the theoretical foundation for a discipline called management, we call their contributions the **classical approach** to management. We can break the classical approach into two subcategories: scientific management and general administrative theorists. Scientific management theory looked at the field from the perspective of how to improve the productivity of operative personnel. The general administrative theorists, on the other hand, were concerned with the overall organization and how to make it more effective.

What Contributions Did Frederick Taylor Make?

scientific management The use of the scientific method to define the "one best way" for a job to be done.

If one had to pinpoint the year that modern management theory was born, one could make a strong case for 1911. That was the year that Frederick Winslow Taylor's *Principles of Scientific Management* was published.[4] Its contents would become widely accepted by managers throughout the world. The book described the theory of **scientific management**—the use of the scientific method to define the "one best way" for a job to be done. The studies conducted before and after the book's publication would establish Taylor as the father of scientific management. Frederick Taylor did most of his work at the Midvale and Bethlehem Steel companies in Pennsylvania (see Details on a Management Classic). As a mechanical engineer with a Quaker-

Details on a Management Classic

Frederick Taylor

Probably the most widely cited example of scientific management is Taylor's pig iron experiment. Workers loaded "pigs" of iron weighing 92 pounds onto rail cars. Their average daily output was 12.5 tons. Taylor believed that if the job was scientifically analyzed to determine the one best way to load pig iron, the output could be increased to 47–48 tons per day.

Taylor began his experiment by looking for a physically strong subject who placed a high value on the dollar. The individual Taylor chose was a big, strong Dutch immigrant, whom he called Schmidt. Schmidt, like the other loaders, earned $1.15 a day, which even at the turn of the century was barely enough for a person to survive on. Taylor offered Schmidt $1.85 a day if he did what Taylor asked.

Using money to motivate Schmidt, Taylor went about having him load the pig irons, alternating various job factors to see what impact the changes had on Schmidt's daily output. For instance, on some days Schmidt would lift the pig irons by bending his knees; on other days he would keep his legs straight and use his back. He experimented with rest periods, walking speed, carrying positions, and other variables. After a long period of scientifically trying various combinations of procedures, techniques, and tools, Taylor succeeded in obtaining the level of productivity he thought possible. By putting the right person on the job with the correct tools and equipment, by having the worker follow his instructions exactly, and by motivating the worker through the economic incentive of a significantly higher daily wage, Taylor was able to reach his 48-ton objective.

It's important to understand what Taylor saw at Midvale Steel that aroused his determination to improve the way things were done in the plant. At the time, there were no clear concepts of worker and management responsibilities. Virtually no effective work standards existed. Workers purposely worked at a slow pace. Management decisions were of the "seat-of-the-pants" variety, based on hunch and intuition. Workers were placed on jobs with little or no concern for matching their abilities and aptitudes with the tasks they were required to do. Most important, management and workers considered themselves to be in continual conflict. Rather than cooperating to their mutual benefit, they perceived their relationship as a zero-sum game—any gain by one would be at the expense of the other.

Puritan background, he was consistently appalled at the inefficiency of workers. Employees used vastly different techniques to do the same job. They were prone to "taking it easy" on the job. Taylor believed that worker output was only about one-third of what was possible. Therefore, he set out to correct the situation by applying the scientific method to jobs on the shop floor. He spent more than two decades pursuing with a passion the "one best way" for each job to be done.

Taylor sought to create a mental revolution among both the workers and management by defining clear guidelines for improving production efficiency. He defined four principles of management, listed in Exhibit AA-1; he argued that following these principles would result in the prosperity of both management and workers. Workers would earn more pay, and management more profits.

Using scientific management techniques, Taylor was able to define the one best way for doing each job. He could then select the right people for the job and train them to do it precisely in this one best way. To motivate workers, he favored incentive

Exhibit AA-1
Taylor's Four Principles of Management

- **1.** Develop a science for each element of an individual's work, which replaces the old rule-of-thumb method.
- **2.** Scientifically select and then train, teach, and develop the worker. (Previously, workers chose their own work and trained themselves as best they could.)
- **3.** Heartily cooperate with the workers so as to ensure that all work is done in accordance with the principles of the science that has been developed.
- **4.** Divide work and responsibility almost equally between management and workers. Management takes over all work for which it is better fitted than the workers. (Previously, almost all the work and the greater part of the responsibility were thrown upon the workers.)

wage plans. Overall, Taylor achieved consistent improvements in productivity in the range of 200 percent or more. And he reaffirmed the role of managers to plan and control and that of workers to perform as they were instructed.

The impact of Taylor's work cannot be overstated.[5] During the first decade of the century, Taylor delivered numerous public lectures to convey scientific management to interested industrialists. Between 1901 and 1911, at least eighteen firms adopted some variants of scientific management. In 1908, the Harvard Business School declared Taylor's approach the standard for modern management and adopted it as the core around which all courses were to be organized. Taylor, himself, began lecturing at Harvard in 1909. Between 1910 and 1912, two events catapulted scientific management into the limelight. In 1910, the Eastern Railroad requested a rate increase from the Interstate Commerce Commission. Appearing before the commission, an efficiency expert claimed that railroads could save a million dollars a day (equivalent to about $16 million a day in 1997 dollars) through the application of scientific management. This assertion became the centerpiece of the hearings and created a national audience for Taylor's ideas. Then in 1911, Taylor published *The Principles of Scientific Management.* It became an instant best seller. By 1914, Taylor's principles had become so popular that an "efficiency exposition" held in New York City, with Taylor as the keynote speaker, drew a crowd estimated at 69,000! Although Taylor spread his ideas not only in the United States but also in France, Germany, Russia, and Japan, his greatest influence was on U.S. manufacturing. His method gave U.S. companies a comparative advantage over foreign firms that made U.S. manufacturing efficiency the envy of the world—at least for fifty years or so.

Who Else, Besides Taylor, Were Major Contributors to Scientific Management? Taylor's ideas inspired others to study and develop methods of scientific management. His most prominent disciples were Frank and Lillian Gilbreth.[6]

A construction contractor by background, Frank Gilbreth gave up his contracting career in 1912 to study scientific management after hearing Taylor speak at a professional meeting. Along with his wife Lillian, a psychologist, he studied work arrangements to eliminate wasteful hand-and-body motions. The Gilbreths also experimented in the design and use of the proper tools and equipment for optimizing work performance.[7] Frank Gilbreth is probably best known for his experiments in reducing the number of motions in bricklaying.

The Gilbreths were among the first to use motion picture films to study hand-and-body motions. They devised a microchronometer that recorded time to 1/2000/second, placed it in the field of study being photographed, and thus determined how long a worker spent enacting each motion. Wasted motions missed by the naked eye could be identified and eliminated. The Gilbreths also devised a classification scheme to label seventeen basic hand motions—such as "search," "select," "grasp," "hold"—which they called **therbligs** (*Gilbreth* spelled backward with the *th* transposed). This scheme allowed the Gilbreths to more precisely analyze the exact elements of any worker's hand movements.

therbligs
A classification scheme for labeling seventeen basic hand motions.

Another notable associate of Taylor at Midvale and Bethlehem Steel was a young engineer named Henry L. Gantt. Like Taylor and the Gilbreths, Gantt sought to increase worker efficiency through scientific investigation. But he extended some of Taylor's original ideas and added a few of his own. For instance, Gantt devised an incentive system that gave workers a bonus for completing their jobs in less time than the allowed standard. He also introduced a bonus for foremen to be paid for each worker who made the standard plus an extra bonus if all the workers under the foreman made it. In so doing, Gantt expanded the scope of scientific management to encompass the work of managers as well as that of operatives.

However, Gantt is probably most noted for creating a graphic bar chart that could be used by managers as a scheduling device for planning and controlling work. We introduced you to this device—the Gantt chart—in our discussion of planning tools in Chapter 4.

Why Did Scientific Management Receive So Much Attention? Many of the guidelines Taylor and others devised for improving production efficiency appear to us today to be common sense. For instance, one can say that it should have been obvious to managers in those days that workers should be carefully screened, selected, and trained before being put into a job.

To understand the importance of scientific management, you have to consider the times in which Taylor, the Gilbreths, and Gantt lived. The standard of living was low. Production was highly labor-intensive. Midvale Steel, at the turn of the century, may have employed twenty or thirty workers who did nothing but load pig iron onto rail cars. Today, their entire daily tonnage could probably be done in several hours by one person with a hydraulic lift truck. But they didn't have such mechanical devices. Similarly, the breakthroughs Frank Gilbreth achieved in bricklaying are meaningful only when you recognize that most quality buildings at that time were constructed of brick, that land was cheap, and that the major cost of a plant or home was the cost of the materials (bricks) and the labor cost to lay them.

What Did Henri Fayol and Max Weber Contribute to Management Thought?

Henri Fayol and Max Weber were two important individuals in developing the General Administrative theory. We mentioned Henri Fayol in Chapter 1 for having designated management as a universal set of functions, specifically, planning, organizing, commanding, coordinating, and controlling. Because his writings were important, let's take a more careful look at what he had to say.[8]

Fayol wrote during the same time as Taylor. However, whereas Taylor was concerned with management at the shop level (or what we today would describe as the job of a supervisor) and used the scientific method, Fayol's attention was directed at the activities of all managers, and he wrote from personal experience. Taylor was a scientist. Fayol, the managing director of a large French coal-mining firm, was a practitioner.

Fayol described the practice of management as something distinct from accounting, finance, production, distribution, and other typical business functions. He argued

principles of management
Fayol's fundamental or universal truths that could be applied to management activities in all human endeavors.

bureaucracy
Weber's ideal type of organization characterized by division of labor, a clearly defined hierarchy, detailed rules and regulations, and impersonal relationships.

that management was an activity common to all human undertakings in business, in government, and even in the home. He then proceeded to state fourteen **principles of management**—fundamental or universal truths—that could be taught in schools and universities. These principles are shown in Exhibit AA-2.

Max Weber (pronounced VAY-ber) was a German sociologist. Writing in the early part of this century, Weber developed a theory of authority structures and described organizational activity on the basis of authority relations.[9] He described an ideal type of organization that he called a **bureaucracy.** It was a system characterized by division of labor, a clearly defined hierarchy, detailed rules and regulations, and impersonal relationships. Weber recognized that this "ideal bureaucracy" didn't exist in reality but, rather, represented a selective reconstruction of the real world. He meant it as a basis for theorizing about work and how work could be done in large groups. His theory became the design prototype for many of today's large organizations. The detailed features of Weber's ideal bureaucratic structure are outlined in Exhibit AA-3.

Exhibit AA-2
Fayol's Fourteen Principles of Management

1. **Division of Work.** This principle is the same as Adam Smith's "division of labor." Specialization increases output by making employees more efficient.
2. **Authority.** Managers must be able to give orders. Authority gives them this right. Along with authority, however, goes responsibility. Wherever authority is exercised, responsibility arises.
3. **Discipline.** Employees must obey and respect the rules that govern the organization. Good discipline is the result of effective leadership, a clear understanding between management and workers regarding the organization's rules, and the judicious use of penalties for infractions of the rules.
4. **Unity of Command.** Every employee should receive orders from only one superior.
5. **Unity of Direction.** Each group of organizational activities that have the same objective should be directed by one manager using one plan.
6. **Subordination of Individual Interests to the General Interest.** The interests of any one employee or group of employees should not take precedence over the interests of the organization as a whole.
7. **Remuneration.** Workers must be paid a fair wage for their services.
8. **Centralization.** Centralization refers to the degree to which subordinates are involved in decision making. Whether decision making is centralized (to management) or decentralized (to subordinates) is a question of proper proportion. The task is to find the optimum degree of centralization for each situation.
9. **Scalar Chain.** The line of authority from top management to the lowest ranks represents the scalar chain. Communications should follow this chain. However, if following the chain creates delays, cross-communications can be allowed if agreed to by all parties and superiors are kept informed.
10. **Order.** People and materials should be in the right place at the right time.
11. **Equity.** Managers should be kind and fair to their subordinates.
12. **Stability of Tenure of Personnel.** High employee turnover is inefficient. Management should provide orderly personnel planning and ensure that replacements are available to fill vacancies.
13. **Initiative.** Employees who are allowed to originate and carry out plans will exert high levels of effort.
14. **Esprit de Corps.** Promoting team spirit will build harmony and unity within the organization.

1. **Division of Labor.** Jobs are broken down into simple, routine, and well-defined tasks.
2. **Authority Hierarchy.** Offices or positions are organized in a hierarchy, each lower one being controlled and supervised by a higher one.
3. **Formal Selection.** All organizational members are to be selected on the basis of technical qualifications demonstrated by training, education, or formal examination.
4. **Formal Rules and Regulations.** To ensure uniformity and to regulate the actions of employees, managers must depend heavily on formal organizational rules.
5. **Impersonality.** Rules and controls are applied uniformly, avoiding involvement with personalities and personal preferences of employees.
6. **Career Orientation.** Managers are professional officials rather than owners of the units they manage. They work for fixed salaries and pursue their careers within the organization.

Exhibit AA-3
Weber's Ideal Bureaucracy

What Were the General Administrative Theorists' Contributions to Management Practice? A number of our current ideas and practices in management can be directly traced to the contributions of the **general administrative theorists.** For instance, the functional view of the manager's job owes its origin to Henri Fayol. Also, although many of his principles may not be universally applicable to the wide variety of organizations that exist today, they became a frame of reference against which many current concepts have evolved.

general administrative theorists
Writers who developed general theories of what managers do and what constitutes good management practice.

Weber's bureaucracy was an attempt to formulate an ideal model around which organizations could be designed. It was a response to the abuses that Weber saw going on within organizations. Weber believed that his model could remove the ambiguity, inefficiencies, and patronage that characterized most organizations at that time. Weber's bureaucracy is not as popular as it was a decade ago, but many of its components are still inherent in large organizations today.

Human Resources Approach

Managers get things done by working with people. This fact explains why some writers and researchers have chosen to look at management by focusing on the organization's human resources. Much of what currently makes up the field of personnel or human resources management, as well as contemporary views on motivation and leadership, has come out of the work of those we have categorized as being part of the **human resources approach** to management.

human resources approach
The study of management that focuses on human behavior.

Who Were Some Early Advocates of the Human Resources Approach?

Undoubtedly, many people in the nineteenth and early part of the twentieth century recognized the importance of the human factor to an organization's success, but five individuals stand out as early advocates of the human resources approach. They are Robert Owen, Hugo Munsterberg, Mary Parker Follett, Chester Barnard, and Elton Mayo.

What Claim to Fame Does Robert Owen Hold? Robert Owen was a successful Scottish businessman who bought his first factory in 1789 when he was just eighteen. Repulsed by the harsh practices he saw in factories across Scotland—such as the employment of young children (many under the age of ten), thirteen-hour workdays, and miserable working conditions—Owen became a reformer. He chided factory owners for treating their equipment better than their employees. He said that they would buy the best machines but then buy the cheapest labor to run them. Owen argued that money spent on improving labor was one of the best investments that business executives could make. He claimed that showing concern for employees was both highly profitable for management and would relieve human misery.

Owen proposed a "utopian" workplace. As one author noted, Owen is not remembered in management history for his successes but rather for his courage and commitment to reducing the suffering of the working class.[10] He was more than a hundred years ahead of his time when he argued, in 1825, for regulated hours of work for all, child labor laws, public education, company-furnished tools and equipment at work, and business involvement in community projects.[11]

For What Is Hugo Munsterberg Best Known? Hugo Munsterberg created the field of industrial psychology—the scientific study of individuals at work to maximize their productivity and adjustment. His text, *Psychology and Industrial Efficiency,* was published in 1913.[12] In it, he argued for the scientific study of human behavior to identify general patterns and to explain individual differences. Munsterberg suggested the use of psychological tests to improve employee selection, the value of learning theory in the development of training methods, and the study of human behavior in order to understand what techniques are most effective for motivating workers. Interestingly, he saw a link between scientific management and industrial psychology. Both sought increased efficiency through scientific work analyses and through better alignment of individual skills and abilities with the demands of various jobs. Much of our current knowledge of selection techniques, employee training, job design, and motivation is built on the work of Munsterberg.

What Contributions Did Mary Parker Follett Make to Management? One of the earliest writers to recognize that organizations could be viewed from the perspective of individual and group behavior was Mary Parker Follett.[13] A transitionalist writing in the time of scientific management but proposing more people-oriented ideas, Follett was a social philosopher. However, her ideas had clear implications for management practice. Follett thought that organizations should be based on a group ethic rather than on individualism. Individual potential, she argued, remained only potential until released through group association. The manager's job was to harmonize and coordinate group efforts. Managers and workers should view themselves as partners—as part of a common group. As such, managers should rely more on their expertise and knowledge to lead subordinates than on the formal authority of their position. Her humanistic ideas influenced the way we look at motivation, leadership, power, and authority.

Who Was Chester Barnard? A transitionalist like Follett, Chester Barnard proposed ideas that bridged classical and human resources viewpoints. Like Fayol, Barnard was a practitioner—he was president of New Jersey Bell Telephone Company. He had read Weber and was influenced by his writings. But unlike Weber, who had an impersonal view of organizations, Barnard saw organizations as social systems that require human cooperation. He expressed his views in his book *The Functions of the Executive,* published in 1938.[14]

Barnard believed that organizations were made up of people who have interacting social relationships. The manager's major roles were to communicate and stimulate subordinates to high levels of effort. A major part of an organization's success, as Barnard saw it, depended on obtaining cooperation from its employees. Barnard also argued that success depended on maintaining good relations with people and institutions outside the organization with whom the organization regularly interacted. By recognizing the organization's dependence on investors, suppliers, customers, and other external stakeholders, Barnard introduced the idea that managers had to examine the external environment and then adjust the organization to maintain a state of equilibrium. Regardless of how efficient an organization's production might be, if management failed either to ensure a continuous input of materials and supplies or to find markets for its outputs, then the organization's survival would be threatened.

The current interest in building cooperative work groups, making business firms more socially responsible, and matching organizational strategies to opportunities in the environment can be traced to ideas originally proposed by Barnard.

What Were the Hawthorne Studies? Without question, the most important contribution to the human resources approach to management came out of the **Hawthorne studies** undertaken at the Western Electric Company's Hawthorne Works in Cicero, Illinois.[15] Scholars generally agree that the Hawthorne studies, under the leadership of Elton Mayo, had a dramatic impact on the direction of management thought. Mayo's conclusions were that behavior and sentiments are closely related, that group influences significantly affect individual behavior, that group standards establish individual worker output, and that money is less a factor in determining output than are group standards, group sentiments, and security. These conclusions led to a new emphasis on the human factor in the functioning of organizations and the attainment of their goals. They also led to increased paternalism by management. (For further information on the Hawthorne studies, see Details on a Management Classic.)

Hawthorne studies
A series of studies during the 1920s and 1930s that provided new insights into group norms and behaviors.

The first published results from the Hawthorne studies appeared in 1930 and then were followed over the next decade by a stream of articles and books written by Mayo and his colleagues.[16] Some of these publications received considerable attention. Mayo's *The Human Problems of an Industrial Civilization,* which came out in 1933, became a best seller and was reviewed favorably in both the popular and academic presses. Another book on the Hawthorne studies, *Management and the Worker,*[17] was considered important enough to be abstracted by *Reader's Digest* in 1939.

The Hawthorne studies, however, have not been without critics. Attacks have been made on procedures, analyses of the findings, and the conclusions drawn.[18] From a historical standpoint, it is of little importance whether the studies were academically sound or their conclusions justified. What is important is that they stimulated an interest in human factors. The Hawthorne studies went a long way in changing the dominant view at the time that people were no different than machines; that is, you put them on the shop floor, cranked in the inputs, and they produced a known quantity of outputs. Furthermore, the legacy of Hawthorne is still with us today. Current organizational practices that owe their roots to the Hawthorne studies include attitude surveys, employee counseling, management training, participative decision making, and team-based compensation systems.

Why Was the Human Relations Movement Important to Management History? Another group within the human resources approach is important to management history for its unflinching commitment to making management practices more humane. Members of the human relations movement uniformly believed in the importance of employee satisfaction—a satisfied worker was believed to be a productive worker. For the most part, names associated with this movement—Dale Carnegie,

Details on a Management Classic

The Hawthorne Studies

The Hawthorne studies, originally begun in 1924 but eventually expanded and carried through the early 1930s, were initially devised by Western Electric industrial engineers to examine the effect of various illumination levels on worker productivity. Control and experimental groups were established. The experimental group was presented with different levels of illumination intensity, while the control group worked under a constant intensity. The engineers expected individual output to be directly related to the intensity of light. However, they found that as the light level was increased in the experimental group, output for both groups rose. To the surprise of the engineers, as the light level was dropped in the experimental group, productivity continued to increase in both groups. In fact, a productivity decrease was observed in the experimental group only when the light intensity had been reduced to that of moonlight. The engineers concluded that illumination intensity was not directly related to group productivity, but they could not explain the behavior they had witnessed.

In 1927, the Western Electric engineers asked Harvard professor Elton Mayo and his associates to join the study as consultants. Thus began a relationship that would last through 1932 and encompass numerous experiments covering the redesign of jobs, changes in the lengths of the workday and workweek, the introduction of rest periods, and individual versus group wage plans.[19] For example, one experiment was designed to evaluate the effect of a group piecework incentive pay system on group productivity. The results indicated that the incentive plan had less effect on workers' output than did group pressure and acceptance and the concomitant security. Social norms or standards of the group, therefore, were concluded to be the key determinants of individual work behavior.

Abraham Maslow, and Douglas McGregor—were individuals whose views were shaped more by their personal philosophies than by substantive research evidence.

Dale Carnegie is often overlooked by management scholars, but his ideas and teachings have had an enormous effect on management practice. His book *How to Win Friends and Influence People*[20] was read by millions in the 1930s, 1940s, and 1950s. In addition, during this same period, tens of thousands of managers and aspiring managers attended his management speeches and seminars. What was the theme of Carnegie's book and lectures? Essentially, he said that the way to succeed was to: (1) make others feel important through a sincere appreciation of their efforts; (2) make a good first impression; (3) win people to your way of thinking by letting others do the talking, being sympathetic, and "never telling a man he is wrong"; and (4) change people by praising good traits and giving the offender the opportunity to save face.[21]

Abraham Maslow, a humanistic psychologist, proposed a theoretical hierarchy of five needs: physiological, safety, social, esteem, and self-actualization.[22] In terms of motivation, Maslow argued that each step in the hierarchy must be satisfied before the next can be activated and that once a need was substantially satisfied it no longer motivated behavior.

A survey of management professors in the early 1970s found that Maslow's 1943 publication on the needs hierarchy was cited as the second most influential article in all of management.[23] The needs hierarchy is arguably still the best-known theory of general motivation, despite the fact that "the available research does not support the Maslow theory to any significant degree."[24] Even today, no author of an introductory textbook in management, organizational behavior, human relations, supervision, psychology, or marketing is likely to omit discussion of the needs hierarchy.

Douglas McGregor is best known for his formulation of two sets of assumptions—Theory X and Theory Y—about human nature.[25] Theory X presents an essentially negative view of people. It assumes that they have little ambition, dislike work, want to avoid responsibility, and need to be closely directed to work effectively. On the other hand, Theory Y offers a positive view. It assumes that people can exercise self-direction, accept responsibility, and consider work to be as natural as rest or play. McGregor believed that Theory Y assumptions best captured the true nature of workers and should guide management practice.

A story about McGregor does a good job of capturing the essence of the human relations perspective. McGregor had taught for a dozen years at the Massachusetts Institute of Technology (M.I.T.). Then he became president of Antioch College. After six years at Antioch, McGregor seemed to recognize that his philosophy had failed to cope with the realities of organizational life.

> I believed, for example, that a leader could operate successfully as a kind of advisor to his organization. I thought I could avoid being a "boss." Unconsciously, I suspect, I hoped to duck the unpleasant necessity of making difficult decisions, of taking the responsibility for one course of action, among many uncertain alternatives, of making mistakes and taking the consequences. I thought that maybe I could operate so that everyone would like me—that "good human relations" would eliminate all discord and disagreement. I couldn't have been more wrong. It took a couple of years but I finally began to realize that a leader cannot avoid the exercise of authority any more than he can avoid responsibility for what happens to his organization.[26]

The irony in McGregor's case was that he went back to M.I.T. and began preaching his humanistic doctrine again. And he continued to do so until his death. The key point here is that, like Maslow's, McGregor's beliefs about human nature have had a strong following among management academics and practitioners. For instance, the previously cited survey on important contributions to management identified McGregor's book as the number one most influential book.[27]

What Was the Common Thread That Linked Advocates of the Human Relations Movement? The common thread that united human relations supporters, including Carnegie, Maslow, and McGregor, was an unshakable optimism about people's capabilities. They believed strongly in their cause and were inflexible in their beliefs, even when faced with contradictory evidence. No amount of contrary experience or research evidence would alter their views. Of course, despite this lack of objectivity, advocates of the human relations movement had a definite influence on management theory and practice.

Who Were the Behavioral Science Theorists?

One final category within the human resources approach encompasses a group of psychologists and sociologists who relied on the scientific method for the study of organizational behavior. Unlike the theorists of the human relations movement, behavioral science theorists engaged in objective research of human behavior in organizations. They carefully attempted to keep their personal beliefs out of their work. They sought to develop rigorous research designs that could be replicated by other behavioral scientists. In so doing, they hoped to build a science of organizational behavior.[28]

A list of important behavioral science theorists and their contributions would number into the hundreds. But beginning after World War II and continuing on to today, they have created a wealth of studies that allow us to make fairly accurate predictions about behavior in organizations. Our current understanding of such issues as leadership, employee motivation, personality differences, the design of jobs and organizations, organizational cultures, high-performance teams, performance appraisals, conflict management, and negotiation techniques are largely due to the contributions of these behavioral scientists.

The Quantitative Approach

The quantitative approach to management (also sometimes referred to as operations research or management science) evolved out of the development of mathematical and statistical solutions to military problems during World War II. For instance, when the British confronted the problem of how to get the maximum effectiveness from their limited aircraft capability against the massive forces of the Germans, they turned to their mathematicians to devise an optimum allocation model. Similarly, U.S. antisubmarine warfare teams used operations research (OR) techniques to improve the odds of survival for Allied convoys crossing the North Atlantic and for selecting the optimal depth-charge patterns for aircraft and surface vessel attacks on German U-boats.

After the war, many of the quantitative techniques that had been applied to military problems were moved into the business sector. One group of military officers, labeled the "Whiz Kids," joined Ford Motor Company in the mid-1940s and immediately began using statistical devices to improve decision making at Ford. Two of the most famous Whiz Kids were Robert McNamara and Charles "Tex" Thornton. McNamara rose to the presidency of Ford and then became U.S. Secretary of Defense. At the Department of Defense, he sought to quantify resource allocation decisions in the Pentagon through cost-benefit analyses. He concluded his career as head of the World Bank. Tex Thornton founded the billion-dollar conglomerate Litton Industries, again relying on quantitative techniques to make acquisition and allocation decisions. Dozens of other operations researchers from the military went into consulting. The consulting firm of Arthur D. Little, for instance, began applying OR techniques to management problems in the early 1950s. By 1954, at least twenty-five firms had established formal OR groups, and as many as 300 OR analysts worked in industry.[29]

What are the quantitative techniques, and how have they contributed to current management practice? The quantitative approach to management includes applications of statistics, optimization models, information models, and computer simulations. Linear programming, for instance, is a technique that managers can use to improve resource allocation choices. Work scheduling can be made more efficient as a result of critical-path scheduling analysis. Decisions on determining the optimum inventory levels a firm should maintain have been significantly influenced by the economic order quantity model. In general, the quantitative approaches have contributed most directly to management decision making, particularly to planning and control decisions.

Analysis: How Times Shape Management Approaches

We conclude this appendix by showing you how the times shape what theorists write about and what practicing managers focus on. Although some management historians may quarrel with the following cause-effect analysis, few would disagree that societal conditions are the primary driving force explaining the emergence of the different management approaches.

What Stimulated the Classical Approach?

The common thread in the ideas offered by people like Taylor, the Gilbreths, Fayol, and Weber was increased efficiency. The world that existed in the late nineteenth and early twentieth century was one of high inefficiency. Most organizational activities were unplanned and unorganized. Job responsibilities were vague and ambiguous. Managers, when they existed, had no clear notion of what they were supposed to do. There was a crying need for ideas that could bring order out of this chaos and improve productivity. And the standardized practices offered by the classicists was a means to achieve that increased productivity. Take the specific case of scientific management. At the turn of the century, the standard of living was low, wages were modest, and few workers owned their own homes. Production was highly labor-intensive. It wasn't unusual, for instance, for hundreds of people to be doing the same repetitive, back-breaking job, hour after hour, day after day. So Taylor could justify spending six months or more studying one job and perfecting a standardized "one best way" to do it because the labor-intensive procedures of the time had so many people performing the same task. And the efficiencies on the production floor could be passed on in lower prices for steel, thus expanding markets, creating more jobs, and making products such as stoves and refrigerators more accessible to working families. Similarly, Gilbreth's breakthroughs in improving the efficiency of bricklayers and standardizing those techniques meant lower costs for putting up buildings and resulted in more buildings being constructed. The cost of putting up factories and homes dropped significantly. So more factories could be built and more people could own their own homes. The end result: The application of scientific management principles contributed to raising the standard of living of entire countries.

What Stimulated the Human Resources Approach?

The human resources approach really began to roll in the 1930s. Two related forces in that decade were instrumental in fostering this interest. First was a backlash to the overly mechanistic view of employees held by the classicists. Second was the emergence of the Great Depression.

The classical view treated organizations and people as machines. In this view, managers were the engineers. They ensured that the inputs were available and that the machine was properly maintained. Any failure by the employee to generate the desired output was viewed as an engineering problem: It was time to redesign the job or grease the machine by offering the employee an incentive wage plan. Unfortunately, this kind of thinking created an alienated work force. Human beings were not machines and did not necessarily respond positively to the cold and regimented work environment of the classicists' perfectly designed organization. The human resources approach offered managers solutions for lessening this alienation and for improving worker productivity.

The Great Depression swept the globe in the 1930s and brought forth a dramatic increase in the role of government in individual and business affairs. For instance, in the United States, Franklin Roosevelt's New Deal sought to restore confidence to a stricken nation. Between 1935 and 1938 alone, the Social Security Act was created to provide old-age assistance; the National Labor Relations Act was passed to legitimize the rights of labor unions; the Fair Labor Standards Act introduced the guaranteed hourly wage; and the Railroad Unemployment Insurance Act established the first national unemployment protection. This New Deal climate raised the importance of the worker. Humanizing the workplace had become congruent with society's concerns at the time.

What Stimulated the Quantitative Approaches?

The major impetus to the quantitative approaches was World War II. Government-funded research programs were created to develop mathematical and statistical aids for solving military problems. The success of these operations research techniques in the military was impressive. After the war, business executives became more open to applying these techniques to their organizational decision making. And, of course, as these techniques proved successful in improving the quality of decisions and increasing profits in those firms that used them, managers in competing firms were forced to adopt these same techniques.

New organizations were additionally being created to disseminate information to managers on these quantitative techniques. "The Operations Research Society of America was founded in 1952, and began publishing its journal, *Operations Research.* In 1953, The Institute of Management Science stated its objectives as 'to identify, extend, and unify scientific knowledge that contributes to the understanding of the practice of management' and began publishing the journal *Management Science.*"[30]

By the late-1960s, course work in mathematics, statistics, and operations management had become required components of most business school curricula. The new generation of managers would be knowledgeable in such techniques as probability theory, linear programming, queuing theory, and games theory.

Appendix B

Understanding Your Career

The career is dead—long live the career. A play on words or an insight into today's careers? Maybe it's a little bit of both. Nonetheless, it's the title of Douglas T. Hall's new book.[1] For several decades, Douglas Hall has been highly regarded for his research about people's careers. And, as we discussed in Chapter 8, careers are changing. The greatest difference is that you, the individual, are responsible for developing and managing your career. In this appendix, we will address some of Hall's early insights into careers. Why? Although they no longer apply "across the board," they provide a foundation of how your career may progress. Second, we will look at suggestions to help enhance your changes of getting into an organization and will offer some tips on developing a successful management career in today's dynamic organizations.

What Are Career Stages?

Previously, one of the most popular ways of analyzing and discussing careers was to view them as a series of stages.[2] Progression from the beginning of a career to its end was viewed as a natural sequence that happened to all individuals. This sequence consisted of five-stages that applied to most people during their adult years, regardless of the type of job they did. Today this model is applicable only among a small set of growing companies, if at all.

Most individuals begin to form ideas about their careers during their elementary and secondary school years. Their careers begin to wind down as they reach "retirement" age. The stages that most individuals will go through during these years are **exploration, establishment, midcareer, late career,** and **decline.** These stages, and the challenges most people will face, are shown in Exhibit AB-1.

The age ranges for each of the five stages in Exhibit AB-1 are provided as general guidelines. They should not be interpreted as ages when events must occur. As such, someone who makes a career change to another line of work at age forty-seven will have many of the same establishment-stage concerns as someone starting at age twenty-five.

exploration career stage
A career stage that usually ends in one's mid-twenties as one makes the transition from school to work.

establishment career stage
A period in which one searches for work and gets a first job.

midcareer stage
A career stage marked by continuous improvement in performance, leveling off in performance, or beginning to deteriorate in performance.

late career stage
A period in which one is no longer learning about his or her job and is not expected to be trying to outdo his or her levels of performance from previous years.

decline career stage
The final stage in one's career, usually marked by retirement.

What Is the Exploration Stage?

Individuals often make decisions about their careers before entering the work force on a paid basis. Information from relatives, teachers, friends, and the media helps them to narrow career choices and leads them in a certain direction.

During the exploration stage, individuals look at potential careers to see what they like or don't like. They form attitudes and prepare themselves for work. The exploration period ends for most individuals when they make the transition from school to work.

How Does One Get Established at Work?

The establishment period begins with the search for work and includes getting that first job, being accepted by peers, learning the job, and gaining the first tangible evidence of success or failure in the "real world." During the establishment stage,

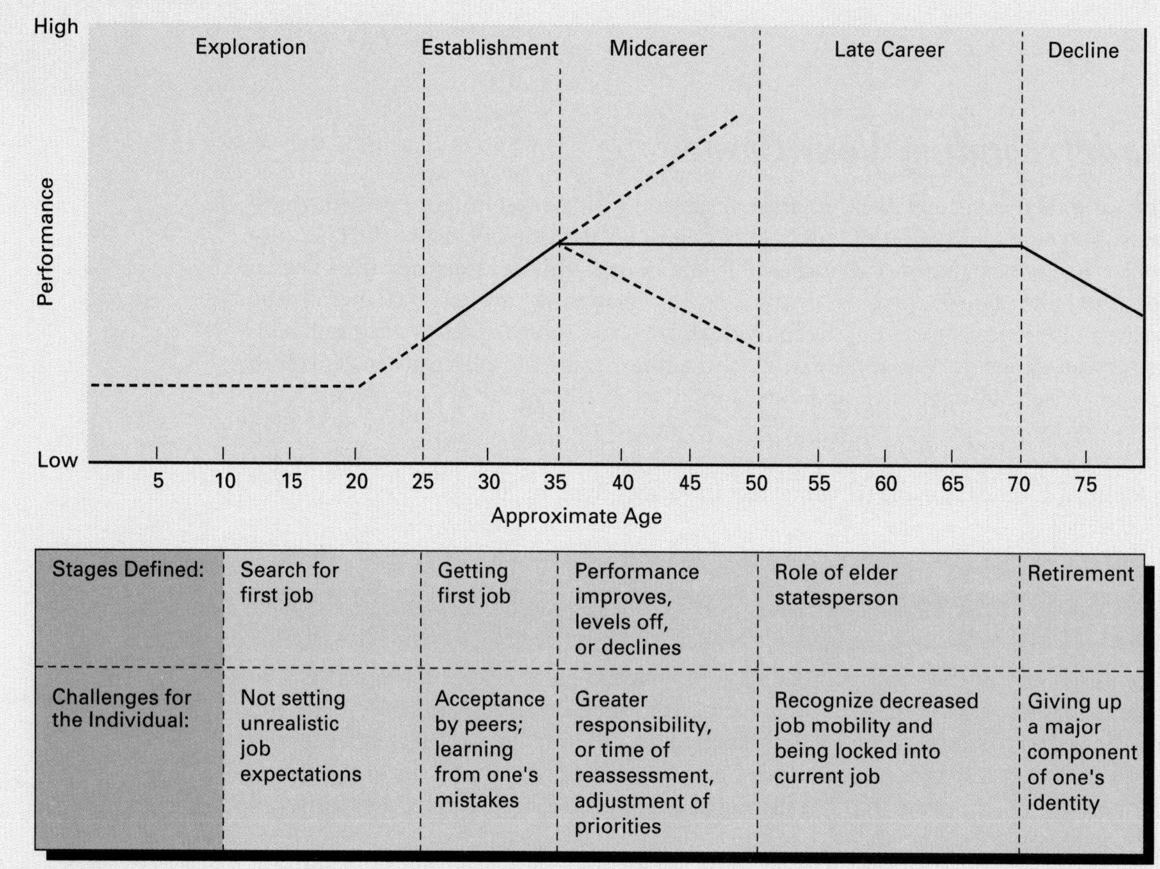

Exhibit AB-1
Career Stages

performance improves, mistakes are made yet learned from, and responsibilities increase. However, individuals in this stage have yet to reach their peak productivity, and rarely are they given work assignments that carry great power or high status. During this stage, one can anticipate expending a lot of time and energy on career goals.

Have You "Made It" by Midcareer?

Many people do not face their first severe career dilemma until they reach the midcareer stage.[3] This is a period when performance improves (the person continues to advance), declines (loses interest), or levels off (plateaus). Those who continue to advance get more responsibility and greater rewards. For some others, it may be a time when they have to reassess what they want out of a career, and possibly make some changes—either in career choice or in personal goals.

In the past fifteen years, a lot of attention has been focused on the career issue of plateauing. Restructuring organizations, downsizing, and reengineering have reduced the upward mobility chances for many employees. The resulting disruption of career plans has led to anxiety and frustration for some.[4]

What Is the Late Career Stage?

For those who continue to grow through the midcareer stage, the late career is usually a pleasant time when one is allowed the luxury of relaxing a bit and enjoying the part of the elder statesperson. During the late career, individuals are no longer expected to outdo their levels of performance from previous years. Their value to the organization lies heavily in their judgment, built up over many years and through varied experiences, and sharing with and teaching others the knowledge they have gained. For those who have stagnated or deteriorated during the midcareer stage, the late career brings the reality that they will not have an everlasting impact or change the world as they once thought.

Do All Careers Eventually Decline?

The final stage in one's career is difficult for everyone, but, ironically, it is probably hardest on those who have had continued successes in the earlier stages. After decades of continued achievements and high levels of performance, the time has come for retirement. These individuals are forced to step out of the limelight and to relinquish a major component of their identity. For those who have seen their performance deteriorate over the years, it may be a pleasant time; the frustrations that have been associated with work are left behind. For the plateaued, it is probably an easy transition to other life activities.

Making a Career Decision

The best career choice is the choice that offers the best match between what you want out of life and what you need. Good career choice outcomes should result in a series of positions that give you an opportunity to be a good performer, make you want to maintain your commitment to your career, lead to highly satisfying work, and give you the proper balance between work and personal life. A good career match, then, is one in which you are able to develop a positive self-concept, to do work that you think is important, and to lead the kind of life you desire.[5] Identifying that balance this is referred to as career planning.

Career planning is designed to assist you in becoming more knowledgeable of your needs, values, and personal goals. This knowledge can be achieved through a three-step, self-assessment process:[6]

1. **Identify and organize your skills, interests, work-related needs, and values.** The best place to begin is by drawing up a profile of your educational record. List each school attended from high school on. What courses do you remember liking most and least? In what courses did you score highest and lowest? In what extracurricular activities did you participate? Are there any specific skills that you acquired? Are there other skills in which you have gained proficiency?

   Next, begin to assess your occupational experience. List each job you have held, the organization you worked for, your overall level of satisfaction, what you liked most and least about the job, and why you left. It's important to be honest in covering each of these points.
2. **Convert this information into general career fields and specific job goals.** Step 1 should have provided some insights into your interests and abilities. What you need to do now is look at how they can be converted into the

kind of organizational setting or field of endeavor with which you will be a good match. Then you can become specific and identify distinct job goals.

What fields are available? In business? In government? In nonprofit organizations? Your answer can be broken down further into areas such as education, financial, manufacturing, social services, or health services. Identifying areas of interest is usually far easier than pinpointing specific occupations. When you are able to identify a limited set of occupations that interest you, you can start to align them with your abilities and skills. Will certain jobs require you to move? If so, would the location be compatible with your geographic preferences? Do you have the educational requirements necessary for the job? If not, what additional schooling will be needed? Does the job offer the status and earning potential that you aspire to? What is the long-term outlook for jobs in this field? Does the career suffer from cyclical employment? Since no job is without its drawbacks, have you seriously considered all the negative aspects? When you have fully answered questions such as these, you should have a relatively short list of specific job goals.

3. **Test your career possibilities against the realities of the organization or the job market.** The final step in this self-assessment process is testing your selection against the realities of the marketplace. This can be done by talking with knowledgeable people in the fields, organizations, or jobs you desire. These informational interviews should provide reliable feedback as to the accuracy of your self-assessment and the opportunities in the fields and jobs that interest you.

How Does One Get into the Organization?

In Chapter 8, we introduced you to the human resource management process. One aspect of that discussion focused on hiring employees. When managers make a decision to hire employees, information is often sent out announcing the job. Seeing that announcement, and feeling that there's a potential match between what you can offer and what the organization wants, you need to throw your hat into the "hiring ring."[7]

One of the more stressful situations you will face happens when you apply for a job. Stress occurs because there are no specific guidelines to follow that can guarantee you success. However, several tips can be offered that may increase your chances of finding employment. Getting an interview is one of the major hurdles in the job-hunting process; it requires hard work. You should view getting a job as your job at the moment.

Competition for most jobs today is fierce. You can't wait until the last minute to enter the job market. Your job hunt must start well in advance of when you plan to start work. So, for seniors in college who plan to graduate in May, we suggest you begin your job search sometime around the previous September.

Why is starting in the fall helpful? There are two advantages. First, it shows that you are taking an interest in your career and that you are planning. You're not waiting until the last minute to begin, and this initiative reflects favorably on you. Second, starting in the fall coincides with many companies' recruiting cycles. If you wait until March to begin the process, some job openings are likely to already have been filled. For specific information regarding the company recruiting cycles in your area, visit your college's career development center.

Given that you will be getting a head start on the hiring process, the next step is to prepare a résumé.

How Do You Prepare a Résumé?

All job applicants need to have information circulating that reflects positively on their strengths. That information needs to be sent to prospective employers in a format that is understandable and consistent with the organization's hiring practices. In most instances, it is presented in the résumé.

No matter who you are or where you are in your career, you need a current résumé. Your résumé is typically the only information source that a recruiter will use in determining whether to grant you an interview. Therefore, your résumé must be a sales tool; it must give key information that supports your candidacy, highlights your strengths, and differentiates you from other job applicants. An example of the type of information that should be included is shown in Exhibit AB-2. Notice, too, that this individual has noted volunteer experience on the résumé.

Exhibit AB-2
A Sample Résumé

CHRIS SMITH
1430 East Avenue
Center City, OK 41111

CAREER OBJECTIVE:	Seeking employment in a marketing department in a progressive organization that provides a challenging opportunity to combine exceptional interpersonal and computer skills.
EDUCATION:	State Community College A.A., Business Administration (May 1995)
	State University B.S., Business Administration (May 1997) Concentration in Marketing
EXPERIENCE: 12/95 to present	State University Campus Bookstore, Assistant Book Buyer *Primary duties:* Responsible for coordinating book purchases with academic departments; placing orders with publishers; invoicing, receiving inventory, pricing, and stocking shelves. Supervised four student employees. Managed annual budget of $25,000.
9/93 to 5/95	State Community College Student Assistant, Business Administration *Primary duties:* Responsible for routine administrative matters in an academic department—including answering phones, word processing faculty materials, and answering student questions.
10/91 to 6/93	State High School Yearbook Staff *Primary duties:* Responsible for coordinating marketing efforts in local community. Involved in fund raising through contacts with community organizations.
SPECIAL SKILLS:	Experienced in Microsoft Word, Netscape, D-Base, and spreadsheet application software. Fluent in speaking and writing Spanish. Certified in CPR.
SERVICE ACTIVITIES:	Vice-president, Student Government Association Volunteer, Meals-On-Wheels Volunteer, United Way
REFERENCES:	Available on request.

It is important to pinpoint a few key themes regarding résumés that may seem like common sense but are frequently ignored. First, your résumé must be printed on a quality printer—or at the very least, professionally typed. The style of type should be easy to read (e.g., Courier type font). Avoid any style that may be hard on the eyes, such as a script or italics font. A recruiter who must review 100 or more résumés a day is not going to look favorably at difficult-to-read résumés. So use a readable font and make the recruiter's job easier.

It is also important to note that some companies today are using computer scanners to make the first pass through résumés. They scan each résumé for specific information such as key job elements, experience, work history, education, or technical expertise.[8] The use of scanners, then, has created two important aspects for résumé writing.[9] The computer matches key words in a job description. Thus, in creating a résumé, you should use typical job description phraseology. Secondly (and this goes back to the issue of type font), the font used should be easily read by the scanner. If it can't be scanned, your résumé may be put in the rejection file.

Your résumé should be copied on good-quality white or off-white paper (no off-the-wall colors). There are certain types of jobs—such as a creative artist position—where this suggestion may be inappropriate. But those are the exceptions. You can't go wrong using a 20-bond-weight paper that has some cotton content (about 20 percent). By all means, don't send standard duplicating paper—it may look as if you are mass-mailing résumés (which you might be doing, but you needn't advertise that fact).

Our last point regarding résumés is related to proofreading. Because the résumé is the only representation of you the recruiter has, a sloppy résumé can be deadly. If it contains misspelled words or is grammatically incorrect, your chances for an interview will be significantly reduced. Proofread your résumé and, if possible, let others proofread it too.

In addition to your résumé, you need a cover letter. Your cover letter should contain information that tells the recruiter why you should be considered for the job. You need to describe why you would be a good job candidate. This means having a cover letter that highlights your greatest strengths and indicates how those strengths can be useful to the company. Your cover letter should also contain some information citing why the organization getting your résumé is of interest to you. Cover letters should be carefully tailored to each organization. Specifics show that you have taken some time and given some thought to the job you're applying for.

Cover letters must be addressed to a real name. Don't send anything out to "To Whom It May Concern"; such letters tell the recruiter that you are on a fishing expedition, mass mailing résumés in hopes that some positive response will be generated. This technique seldom works in job hunting. You may not always have the recruiter's name and title, but with some work you can get that information. Telephone the company in question and ask for it; most receptionists in employment will give out the recruiter's name and title. If you just can't get a name, go to the reference section of a library (you may also find this information on the Internet) and locate a copy of a publication such as the *Standard and Poor's Register Manual* or *Moody's*. These publications usually list the names and titles of officers in the organization. If everything else fails, send your résumé to one of the officers, preferably the officer in charge of employment or administration, or even to the president of the organization.

Like the résumé, the cover letter should be flawless. Proofread it as carefully as you do the résumé. Finally, sign each cover letter individually.

How Can You Excel at the Interview?

Once you have made it through the initial screening process, you are likely to be called in for an interview. Interviews play a critical role in determining whether you will get the job. Up to now, all the recruiter has seen are your well-polished cover letter and résumé. Remember, however, what was said in Chapter 8 regarding hiring. Few individuals, if any, get a job without an interview. No matter how qualified you are for a position, if you perform poorly in the interview, you're not likely to be hired!

The reason interviews are so popular is that they help the recruiter determine if you are a "good fit" for the organization, in terms of your level of motivation and interpersonal skills.[10] Popularity aside, however, how interviews are conducted can be problematic. We presented in Chapter 8 a summary of the research conducted on interviews (see page 240). Although interviewer mistakes or bias shouldn't be part of your interview, it's important for you to understand that they may exist. Why is this knowledge important? Knowing how the interviewer may react in the hiring process can help you avoid making a costly mistake. In addition, many of the biases that may exist in the interview can be overcome through a technique called impression management. *Impression management* refers to attempts to project an image that will result in achieving a favorable outcome.[11] For example, if you can say or do something that is viewed favorably by the interviewer, then you may create a more favorable impression of yourself. Take a situation in which you find out early in the interview that your interviewer values workers who are capable of balancing work and personal responsibilities. Making statements of being an individual who likes to work hard but also reserves time to spend with family and friends may create a positive impression. You need to understand, too, that interviewers generally have short and inaccurate memories.[12] Research has shown that most remember only about half of what you say. Taking notes can help them remember more, but what they remember most will be those impressions you make—both favorable and unfavorable.[13] Given this background information on interviews and interviewers, what can you do to increase your chances of excelling in the interview?

First, do some homework. Go to your library—or do a search for the company on the Internet—and get as much information as possible on the organization. Don't fall into the trap that one applicant did when interviewing for a job at IBM—he didn't even know what IBM stood for. Develop a solid grounding in the company, its history, markets, financial situation—and the industry in which it competes.

The night before the interview, get a good night's rest. Eat a good breakfast to build your energy level, as the day's events will be grueling. As you prepare for the interview, keep in mind that your appearance is going to be the first impression you make. Dress appropriately. Even though appearance generally is not supposed to enter into the hiring decision, incorrect attire can result in a negative impression. In fact, one study suggests that 80 percent of the interviewer's perception of you in the interview comes from his or her initial perception of you, based primarily on your appearance and body language.[14] Therefore dress appropriately and be meticulous in your attire.

Arrive early—about thirty minutes ahead of your scheduled interview. It is better for you to wait than to have to contend with something unexpected, like a traffic jam, that could make you late. Arriving early also gives you an opportunity to survey the office environment and possibly gather some clues about the organization. You should use any clues you can pick up to increase your chances of making a favorable impression.

As you meet the recruiter, give him or her a firm handshake. Make good eye contact and maintain it throughout the interview. Remember, your body language may be giving away secrets about you that you don't want an interviewer to pick up. Sit erect and maintain good posture. At this point, you are probably as nervous as you have ever been. It is natural to be nervous, but try your best to relax. Recruiters know you'll be anxious, and a good one will try to put you at ease. Being prepared for an interview can also help build confidence and reduce the nervousness. You can start building that confidence by reviewing a set of questions most frequently asked by interviewers. You can usually get a copy of these from the career center at your college. More important, however, since you may be asked these questions, you should have developed responses beforehand. But let's add a word of caution here. The best advice is to be yourself. Don't go into an interview with a prepared text and recite it from memory. Have an idea of what you would like to say, but don't rely on verbatim responses. Experienced interviewers will see through this "over-preparedness" and downgrade their evaluation of you.

You should also try to go through several "practice" interviews if possible. Universities often have career days on campus, when recruiters from companies are on-site to interview students. Take advantage of them. Even if the job does not fit what you want, the process will at least serve to help you become more skilled at dealing with interviews. You can also practice with family, friends, career counselors, student groups to which you belong, or your faculty adviser.

When the interview ends, thank the interviewer for his or her time and for giving you this opportunity to talk about your qualifications. But don't think that "selling" yourself has stopped there. As soon as you get home, send a thank you letter to the recruiter for taking the time to interview you and giving you the opportunity to discuss your job candidacy. You'd be amazed at how many people fail to do this! This little act of courtesy has an impact—use it to your advantage.

What Happens When the Good News Arrives?

A successful job search culminates with the inevitable—it's time to go to work. Although there's a natural excitement associated with starting a job, there are some aspects of those first few months that you should be aware of. In the next section, we'll look at some suggestions on how to survive in the organization and suggest ways that you can use to make inroads toward building a successful management career.

Are There Keys to a Successful Management Career?

If you choose a career in management, there are certain keys to success you should consider (see Exhibit AB-3). The following thirteen suggestions are based on proven tactics that managers have used to advance their careers.[15]

Select Your First Job Judiciously. All first jobs are not alike. Where managers begin in the organization has an important effect on their subsequent career progress. Specifically, evidence suggests that if you have a choice, you should select a powerful department as the place to start your management career.[16] A power department is one in which crucial and important organizational decisions are made. If you start out in departments that are high in power within the organization, you're more likely to advance rapidly throughout your management career.

Do Good Work. Good work performance is a necessary (but not sufficient) condition for managerial success. The marginal performer may be rewarded in the short term, but his or her weaknesses are bound to surface eventually and cut off career advance-

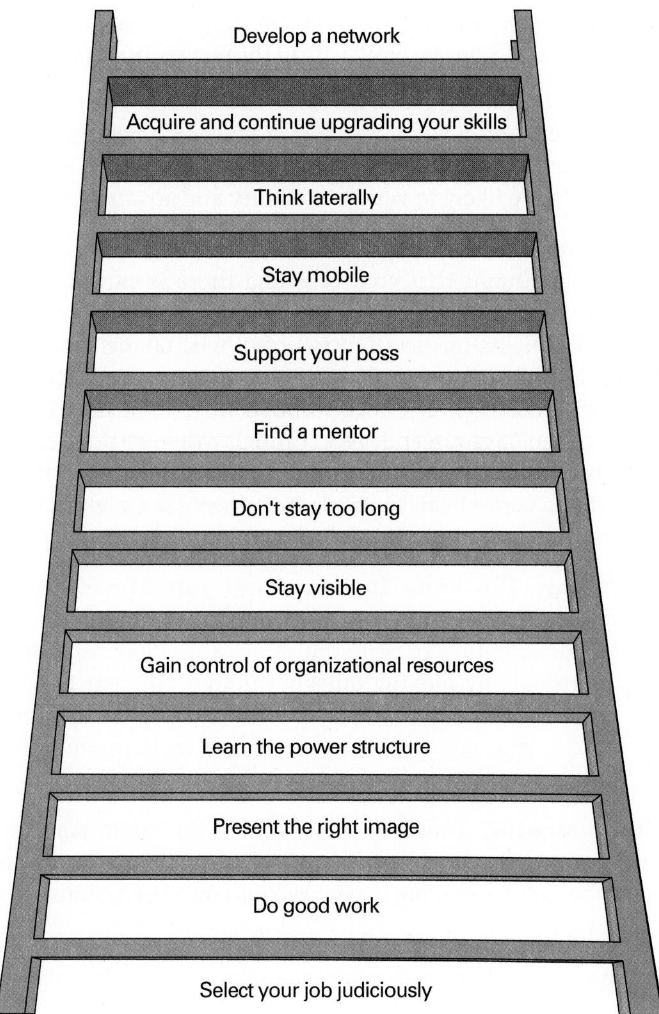

Exhibit AB-3
Steps of a Successful Management Career

ment. Your good work performance is no guarantee of success, but without it, the probability of a successful management career is low.

Present the Right Image. Assuming that your work performance is in line with that of other successful managers, the ability to align your image with that sought by the organization is certain to be interpreted positively. You should assess the organization's culture so that you can determine what the organization wants and values. Then you need to project that image in terms of style of dress; organizational relationships that you should and should not cultivate; whether you should project a risk-taking or risk-averse stance; the leadership style you should use; whether you should avoid, tolerate, or encourage conflict; the importance of getting along well with others; and so forth.

Learn the Power Structure. The authority relationships defined by the organization's formal structure shown by an organizational chart explain only part of the influence patterns within an organization. It's of equal or greater importance to know and understand the organization's power structure. You need to learn "who's really in charge, who has the goods on whom, what are the major debts and dependencies"—all things that won't be reflected in neat boxes on the organizational chart. Once you have this knowledge, you can work within the power structure with more skill and ease.[17]

Gain Control of Organizational Resources. The control of scarce and important organizational resources is a source of power. Knowledge and expertise are particularly effective resources to control. They make you more valuable to the organization and therefore more likely to gain job security and advancement.

Stay Visible. Because the evaluation of managerial effectiveness can be very subjective, it's important that your boss and those in power in the organization be made aware of your contributions. If you're fortunate enough to have a job that brings your accomplishments to the attention of others, taking direct measures to increase your visibility might not be needed. But your job may require you to handle activities that are low in visibility, or your specific contribution may be indistinguishable because you're part of a group endeavor. In such cases, without creating the image of a braggart, you'll want to call attention to yourself by giving progress reports to your boss and others. Other tactics include being seen at social functions, being active in your professional associations, and developing powerful allies who speak positively of you.

Don't Stay Too Long in Your First Job. The evidence indicates that, given a choice between staying in your first management job until you've "really made a difference" or accepting an early transfer to a new job assignment, you should go for the early transfer.[18] By moving quickly through different jobs, you signal to others that you're on the fast track. This, then, often becomes a self-fulling prophecy. The message for you is to start fast by seeking early transfers or promotions from your first management job.

Find a Mentor. A mentor is someone from whom you can learn and who can encourage and help you. The evidence indicates that finding a sponsor who is part of the organization's power core is essential for you to make it to top levels of management.[19]

Support Your Boss. Your immediate future is in the hands of your current boss. He or she evaluates your performance, and you are unlikely to have enough power to successfully challenge this manager. Therefore, you should make the effort to help your boss succeed, be supportive if your boss is under siege from other organizational members, and find out what he or she will be using to assess your work effectiveness. Don't undermine your boss. Don't speak negatively of your boss to others. If your boss is competent and visible and possesses a power base, he or she is likely to be on the way up in the organization. Being perceived as supportive, you might find yourself pulled along too. If your boss's performance is poor and his or her power is low, you need to transfer to another unit. A mentor may be able to help you arrange a transfer. It's hard to have your competence recognized or your positive performance evaluation taken seriously if your boss is perceived as incompetent.

Stay Mobile. You're likely to move upwardly more rapidly if you indicate your willingness to move to different geographical locations and across functional lines within the organization. Career advancement may also be facilitated by your willingness to change organizations. Working in a slow-growth, stagnant, or declining organization should make mobility even more important to you.

Think Laterally. The suggestion to think laterally acknowledges the changing world of management. Because of organizational restructurings and downsizings, there are fewer rungs on the promotion ladder in many large organizations. To survive in this environment, you should think in terms of lateral career moves.[20] It's important to recognize that lateral movers in the 1960s and 1970s were presumed to be mediocre performers. That presumption doesn't hold today. Lateral shifts are now a viable career consideration. They give you a wider range of experiences, which enhances your long-term mobility. In addition, these moves can help energize you by making your work more interesting and satisfying. So if you're not moving ahead in your organization, consider a lateral move internally or a lateral shift to another organization.

Think of Your Career in Terms of Skills You're Acquiring and Continue Upgrading Those Skills. Organizations need employees who can readily adapt to the demands of the rapidly changing marketplace. Focusing on skills that you currently have and continuing to learn new skills can establish your value to the organization. It's employees who don't add value to an organization whose jobs (and career advancement) are in jeopardy.

Work Harder Than Ever at Developing a Network. Our final suggestion is based on the recognition that having a network of friends, colleagues, neighbors, customers, suppliers, and so on can be a useful tool for career development. If you spend some time cultivating relationships and contacts throughout your industry and community, you'll be prepared if worse comes to worse and your current job is eliminated. Even if your job is in no danger of being cut, having a network can prove beneficial in getting things done.

Answer Key

TESTING YOUR COMPREHENSION

Chapter 1: pp. 25–6

1. **b**	10. **a**
2. **a**	11. **c**
3. **c**	12. **d**
4. **b**	13. **c**
5. **b**	14. **c**
6. **d**	15. **b**
7. **c**	16. **b**
8. **b**	17. **c**
9. **d**	18. **d**

Chapter 2: pp. 62–3

1. **b**	10. **d**
2. **c**	11. **a**
3. **a**	12. **b**
4. **c**	13. **c**
5. **d**	14. **b**
6. **c**	15. **b**
7. **c**	16. **a**
8. **d**	17. **d**
9. **b**	

Chapter 3: pp. 95–6

1. **c**	10. **a**
2. **d**	11. **c**
3. **c**	12. **b**
4. **a**	13. **a**
5. **b**	14. **b**
6. **c**	15. **d**
7. **b**	16. **a**
8. **c**	17. **b**
9. **d**	18. **c**

Chapter 4: pp. 127–28

1. **c**	10. **c**
2. **d**	11. **b**
3. **c**	12. **c**
4. **b**	13. **d**
5. **a**	14. **b**
6. **d**	15. **d**
7. **a**	16. **a**.
8. **b**	17. **c**
9. **c**	18. **d**

Chapter 5: pp. 156–57

1. **b**	10. **b**
2. **a**	11. **a**
3. **c**	12. **c**
4. **d**	13. **d**
5. **a**	14. **a**
6. **c**	15. **c**
7. **b**	16. **b**
8. **c**	17. **d**
9. **d**	18. **a**

Chapter 6: pp. 190–91

1. **b**	9. **d**
2. **c**	10. **b**
3. **a**	11. **c**
4. **d**	12. **d**
5. **b**	13. **a**
6. **a**	14. **c**
7. **c**	15. **b**
8. **a**	16. **d**

Chapter 7: pp. 224–25

1. **c**	10. **c**
2. **a**	11. **d**
3. **b**	12. **a**
4. **a**	13. **c**
5. **d**	14. **d**
6. **b**	15. **b**
7. **d**	16. **c**
8. **c**	17. **a**
9. **a**	

Chapter 8: pp. 260–61

1. **d**	10. **b**
2. **c**	11. **d**
3. **c**	12. **b**
4. **a**	13. **a**
5. **b**	14. **c**
6. **c**	15. **b**
7. **d**	16. **d**
8. **a**	
9. **c**	

Chapter 9: pp. 290–91

1. **c**	9. **b**
2. **a**	10. **c**
3. **b**	11. **a**
4. **a**	12. **d**
5. **a**	13. **c**
6. **c**	14. **d**
7. **d**	15. **b**
8. **a**	16. **a**

Chapter 10: pp. 326–27

1. **b**	10. **c**
2. **d**	11. **a**
3. **c**	12. **d**
4. **d**	13. **c**
5. **b**	14. **b**
6. **c**	15. **c**
7. **d**	16. **b**
8. **a**	17. **a**
9. **b**	18. **d**

Chapter 11: pp. 351–52

1. **b**	10. **b**
2. **c**	11. **c**
3. **d**	12. **d**
4. **b**	13. **a**
5. **d**	14. **b**
6. **a**	15. **c**
7. **c**	16. **a**
8. **a**	17. **c**
9. **d**	18. **d**

Chapter 12: pp. 382–83

1. **d**	10. **c**
2. **b**	11. **d**
3. **a**	12. **b**
4. **c**	13. **d**
5. **a**	14. **c**
6. **d**	15. **d**
7. **b**	16. **a**
8. **a**	17. **c**
9. **d**	18. **b**

Chapter 13: pp. 417–18

1. **d**
2. **b**
3. **c**
4. **a**
5. **c**
6. **b**
7. **a**
8. **d**
9. **a**
10. **c**
11. **a**
12. **b**
13. **c**
14. **a**
15. **d**
16. **c**
17. **b**

Chapter 14: pp. 454–55

1. **b**
2. **c**
3. **d**
4. **c**
5. **a**
6. **d**
7. **d**
8. **c**
9. **a**
10. **a**
11. **c**
12. **a**
13. **b**
14. **d**
15. **b**
16. **c**
17. **d**
18. **a**

Chapter 15: pp. 482–83

1. **a**
2. **d**
3. **d**
4. **b**
5. **c**
6. **a**
7. **c**
8. **a**
9. **b**
10. **d**
11. **a**
12. **c**
13. **b**
14. **c**
15. **a**
16. **c**
17. **d**
18. **c**

Chapter 16: pp. 511–12

1. **c**
2. **d**
3. **a**
4. **b**
5. **c**
6. **d**
7. **c**
8. **b**
9. **c**
10. **d**
11. **a**
12. **b**
13. **c**
14. **d**
15. **a**
16. **d**
17. **c**
18. **b**

Endnotes

Chapter 1

1. M. A. Verespej, "Growth by Design," *Industry Week,* January 8, 1996, pp. 39–42.
2. U.S. Bureau of the Census, *Statistical Abstracts of the United States: 1993,* 113th ed. (Washington, D.C.: Government Printing Office, 1993), p. 405.
3. L. Smith, "Rubbermaid Goes Thump," *Fortune,* October 2, 1995, p. 91.
4. A. Taylor III, "Boeing: Sleepy in Seattle," *Fortune,* August 7, 1995, p. 92.
5. H. Fayol, *Industrial and General Administration* (Paris: Dunod, 1916).
6. H. Koontz and C. O'Donnell, *Principles of Management: An Analysis of Managerial Functions* (New York: McGraw-Hill, 1955).
7. For a comprehensive review of this question, see C. P. Hales, "What Do Managers Do? A Critical Review of the Evidence," *Journal of Management Studies,* January 1986, pp. 88–115.
8. H. Mintzberg, *The Nature of Managerial Work* (New York: Harper & Row, 1973).
9. See, for example, L. D. Alexander, "The Effect Level in the Hierarchy and Functional Area Have on the Extent Mintzberg's Roles Are Required by Managerial Jobs," *Academy of Management Proceedings, 1979,* pp. 186–89; A. W. Lau and C. M. Pavett, "The Nature of Managerial Work: A Comparison of Public and Private Sector Managers," *Group and Organization Studies,* December 1980, pp. 453–66; M. W. McCall Jr., and C. A. Segrist, *In Pursuit of the Manager's Job: Building on Mintzberg.* Technical Report No. 14 (Greensboro, N.C.: Center for Creative Leadership, 1980); C. M. Pavett and A. W. Lau, "Managerial Work: The Influence of Hierarchical Level and Functional Specialty," *Academy of Management Journal,* March 1983, pp. 170–77; Hales, "What Do Managers Do?"; A. I. Kraut, P. R. Pedigo, D. D. McKenna, and M. D. Dunnette, "The Role of the Manager: What's Really Important in Different Management Jobs," *Academy of Management Executive,* November 1989, pp. 286–93; and M. J. Martinko and W. L. Gardner, "Structured Observation of Managerial Work: A Replication and Synthesis," *Journal of Management Studies,* May 1990, pp. 330–57.
10. Pavett and Lau, "Managerial Work."
11. S. J. Carroll and D. A. Gillen, "Are the Classical Management Functions Useful in Describing Managerial Work?" *Academy of Management Review,* January 1987, p. 48.
12. See, for example, H. Koontz, "Commentary on the Management Theory Jungle: Nearly Two Decades Later," in H. Koontz, C. O'Donnell, and H. Weihrich, eds., *Management: A Book of Readings,* 6th ed. (New York: McGraw-Hill, 1984), pp. 10–14; and Carroll and Gillen, "Are the Classical Management Functions Useful in Describing Managerial Work?" pp. 38–51.
13. Koontz, "Commentary on the Management Theory Jungle"; and P. Allan, "Managers at Work: A Large-Scale Study of the Managerial Job in New York City Government," *Academy of Management Journal,* September 1981, pp. 613–19.
14. F. Luthans, S. A. Rosenkrantz, and H. W. Hennessey, "What Do Successful Managers Really Do? An Observation Study of Managerial Activities," *Journal of Applied Behavioral Science* 21, No. 3 (1985), pp. 255–70; F. Luthans, "Successful vs. Effective Real Managers," *Academy of Management Executive,* May 1988, pp. 127–32; F. Luthans, R. M. Hodgetts, and S. A. Rosenkrantz, *Real Managers* (Cambridge, Mass.: Ballinger Publishing, 1988); and F. Luthans, D. H. B. Welsh, and L. A. Taylor III, "A Descriptive Model of Managerial Effectiveness," *Group & Organization Studies,* June 1988, pp. 148–62.
15. R. L. Katz, "Skills of an Effective Administrator," *Harvard Business Review,* September–October, 1974, pp. 90–102.
16. See, for example, J. W. Driscoll, G. Cowger, and R. Egan, "Private Managers and Public Myths: Public Managers and Private Myths," *Sloan Management Review,* Fall 1979, pp. 53–57; D. Rogers, "Managing in the Public and Private Sectors: Similarities and Differences," *Management Review,* May 1981, pp. 48–54; G. Allison, "Public and Private Management: Are They Fundamentally Alike in All Unimportant Respects?" in F. S. Lane, ed., *Current Issues in Public Administration,* 2nd ed. (New York: St. Martin's Press, 1982); D. Yates Jr., *The Politics of Management* (San Francisco: Jossey-Bass, 1985), pp. 12–39; J. N. Baldwin, "Public vs. Private: Not That Different, Not That Consequential," *Public Personnel Management,* Summer 1987, pp. 181–91; and H. G. Rainey, "Public Management: Recent Research on the Political Context and Managerial Roles, Structures, and Behaviors," *Journal of Management,* June 1989, pp. 229–50.
17. J. Case, "The Wonderland Economy," U.S. Small Business Administration, *The State of Small Business: A Report of the President, Small Business Administration, 1995* (Washington, D.C.: Government Printing Office, 1995), p. 16; and A. Barrett, "It's a Small (Business) World," *Business Week,* April 17, 1995, pp. 96–101.
18. W. Sengenberger, G. Loveman, and M. J. Piore, eds., *The Reemergence of Small Enterprises: Industrial Restructuring in Industrial Countries* (Geneva: International Institute of Labour Studies, 1990); and "Entrepreneurs Pop Up in China," *Wall Street Journal,* April 7, 1994, p. A10.
19. J. G. P. Paolillo, "The Manager's Self-Assessments of Managerial Roles: Small vs. Large Firms," *American Journal of Small Business,* January–March 1984, pp. 58–64.
20. See, for example, G. d'Amboise and M. Muldowney, "Management Theory for Small Business: Attempts and Requirements," *Academy of Management Review,* April 1988, pp. 226–40.

21. See for example, R. Calori and B. Dufour, "Management European Style," *Academy of Management Executive,* February 1995, pp. 61–71.
22. Based on S. Glain, "Milton Kim's Reforms at Seoul Firm Outrage Conservative Securities Rivals," *Wall Street Journal,* April 4, 1994, p. A8.
23. J. A. Byrne and L. Bongiorno, "CEO Pay: Ready for Take-off," *Business Week,* April 24, 1995, p. 90.
24. K. Greene and R. Greene, "The 20 Top-Paid Women in Corporate America," *Working Woman,* January 1997, p. 28.
25. See, for example, P. Burrows, "An Insanely Great Paycheck," *Business Week,* February 26, 1996, p. 42.
26. H. Koontz, "The Management Theory Jungle," *Journal of the Academy of Management,* December 1961, pp. 174–88.
27. H. Koontz, ed., *Toward a Unified Theory of Management* (New York: McGraw-Hill, 1964).
28. See for example, W. J. Cook, "On Track in the Slowdown," *U.S. News & World Report,* May 29, 1995, pp. 47–52.
29. See, for example, L. W. Fry and D. A. Smith, "Congruence, Contingency, and Theory Building," *Academy of Management Review,* January 1987, pp. 117–32.
30. The idea for this exercise came from B. Goza, "Graffiti Needs Assessment: Involving Students in the First Class Session," *Journal of Management Education* 17, No. 1 (February 1993), pp. 99–106.
31. "The Fan versus the Businessman," *Inc. 500,* (1995), pp. 34–35.

Chapter 2

1. D. Fenn, "Leader of the Pack," *Inc.,* February 1996, pp. 31–38.
2. See for example, A. Toffler, *The Third Wave* (New York: Bantam Books, 1981).
3. B. Zajak, "The 100 Largest U.S. Multinationals: Weak Dollar, Strong Results," *Forbes,* July 17, 1995, pp. 274–76.
4. S. Toy, P. Dwyer, J. Templeman, and S. Browder, "A Stronger Tailwind for Airbus," *Business Week,* March 18, 1996, p. 51.
5. R. L. Rose, "For Whirlpool, Asia Is the New Frontier," *Wall Street Journal,* April 25, 1996, p. B1.
6. N. Adler, *International Dimensions of Organizational Behavior,* 2nd ed. (Boston: PWS-Kent, 1991), p. 11.
7. See, for example, C. Hampden-Turner and A. Trompenaars, *The Seven Cultures of Capitalism* (New York: Bantam Doubleday Dell Publishing Group, 1993).
8. Ibid., p. 347.
9. "Denty vs. SmithKline Beecham Corp., (DC EPA, No. 93-6978, November 6, 1995), in "ADEA Claim Is Not Applicable Overseas," *HRNews,* December 1995, p. 24.
10. G. Hofstede, *Culture's Consequences: International Differences in Work-Related Values* (Beverly Hills, Calif.: Sage Publications, 1980), pp. 25–26; and Hofstede, "The Cultural Relativity of Organizational Practices and Theories," *Journal of International Business Studies,* Fall 1983, pp. 75–89.
11. Hofstede called this last dimension masculinity-femininity. We have changed it because of the strong sexist connotation in his choice of terms.
12. G. Hofstede, *Culture's Consequences: International Differences in Work-Related Values,* pp. 25–26; and Hofstede, "The Cultural Relativity of Organizational Practices and Theories," pp. 75–89.
13. See, "Don't Be an Ugly-American Manager," *Fortune,* October 16, 1995, p. 225; and S. Overman, "Managing the Diverse Work Force," *HRMagazine,* April 1991, p. 31.
14. C. Johnson, "Cultural Sensitivity Adds Up to Good Business Sense," *HRMagazine,* November 1995, pp. 82–85.
15. F. Rice, "How to Make Diversity Pay," *Fortune,* August 8, 1994, p. 79; R. Mitchell and M. Oneal, "Managing by Values," *Business Week,* August 1, 1994, p. 46; B. McMenamin, "Diversity Hucksters," *Forbes,* May 22, 1995, p. 174; and Johnson, "Cultural Sensitivity Adds Up to Good Business Sense."
16. See, for example, J. C. Collins and J. I. Porras, "A Theory of Evolution," *Audacity,* Winter 1996, pp. 5–11.
17. J. H. Sheridan, "Betting on a Smart Mill," *Industry Week,* February 5, 1996, p. 39.
18. J. Rothfeder and J. Bartimo, "How Software Is Making Food Sales a Piece of Cake," *Business Week,* July 2, 1990, pp. 54–55.
19. S. E. O'Connell, "The Virtual Workplace Moves at Warp Speed," *HRMagazine,* March 1996, pp. 51–53; and "Managing the Reinvented Work Place Becomes a Hot Topic," *Wall Street Journal,* March 20, 1996, p. A1.
20. A. B. Carroll, "A Three-Dimensional Conceptual Model of Corporate Performance," *Academy of Management Review,* October 1979, p. 499.
21. For an interesting discussion on the "profit motive" of social responsibility, see A. Underwood, "Being Cruel to Be Kind," *Newsweek,* October 17, 1994, p. 51.
22. See, for example, R. A. Buchholz, *Essentials of Public Policy for Management,* 2nd. ed (Englewood Cliffs, N.J.: Prentice Hall, 1990).
23. See S. Prakash Sethi, "A Conceptual Framework for Environmental Analysis of Social Issues and Evaluation of Business Response Patterns," *Academy of Management Review,* January 1979, pp. 68–74.
24. See, for example, D. J. Wood, "Corporate Social Performance Revisited," *Academy of Management Review,* October 1991, pp. 703–08.
25. Based on T. Ehrenfeld, "Socially Responsible Entrepreneur of the Year: Friend of the Family," *Inc.,* December 1994, pp. 93–96.
26. "Franchise Superstars: The Top 100 Fastest Growing Franchises," *Entrepreneur,* April 1996, pp. 150–53.
27. R. D. Hisrich, "Entrepreneurship/Intrapreneurship," *American Psychologist,* February 1990, p. 218; and S. Baker, "This Is My Last Startup. Honest," *Business Week,* March 25, 1996, pp. 81–82.
28. See, for instance, T. M. Begley and D. P. Boyd, "A Comparison of Entrepreneurs and Managers of Small Busi-

ness Firms," *Journal of Management,* Spring 1987, pp. 99–108.

29. P. E. Drucker, *Innovation and Entrepreneurship* (New York: Harper & Row, 1985).

30. K. H. Vesper, *New Venture Strategies* (Englewood Cliffs, N.J.: Prentice Hall, 1980), p. 14.

31. G. W. Loveman and J. J. Gabarro, "The Managerial Implications of Changing Work Force Demographics: A Scoping Study," *Human Resource Management,* Spring 1991, pp. 7–29.

32. S. Pedigo, "Diversity in the Work Force: Riding the Tide of Change," *The Wyatt Communicator,* Winter 1991, p. 9. See also, J. Dreyfuss, "Get Ready for the New Workforce," *Fortune,* April 23, 1990, p. 176.

33. F. Rice, "How to Make Diversity Pay," *Fortune,* August 8, 1994, p. 79.

34. See for example, S. Shellenbarger, "Flexible Workers Come under the Umbrella of Family Programs," *Wall Street Journal,* February 8, 1995, p. B1.; and S. Hand and R. A. Zwacki, "Family-Friendly Benefits: More Than a Frill," *HRMagazine,* October 1994, pp. 79–84.

35. See, for example, Hand and Zawacki, "Family-Friendly Benefits; S. Nelton, "A Flexible Style of Management," *Nation's Business,* December 1993, pp. 24–31; and B. P. Nobel, "Making the Case for Family Friendly Programs," *New York Times,* May 2, 1993, p. F25.

36. R. Levine, "Childcare: Inching Up the Corporate Agenda," *Management Review,* January 1989, pp. 43–47.

37. See, for example, B. Krone, "Total Quality Management: An American Odyssey," *Bureaucrat,* Fall 1990, pp. 35–38; A. Gabor, *The Man Who Discovered Quality* (New York: Random House, 1990); J. Clemmer, "How Total Is Your Quality Management?" *Canadian Business Review,* Spring 1991, pp. 38–41; and M. Sashkin and K. J. Kiser, *Total Quality Management* (Seabrook, Md.: Ducochon Press, 1991).

38. For an excellent review of the theory of development and the implications of Deming's TQM, see J. W. Dean Jr. and D. E. Bowen, "Management Theory and Total Quality: Improving Research and Practice through Theory Development," *Academy of Management Review,* July 1994, pp. 392–418; and J. C. Anderson, M. Rungtusanatham, and R. G. Schroeder, "A Theory of Quality Management Underlying the Deming Management Method," *Academy of Management Review,* July 1994, pp. 472–509.

39. A. C. Hyde, "Rescuing Quality Management from TQM," *Bureaucrat,* Winter 1990–91, p. 16.

40. M. Hendricks, "Step by Step," *Entrepreneur,* March 1996, p. 70.

41. T. A. Stewart, "Reengineering: The Hot New Managing Tool," *Fortune,* August 23, 1993, pp. 41–48.

42. A. B. Shani and Y. Mitki, "Reengineering, Total Quality Management, and Sociotechnical Systems Approaches to Organizational Change: Towards an Eclectic Approach?" *Journal of Quality Management,* 1996, pp. 133–34; and M. Hammer and S. A. Stanton, *The Reengineering Revolution* (New York: Harper Business, 1995).

43. Hammer and Stanton, *The Reengineering Revolution,* pp. 41–43; and B. S. Moskal, "Reengineering without Downsizing," *Industry Week,* February 19, 1996, p. 23.

44. Hammer and Stanton, *The Reengineering Revolution,* p. 42.

45. J. Flint, "No Pain, No Gain," *Forbes,* April 24, 1995, p. 116.

46. R. Henkoff, "New Secrets from Japan," *Fortune,* November 27, 1995, p. 140.

47. A. E. Serwer, "Layoffs Trail Off—But Only for Some," *Fortune,* March 20, 1995, p. 14; and B. Wysocki Jr., "Big Corporate Layoffs Are Slowing Down," *Wall Street Journal,* June 12, 1995, p. A1.

48. C. Arnst, "The Bloodletting at AT&T Is Just the Beginning," *Business Week,* January 15, 1996, p. 30; A. K. Naj, "AlliedSignal Posts 15% Profit Rise, Plans to Eliminate 3000 Auto Jobs," *Wall Street Journal,* October 30, 1995, p. B4; J. Nocera, "Living with Layoffs," *Fortune,* April 1, 1996, pp. 69–71; and L. S. Richman, "Managing through a Downturn," *Fortune,* August 7, 1995, p. 59.

49. A. Taylor III, "New Ideas from Europe's Automakers," *Fortune,* March 21, 1994, p. 166.

50. S. Z. Reifman, "Jobs and Productivity," *Forbes,* April 24, 1995, p. 254.

51. J. A. Byrne, "Why Downsizing Looks Different These Days," *Fortune,* October 19, 1994, p. 43.

52. This vignette is adapted from A. Crittenden, "Temporary," *Working Woman,* February 1994, p. 32.

53. Ibid., p. 32.

54. S. F. Cooper, "The Expanding Use of the Contingent Workforce in the American Economy: New Opportunities for Employers," *Employee Relations Law Journal,* Spring 1995, pp. 525–59.

55. J. Templemann, M. Trinephi, and S. Toy, "A Contingent Swarming With Temps," *Business Week,* April 8, 1996, p. 54; and B. Rogers, "Temporary Help Industry Evolves as It Grows," *HRNews,* January 1995, p. 4.

56. Based on W. Bridges, "The End of the Job," *Fortune,* September 19, 1994, p. 62–74; P. F. Drucker, "The Age of Social Transformation," *Atlantic Monthly,* November 1994, pp. 53–80; and S. Shellenbarger, "In Reengineering, What Really Matters Are Workers' Lives," *Wall Street Journal,* March 1, 1995, p. B1.

57. R. Norton, "Job Destruction/Job Creation," *Fortune,* April 1, 1996, p. 55.

58. W. Bridges, "A Nation of Owners," *The State of Small Business* (Annual, 1995), pp. 89–91.

59. See K. W. Thomas and B. A. Velthouse, "Cognitive Elements of Empowerment: An 'Interpretive' Model of Intrinsic Task Motivation," *Academy of Management Review,* October 1990, pp. 666–81.

60. See for example, P. LaBarre, "Lighten Up," *Industry Week,* February 5, 1996, p. 53; and J. Rossant, "The Man Who's Driving Fiat Like a Ferrari," *Business Week,* January 23, 1993, pp. 82–83.

61. A. Bennett, *The Death of the Organization Man* (New York: William Morrow, 1990), p. 205.

62. See J. E. Ellis, "Monsanto's New Challenges: Keeping Minority Workers," *Business Week,* July 8, 1991, p. 61; and T. Cox Jr. and S. Blake, "Managing Cultural Diversity: Implications for Organizational Competitiveness," *Academy of Management Executive,* August 1991, pp. 45–56.

63. See for example, D. Stipp, "Lotus Extends Company Benefits to Cover Domestic Partners of Homosexual Staff," *Wall Street Journal,* September 9, 1991, p. B6.

64. R. Tetzeli, "Business Students Cheat Most," *Fortune,* July 1, 1991, p. 14.

65. See, for example, L. G. Russell and R. F. Scherer, "Debating Ethics Issues: Using the Forensic Model for Analysis and Presentation," *Journal of Management Education,* August 1995, pp. 399–403.

66. D. L. Boroughs, "The Bottom Line on Ethics," *U.S. News & World Report,* March 20, 1995, pp. 61–66.

67. Questions adapted from R. M. Snow and A. J. Bloom, "A Survey-Based Pedagogical Approach to Ethics in the Workplace," *Journal of Applied Behavior Sciences,* March 1996, p. 89.

68. K. Davis and W. C. Frederick, *Business and Society: Management, Public Policy, Ethics,* 5th ed. (New York: McGraw-Hill, 1984), p. 76.

69. G. F. Cavanagh, D. J. Moberg, and M. Valasquez, "The Ethics of Organizational Politics," *Academy of Management Journal,* June 1981, pp. 363–74. See E. N. Brady, "Rules for Making Exceptions to Rules," *Academy of Management Review,* July 1987, pp. 436–44 for an argument that the theory of justice is redundant with the utilitarian and rights theories.

70. B. Dumaine, "Exporting Jobs and Ethics," *Fortune,* October 5, 1992, p. 10.

71. See, for example, M. C. Mathews, "Codes of Ethics: Organizational Behavior and Misbehavior," in W. C. Frederick and L. E. Preston, eds., *Business Ethics: Research Issues and Empirical Studies* (Greenwich, Conn.: JAI Press, 1990), pp. 99–122.

72. K. Walter, "Ethics Hot Lines Tap into More Than Wrongdoing," *HRMagazine,* September 1995, pp. 79–81.

73. P. Richter, "Big Business Puts Ethics in Spotlight," *Los Angeles Times,* June 19, 1986, p. 29.

74. K. Walter, "Values Statements That Augment Corporate Success," *HRMagazine,* October 1995, p. 87.

75. T. Peters, *Thriving on Chaos: Handbook for a Management Revolution* (New York: Knopf, 1987).

76. J. Teresko, "Data Warehouses: Build Them for Decision-Making Power," *Industry Week,* March 18, 1996, pp. 43–45.

77. Case adapted from "Jack Welch's Nightmare on Wall Street," *Fortune,* September 5, 1994, pp. 40–48.

Chapter 3

1. Based on D. Darlin, "Still Running Scared," *Forbes,* September 26, 1994, pp. 127–28.

2. H. Mintzberg, *The Rise and Fall of Strategic Planning* (New York: Free Press, 1994).

3. S. McKay, "A Paper Tiger in the Paperless World," *Canadian Business,* April 1996, pp. 25–26.

4. Mintzberg, *The Rise and Fall of Strategic Planning.*

5. Ibid.

6. K. Rebello and P. Burrows, "The Fall of an American Icon," *Business Week,* February 5, 1996, pp. 34–42.

7. G. Hamel, and C. K. Prahalad, *Competing for the Future* (Boston: Harvard Business School Press, 1994).

8. J. Moore, "The Death of Competition," *Fortune,* April 15, 1996, pp. 142–43.

9. D. Miller, "The Architecture of Simplicity," *Academy of Management Review,* January 1993, pp. 116–38.

10. E. Brown, "Can the Body Shop Shape Up?" *Fortune,* April 15, 1996, pp. 118–20; and J. Conlin, "Battle for the Soul of the Body Shop," *Working Woman,* April 1996, pp. 11–12.

11. See, for example, J. A. Pearce II, K. K. Robbins, and R. B. Robinson Jr., "The Impact of Grand Strategy and Planning Formality on Financial Performance," *Strategic Management Journal,* March–April 1987, pp. 125–34; L. C. Rhyne, "Contrasting Planning Systems in High, Medium, and Low Performance Companies," *Journal of Management Studies,* July 1987, pp. 363–85; R. Brahm and C. B. Brahm, "Formal Planning and Organizational Performance: Assessing Emerging Empirical Research Trends," paper presented at the National Academy of Management Conference, New Orleans, August 1987; J. A. Pearce II, E. B. Freeman, and R. B. Robinson Jr., "The Tenuous Link between Formal Strategic Planning and Financial Performance," *Academy of Management Review,* October 1987, pp. 658–75; D. K. Sinha, "The Contribution of Formal Planning to Decisions," *Strategic Management Journal,* October 1990, pp. 479–92; N. Capon, J. U. Farley, and J. M. Hubert, "Strategic Planning and Financial Performance," *Journal of Management Studies,* January 1994, pp. 22–38; and C. C. Miller and L. B. Cardinal, "Strategic Planning and Firm Performance: A Synthesis of More Than Two Decades of Research," *Academy of Management Journal,* March 1994, pp. 1649–85.

12. G. McWilliams, S. Moshavi, and M. Shari, "Enron: Maybe Megadeals Mean Megarisk," *Business Week,* September 4, 1995, pp. 52–53.

13. R. Ackoff, "A Concept of Corporate Planning," *Long Range Planning,* September 1970, p. 3.

14. M. B. McCaskey, "A Contingency Approach to Planning: Planning with Goals and Planning without Goals," *Academy of Management Journal,* June 1974, pp. 281–91.

15. L. Cauley, "Cellular-Phone Spinoff Marked Start of Slide Leading to PacTel Deal," *Wall Street Journal,* April 2, 1996, pp. A1, A8.

16. S. Kaufman, "Going for the Goals," *Success,* January 1988, pp. 38–41.

17. The concept is generally attributed to Peter F. Drucker, *The Practice of Management,* (New York: Harper & Row, 1954).

18. See, for example, E. A. Locke, "Toward a Theory of Task Motivation and Incentives," *Organizational Behavior and Human Performance,* May 1968, pp. 157–89; E. A. Locke, K. N. Shaw, L. M. Saari, and G. P. Latham, "Goal Setting and Task Performance: 1969–1980," *Psychological Bulletin,* July 1981, pp. 125–52; M. E. Tubbs, "Goal Setting: A Meta-

Analytic Examination of the Empirical Evidence," *Journal of Applied Psychology,* August 1986, pp. 474–83; A. J. Mento, R. P. Steel, and R. J. Karren, "A Meta-Analytic Study of the Effects of Goal Setting on Task Performance: 1966–1984," *Organizational Behavior and Human Decision Processes,* February 1987, pp. 52–83; and E. A. Locke and G. P. Latham, *A Theory of Goal Setting and Task Performance* (Englewood Cliffs, N.J.: Prentice Hall, 1990).

19. See, for example, G. P. Latham and L. M. Saari, "The Effects of Holding Goal Difficulty Constant on Assigned and Participatively Set Goals," *Academy of Management Journal,* March 1979, pp. 163–68; M. Erez, P. C. Earley, and C. L. Hulin, "The Impact of Participation on Goal Acceptance and Performance: A Two-Step Model," *Academy of Management Journal,* March 1985, pp. 50–66; and G. P. Latham, M. Erez, and E. A. Locke, "Resolving Scientific Disputes by the Joint Design of Crucial Experiments by the Antagonists: Application to the Erez-Latham Dispute Regarding Participation in Goal Setting," *Journal of Applied Psychology,* November 1988, pp. 753–72.
20. G. P. Latham, T. R. Mitchell, and D. L. Dossett, "Importance of Participative Goal Setting and Anticipated Rewards on Goal Difficulty and Job Performance," *Journal of Applied Psychology,* April 1978, pp. 163–71.
21. R. Rodgers and J. E. Hunter, "Impact of Management by Objectives on Organizational Productivity," *Journal of Applied Psychology,* April 1991, pp. 322–36.
22. W. E. Deming, *Out of Crisis* (Cambridge, Mass.: MIT Center for Advanced Engineering Study, 1986).
23. S. Kaufman, "Going for the Goals," *Success,* January 1988, pp. 38–41.
24. See, for instance, P. P. Carson, and K. D. Carson, "Deming versus Traditional Management Theorists on Goal Setting: Can Both be Right?" *Business Horizons,* September–October 1993, pp. 79–84.
25. See for example, L. J. Rosenberg and C. D. Schewe, "Strategic Planning: Fulfilling the Promise," *Business Horizons,* July–August, 1985, pp. 54–62; and W. Kiechel III, "Corporate Strategy for the 1990s," *Fortune,* February 29, 1989, pp. 34–42.
26. See for example, S. Hart and C. Banbury, "How Strategy Making Processes Can Make a Difference," *Strategic Management Journal,* May 1994, pp. 251–69.
27. "A Solid Strategy Helps Companies' Growth," *Nation's Business,* October 1990, p. 10.
28. C. C. Miller and L. B. Cardinal, "Strategic Planning and Firm Performance: A Synthesis of More Than Two Decades of Research," *Academy of Management Journal,* March 1994, pp. 16–61.
29. "Colleges Undergo Reassessment," *Time,* April 14, 1992, p. 81.
30. P. LaBarre, "Knowledge Brokers," *Industry Week,* April 1, 1996, p. 52.
31. N. Venkatraman and J. E. Prescott, "Environment-Strategy Coalignment: An Empirical Test of Its Performance Implications," *Strategic Management Journal,* January 1990, pp. 1–23.
32. J. Hyatt and J. Useem, "Competition: It's against Regulations," *Inc.,* April 1996, p. 57.
33. See, for example, D. Marline, B. T. Lamont, and J. J. Hoffman, "Choice Situation, Strategy, and Performance: A Reexamination," *Strategic Management Journal,* March 1994, pp. 229–39.
34. B. Dumaine, "Payoff from the New Management," *Fortune,* December 13, 1993, pp. 103–10.
35. See S. E. Jackson and J. E. Dutton, "Discerning Threats and Opportunities," *Administrative Science Quarterly,* September 1988, pp. 370–87.
36. J. B. Barney, "Looking Inside for Competitive Advantage," *Academy of Management Executive,* February 1995, p. 49.
37. A. Taylor III, "New Ideas from Europe's Automakers," *Fortune,* March 21, 1994, pp. 159–72.
38. "Sounds Awful, Tastes Great," *Canadian Business,* December 1995, p. 79.
39. See, for example, J. B. Barney, "Organizational Culture: Can It Be a Source of Sustained Competitive Advantage?" *Academy of Management Review,* July 1986, pp. 656–65; C. Scholz, "Corporate Culture and Strategy—The Problem of Strategic Fit," *Long Range Planning,* August 1987, pp. 78–87; S. Green, "Understanding Corporate Culture and Its Relation to Strategy," *International Studies of Management and Organization,* Summer 1988, pp. 6–28; T. Kono, "Corporate Culture and Long-Range Planning," *Long Range Planning,* August 1990, pp. 9–19; and C. M. Fiol, "Managing Culture as a Competitive Resource: An Identity-Based View of Sustainable Competitive Advantage," *Journal of Management,* March 1991, pp. 191–211.
40. M. Maremount, "Kodak's New Focus," *Business Week,* January 30, 1995, p. 63.
41. "Bigger Is Better: Success Isn't Spelled S-M-A-L-L," *Industry Week,* April 1, 1996, p. 27.
42. M. Magnet, "Let's Go for Growth," *Fortune,* March 7, 1994, pp. 60–72, and H. Rudnitsky, "Leaner Cuisine," *Forbes,* March 27, 1995, p. 43.
43. L. Nakarmi, K. Kelly, and L. Armstrong, "Look Out, World—Samsung Is Coming," *Business Week,* July 10, 1995, pp. 52–53.
44. K. Harris, "Edgar in Hollywood," *Fortune,* April 15, 1996, p. 102.
45. See for example, K. S. Cameron, S. J. Freeman, and A. K. Mishra, "Best Practices in White Collar Downsizing: Management Contradictions," *Academy of Management Executive,* August 1991, pp. 57–73.
46. P. Burrows, "Pennzoil Switches on Its Searchlight," *Business Week,* February 13, 1995, pp. 74–75.
47. See, for example, M. E. Porter, *Competitive Strategy: Techniques for Analyzing Industries and Competitors* (New York: Free Press, 1980); Porter, *Competitive Advantage: Creating and Sustaining Superior Performance* (New York: Free Press, 1985); "From Competitive Advantage to Corporate Strategy," *Harvard Business Review,* May–June 1987, pp. 43–59; Porter, "Know Your Place," *Inc.,* September 1991, pp. 90–93; G. G. Dess and P. S. Davis, "Porter's (1980) Generic Strategies as Determinants of Strategic Group Membership

and Organizational Performance," *Academy of Management Journal,* September 1984, pp. 467–88; Dess and Davis, "Porter's (1980) Generic Strategies and Performance: An Empirical Examination with American Data. Part I: Testing Porter," *Organization Studies,* 1986, pp. 37–55; Dess and Davis, "Porter's (1980) Generic Strategies and Performance: An Empirical Examination with American Data. Part II: Performance Implications," *Organization Studies,* June 1986, pp. 255–61; A. I. Murray, "A Contingency View of Porter's 'Generic Strategies'," *Academy of Management Review,* July 1988, pp. 390–400; C. W. L. Hill, "Differentiation versus Low Cost or Differentiation and Low Cost: A Contingency Framework," *Academy of Management Review,* July 1988, pp. 401–12; and I. Bamberger, "Developing Competitive Advantage in Small and Medium-Sized Firms," *Long Range Planning,* October 1989, pp. 80–88.

48. J. Templeman and D. Woodruff, "Mercedes Can't Shift into Cruise Control Yet," *Business Week,* April 17, 1995, p. 58; and Taylor, "New Ideas from Europe's Automakers," pp. 168, 172.
49. W. Zellner, "Back to 'Coffee, Tea, or Milk'?" *Business Week,* July 3, 1995, p. 52; and J. Loric, "Road Warriors," *Canadian Business,* October 1995, pp. 26–28.
50. K. Riley, "Patenting New Laser, Gas Process Lets Business Clean Up in Computer Chips," *Washington Times,* January 29, 1996, pp. B17, B20.
51. R. T. King Jr., "Grapes of Wrath: Kendall-Jackson Sues Gallo Winery in a Battle Over a Bottle," *Wall Street Journal,* April 5, 1996, p. B1.
52. D. M. Schroeder and A. G. Robinson, "America's Most Successful Export to Japan: Continuous Improvement Programs," *Sloan Management Review,* Spring 1991, pp. 67–81; and R. J. Schonenberger, "Is Strategy Strategic? Impact of Total Quality Management on Strategy," *Academy of Management Executive,* August 1992, pp. 80–87.
53. M. Barrier, "Learning the Meaning of Measurement," *Nation's Business,* June 1994, pp. 72–74; and J. Case, "The Change Masters," *Inc.,* March 1992, p. 60.
54. L. McMillen, "To Boost Quality and Cut Costs, Oregon State University Adopts a Customer-Oriented Approach to Campus Services," *Chronicle of Higher Education,* February 6, 1991, p. A27.
55. A. L. Spout, "Packard Bell Sells More PCs in the U.S. Than Anyone. So Just Who Are These Guys?" *Fortune,* June 12, 1994, pp. 82–88.
56. See, for example, J. B. Cunningham and J. Lischeron, "Defining Entrepreneurship," *Journal of Small Business Management,* January 1991, pp. 45–61.
57. Adapted from H. H. Stevenson, M. J. Roberts, and H. I. Grousbeck, *New Business Ventures and the Entrepreneur* (Homewood, Ill.: Irwin, 1989).
58. See, for instance, T. M. Begley and D. P. Boyd, "A Comparison of Entrepreneurs and Managers of Small Business Firms," *Journal of Management,* Spring 1987, pp. 99–108.
59. J. A. Hornaday, "Research about Living Entrepreneurs," in C. A. Kent, D. L. Sexton, and K. H. Vesper, eds., *Encyclopedia of Entrepreneurship* (Englewood Cliffs, N.J.: Prentice Hall, 1982), p. 28.
60. B. Bowers and U. Gupta, "New Entrepreneurs Offer a Simple Lesson in Building a Fortune," *Wall Street Journal,* October 19, 1994, p. A1.
61. R. H. Brockhaus Sr., "The Psychology of the Entrepreneur," in Kent, Sexton, and Vesper, eds., *Encyclopedia of Entrepreneurship,* pp. 41–49.
62. M. Frese, W. Kring, A. Soose, and J. Zemple, "Personal Initiative at Work: Differences between East and West Germany," *Academy of Management Journal,* January 1996, p. 37.
63. This exercise is based on J. P. Sheppard, "When the Going Gets Tough, the Tough Go Bankrupt," *Journal of Management Inquiry,* September 1992, pp. 183–92.
64. Based on B. G. Posner, "Targeting the Giant," *Inc.,* October 1993, pp. 92–100.

Chapter 4

1. Based on S. Sansomi, "Full Steam Ahead For Diesel," *Business Week,* April 29, 1996, p. 58.
2. M. Schuman, "Thin Is Out, Fat Is In," *Forbes,* May 9, 1994, pp. 92–94.
3. J. Diffenbach, "Corporate Environmental Analysis in Large U.S. Corporations," *Long Range Planning,* June 1983, pp. 107–16; S. C. Jain, "Environmental Scanning in U.S. Corporations," *Long Range Planning,* April 1984, pp. 117–28; L. M. Fuld, *Monitoring the Competition* (New York: John Wiley & Sons, 1988); and E. H. Burack and N. J. Mathys, "Environmental Scanning Improves Strategic Planning," *Personnel Administrator,* April 1989, pp. 82–87.
4. R. Subramanain, N. Fernandes, and E. Harper, "Environmental Scanning in U.S. Companies: Their Nature and Their Relationship to Performance," *Management International Review,* July 1993, pp. 271–86.
5. W. L. Renfro and J. L. Morrison, "Detecting Signals of Change," *Futurist,* August 1984, p. 49.
6. B. Gilad, "The Role of Organized Competitive Intelligence in Corporate Strategy," *Columbia Journal of World Business,* Winter 1989, pp. 29–35; B. D. Gelb, M. J. Saxton, G. M. Zinkhan, and N. D. Albers, "Competitive Intelligence: Insights from Executives," *Business Horizons,* January–February 1991, pp. 43–47; L. Fuld, "A Recipe for Business Intelligence," *Journal of Business Strategy,* January–February 1991, pp. 12–17; G. B. Roush, "A Program for Sharing Corporate Intelligence," *Journal of Business Strategy,* January–February 1991, pp. 4–7; and R. S. Teitelbaum, "The New Role for Intelligence," *Fortune,* November 2, 1992, pp. 104–07.
7. Based on D. Woodruff, "Talk about Life in the Fast Lane," *Business Week,* October 17, 1994, pp. 155–66.
8. M. Robichaux, "'Competitor Intelligence': A Grapevine to Rivals' Secrets," *Wall Street Journal,* April 12, 1989, p. B2.
9. W. H. Davidson, "The Role of Global Scanning in Business Planning," *Organizational Dynamics,* Winter 1991, pp. 5–16.
10. M. Werner, "Planning for Uncertain Futures: Building Commitment through Scenario Planning," *Business Horizons,* May–June 1990, pp. 55–58.

11. This section is based on B. Brocka and M. S. Brocka, *Quality Management* (Homewood, Ill.: Business One Irwin, 1992), pp. 231–36; G. A. Weimer, "Benchmarking Maps the Route to Quality," *Industry Week,* July 20, 1992, pp. 54–55; J. Main, "How to Steal the Best Ideas Around," *Fortune,* October 19, 1992, pp. 102–06; and H. Rothman, "You Need Not Be Big to Benchmark," *Nation's Business,* December 1992, pp. 64–65.
12. O. Suris, "Honda Accord Pulls Up Alongside Ford Taurus," *Wall Street Journal,* April 13, 1996, p. B1.
13. See, for example, R. Henkoff, "The Hot New Seal of Quality," *Fortune,* June 28, 1993, pp. 116–20; D. Fenn, "The Prevention Corrective-Action Report," *Inc.,* January 1996, pp. 67–69; J. Becker, "Passing the Quality Test," *Plant Engineering and Maintenance,* June 1994, p. 4; "Passenger Focus Keeps Railway on Track," *International Journal of Health Care Quality,* June 1995, p. 15; E. Kirschner, "Betz Laboratories—All or Nothing, Every Plant, Every Product," *Chemical Week,* April 28, 1993, p. 66; W. Ferguson, "EC Product and Service Standards," *Journal of Small Business,* October 1994, pp. 84–88; and Q. R. Skrabec Jr., "Maximizing the Benefits of Your ISO 9000 Campaign," *Industrial Engineering,* April 1995, pp. 34–38.
14. Henkoff, "The Hot New Seal of Quality," p. 116.
15. It is important to recognize that components of the ISO 9000 series focus on different areas. For example, ISO 9000 represents the guidelines to aid in selection and use of applying ISO standards. ISO 9001, the most comprehensive standard, applies to organizations that research, design, manufacture, ship, or install service products. ISO 9002 are standards for organizations that manufacture and install products; 9003 is for organizations in the warehousing and distribution business. ISO 9004 covers quality management systems applications, and, with 9004-2, its guidelines. See, for examples, Skrabec, "Maximizing the Benefits of Your ISO 9000 Campaign," and Ferguson, "EC Product and Service Standards."
16. D. S. Holter, "Squeaky Clean: How Companies Prepare for ISO 14000," *Machine Design,* January 11, 1996, pp. 42–44.
17. M. Larson, "The Long Road Ahead: A Certification ISO Chronicle," *Quality,* January 1996, p. 34.
18. L. J. Shinn and M. S. Sturgeon, "Budgeting from Ground Zero," *Association Management,* September 1990, pp. 45–58.
19. R. D. Behn, *Policy Termination: A Survey of the Current Literature and an Agenda for Future Research* (Washington, D.C.: Ford Foundation, 1977).
20. J. V. Pearson and R. J. Michael, "Zero-Based Budgeting: A Technique for Planned Organizational Decline," *Long Range Planning,* June 1981, pp. 68–76.
21. P. A. Pyhrr, "Zero-Based Budgeting," *Harvard Business Review,* November–December 1970, pp. 111–18.
22. V. S. Sherlekar and B. V. Dean, "An Evaluation of the Initial Year of Zero-Based Budgeting in the Federal Government," *Management Science,* August 1980, pp. 750–72.
23. See H. E. Fearon, W. A. Ruch, V. G. Reuter, C. D. Wieters, and R. R. Reck, *Fundamentals of Production/Operations Management,* 3rd ed. (St. Paul, Minn.: West Publishing, 1986), p. 97.
24. E. Hazen, "Project Management Ensures On-Time Completion," *Transmission and Distribution,* April 1989, pp. 24–27.
25. L. Nakarmi, "Seoul Yanks the Chaebol's Leash," *Business Week,* October 30, 1995, p. 58.
26. See, for example, S. Stiansen, "Breaking Even," *Success,* November 1988, p. 16.
27. S. E. Barndt and D. W. Carvey, *Essentials of Operations Management* (Englewood Cliffs, N.J.: Prentice Hall, 1982), p. 134.
28. See, for example, H. G. DeYoung, "Thieves among Us," *Industry Week,* June 17, 1996, pp. 12–16.
29. A. Murphy, "Inc. 500: Masters of the Ordinary," *Inc.,* October 1993, p. 49.

Chapter 5

1. J. Solomon, "Operation Rescue," *Working Woman,* May 1996, pp. 54–59; and E. Schmuckler, "The Top 50 Women Business Owners," *Working Woman,* May 1996, p. 32.
2. See, for example, J. W. Dean Jr. and M. P. Sharfman, "Does Decision Process Matter? A Study of Strategic Decision-Making Effectiveness," *Academy of Management Journal,* March 1996, pp. 368–96.
3. W. Pounds, "The Process of Problem Finding," *Industrial Management Review,* Fall 1969, pp. 1–19.
4. R. J. Volkema, "Problem Formulation: Its Portrayal in the Texts," *Organizational Behavior Teaching Review,* 1986–87, pp. 113–26.
5. See H. A. Simon, "Rationality in Psychology and Economics," *Journal of Business,* October 1986, pp. 209–24; and A. Langley, "In Search of Rationality: The Purposes Behind the Use of Formal Analysis in Organizations," *Administrative Science Quarterly,* December 1989, pp. 598–631.
6. F. A. Shull Jr., A. L. Delbecq, and L. L. Cummings, *Organizational Decision Making* (New York: McGraw-Hill, 1970), p. 151.
7. A few of the more enlightening include M. D. Cohen, J. G. March, and J. P. Olsen, "A Garbage Can Model of Organizational Choice," *Administrative Science Quarterly,* March 1972, pp. 1–25; H. Mintzberg, D. Raisinghani, and A. Theoret, "The Structure of 'Unstructured' Decision Processes," *Administrative Science Quarterly,* June 1976, pp. 246–75; K. E. Weick, *The Social Psychology of Organizing,* rev. ed. (Reading, Mass.: Addison-Wesley, 1979); A. Grandori, "A Prescriptive Contingency View of Organizational Decision Making," *Administrative Science Quarterly,* June 1984, pp. 192–209; and P. C. Nutt, "Types of Organizational Decision Processes," *Administrative Science Quarterly,* September 1984, pp. 414–50.
8. J. G. March, "Decision-Making Perspective: Decisions in Organizations and Theories of Choice," in A. H. Van de Ven and W. F. Joyce, eds., *Perspectives on Organization Design and Behavior* (New York: Wiley-Interscience, 1981), pp. 232–33.

9. See N. McK. Agnew and J. L. Brown, "Bounded Rationality: Fallible Decisions in Unbounded Decision Space," *Behavioral Science,* July 1986, pp. 148–61; B. E. Kaufman, "A New Theory of Satisficing," *Journal of Behavioral Economics,* Spring 1990, pp. 35–51; and D. R. A. Skidd, "Revisiting Bounded Rationality," *Journal of Management Inquiry,* December 1992, pp. 343–47.

10. D. A. Duchon, and K. J. Donde-Dunegan, "Avoid Decision Making Disaster By Considering Psychological Biases," *Review of Business,* Summer/Fall 1991, pp. 13–18.

11. H. A. Simon, *Administrative Behavior,* 3rd ed. (New York: Free Press, 1976).

12. J. Cole and A. Pasztor, "The Safety Wall—Airlines Are Grappling with a Complex Task: Avoiding Catastrophe," *Wall Street Journal,* May 13, 1996, p. A1.

13. See for example, B. M. Staw, "The Escalation of Commitment to a Course of Action," *Academy of Management Review,* October 1981, pp. 577–87; and D. R. Bobocel and J. P. Meyer, "Escalating Commitment to a Failing Course of Action: Separating the Roles of Choice and Justification," *Journal of Applied Psychology,* June 1994, pp. 360–63.

14. M. R. Beschloss, "Fateful Presidential Decisions," *Forbes FYI,* vol. 1 1995, pp. 171–72.

15. S. McKay, "When Good People Make Bad Choices," *Canadian Business,* February 1994, pp. 52–55.

16. G. White, "Escalating Commitment to a Course of Action: A Reinterpretation," *Academy of Management Review,* April 1986, pp. 311–21.

17. P. Coy, "Shades of Isaac Newton," *Business Week,* November 27, 1995, pp. 110–12.

18. A. J. Rowe, J. D. Boulgarides, and M. R. McGrath, *Managerial Decision Making: Modules in Management Series,* (Chicago: SRA, 1994), pp. 18–22.

19. L. W. Busenitz, and J. B. Barney, "Biases and Heuristics in Strategic Decision Making: Differences between Entrepreneurs and Managers in Large Organizations," in D. P. Moore, ed., *Academy of Management Best Papers Proceedings,* August 14–17, 1994, pp. 85–89.

20. S. Wally, and J. R. Baum, "Personal and Structural Determinants of the Pace of Strategic Decision Making," *Academy of Management Journal,* June 1994, pp. 932–56.

21. "Meaningful Meetings," *Inc.,* September 1994, p. 122.

22. I. L. Janis, *Victims of Groupthink* (Boston: Houghton Mifflin, 1972).

23. See, for example, L. K. Michaelson, W. E. Watson, and R. H. Black, "A Realistic Test of Individual vs. Group Consensus Decision Making," *Journal of Applied Psychology,* June 1989, pp. 834–39; P. W. Pease, M. Bieser, and M. E. Tubbs, "Framing Effects and Choice Shifts in Group Decision Making," *Organizational Behavior and Human Decision Processes,* October 1993, pp. 149–65; and S. Strauss and J. E. McGrath, "Does the Medium Matter? The Interaction of Task Type and Technology on Group Performance and Member Reactions," *Journal of Applied Psychology,* February 1994, pp. 87–97.

24. I. L. Janis, *Groupthink* (Boston: Houghton Mifflin, 1982); C. R. Leana, "A Partial Test of Janis' Groupthink Model: Effects of Group Cohesiveness and Leader Behavior on Defective Decision Making," *Journal of Management,* Spring 1985, pp. 5–17; and G. Morehead and J. R. Montanari, "An Empirical Investigation of the Groupthink Phenomenon," *Human Relations,* May 1986, pp. 399–410.

25. See, for example, T. W. Costello and S. S. Zalkind, eds., *Psychology in Administration: A Research Orientation* (Englewood Cliffs, N.J.: Prentice Hall, 1963), pp. 429–30; R. A. Cooke and J. A. Kernaghan, "Estimating the Difference between Group versus Individual Performance on Problem-Solving Tasks," *Group and Organization Studies,* September 1987, pp. 319–42; and L. K. Michaelsen, W. E. Watson, and R. H. Black, "A Realistic Test of Individual versus Group Consensus Decision Making," *Journal of Applied Psychology,* October 1989, pp. 834–39.

26. A. L. Delbecq, A. H. Van de Ven, and D. H. Gustafson, *Group Techniques for Program Planning and a Guide to Nominal and Delphi Processes* (Glenview, Ill.: Scott, Foresman, 1975).

27. Shull, Delbecq, and Cummings, *Organizational Decision Making,* p. 151.

28. A. E. Osborn, *Applied Imagination: Principles and Procedures of Creative Thinking* (New York: Scribners, 1941).

29. The following discussion is based on Delbecq, Van de Ven, and Gustafson, *Group Techniques for Program Planning and a Guide to Nominal and Delphi Processes.*

30. See A. R. Dennis, J. E. George, L. M. Jessup, J. E. Nunamaker Jr., and D. R. Vogel, "Information Technology to Support Group Work," *MIS Quarterly,* December 1988, pp. 591–619; D. W. Straub and R. A. Beauclair, "Current and Future Uses of Group Decision Support System Technology: Report on a Recent Empirical Study," *Journal of Management Information Systems,* Summer 1988, pp. 101–16; J. Bartimo, "At These Shouting Matches, No One Says a Word," *Business Week,* June 11, 1990, p. 78; and M. S. Poole, M. Holmes, and G. DeSanctis, "Conflict Management in a Computer-Supported Meeting Environment," *Management Science,* August 1991, pp. 926–53.

31. See W. M. Bulkeley, "'Computerizing' Dull Meetings Is Touted as an Antidote to the Mouth That Bored," *Wall Street Journal,* January 28, 1992, p. B1.

32. See, for example, E. F. Jackofsky, J. W. Slocum Jr., and S. J. McQuaid, "Cultural Values and the CEO: Alluring Companions?" *Academy of Management Executive,* February 1988, pp. 39–49; S. P. Robbins, *Organizational Behavior: Concepts, Controversies, Applications,* 7th ed. (Upper Saddle River, N.J.: Prentice Hall, 1996), pp. 158–59; N. Sumihara, "A Case Study of Cross-Cultural Interaction in a Japanese Multinational Corporation Operating in the United States: Decision-Making Processes and Practices," in R. R. Sims and R. F. Dennehy, eds., *Diversity and Differences in Organizations: An Agenda for Answers and Questions* (Westport, Conn.: Quorum Books, 1993), pp. 135–47.

33. Jackofsky, Slocum, and McQuaid, "Cultural Values and the CEO."

34. Based on J. Hancock, "Made in the Shade No Longer," *The Sun: Business,* January 26, 1996, pp. E1, E2.

35. K. Labich, "Nike vs. Reebok," *Fortune,* September 18, 1995, pp. 90–106.

Chapter 6

1. Based on "Creating a 21st-Century Business," *Industry Week,* April 19, 1993, p. 38; and O. Port, "Custom-Made, Direct from the Plant," *Business Week/21st Century Capitalism,* November 18, 1994, pp. 158–59.
2. E. E. Adam Jr. and R. J. Ebert, *Production & Operations Management,* 5th ed. (Englewood Cliffs, N.J.: Prentice Hall, 1992), p. 46.
3. H. Plotkin, "Riches to Rags," *Inc. Technology,* Summer 1995, pp. 62–67.
4. P. Engardio, "There's More Than One Way to Play Leapfrog," *Business Week/21st Century Capitalism,* November 18, 1994, pp. 162–65.
5. Adam and Ebert, *Production & Operations Management,* 5th ed., p. 137.
6. J. Teresko, "Speeding the Product Development Cycle," *Industry Week,* July 18, 1988, p. 41.
7. G. Bylinsky, "The Digital Factory," *Fortune,* November 14, 1994, pp. 96–100.
8. J. E. Halpert, "One Car, Worldwide, with Strings Pulled from Michigan," *New York Times,* August 29, 1993, p. F7.
9. P. Fuhrman, "New Way to Roll," *Forbes,* April 24, 1995, pp. 180–82.
10. G. Bock, "Limping Along in Robot Land," *Time,* July 13, 1987, p. 43.
11. N. Gross, "Why They Call Japan 'Robot Paradise'," *Business Week,* August 20, 1990, p. 93.
12. See, for instance, E. H. Hall Jr., "Just-in-Time Management: A Critical Assessment," *Academy of Management Executive,* November 1989, pp. 315–18.
13. J. Flint, "King Lear," *Forbes,* May 22, 1995, pp. 43–44.
14. See, for instance, O. Port, "Moving Past the Assembly Line," *Business Week/Reinventing America Special Issue,* November 1992, pp. 177–80; D. M. Upton, "The Management of Manufacturing Flexibility," *California Management Review,* Winter 1994, pp. 72–89; Bylinsky, "The Digital Factory"; and N. Gross and P. Coy, "The Technology Paradox," *Business Week,* March 6, 1995, pp. 76–84.
15. S. Moffat, "Japan's New Personalized Production," *Fortune,* October 22, 1990, p. 44.
16. S. M. Silverman, "Retail Retold," *INC. Technology,* Summer 1995, pp. 23–24.
17. B. Ives and R. O. Mason, "Can Information Technology Revitalize Your Customer Service?" *Academy of Management Executive,* November 1990, pp. 52–69.
18. Ibid.
19. See, for instance, S. Dentzer, "Death of the Middleman?" *U.S. News & World Report,* May 22, 1995, p. 56.
20. See, for instance, J. W. Verity, "Planet Internet," *Business Week,* April 3, 1995, pp. 118–24; and B. Ziegler, "In Cyberspace the Web Delivers Junk Mail," *Wall Street Journal,* June 13, 1995, p. B1.
21. "The Internet: Instant Access to Information," *Canadian Business,* May 1995, pp. 41–43.
22. See, for example, T. H. Berry, *Managing the Total Quality Transition* (New York: McGraw-Hill, 1991); N. Gabel, "Is 99.9% Good Enough?" *Training,* March 1, 1991, p. 40; D. Ciampa, *Total Quality* (Reading, Mass.: Addison-Wesley, 1992); W. H. Schmidt and J. P. Finnegan, *The Race without a Finish Line* (San Francisco: Jossey-Bass, 1992); and T. B. Kinni, "Process Improvement," *Industry Week,* January 23, 1995, pp. 52–58.
23. M. Sashkin and K. J. Kiser, *Putting Total Quality Management to Work* (San Francisco: Berrett-Koehler, 1993), p. 44.
24. T. F. O'Boyle, "A Manufacturer Grows Efficient by Soliciting Ideas from Employees," *Wall Street Journal,* June 5, 1992, p. A1.
25. M. Hammer and J. Champy, *Reengineering the Corporation: A Manifesto for Business Revolution* (New York: Harper Business, 1993). See also J. Champy, *Reengineering Management: The Mandate for New Leadership* (New York: Harper Business, 1995); and M. Hammer and S. A. Stanton, *The Reengineering Revolution* (New York: Harper Business, 1995).
26. R. Karlgaard, "ASAP Interview: Mike Hammer," *Forbes ASAP,* September 13, 1993, p. 70.
27. Ibid.
28. "The Age of Reengineering," *Across the Board,* June 1993, pp. 26–33.
29. R. Hotch, "In Touch through Technology," *Nation's Business,* January 1994, pp. 33–35.
30. This section is based on J. W. Verity, "Getting Work to Go with the Flow," *Business Week,* June 21, 1993, pp. 156–61.
31. See, for example, R. Hotch, "Communications Revolution," *Nation's Business,* May 1993, pp. 20–28.
32. Ibid., pp. 21–22.
33. B. Ziegler, "Building a Wireless Future," *Business Week,* April 5, 1993, p. 57.
34. See, for example, B. Enslow, "The Payoff from Expert Systems," *Across the Board,* January–February 1989, pp. 54–58; and E. I. Schwartz, "Smart Programs Go to Work," *Business Week,* March 2, 1992, pp. 97–105.
35. F. L. Luconi, T. W. Malone, and M. S. S. Morton, "Expert Systems: The Next Challenge for Managers," *Sloan Management Review,* Summer 1996, pp. 3–14.
36. M. W. Davis, "Anatomy of Decision Support," *Datamation,* June 15, 1985, p. 201.
37. Cited in T. A. Stewart, "Brainpower," *Fortune,* June 3, 1991, p. 44.
38. G. Bylinsky, "Computers That Learn by Doing," *Fortune,* September 6, 1993, pp. 96–102; R. E. Calem, "To Catch a Thief," *Forbes ASAP,* June 5, 1995, pp. 44–45; and O. Port, "Computers That Think Are Almost Here," *Business Week,* July 17, 1995, pp. 68–73.
39. Bylinsksy, "Computers That Learn by Doing."
40. J. Bartimo, "At These Shouting Matches, No One Says a Word," *Business Week,* June 11, 1990, p. 78; M. S. Poole, M. Holmes, and G. DeSanctis, "Conflict Management in a Computer-Supported Meeting Environment," *Management Science,* August 1991, pp. 926–53; A. R. Dennis and J. S.

Valacich, "Computer Brainstorms: More Heads Are Better Than One," *Journal of Applied Psychology,* August 1993, pp. 531–37; R. B. Gallupe and W. H. Cooper, "Brainstorming Electronically," *Sloan Management Review,* Fall 1993, pp. 27–36; and R. B. Gallupe, W. H. Colper, M. L. Grise, and L. M. Bastianutti, "Blocking Electronic Brainstorms," *Journal of Applied Psychology,* February 1994, pp. 77–86.

41. W. R. Pape, "Beyond E-Mail," *INC. Technology,* Summer 1995, p. 28.
42. "A High-Technology Meeting of Minds," *U.S. News & World Report,* June 5, 1995, p. 46.
43. M. E. Flatley and J. Hunter, "Electronic Mail, Bulletin Board Systems, Conferences: Connections for the Electronic Teaching/Learning Age," in N. J. Groneman, ed., *Technology in the Classroom* (Reston, Va.: National Business Education Association, 1995), pp. 73–85.
44. A. L. Sprout, "Surprise! Software to Help You Manage," *Fortune,* April 17, 1995, pp. 197–202.
45. H. Schachter, "The Dispossessed," *Canadian Business,* May 1995, pp. 30–40.
46. J. E. Rigdon, "Give and Take," *Wall Street Journal,* November 14, 1994, p. A24.
47. P. E. Ross, "Software as Career Threat," *Forbes,* May 22, 1995, pp. 240–46.
48. This description is based on J. O'C. Hamilton, S. Baker, and B. Vlasic, "The New Workplace," *Business Week,* April 29, 1996, pp. 105–17; and L. Jaroff, "Age of the Road Warrior," *Time,* Spring 1995, pp. 38–40.
49. See J. R. Hackman and G. R. Oldham, "Motivation through the Design of Work: Test of a Theory," *Organizational Behavior and Human Performance,* August 1976, pp. 250–79; Y. Fried and G. R. Ferris, "The Validity of the Job Characteristics Model: A Review and Meta-Analysis," *Personnel Psychology,* Summer 1987, pp. 287–322; S. J. Zaccaro and E. F. Stone, "Incremental Validity of an Empirically Based Measure of Job Characteristics," *Journal of Applied Psychology,* May 1988, pp. 245–52; and R. W. Renn and R. J. Vandenberg, "The Critical Psychological States: An Underrepresented Component in Job Characteristics Model Research," *Journal of Management,* February 1995, pp. 279–303.
50. See "Job Characteristics Theory of Work Redesign," in J. B. Miner, *Theories of Organizational Behavior* (Hinsdale, Ill.: Dryden Press, 1980), pp. 231–66; Fried and Ferris, "The Validity of the Job Characteristics Model"; and Zaccaro and Stone, "Incremental Validity of an Empirically Based Measure of Job Characteristics."
51. See R. B. Dunham, "Measurement and Dimensionality of Job Characteristics," *Journal of Applied Psychology,* August 1976, pp. 404–09; J. L. Pierce and R. B. Dunham, "Task Design: A Literature Review," *Academy of Management Review,* January 1976, pp. 83–97; D. M. Rousseau, "Technological Differences in Job Characteristics, Employee Satisfaction, and Motivation: A Synthesis of Job Design Research and Sociotechnical Systems Theory," *Organizational Behavior and Human Performance,* October 1977, pp. 18–42.
52. All of the sources in note 51; and Y. Fried and G. R. Ferris, "The Dimensionality of Job Characteristics: Some Neglected Issues," *Journal of Applied Psychology,* August 1986, pp. 419–26.
53. R. B. Tiegs, L. E. Tetrick, and Y. Fried, "Growth Need Strength and Context Satisfactions as Moderators of the Relations of the Job Characteristics Model," *Journal of Management,* September 1992, pp. 575–93.
54. C. A. O'Reilly and D. F. Caldwell, "Informational Influence as a Determinant of Perceived Task Characteristics and Job Satisfaction," *Journal of Applied Psychology,* April 1979, pp. 157–65; R. V. Montagno, "The Effects of Comparison Others and Prior Experience on Response to Task Design," *Academy of Management Journal,* June 1985, pp. 491–98; and P. C. Bottger and I. K.-H. Chew, "The Job Characteristics Model and Growth Satisfaction: Main Effects of Assimilation of Work Experience and Context Satisfaction," *Human Relations,* June 1986, pp. 575–94.
55. Fried and Ferris, "The Validity of the Job Characteristics Model; and Hackman, "Work Design," pp. 132–33.
56. J. R. Hackman and G. R. Oldham, "Development of the Job Diagnostic Survey," *Journal of Applied Psychology,* April 1975, pp. 159–70.
57. J. R. Hackman, "Work Design," in J. R. Hackman and J. L. Suttle, eds., *Improving Life at Work* (Glenview, Ill.: Scott, Foresman, 1977), p. 129.
58. General support for the JCM is reported in Fried and Ferris, "The Validity of the Job Characteristics Model."
59. Ibid.
60. G. R. Salancik and J. Pfeffer, "A Social Information Processing Approach to Job Attitudes and Task Design," *Administrative Science Quarterly,* June 1978, pp. 224–53; J. G. Thomas and R. W. Griffin, "The Power of Social Information in the Workplace," *Organizational Dynamics,* Autumn 1989, pp. 63–75; and M. D. Zalesny and J. K. Ford, "Extending the Social Information Processing Perspective: New Links to Attitudes, Behaviors, and Perceptions," *Organizational Behavior and Human Decision Processes,* December 1990, pp. 205–46.
61. See, for instance, J. Thomas and R. W. Griffin, "The Social Information Processing Model of Task Design: A Review of the Literature," *Academy of Management Journal,* September 1987, pp. 501–23; and G. W. Meyer, "Social Information Processing and Social Networks: A Test of Social Influence Mechanisms," *Human Relations,* September 1994, pp. 1013–45.
62. R. W. Griffin and G. C. McMahan, "Motivation through Job Design," in J. Greenberg, ed., *Organizational Behavior: The State of the Science* (Hillsdale, N.J.: Lawrence Erlbaum Associates, 1994), pp. 36–38.
63. J. R. Hackman, "The Design of Work Teams," in J. W. Lorsch, ed., *Handbook of Organizational Behavior* (Englewood Cliffs, N.J.: Prentice Hall, 1987), pp. 324–27.
64. See, for instance, A. Saltzman, "Family Friendliness," *U.S. News & World Report,* February 22, 1993, pp. 59–66; M. A. Verespej, "People-First Policies," *Industry Week,* June 21, 1993, p. 20; and D. Stamps, "Taming Time with Flexible Work," *Training,* May 1995, pp. 60–66.
65. J. R. Hackman, "Work Design," pp. 136–40.

66. Cited in C. M. Solomon, "Job Sharing: One Job, Double Headache?" *Personnel Journal,* September 1994, p. 90.

67. D. R. Dalton and D. J. Mesch, "The Impact of Flexible Scheduling on Employee Attendance and Turnover," *Administrative Science Quarterly,* June 1990, pp. 370–87; and K. S. Kush and L. K. Stroh, "Flextime: Myth or Reality?" *Business Horizons,* September–October 1994, p. 53.

68. Kush and Stroh, "Flextime."

69. Solomon, "Job Sharing," p. 90.

70. "Teaming Up to Manage," *Working Woman,* September 1993, pp. 31–32.

71. S. Shellenbarger, "Two People, One Job: It Can Really Work," *Wall Street Journal,* December 7, 1994, p. B1.

72. "Job-Sharing: Widely Offered, Little Used," *Training,* November 1994, p. 12.

73. Shellenbarger, "Two People, One Job."

74. See, for example, R. Maynard, "The Growing Appeal of Telecommuting," *Nation's Business,* August 1994, pp. 61–62; and F. A. E. McQuarrie, "Telecommuting: Who Really Benefits?" *Business Horizons,* November–December 1994, pp. 79–83.

75. Cited in A. Dunkin, "Taking Care of Business—Without Leaving the House," *Business Week,* April 17, 1995, pp. 106–07.

76. Cited in "Portrait of a Telecommuter," *INC. Technology,* November 1994, p. 18.

77. "American Express: Telecommuting," *Fortune,* Autumn 1993, pp. 24–28.

78. S. Silverstein, "Telecommuting Boomlet Has Few Follow-Up Calls," *Los Angeles Times,* May 16, 1994, p. A1.

79. Company data are based on a story by J. Useem, in J. Hyatt and J. Useem, "The Defiant Ones: Succession—It's All Relative," *Inc.,* April 1996, p. 60. Issues raised for production workers are for class exercise purposes only and are not reflective of actual practices at Indas.

80. Adapted from L. Smith, "What the Boss Knows about You," *Fortune,* August 9, 1993, pp. 88–93.

81. R. Tomsho, "How Greyhound Lines Re-engineered Itself Right into a Deep Hole," *Wall Street Journal,* October 20, 1994, p. A1.

Chapter 7

1. M. S. Egan, "Reorganization as Rebirth," *HRMagazine,* January 1995, pp. 84–88.

2. See, for instance, B. S. Moskal, "Supervisors, Begone!" *Industry Week,* June 20, 1988, p. 32; and G. A. Patterson, "Auto Assembly Lines Enter a New Era," *Wall Street Journal,* December 28, 1988, p. A2.

3. See for example, R. Roher, "Keep the Right Hand Informed," *Supervision,* October 1995, pp. 3–5. See also, W. Vastino, "A Chart Does Not an Organization Make," *National Petroleum News,* September 1995, p. 58.

4. The matrix organization is an obvious example of an organization design that breaks the chain of command. See, for instance, D. I. Cleland, ed., *Matrix Management Systems Handbook* (New York: Van Nostrand Reinhold, 1984); and E. W. Larson and D. H. Gobeli, "Matrix Management: Contradictions and Insights," *California Management Review,* Summer 1987, pp. 126–38.

5. L. Urwick, *The Elements of Administration* (New York: Harper & Row, 1944), pp. 52–53.

6. J. S. McClenahen, "Managing More People in the '90s," *Industry Week,* March 20, 1989, p. 30.

7. G. M. Spreitzer, "Social Structural Characteristics of Psychological Empowerment," *Academy of Management Journal,* April 1996, pp. 483–504.

8. D. Van Fleet, "Span of Management Research and Issues," *Academy of Management Journal,* September 1983, pp. 546–52.

9. Stanley Milgram, *Obedience to Authority* (New York: Harper & Row, 1974).

10. See, for instance, D. Kipnis, *The Powerholders* (Chicago: University of Chicago Press, 1976); J. Pfeffer, *Power in Organizations* (Marshfield, Mass.: Pitman Publishing, 1981); H. Mintzberg, *Power In and Around Organizations* (Englewood Cliffs, N.J.: Prentice Hall, 1983); and D. W. Ewing, *"Do It My Way or You're Fired": Employee Rights and the Changing Role of Management Prerogatives* (New York: John Wiley, 1983).

11. See J. R. P. French and B. Raven, "The Bases of Social Power," in D. Cartwright and A. F. Zander, eds., *Group Dynamics: Research and Theory* (New York: Harper & Row, 1960), pp. 607–23; P. M. Podsakoff and C. A. Schriesheim, "Field Studies of French and Raven's Bases of Power: Critique, Reanalysis, and Suggestions for Future Research," *Psychological Bulletin,* May 1985, pp. 387–411; R. K. Shukla, "Influence of Power Bases in Organizational Decision Making: A Contingency Model," *Decision Sciences,* July 1982, pp. 450–70; D. E. Frost and A. J. Stahelski, "The Systematic Measurement of French and Raven's Bases of Social Power in Workgroups," *Journal of Applied Social Psychology,* April 1988, pp. 375–89; and T. R. Hinkin and C. A. Schriesheim, "Development and Application of New Scales to Measure the French and Raven (1959) Bases of Social Power," *Journal of Applied Psychology,* August 1989, pp. 561–67.

12. See, for example, D. Benton, *Applied Human Relations: An Organizational Approach,* 5th ed. (Englewood Cliffs, N.J.: Prentice Hall, 1995), pp. 267–70; and A. J. DuBrin, *Human Relations: A Job-Oriented Approach,* 5th ed. (Englewood Cliffs, N.J.: Prentice Hall, 1992), pp. 313–14.

13. See, for example, H. Lancaster, "When Your Boss Doesn't Like You, It's Detente or Departure," *Wall Street Journal,* August 15, 1995, p. B1.

14. Henri Fayol, *General and Industrial Management,* trans. C. Storrs (London: Pitman Publishing, 1949), pp. 19–42.

15. R. E. Daft, *Management,* 3rd ed. (Fort Worth: Dryden Press, 1994), p. 298.

16. K. Kelly, "Who Says Big Companies Are Dinosaurs?" *Business Week,* July 25, 1994, p. 14.

17. J. H. Sheridan, "What's Your Story?" *Industry Week,* May 20, 1996, p. 118.

18. J. H. Sheridan, "Sizing Up Corporate Staffs," *Industry Week,* November 21, 1988, p. 47.

19. T. Burns and G. M. Stalker, *The Management of Innovation* (London: Taristock, 1961).

20. A. D. Chandler Jr., *Strategy and Structure: Chapters in the History of the Industrial Enterprise* (Cambridge, Mass.: MIT Press, 1962).

21. See, for instance, R. E. Miles and C. C. Snow, *Organizational Strategy, Structure, and Process* (New York: McGraw-Hill, 1978); and H. L. Boschken, "Strategy and Structure: Reconceiving the Relationship," *Journal of Management,* March 1990, pp. 135–50.

22. See, for instance, P. M. Blau and R. A. Schoenherr, *The Structure of Organizations* (New York: Basic Books, 1971); D. S. Pugh, "The Aston Program of Research: Retrospect and Prospect," in A. H. Van de Ven and W. F. Joyce, eds., *Perspectives on Organization Design and Behavior* (New York: John Wiley, 1981), pp. 135–66; and R. Z. Gooding and J. A. Wagner III, "A Meta-Analytic Review of the Relationship between Size and Performance: The Productivity and Efficiency of Organizations and Their Subunits," *Administrative Science Quarterly,* December 1985, pp. 462–81.

23. C. C. Miller, W. H. Glick, Y.-D. Wang, and G. Huber, "Understanding Technology-Structure Relationships: Theory Development and Meta-Analytic Theory Testing," *Academy of Management Journal,* June 1991, pp. 370–99.

24. R. Karlgaard, "Percy Barnevik," *Forbes ASAP,* December 5, 1994, pp. 65–68; and C. Rapoport, "A Tough Swede Invades the U.S.," *Fortune,* June 29, 1992, pp. 76–79.

25. J. Woodward, *Industrial Organization: Theory and Practice* (London: Oxford University Press, 1965); and C. Perrow, *Organizational Analysis: A Sociological Perspective* (Belmont, Calif.: Wadsworth, 1970).

26. D. Gerwin, "Relationships between Structure and Technology," in P. C. Nystrom and W. H. Starbuck, eds., *Handbook of Organizational Design,* vol. 2 (New York: Oxford University Press, 1981), pp. 3–38; and D. M. Rousseau and R. A. Cooke, "Technology and Structure: The Concrete, Abstract, and Activity Systems of Organizations," *Journal of Management,* Fall/Winter 1984, pp. 345–61.

27. S. P. Robbins, *Organization Theory: Structure, Design, and Applications,* 3rd ed. (Englewood Cliffs, N.J.: Prentice Hall, 1990), pp. 210–32.

28. See, for example, H. M. O'Neill, "Restructuring, Reengineering and Rightsizing: Do the Metaphors Make Sense?" *Academy of Management Executive* 8, No. 4 (1994), pp. 9–30; and R. K. Reger, J. V. Mullane, L. T. Gustafson, and S. M. DeMarie, "Creating Earthquakes to Change Organizational Mindsets," *Academy of Management Executive* 8, No. 4 (1994), pp. 31–46.

29. S. Lubove, "It Ain't Broke, But Fix It Anyway," *Forbes,* August 1, 1994, p. 56.

30. H. Mintzberg, *Structure in Fives: Designing Effective Organizations* (Englewood Cliffs, N.J.: Prentice Hall, 1983), p. 157.

31. See, for instance, J. Galbraith, "Matrix Organization Designs: How to Combine Functional and Project Forms," *Business Horizons,* February 1971, pp. 29–40; and L. R. Burns, "Matrix Management in Hospitals: Testing Theories of Structure and Development," *Administrative Science Quarterly,* September 1989, pp. 349–68.

32. J. Brikinghaw, "Encouraging Entrepreneurial Activity in Multinational Corporations," *Business Horizons,* May–June 1995, pp. 32–38; and J. C. Spender and E. H. Kessler, "Managing the Uncertainties of Innovation," *Human Relations,* January 1995, pp. 35–56.

33. See, for example, H. Rothman, "The Power of Empowerment," *Nation's Business,* June 1993, pp. 49–52; and L. Grant, "New Jewel in the Crown," *U.S. News & World Report,* February 28, 1994, pp. 55–57.

34. B. Dumaine, "Payoff from the New Management," *Fortune,* December 13, 1993, pp. 103–10.

35. See, for example, G. G. Dess, A. M. A. Rasheed, K. J. McLaughlin, and R. L. Priem, "The New Corporate Architecture," *Academy of Management Executive* 9, No. 3 (1995), pp. 7–20.

36. For additional readings on boundaryless organizations, see "The Boundaryless Organization: Break the Chains of Organizational Structures," *HR Focus,* April 1996, p. 21; R. M. Hodgetts, "A Conversation with Steve Kerr," *Organizational Dynamics,* Spring 1996, pp. 68–79; J. Gebhardt, "The Boundaryless Organization," *Sloan Management Review,* Winter 1996, pp. 117–19. For another view of boundaryless organizations, see B. Victor, "The Dark Side of the New Organizational Forms: An Editorial Essay," *Organization Science,* November 1994, pp. 479–82.

37. See, for example, N. A. Wishart, J. J. Elam, and D. Robey, "Redrawing the Portrait of a Learning Organization: Inside Knight-Ridder, Inc.," *Academy of Management Executive* 10, No. 1 (1996), pp. 7–20; G. G. Dess, A. M. A. Rasheed, K. J. McLaughlin, and R. L. Priem, "The New Corporate Architecture," *Academy of Management Executive* 9, No. 3 (1995), pp. 7–20; J. C. Hyatt, "GE's Chairman's Annual Letter Notes Strides by 'Stretch' of the Imagination," *Wall Street Journal,* March 8, 1994, p. B6; and J. Lipnack and J. Stamps, "The Best of Both Worlds," *Inc.,* March 1994, p. 33; and R. Keidel, "Rethinking Organizational Design," *Academy of Management Executive* November 1994, pp. 12–27.

38. J. A. Byrne, "The Horizontal Corporation," *Business Week,* December 20, 1993, pp. 76–81.

39. R. Jacob, "The Struggle to Create an Organization for the 21st Century," *Fortune,* April 3, 1995, pp. 98–99. See also R. P. Vecchio, "A Cross National Comparison of the Influence of Span of Control," *International Journal of Management,* September 1995, pp. 261–70.

40. T. A. Stewart. "Welcome to the Revolution," *Fortune,* December 13, 1993, p. 66; and N. M. Tichey, "Revolutionize Your Company," *Fortune,* December 13, 1993, pp. 114–18.

41. "A Master Class of Radical Change," *Fortune,* December 13, 1993, p. 83; and Byrne, "The Horizontal Corporation," p. 78.

42. L. Smircich, "Concepts of Culture and Organizational Analysis," *Administrative Science Quarterly,* September 1983, p. 339.

43. A. M. Sapienza, "Believing Is Seeing: How Culture Influences the Decisions Top Managers Make," in R. H. Kil-

mann et al., eds., *Gaining Control of the Corporate Culture* (San Francisco: Jossey-Bass, 1985), p. 68.

44. Based on G. Hofstede, B. Neuijen, D. D. Ohayv, and G. Sanders, "Measuring Organizational Culture: A Qualitative and Quantitative Study across Twenty Cases," *Administrative Science Quarterly,* June 1990, pp. 286–316; and C. A. O'Reilly III, J. Chatman, and D. F. Caldwell, "People and Organizational Culture: A Profile Comparison Approach to Assessing Person-Organization Fit," *Academy of Management Journal,* September 1991, pp. 487–516.
45. D. C. Hambrick and S. Finkelstein, "Managerial Discretion: A Bridge between Polar Views of Organizational Outcomes," in L. L. Cummings and B. M. Staw, eds., *Research in Organizational Behavior* (Greenwich, Conn.: JAI Press, 1987), pp. 384–85.
46. L. Hays, "Blue Period: Gerstner Is Struggling as He Tries to Change Ingrained IBM Culture," *Wall Street Journal,* May 13, 1994, p. A1.
47. Ibid., p. A8.
48. F. E. Whittlesey, "CEO Herb Kelleher Discusses Southwest Airlines' People Culture," *American Compensation Association Journal,* Winter 1995, p. 8.
49. S. N. Brenner and E. A. Molander, "Is the Ethics of Business Changing?" *Harvard Business Review,* January–February 1977, pp. 57–71.
50. H. C. Kelman and L. H. Lawrence, "American Response to the Trial of Lt. William L. Calley," *Psychology Today,* June 1972, pp. 41–45.
51. B. S. Moskal, "A Shadow between Values and Reality," *Industry Week,* May 16, 1994, pp. 23–26.
52. Based on L. Brokaw, "Thinking Flat," *Inc.,* October 1993, p. 86.
53. Ibid.

Chapter 8

1. K. Rebello, "We Humbly Beg You to Take This Job, Please," *Business Week,* June 17, 1996, p. 40.
2. "European News in Brief," *Facts on File,* (Chicago: Rand McNally, 1993), p. 672.
3. "Why Labor Keeps Losing," *Fortune,* July 11, 1994, p. 178.
4. B. Leonard, "EEOC Call for Males Is a Drag, Hooters Claims," *HRNews,* December 1995, pp. 1–2.
5. E. H. Burack, "Corporate Business and Human Resource Planning Practices: Strategic Issues and Concerns," *Organizational Dynamics,* Summer 1986, pp. 73–87.
6. A. S. Bargerstock and G. Swanson, "Four Ways to Build Cooperative Recruitment Alliances," *HRMagazine,* March 1991, p. 49; and T. J. Bergmann and M. S. Taylor, "College Recruitment: What Attracts Students to Organizations?" *Personnel,* May–June 1984, pp. 34–46.
7. J. R. Gordon, *Human Resource Management: A Practical Approach* (Boston: Allyn and Bacon, 1986), p. 170.
8. See, for example, J. Powell Kirnan, J. A. Farley, and K. F. Geisinger, "The Relationship between Recruiting Source, Applicant Quality, and Hire Performance: An Analysis by Sex, Ethnicity, and Age," *Personnel Psychology,* Summer 1989, pp. 293–308.
9. J. Spiers, "Upper Middle Class Woes," *Fortune,* December 27, 1993, p. 80.
10. See, for example, L. Greenhalgh, A. T. Lawrence, and R. I. Sutton, "Determinants of Work Force Reduction Strategies in Declining Organizations," *Academy of Management Review,* April 1988, pp. 241–54.
11. J. J. Asher, "The Biographical Item: Can It Be Improved?" *Personnel Psychology,* Summer 1972, p. 266.
12. G. W. England, *Development and Use of Weighted Application Blanks,* rev. ed. (Minneapolis: Industrial Relations Center, University of Minnesota, 1971).
13. J. Aberth, "Pre-Employment Testing Is Losing Favor," *Personnel Journal,* September 1986, pp. 96–104.
14. C. Lee, "Testing Makes a Comeback," *Training,* December 1988, pp. 49–59.
15. E. E. Ghiselli, "The Validity of Aptitude Tests in Personnel Selection," *Personnel Psychology,* Winter 1973, p. 475.
16. G. Grimsley and H. E. Jarrett, "The Relation of Managerial Achievement to Test Measures Obtained in the Employment Situation: Methodology and Results," *Personnel Psychology,* Spring 1973, pp. 31–48; and A. K. Korman, "The Prediction of Managerial Performance: A Review," *Personnel Psychology,* Summer 1968, pp. 295–322.
17. R. L. Dipboye, *Selection Interviews: Process Perspectives* (Cincinnati: South-Western Publishing, 1992), p. 6.
18. See, for instance, R. D. Arvey and J. E. Campion, "The Employment Interview: A Summary and Review of Recent Research," *Personnel Psychology,* Summer 1982, pp. 281–322; and M. M. Harris, "Reconsidering the Employment Interview: A Review of Recent Literature and Suggestions for Future Research," *Personnel Psychology,* Winter 1989, pp. 691–726.
19. Dipboye, *Selection Interviews,* p. 180.
20. See, for instance, H. G. Baker and M. S. Spier, "The Employment Interview: Guaranteed Improvement in Reliability," *Public Personnel Management,* Spring 1990, pp. 85–87; and Dipboye, *Selection Interviews,* pp. 6–9.
21. "What Personnel Offices Really Stress in Hiring," *Wall Street Journal,* March 6, 1991, p. A1.
22. See, for example, M. A. McDaniel, "Biographical Constructs for Predicting Employee Suitability," *Journal of Applied Psychology,* December 1989, pp. 964–70; and M. Tadman, "The Past Predicts the Future," *Security Management,* July 1989, pp. 57–61.
23. Commerce Clearing House, *Human Resource Management: Ideas and Trends,* May 17, 1992, p. 85.
24. N. D. Bates, "Understanding the Liability of Negligent Hiring," *Security Management Supplement,* July 1990, p. 7A.
25. Cited in "The Five Factors That Make for Airline Accidents," *Fortune,* May 22, 1989, p. 80.
26. R. G. Zalman, "The Basics of In-House Skills Training," *HRMagazine,* February 1991, p. 1.

27. B. Leonard, "Cover Story," *HRMagazine,* July 1996, pp. 75–82; and J. S. DeMatteo, G. H. Dobbins, and K. M. Luindby, "The Effects of Accountability on Training Effectiveness," in D. P. Moore, ed., *Academy of Management Best Papers Proceedings,* August 14–17, 1994, p. 122.
28. See, for example, S. L. Premack and J. P. Wanous, "A Meta-Analysis of Realistic Job Preview Experiments," *Journal of Applied Psychology,* November 1985, pp. 706–20.
29. M. P. Cronin, "Training: Asking Workers What They Want," *Inc.,* August 1994, p. 103.
30. D. E. Super and D. T. Hall, "Career Development: Exploration and Planning," in M. R. Rosenzweig and L. W. Porter, eds., *Annual Review of Psychology,* vol. 29 (Palo Alto, Calif.: Annual Reviews, 1978), p. 334.
31. "Three Million U.S. Jobs Cut in Seven Years," *Manpower Argus* (Milwaukee: Manpower, March 1996), p. 3.
32. See, for example, D. A. De Cenzo and S. P. Robbins, *Human Resource Management,* 5th ed. (New York: John Wiley & Sons, 1996), pp. 328–43.
33. The BARS method has not been without its critics. See, for example, L. R. Gomez-Mejia, "Evaluating Employee Performance: Does the Appraisal Instrument Make a Difference?" *Journal of Organizational Behavior Management,* Winter 1988, pp. 155–71.
34. R. D. Bretz Jr., G. T. Milkovich, and W. Read, "The Current State of Performance Appraisal Research and Practice: Concerns, Directions, and Implications," *Journal of Management,* June 1992, p. 331.
35. See, for example, J. Alley, "Where the Jobs Are," *Fortune,* September 18, 1995, pp. 53–55.
36. U.S. Department of Commerce, Bureau of the Census, *Statistical Abstracts of the United States: 1991* (Washington, D.C.: Government Printing Office, 1994), p. 434.
37. "Falling Behind: The U.S. Is Losing the Job Safety War to Japan, Too," *Wall Street Journal,* May 16, 1992, p. A1.
38. Interview with Bill Gates, "Bill Gates on Rewiring the Power Structure," *Working Woman,* April 1994, p. 62.
39. R. Leger, "Linked by Differences," *Springfield News-Leader,* December 31, 1993, p. B6.
40. B. R. Ragins and T. A. Scandura, "Gender and the Termination of Mentoring Relationships," in Moore, ed., *Academy of Management Best Papers Proceedings,* pp. 361–65.
41. A. B. Fisher, "Sexual Harassment: What to Do," *Fortune,* August 23, 1993, p. 85.
42. C. M. Keon Jr., "Sexual Harassment Claims Stem from a Hostile Work Environment," *Personnel Journal,* August 1990, p. 89.
43. "U.S. Leads Way in Sex Harassment Laws, Study Says," *Evening Sun,* November 30, 1992, pp. A1, A7.
44. S. Webb, *The Webb Report: A Newsletter on Sexual Harassment* (Seattle: Premier Publishing, January 1994), pp. 4–7, and (April 1994), pp. 2–5.
45. See D. E. Terpstra and D. D. Baker, "Outcomes of Federal Court Decisions on Sexual Harassment," *Academy of Management Journal,* March 1992, pp. 181–90.
46. See A. Deutschman, "Dealing with Sexual Harassment," *Fortune,* November 4, 1991, pp. 145–48; R. T. Gray, "How to Deal with Sexual Harassment," *Nation's Business,* December 1991, pp. 28–31; T. Segal, "Getting Serious about Sexual Harassment," *Business Week,* November 9, 1992, pp. 78–82; T. R. Haggard and M. G. Alexander Jr., "Tips on Drafting and Enforcing a Policy on Sexual Harassment," *Industrial Management,* January–February 1994, pp. 2–5; and S. Nelton, "Sexual Harassment: Reducing the Risks," *Nation's Business,* March 1995, pp. 24–26.
47. Fisher, "Sexual Harassment."
48. See for example, P. Ingram and T. Simons, "Institutional and Resource Dependence Determinants of Responsiveness to Work-Family Issues," *Academy of Management Journal* 38, No. 5 (1995), pp. 1446–82.
49. B. P. Nobel, "Making the Case for Family-Friendly Programs," *New York Times,* May 2, 1993, p. F25.
50. S. Hand and R. A. Zawacki, "Family-Friendly Benefits: More Than a Frill," *HRMagazine,* October 1994, pp. 82–83; and S. Shellenbarger, "A Tangible Commitment to Work-Family Issues," *Wall Street Journal,* September 21, 1994, p. B1.
51. Based on L. Bernier, "I Don't Want to Fight Anymore," *Business Week,* April 15, 1996, p. 93.
52. S. Nelton, "A Flexible Style of Management," *Nation's Business,* December 1993, pp. 24–31; and A. Saltzman, "Family-Friendliness," *U.S. News & World Report,* February 22, 1993, pp. 59–66.
53. C. A. Higgins, L. E. Duxburey, and R. H. Irving, "Work-Family Conflict in the Dual Career Family," *Organizational Behavior and Human Decision Process,* January 1992, pp. 51–75.
54. K. E. Newgren, C. E. Kellogg, and W. Gardner, "Corporate Responses to Dual-Career Couples: A Decade of Transformation," *Akron Business and Economic Review,* Summer 1988, pp. 85–96.
55. See, for instance, D. M. Noer, *Healing the Wounds* (San Francisco: Jossey-Bass, 1993).
56. Ibid., p. 11.
57. Ibid., p. 13.
58. The idea for this application was directly influenced by the experiential exercise in De Cenzo and Robbins, *Human Resource Management,* 5th ed., pp. 152–53.
59. M. Mannix, "A Paper Résumé? It's Passé," *U.S. News & World Report,* October 30, 1995, p. 90.
60. "Hottest Corporate Jobs Are Unheard Of," *The Sun: Business,* February 11, 1996, p. E8. See also, P. Scheetz, "Best, Worst Majors for Job-Hunting Grads," *Employment Research Institute,* (East Lansing, Mich.: Michigan State University), quoted in *USA Today,* May 29, 1996, p. B11.

Chapter 9

1. N. Sandler, "A New Face for Bank Leumi," *Business Week,* August 28, 1995, p. 69.
2. R. Mitchell, J. M. Laderman, L. Nathans Spiro, G. Smith, and S. Atchison, "The Schwab Revolution," *Business Week,* December 19, 1994, p. 91.

3. S. Toy, "Can the Queen of Cosmetics Keep Her Crown?" *Business Week,* January 17, 1994, pp. 90–92.

4. R. Koselka, "The Daily Entrepreneur," *Forbes,* October 10, 1994, p. 144.

5. The idea for these metaphors came from Vaill, *Managing as a Performing Art.*

6. K. Lewin, *Field Theory in Social Science* (New York: Harper & Row, 1951).

7. See, for instance, T. Peters, *Thriving on Chaos* (New York: Alfred A. Knopf, 1987).

8. P. Berman, "Harry's a Great Story Teller," *Forbes,* February 27, 1995, pp. 112–16; J. Bamford, "Changing Business as Usual," *Working Woman,* November 1993, p. 62; "Interview with Harry V. Quadracci," *Business Ethics,* May–June 1993, pp. 19–21; and D. M. Kehrer, "The Miracle of Theory Q," *Business Month,* September 1989, pp. 45–49.

9. Peters, *Thriving on Chaos,* p. 3.

10. Ibid.

11. See, for example, C.-M. Lau and R. Woodman, "Understanding Organizational Change: A Schematic Perspective," *Academy of Management Journal* 38, No. 2 (1995), pp. 537–54; A. B. Fisher, "Making Change Stick," *Fortune,* April 17, 1995, pp. 121–31; and B. M. Staw, "Counterforces to Change," in P. S. Goodman and Associates, eds., *Change in Organizations* (San Francisco: Jossey-Bass, 1982), pp. 87–121.

12. J. P. Kotter and L. A. Schlesinger, "Choosing Strategies for Change," *Harvard Business Review,* March–April 1979, pp. 107–09.

13. L. Coch and J. R. P. French Jr., "Overcoming Resistance to Change," *Human Relations,* November 1948, pp. 512–32.

14. J. P. Kotler and L. A. Schlesinger, "Choosing Strategies for Change," *Harvard Business Review,* March to April 1979, pp. 106–14.

15. J. P. Daly, "Explaining Changes to Employees: The Influence of Justifications and Change Outcomes on Employees' Fairness Judgements," *Journal of Applied Behavioral Sciences,* December 1995, pp. 415–28.

16. D. Ciampa, *Total Quality: A User's Guide for Implementation* (Reading, Mass.: Addison-Wesley, 1992), pp. 100–04.

17. K. H. Hammonds, "Where Did We Go Wrong?" *Business Week,* Quality 1991 Special Issue, p. 38.

18. F. J. Barrett, G. Fann Thomas, and S. P. Hocevar, "The Central Role of Discourse in Large-Scale Change: A Social Construction Perspective," *Journal of Applied Behavioral Science,* September 1995, p. 370.

19. See, for example, T. Galpin, "Connecting Culture to Organizational Change," *HRMagazine,* March 1996, pp. 84–90.

20. R. T. Golembiewski, *Organization Development: Ideas and Issues* (New Brunswick, N.J.: Transaction Books, Rutgers University, 1989).

21. E. H. Schein, *Process Consultation: Its Role in Organizational Development* (Reading, Mass.: Addison-Wesley, 1969), p. 9.

22. See, for instance, "Workplace Stress Is Rampant, Especially with the Recession," *Wall Street Journal,* May 5, 1992, p. A1; and C. L. Cordes and T. W. Dougherty, "A Review and an Integration of Research on Job Burnout," *Academy of Management Review,* October 1993, pp. 621–56.

23. Adapted from R. S. Schuler, "Definition and Conceptualization of Stress in Organizations," *Organizational Behavior and Human Performance,* April 1980, p. 189.

24. Ibid.

25. See for example, R. L. Kahn, B. N. Wolfe, R. P. Quinn, and J. D. Snook, *Organizational Stress: Studies in Role Conflict and Ambiguity* (New York: John Wiley & Sons, 1964); and C. S. Smith and J. Tisak, "Discrepancy Measures of Role Stress Revisited: New Perspectives on Old Issues," *Organizational Behavior and Human Decisions,* November 1993, pp. 285–307.

26. R. McGarvey, "On the Edge," *Entrepreneur,* August 1995, p. 76.

27. This information is adapted from a newswire report by M. Yamaguchi as cited in "Stress in Japanese Business," *Audio Human Resource Report,* March 1991, pp. 6–7.

28. McGarvey, "On the Edge"; and K. L. Miller, "Now Japan Is Admitting It: Work Kills Executives," *Business Week,* August 3, 1992, p. 17.

29. T. H. Holmes and M. Masuda, "Life Change and Illness Susceptibility," in J. P. Scott and E. C. Senay, eds., *Separation and Depression* (Washington, D.C.: American Association for the Advancement of Science, 1973), pp. 176–79.

30. See for example, M. Friedman and R. H. Rosenman, *Type A Behavior and Your Heart* (New York: Alfred Knopf, 1974).

31. A. A. Brott, "New Approaches to Job Stress," *Nation's Business,* May 1994, pp. 81–82; and C. J. Bacher, "Workers Take Leave of Job Stress," *Personnel Journal,* January 1995, pp. 38–48.

32. V. Howell, "The Groggy Beginnings of EAPs," *JEMS,* November 1988, p. 43.

33. "EAPs Evolve to Health Plan Gatekeeper," *Employee Benefit Plan Review,* February 1992, p. 18.

34. E. Stetzer, "Bringing Sanity to Mental Health Costs," *Business and Health,* February 1992, p. 72.

35. See G. Nicholas, "How to Make Employee Assistance Programs More Productive," *Supervision,* July 1991, pp. 3–6; and "EAPs to the Rescue," *Employee Benefit Plan Review,* February 1991, pp. 26–27.

36. S. L. Hyland, "Health Care Benefits Show Cost-Containment Strategies," *Monthly Labor Review,* February 1992, p. 42; T. R. Welter, "Wellness Programs: Not a Cure-All," *Industry Week,* February 15, 1988, p. 42.

37. L. Ingram, "Many Healthy Returns," *Entrepreneur,* September 1994, p. 84; H. Harrington, "Retiree Wellness Plan Cuts Health Costs," *Personnel Journal,* August 1990, p. 60.

38. See for example, T. Stevens, "Converting Ideas into Profits," *Industry Week,* June 3, 1996, p. 21; T. Stewart, "3M Fights Back," *Fortune,* February 5, 1996, pp. 94–99; K. Kelly, "3M Run Scared? Forget About It," *Business Week,* September 16, 1991, pp. 59–62; and R. Mitchell, "Masters of Innovation," *Business Week,* April 10, 1989, p. 58.

39. J. C. Collins and J. I. Porras, "A Theory of Evolution," *Audacity,* Winter 1996, pp. 5–11.

40. These definitions are based on T. M. Amabile, "A Model of Creativity and Innovation in Organizations," in B. M. Staw and L. L. Cummings, eds., *Research in Organizational Behavior* (Greenwich, Conn.: JAI Press, 1988), p. 126.

41. J. Calano and J. Salzman, "Ten Ways to Fire Up Your Creativity," *Working Woman,* July 1989, p. 94.

42. A. Bianchi, "Innovation: The Ultimate Frequent Flyer," *Inc.,* May 1996, p. 125.

43. J. Flynn, Z. Schiller, J. Carey, and R. Coxeter, "Novo Nordisk's Mean Green Machine," *Business Week,* November 14, 1994, p. 72.

44. See, for example, G. R. Oldham and A. Cummings, "Employee Creativity: Personal and Contextual Factors at Work," *Academy of Management Journal* 39, No. 3 (1996), pp. 607–34.

45. "Be Creative Now: Companies Try to Inspire Creativity in a Leaner Work Place," *Wall Street Journal,* June 13, 1996, p. A1; and S. G. Scott and R. A. Bruce, "Determinants of Innovative Behavior: A Path Model of Individual Innovation in the Workplace," *Academy of Management Journal* 37, No. 3 (1994), pp. 580–607.

46. E. Glassman, "Creative Problem Solving," *Supervisory Management,* January 1989, pp. 21–22.

47. F. Damanpour, "Organizational Innovation: A Meta-Analysis of Effects of Determinants and Moderators," *Academy of Management Journal,* September 1991, pp. 555–90.

48. Stevens, "Converting Ideas into Profits," p. 20.

49. Adapted from M. Henricks, "Good Thinking," *Entrepreneur,* May 1996, pp. 70–73; M. Loeb, "Ten Commandments for Managing Creative People," *Fortune,* January 16, 1995, pp. 135–36; and Calano and Salzman, "Ten Ways to Fire Up Your Creativity," pp. 94–95.

50. P. R. Monge, M. D. Cozzens, and N. S. Contractor, "Communication and Motivation Predictors of the Dynamics of Organizational Innovation," *Organizational Science,* September 1991, pp. 250–74.

51. See, for example, T. S. Schoenecker, U. S. Daellenbach, and A. M. McCarthy, "Factors Affecting a Firm's Commitment to Innovation," in D. Perrin More, ed., *Best Paper Proceedings: Fifty-Fifth Annual Meeting of the Academy of Management,* August 6–9, 1996, pp. 52–56.

52. See, for instance, Amabile, "A Model of Creativity and Innovation in Organizations," p. 147; M. Tushman and D. Nadler, "Organizing for Innovation," *California Management Review,* Spring 1986, pp. 74–92; R. Moss Kanter, "When a Thousand Flowers Bloom: Structure, Collective, and Social Conditions for Innovation in Organizations," in Staw and Cummings, *Research in Organizational Behavior,* pp. 169–211; and G. Morgan, "Endangered Species: New Ideas," *Business Month,* April 1989, pp. 75–77; S. G. Scott and R. A. Bruce, "Determinants of Innovative People in the Work Place," *Academy of Management Journal,* June 1994, pp. 580–607; Loeb, "Ten Commandments for Managing Creative People"; and T. Stevens, "Creativity Killers," *Industry Week,* January 23, 1995, pp. 63, 126.

53. Stevens, "Converting Ideas into Profits," p. 21.

54. J. M. Howell, and C. A. Higgins, "Champions of Change," *Business Quarterly,* Spring 1990, pp. 31–32.

55. Information and quotes come from B. Schlender, "Paradise Lost: Apple's Quest for Life after Death," *Fortune,* February 19, 1996, pp. 64–74.

Chapter 10

1. Based on P. Galuszka, P. Kranz, and S. Reed, "Russia's New Capitalism," *Business Week,* October 10, 1994, pp. 68, 70.

2. S. J. Becker, "Empirical Validation of Affect, Behavior, and Cognition as Distinct Components of Attitude," *Journal of Personality and Social Psychology,* May 1984, pp. 1191–205.

3. R. McGarvey, "Power of One," *Entrepreneur,* April 1995, p. 76.

4. P. P. Brooke Jr., D. W. Russell, and J. L. Price, "Discriminant Validation of Measures of Job Satisfaction, Job Involvement, and Organizational Commitment," *Journal of Applied Psychology,* May 1988, pp. 139–45.

5. I. Ajzen and M. Fishbein, *Understanding Attitudes and Predicting Behavior* (Englewood Cliffs, N.J.: Prentice Hall, 1980).

6. L. Festinger, *A Theory of Cognitive Dissonance* (Stanford, Calif.: Stanford University Press, 1957).

7. J. B. Rotter, "Generalized Expectancies for Internal versus External Control of Reinforcement," *Psychological Monographs* 80, No. 609 (1966). See also, T. E. Becker, R. S. Billings, D. M. Eveleth, and N. L. Gilbert, "Foci and Bases of Employee Commitment: Implications for Job Performance," *Academy of Management Journal* 39, No. 2 (1996), pp. 464–82.

8. See, for example, J. B. Herman, "Are Situational Contingencies Limiting the Job Attitude–Job Performance Relationship?" *Organizational Behavior and Human Performance,* October 1973, pp. 208–24; M. M. Petty, G. W. McGee, and J. W. Cavender, "A Meta-Analysis of the Relationships between Individual Job Satisfaction and Individual Performance," *Academy of Management Review,* October 1984, pp. 712–21; C. N. Greene, "The Satisfaction–Performance Controversy," *Business Horizons,* February 1972, pp. 31–41; E. E. Lawler III, *Motivation and Organizations* (Monterey, Calif.: Brooks/Cole, 1973); A. H. Brayfield and W. H. Crockett, "Employee Attitudes and Employee Performance," *Psychological Bulletin,* September 1955, pp. 396–428; F. Herzberg, B. Mausner, R. O. Peterson, and D. F. Capwell, *Job Attitudes: Review of Research and Opinion* (Pittsburgh: Psychological Service of Pittsburgh, 1957); V. H. Vroom, *Work and Motivation* (New York: John Wiley & Sons, 1964); and G. P. Fournet, M. K. Distefano Jr., and M. W. Pryer, "Job Satisfaction: Issues and Problems," *Personnel Psychology,* Summer 1966, pp. 165–83.

9. Greene, "The Satisfaction–Performance Controversy"; Lawler, *Motivation and Organizations;* and Petty, McGee, and Cavender, "A Meta-Analysis of the Relationships between Individual Job Satisfaction and Individual Performance."

10. All the works cited in note 9.

11. C. Ostroff, "The Relationship between Satisfaction, Attitudes, and Performance: An Organizational Level Analy-

sis," *Journal of Applied Psychology,* December 1992, pp. 963–74.

12. See for example, W. Gallagher, "How We Become What We Are," *Atlantic Monthly,* September 1994, pp. 39–55.
13. See, for example, A. H. Buss, "Personality as Traits," *American Psychologist,* November 1989, pp. 1378–88. See also D. B. Turban and T. W. Dougherty, "Role of Protégé Personality in Receipt of Mentoring and Career Success," *Academy of Management Journal* 37, No. 3 (1994), pp. 588–702.
14. I. Briggs-Myers, *Introduction to Type* (Palo Alto, Calif.: Consulting Psychologists Press, 1980).
15. S. P. Robbins, *Organizational Behavior: Concepts, Controversies, Applications,* 7th ed. (Upper Saddle River, N.J.: Prentice Hall, 1996), p. 93.
16. Ibid., pp. 7–8.
17. J. M. Digman, "Personality Structure: Emergence of the Five-Factor Model," in M. R. Rosenweig and L. W. Porter, eds., *Annual Review of Psychology,* vol. 41 (Palo Alto, Calif.: Annual Reviews, 1990), pp. 417–40; O. P. John, "The Big Five Factor Taxonomy: Dimensions of Personality in the Natural Language and in Questionnaires," in L. A. Pervin, ed., *Handbook of Personality Theory and Research* (New York: Guilford Press, 1990), pp. 66–100; and M. K. Mount, M. R. Barrick, and J. P. Strauss, "Validity of Observer Ratings of the Big Five Personality Factors," *Journal of Applied Psychology,* April 1996, pp. 272–80.
18. See, for example, M. R. Barrick and M. K. Mount, "The Big Five Personality Dimensions and Job Performance: A Meta-Analysis," *Personnel Psychology* 44 (1991), pp. 1–26; and Barrick and Mount, "Autonomy as a Moderator of the Relationship between the Big Five Personality Dimensions and Job Performance," *Journal of Applied Psychology,* February 1993, pp. 111–18.
19. Barrick and Mount, "Autonomy as a Moderator of the Relationship between the Big Five Personality Dimensions and Job Performance."
20. J. M. Graves, "Building a Fortune on Free Data," *Fortune,* February 6, 1995, p. 31.
21. See, for instance, D. W. Organ and C. N. Greene, "Role Ambiguity, Locus of Control, and Work Satisfaction," *Journal of Applied Psychology,* February 1974, pp. 101–02; T. R. Mitchell, C. M. Smyser and S. E. Weed, "Locus of Control: Supervision and Work Satisfaction," *Academy of Management Journal,* September 1975, pp. 623–31; and J. Fierman, "What's Luck Got to Do with It?" *Fortune,* October 16, 1995, p. 149.
22. R. G. Vleeming, "Machiavellianism: A Preliminary Review," *Psychology Reports,* February 1979, pp. 295–310; see also J. Weber and G. McWilliams, "Cathy Abbott Is No Good Ol' Boy," *Business Week,* February 12, 1996, pp. 94–96; and R. D. Hof, K. Rebello, and P. Burrows, "Scott McNealy's Rising Sun," *Business Week,* January 22, 1996, pp. 68–73.
23. Based on J. Brockner, *Self-Esteem at Work* (Lexington, Mass.: Lexington Books, 1988), chapters 1–4.
24. See K. Onstad, "No Jobs? No Problem!" *Canadian Business,* December 1995, p. 21; and J. Aley, "Wall Street's King Quant," *Fortune,* February 5, 1996, pp. 108–12.
25. T. Dalrymple, "Letting the Steam Out of Self-Esteem," *Psychology Today,* September–October 1995, pp. 24–26.
26. M. Snyder, *Public Appearances/Private Realities: The Psychology of Self-Monitoring* (New York: W. H. Freeman, 1987).
27. Ibid.
28. See, for example, A. E. Sewer, "The Simplot Saga," *Fortune,* November 27, 1995, pp. 69–86.
29. M. Ballon, "Pretzel Queen," *Forbes,* March 13, 1995, pp. 112–13.
30. R. N. Taylor and M. D. Dunnette, "Influence of Dogmatism, Risk-Taking Propensity, and Intelligence on Decision-Making Strategies for a Sample of Industrial Managers," *Journal of Applied Psychology,* August 1974, pp. 420–23.
31. I. L. Janis and L. Mann, *Decision Making: A Psychological Analysis of Conflict, Choice, and Commitment* (New York: Free Press, 1977).
32. N. Kogan and M. A. Wallach, "Group Risk Taking as a Function of Members' Anxiety and Defensiveness," *Journal of Personality,* March 1967, pp. 50–63.
33. J. L. Holland, *Making Vocational Choices: A Theory of Vocational Personalities and Work Environments,* 2nd ed. (Englewood Cliffs, N.J.: Prentice Hall, 1985).
34. See, for example, A. R. Spokane, "A Review of Research on Person-Environment Congruence in Holland's Theory of Careers," *Journal of Vocational Behavior,* June 1985, pp. 306–43; and D. Brown, "The Status of Holland's Theory of Career Choice," *Career Development Journal,* September 1987, pp. 13–23.
35. See, for example, L. Brokaw, "Case in Point," *Inc.,* December 1995, pp. 88–92.
36. H. H. Kelley, "Attribution in Social Interaction," in E. Jones, et al., eds., *Behavior* (Morristown, N.Y.: General Learning Press, 1972).
37. See A. G. Miller and T. Lawson, "The Effect of an Informational Option on the Fundamental Attribution Error," *Personality and Social Psychology Bulletin,* June 1989, pp. 194–204.
38. See, for example, L. Jussim, "Self-fulfilling Prophesies: A Theoretical and Integrative Review," *Psychological Review,* October 1986, pp. 429–45; and D. Eden, *Pygmalion in Management* (Lexington, Mass.: Lexington Books, 1990).
39. B. F. Skinner, *Contingencies of Reinforcement* (East Norwalk, Conn.: Appleton-Century-Crofts, 1971).
40. A. Bandura, *Social Learning Theory* (Englewood Cliffs, N.J.: Prentice Hall, 1977).
41. S. E. Asch, "Effects of Group Pressure upon the Modification and Distortion of Judgements," in H. Guetzkow, ed., *Groups, Leadership, and Men* (Pittsburgh: Carnegie Press, 1951), pp. 177–90.
42. Ibid.
43. See, for instance, E. J. Thomas and C. F. Fink, "Effects of Group Size," *Psychological Bulletin,* July 1963, pp. 371–84; and M. E. Shaw, *Group Dynamics: The Psychology of Small Group Behavior,* 3rd ed. (New York: McGraw-Hill, 1981).

44. See R. Albanese and D. D. Van Fleet, "Rational Behavior in Groups: The Free-Riding Tendency," *Academy of Management Review,* April 1985, pp. 244–55.

45. L. Berkowitz, "Group Standards, Cohesiveness, and Productivity," *Human Relations,* November 1954, pp. 509–19; and B. Mullen and C. Copper, "The Relation between Group Cohesiveness and Performance: An Integration," *Psychological Bulletin,* March 1994, pp. 210–17.

46. S. E. Seashore, *Group Cohesiveness in the Industrial Work Group* (Ann Arbor: University of Michigan, Survey Research Center, 1954).

47. The idea for this exercise came from J. Gandz and J. M. Howell, "Confronting Sex Role Stereotypes: The Janis/Jack Jerome Cases," *Organizational Behavior Teaching Review* 13, No. 4 (1988–1989), pp. 103–11.

48. Based on A. B. Fisher, "Japanese Working Women Strike Back," *Fortune,* May 31, 1993, p. 22.

Chapter 11

1. M. MacIsaac, "Born Again Basket Case," *Canadian Business,* May 1993, pp. 34–37.

2. See, for example, D. W. Tjosvold, *Working Together to Get Things Done: Managing for Organizational Productivity* (Lexington, Mass.: Lexington Books, 1986); Tjosvold, *Organization: An Enduring Competitive Advantage* (Chichester, England: John Wiley & Sons, 1991); J. Lipnack and J. Stamps, *The TeamNet Factor* (Essex Junction, Vt.: Oliver Wright, 1993); and J. R. Katzenbach and D. K. Smith, *The Wisdom of Teams* (Boston: Harvard Business School Press, 1993); see also D. Richardson, "Teams Not Always the Best Way to Get Work Done," *HRNews,* August 1996, p. 11.

3. "Teams Rule According to U.S. Manufacturers," *Wall Street Journal,* May 28, 1996, p. A1.

4. M. A. Campion, and A. C. Higgs, "Design Work Teams to Increase Productivity and Satisfaction," *HRMagazine,* October 1995, pp. 101–07.

5. S. P. Robbins, *Organizational Behavior: Concepts, Controversies, Applications,* 7th ed (Upper Saddle River, N.J.: Prentice Hall, 1996), p. 347. See also, G. M. Spreitzer, "Psychological Empowerment in the Workplace: Dimensions, Measurement, and Validation," *Academy of Management Journal* 38, No. 5 (1995), pp. 1442–65.

6. B. W. Tuckman and M. A. C. Jensen, "Stages of Small-Group Development Revisited," *Group and Organizational Studies* 2, No. 3 (1977), pp. 419–27; and P. Buhler, "Group Membership," *Supervision,* May 1994, pp. 8–10.

7. L. N. Jewell, and H. J. Reitz, *Group Effectiveness in Organizations* (Glenview, Ill.: Scott, Foresman, 1981); and M. Kaeter, "Repotting Mature Work Teams," *Training,* April 1994, pp. 54–56.

8. See, for instance, V. I. Sessa, "Using Perspective Taking to Manage Conflict and Affect in Teams," *Journal of Applied Behavioral Science,* March 1996, pp. 110–15.

9. Information for this section is based on Katzenbach and Smith, *The Wisdom of Teams,* pp. 21, 45, 85; and D. C. Kinlaw, *Developing Superior Work Teams* (Lexington, Mass.: Lexington Books, 1991), pp. 3–21.

10. Katzenbach and Smith, *The Wisdom of Teams,* p. 45.

11. "Where Teams Trip Up," *Inc.,* November 1995, p. 94.

12. H. Rothman, "The Power of Empowerment," *Nation's Business,* June 1993, pp. 49–51.

13. P. W. Mulvey, J. F. Veiga, and P. M. Elsass, "When Teammates Raise a White Flag," *Academy of Management Executive* 10, No. 1 (1996), pp. 40–50; J. H. Shonk, *Team-Based Organizations* (Homewood, Ill.: Business One Irwin, 1992); and M. A. Verespej, "When Workers Get New Roles," *Industry Week,* February 3, 1992, p. 11.

14. S. Sherman, "Secrets of HP's 'Muddled' Team," *Fortune,* March 18, 1996, pp. 116–20.

15. E. Hill Updike, D. Woodruff, and L. Armstrong, "Honda's Civic Lesson," *Business Week,* September 18, 1995, p. 71.

16. See, for example, R. C. Ford and M. D. Fottler, "Empowerment: A Matter of Degree," *Academy of Management Executive* 9, No. 3 (1995), pp. 21–28; D. Barry, "Managing the Bossless Team," *Organizational Dynamics 1* (Summer 1991), pp. 31–47; and J. R. Barker, "Tightening the Iron Cage: Concertive Control in Self-Managing Teams," *Administrative Science Quarterly,* September 1993, pp. 408–37.

17. See R. C. Liden, S. J. Wayne, and L. Bradway, "Connections Make the Difference," *HRMagazine,* February 1996, pp. 73–79; R. McGarvey, "More Power to Them," *Entrepreneur,* February 1995, pp. 73–75; J. Hillkirk, "Self-Directed Work Teams Give TI a Life," *USA Today,* December 20, 1993, p. B8; and M. A. Verespej, "Worker-Managers," *Industry Week,* May 16, 1994, p. 30.

18. See, for example, K. Labich, "Elite Teams Get the Job Done," *Fortune,* February 19, 1996, pp. 90–99; Sherman, "Secrets of HP's 'Muddled' Team"; and B. Dumaine, "The Trouble with Teams," *Fortune,* September 5, 1994, p. 92.

19. G. Taninecz, "Team Players," *Industry Week,* July 15, 1996, pp. 28–31; S. S. Brooks, "Managing Horizontal Revolution," *HRMagazine,* June 1995, pp. 52–58; and Lipnack and Stamps, *The TeamNet Factor,* pp. 14–17.

20. M. Loeb, "Empowerment That Pays Off," *Fortune,* March 20, 1995, p. 145.

21. T. B. Kinni, "Boundary-Busting Teamwork," *Industry Week,* March 21, 1994, pp. 72–78.

22. See M. R. Manning, and P. J. Schmidt, "Building Effective Work Teams: A Quick Exercise Based on a Scavenger Hunt," *Journal of Management Education,* August 1995, pp. 392–98; D. Vinokur-Kaplan, "Treatment Teams That Work (and Those That Don't): An Application of Hackman's Group Effectiveness Model to Interdisciplinary Teams in Psychiatric Hospitals," *Journal of Applied Behavior Science,* September 1995, pp. 303–27; B. Nelson, "Ways to Foster Team Spirit," *HRMagazine,* November 1995, pp. 47–50; E. Sundstrom, K. P. DeMeuse, and D. Futrell, "Work Teams," *American Psychologist,* February 1990, p. 120; C. E. Larson and F. M. J. LaFasto, *Teamwork* (Newbury Park, Calif.: Sage Publications, 1992); J. R. Hackman, ed., *Groups That Work (and Those That Don't)* (San Francisco: Jossey-Bass, 1990), and D. W. Tjosvold and M. M. Bass, *Leading the Team Organization* (Lexington, Mass.: Lexington Books, 1991).

23. "Job Morphing," *Wall Street Journal,* June 29, 1995, p. A1.
24. Larson and LaFasto, *Teamwork,* p. 75.
25. See, for example, "Effects of Distribution of Feedback in Work Groups," *Academy of Management Journal* 37, No. 3 (1994), pp. 635–41.
26. Based on F. Bartolome, "Nobody Trusts the Boss Completely—Now What?" *Harvard Business Review,* March–April 1989, pp. 135–42; and P. Pascarella, "15 Ways to Win People's Trust," *Industry Week,* February 1, 1993, pp. 47–51.
27. Dumaine, "The Trouble with Teams," *Fortune.*
28. D. Harrington-Mackin, *The Team Building Tool Kit* (New York: AMACOM, 1994), p. 53.
29. T. D. Shellhardt, "To Be a Star among Equals, Be a Team Player," *Wall Street Journal,* April 20, 1994, p. B1.
30. Ibid.
31. Based on C. Margerison and D. McCann, *Team Management: Practical New Approaches* (London: Mercury Books, 1990).
32. Ibid.
33. "Teaming for Success," *Training,* January 1994, p. 541.
34. Information in this section is based on Kaeter, "Repotting Mature Work Teams." See also K. Dow Scott and A. Townsend, "Teams: Why Some Succeed and Others Fail," *HRMagazine,* August 1994, pp. 62–67.
35. "Teamwork for Employees and Managers (TEAM) Act," *HR Legislative Fact Sheet,* June 1996, pp. 28–29; and R. Hanson, R. I. Porterfield, and K. Ames, "Employee Empowerment at Risk: Effects of Recent NLRB Rulings," *Academy of Management Executive* 9, No. 2 (1995), pp. 45–56.
36. See L. Rubis, "Team Act Sent to Clinton," *HRNews,* August 1996, p. 1; A. Berstein, "Making Teamwork Work—And Appeasing Uncle Sam," *Business Week,* January 25, 1993, p. 101; K. G. Salwen, "DuPont Is Told It Must Disband Nonunion Panels," *Wall Street Journal,* June 7, 1993, p. A2; and "Study Commends Worker Participation, But Says Labor Laws May Be Limiting," *Wall Street Journal,* June 3, 1994, p. A2.
37. Legislation, called the "Teamwork for Employees and Managers (TEAM) Act" has been proposed in both the House of Representatives and the Senate. The act, as proposed, was designed to "permit employers and employees to establish and maintain employee involvement programs—including various approaches to problem-solving, communication enhancement, productivity improvement programs." In May 1996, the act was passed in the House and sent to the Senate for approval. By a vote of 53 to 46, the Senate approved the act in principal but did not agree to some of its language. Accordingly, the bill returned to the House for its review. Whatever that outcome, it's important to note that President Clinton has publicly stated he would veto any such bill if it came to the White House for his signature. ["Teamwork For Employees and Managers (TEAM) Act." *HR Legislative Fact Sheet,* June 1996, pp. 28–29.]
38. D. C. Kinlaw, *Developing Superior Work Teams* (Lexington, Mass.: Lexington Books, 1991), p. 43.
39. B. Krone, "Total Quality Management: An American Odyssey," *Bureaucrat,* Fall 1990, p. 37.
40. *Profiles in Quality: Blueprints for Action from 50 Leading Companies* (Boston: Allyn & Bacon, 1991), p. 37.
41. Based on M. Selz, "Testing Self-Managed Teams, Entrepreneur Hopes to Lose Job," *Wall Street Journal,* January 11, 1994, pp. B1.

Chapter 12

1. D. Fenn, "Compensation: Bonuses That Make Sense," *Inc.* March 1996, p. 95.
2. R. Katerberg and G. J. Blau, "An Examination of Level and Direction of Effort and Job Performance," *Academy of Management Journal,* June 1983, pp. 249–57.
3. A. Maslow, *Motivation and Personality* (New York: Harper & Row, 1954).
4. M. Henricks, "Motivating Force," *Entrepreneur,* December 1995, pp. 70–72.
5. See, for example, E. E. Lawler III and J. L. Suttle, "A Causal Correlational Test of the Need Hierarchy Concept," *Organizational Behavior and Human Performance,* April 1972, pp. 265–87; and D. T. Hall and K. E. Nongaim, "An Examination of Maslow's Need Hierarchy in an Organizational Setting," *Organizational Behavior and Human Performance,* February 1968, pp. 12–35.
6. D. McGregor, *The Human Side of Enterprise* (New York: McGraw-Hill, 1960).
7. F. Herzberg, B. Mausner, and B. Snyderman, *The Motivation to Work* (New York: John Wiley & Sons, 1959); and F. Herzberg, *The Managerial Choice: To Be Effective or To Be Human,* rev. ed. (Salt Lake City: Olympus, 1982).
8. See, for instance, M. F. Gordon, N. M. Pryor, and B. V. Harris, "An Examination of Scaling Bias in Herzberg's Theory of Job Satisfaction," *Organizational Behavior and Human Performance,* February 1974, pp. 106–21; E. A. Locke and R. J. Whiting, "Sources of Satisfaction and Dissatisfaction among Solid Waste Management Employees," *Journal of Applied Psychology,* April 1974, pp. 145–56; and J. B. Miner, *Theories of Organizational Behavior* (Hinsdale, Ill.: Dryden Press, 1980), pp. 76–105.
9. D. C. McClelland, *The Achieving Society* (New York: Van Nostrand Reinhold, 1961); J. W. Atkinson and J. O. Raynor, *Motivation and Achievement* (Washington, D.C.: Winston, 1974); and D. C. McClelland, *Power: The Inner Experience* (New York: Free Press, 1969).
10. McClelland, *The Achieving Society.*
11. J. S. Adams, "Inequity in Social Exchanges," in L. Berkowitz, ed., *Advances in Experimental Social Psychology,* vol. 2 (New York: Academic Press, 1965), pp. 267–300.
12. D. C. McClelland and D. G. Winter, *Motivating Economic Achievement* (New York: Free Press, 1969).
13. McClelland, *Power;* D. C. McClelland and D. H. Burnham, "Power Is the Great Motivator," *Harvard Business Review,* March–April 1976, pp. 100–10.
14. "McClelland: An Advocate of Power," *International Management,* July 1975, pp. 27–29.

15. D. Miron and D. C. McClelland, "The Impact of Achievement Motivation Training on Small Businesses," *California Management Review,* Summer 1979, pp. 13–28.

16. P. S. Goodman, "An Examination of Referents Used in the Evaluation of Pay," *Organizational Behavior and Human Performance,* October 1974, pp. 170–95; S. Ronen, "Equity Perception in Multiple Comparisons: A Field Study," *Human Relations,* April 1986, pp. 333–46; R. W. School, E. A. Cooper, and J. F. McKenna, "Referent Effects on Behavioral and Attitudinal Outcomes," *Personnel Psychology,* Spring 1987, pp. 113–27; and C. T. Kulik and M. L. Ambrose, "Personal and Situational Determinants of Referent Choice," *Academy of Management Review,* April 1992, pp. 212–37.

17. P. S. Goodman and A. Friedman, "An Examination of Adams' Theory of Inequity," *Administrative Science Quarterly,* September 1971, pp. 271–88.

18. See, for example, M. R. Carrell, "A Longitudinal Field Assessment of Employee Perceptions of Equitable Treatment," *Organizational Behavior and Human Performance,* February 1978, pp. 108–18; R. G. Lord and J. A. Hohenfeld, "Longitudinal Field Assessment of Equity Effects on the Performance of Major League Baseball Players," *Journal of Applied Psychology,* February 1979, pp. 19–26; and J. E. Dittrich and M. R. Carrell, "Organizational Equity Perceptions, Employee Job Satisfaction, and Department Absence and Turnover Rates," *Organizational Behavior and Human Performance,* August 1979, pp. 97–132.

19. P. S. Goodman, "Social Comparison Process in Organizations," in B. M. Staw and G. R. Salancik, eds., *New Directions in Organizational Behavior* (Chicago: St. Clair, 1977), pp. 97–132.

20. V. H. Vroom, *Work and Motivation* (New York: John Wiley & Sons, 1964).

21. See, for example, H. G. Henneman III and D. P. Schwab, "Evaluation of Research on Expectancy Theory Prediction of Employee Performance," *Psychological Bulletin,* July 1972, pp. 1–9; and L. Reinharth and M. Wahba, "Expectancy Theory as a Predictor of Work Motivation, Effort Expenditure, and Job Performance," *Academy of Management Journal,* September 1975, pp. 502–37.

22. See, for example, V. H. Vroom, "Organizational Choice: A Study of Pre- and Postdecision Processes," *Organizational Behavior and Human Performance,* April 1966, pp. 212–25; and L. W. Porter and E. E. Lawler III, *Managerial Attitudes and Performance* (Homewood, Ill.: Richard D. Irwin, 1968).

23. Among academicians these three variables are typically referred to as valence, instrumentality, and expectancy, respectively.

24. This four-step discussion was adapted from K. F. Taylor, "A Valence-Expectancy Approach to Work Motivation," *Personnel Practice Bulletin,* June 1974, pp. 142–48.

25. See also, N. H. Leonard, L. L. Beauvais, and R. W. School, "A Self-Concept–Based Model of Work Motivation," in D. P. Moore, ed., *Best Papers Proceedings: Academy of Management,* Vancouver, British Columbia, Canada, August 6–9, 1995, pp. 322–26.

26. See, for instance, M. Siegall, "The Simplistic Five: An Integrative Framework for Teaching Motivation," *Organizational Behavior Teaching Review* 12, No. 4 (1987–1988), pp. 141–43.

27. See, for instance, J. L. Xie and G. Johns, "Job Scope and Stress: Can Job Scope Be Too High?" *Academy of Management Journal* 38, No. 5 (1995), pp. 1288–309.

28. "The Value of Flexibility," *Inc.,* April 1996, p. 114; and B. J. Wixom Jr., "Recognizing People in a World of Change," *HRMagazine,* June 1995, p. 65.

29. P. LaBarre, "Lighten Up!" *Industry Week,* February 5, 1996, p. 53.

30. I. Harpaz, "The Importance of Work Goals: An International Perspective," *Journal of International Business Studies,* First Quarter 1990, pp. 75–93.

31. S. Shellenbarger, "Enter the 'New Hero': A Boss Who Knows You Have a Life," *Wall Street Journal,* May 8, 1996, p. B1.

32. See also, A. Kindelan, "Dependent-Care Accounts Top Family-Friendly Benefits," *HR News,* April 1996, p. 14; and E. Sheley, "Job Sharing Offers Unique Challenges," *HRMagazine,* January 1996, pp. 46–49.

33. G. Hofstede, "Motivation, Leadership, and Organizations: Do American Theories Apply Abroad?" *Organizational Dynamics,* Summer 1980, p. 55.

34. D. H. B. Walsh, F. Luthens, and S. M. Sommer, "Organizational Behavior Modification Goes to Russia: Replicating an Experimental Analysis across Cultures and Tasks," *Journal of Organizational Behavior Management,* Fall 1993, pp. 15–35; and J. R. Baum, J. D. Olian, M. Erez, and E. R. Schnell, "Nationality and Work Role Interactions: A Cultural Contrast of Israel and U.S. Entrepreneurs' versus Managers' Needs," *Journal of Business Venturing,* November 1993, pp. 499–512.

35. See, for instance, J. K. Giacobbe-Miller and D. J. Miller, "A Comparison of U.S. and Russian Pay Allocation Decisions and Distributive Justice Judgements," in Moore, ed., *Best Papers Proceedings: Academy of Management,* pp. 177–81.

36. A. Ignatius, "Now If Ms. Wong Insults a Customer, She Gets an Award," *Wall Street Journal,* January 24, 1989, p. A1.

37. R. K. Abbott, "Performance-Based Flex: A Tool for Managing Total Compensation Costs," *Compensation and Benefits Review,* March–April 1993, pp. 18–21; J. R. Schuster and P. K. Zingheim, "The New Variable Pay: Key Design Issues," *Compensation and Benefits Review,* March–April 1993, pp. 27–34; C. R. Williams and L. P. Livingstone, "Another Look at the Relationship between Performance and Voluntary Turnover," *Academy of Management Journal,* April 1994, pp. 269–98; and A. M. Dickinson and K. L. Gillette, "A Comparison of the Effects on Productivity: Piece Rate Pay versus Base Pay Plus Incentives," *Journal of Organizational Behavior Management,* Spring 1994, pp. 3–82.

38. See, for example, Fenn, "Compensation"; J. H. Sheridan, "Yes to Team Incentives," *Industry Week,* March 4, 1996, p. 64; and H. N. Altmansberger and M. J. Wallace Jr., "Strategic Use of Goalsharing at Corning," *ACA Journal,* Winter 1995, pp. 64–71.

39. D. A. De Cenzo and S. P. Robbins, *Human Resource Management,* 5th ed. (New York: John Wiley & Sons, 1996), p. 354.

40. G. Grib and S. O'Donnell, "Pay Plans That Reward Employee Achievement," *HRMagazine,* July 1995, pp. 49–50.

41. S. Tully, "Your Paycheck Gets Exciting," *Fortune,* November 1, 1993, p. 83.

42. "Compensation: Sales Managers as Team Players," *Inc.,* August 1994, p. 102.

43. D. Fenn, "Compensation: Goal-Driven Incentives," *Inc.,* August 1996, p. 91; and M. A. Verespej, "More Value for Compensation," *Industry Week,* June 17, 1996, p. 20.

44. S. Overman, "Saturn Teams Working and Profiting," *HRMagazine,* March 1995, p. 72.

45. M. E. Lattoni and A. Mercier, "Developing Competency-Based Organizations and Pay Systems," *Focus: A Review of Human Resource Management Issues in Canada* (Calgary, Canada: Towers Perrin, Summer 1994), p. 18.

46. Ibid.

47. K. Capell, "Options for Everyone," *Business Week,* July 22, 1996, pp. 80–88; A. Bernstein, "United We Own," *Business Week,* March 18, 1996, pp. 96–102; and R. McGarvey, "Something Extra," *Entrepreneur,* May 1995, p. 70.

48. See, for example, T. R. Stenhouse, "The Long and the Short of Gainsharing," *Academy of Management Executive* 9, No. 1 (1995), pp. 77–78.

49. C. M. Rosen and M. Quarrey, "How Well Is Employee Ownership Working?" *Harvard Business Review,* September–October 1987, pp. 126–32.

50. S. C. Kumbhakar and A. E. Dunbar, "The Elusive ESOP-Productivity Link: Evidence from U.S. Firm-Level Data," *Journal of Public Economics,* September 1993, pp. 273–83; and S. A. Lee, "ESOP Is a Powerful Tool to Align Employees with Corporate Goals," *Pension World,* April 1994, pp. 40–42.

51. Bernstein, "United We Own," p. 102.

52. J. L. Pierce and C. A. Furo, "Employee Ownership: Implications For Management," *Organizational Dynamics,* Winter 1990, pp. 32–43.

53. Ibid, p. 38.

54. S. W. Kelley, "Discretion and the Service Employee," *Journal of Retailing,* Spring 1993, pp. 104–26; S. S. Brooks, "Noncash Ways to Compensate Employees," *HRMagazine,* April 1994, pp. 38–43; and S. Greengard, "Leveraging a Low-Wage Work Force," *Personnel Journal,* January 1995, pp. 90–102.

55. R. McGarvey, "Fire 'Em Up," *Entrepreneur,* March 1996, pp. 76–79.

56. Based on "Get 'Em While They're Hot," *Canadian Business,* April 1996, pp. 52–54.

57. R. Henkoff, "Finding, Training, and Keeping the Best Service Workers," *Fortune,* October 5, 1994, pp. 110–22.

58. M. P. Cronin, "No More Clock Watchers," *Inc.,* February 1994, p. 83.

Chapter 13

1. P. Engardio, "Live-Wire Management at Johnson Electric," *Business Week,* November 27, 1995, p. 80.

2. N. Tichy and C. DeRose, "Roger Enrico's Master Class," *Fortune,* November 27, 1995, pp. 105–06.

3. See S. A. Kirkpatrick and E. A. Locke, "Leadership: Do Traits Matter?" *Academy of Management Executive,* May 1991, pp. 48–60. See also M. D. Mumford, T. L. Gessner, M. S. Connelly, J. A. O'Connor, and T. C. Clifton, "Leadership and Destructive Acts: Individual and Situational Influences," *Leadership Quarterly* 4, No. 2 (1993), pp. 115–47.

4. S. Sherman, "How Tomorrow's Best Leaders Are Learning Their Stuff," *Fortune,* November 27, 1995, pp. 90–102.

5. K. Lewin and R. Lippitt, "An Experimental Approach to the Study of Autocracy and Democracy: A Preliminary Note," *Sociometry* 1 (1938), pp. 292–300; K. Lewin, "Field Theory and Experiment in Social Psychology: Concepts and Methods," *American Journal of Sociology* 44 (1939), pp. 868–96; K. Lewin, R. Lippitt, and R. K. White, "Patterns of Aggressive Behavior in Experimentally Created Social Climates," *Journal of Social Psychology* 10 (1939), pp. 271–301; and R. Lippitt, "An Experimental Study of the Effect of Democratic and Authoritarian Group Atmospheres," *University of Iowa Studies in Child Welfare* 16 (1940), pp. 43–95.

6. B. M. Bass, *Stodgill's Handbook of Leadership* (New York: Free Press, 1981), pp. 298–99.

7. R. Tannenbaum and W. H. Schmidt, "How to Choose a Leadership Pattern," *Harvard Business Review,* May–June 1973, pp. 162–80.

8. R. M. Stogdill and A. E. Coons, eds., *Leader Behavior: Its Description and Measurement,* Research Monograph No. 88 (Columbus: Ohio State University, Bureau of Business Research, 1951). For a more recent literature review of the Ohio State research, see S. Kerr, C. A. Schriesheim, C. J. Murphy, and R. M. Stogdill, "Toward a Contingency Theory of Leadership based upon the Consideration and Initiating Structure Literature," *Organizational Behavior and Human Performance,* August 1974, pp. 62–82; and B. M. Fisher, "Consideration and Initiating Structure and Their Relationships with Leader Effectiveness: A Meta-Analysis," in F. Hoy, ed., *Proceedings of the 48th Annual Academy of Management Conference,* (Anaheim, Calif.: 1988), pp. 201–05.

9. R. Kahn and D. Katz, "Leadership Practices in Relation to Productivity and Morale," in D. Cartwright and A. Zander, eds., *Group Dynamics: Research and Theory,* 2nd ed. (Elmsford, N.Y.: Pow, Paterson, 1960).

10. R. R. Blake and J. S. Mouton, *The Managerial Grid III* (Houston: Gulf Publishing, 1984).

11. L. L. Larson, J. G. Hunt, and R. N. Osborn, "The Great Hi-Hi Leader Behavior Myth: A Lesson from Occam's Razor," *Academy of Management Journal,* December 1976, pp. 628–41; and P. C. Nystrom, "Managers and the Hi-Hi Leader Myth," *Academy of Management Journal,* June 1978, pp. 325–31.

12. See for example, "The 3-D Theory of Leadership," in W. J. Reddin, *Managerial Effectiveness* (New York: McGraw-Hill, 1967).

13. F. E. Fiedler, *A Theory of Leadership Effectiveness* (New York: McGraw-Hill, 1967).

14. L. H. Peters, D. D. Hartke, and T. J. Pholman, "Fiedler's Contingency Theory of Leadership: An Application of the Meta-Analysis Procedures of Schmidt and Hunter," *Psychological Bulletin,* March 1985, pp. 274–85.

15. See, for instance, R. W. Rice, "Psychometric Properties of the Esteem for the Least Preferred Co-Worker (LPC) Scale," *Academy of Management Review,* January 1978, pp. 106–18; C. A. Schriesheim, B. D. Bannister, and W. H. Money, "Psychometric Properties of the LPC Scale: An Extension of Rice's Review," *Academy of Management Review,* April 1979, pp. 287–90; E. H. Schein, *Organizational Psychology,* 3rd ed. (Englewood Cliffs, N.J.: Prentice Hall, 1980), pp. 116–17; and B. Kabanoff, "A Critique of Leader Match and Its Implications for Leadership Research," *Personnel Psychology,* Winter 1981, pp. 749–64.

16. R. J. House, "A Path-Goal Theory of Leader Effectiveness," *Administrative Science Quarterly* September 1971, pp. 321–38; R. J. House and T. R. Mitchell, "Path-Goal Theory of Leadership," *Journal of Contemporary Business,* Autumn 1974, p. 86; and R. J. House, "Retrospective Comment," in L. E. Boone and D. D. Bowen, eds., *The Great Writings in Management and Organizational Behavior,* 2nd ed. (New York: Random House, 1987), pp. 354–64.

17. J. Seltzer and J. W. Smither, "A Role Play Exercise to Introduce Students to Path-Goal Leadership," *Journal of Management Education,* August 1995, p. 381.

18. J. Indrik, "Path-Goal Theory of Leadership: A Meta-Analysis," paper presented at the National Academy of Management Conference, Chicago, August 1986; R. T. Keller, "A Test of the Path-Goal Theory of Leadership with Need for Clarity as a Moderator in Research and Development Organizations," *Journal of Applied Psychology,* April 1989, pp. 208–12; J. C. Wofford and L. Z. Liska, "Path-Goal Theories of Leadership: A Meta-Analysis," *Journal of Management,* Winter 1993, pp. 857–76; and S. Sagie and M. Koslowsky, "Organizational Attitudes and Behaviors as a Function of Participation in Strategic and Tactical Change Decisions: An Application of Path-Goal Theory," *Journal of Organizational Behavior,* January 1994, pp. 37–47.

19. V. H. Vroom and P. W. Yetton, *Leadership and Decision-Making* (Pittsburgh: University of Pittsburgh Press, 1973).

20. V. H. Vroom and A. G. Yago, *The New Leadership: Managing Participation in Organizations* (Englewood Cliffs, N.J.: Prentice Hall, 1988). See especially Chapter 8.

21. See for example, R. H. G. Field, "A Test of the Vroom-Yetton Normative Model of Leadership," *Journal of Applied Psychology,* October 1982, pp. 523–32; C. R. Leana, "Power Relinquishment versus Power Sharing: Theoretical Clarification and Empirical Comparison of Delegation and Participation," *Journal of Applied Psychology,* May 1987, pp. 228–33; J. T. Ettling and A. G. Yago, "Participation under Conditions of Conflict: More on the Validity of the Vroom-Yetton Model," *Journal of Management Studies,* January 1988, pp. 73–83; and R. H. G. Field and R. J. House, "A Test of the Vroom-Yetton Model Using Manager and Subordinate Reports," *Journal of Applied Psychology,* June 1990, pp. 362–66.

22. For additional information about the exchanges that occur between the leader and the follower, see A. S. Phillips and A. G. Bedeian, "Leader-Follower Exchange Quality: The Role of Personal and Interpersonal Attributes," *Academy of Management Journal* 37, No. 4 (1994), pp. 990–1001; and T. A. Scandura and C. A. Schriesheim, "Leader-Member Exchange and Supervisor Career Mentoring as Complementary Constructs in Leadership Research," *Academy of Management Journal* 37, No. 6 (1994), pp. 1588–1602.

23. P. Hersey and K. H. Blanchard, "So You Want to Know Your Leadership Style?" *Training and Development Journal,* February 1974, pp. 1–15; and Hersey and Blanchard, *Management of Organizational Behavior: Utilizing Human Resources,* 5th ed. (Englewood Cliffs, N.J.: Prentice Hall, 1988).

24. Hersey and Blanchard, *Management of Organizational Behavior,* p. 171. Readers who wish to look at both sides of the debate on the validity of situational leadership are encouraged to read W. R. Norris and R. P. Vecchio, "Situational Leadership Theory: A Replication," *Group and Organization Management,* September 1992, pp. 331–42; and W. Blank, J. R. Weitzel, and S. G. Green, "A Test of the Situational Leadership Theory," *Personnel Psychology,* Autumn 1990, pp. 579–97.

25. P. Hersey and K. H. Blanchard, "Grid Principles and Situationalism: Both! A Response to Blake and Mouton," *Group and Organization Studies,* June 1982, pp. 207–10.

26. See R. H. Hambleton and R. Gumpert, "The Validity of Hersey and Blanchard's Theory of Leader Effectiveness," *Group and Organization Studies,* June 1982, pp. 225–42; C. L. Graeff, "The Situational Leadership Theory: A Critical Review," *Academy of Management Review,* April 1983, pp. 285–91; R. P. Vecchio, "Situational Leadership Theory: An Examination of a Prescriptive Theory," *Journal of Applied Psychology,* August 1987, p. 444–51; J. R. Goodson, G. W. McGee, and J. F. Cashman, "Situational Leadership Theory: A Test of Leadership Prescriptions," *Group and Organizational Studies,* December 1989, pp. 446–61; Blank, Weitzel, and Green, "A Test of the Situational Leadership Theory"; Norris, and Vecchio, "Situational Leadership Theory"; and P. R. Lucas, P. E. Messner, C. W. Ryan, and G. P. Sturm, "Preferred Leadership Style Differences: Perceptions of Defence Industry Labour and Management," *Leadership and Organization Development Journal,* December 1992, pp. 19–22.

27. J. A. Conger and R. N. Kanungo, "Behavioral Dimensions of Charismatic Leadership," in J. A. Conger, R. N. Kanungo, and Associates, *Charismatic Leadership* (San Francisco: Jossey-Bass, 1988), p. 79.

28. P. Sellers, "What Exactly Is Charisma?" *Fortune,* January 15, 1996, pp. 68–75.

29. R. J. House, "A 1976 Theory of Charismatic Leadership," in J. G. Hunt and L. L. Larson, eds., *Leadership: The Cutting Edge,* (Carbondale, Ill.: Southern Illinois University Press, 1977), pp. 189–207.

30. W. Bennis, "The Four Competencies of Leadership," *Training and Development Journal,* August 1984, pp. 15–19; and M. Loeb, "Where Leaders Come From," *Fortune,* September 19, 1994, p. 241.

31. Conger and Kanungo, "Behavioral Dimensions of Charismatic Leadership," pp. 78–97.

32. R. J. House, J. Woycke, and E. M. Fodor, "Charismatic and Noncharismatic Leaders: Differences in Behavior and Ef-

fectiveness," in Conger, Kanungo, *Charismatic Leadership,* pp. 103–04; and B. R. Agle and J. A. Sonnenfeld, "Charismatic Chief Executive Officers: Are They More Effective? An Empirical Test of Charismatic Leadership Theory," in D. P. Moore, ed., *Academy of Management Best Papers Proceedings 1994,* August 14–17, 1994), pp. 2–6.

33. Sellers, "What Exactly Is Charisma?" p. 75.
34. House, "A 1976 Theory of Charismatic Leadership."
35. Sellers, "What Exactly Is Charisma?" p. 68; R. Pillai, "Context and Charisma: The Role of Organic Structure, Collectivism, and Crisis in the Emergence of Charismatic Leadership," in D. P. Moore, ed., *Academy of Management Best Papers Proceedings,* August 6–9, 1995, p. 332; and D. Machan, "The Charisma Merchants," *Forbes,* January 23, 1989, pp. 100–01.
36. See, J. M. Burns, *Leadership,* (New York: Harper & Row, 1978); B. M. Bass, *Leadership and Performance beyond Expectations,* (New York: Free Press, 1985); and B. M. Bass, "From Transactional to Transformational Leadership: Learning to Share the Vision," *Organizational Dynamics,* Winter 1990, pp. 19–31.
37. Sellers, "What Exactly Is Charisma?"; and M. A. Verespej, "Lead, Don't Manage," *Industry Week,* March 4, 1996, p. 55.
38. B. M. Bass, "Leadership: Good, Better, Best," *Organizational Dynamics,* Winter 1985, pp. 26–40; and J. Seltzer and B. M. Bass, "Transformational Leadership: Beyond Initiation and Consideration," *Journal of Management,* December 1990, pp. 693–703.
39. See B. J. Tepper, "Patterns of Downward Influence and Follower Conformity in Transactional and Transformational Leadership," in D. P. Moore, ed., *Academy of Management Best Papers Proceedings 1994,* August 14–17, 1994, pp. 267–71.
40. B. J. Avolio and B. M. Bass, "Transformational Leadership, Charisma and Beyond," working paper, School of Management, State University of New York, Binghamton, N.Y., 1985, p. 14; and S. Caminiti, "What Team Leaders Need to Know," *Fortune,* February 20, 1995, pp. 93–98.
41. Cited in B. M. Bass and B. J. Avolio, "Developing Transformational Leadership: 1992 and Beyond," *Journal of European Industrial Training,* January 1990, p. 23.
42. J. J. Hater and B. M. Bass, "Supervisors' Evaluation and Subordinates' Perceptions of Transformational and Transactional Leadership," *Journal of Applied Psychology,* November 1988, pp. 695–702.
43. Bass and Avolio, "Developing Transformational Leadership."
44. Based on a CBS *60 Minutes* segment, September 24, 1995.
45. J. M. Kouzes and B. Z. Posner, *Credibility: How Leaders Gain and Lose It, and Why People Demand It* (San Francisco: Jossey-Bass, 1993), p. 14.
46. Ibid.
47. Ibid.
48. Ibid., p. 37.
49. Based on L. T. Hosmer, "Trust: The Connecting Link between Organizational Theory and Philosophical Ethics," *Academy of Management Review,* April 1995, p. 393; and R. C. Mayer, J. H. Davis, and F. D. Shoorman, "An Integrative Model of Organizational Trust," *Academy of Management Review,* July 1995, p. 712.
50. P. L. Schindler and C. C. Thomas, "The Structure of Interpersonal Trust in the Workplace," *Psychological Reports,* October 1993, pp. 563–73.
51. J. K. Butler Jr. and R. S. Cantrell, "A Behavioral Decision Theory Approach to Modeling Dyadic Trust in Superiors and Subordinates," *Psychological Reports,* August 1984, pp. 19–28.
52. T. A. Stewart, "The Nine Dilemmas Leaders Face," *Fortune,* March 18, 1996, p. 113.
53. See for example, W. H. Miller, "Leadership at a Crossroads," *Industry Week,* August 19, 1996, pp. 43–44.
54. "Rambos in Pinstripes: Why So Many CEOs Are Lousy Leaders," *Fortune,* June 24, 1996, p. 147.
55. Cited in Kouzes and Posner, *Credibility,* pp. 278–83.
56. Based on F. Bartolome, "Nobody Trusts the Boss Completely—Now What?" *Harvard Business Review,* March–April 1989, pp. 135–42; and J. K. Butler Jr., "Toward Understanding and Measuring Conditions of Trust: Evolution of a Condition of Trust Inventory," *Journal of Management,* September 1991, pp. 643–63.
57. W. W. Burke, "Leadership as Empowering Others," in S. Srivastva and Associates, *Executive Power* (San Francisco: Jossey-Bass, 1986); J. A. Conger and R. N. Kanungo, "The Empowerment Process: Integrating Theory and Practice," *Academy of Management Review,* July 1988, pp. 471–82; J. Greenwald, "Is Mr. Nice Guy Back?" *Time,* January 27, 1992, pp. 42–44; J. Weber, "Letting Go Is Hard to Do," *Business Week,* November 1, 1993, pp. 218–19; and L. Holpp, "Applied Empowerment," *Training,* February 1994, pp. 39–44.
58. See, for example, R. Wellins and J. Worklan, "The Philadelphia Story," *Training,* March 1994, pp. 93–100.
59. S. M. Puffer and D. J. McCarthy, "A Framework for Leadership in a TQM Context," *Journal of Quality Management,* January 1996, pp. 109–30; and D. A. Waldman, "A Theoretical Consideration of Leadership and Total Quality Management," *Leadership,* Spring 1993, pp. 65–79.
60. Gary N. Powell, *Women and Men in Management,* 2nd ed. (Thousand Oaks, Calif.: Sage, 1993). See also, R. L. Kent and S. E. Moss, "Effects of Sex and Gender Role on Leader Emergence," *Academy of Management Journal* 37, No. 6 (1994), pp. 1335–46.
61. S. P. Robbins. *Organizational Behavior: Concepts, Controversies, and Applications,* 7th ed. (Englewood Cliffs, N.J.: Prentice Hall, 1996), p. 441; K. Onstad, "You Say 'Tomato'," *Canadian Business,* June 1996, p. 33; H. Collingwood, "Women as Managers: Not Just Different—Better," *Working Woman,* November 1995, p. 14; and D. Phillips, "The Gender Gap," *Entrepreneur,* May 1995, pp. 108–13.
62. H. Collingwood, "Women as Managers: Not Just Different—Better."
63. Based on M. Mallory, "What Do Women Want? Warnaco's Linda Wachner Knows," *U.S. News & World Report,* November 6, 1995, p. 75; B. Dumaine, "America's Toughest Bosses," *Fortune,* October 18, 1993, p. 41; S. Caminiti, "America's Most Successful Businesswoman," *Fortune,* June

15, 1992, pp. 102–08; M. Mahar, "The Measure of Success," *Working Woman,* May 1992, pp. 70–77; and D. W. Johnson, "Leaders of Corporate Change," *Fortune,* December 14, 1992, pp. 106–07.

64. Dumaine, "America's Toughest Bosses," p. 41.
65. G. Hofstede, "Motivation, Leadership, and Organization: Do American Theories Apply Abroad?" *Organizational Dynamics,* Summer 1980, p. 57, and A. Ede, "Leadership and Decision Making: Management Styles and Culture," *Journal of Managerial Psychology,* July 1992, pp. 28–31.
66. S. Kerr and J. M. Jermier, "Substitutes for Leadership: Their Meaning and Measurement," *Organization Behavior and Human Performance,* December 1978, pp. 375–403; J. P. Howell and P. W. Dorfman, "Substitutes for Leadership: Test of a Construct," *Academy of Management Journal,* December 1981, pp. 714–28; P. W. Howard and W. F. Joyce, "Substitutes for Leadership: A Statistical Refinement," paper presented at the 42nd Annual Academy of Management Conference, New York, August 1982; J. P. Howell, P. W. Dorfman, and S. Kerr, "Leadership and Substitutes for Leadership," *Journal of Applied Behavioral Science* 22, No. 1 (1986), pp. 29–46; and J. P. Howell, D. E. Bowen, P. W. Dorfman, S. Kerr, and P. M. Podsakoff, "Substitutes for Leadership: Effective Alternatives to Ineffective Leadership," *Organizational Dynamics,* Summer 1990, pp. 21–38.
67. K. Davis, *Human Behavior at Work: Organizational Behavior,* 6th ed. (New York: McGraw-Hill, 1981), pp. 141–44.
68. Sellers, "What Exactly Is Charisma?" pp. 70–71.

Chapter 14

1. M. P. Cronin, "Plaudits for the Buddy System," *Inc.,* March 1994, p. 137.
2. N. K. Austin, "The Skill Every Manager Must Master," *Working Woman,* May 1995, p. 29; and L. E. Penley, E. R. Alexander, I. E. Jernigan, and C. I. Henwood, "Communication Abilities of Managers: The Relationship to Performance," *Journal of Management,* March 1991, pp. 57–76.
3. C. O. Kursh, "The Benefits of Poor Communication," *Psychoanalytic Review,* Summer–Fall, 1971, 189–208.
4. D. K. Berlo, *The Process of Communication* (New York: Holt, Rinehart, & Winston, 1960), pp. 30–32.
5. Ibid., p. 54.
6. Ibid., p. 103.
7. R. T. Baker and B. S. Hall, "Using the Business Briefing to Develop Communication Skills," *Journal of Management Education,* November 1995, p. 513.
8. "Psst: Pass It On," *Entrepreneur,* April 1995, p. 64.
9. M. Henricks, "More Than Words," *Entrepreneur,* August 1995, pp. 54–57.
10. A. Mehrabian, "Communication without Words," *Psychology Today,* September 1968, pp. 53–55.
11. A. Markels, "Managers Aren't Always Able to Get the Right Message across with E-Mail," *Wall Street Journal,* August 6, 1996, p. B1; and W. R. Pape, "Beyond E-Mail," *Inc. Technology,* Summer 1995, p. 27.
12. Henricks, "More Than Words."
13. J. Mariotti, "The New Vocabulary," *Industry Week,* March 18, 1996, p. 38.
14. Ibid.
15. "Communication: Open Book Management 101," *Inc.,* August 1996, p. 92.
16. See, for instance, G. M. McEvoy, "Student Diary Keeping: Tool for Instructional Improvement," *Journal of Management Education,* May 1996, pp. 206–29.
17. T. D. Lewis and G. H. Graham, "Six Ways to Improve Your Communication Skills," *Internal Auditor,* May 1988, p. 25.
18. This section on gender differences in communications is based on D. Tannen, *You Just Don't Understand: Women and Men in Conversation* (New York: Ballantine Books, 1991); D. Tannen, *Talking from 9 to 5* (New York: Morrow, 1994); J. C. Tingley, *Genderflex: Men & Women Speak Other's Language at Work* (New York: American Management Association, 1994); C. Baher, "How to Avoid Communication Clashes," *HR Focus,* April 1994, p. 3; and "Communication: Bridging the Gender Gap," *HR Focus,* April 1994, p. 22.
19. See, for example, L. K. Larkey, "Toward a Theory of Communicative Interactions in Culturally Diverse Workgroups," *Academy of Management Review,* June 1996, pp. 463–91; R. V. Lindahl, "Automation Breaks the Language Barrier," *HRMagazine,* March 1996, pp. 79–82; D. Lindorff, "In Beijing, the Long March Is Just Starting," *Business Week,* February 12, 1996, p. 68; and L. Miller, "Two Aspects of Japanese and American Co-Worker Interaction: Giving Instructions and Creating Rapport," *Journal of Applied Behavioral Science,* June 1995, pp. 141–61.
20. Based on S. D. Saleh, "Relational Orientation and Organizational Functioning: A Cross-Cultural Perspective," *Canadian Journal of Administrative Sciences,* September 1987, pp. 276–93.
21. See, for example, J. D. Pettit Jr., B. C. Vaught, and R. L. Trewatha, "Interpersonal Skill Training: A Perspective for Success," *Business,* April–June 1990, pp. 8–14; and D. Milbank, "Managers Are Sent to 'Charm Schools' to Discover How to Polish Up Their Acts," *Wall Street Journal,* December 14, 1990, p. B1.
22. C. Hymowitz, "Five Main Reasons Why Managers Fail," *Wall Street Journal,* May 2, 1988, p. B25.
23. D. Milbank, "Interpersonal Skills: Most Appreciated and Sought After in the 1990s," *Canadian Manager,* Spring 1993, p. 26.
24. L. Porter and L. E. McKibbin, *Future of Management Education and Development: Drift or Thrust into the 21st Century* (New York: McGraw-Hill, 1988).
25. S. P. Robbins and P. L. Hunsaker, *Training in Interpersonal Skills: TIPS for Managing People at Work,* 2nd ed. (Upper Saddle River, N.J.: Prentice Hall, 1996); C. T. Lewis, J. E. Garcia, and S. M. Jobs, *Managerial Skills in Organizations* (Boston: Allyn & Bacon, 1990); D. A. Whetten and K. Cameron, *Developing Management Skills,* 2nd ed. (New York: HarperCollins, 1992); and A. C. Yrle, and W. P. Gale, "Using Interpersonal Skills to Manage More Effectively," *Supervisory Management,* April 1993, p. 4.

26. R. McGarvey, "Now Hear This," *Entrepreneur,* June 1996, pp. 87–89.
27. C. R. Rogers and R. E. Farson, *Active Listening* (Chicago: Industrial Relations Center of the University of Chicago, 1976).
28. S. P. Robbins, and P. L. Hunsaker, *Training in Interpersonal Skills,* 2nd ed., pp. 37–39.
29. C. Fisher, "Transmission of Positive and Negative Feedback to Subordinates," *Journal of Applied Psychology,* October 1979, pp. 433–540.
30. D. Llgen, C. D. Fisher, and M. S. Taylor, "Consequences of Individual Feedback on Behavior in Organizations," *Journal of Applied Psychology,* August 1979, pp. 349–71.
31. F. Bartolome, "Teaching about Whether to Give Negative Feedback," *The Organizational Behavior Teaching Review* 9, No. 2 (1986–1987), pp. 95–104.
32. K. Halperin, C. R. Snyder, R. J. Schenkel, and B. K. Houston, "Effect of Source Status and Message Favorability on Acceptance of Personality Feedback," *Journal of Applied Psychology,* February 1976, pp. 85–88.
33. C. R. Mill, "Feedback: The Art of Giving and Receiving Help," in L. Porter and C. R. Mill, eds., *The Reading Book for Human Relations Training* (Bethel, Maine: NTL Institute for Applied Behavioral Science, 1976), pp. 18–19.
34. Ibid.
35. Ibid.
36. Ibid.
37. K. S. Verderber and R. F. Verderber, *Inter-Act: Using Interpersonal Communication Skills,* 4th ed. (Belmont, Calif.: Wadsworth, 1986).
38. L. E. Bourne Jr. and C. V. Bunderson, "Effects of Delay of Information Feedback and Length of Post-Feedback Interval on Concept Identification," *Journal of Experimental Psychology,* January 1963, pp. 1–5.
39. Mill, "Feedback," pp. 18–19.
40. Verderber and Verderber, *Inter-Act.*
41. B. K. Hackman and D. C. Dunphy, "Managerial Delegation," in G. C. Cooper and I. T. Robertson, eds., *International Review of Industrial and Organizational Psychology* (Chichester, England: John Wiley & Sons, 1990), pp. 35–37; and B. Marquand, "Effective Delegation," *Manage,* July 1993, pp. 10–12.
42. C. R. Leana, "Predictors and Consequences of Delegation," *Academy of Management Journal,* December 1986, pp. 754–74.
43. L. L. Steinmetz, *The Art and Skill of Delegation* (Boston: Addison-Wesley, 1976).
44. C. D. Pringle, "Seven Reasons Why Managers Don't Delegate," *Management Solutions,* November 1986, pp. 26–30.
45. Robbins and Hunsaker, *Training in Interpersonal Skills, 2nd ed.,* pp. 93–95; R. T. Noel, "What You Say to Your Employees When You Delegate," *Supervisory Management,* December 1993, p. 13; and S. Caudron, "Delegate for Results," *Industry Week,* February 6, 1995, pp. 27–30.
46. K. W. Thomas and W. H. Schmidt, "A Survey of Managerial Interests with Respect to Conflict," *Academy of Management Journal,* June 1976, pp. 315–18.
47. Ibid.
48. J. Graves, "Successful Management and Organizational Mugging," in J. Papp, ed., *New Directions in Human Resource Management* (Englewood Cliffs, N.J.: Prentice Hall, 1974).
49. This section is adapted from S. P. Robbins, *Managing Organizational Conflict: A Non-traditional Approach* (Englewood Cliffs, N.J.: Prentice Hall, 1977), pp. 11–14.
50. R. H. Killman and K. W. Thomas, "Developing a Forced-Choice Measure of Conflict Handling Behavior: The MODE Instrument," *Educational and Psychological Measurement,* Summer 1977, pp. 309–25.
51. L. Greenhalgh, "Managing Conflict," *Sloan Management Review,* Summer 1986, pp. 45–51.
52. Robbins, *Managing Organizational Conflict,* pp. 31–55.
53. Kursh, "The Benefits of Poor Communication."
54. K. W. Thomas, "Conflict and Conflict Management," in M. Dunnette, ed., *Handbook of Industrial and Organizational Psychology,* (Chicago: Rand McNally, 1976), pp. 889–935.
55. See, for instance, D. Tjosvold and D. W. Johnson, *Productive Conflict Management Perspectives for Organizations* (New York: Irvington Publishers, 1983).
56. This section is drawn from K. W. Thomas, "Toward Multidimensional Values in Teaching: The Example of Conflict Behaviors," *Academy of Management Review,* July 1977, p. 487.
57. S. P. Robbins, "Conflict Management and Conflict Resolution Are Not Synonymous Terms," *California Management Review,* Winter 1978, p. 71.
58. Robbins, *Managing Organizational Conflict,* pp. 78–89.
59. R. E. Walton and R. B. McKersie, *A Behavioral Theory of Labor Negotiations: An Analysis of a Social Interaction System* (New York: McGraw-Hill, 1965).
60. K. W. Thomas, "Conflict and Negotiation Processes in Organizations," in M. D. Dunnette and L. M. Hough, eds. *Handbook of Industrial and Organizational Psychology,* vol. 3, 2nd ed. (Palo Alto, Calif.: Consulting Psychologists Press, 1992), pp. 651–717.
61. Based on R. Fisher and W. Ury, *Getting to Yes: Negotiating Agreement without Giving In* (Boston: Houghton Mifflin, 1981); J. A. Wall Jr. and M. W. Blum, "Negotiations," *Journal of Management,* June 1991, pp. 295–96; and M. H. Bazerman and M. A. Neale, *Negotiating Rationally* (New York: Free Press, 1992).
62. "How to Negotiate with Really Tough Guys," *Fortune,* May 27, 1996, pp. 173–74.
63. Case based on J. Cushman, "Avianca Flight 52: The Delays that Ended in Disaster," *New York Times,* February 5, 1990, p. B1; and E. Weiner, "Right Word is Crucial in Air Control," *New York Times,* January 1990, p. B5.

Chapter 15

1. G. Lesser, "A Hard Rain's Gonna Fall," *Sky,* August 1996, p. 22.
2. Vignette based on Lesser, "A Hard Rain's Gonna Fall," pp. 22–27.

3. K. A. Merchant, "The Control Function of Management," *Sloan Management Review,* Summer 1982, pp. 43–55.

4. E. Flamholtz, "Organizational Control Systems as a Managerial Tool," *California Management Review,* Winter 1979, p. 55.

5. W. G. Ouchi, "A Conceptual Framework for the Design of Organizational Control Mechanisms," *Management Science,* August 1979, pp. 833–38; and Ouchi, "Markets, Bureaucracies, and Clans," *Administrative Science Quarterly,* March 1980, pp. 129–41.

6. S. Tully, "Purchasing's New Muscle," *Fortune,* February 20, 1995, pp. 78–79.

7. W. Zellner, "Leave the Driving to Lentzsch," *Business Week,* March 18, 1996, pp. 66–67.

8. S. Kerr, "On the Folly of Rewarding A, While Hoping for B," *Academy of Management Journal,* December 1975, pp. 769–83.

9. R. Stodghill, "Combat-Ready at McDonnell," *Business Week,* April 29, 1996, p. 39; and S. Greco, "Are We Making Money Yet?" *Inc.,* July 1996, pp. 53–61.

10. See, for instance, Zellner, "Leave the Driving to Lentzsch."

11. H. Koontz and R. W. Bradspies, "Managing through Feedforward Control," *Business Horizons,* June 1972, pp. 25–36.

12. G. Pitts, "From Potholes to Profits," *The Globe and Mail,* April 4, 1995, p. 18.

13. W. H. Newman, *Constructive Control: Design and Use of Control Systems,* (Englewood Cliffs, N.J.: Prentice Hall, 1975), p. 33.

14. Ibid.

15. See, for example, Tully, "Purchasing's New Muscle," pp. 75–83.

16. See for instance, S. Chandler, "How TWA Faced the Nightmare," *Business Week,* August 5, 1996, p. 30.

17. See, for instance, M. Kripalani, "A Traffic Jam of Auto Makers," *Business Week,* August 5, 1996, pp. 46–47.

18. Kripalani, "A Traffic Jam of Auto Makers," p. 46.

19. D. Freedman, "Bits to Ship," *Forbes ASAP,* December 5, 1994, pp. 28–31.

20. Based on a tape recording made by the Dallas Fire Department and made available under the Texas Open Records Act.

21. Cited in A. B. Carroll, "In Search of the Moral Manager," *Business Horizons,* March–April 1987, p. 7.

22. See, for instance, B. J. Jaworski and S. M. Young, "Dysfunctional Behavior and Management Control: An Empirical Study of Marketing Managers," *Accounting, Organizations, and Society,* January 1992, pp. 17–35.

23. E. E. Lawler III and J. G. Rhode, *Information and Control in Organizations* (Santa Monica, Calif.: Goodyear, 1976), p. 108.

24. J. D. Thompson, *Organizations in Action* (New York: McGraw-Hill, 1967), p. 124.

25. J. Teresko, "Opening Up the Plant Floor," *Industry Week,* May 20, 1996, p. 172; S. Lubove, "High-Tech Cops," *Forbes,* September 25, 1995, pp. 44–45; M. Meyer, "The Fear of Flaming," *Newsweek,* June 20, 1994, p. 54; and J. Ubois, "Plugged in Away from the Office," *Working Woman,* June 1994, pp. 60–61.

26. F. Jossi, "Eavesdropping in Cyberspace," *Business Ethics,* May–June 1994, pp. 22–25.

27. Ibid.

28. L. Smith, "What the Boss Knows about You," *Fortune,* August 1993, pp. 88–93.

29. Based on "Is Nothing Private Anymore?" ABC's *20/20,* January 24, 1992.

30. Ibid.

31. Smith, "What the Boss Knows about You"; Z. Schiller and W. Konrad, "If You Light Up on Sunday, Don't Come In on Monday," *Business Week,* August 26, 1991, pp. 68–72; and G. Bylinsky, "How Companies Spy on Employees," *Fortune,* November 4, 1991, pp. 131–40.

32. J. Rothfeder and J. Bartimo, "How Software Is Making Food Sales a Piece of Cake," *Business Week,* July 2, 1990, pp. 54–55.

Chapter 16

1. Based on B. Little, "Stock Answers," *The Globe and Mail,* June 6, 1995, p. 12.

2. For a good overview of information processing in organizations, see T. A. Stewart, "Managing in a Wired Company," *Fortune,* July 11, 1994, pp. 44–56.

3. See, for example, R. A. Mamis, "Crash Course," *Inc.,* February 1995, pp. 54–63.

4. J. T. Small and W. B. Lee, "In Search of an MIS," *MSU Business Topics,* Autumn 1975, pp. 47–55.

5. H. A. Simon, *Administrative Behavior,* 3rd ed. (New York: Free Press, 1976), p. 294; and J. Teresko, "Data Warehouses: Build Them for Decision-Making Power," *Industry Week,* March 18, 1996, pp. 43–46.

6. J. C. Carter and F. N. Silverman, "Establishing an MIS," *Journal of Systems Management,* January 1980, p. 15.

7. D. H. Freedman, "Through the Looking Glass," *The State of Small Business* 1 (1996), p. 47; and L. Hayes, "Using Computers to Divine Who Might Buy a Gas Grill," *Wall Street Journal,* August 16, 1994, p. B1.

8. Adapted from S. P. Robbins and M. Coulter, *Management,* 5th ed. (Upper Saddle River, N.J.: Prentice Hall, 1996), pp. 735–38.

9. See, for example, G. Bylinsky, "Saving Time with New Technology," *Fortune,* December 30, 1991, pp. 98–104; and P. F. Drucker, "The Information Executives Truly Need," *Harvard Business Review,* January–February 1995, pp. 54–62.

10. R. D. Hof, "How to Kick the Mainframe Habit," *Business Week,* June 26, 1995, pp. 102–04; A. L. Sprout, "Surprise! Software to Help You Manage," *Fortune,* April 17, 1995, pp 197–200; S. A. Stanton, "End-User Computing: Power to the People," *Journal of Information Systems Management,* Summer 1988, pp. 79–81; and G. L. Boyer and D. McKinnon, "End-User Computing Is Here to Stay," *Supervisory Management,* October 1989, pp. 17–22.

11. J. Bell, "Corporate Chain Gangs," *Industry Week,* April 15, 1996, pp. 51–56; P. Coy, "The New Realism in Office Systems," *Business Week,* June 15, 1992, pp. 128–33; and M.

Magnet, "Who's Winning the Information Revolution," *Fortune,* November 30, 1992, pp. 110–17.

12. "Cutting Out the Middleman," *Forbes,* January 6, 1992, p. 169.
13. T. Petzinger Jr., "Phil Wilkerson Leads Levi into Radical Shift in Computer Culture," *Wall Street Journal,* August 4, 1995, p. B1.
14. D. L. Boroughs, "Paperless Profits," *U.S. News & World Report,* July 17, 1995, pp. 40–42.
15. See, for example, S. W. Quickel, "Management Joins the Computer Age," *Business Month,* May 1989, pp. 42–46; G. P. Huber, "A Theory of the Effects of Advanced Information Technology on Organizational Design, Intelligence, and Decision Making," *Academy of Management Review,* January 1990, pp. 47–71; and U. G. Gupta, "An Empirical Investigation of the Contribution of Information Systems to Productivity," *Industrial Management,* March–April 1994, pp. 15–18.
16. See, for instance, J. de Jong, "Improving Customer Service for the Crucial Few," *Inc. Technology,* No. 2 (1995), p. 38.
17. R. Karlgaard, "ASAP Interview with Susan Cramm and John Martin," *Forbes ASAP,* Summer 1994, pp. 67–70.
18. L. M. Applegate, J. I. Cash, and D. Q. Mills, "Information Technology and Tomorrow's Manager," *Harvard Business Review,* November–December 1988, pp. 128–36.
19. J. H. Boyett and H. P. Conn, *Workplace 2000* (New York: Dutton, 1991), p. 25.
20. Ibid.
21. M. Newman and D. Rosenberg, "Systems Analysts and the Politics of Organizational Control," *Omega* 13, No. 5 (1985), pp. 393–406.
22. This section is based on R. C. Huseman and E. W. Miles, "Organizational Communication in the Information Age: Implications of Computer-Based Systems," *Journal of Management,* Summer 1988, pp. 181–204.
23. R. B. Lieber, "Here Comes SAP," *Fortune,* October 2, 1995, pp. 122–24.
24. R. Henkoff, "Some Hope for Troubled Cities," *Fortune,* September 9, 1991, pp. 121–28.
25. *Fortune,* October 28, 1985, p. 47.
26. S. E. Barndt and D. W. Carvey, *Essentials of Operations Management* (Englewood Cliffs, N.J.: Prentice Hall, 1982), p. 112.
27. J. Dreyfuss, "Shaping Up Your Suppliers," *Fortune,* April 10, 1989, pp. 116–22; and T. M. Rohan, "Supplier-Customer Links Multiplying," *Industry Week,* April 17, 1989, p. 20.
28. Rohan, "Supplier-Customer Links Multiplying."
29. See, for example, B. B. Flynn, S. Sakakibara, and R. G. Schroeder, "Relationship between JIT and TQM: Practices and Performance," *Academy of Management Journal* 38, No. 5 (1995), pp. 1325–60.
30. R. B. Chase and N. J. Aquilano, *Production and Operations Management: A Life-Cycle Approach,* 3rd ed. (Homewood, Ill.: Irwin, 1981), pp. 551–52.
31. J. A. Miller, *Implementing Activity-Based Management in Daily Operations* (New York: John Wiley & Sons, 1996); J. Thomas, "As Easy as ABC," *Chilton Distribution,* January 1994, p. 40; and R. J. Schonberger, "World-Class Manufacturing: The Next Decade," *Industry Week,* March 18, 1996, p. 24.
32. P. Elmer-Dewitt, "Nabbing the Pirates of Cyberspace," *Time,* June 13, 1994, pp. 62–63; and J. Martin, "Freeze, It's the Cyber Fuzz," *Fortune,* May 2, 1994, pp. 14–15.
33. Martin, "Freeze, It's the Cyber Fuzz."
34. S. Oliver, "Virtual Retailer," *Forbes,* April 24, 1995, pp. 126–27; "Information Technology," *Fortune,* April 18, 1994, p. 106; and information available from CUC International's home page (1996) on the Internet.

Appendix A

1. C. S. George Jr., *The History of Management Thought,* 2nd ed. (Englewood Cliffs, N.J.: Prentice Hall, 1972), p. 4.
2. W. E. Wallace, "Michelangelo, C.E.O.," *New York Times,* April 16, 1994, p. Y11.
3. A. Smith, *An Inquiry into the Nature and Causes of Wealth of Nations* (New York: Modern Library, 1937). Originally published in 1776.
4. F. W. Taylor, *The Principles of Scientific Management* (New York: Harper, 1911).
5. These facts about the dissemination of Taylor's ideas are from S. R. Barley and G. Kunda, "Design and Devotion: Surges of Rational and Normative Ideologies of Control in Managerial Discourse," *Administrative Science Quarterly,* September 1992, pp. 369–71. See also M. Banta, *Taylored Lives: Narrative Productions in the Age of Taylor, Veblen, and Ford* (Chicago: University of Chicago Press, 1993).
6. F. B. Gilbreth, *Motion Study* (New York: D. Van Nostrand, 1911); and F. B. Gilbreth and L. M. Gilbreth, *Fatigue Study* (New York: Sturgis and Walton, 1916).
7. Gilbreth, *Motion Study.*
8. H. Fayol, *Industrial and General Administration* (Paris: Dunod, 1916).
9. M. Weber, *The Theory of Social and Economic Organizations,* ed. T. Parsons, trans. A. M. Henderson and T. Parsons (New York: Free Press, 1947).
10. W. J. Duncan, *Great Ideas in Management* (San Francisco: Jossey-Bass, 1989), p. 137.
11. R. A. Owen, *A New View of Society* (New York: E. Bliss and White, 1825).
12. H. Munsterberg, *Psychology and Industrial Efficiency* (Boston: Houghton Mifflin, 1913).
13. M. P. Follet, *The New State: Group Organization the Solution of Popular Government* (London: Longmans, Green, 1918).
14. C. I. Barnard, *The Functions of the Executive* (Cambridge, Mass.: Harvard University Press, 1938).
15. E. Mayo, *The Human Problems of an Industrial Civilization* (New York: Macmillan, 1933); and F. J. Roethlisberger and W. J. Dickson, *Management and the Worker* (Cambridge, Mass.: Harvard University Press, 1939).
16. The facts of this paragraph are from Barley, and Kunda, "Design and Devotion," p. 374.
17. Roethlisberger and Dickson, *Management and the Worker.*
18. A. Carey, "The Hawthorne Studies: A Radical Criticism," *American Sociological Review,* June 1967, pp. 403–16; R. H.

Franke and J. Kaul, "The Hawthorne Experiments: First Statistical Interpretations," *American Sociological Review,* October 1978, pp. 623–43; B. Rice, "The Hawthorne Defect: Persistence of a Flawed Theory," *Psychology Today,* February 1982, pp. 70–74; J. A. Sonnenfeld, "Shedding Light on the Hawthorne Studies," *Journal of Occupational Behavior,* April 1985, pp. 111–30; S. R. G. Jones, "Worker Interdependence and Output: The Hawthorne Studies Reevaluated," *American Sociological Review,* April 1990, pp. 176–90; and S. R. G. Jones, "Was There a Hawthorne Effect?" *American Journal of Sociology,* November 1992, pp. 451–68.

19. Mayo, *The Human Problems of an Industrial Civilization.*
20. D. Carnegie, *How to Win Friends and Influence People* (New York: Simon & Schuster, 1936).
21. D. Wren, *The Evolution of Management Thought,* 3rd ed. (New York: John Wiley & Sons, 1987), p. 422.
22. A. Maslow, "A Theory of Human Motivation," *Psychological Review,* July 1943, pp. 370–96. See also Maslow, *Motivation and Personality* (New York: Harper & Row, 1954).
23. M. T. Matteson, "Some Reported Thoughts on Significant Management Literature," *Academy of Management Journal,* June 1974, pp. 386–89.
24. J. B. Miner, *Theories of Organizational Behavior* (Hinsdale, Ill.: Dryden, 1980), p. 41.
25. D. McGregor, *The Human Side of Enterprise* (New York: McGraw-Hill, 1960).
26. Wren, *The Evolution of Management Thought,* 3rd ed., p. 127.
27. Matteson, "Some Reported Thoughts on Significant Management Literature."
28. M. Warner, "Organizational Behavior Revisited," *Human Relations,* October 1994, p. 1153.
29. Cited in E. Burack and R. B. D. Batlivala, "Operations Research: Recent Changes and Future Expectation in Business Operations," *Business Perspectives,* June 1972, pp. 15–22.
30. Wren, *The Evolution of Management Thought,* 3rd ed., p. 51.

Appendix B

1. D. T. Hall and Associates, *The Career Is Dead—Long Live the Career: A Relational Approach to Careers* (San Francisco: Jossey-Bass, 1996).
2. See, for example, D. E. Super, *The Psychology of Careers* (New York: Harper & Row, 1957); E. Schein, *Career Dynamics: Matching Individual and Organizational Needs* (Reading, Mass.: Addison-Wesley, 1978); and D. J. Levinson, C. N. Darrow, E. B. Klein, M. H. Levinson, and B. McKee, *A Man's Life* (New York: Knopf, 1978).
3. J. Fierman, "Beating the Midlife Career Crisis," *Fortune,* September 6, 1993, p. 51.
4. F. M. Hudson, "When Careers Turn Stale," *Next* (Lakewood, Calif.: American Association of Retired Persons, 1994), p. 3.
5. D. E. Super, "A Life-Span Life Space Approach to Career Development," *Journal of Vocational Behavior* 16 (Spring 1980), pp. 282–98; see also pp. 99–131 in E. P. Cook and M. Arthur, *Career Theory Handbook* (Englewood Cliffs, N.J.: Prentice Hall, 1991); and L. S. Richman, "The New Worker Elite," *Fortune,* August 22, 1994, pp. 56–66.
6. I. R. Schwartz, "Self-Assessment and Career Planning: Matching Individuals and Organizational Goals," *Personnel,* January–February 1979, p. 48.
7. Material for this section is adapted from D. A. De Cenzo and S. P. Robbins, *Human Resource Management,* 5th ed. (New York: John Wiley & Sons, 1996), Appendix A and Appendix B.
8. See, for example, J. Lawlor, "Scanning Résumés: The Impersonal Touch," *USA Today,* October 7, 1991, p. 7B.
9. T. Mullins, "How to Land a Job," *Psychology Today,* September/October 1994, pp. 12–13.
10. For a discussion on fit and its appropriateness to the interviewing process, see "The Right Fit," *Small Business Reports,* April 1993, p. 28.
11. For a more detailed discussion of impression management, see A. L. Kristof and C. K. Stevens, "Applicant Impression Management Tactics: Effects on Interviewer Evaluations and Interview Outcomes," in D. P. Moore, ed., *Academy of Management Best Papers Proceedings,* August 14–17, 1994, pp. 127–31.
12. Reported in R. E. Carlson, P. W. Thayer, E. C. Mayfield, and D. A. Peterson, "Improvements in the Selection Interview," *Personnel Journal,* April 1971, p. 272.
13. R. L. Dipboye, *Selection Interviews: Process Perspectives* (Cincinnati, Ohio: South-Western Publishing, 1992), p. 201.
14. K. Schabacker, "Tips on Making a Great First Impression," *Working Woman,* February 1992, p. 55.
15. A. N. Schoonmaker, *Executive Career Strategy* (New York: American Management Association, 1971); A. J. DuBrin, *Fundamentals of Organizational Behavior: An Applied Perspective,* 2nd ed. (Elmsford, N.Y.: Pergamon Press, 1978), Chapter 5; E. E. Jennings, "Success Chess," *Management of Personnel Quarterly,* Fall 1980, pp. 2–8; and R. Henkoff, "Winning the New Career Game," *Fortune,* July 12, 1993, pp. 46–49.
16. J. E. Sheridan, J. W. Slocum Jr., R. Buda, and R. C. Thompson, "Effects of Corporate Sponsorship and Departmental Power on Career Tournaments," *Academy of Management Journal,* September 1990, pp. 578–602.
17. C. Perrow, *Complex Organizations: A Critical Essay* (Glenwood, Ill.: Scott, Foresman, 1972), p. 43.
18. Sheridan et al., "Effects of Corporate Sponsorship and Departmental Power on Career Tournaments."
19. G. F. Dreher and R. A. Ash, "A Comparative Study of Mentoring among Men and Women in Managerial, Professional, and Technical Positions," *Journal of Applied Psychology,* October 1990, pp. 539–46.
20. See, for example, D. Kirkpatrick, "Is Your Career on Track?" *Fortune,* June 2, 1990, pp. 38–48; A. Saltzman, "Sidestepping Your Way to the Top," *U.S. News & World Report,* October 17, 1990, pp. 60–61; and B. Nussbaum, "I'm Worried about My Job," *Business Week,* October 7, 1991, pp. 94–97.

Illustration Credits

Chapter 1

page 2 Autodesk, Inc.
page 3 Joe Traver/Gamma-Liaison, Inc.
page 5 Michael A. Schwarz/The Image Works
page 9 John Abbott/John Abbott Photography
page 16 Mark Tucker Photography
page 18 Courtesy of Ssangyong Investment & Securities Company
page 19 John Abbott/John Abbott Photography
page 22 Mark C. Burnett/Stock Boston

Chapter 2

page 31 Edward Santalone
page 33 Courtesy of International Business Machines Corporation. Unauthorized use not permitted.
page 39 Courtesy Lukens, Inc.
page 43 Allan Penn/Allan Penn Photography
page 45 Steve Mellon
page 52 John Witmer/*Dayton Daily News*/Gamma-Liaison, Inc.
page 55 John Abbott Photography

Chapter 3

page 70 Amy C. Etra
page 73 Paul Bowen Photography, Inc.
page 74 Chris Buck/Outline Press Syndicate Inc.
page 75 Dan Ford Connolly/Mercury Pictures
page 81 ©James Schnepf
page 83 Sjaak Ramakers/Sjaak Ramakers Fotograaf
page 86 Terry Parke/Terry Parke Photography
page 87 Michelle Litvin
page 90 Amy C. Etra

Chapter 4

page 101 Elizabeth Garvy/Elizabeth Garvey Photography
page 102 Frank LaBua/Simon & Schuster/PH College
page 103 David Fields Photography
page 107 Scott Montgomery/Scott Montgomery Photography
page 111 DiMaggio/Kalish/The Stock Market
page 114 Ki Ho Park/Kistone Photography
page 118 Stephen Homer
page 120 Robbie McClaran

Chapter 5

page 133 Jim Cooper/AP/Wide World Photos
page 135 Llewellyn/Uniphoto Picture Agency
page 140 A. De Wilderberg/Gamma-Liaison, Inc.
page 142 Roberto Borea/AP/Wide World Photos
page 143 Lou DeMatteis
page 145 Will and Deni McIntyre
page 153 Katherine Lambert

Chapter 6

page 163 Chris Corsmeier/Chris Corsmeier Photography
page 165 Brian Leng Photography
page 168 Courtesy Diamond Star Motors
page 169 Kelley McMannis/Parker Hannifin Corp., Compumotor Division
page 171 Jacques M. Chenet/*Newsweek*/Gamma-Liaison, Inc.
page 177 Jeffery MacMillan
Page 179 Mark Richards

Chapter 7

page 197 Via Christi Health System
page 198 Philip Gordon/REA/SABA Press Photos, Inc.
page 201 Chris Usher/Chris Usher Photography
page 209 Claudio Vazquez
page 214 Gale Zucker/Gale Zucker Photography
page 215 Hans J. Ellerbrock/Bilderberg Archiv der Fotografen
page 221 Mike Greenlar

Chapter 8

page 230 Mark Richards
page 233 Lee Malis/Spectrum Pictures
page 236 Alexandra Boulat/SIPA Press
page 239 Courtesy of International Business Machines Corporation. Unauthorized use not permitted.
page 254 David Quinney
page 256 Susan Ragan/AP/Wide World Photos
page 257 Peter Schinzler/Bildagentur Anne Hamann

Chapter 9

page 267 Reuven Kopitchinski
page 272 Richard Schultz
page 274 David Stoecklein/The Stock Market
page 278 Doug Knutson/Knutson Photography Inc.
page 281 Tony Savino/The Image Works
page 285 Northstar-at-Tahoe
page 287 Courtesy of Toyota Inc.

Chapter 10

page 297 Nikolai Ignatiev/Network Matrix
page 301 Najlah Feanny/SABA Press Photos, Inc.

page 305 Chris Usher/Chris Usher Photography
page 308 Erica Freudenstein/SABA Press Photos, Inc.
page 312 Ron McMillan/Gamma Liaison
page 316 Courtesy of Siemens Corp.
page 320 Paul H. Henning/Uniphoto Picture Agency

Chapter 11

page 332 Joseph Robichaud Photography/Imperial Oil, Products and Chemicals Division
page 333 Robbie McClaran
page 337 Andy Freeberg/Andy Freeberg Photography
page 338 L. Kolvoord/The Image Works
page 340 Eligio Paoni/Contrasto/SABA Press Photos, Inc.
page 348 Michael L. Abramson

Chapter 12

page 357 ©Bruce Zake
page 359 Mel L. Russell
page 365 Ben Van Hook
page 367 Sylvia Plachy
page 372 Gary Laufman Photography
page 377 Courtesy Southwest Airlines
page 379 Perry Zavitz Photography, Inc.

Chapter 13

page 388 Greg Girard/Contact Press Images
page 390 Dana Fineman/Sygma
page 395 Terry Parke/Terry Parke Photography
page 400 ©Donald C. Johnson. All rights reserved.
page 405 Nortel/Northern Telecom Ltd.
page 407 Miles Ladin Photography
page 412 John Abbott/John Abbott Photography

Chapter 14

page 423 Ann States/Voldi Tanner
page 425 Art Attack/Monkmeyer Press
page 428 K.C. Kratt/K.C. Kratt Photography, Inc.
page 430 Jim Judkis
page 434 Zimbel/Monkmeyer Press
page 441 Bruce Ayres/Tony Stone Images
page 449 Molly Roberts

Chapter 15

page 460 Alan Copson
page 462 Axel Koester Photography
page 465 Tom Campbell/FPG International
page 468 Anthony Edgeworth
page 469 Suzanne Ahearne
page 475 Hormazd Sorabjee
page 478 Frederick Charles/Frederick Charles Photography

Chapter 16

page 487 Courtesy Mount Sinai Hospital Toronto, Ontario
page 491 Courtesy Levi Strauss & Co.
page 490 Archambault Photography, Inc.
page 494 Robert Holmgren
page 496 Erik Freeland
page 502 Tom Wagner/SABA Press Photos, Inc.
page 508 ©Mitsuhiro Wada, courtesy of Business Week Tokyo.

Name/Organization Index

C

N

O

X, Y, Z

Glindex

a combined glossary/subject index

Q

Quality control *Ensuring that what is produced meets some preestablished standard,* 503
versus continuous improvement, 503

Quality of life *A national culture attribute that reflects the emphasis placed upon relationships and concern for others,* 37, 38

Quantitative approach, management, A-12
stimulus, A-14

Quantitative forecasting *Applies a set of mathematical rules to a series of past data to predict future outcomes,* 105

Quantity of life *A national culture attribute describing the extent to which societal values are characterized by assertiveness and materialism,* 37, 38

Queuing theory *A technique that balances the cost of having a waiting line against the cost of service to maintain that line; also called waiting-line theory,* 119

R

Range of variation *The acceptable parameters of variance between actual performance and the standard,* 463

Ratio analyses, financial control, 505–7

Rational *Describes choices that are consistent and value-maximizing within specified constraints,* 138

Rational decision making, 138, 139

Rationality, bounded, 140, 141

Readiness *The situational leadership model term for a follower's ability and willingness to perform,* 403

Realistic job preview, 244

Receiver, communication, 424–6

Recruiting sources, 237
and WWW, 236, 265

Recruitment *The process of locating, identifying, and attracting capable applicants,* 236

Reducing stress, 283, 284

Reengineering *Radical, quantum change in an organization,* 50, 172, 173, 178
key elements, 173

Referent *In equity theory, the other persons, the systems, or the personal experiences against which individuals compare themselves to assess equity,* 369

Referent power, 207

Referrals, employee, 236, 237

Reinforcement, 317, 318
process, 317

Reject error, 238

Reliability *The degree to which a selection device measures the same thing consistently,* 239

Remedial maintenance *Maintenance that calls for the overhaul, replacement, or repair of equipment when it breaks down,* 503

Repetitive tasks, 178
and automation, 178

Representative heuristics *The tendency for people to base judgments of probability on things with which they are familiar,* 141, 142

Resistance to change, 275–7

Resource allocator role, 9, 10

Responsibility *An obligation to perform assigned activities,* 201
and delegation, 438, 439

Restraining forces, 273

Retention processes, 317

Retrenchment strategy *A strategy characteristic of a company that is reducing its size, usually in an environment of decline,* 86

Return-on-investment ratios *[Revenues divided by investments] multiplied by [profit divided by revenues],* 507

Revenue forecasting *Predicting future revenues,* 104

Reward power, 207

Rights view of ethics, 57

Rightsizing *Linking staffing levels to organizational goals,* 51, 53

Ringisei, 154

Risk *The probability that a particular outcome will result from a given decision,* 139

RJP, 244

Robotics *Computer-controlled machines that manipulate materials and perform complex functions,* 40, 167, 168

Role *A set of expected behavior patterns attributed to someone who occupies a given position in a social unit,* 320

Roles, management, 9–11

Roles, teams, 345

Rule *An explicit statement that tells managers what they ought or ought not to do,* 144

S

Safety and health, 253

Safety needs, 359

Sampling techniques, quality control, 504

Satisfaction-dissatisfaction continuum, 365

Scenario *A visualization of what the future is likely to be,* 104

Scheduling *A listing of what activities have to be done, the order in which they are to be done, who is to do each, and when they are to be completed,* 111

Scheduling options, work, 186–8

School placements, 237

Scientific management *The use of the scientific method to define the "one best way" for a job to be done,* A-2–4

Security and groups, 319

Selection process *The process of screening job applicants to ensure that the most appropriate candidates are hired,* 236–8

Selective perception, communication, 430

Selectivity, judging, 314

Self-actualization needs, 359

Self-esteem *An individual's degree of like or dislike for him- or herself,* 305
and groups, 319

Self-fulfilling prophesy, 314

Self-managed work teams *A formal group of employees who operate without a manager and are responsible for a complete work process or segment that delivers a product or service to an external or internal customer,* 338

Self-monitoring *A measure of an individual's ability to adjust his or her behavior to external, situational factors,* 307

Self-serving bias *The tendency for individuals to attribute their own successes to internal factors while putting the blame for failures on external factors,* 313

Selling style, leadership, 403, 404

Sensitivity to differences, 56

Service organization *An organization that produces nonphysical outputs such as educational, medical, or transportation services,* 495

Sexual harassment *Sexually suggestive remarks, unwanted touching and sexual advances, requests for sexual favors, or other verbal and physical conduct of a sexual nature,* 255

Shaping behavior *Systematically reinforcing each successive step that moves an individual closer to a desired behavior,* 317

Short-term plans *Plans that cover less than one year,* 77

U

V